# NATIONS WITHOUT STATES

# NATIONS WITHOUT STATES

*A Historical Dictionary of Contemporary National Movements*

**James Minahan**

**Foreword by Leonard W. Doob**

**Greenwood Press**
Westport, Connecticut • London

**Library of Congress Cataloging-in-Publication Data**

Minahan, James.
    Nations without states : a historical dictionary of contemporary
national movements / James Minahan, foreword by Leonard W. Doob.
        p.   cm.
    Includes bibliographical references.
    ISBN 0–313–28354–0 (alk. paper)
    1. World politics—1989–   .  2. Nationalism—History—20th century.
I. Title.
D860.M56   1996
909.82'9'03—dc20          95–6626

British Library Cataloguing in Publication Data is available.

Library of Congress Catalog Card Number: 95–6626
ISBN: 0–313–28354–0

First published in 1996

Greenwood Press, 88 Post Road West, Westport, CT 06881
An imprint of Greenwood Publishing Group, Inc.

Printed in the United States of America

The paper used in this book complies with the
Permanent Paper Standard issued by the National
Information Standards Organization (Z39.48–1984).

10 9 8 7 6 5 4 3 2

# Contents

# Foreword

## Leonard W. Doob

*Sterling Professor Emeritus*

You and I are fortunate to have this book available to us. In it we can gracefully and effortlessly find critical information concerning 210 "nations" on our planet, each of whose inhabitants share a common heritage, take pride in their distinctive culture and present-day beliefs and habits, and have been, or are now, subservient to a larger state or states. In varying degrees these people resent their subservience, and they struggle, sometimes covertly, often overtly, to achieve political independence and hence, in their view, to control their own lives and destinies.

Concisely and clearly, every entry contains the essential facts about the "nations" without states. Provided for each are the names of its leaders, the language of the people, geographic and other demographic data, a description of the precious flag, and especially a sufficiently detailed historical account to explain the background and continuing contacts they have had, and are continuing to have, with other ethnic or culture groups and with the larger and more or less powerful state or states of which they may be unwillingly a part. For better or worse, thus adding to our joy or gloom, almost every day and sometimes throughout the day our mass media report news or views about these cultural "nations."

This book can be used quickly whenever we discover or realize that, as alert individuals or as scholars, we are not omniscient. We can or must consult a reliable source about a "nation" when we read or hear that one of them or its members have proudly publicized its identity by staging a demonstration or celebrating an anniversary, by protesting a grievance or petitioning some organization such as a church or the United Nations, or by committing a noble or atrocious act. This "dictionary" is veritably encyclopedic in its scope; even references for additional reading are provided.

The very existence of these "nations" challenges and stimulates us to raise pressing and not completely solvable questions that forever bounce upon our philosophies and existence. Why do these 210 "nations," which, in the author's words are "only a fraction of the world's stateless nations," continue to exist? We must delve into history and wonder why the differences have emerged and evolved, why they have given rise to conflicts. The questions are not trivial: they make us ask again and again whether economic or some other factors have affected the societies and whether their leaders or other outstanding persons have played crucial roles in formulating or shouting about the issues they feature and press upon their contemporaries. Posed here, too, is the clash between the eternal values of diversity and conformity: is it more important to treasure diversities than uniformities among human beings; or both, depending on goodness knows what? About the future, some of the 210 are dangerous to themselves or to others; how can we advance the struggle, to reduce present or possible violence for ourselves, for them, and for all children, including our own? Finally, are any of the 210 "nations" endangered species like some of our plants and animals, and, if so, should they be protected and preserved? Is the abstract or concrete goal of sustainability relevant for any of the 210? In our effort to reply to these and other profound or trivial questions, at least we can be guided by what the entries in this volume conveniently report.

# Preface

The end of the Cold War, the twentieth century's most protracted conflict, began a process of change that has profoundly altered the world. This volume addresses that change and the stateless nations that have played a vital part in it. *Nations without States: A Historical Dictionary of Contemporary National Movements* follows the development of these nations from the earliest periods of their national histories to the present. This collection of national surveys is an essential guide to the emerging nations that the world ignored or suppressed during the decades of the Cold War, the longest and most stable peace in the history of the modern world. The Cold War did give the world relative peace and stability, but it was a fragile peace and a stability imposed by force. Until now there has not been a reference book that has addressed the post–Cold War nationalist resurgence by focusing on the most basic element of any nationalism, the nation itself.

This dictionary was prepared to fill that void. It contains over 200 national surveys, short articles highlighting the historical, political, social, and economic evolution of the many stateless nations that are now emerging to claim a role in the post–Cold War world order. The worth of the dictionary, in part, derives from its up-to-date information on the virtually unknown nations that are currently making news and those that will produce future headlines, controversies, and conflicts.

Selecting the national surveys to be included in the dictionary presented numerous problems, not the least of which was the difficulty of applying a uniform criterion to the many nationalisms. These new, or newly rediscovered, nations represent a perplexing diversity of national groups that share just one characteristic: they identify themselves as separate nations.

The arduous task of researching this diversity has been made more complicated by the lack of a consensus on what constitutes a nation or nation-state. There is no universally accepted definition of nation, country, or state. The subject continues to generate endless debate and numerous conflicts.

An attempt to apply the criteria used to distinguish independent states floundered on the numerous anomalies encountered. Size is definitely not a criterion. Over forty states recognize a building in Rome, covering just 108.7 acres, as an independent state. Nor is United Nations membership the measure of independence: Ukraine and Belarus (Byelorussia) were founding members of the United Nations in 1945 yet became independent only in 1991. Membership in such international organizations as the International Olympic Committee (IOC) or the Organization of African Unity (OAU) does not necessarily signify political independence. Antarctica issues postage stamps but has no citizens, Palestine has citizens and embassies in dozens of countries but is not, in practice, an independent state, and so on.

*Webster's Unabridged Dictionary* defines the word nation as "a body of people, associated with a particular territory, that is sufficiently conscious of its unity to seek or possess a government particularly its own." Building on this definition the criterion used for selecting the nations for inclusion was narrowed to just three important factors, modified by the diversity of the nations themselves. The three factors are a national claim to a recognizable geographic area; the display of the outward trappings of national consciousness, particularly the adoption of a flag, a very important and very emotional part of any nationalism; and the formation of a specifically nationalist organization or policial grouping that reflects the nation's claim to self-determination. Many stateless nations were eliminated from *Nations without States* when one of these three factors could not be found during the exhaustive research process.

The only exception to the criterion for inclusion is Romanistan. The Rom or Gypsies have evolved a strong national sentiment but, uniquely, without a definite geographic base. The decision to include Romanistan is based on the well-developed Rom national movement that works for an autonomous Rom homeland to be called Romanistan and the fact that the Rom may well constitute the world's largest nation without a state. The proposal by the Rom of Europe that they be recognized as a transnational European national group is a unique approach to their stateless condition and could become the model for other dispersed peoples.

A word also needs to be added about the Native American nations included in the dictionary. These nations fit the criterion used; however, the pending land claims create some geographical confusion. Where the claims remain unsettled or disputed, the territory presently controlled by these nations, usually in the form of reservations, is the territorial extent cited in the pertinent national entries.

In any compilation, the selection process for choosing which material to include is a complex evolution of subtraction and addition. Estimates of the number of stateless nations in the world run as high as 9,000, making the selection process truly a process of elimination. The nations included in this volume therefore represent only a fraction of the world's stateless nations. National sentiment is often difficult to define and is very tricky to measure. For that reason, this pioneering volume contains only those stateless nations that have demonstrated a political mobilization in pursuit of a goal, the status of a self-governing political entity.

Each national entry is divided into several parts or headings: the name and alternative names; simple line drawings of the pertinent flag and maps; the capital city; population statistics, incorporating the total population, the largest national groups, the major languages and religions, and the largest cities and urban areas; geography, including size, location, and political status; independence declarations; the national and other pertinent flags; a brief sketch of the primary national group or groups; and the nation, including the history and national development to the present.

The majority of the nations included in this volume played little or no role in international politics before the end of the Cold War. Some of the nations will be familiar, historically or more recently as news items, but the majority are so unfamiliar that many do not have standardized names or spellings in English. Familiar territorial names often were, or are, the colonial or imposed names that represented a particularly harsh form of cultural suppression. That situation is now being reversed, with cartographers and geographers attempting to settle on the definitive forms of the names of nations, national groups, and languages. Until that process is completed, many of the names used in this volume not only will be unfamiliar but may not appear in even the most comprehensive reference sources.

The capital city, although sometimes not officially recognized as such, is most often the historic and cultural center of the nation. Since one of the primary issues common to a majority of the stateless nations is the right to use their language, the name of the capital and other cities is given, where applicable, in the local language form and is followed by the official, more familiar, or English-language version in parenthesis.

The population figures are the author's estimates for the year 1995. The figures are designated by the abbreviation (95e) before the appropriate statistics. The figures were gleaned from a vast number of sources, both official and unofficial, representing the latest censuses, official estimates, and, where no other sources were available, nationalist claims. Official rates of population growth, urban expansion, and other variables were applied to the figures to arrive at the statistics included in the dictionary.

The population statistics are accompanied by the national breakdown of the total population of the national territory. All the nations included in the dictionary, like the vast majority of the world's independent states, are inhabited by more than one national group. Along with the population of the primary national group, the national and religious divisions within each nation are detailed in percentages. The population figures for the major cities cover the population within the city limits and, where appropriate, the population of the surrounding urban or metropolitan area in parenthesis. The two figures are included in an effort to reconcile the vastly different methods of enumerating urban populations used by the various governments and international agencies. A list of the principal statistical sources is provided at the end of this preface.

The geographic information incorporates the size of the territory, in both square miles (sq.mi.) and square kilometers (sq.km.). Where important disparities over territorial size occur, both the official and claimed territorial extents are included. The geographic location of the territory, in relation to the state, and the current political status of the national territory are covered in the geography section.

A surprising number of the stateless nations have, at some time over the last century, been declared independent states. These declarations, one of the research tools used to investigate the stateless nations, highlight the cyclical nature of world politics. Instability or war prompted most of the past declarations, just as the present world situation has instigated the current spate of declarations and the astonishing number of newly recognized states. More detailed information, state names, and the pertinent dates can be found in Appendix A.

The people, the national group associated with the national territory, for various reasons, often form only a minority of the total population. Territorial claims are invariably based on historic association, not modern ethnic demographic patterns or international borders. Current political events have graphically demonstrated that the overall numbers are much less important than the level of national sentiment and political mobilization. A brief sketch of the population accompanies each entry, highlighting the linguistic, religious, cultural, and national influences that have shaped the primary national group.

Each of the stateless nations has its own particular history, the events and conflicts that have shaped its national characteristics and level of mobilization. The largest part of each national survey is therefore devoted to the historical development of the primary national group. The historical survey follows the evolution and consolidation of the nation from its earliest history to the present. Although meticulous attention has been paid to the content and objectivity of each national survey, the polemic nature of the subject and, in many cases, the lack of official information have made it impossible to eliminate all the unsubstantiated material. The author apologizes for the unintentional inclusion of controversial, dubious, or distorted information gathered from myriad and often unsatisfactory sources.

The two appendixes included in this volume allow the reader to develop a better understanding of the historical evolution of national sentiment over the past century and the rapid proliferation of national organizations that has attended the post–Cold War wave of nationalism. Appendix A sets the numerous declarations of independence in a historical and chronological context, explicitly illustrating the waves of nationalism that have paralleled or accompanied the momentous trends and events of contemporary history. Appendix B provides a geographic listing, by region and nation, of the ever-expanding number of national organizations that herald the mobilization of national sentiment. The number of groups that exist within each national movement graphically illustrates the range of nationalist opinion, although little is known or published about the ideologies, aims, or methods of the majority of these national organizations.

Few of the stateless nations developed in isolation; instead, they were shaped by their relations with governments and neighboring peoples. To facilitate the reader's identification of nations mentioned in the text that are included as a separate national survey in the dictionary, the name of the nation appears with an asterisk (*). An extensive subject index at the end of the volume provides a convenient way to access desired information. Each entry also includes a short bibliographic list as a guide to sources that pertain to the nation in question.

This dictionary was compiled to provide a guide to the nations in the forefront of the post–Cold War nationalist resurgence, a political process all too often considered synonymous with the more extreme and violent aspects of nationalism. This volume is not presented as an assertion that a multitude of new states is about to appear, even though political self-rule is the ultimate goal of the stateless nations included. This dictionary is presented as a unique reference source to the nonstate nations that are spearheading one of the most powerful and enduring political movements of the twentieth century, the pursuit of democracy's basic tenet, self-determination.

## PRINCIPAL STATISTICAL SOURCES

1. National Censuses 1990–1994.
2. World Population Chart 1990 (United Nations).
3. Populations and Vital Statistics 1994 (United Nations).
4. World Tables 1994 (World Bank).
5. World Demographic Estimates and Projections, 1950–2025, 1988 (United Nations).
6. UNESCO Statistical Annual 1990.
7. World Bank Atlas 1993.
8. The Economist Intelligence Unit (Country Report series 1994).
9. World Population Prospects, the 1992 Revision (United Nations).
10. Europa Yearbook 1994.
11. U.S. Department of State publications.
12. The World Factbook.
13. United Nations Statistical Yearbook 1993.
14. United Nations Demographic Yearbook 1993.
15. The Statesman's Yearbook 1994.
16. Encyclopedia Britannica.
17. Encyclopedia Americana.

18. Bureau of the Census, U.S. Department of Commerce 1990.

19. National Geographic Society.

20. Royal Geographical Society.

21. Webster's New Geographical Dictionary 1988.

22  Political Handbook of the World.

23. The Urban Foundation.

24. The Blue Plan.

25. Eurostat, the European Union Statistical Office.

26. Indigenous Minorities Research Council.

27. The Minority Rights Group.

28. Cultural Survival.

29. World Council of Indigenous Peoples.

30. Survival International.

31. China Statistical Yearbook, State Statistical Bureau of the People's Republic of China.

32. Arab Information Center.

33. CIEMEN, Escarré's International Centre for Ethnical Minorities and Nations, Barcelona.

34. International Monetary Fund.

35. American Geographic Society.

# Introduction

Over the last century, perhaps no subject has inspired the passions that surround nationalism and national sentiment. Nationalism, in its most virulent forms, has provoked wars, massacres, terrorism, and genocide. The majority of the world's stateless nations have embraced nationalism but seek greater autonomy or independence through peaceful methods. Although the nationalist resurgence has spawned numerous conflicts, nationalism is not automatically a divisive force, as it provides citizens with an identity and a sense of responsibility and involvement.

An offshoot of the eighteenth-century doctrine of popular sovereignty, nationalism became a driving force in the nineteenth century, shaped and invigorated by the principles of the American and French revolutions. The first wave of modern nationalism culminated in the breakup of Europe's multinational empires after World War I. The second wave began during World War II and continued as the very politicized decolonization process that engulfed the remaining colonial empires as a theater of the Cold War after 1945. The removal of Cold War factionalism has now released a third wave of nationalism, of a scale and diffusion unprecedented in modern history.

The conflicts resulting from this latest nationalist upsurge have reinforced the erroneous beliefs that nationalism is synonymous with extremism and separatism and is confined to the historical "hot spots" in Europe and Asia. One of the basic premises of this volume is that the nationalist resurgence at the end of the twentieth century is spreading to all corners of the world and is set to mold the world's political agenda for decades to come.

The revival of nationalism is not limited to any one continent, nor is it a product of any particular ideology, geographic area, or combination of political or historical factors. The latest wave of nationalism affects rich and poor, large and small, developed and developing. The upsurge of nationalism has already sundered the Soviet Union, Yugoslavia, Czechoslovakia, and Ethiopia and threatens the territorial integrity of most of the world's recognized nation-states.

Nationalism has become an ascendant ideology that is increasingly challenging the nineteenth-century definition of the unitary nation-state. The worldwide nationalist revival is an amplified global echo of the nationalism that swept Europe's stateless nations in the late nineteenth and early twentieth centuries. The belief that political and economic security could be guaranteed only by the existing political order faded as quickly as the ideological and political divisions set in place after World War II. The world's insistence that national structures conform to the existing international borders for the sake of world peace was one of the first casualties of the revolution brought on by the world's new enthusiasm for democracy and self-determination.

The growth of national sentiment can be based on language, history, culture, territorial claims, geographical location, religion, economics, ethnicity, racial background, opposition to another group, or opposition to bad or oppressive government. The mobilization of national sentiment is most often a complicated mixture of some or all of these components. No one of these factors is essential; however, some must be present for group cohesion to be strong enough to evolve a self-identifying nationalism.

Democracy, although widely accepted as the only system that is able to provide the basis of humane political and economic activity, can be a subversive force. Multiparty democracy often generates chaos and instability as centrifugal forces, an inherent part of a free political system, are set loose. The post–Cold War restoration of political pluralism and democratic process has given rise to a rebirth of ethnicity and politicized national identity, while the collapse of Communism in much of the world has shattered the political equilibrium that prevailed for over four decades. The Cold War blocks had mostly succeeded in suppressing or controlling the regional nationalisms in their respective spheres, nationalisms that now have begun to reignite old national desires and ethnic rivalries. Around the globe numerous stateless nations, their identities and aspirations long buried under decades of Cold War tensions, are emerging to claim for themselves the basic principle of democracy: self-determination.

The world has a tendency to simplify national reality and to identify it with state structures, but this century's last and most powerful resurgence of nationalism is a movement against the existing state structures. The nationalism of the stateless nations is rooted in the mismatch of state frontiers relative to the peoples claiming national status. Very few of the so-called nation-states are homogeneous, made up of just one nation, but are, in fact, multiethnic, multinational, and multireligious political entities increasingly threatened by the aspiration of their constituent nations.

The centrifugal forces, held in check by the Cold War, have emerged to challenge the accepted definition of what constitutes a nation and its rights. The doctrine of statism is slowly being superseded by a post–Cold War internationalism that is reshaping the world's view of the unitary nation-state and, what is more important, the world's view of who or what constitutes a nation.

The emphasis on the rights of states, rather than the rights of the individuals and nations within them, has dictated international attitudes to nationalism, buttressed by ignorance and failure to understand the nation versus the nation-state. The use of condemnatory labels—separatist, secessionist, rebel, splittist, and so on—has been a powerful state weapon against those who seek a different state structure on behalf of their nations.

Two main trends are vying to shape the post–Cold War world. One is the movement to form continental or regional economic-political groupings that would allow for smaller political units as members. The other is the emergence of smaller and smaller national units as older states are broken up. The two trends are not mutually exclusive. The nation-state and its absolute sovereignty are fading and giving way to historical trends—the nation, rather than the nation-state, in one direction, and supranational bodies, such as the United Nations, European Union, and even the North American Free Trade Area (NAFTA), in the other.

The rapidly changing political and economic realities have swept aside the old arguments that population size, geographic location, and economic viability are deterrents to national self-determination. The revival of nationalism is converging with the emergence of continental political and economic units theoretically able to accommodate smaller national units within overarching political, economic, and security frameworks. The nationalist resurgence is inexorably moving global politics away from the present state system to a new political order more closely resembling the world's ethnic and historical geography.

The rapid spread of national sentiment, affecting even nations long considered assimilated or quiescent, is attracting considerable attention, but the focus of this attention is invariably on its impact on established governments and its effect on international relations. As the Cold War withered away, it was replaced by a bewildering number and variety of nationalisms that, in turn, spawned a global movement toward the breakdown of the existing system of nation-states.

The global impact of the worldwide nationalist upsurge has only begun to be felt or studied. The biggest impulse to the recent explosion of nationalism was the end of the Cold War. The fall of Communist dictatorships released nationalisms across Europe and the former Soviet Union. That nationalism is now feeding on itself as the freedom won by many historically stateless nations has emboldened others to demand greater self-determination.

The third wave of twentieth-century nationalism, with its emphasis on democratic self-determination, is set to top the international agenda well into the twenty-first century. The nationalist revival, global in scope, has strengthened submerged national, ethnic, and regional identities and has shattered the conviction that assimilation would eventually homogenize the existing nation-states.

A unique feature of this current wave of nationalism is the growing mutual cooperation and support among and between the stateless nations internationally.

Most of the nations selected for inclusion in the dictionary are members or aspiring members of two organizations that, for the first time, provide a legitimate forum in which to gain strength through numbers and to publicize their causes without recourse to violence. The larger of the organizations, the Unrepresented Nations and Peoples Organization (UNPO), was formed in 1991 by six stateless nations, four of which have since been recognized as independent states. The organization, its membership swollen by the representatives of dozens of stateless nations, is already referred to as an alternative United Nations. The second group, the Free Europe Alliance, is less global in scale but, like the UNPO, is inundated by membership applications.

The political and cultural renaissance spreading through the world's stateless nations is inexorably moving global politics away from the present system of sovereign states, each jealously defending its authority, to a new world order more closely resembling the world's true national and historical geography. A world community dominated by democracy must inevitably recognize the rights of the stateless nations, including the right to choose their own future. The diffusion and force of contemporary national movements make it imperative that the nationalist phenomenon is studied and understood.

# NATIONS WITHOUT STATES

# ABKHAZIA

## Apsny; Abkhazskaya

*CAPITAL: Sukhumi*

*POPULATION:* (All population figures are estimates for early 1992, prior to the outbreak of fighting in the region.) (92e) 544,000 : 150,000 Abkhaz and Abaza in Georgia and adjacent areas of Russia. MAJOR NATIONAL GROUPS: (92e) Georgian 44%, Abkhaz 20%, Russian 16%, Armenian 6%, Ukrainian 2%, Pontian Greek 2%. MAJOR RELIGIONS: Georgian Orthodox, Sunni Muslim, Russian Orthodox, Armenian Orthodox. MAJOR CITIES: (92e) Sukhumi 138,000 (166,000), Tkvarceli 45,000, Gagra 37,000, Ochamchira 30,000, Gudauta 27,000, Gali 20,000.

*GEOGRAPHY:* AREA: 3,299 sq.mi.-8,547 sq.km. LOCATION: Abkhazia occupies a narrow coastal plain, backed by a spur of the western Caucasus Mountains, in northwestern Georgia. Abkhazia borders the Russian Federation on the north, the Black Sea on the southwest, and the Georgian region of Mingrelia on the southeast. POLITICAL STATUS: The status of Abkhazia, called Apsny by the Abkhaz, is disputed. In 1992 Abkhazia was declared an independent republic; however, officially it remains an autonomous republic within the Republic of Georgia.

*INDEPENDENCE DECLARED:* 8 March 1918; 4 March 1921; 23 July 1992.

*FLAG:* The Abkhaz national flag, the official flag of the breakaway republic, has seven green and white stripes with a red canton on the upper hoist bearing a white hand below an arch of seven white, five-pointed stripes.

*PEOPLE:* The Abkhaz, including the 35,000 Abaza living in the Karachai-Balkaria* region of the adjoining Russian Federation, are a North Caucasian nation encompassing four major geographical and cultural groups, the Muslim Gudauta, Abzhui and Abaza, and the Orthodox Samurzakan. The Abkhaz and Abaza, both groups calling themselves Apsua, speak a Caucasian language of the Abkhazo-Adygheian language group, an extremely complicated mixture of Caucasian and archaic Latin elements with its own alphabet. The language, considered the world's fastest phonetically, has complete information, such as word root and tense, often conveyed by a single consonant. Until the secessionist violence erupted in 1992, the Georgian population constituted the largest of the ten national groups living in the region.

*THE NATION:* Abkhazia, forming part of the region thought to be the original home of the Caucasian race, was known to the ancient maritime peoples of the Mediterranean. Greeks colonized the coastal regions as early as the sixth century B.C. Latinized following the Roman conquest of the Greek cities in 65 B.C., the Abkhaz adopted much of the Romans' Latin culture and language. In the sixth century A.D., in compliance with an imperial decree commanding all pagans in the empire to convert, the Abkhaz adopted Christianity as their national religion.

Abkhaz kings in the eighth century united all of western Georgia under their rule to form the region's first independent Abkhaz kingdom. Weakened by wars and internal strife, the kingdom declined, and by the tenth century most of its territory had come under the rule of the expanding Georgian kingdom. In the early sixteenth century, the Turks began to raid the coast, finally annexing Abkhazia to their Ottoman Empire in 1578. Over the next decades a majority of the Abkhaz abandoned Christianity for the Islamic religion of the Turks.

In 1810 several Abkhaz dukes signed a protectorate treaty with the Russians, then expanding into the Caucasian territories of the decaying Ottoman Empire. Repressive Russian rule sparked sporadic revolts and drove thousands of Abkhaz to migrate to Turkish territory. In 1864 the Russian authorities deposed the Abkhaz dukes and formally annexed the region. Russian attempts to promote assimilation, particularly official efforts to convert the Muslim Abkhaz to Orthodox Christianity, incited a popular uprising in 1866. The Russian military quickly defeated the poorly armed Abkhaz army of 20,000 and subjected the majority of the defeated Abkhaz to virtual serfdom on the Russian and Georgian estates established on confiscated Abkhaz lands.

The Russian Empire, devastated by nearly three years of war, was swept by revolution in February 1917, leaving Abkhazia effectively independent as local government collapsed. Abkhaz leaders formed the Abkhaz National Council and asserted their nation's right to autonomy within a democratic Russia. Occupied by Georgian troops following the Bolshevik coup that ended Russia's democratic experiment in October 1917, the Abkhaz organized resistance and, in February 1918, rose to expel the Georgians. The rebels proclaimed Abkhazia independent on 8 March 1918. Their independent state lasted just forty-two days before Bolshevik troops invaded. In desperation the Abkhaz leaders appealed to neighboring Georgia for military aid. Once having driven the Bolsheviks out of

Abkhazia, the Georgians stayed to incorporate unwilling Abkhazia into their newly independent republic.

The Abkhaz revolted against Georgian rule in early 1921 and again declared their homeland an independent state on 4 March 1921. The resulting chaos within Georgia provided a pretext for the Red Army's subsequent invasion and conquest of both Abkhazia and Georgia. In 1930, as part of the Soviet's nationalities policy, Abkhazia became an autonomous republic within the Georgian Soviet Socialist Republic.

Stalin, himself an ethnic Georgian and particularly suspicious of the small Muslim nations of the Caucasus, in 1943 prepared a plan to deport the Abkhaz to Central Asia, but the plan was later postponed. Preparations for the mass deportation of the Abkhaz began again in 1953, but due to Stalin's death in that year the Abkhaz were spared the horrors experienced by other Caucasian peoples deported from their homelands on Stalin's orders.

Massive Georgian immigration to Abkhazia, undertaken under Stalin's long dictatorial rule, reduced the Abkhaz to minority status in their homeland by the end of World War II. Resentment of the Georgian's dominant status fanned tense ethnic relations in the region and stimulated an Abkhaz national revival in the 1970s and 1980s.

The liberalization of Soviet life in the late 1980s accelerated the growth of Abkhaz nationalism. In 1988 a nationalist popular front organization, Aiglara (Unity), formed, and, for the first time since 1921, the Abkhaz National Council convened. On 18 March 1989 the council called for Abkhaz secession from Georgia, which provoked a strong Georgian nationalist reaction and violent confrontations in Sukhumi and other Abkhaz cities.

The Georgian republic regained its independence at the disintegration of the Soviet Union in 1991, claiming Abkhazia as part of its national territory. An ethnocentric Georgian national government exacerbated tensions between Georgians and Abkhazians, whose sense of national identity is as strong as that of the Georgians. On 23 July 1992 the Abkhaz legislature reinstated the republic's 1925 constitution, effectively declaring Abkhazia an independent republic. In August the Georgian military occupied the region, setting off a bitter war of secession.

The separatist forces slowly drove the Georgian military from the region and, in September 1993, took the capital, Sukhumi. Some 200,000 Georgians fled from Abkhazia into western Georgia. In June 1994 the Georgian government reluctantly accepted 3,000 Russian troops on the Abkhaz border, effectively bringing independent Abkhazia under de facto Russian protection.

*SELECTED BIBLIOGRAPHY:*

Boyette, William. *Soviet Georgia.* 1988.
Colton, Timothy, and Robert Levgold, eds. *After the Soviet Union.* 1992.
Dins, Sham. *Perestroika and the Nationalities Quest in the USSR.* 1991.
Seton-Watson, Hugh. *The Russian Empire, 1801–1917.* 1967.

# ACEH

**Achin; Atchin; Atjeh**

*CAPITAL: Kutaradja (Banda Aceh)*

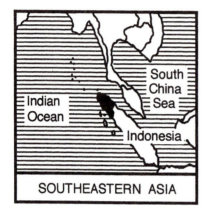

SOUTHEASTERN ASIA

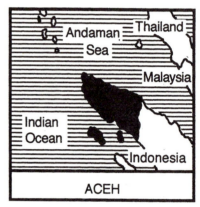

ACEH

*POPULATION:* (95e) 3,799,000 : 3,425,000 Acehnese in Indonesia. MAJOR NATIONAL GROUPS: (95e) Acehnese 86%, other Indonesian. MAJOR LANGUAGES: Acehnese, Batak, Bahasa Indonesia. MAJOR RELIGIONS: (95e) Sunni Muslim 99%. MAJOR CITIES: (95e) Kutaradja 126,000, Langsa 91,000, Lhoksennane 55,000, Sinabang 28,000, Sabang 20,000.

*GEOGRAPHY:* AREA: 21,381 sq.mi.-55,392 sq.km. LOCATION: Aceh occupies a strategic position on the northwestern tip of the island of Sumatra, the farthest west of the islands of the Malay Archipelago, lying in the Indian Ocean just southwest of the Malay Peninsula. POLITICAL STATUS: Aceh forms a special autonomous district of the Republic of Indonesia, the only one of its kind in the country.

*INDEPENDENCE DECLARED:* 11 February 1950.

*FLAG:* The Acehnese national flag, the flag of the national movement, is a red field bearing a centered white crescent moon and five-pointed star and with black horizontal stripes, outlined in white, at the top and bottom.

*PEOPLE:* The Acehnese are a nation of mixed Malay, Arabic, and Indian ancestry, physically resembling the other Malay peoples but with pronounced Indian and Arabic features, almond-shaped eyes, and long, straight Semitic noses. The Acehnese speak a Malayo-Polynesian language, with a marked Arabic admixture, written in its own alphabet, a modified Arabic script. The Acehnese homeland is subject to the Bohorok, a hot, dry wind that blows during the monsoon season, a wind the Acehnese claim has shaped their national character.

*THE NATION:* A powerful ancient Malay state, Aceh often controlled parts of the nearby Malay Peninsula, its power eventually curbed by the Indianized states established on Java and Sumatra by Hindu immigrants in the seventh century A.D. Muslim Arabs settled the Acehnese coast in the twelfth century, soon converting the Acehnese to their Islamic religion. An independent sultanate, established on the Muslim model, maintained strong ties to the west, ties strengthened by continued Arabic immigration and the arrival of Gujarati Muslims from northwestern India.

The sultanate's political and military power, gradually diminished by wars with neighboring states, recovered under the rule of Ali Mubhayat Syah in the early sixteenth century. During the reign of Iskander Shah, in the seventeenth century, Aceh experienced a great flowering of culture and political power, a golden age financed by a virtual monopoly on the lucrative Sumatra pepper trade.

Wealthy Aceh, visited by Portuguese fleets under DeCunha in 1506 and Sequeira in 1509, was the goal of the first Dutch expedition to the Indies in 1599 and of an English East India Company expedition in 1602. European encroachments and a devastating civil war began a long period of Acehnese decline. The state, in an occurence unusual in the East, was ruled by a succession of four female monarchs between 1641 and 1699.

The sultanate established formal treaty relations with Great Britain in 1819 and was recognized as a sovereign state by both Britain and the Dutch in 1824. The two European powers, despite their formal recognition of the sultanate, continued to vie for influence and for control of the important spice trade. An Anglo-Dutch treaty of 1871 acknowledged Dutch supremacy in the Indies and effectively relegated Aceh to the Dutch sphere of influence.

Negotiations between the American consul in Singapore and Acehnese ministers in 1873 provided the pretext for Dutch aggression. Dutch gunboats shelled the Acehnese capital while colonial troops landed on the coast, thus setting off the longest and bloodiest colonial war in Dutch history, a war that continued up to World War I.

Japanese forces, advancing on the islands in 1942, inspired an Acehnese uprising, and, even though the Japanese drove the Dutch forces from the sultanate, the conservative Acehnese rejected Japanese overtures. Following the Japanese surrender in 1945, many Acehnese joined the anticolonial forces fighting Dutch attempts to regain control of their colonial possessions in the East Indies.

Initially rejecting inclusion in a united Indonesia, the Acehnese were finally persuaded to accept the status of an autonomous state within a federal Indonesia in 1949. The United States of Indonesia, dominated by the numerically predominant Javanese of the central island, soon began to disintegrate as opposition mounted to attempts to abolish the autonomy of the member states. Rejecting direct rule from Java, the Acehnese rebelled in early 1950. The Acehnese rebel leaders declared Aceh independent of Indonesia on 11 February 1950, but, in spite of fierce Acehnese resistance, the secession collapsed as Indonesian troops overwhelmed the poorly armed rebels.

The Indonesian central government, to undermine the nationalist movement, granted Aceh some autonomy in 1956. Two years later, alarmed by the growing Communist influence in Java, Acehnese leaders demanded full autonomy. Militant nationalists mobilized in the 1960s, but gained majority support only following the imposition of a new transmigration policy, the government-sponsored resettlement of population from the seriously overcrowded central island of Java to the less populated islands.

The Acehnese separatists, led by Hassan di Tiro, the eighth head of the dynasty established in Aceh in 1874, fought bloody battles with government forces throughout the 1970s. In 1980 di Tiro died in battle with the Indonesian military. His memory is revered as a national hero and a martyr to Acehnese nationalism and freedom.

The Indonesian government announced the end of the separatist movement in 1986, but fighting soon resumed and by 1990 had assumed the aspect of a full-scale war, leaving over 2,000 dead, many killed in atrocities carried out by government troops. Acehnese nationalists, in 1991, asserted that the advantage of Indonesian citizenship is now outweighed by mistrust and the strong reaction to the indiscriminate violence of the government forces, with the only solution independence for Aceh.

The Acehnese point to their extensive natural gas reserves, vast forests, and mineral deposits as the natural wealth that holds the promise of an independent Aceh. The uncontrolled exploitation of these natural resources by the Indonesian government has become one of the main nationalist issues in the region.

*SELECTED BIBLIOGRAPHY:*
Hawthorne, Daniel. *Islands of the East Indies.* 1977.
Hyma, Albert. *History of the Dutch in the Far East.* 1953.
Schnitger, F. M. *Forgotten Kingdoms in Sumatra.* 1989.

# ADAL

**Dankalia; Dancalia; Danakilia**

*Capital: Desse (Dese)*

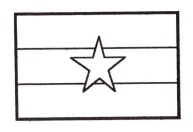

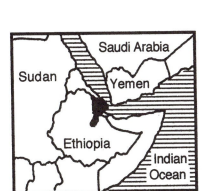

NORTHEASTERN AFRICA

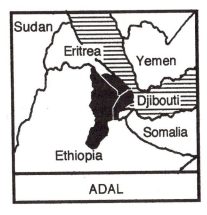

ADAL

*POPULATION:* (95e) 2,280,000 : 2,370,000 Afar and Saho in Ethiopia, Djibouti, and Eritrea. MAJOR NATIONAL GROUPS: (95e) Afar-Saho 85%, Arab, Somali, other Ethiopian, other Djiboutian, other Eritrean. MAJOR LANGUAGES: Afar-Saho, Arabic, Tigrinya, Somali. MAJOR RELIGIONS: Sunni Muslim, Ethiopian Orthodox. MAJOR CITIES: (95e) ETHIOPIA: Desse (Dese) 137,000, Serdo 14,000, Aussa (Asyita) 10,000. DJIBOUTI: Tadjoura 20,000, Obock 13,000. ERITREA: Assab (Aseb) 60,000, Beylul 15,000.

*GEOGRAPHY:* AREA: 31,246 sq.mi.-80,948 sq.km. LOCATION: Adal lies in the Danakil Basin of East Africa's Great Rift Valley in eastern Ethiopia, northern Djibouti, and southern Eritrea. The so-called Afar Triangle is one of the world's hottest regions, at its lowest point 383 feet below sea level, and is mostly desert east of the coastal mountains that front the Red Sea. POLITICAL STATUS: Adal has no official status; the region claimed by nationalists forms the Afar autonomous region of Ethiopia, the *cercles* (districts) of Djibouti north and west of the Gulf of Tadjoura, and the districts of Eritrea south of the Gulf of Zula.

*FLAG:* The Afar-Saho flag, the flag of the largest national organization, the Afar Liberation Front (ALF), is a horizontal tricolor of pale blue, white, and green bearing a centered, five-pointed red star. OTHER FLAG(S): The traditional Afar-Saho flag is a green or black field charged with the Shahada in white Arabic script centered and a small white crescent moon and five-pointed star on the upper hoist.

*PEOPLE:* The Afar, including the closely related Saho, are a nation of mixed ancestry, the descendants of ancient Semitic and Hamitic peoples with a later Arabic admixture. The Afar speak a Cushitic language of the Hamitic group of the Hamito-Semitic languages considerably altered by exposure to Arabic. Divided into tribes, subtribes, and clans, the Afar are also identified by a class system that segregates the population into two distinct divisions, the Asimara (Red) nobles and the Adoimara (White) commoners. The Saho, although often considered a branch of the Afar people, form ten small tribal groups and account for some 10% of the national population.

*THE NATION:* An ancient Semitic people, migrants from southern Arabia, settled the Danakil Basin thousands of years ago. Mixing with the indigenous Hamitic peoples, the migrants developed a nomadic, tribal culture in the hot, dry desert. The forbidding landscape of their homeland discouraged most invaders, although at times the tribes came under the nominal rule of the ancient Ethiopian Empire.

Seafaring Arabs, spurred by missionary zeal to spread their new Islamic religion, converted the coastal tribes to Islam in the seventh century. Carried by caravans and raiders, the new religion spread to the isolated interior tribes between the tenth and twelfth centuries. Modeled on the Muslim tradition, small Afar sultanates flourished, eventually forming a powerful confederation, called Adal, in the twelfth century.

A gifted Afar military leader, Ahmad ibn Ghazi, organized a *jihad* (holy war) against Christian Ethiopia in the sixteenth century. Leading a great army of Afars, Sahos, Somalis, and other Muslim peoples, Ghazi scored a decisive victory in 1529, utterly destroying the Ethiopian states except for a few mountain strongholds. With the assistance of Portuguese soldiers, a resurgent Ethiopia defeated the Muslims in 1541, causing the Afar-Saho to withdraw to their desert homeland and to avoid contacts with outsiders over the next century.

Italian colonial forces established a base on the coast at Assab in 1869 and slowly expanded their conquests at the expense of the Egyptians and Turks. In 1882 the Italians created a colonial administration for the region; however, the forbidding desert confined their authority to the Red Sea coast. Christian Ethiopia, fearing further European expansion, conquered the Muslim stronghold of Harar and sent an army against the Afar Sultanate of Aussa, thus adding the first Afar territory in the eastern lowlands to their expanding empire. The Afar-Saho homeland was eventually divided by three colonial powers, Italy in the northern coastal area, Ethiopia in the lowlands, and France, which gained control of the Afar Sultanate of Tadjoura. The three powers agreed to new boundaries that effectively divided Adal into three parts, the partition reflected by a new name, the Afar Triangle.

The Afar tribes, nominally ruled by three sultanates, one of which, Tadjoura, lay wholly within French territory, refused to recognize the imposed international borders, continued to move their herds across the colonial frontiers, and, except for those living near the larger towns, were little affected by the colonial administrations. Not until 1928 did the first European cross the huge Danakil

Basin, while most of the enormous natural depression remained outside government controls until after World War II.

The Afars of Italian Eritrea, under British administration after World War II, were the first of their nation to encounter modern education and ideas, and they later provided the leadership of the Afar national movement that formed after Eritrea was federated with feudal, Christian Ethiopia in 1952. Afar nationalism gained some support over the next two decades but became a popular movement only after the 1974 Ethiopian revolution.

The Afar, having initially backed the overthrow of Ethiopia's feudal monarchy, were outraged by the new Marxist government's response to an Afar petition for famine aid and protection of their traditional grazing lands. The official answer was to order Marxist land reform, parceling out the best of the Afar grazing lands to farmers, many from outside the region. The violent suppression of Afar protests provoked a mass exodus. Led by Sultan Ali Mirah, thousands of Afar fled to French territory, where they formed the first openly separatist national organization, the Afar Liberation Front (ALF).

The collapse of Ethiopia's Marxist government in 1991 was followed by the creation of an autonomous Afar state within newly democratic Ethiopia, but autonomy has failed to satisfy the growing Afar demands for unification and independence. A serious Afar revolt in northern Djibouti, launched in November 1991, has mobilized Afar nationalists in all three areas of the divided nation. The independence, from Ethiopia, of Eritrea, in May 1993, and a major offensive against the Afars in Djibouti, in July 1993, have strengthened demands for a united, independent Afar state.

*SELECTED BIBLIOGRAPHY:*
Hancock, Graham. *African Ark: People and Ancient Culture of Ethiopia and the Horn of Africa.* 1990.
Legum, Colin. *Horn of Africa in Continuing Crisis.* 1979.
Lewis, I. M. *Nationalism and Self-Determination in the Horn of Africa.* 1984.
Thompson, Virginia, and Richard Adloff. *Djibouti: Pawn of the Horn of Africa.* 1981.

# AJARISTAN

**Adjaria; Adzharistan; Adzharia**

*CAPITAL: Batumi*

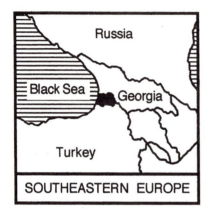

*POPULATION:* (95e) 389,000 : 250,000 Ajars (Ajarians) in Georgia and another 55,000, called Laz, in adjacent areas of Turkey. MAJOR NATIONAL GROUPS: (95E) Ajar 65%, Georgian 14%, Russian 8%, Armenian 5%, Pontian Greek 2%. MAJOR LANGUAGES: Georgian, Russian, Armenian. MAJOR RELIGIONS: (95e) Sunni Muslim 68%, Georgian Orthodox, Russian Orthodox, Armenian Orthodox. MAJOR CITIES: (95e) Batumi 141,000 (171,000), Kobuleti 36,000.

*GEOGRAPHY:* AREA: 1,160 sq.mi.-3,005 sq.km. LOCATION: Ajaristan lies in southwestern Georgia, a mountainous region sloping down to a narrow, subtropical plain on the Black Sea just north of the international border between Turkey and Georgia. POLITICAL STATUS: Ajaristan forms an autonomous republic within the Republic of Georgia.

*INDEPENDENCE DECLARED:* 18 April 1918; 12 February 1921.

*FLAG:* The Ajar national flag, the flag of the national movement, is a green field with a narrow red border charged with a centered white crescent moon and five-pointed star.

*PEOPLE:* The Ajarians are a South Caucasian people of Georgian ancestry who speak a Gurian dialect of the Georgian language called Guruli, which utilizes many borrowings from Turkish. The Ajar nation is traditionally divided into the Ajars in the south and east and the Kabuletians in the north and west. The majority adhere to the Hanafite rite of Sunni Islam, and, even though their religion and culture separates them from the Georgians, they have not been recognized as a separate national group since the 1930s.

*THE NATION:* Ajaristan, known to the ancient world as Colchis, flourished following the colonization of the region by the ancient Greeks between the sixth and fourth centuries B.C. Celebrated in the Greek legends of *Jason and the Argonauts* and *Medea*, Colchis remained part of the Greek world for centuries. In the first century B.C. Colchis formed an important part of the Greek kingdom of Pontus.

Conquered by the Romans in 62 B.C., Colchis, called Iberia, became a prosperous, Latinized province that eventually adopted the new Christian religion that spread through the Roman Empire. Following the decline of Roman power, in the sixth century A.D., the region formed part of the Christian Armenian kingdom and in the ninth century became part of the expanding Georgian kingdom.

The inhabitants, concentrated in the coastal plain and protected by high mountains, remained semi-independent until the fifteenth-century Turkish conquest. Over the next two centuries a majority adopted the Turks' Islamic culture and religion, their homeland forming an important part of the administrative district called Lazistan.

Expanding at the expense of the decaying Ottoman Empire in the nineteenth century, Russia finally forced Turkey to cede the last Ajar territory, Batumi, in 1878. Undeterred by the frequent disturbances in the region, the Russians developed Batumi as a major Black Sea port and fostered the growth of subtropical agriculture in the region.

The Muslim Ajars, restive under Christian rule, rose during the 1905 Russian Revolution and attacked the estates of the Georgian and Russian landlords who dominated their homeland. Subdued by imperial troops, Ajar resentment of the privileges enjoyed by their Christian overlords continued to grow, reinforced by their pro-Turkish sentiment as tensions mounted prior to World War I.

Ajaristan formed part of the front line when war began in August 1914. Ajar nationalists, in December 1914, rebelled in support of a Turkish invasion, and their people suffered severe reprisals when the Turkish troops withdrew under Russian pressure.

The onset of the Russian Revolution in February 1917 threw the region into chaos as the local government collapsed. Armed bands of Russian soldiers and Ajar, Georgian, and Armenian nationalists roamed the area at will. Turkish troops took Ajaristan in April 1918 with the active assistance of the Ajar nationalists. With Turkish encouragement the nationalists declared Ajaristan independent of Russia on 18 April 1918, calling their new state the Southwestern Caucasian Republic. An Ajar national council, the Showra, formally claimed the Muslim majority districts of Batumi, Kars, Akhaltsikh, Skhalkalaki, Sharur, and Nakichevan, areas also claimed by newly independent Georgia and Armenia.

British troops, amid the escalating Russian civil war, occupied Batumi in December 1918, the British authorities promising to protect the new republic until its fate could be decided by the Paris Peace Conference. In April 1919, pressured by the governments of Georgia and Armenia, the British forcibly disbanded the Showra and in June 1920 evacuated all British troops from the area. Quickly overcoming Ajar resistance, the Georgians took Batumi and the north while the Armenians incorporated Kars and the south.

The Soviet Red Army, victorious in the civil war, invaded independent Georgia in early 1921. Amid the ensuing disorder, the Ajars declared their homeland independent on 12 February 1921 and requested Turkish military aid. In March Turkish troops occupied the region and over vehement Ajar protests attempted to annex the region to Turkey. Pressed by the Soviet government, the Turks withdrew in May but retained control of Kars and the southern districts. Soviet Ajaristan, given the status of an autonomous republic, was incorporated into Soviet Georgia.

Counted as ethnic Georgians in Soviet censuses since the 1930s, the loyalty of the Muslim Ajars remained suspect. Stalin drew up a plan for their deportation during World War II, but the plan was postponed and finally abandoned at Stalin's death in 1953. Spared by Stalin's death, the Ajars experienced a modest national revival that strengthened Ajar resistance to Georgian attempts to eliminate their autonomy and to promote assimilation during the 1960s and 1970s.

In the wake of the failed Soviet coup in August 1991, Georgia regained its independence under a nationalist, ethnocentric government that fanned ethnic and religious tensions in the state before its overthrow in January 1992. In spite of the overtures of the new Georgian government, the attitude of the radical Georgian nationalists (that the Ajars represent a threat to the Christian Georgian state) has come to dominate the Ajars' relations with the Georgian government.

The only area of Georgia not to have experienced violent confrontations since Georgia regained its independence, Ajaristan is increasingly going its own way. Led by Aslan Abashidze, the Ajar government has tried to isolate the region from the chaos overtaking Georgia. In late 1993 the government refused to take all but a few thousand of the refugees fleeing the separatist war in Abkhazia,* fearing that the delicate ethnic balance in the republic would be damaged and Ajaristan, like the other areas of Georgia, would collapse in chaos and violence.

*SELECTED BIBLIOGRAPHY:*

Allen, W. E. *A History of the Georgian People.* 1978.
Boyette, William. *Soviet Georgia.* 1988.
Minorsky, Vladimir. *Studies in Caucasian History.* 1953.

# ALAND

Åland; Ålandöerna; Ahvenanmaa;
Aland Islands

*CAPITAL: Mariehamm (Maarianhamina)*

NORTHEASTERN EUROPE

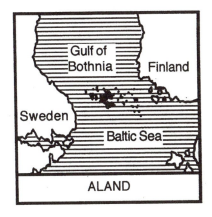

ALAND

*POPULATION:* (95e) 25,000 : 30,000 Alanders in Finland. MAJOR NA-
TIONAL GROUPS: (95e) Alander 96%, other Finn 3%. MAJOR LAN-
GUAGES: Swedish, Finnish. MAJOR RELIGION: Lutheran. MAJOR CITY:
(95e) Mariehamm (Maarianhamina) 11,000.

*GEOGRAPHY:* AREA: 581 sq.mi.-1,505 sq.km. LOCATION: Aland, called
Ahvenanmaa, the Land of Streams, in Finnish, is an archipelago of 6,544 islands
and islets in the Baltic Sea at the mouth of the Gulf of Bothnia fifteen miles
west of the Finnish mainland and fifteen miles east of Sweden. The islands,
only some 700 of which are inhabited, take their name from the largest and
most important island of the group, Aland. POLITICAL STATUS: Aland forms
an autonomous province of the Republic of Finland.

*FLAG:* The Aland national flag, the official flag of the autonomous state, is
a blue field bearing a red Scandinavian cross outlined in yellow.

*PEOPLE:* The Alanders, overwhelmingly of Swedish descent, are a separate
Scandinavian nation whose unique culture incorporates both Swedish and Finnish influences. The population of the islands, following a sharp decline from
nearly 30,000 in the 1950s, mostly due to immigration to Sweden, has stabilized
over the last decade. The Alanders, following a long dispute between Sweden
and Finland, have been recognized as a separate Scandinavian nation by the
Nordic Council, a regional grouping of the Scandinavian states.

*THE NATION:* Inhabited from prehistoric times, the island's original inhabitants were absorbed by Finns migrating from the east in the eighth century A.D.
The Christian Swedes launched a crusade to conquer and Christianize the pagan

Finns in 1154. The islands, colonized by the victorious Swedes, became thoroughly Swedish in culture and language and remained an integral part of the Swedish kingdom for over 600 years.

The strategically important islands, contested by Sweden and Russia during the eighteenth-century wars for supremacy in the north, were ceded, along with Swedish Finland, to the Russian Empire in 1809. The Russian government militarized and fortified the islands, which remained the center of international disputes and treaties through much of the next century. Shelled by an Anglo-French fleet in 1854, during the Crimean War, the island's fortifications were later destroyed, and remilitarization was forbidden under the terms of the 1856 Treaty of Paris.

The energetic Alanders, stifled by the unpopular and repressive Russian bureaucracy, looked beyond their islands to sustain themselves. A huge Alander merchant fleet dominated the nineteenth-century European grain trade and engendered a tradition of independence and self-reliance that has become an important part of the Alander national character.

Affected by the wave of nationalist sentiment that swept Europe in the late nineteenth century, the islanders developed a particular Alander self-awareness fanned by opposition to repressive Russian rule. Alander resentment erupted in open conflict during the 1905 Russian Revolution, the rebellion quickly crushed by troops hastily dispatched from the mainland.

The outbreak of war in 1914 emphasized Aland's strategic military importance. With British and French consent, the Russians refortified the islands in 1915. The remilitarization of their islands spurred the growth of nationalism and pro-Swedish sentiment during the war.

The Republic of Finland, independent of Russia in 1917, claimed the islands as part of its national territory. Asserting their right to self-determination, the Alanders voted to secede from Finland and to unite with Sweden. The conflicting claims to the islands brought Sweden and Finland close to war in 1920. In September of that year the dispute was referred to the new League of Nations, which decided in Finland's favor in June 1921. The agreement provided for an autonomous Aland state in union with the Finnish Republic.

The Alander economy, based on tourism, is buoyed by the duty-free goods sold on ships moving between Aland and the mainland ports in Finland and Sweden. The tourist income gave the Alanders one of the highest incomes in the region in the 1980s.

Alander nationalism, dormant for decades under liberal Finnish authority, again became an issue in the late 1980s, stimulated by the disintegration of the Soviet Union and Finland's application to join the European Union. The Alanders, already enjoying most of the trappings of independence, took a step closer in March 1991 with the endorsement of a proposal to introduce their own currency, the Aland daler. A revised autonomy statute, effective on 1 January 1993, provides for greater economic and legislative freedom.

Finland's entry in the European Union has raised fears that membership will affect the island's demilitarized status and the duty-free tourism that contributes 70% of the Alanders' national income. The Alanders negotiated and won special concessions from the European Union. For tax purposes Aland will count as a country outside the Union, allowing them to go on selling duty-free goods after 1999, when that becomes illegal. The deal also allows the Alanders to block other Europeans from buying properties or setting up industries in the islands. The negotiated concessions, finalized in November 1994, brought the Alanders a step closer to full independence within the European Union.

*SELECTED BIBLIOGRAPHY:*

Hamalainen, P. K. *In Time of Storm: Revolution, Civil War and the Ethnolinguistic Issue in Finland.* 1979.

Matts, Dreijer. *History of the Aland People: From the Stone Age to Gustavus Wasa.* 1986.

Mead, W. R. *A Historic Geography of Scandinavia.* 1981.

# ALSACE

**Alsace-Lorraine; Elsass-Lotharingen**

*CAPITAL: Strassburg (Strasbourg)*

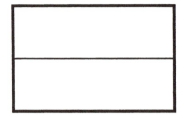

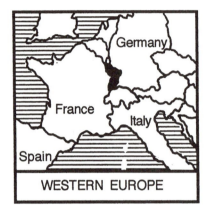

WESTERN EUROPE

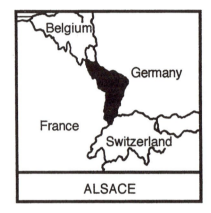

ALSACE

*POPULATION:* (95e) 2,431,000 : 2,120,000 Alsatians in France. MAJOR NATIONAL GROUPS: (95e) Alsatian (including Lorrainers) 75%, other French, German. MAJOR LANGUAGES: French, Alsatian (Elsaessisch), standard German. MAJOR RELIGIONS: Roman Catholic 74%, Protestant 23%. MAJOR CITIES: (95e) ALSACE: Strassburg (Strasbourg) 243,000 (477,000), Mülhausen (Mulhouse) 109,000 (251,000), Kolmar (Colmar) 68,000 (99,000), Sarreguemines (Sarregemund) 25,000, Haguenau 24,000 (40,000). LORRAINE: Metz 121,000 195,000), Diedenhofen (Thionville) 44,000 (156,000), Forbach 29,000 (73,000), Hayingen (Hayange) 24,000 (89,000), Grossmoyluvre (Moyeurve-Grande) 10,000 (87,000). FRANCHE-COMTÉ: Belfurt (Belfort) 49,000 (86,000).

*GEOGRAPHY:* AREA: 5,842 sq.mi.-15,134 sq.km. LOCATION: Alsace lies in northeastern France in the valley of the Rhine River, which forms the frontier between France and Germany. Alsace borders Germany on the east and north, Luxembourg on the northwest, and Switzerland on the south. POLITICAL STATUS: Alsace, the historic region of Alsace-Lorraine, forms the French administrative region of Alsace, the northern departments of the region of Lorraine, and the Territory of Belfort, which forms part of Franche-Comté Region.

*FLAG:* The Alsatian national flag, the flag of the national movement, is a horizontal bicolor of red over white.

*PEOPLE:* The Alsatians, descendants of early Germanic peoples, are closely related to the inhabitants of Luxembourg and neighboring parts of Germany.

Historically, the Alsatians are 90% German-speaking, with a small, traditionally French-speaking minority. The Alsatians are now effectively bilingual, speaking both French and one of the German vernaculars collectively called Elsasserdeutsch or Elsaessisch (Alsatian), a Franconian dialect in the north and an Alemannic dialect in the south. The Alsatian dialects are akin to the Rhinish dialects spoken in the adjoining German states, but differ considerably from standard spoken German. The linguistic division of Alsace approximates the region's religious division, the Roman Catholic Franconian majority in the north and the large Protestant Alemannic minority concentrated in the south.

*THE NATION:* Various Germanic tribes occupied the Roman frontier district west of the Rhine River as Roman power declined in the fifth century. An early Frankish duchy, Alsace was eventually absorbed by Charlemagne's Frankish empire. Following Charlemagne's death in 814, control of the empire fell to squabbling heirs, and three grandsons divided the empire among themselves in 843. The division of the empire, formalized by the Treaty of Verdun, was written in the earliest recorded examples of the French and German languages. By the terms of the treaty, Alsace formed part of the middle kingdom of Lotharingia, later called Lorraine.

The Alsatian lands, incorporated by the Holy Roman Empire in 870, were gradually partitioned and, by the fourteenth century, formed a number of tiny states while some southern districts came under Hapsburg rule. A noted center of secular and ecclesiastical learning, Alsace produced many noted medieval scholars, including Martin Waldseemuller, who proposed naming the New World after Amerigo Vespucci in 1507.

The French kingdom began to subjugate the numerous small states on its borders at the end of the Thirty Years' War in 1648 and annexed the last independent holdings in Alsace during the French Revolution. Under Napoleon's highly centralized government Alsace lost its former autonomy, and the historic provinces disappeared into small administrative departments while its German-speaking inhabitants were subjected to intense assimilation pressures.

The unification of Germany, the goal of the most powerful of the numerous German states, Prussia, threatened France's hegemony in Europe and escalated the cultural and linguistic tensions in Alsace. Overrun by German troops when war between Germany and France broke out in 1870, the predominantly German-speaking districts of Alsace and Lorraine were annexed in 1871. Germany allowed France to retain Belfort and the surrounding territory as a gesture to the French garrison's brave resistance to a long German siege, the only part of Alsace retained by France.

The Alsatians resisted official German efforts to eradicate their unique culture and dialects and developed a strong anti-German sentiment. In 1911 the German government granted autonomy to the region to counter rising Alsatian nationalism. After serious nationalist rioting in 1913, new restrictions were imposed on the region that heightened Alsatian resentment and exacerbated tensions between France and Germany. France's refusal to accept the loss of Alsace-

Lorraine or to refrain from meddling in the region caused one of the continuing conflicts that eventually led to war in 1914.

Retroceded to France by defeated Germany in 1919, the Alsatians were again subjected to intense assimilation pressures despite government assurances of cultural and linguistic autonomy. Separatist sentiment, fanned by the suppression of Alsatian newspapers, cultural institutions, schools, and local government, pro-voked massive demonstrations demanding that U.S. president Wilson's principle of self-determination for Europe's minorities be applied to Alsace. In spite of the French government's attempts to crush the movement, Alsatian nationalism retained widespread support up to World War II.

Victorious Germany again annexed Alsace-Lorraine following France's ac-ceptance of surrender terms in 1940. The Nazi authorities sent thousands of reluctant Alsatian conscripts to the German military and many Alsatian nation-alists to concentration camps.

Generally hailed as liberators, French and American troops occupied Alsace in 1944 and the region officially reverted to French rule when the war in Europe ended. As in 1919–1920, the French government stressed assimilation in an effort to eliminate the "Alsatian question" that had plagued Franco-German relations since 1870.

Alsatian nationalist sentiment declined with rising prosperity and the begin-nings of European integration and Franco-German cooperation in the 1950s. A national revival, a decade later, spurred by the collapse of the important steel industry, accelerated as a united Europe became a viable reality. In 1980 the highly centralized French government began to devolve some autonomous pow-ers to twenty-two newly created administrative regions that loosely mirrored France's historic regions.

The continuing process of European unification has given the Alsatians a new focus, a Europeanized Alsace, a bilingual and bicultural federal state at the heart of united Europe. Considered too French by the Germans and too German by the French, and having been forced to change nationality four times in this century, the fervently pro-European Alsatians look to a continental federation that will allow them to finally be themselves, a distinct European nation.

*SELECTED BIBLIOGRAPHY:*

Brustein, William. *The Social Origins of Political Regionalism: France 1849–1981.* 1982.

Kahn, Bonnie M. *My Father Spoke French: Nationalism and Legitimacy in Alsace, 1871–1914.* 1970.

Morgan, Roger, and Caroline Bray. *Partners and Rivals in Western Europe: Britain, France and Germany.* 1986.

# ALTAI-KHAKASSIA

**Altay-Khakass, Altai and Khakassia**

*CAPITAL: Ulala (Gorno-Altaisk)*

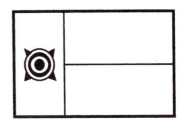

Russia (Siberia)

Kazakh-stan

Mongolia

China

**NORTH-CENTRAL ASIA**

Russia

Kazakhstan

Mongolia

China

**ALTAI-KHAKASSIA**

*POPULATION:* (95e) 794,000 : 215,000 Altaians in Russia, including 85,000 Khakas, 73,000 Altai, 21,000 Shor, and several smaller groups. MAJOR NATIONAL GROUPS: (95e) Russian (including Raskolniki) 43%, Altaian 24% (Oirot, Khakass, Shor, Temut, Tilemut, Soyon, Kumand), Kazakh 11%, Ukrainian 8%, Tuvan 4%, Mongol, Uighur. MAJOR LANGUAGES: Russian, Khakas, Altai, Kazakh, Tuvan. MAJOR RELIGIONS: Russian Orthodox (including Old Believers), Buddhist (Tibetan Lamaism), Burkhanism. MAJOR CITIES: (95e) ALTAI: Ulala (Gorno-Atlaisk) 59,000, Akhtas 22,000. KHAKASSIA: Abakan 174,000, Chernogorsk 88,000, Sarala (Sira) 33,000, Abaza 24,000.

*GEOGRAPHY:* AREA: 59,595 sq.mi.-154,391 sq.km. LOCATION: Altai-Khakassia lies in Central Asia on the Russian Federation's southern border. A mountainous region sloping down to the Abakan Steppe in the north, Altai-Khakassia includes Russia's highest mountain, Mt. Belukha, so sacred to the Altaians that no one would dare to climb it. Altai-Khakassia borders Kazakhstan on the southwest, Mongolia and China on the south, Tuva (Tannu Tuva*) on the east, and the southern provinces of Siberia* on the north. POLITICAL STATUS: The region claimed by nationalists, Altai-Khakassia, has no official status as a united political entity but forms the republics of Altai and Khakassia, member states of the Russian Federation.

*INDEPENDENCE DECLARED:* 26 January 1918.

*FLAG:* The Altaian flag, the flag of the national movement, is a horizontal bicolor of white over light blue with a green vertical stripe at the hoist bearing the national symbol, a black and white circle resembling a target, centered.

*PEOPLE:* The Altaian peoples are of mixed Turkic and Mongol background, physically resembling the Mongols but speaking North Turkic languages of the West Altaic group of languages. Altai, including the dialects Oirot and Soyon, is spoken in the south, and Khakas, with its major dialect, Abakan, in the Abakan Steppe and the basin of the Yenisei River in the north. The Altaian peoples are mostly Orthodox Christian or adhere to an indigenous religion, Burkhanism, which combines aspects of early shamanist beliefs with later Christian and Buddhist influences. In rural areas many Altaians, mostly sheepherders, still worship fire and milk and continue to respect the wisdom of the traditional shamans.

*THE NATION:* Remains have been found of a primitive communal society that existed in the Altai Mountains as early as the third millennium B.C., however little is known of the area's ancient history. It was first mentioned in the early fifth century A.D. in Chinese records as a region inhabited by nomadic Mongol tribes. Overrun and settled by migrating Turkic peoples, a Turkic khanate dominated the tribes from the fifth to the eighth centuries. The Mongol peoples gradually adopted the language and many of the cultural traits of their Turkic rulers.

The expanding Mongol Empire absorbed the Altai lands in the thirteenth century, and the Altaian tribes remained under nominal Mongol rule for over two centuries. A powerful tribal federation, dominated by the Oirot tribe, formed in the sixteenth century and eventually extended its sway far into Central Asia.

Slavic Cossacks, the vanguard of Russian expansion, began to penetrate the federation and by the late sixteenth century regularly collected a fur tax from the northern tribes. Drawn to the rich copper mines of the Yenisei River valley, the Russians extended their rule to Khakassia in the seventeenth century. Control of the growing trade in furs and animal products allowed the Russians to slowly extend their influence among the southern mountain tribes over the next century.

The Oirot federation, under attack by Manchu China and various Mongol groups, collapsed in the early 1750s. The tribes, pressed by the powerful invaders, turned to the Russians for protection. In 1756 the Altaians voluntarily placed themselves under Russian rule. The Russians established a civil government in the region, collected taxes in the form of furs, and occasionally put down uprisings but generally left the nomadic tribes to govern themselves under their traditional rulers.

A new religion, called Burkhanism, anti-Russian and antipagan, spread through the tribes in 1904, its popularity marking the beginning of Altai nationalism. Russian colonization, facilitated by the completion of the Trans-Siberian Railroad, further aggravated ethnic tensions in the region. In 1911 the related people of Tannu Tuva declared their independence as revolution swept the Manchus from power in China, the move greatly affecting the growth of Altai nationalism and leading to the first attempts to unite the related tribes.

Virtually untouched by World War I, the Altaian tribes were left effectively independent as Russian civil government collapsed in the wake of the Russian Revolution in February 1917. United for the first time, the tribes organized to resist the attempt by local Bolsheviks to take power as chaos and civil war spread throughout the disintegrating Russian Empire. On 26 January 1918 the victorious Altaians declared their homeland independent of Russia and laid claim to the lower Yenisei River valley, the Abakan Steppe, the Altai Mountains, and the huge Altai Steppe to the west.

Allied to the anti-Bolshevik White forces of Admiral Kolchak, the Altaians participated in some of the fiercest battles of the Russian civil war. In 1920 the Red Army finally defeated the Whites, leaving the Altaians to fight on alone against the advancing Reds. Continuing to harass the Red Army units from mountain strongholds, the Altaian tribes held out against overwhelming odds until 1922.

Partly as punishment for their support of the Whites, the new Soviet government designated the Altai Steppe a Russian settlement area. In 1922 the opening of the Steppe to Slav colonists restricted the tribes to a newly created autonomous province, called Oirot for the largest of the tribes, in the southern Altai Mountains. In 1930 the Soviet authorities created a separate, autonomous region for the Khakas of the Abakan Steppe and the Yenisei River valley.

The small nomadic nation, devastated by war and divided and forced to settle during collectivization in the 1930s, began to decline, rapidly losing population. Alcohol abuse became a major social problem as pressure increased to embrace a universal Soviet culture. In spite of the problems created by Soviet rule, the Altaians made great gains in education and gradually produced a new generation of leaders well aware of past glories and injustices. A modest national revival took hold in the more relaxed atmosphere following Stalin's death in 1953, a revival that began to reverse the long Altaian decline. In the 1960s the Altaian nation again began to increase in numbers.

The liberalization of the late 1980s prompted Altaian demands for reunification and an end to the artificial divisions imposed by Stalin. Following the disintegration of the Soviet Union in 1991, the regions of Gorno-Altai and Khakassia demanded full republic status within the newly democratic Russian Federation. Under the terms of Russia's new constitution, in March 1992, Altai and Khakassia gained republic status, but nationalist demands for reunification and greater autonomy continue to be ignored.

*SELECTED BIBLIOGRAPHY:*

Hauner, Milan. *Heartland Yesterday and Today.* 1990.
Kozlov, Viktor. *The Peoples of the Soviet Union.* 1988.
McCagg, William O., and Brian D. Silver, eds. *Soviet Asian Ethnic Frontiers.* 1979.

# ANKOLE

**Ankole-Kigezi**

*CAPITAL: Mbarara*

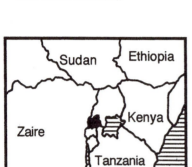

EAST-CENTRAL AFRICA

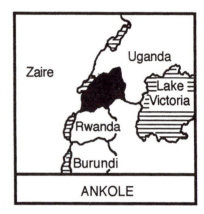

ANKOLE

*POPULATION:* (95e) 2,541,000 : 1,520,000 Banyankole (Ankole) and 1,165,000 Bakiga (Kiga) in Uganda. MAJOR NATIONAL GROUPS: (95e) Banyankole 58%, Bakiga 39%, other Ugandan. MAJOR LANGUAGES: Luyankore (Nkole/Nkore), Lukiga (Chiga), Swahili, English. MAJOR RELIGIONS: Roman Catholic, Protestant, animist. MAJOR CITIES: (95e) Kabale 60,000, Mbarara 40,000, Bushenyi 27,000, Kisoro 22,000.

*GEOGRAPHY:* AREA: 8,062 sq.mi.-20,886 sq.km. LOCATION: Ankole occupies a fertile plateau region in southwestern Uganda just east of Lake Edward in the highland lakes area of East Africa. POLITICAL STATUS: Officially, Ankole forms the southern province of Uganda. In November 1993 nationalists unilaterally proclaimed the restoration of the Kingdom of Ankole within Uganda.

*FLAG:* The Ankole national flag, the flag of the former kingdom, is a green field bearing a crouching white lion surmounted by two white drumheads crossed by horizontal black stripes and backed by crossed white spears.

*PEOPLE:* The Banyankole, called Ankole or Nkole, are an amalgamation of two distinct peoples, the Bairu (Iru), a Bantu agricultural people, and the Bahima (Hima), Nilotic pastoralists who account for some 5% of the population. The Bakiga (Kiga), concentrated in the southwest region of Kigezi, are a Bantu people closely related to the Bairu. Both the Ankole and the Kiga speak Bantu languages of the Benue-Niger language group and are mostly Christian. The three peoples of the region mixed very little, and intermarriage was forbidden until after Ugandan independence in 1962.

*THE NATION:* Bantu peoples, farmers and fishermen, originally organized in village and clan groups, formed a unified state in the region in the fourteenth century. Part of the semilegendary Bacwezi kingdom thought to have incorporated lands now in Uganda and northwestern Tanzania, the region grew rich on agriculture and trade. Around 1500, tall Nilotic herdsmen, the Hima, conquered the kingdom from the north and relegated the more advanced Bantu peoples to a serflike condition, forbidden to own cattle, the measure of wealth, or to intermarry with the Hima aristocracy.

The Hima Abahinda dynasty based their wealth on herds of long-horned Ankole cattle tended by Iru herdsmen. The Hima aristocracy, headed by a king, the Omugabe, formed a relationship with the Iru similar to that of the Tutsi and Hutu peoples of neighboring Rwanda. The Hima vested power in a royal drum called the Bahyendanwa, revered as the symbol of Ankole nationhood and for the belief that as long as the drum remained in the kingdom, Ankole would prosper.

European explorers visited the kingdom in the 1860s, amazed at the sophisticated and cultured societies they encountered in Ankole and the neighboring kingdoms. European missionaries followed the explorers and converted a majority of the population to Christianity, the Hima generally adopting Protestant beliefs, and the Iru, mostly Roman Catholic.

British officials, in an attempt to cut off the arms trade from German East Africa, signed a treaty with Ankole in 1894, then proceeded to proclaim the kingdom a British protectorate. The Ankole bitterly opposed British attempts to extend their authority to the kingdom and sporadic skirmishes culminated in a general uprising in 1897. Crushed by British troops sent from nearby colonies, Ankole's leaders signed a formal protectorate agreement that left most government functions to the Omugabe and a partially elected assembly, the Eishengyero.

British colonial policy in the 1920s and 1930s greatly reduced the power of the king and the political independence of the kingdom. Unpopular British rule, more concerned with the economy than with the trappings of monarchy, reduced Ankole to a vast labor pool. Less developed than other parts of British Uganda, Ankole resentment fostered the rise of nationalism during World War II. Iru activists, seeking to exploit British rule, formed the Kumayana movement in the early 1950s and demanded that the British authorities end Hima domination and the disparities in the allocation of local government jobs and in education. The Iru rights movement later merged with the growing Ankole national movement.

The kingdoms of southern Uganda increasingly opposed inclusion in Uganda as the British territory moved toward independence in the decade after World War II. The growing opposition to domination by Uganda's non-Bantu northern tribes pushed the Hima and Iru to bury old differences and begin to identify with Ankole nationalism. In the late 1950s agitation for autonomy or separate independence swept the kingdom, but after extensive negotiations the Ankole finally accepted semifederal status within independent Uganda.

The independence government of Milton Obote, a non-Bantu northerner, quickly moved to curtail the powers of the southern kingdoms over vehement Bantu opposition. In 1966, amid growing tensions and moves toward secession, the Obote government ended all Ankole autonomy and in 1967 abolished the four southern kingdoms.

Firmly opposed to the Obote government, most Ankole supported the revolt, led by Idi Amin, that overthrew Obote in 1971. Quickly disillusioned with the mercurial Amin, the Ankole withdrew their support as Amin's administration became even more repressive than Obote's. Following an abortive secessionist revolt in 1972, Amin loosed his mainly Muslim army on Ankole. Thousands died in brutal massacres, and refugees streamed across the borders into Zaire and Rwanda. Its leadership decimated, murdered or disappeared, the Ankole national movement collapsed.

Idi Amin Dada, one of Africa's most brutal dictators, finally overthrown in April 1979, fled the country, but several successor governments lasted only short periods until Milton Obote again became president of Uganda in 1980. The Ankole, with vivid memories of Obote's earlier rule, gave their support to a southern Bantu rebel movement led by an ethnic Ankole, Yoweri Musaveni. The rebels drove Obote from office in 1986 and installed Musaveni as the head of Uganda's first Bantu-dominated government.

Relative peace since 1986 paradoxically has allowed Ankole nationalism to resurface, even though firmly opposed by President Musaveni. Led by the more militant Protestant minority, the nationalist movement is buoyed by nostalgia for the former monarchy and the memories of the peace and prosperity the kingdom enjoyed until 1967. Ankole nationalism is sustained by the belief that an independent Ankole would have been spared the horrors and desolation of the years since 1962.

In 1992 the Ugandan government announced a radical decentralization of government to councils in local areas, prompting calls for the restoration of the Ankole kingdom. In July 1993 a new law restored the former kingdoms except for Ankole. Firmly opposed to the restoration of the Ankole kingdom, President Musaveni refused to listen to Ankole arguments. In November 1993, in defiance of the president, John Barigye was crowned king, and the restoration of the kingdom was declared. The declaration, declared illegal by the government, set off a serious crisis between the Ankole government, backed by the nationalists, and Uganda's central government.

*SELECTED BIBLIOGRAPHY:*

Bwengye, Francis. *The Agony of Uganda: From Idi Amin to Obote.* 1986.

Karugire, Samuel R. *A Political History of Uganda.* 1980.

Mukherjee, Ramkrishna. *Uganda: A Historical Accident? Class, Nation, State Formation.* 1985.

# ANTIOQUIA

*CAPITAL: Medellin*

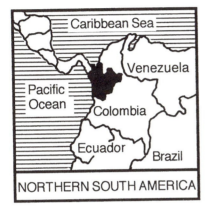

*POPULATION:* (95e) 7,966,000 : 8,350,000 Antioquians in Colombia. MAJOR NATIONAL GROUPS: (95e) Antioquian 89%, other Colombian. MAJOR LANGUAGE: Spanish. MAJOR RELIGIONS: Roman Catholic, Protestant, Jewish. MAJOR CITIES: (95e) Medellin 1,783,000 (2,545,000), Manizales 311,000 (518,000), Pereira 250,000 (490,000), Bello 246,000, Armenia 215,000 (326,000), Itague 190,000, Taluá 109,000 (143,000), Cartago 111,000, Santa Rosa de Cabal 95,000 (124,000), Buga 91,000 (120,000), La Dorada 88,000 (112,000).

*GEOGRAPHY:* AREA: 47,516 sq.mi.-123,098 sq.km. LOCATION: Antioquia lies in northwestern Colombia, a mountainous region of high valleys in the Andes Mountains and extending west and north into the coastal lowlands on the Atlantic Ocean and the Caribbean Sea. POLITICAL STATUS: Antioquia, as defined by nationalists, forms the Colombian departments of Antioquia, Caldas, Chocó, Quindío, Risaralda, and the northeastern districts of Valle Department.

*FLAG:* The Antioquian flag, the flag of the national movement, is a horizontal bicolor of white over green.

*PEOPLE:* The Antioquians, popularly called Paisas, are mostly descended from sixteenth-century Basque and Jewish refugees from Spain. Isolated in the valleys of the high Andes, the Antioquians developed a unique culture and preserved the purest Spanish spoken in the Americas. The Antioquian birthrate, possibly the world's highest, with families of up to sixteen children the norm, has rapidly increased the population and led to the expansion of the Antioquians from their core area, but, without intermarriage with other Colombians or the loss of population at the center, a highly unusual phenomenon in Latin America.

*THE NATION:* Refugee Basques and Jews forced to convert to Catholicism, fleeing persecution in Spain, arrived in the New World in the 1530s. Deliberately choosing isolation in the Andean highlands, the refugees settled in high valleys accessible only by mule trails through difficult mountain passes. The immigrants founded the town of Antioquia in 1541 and took the name of the town as the name of their new homeland. The isolated Antioquians were unusual in several ways: a very high birthrate, a refusal to intermarry, and their rejection of slavery from the start. Dividing the land in the European manner, the Antioquians settled on small family farms that they worked themselves.

For over three centuries the Antioquians lived in isolation, a prosperous farming and mining community that received no new immigrants after the first wave of arrivals. Unusually large families increased the population rapidly. In their first century they increased from less than 100,000 to over 2 million. The prolific Antioquians soon expanded in all directions from the original settlements, taking with them their unique culture and their strong ties to the Antioquian heartland.

The region, rich in minerals, particularly gold, became an important mining center in the seventeenth century. Smuggling developed as a means to avoid paying the Spanish king his fifth on gold exports and remains a tradition in the area to the present.

Antioquia, included in the Federation of New Granada when Spanish rule ended in 1819, at first moved to separate from the new state, but the Antioquian leaders were persuaded to accept substantial autonomy rather than to follow Ecuador and Venezuela into secession. The Colombian constitution of 1855 created a loose confederation of autonomous states, satisfying Antioquian demands for extensive self-government.

Antioquian expansion continued to spread along the fertile mountain valleys. Manizales was founded in 1848, Pereira in 1863, and Armenia as late as 1889. To dilute the power of the expanding Antioquian homeland and to undermine national sentiment in the region, the Colombian government instituted a policy of separation. The regions of Caldas, Risaralda, and Quindío were separated from Antioquia as they became settled; however, the inhabitants of these new departments retained their sense of Antioquian identity.

The abolition of state sovereignty in 1886 led to a sharp deterioration in the relations between the Antioquian provinces and the centralizing government in Bogotá. In 1899 civil war erupted between the advocates of a loose confederation and the supporters of a strong central government. Antioquian rebels, many demanding secession, continued to fight government troops until they were finally subdued in 1902. Government suppression of nationalist and regionalist tendencies escalated following civil war and the secession of neighboring Panama in 1903.

Coffee, introduced around 1900, brought stability to the Antioquian expansion, and within twenty years the Antioquian provinces produced a majority of

Colombia's coffee exports. Industrialization followed the construction of railroads and the end of Antioquia's long isolation. Textiles, produced in Antioquia's growing industrial cities, followed the coffee boom as the region's major product.

Antioquian society, devoutly Roman Catholic, prosperous, and middle-class, was profoundly shaken by La Violencia, the civil war that engulfed Colombia from 1946 to 1958. The conflict marked the beginning of modern Antioquian nationalism and raised demands for autonomy, even independence, to escape Colombia's chronic instability.

In the 1960s, the Antioquians spread into the highlands above Cali in the Cauca Valley. The growing industrialization of their provinces was notable for some highly progressive social schemes, including model housing estates for industrial workers. The Antioquian economy began to falter in the late 1970s, damaged by industrial recession and the end of the coffee boom. Drawing on the Antioquian tradition of smuggling contraband, a new boom crop appeared: drugs.

Drug trafficking, taken up by the lowest rungs of Antioquian society in the 1960s, spread through the Antioquian provinces during the economic recession of the late 1970s and by the 1980s involved all social classes. Developed, prosperous Antioquia rapidly degenerated into a killing ground for various armed groups connected with the military, leftist guerrillas, and the gangs in the pay of local drug barons.

Antioquians generally blame successive governments and past errors for the violence that has overwhelmed their homeland. Antioquian nationalists, who claim that their homeland is paying for these past government mistakes, admit that independence and the elimination of the drug trade would bring a massive economic depression but are adamant that with international assistance Antioquia would rank among the hemisphere's richest states within three to five years.

*SELECTED BIBLIOGRAPHY:*

Fluharty, V. L. *Dance of the Millions: Military Rule and the Social Revolution in Colombia.* 1957.

Kline, Harvey F. *Colombia: Portrait of Unity and Diversity.* 1983.

Niles, B. *Colombia.* 1976.

Oquist, Paul. *Violence, Conflict and Politics in Colombia.* 1980.

# ARABISTAN

**Arabestan; Ahvaz; Khuzestan**

*CAPITAL: Ahvaz (Ahwaz)*

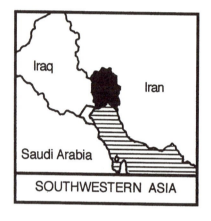

SOUTHWESTERN ASIA

ARABISTAN

*POPULATION:* (95e) 3,165,000 : 2,977,000 Arabistanis in Iran. MAJOR NATIONAL GROUPS: (95e) Arabistani 81%, other Iranian. MAJOR LANGUAGES: Arabic, Farsi. MAJOR RELIGIONS: Shia Muslim, Sunni Muslim. MAJOR CITIES: (95e) Ahvaz (Ahwaz) 625,000, Abadan 521,000 (875,000), Huhammarrah (Khorramshahr) 312,000, Bandar-e-Mah Shahr 195,000, Dezful 185,000 (320,000), Masjed Soleyman 171,000, Behbehan 155,000, Agha Jari 122,000, Ramhormoz 118,000 Andimeshk 104,000.

*GEOGRAPHY:* AREA: 24,962 sq.mi.-64,668 sq.km. LOCATION: Arabistan lies in southwestern Iran, a lowland region forming part of the Tigris-Euphrates Valley between the Iraqi border and the Zargos Mountains at the head of the Persian Gulf. POLITICAL STATUS: Arabistan has no official status; the region called Arabistan by nationalists forms the province of Khuzestan in the Islamic Republic of Iran.

*FLAG:* The Arabistani flag, the flag of the national movement, is a vertical tricolor of red, white, and black bearing a centered green, five-pointed star surrounded by a green circle.

*PEOPLE:* The Arabistanis are a Semitic Arab people made up of thirty tribal groups that are ethnically and culturally related to the Arab peoples to the west but are not closely related to Iran's majority Aryan population. The Arabistanis, who speak an Arabic dialect with a marked Farsi (Iranian) admixture, are mostly Shia Muslims, adhering to the branch of Islam predominant in Iran, with a Sunni Muslim minority concentrated in the coastal areas.

*THE NATION:* The land known to the ancients as Elam has been conquered many times and by many nations, including the Greeks of Alexander the Great, who called the area Susiana after its ancient capital at Susa. Under the rule of the ancient Persians, the region's name changed to Khuzestan, the Land of the Khuz, the name of the descendants of the ancient Elamites of the biblical era.

Invading Arabs added Khuzestan to the Muslim caliphate in the seventh century. To ensure the loyalty of the frontier district, the Arab authorities settled Arab colonists among the native Khuz, and the name of the region was changed from Khuzestan to Arabistan, the Land of the Arabs. Forming the eastern extension of Arab culture, the region became one of the wealthiest districts of the Arabs' extensive empire. The region boasted a vast irrigation system that sustained a large, settled population and wealthy, sophisticated cities, renowned seats of Muslim learning. By the eleventh century the native Khuz had disappeared, having either died out or been absorbed by the Arab majority.

Arabistan's prosperity ended with the thirteenth-century Mongol invasion. The marauding Mongols slaughtered much of the population, laid waste vast stretches of fertile farmland, and destroyed the region's renowned irrigation network. The region eventually recovered, but it never regained its former glory. Without irrigation most of the area reverted to barren desert, with agriculture restricted to the wetlands along the rivers.

The Arab's Muslim empire, weakened by conflicts with the growing might of the Turkish Ottoman Empire, lost Arabistan to the Persians in the sixteenth century. The region eventually formed a frontier district between the Persians and the Turkish-ruled Arab lands. Backward and neglected, Arabistan's long decline continued, and by the nineteenth century it was one of the poorest and least developed areas of the Middle East.

Persian settlers, favored by the government, enjoyed the benefits of Persia's late nineteenth-century modernization, leaving the Arabistanis economically deprived, and thus exacerbating the traditional hostility between the two peoples. Oil, discovered in 1908, radically changed the province's historic population pattern as the mainly rural Arabistanis migrated to the rapidly growing cities near the oil fields.

Arab liberation, supported by the Allies as a way to undermine the Ottoman Empire when war began in 1914, reverberated in Arabistan, one of the few Arab-populated territories not under Turkish rule. After centuries of harsh Persian domination, the Arabistanis enthusiastically embraced the call for Arab emancipation. After the war the Arabistanis received aid and support from the Arab countries that emerged from the collapse of the Ottoman Empire in 1918.

Reza Shah Pahlevi, a military officer, overthrew the old Persian dynasty in 1925 and proclaimed himself the new ruler of the country, which he renamed Iran. The centralization of government, under the Pahlevi dynasty, included the official elimination of the privileges of the Iranian state's numerous ethnic and religious minorities. In 1928 the inhabitants of Arabistan, again rechristened Khuzestan, came under intense pressure to assimilate, with ethnic clothing outlawed, Arabic language publications banned, and all schools ordered to teach only in Farsi, Iran's official language.

The Arab League, founded in 1945, demanded independence for Arabistan, and the province remained one of the focal points of Arab nationalism throughout the 1950s. In 1958 a radical Arab nationalist government took power in neighboring Iraq and drastically increased the outside support for the nascent Arabistani nationalist movement. Exile nationalist organizations, based in the Iraqi capital, Baghdad, directed operations in the province, with strikes, demonstrations, and the sabotage of pipelines and oil refineries becoming common practice.

The Iraqi government temporarily suspended overt aid to the national movement following the resolution of a long-standing border dispute with Iran in 1975. However, in 1979 Iraq resumed its support of the Arabistani nationalists following the revolution that brought a radical Islamic government to power in Iran. The Arabistanis, viewed by the new Islamic government as potential agents for rival Iraq, suffered severe suppression even though they had initially supported the revolution. Betrayed by the revolutionary government, the Arabistanis launched a renewed campaign of sabotage.

The Iraqi dictator, Saddam Hussein, citing the harsh treatment of the Arabistanis, declared the 1975 border agreement void and, on the same day, 22 September 1980, launched a military invasion of Iranian Khuzestan. The conflict soon bogged down and became an eight-year war of attrition. By 1988 Arabistan's cities, ports, and oil fields lay in ruins, but still under Iranian control.

Abandoned by Saddam Hussein's Iraq, which turned its attention to nearby Kuwait in 1990, the Arabistanis have looked beyond Iraq to the other Arab states for support. Drawing on Arab sympathy and monetary aid, the Arabistani nationalists compare their situation to that of the people of Palestine,* another Arab nation under foreign military rule.

*SELECTED BIBLIOGRAPHY:*

El Azhary, M. S., ed. *The Iran-Iraq War: Historic, Economic and Political Analysis.* 1984.

Hume, Cameron. *The United Nations, Iran, and Iraq.* 1994.

Marlowe, John. *The Persian Gulf in the Twentieth Century.* 1962.

Tapper, Richard, ed. *The Conflict of Tribe and State in Iran and Afghanistan.* 1983.

# ARAKAN

**Rakhine**

*CAPITAL: Akyab (Sittwe)*

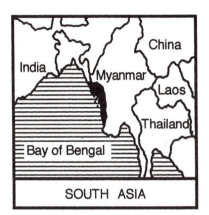

SOUTH ASIA

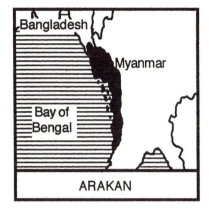

ARAKAN

*POPULATION:* (95e) 4,330,000 : 3,200,000 Arakanese and Rohingya in Myanmar. MAJOR NATIONAL GROUPS: (95e) Arakanese 55%, Rohingya 22%, Bengali 6%, Chin (Zomi) 5%, other Burmese. MAJOR LANGUAGES: Arakanese, Burmese, Bengali, English. MAJOR RELIGIONS: (95e) Sunni Muslim 70%, Buddhist 20%. MAJOR CITIES: (95e) Akyab (Sittwe) 230,000 (405,000), Sandoway (Thandwe) 145,000, Kyaukpyu 70,000, Myohaung 60,000, Sindingala 50,000.

*GEOGRAPHY:* AREA: 14,194 sq.mi.-36,772 sq.km. LOCATION: Arakan occupies a long, narrow plain on the Bay of Bengal in northwest Myanmar (Burma), separated from the rest of the Myanmar by the mountain range called the Arakan Yoma. POLITICAL STATUS: Arakan, officially called Rakhine, forms a state of the Socialist Republic of the Union of Myanmar, formerly known as Burma.

*FLAG:* The Arakanese national flag, the flag of the national movement, is a horizontal bicolor of white over red charged with a five-pointed red star on the upper hoist.

*PEOPLE:* The Arakanese are a people of Bengali, Arab, and Burman ancestry who speak a hybrid language that combines archaic Burmese, Bengali, and Arabic forms. Generally darker than Myanmar's dominant Burmans, racial animosity is aggravated by religious conflicts, as the Arakanese and the related Rohingyas are predominantly Muslim, unlike Myanmar's Buddhist majority. The Rohingyas, descendants of Bengalis who settled the region under British rule, have been declared illegal immigrants, and their Burmese citizenship has been denied. The traditional animosity between the Arakanese and the Burmans is illustrated by a popular Burman proverb, "If you meet an Arakanese and a poisonous snake, first kill the Arakanese."

*THE NATION:* Arakan, thought to have originally been settled from India's Coromandel Coast in the fourth century A.D., was an ancient maritime state with strong ethnic, economic, and religious ties to India. Islam, introduced by Arab invaders in the late seventh century, soon became the religion of the majority, further separating Arakan from the Buddhist nations on the eastern side of the Arakan Yoma.

Invading Burmans, a warrior people related to the Tibetans, conquered the Arakanese state in the eleventh century. After several unsuccessful rebellions, the victorous Arakanese drove the Burmans from their homeland in 1238. Resurgent Arakan quickly expanded to eventually control an extensive empire on the northern shore of the Bay of Bengal in the fifteenth century. In 1495 the Arakanese kingdom extended its borders westward and took control of the important port city of Chittagong, but Arakan's expansion was then checked by the rise of the powerful Mogul Empire on the kingdom's western border.

Defeated and annexed by the Moguls in 1666, the Arakanese kingdom retained considerable autonomy, again becoming virtually independent as Mogul power declined in the late eighteenth century. In 1793 the Burmans returned to conquer the kingdom, but, after only two years of harsh Burman rule, the Arakanese rebelled. After brutally crushing the rebellion, the Burmans deported over 20,000 to slavery in Upper Burma. Thousands fled Burman reprisals by crossing the Naaf River to seek protection in British Bengal.

A second Arakanese rebellion, 1811–15, greatly increased tensions on the frontier between British territory and the Burmese kingdom. Repeated border clashes culminated in the first Anglo-Burmese war in 1824. The terms of the 1826 Treaty of Yanbu forced the defeated Burmans to cede Arakan to the British Empire.

The territories of the former Burmese kingdom, reunited under British rule in 1886, formed part of British India for decades. Pressured by the majority Burmans, the British authorities separated the province of Burma, including Arakan, from India in 1937.

The outbreak of World War II pitted the British, aided by the Arakanese and other minority peoples, against the invading Japanese and the initially pro-Japanese Burmans. Arakanese nationalists, promised separate administration at war's end, felt betrayed when the British ignored the promise following the Burman's defection to the Allied cause in 1943.

Postwar preparations for the independence of Burma motivated Arakanese demands for separate independence. A negotiated compromise, autonomy within a Burmese federation, was abrogated soon after Burmese independence in 1948.

Arakanese nationalism, particularly after the military takeover of Burma in 1962, became a potent force in the region. The formation of the Arakan Liberation Front (ALF) in 1974 marked a major escalation of the sporadic Arakanese rebellion against Burman domination. Led by Khaing Mo Lin, the ALF launched a coordinated military campaign against the powerful and ruthless Burmese army.

The death of Khaing Mo Lin, killed in battle in 1977, provoked a massive exodus of 200,000 rebels and their supporters to sanctuary in neighboring Bangladesh. In 1979 the majority returned to their homes, but the Burmese military government refused to accept some 50,000 Arakanese separatists.

Staggering economic problems, the result of decades of inept military rule, have impoverished potentially rich Arakan. Over half the Arakanese population leads a miserable existence as sharecroppers on estates owned by mostly ethnic Burman absentee landlords. In 1982 Burma's ethnocentric military rulers, following an announcement that only Buddhists are eligible for citizenship, declared Arakan's Rohingya minority a stateless people, charging that they are illegal immigrants from Bengal, now independent Bangladesh. Theoretically unprotected by state institutions, the Rohingya and some Arakanese suffered confiscation of property, forced labor, and religious persecution.

The Burmese military government, claiming that Arakanese nationalists were preparing to declare independence in 1991, launched a massive military offensive. Unable to locate the elusive nationalists, the military turned on the most visible target, the unarmed Rohingyas. Rohingya refugees, numbering over 200,000 by the end of 1992, streamed across the Bangladesh border, bringing with them tales of persecutions and horrors.

The government of Myanmar, seeking to improve its international image as one of the world's most brutal regimes, made some concessions to the sensibilities of Arakan's Muslim population. In spite of its new attitude to Arakanese nationalism, the Myanmar government failed in a bid to persuade the growing number of armed national organizations to begin negotiations. Sporadic fighting continues in the region in the mid-1990s.

In February 1994 the United Nations began the repatriation of some of the Rohingyas in the dismal refugee camps on the Bangladeshi border. The government of Myanmar has agreed to accept some 130,000 of the over 200,000 refugees but continues to claim the remainder are illegal immigrants and must stay in Bangladesh, where the Myanmar government claims they originated.

*SELECTED BIBLIOGRAPHY:*
Lintner, Bertil. *Land of Jade: A Journey through Insurgent Burma.* 1990.
Silverstein, J. *Burmese Politics: The Dilemma of National Unity.* 1980.
Von der Mehden, Frederick R. *Religion and Nationalism in Southeast Asia: Burma, Indonesia, and the Philippines.* 1968.

# ARAUCANIA

**Mapu**

*CAPITAL: Temuco*

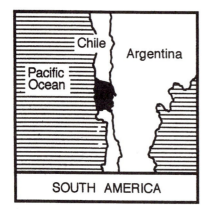

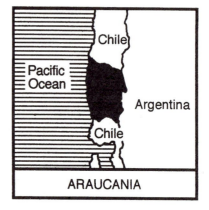

*POPULATION:* (95e) 1,503,000 : 1,404,000 Araucanians in Chile; another 155,000 live in adjacent areas of Argentina. MAJOR NATIONAL GROUPS: (95e) Araucanian (Mapuche) 77%, other Chilean. MAJOR LANGUAGES: Araucanian, Spanish. MAJOR RELIGIONS: animist, Roman Catholic. MAJOR CITIES: (95e) Temuco 197,000 (262,000), Valdivia 125,000, Villarica 56,000, Angol 45,000, Lebu 40,000, Victoria 38,000, Lautaro 29,000.

*GEOGRAPHY:* AREA: 21,209 sq.mi.-54,946 sq.km. LOCATION: Araucania occupies a fertile plain in south-central Chile between the Bío-bío River on the north, the Bueno River and Lake Puyehue on the south, the Pacific Ocean on the west, and the Andes Mountains, which form the international border with Argentina, on the east. POLITICAL STATUS: Araucania, the area claimed by nationalists, forms the Chilean region of La Araucania, the districts of the region of Los Lagos north of the Bueno River, and the districts of the region of Bío-bío south of the Bío-bío River and the Gulf of Arauco.

*FLAG:* The Araucanian flag, the flag of the national movement, is a horizontal tricolor of light blue, green, and red bearing narrow black stripes, with white geometric designs at the top and bottom and charged with a centered yellow disc bearing the national symbols, in brown.

*PEOPLE:* The Araucanians, often called Mapuche, are a Native American people traditionally divided into a number of distinct castes or tribes. The most important of the Araucanian peoples are the Mapuche, the People of the Land, traditionally farmers; the Moluche, the People of O, traditionally warriors; the Pipuche, the People of the Pines, mountain dwellers; the Huilinche, the People of the South; the Pepuenche, the People of the North; and the Laiquenche, the People of the Coast. The Araucanians speak a number of related dialects that make up a separate language family of the Andean branch of the Andean-Equatorial languages. The Araucanians have retained their traditional religious beliefs and traditions, including holding their lands in common, an important part of Araucanian culture.

*THE NATION:* The Araucanian tribes, living in the southern part of the South American continent between the Pacific and Atlantic Oceans, halted the southern expansion of the Inca Empire by defeating invasions launched by Tupai Yu-panqui between 1448 and 1482. The Incas, unable to penetrate the area, finally withdrew in the face of fierce Araucanian resistance, leaving the Araucanians the most powerful nation in the southern part of the continent prior to the arrival of the Europeans, their territory reaching east to the Altantic.

A vigorous and warlike farming people, the Araucanians dominated a large area on both sides of the Andes Mountains when the Spanish, under Pedro de Valdivia, moved south from Peru in 1540. The Spanish crossed the Bío-bío River, which marked the northern border of Araucanian territory, meeting only minimal resistance. The Spaniards founded Concepcíon in 1550, and Valdivia, farther south, in 1552. The Spanish, with the establishment of permanent set-tlements in the region, considered the conquest of Chile complete.

The Araucanians, led by their warrior chief, Lautaro, struck back at Spanish encroachment in 1553. The warriors surged north and destroyed the settlements south of the Bío-bío and in December 1553 defeated Valdivia's Spanish army. In a later battle the Araucanians captured and killed Valdivia. The victorious Araucanians, intent on driving the Spanish back to Peru, marched on the major Spanish base at Santiago.

Betrayed to the Spanish by an Araucanian renegade, Lautaro died fighting his attackers. Deprived of Lautaro's leadership, the Araucanian offensive faltered. The demoralized warriors soon withdrew to return to their homeland south of the Bío-bío River. While continuing to repulse Spanish incursions from the north, the Araucanians eradicated all signs of the Spanish presence in their homeland by 1598.

The Spanish authorities, unable to militarily defeat the Araucanians, negoti-ated a treaty in 1641. The treaty guaranteed Araucanian control of the lands south of the Bío-bío and prohibited further Spanish attempts to conquer the region. In spite of the treaty guarantees the Araucanians rallied to repulse re-newed Spanish incursions in 1725, 1740, and 1766. Pressure on the Araucanians decreased as the Spanish turned their attention to the wars in Europe and to the increasingly restive colonial populations in the Americas.

Chile won its independence from Spain in 1818, the new government reviving the struggle to conquer Araucania, claimed as part of Chile's national territory. Unlike their kin, conquered and nearly exterminated in neighboring Argentina, the Araucanians west of the Andes Mountains repeatedly defeated Chilean mil-itary offensives.

A French adventurer, Aurelio de Toumens, landed on the Araucanian coast in 1859. Promising protection from Chilean attacks, de Toumens declared Araucania independent on 17 November 1861, with himself as its king. Three days later de Toumens announced the annexation of Argentine Patagonia to his new kingdom, thus becoming a wanted man in both Chile and Argentina. Captured and deported in 1863, de Toumens attempted to regain Araucanian support in 1869 and 1873, but, his entreaties rebuffed, he eventually returned to France and obscurity.

The Chilean government, determined to take control of Araucania, sent a large military force south in 1873, but once again the Araucanians defeated the invaders. In 1880 the Chileans returned, this time with their entire national army. Unable to hold out against such a large force, the Araucanians were finally defeated in 1881, ending over three centuries of resistance to the Spanish expansion.

The defeated Araucanians, many of their most productive lands confiscated and colonized by Chileans and immigrants newly arrived from Europe, settled on small farms on their remaining communal lands. Over the next decades the Araucanians lost control of most of their lands except for a compact region in the foothills of the Andes, ultimately to be restricted to reservations under direct Chilean government control.

Rapid population growth and limited opportunities forced many young Araucanians to migrate to the cities in search of work during the 1950s and 1960s. Increasingly politicized, urban activists formed cultural and national organizations, many decidedly pro-Communist, an ideology that appealed to the Araucanians' ancient communal tradition.

The Araucanians suffered disproportionately following the overthrow of the hemisphere's first freely elected Communist government in 1973. During the sixteen-year dictatorship that followed, the Araucanians lost most of the benefits accrued under Communist rule. In 1978 young nationalists rejected the Araucanians' long struggle for acceptance in Chile and formed the Mapuche People's Liberation Organization (Ad Mapu). In 1984 the nationalists adopted a program aimed at eventual independence for Araucania. Several radical organizations turned to violence, while others began a program of occupying lands they claim as traditional Araucanian national territory.

A democratic Chilean government, elected in 1989, has attempted to redress some of the past injustices, but with little success. In 1991 nationalists threatened a secessionist uprising unless preparations were initiated to return 600,000 acres of land taken from the Araucanians since 1881.

Disappointed by their failure to win justice for their land claims in the Chilean courts, many young Araucanians have embraced a more radicalized form of nationalism. In late 1992 most of the nationalist organizations supported a demand that the Spanish, Chilean, and Argentine governments recognize and honor past treaties with the Araucanians, which would, in effect, give legal sanction to Araucanian independence.

*SELECTED BIBLIOGRAPHY:*

Berdichewsky, Bernardo. *The Araucanian Indians of Chile.* 1987.

Church, George E. *Aborigines of South America.* 1977.

Elliott, L. E., ed. *Chile Today and Tomorrow.* 1976.

Lyon, Patricia. *Native South Americans: Ethnology of the Least Known Continent.* 1985.

# ARTSAKH

### Nagorno-Karabakh; Eastern Armenia

*CAPITAL: Stepanakert (Khankendi)*

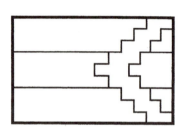

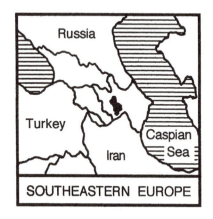

*POPULATION:* (95e) 201,000 : 182,000 Artsakh Armenians in Azerbaidzhan. MAJOR NATIONAL GROUPS: (95e) Artsakh Armenian 90%, Azeri 10%. MAJOR LANGUAGES: Armenian, Azeri, Russian. MAJOR RELIGIONS: (95e) Armenian Orthodox 75%, Shia Muslim, Sunni Muslim. MAJOR CITIES: (95e) Stepanakert (Khankendi) 35,000 (62,000), Shusha 20,000.

*GEOGRAPHY:* AREA: 1,699 sq.mi.-4,402 sq.km. LOCATION: Artsakh occupies a mountainous region around the valley of the Kura River in western Azerbaidzhan and is separated by some fifteen miles of territory from the international border between Azerbaidzhan and Armenia. POLITICAL STATUS: Artsakh's status remains unsettled. Officially, the region forms an autonomous district of the Republic of Azerbaidzhan.

*INDEPENDENCE DECLARED:* 31 December 1991.

*FLAG:* The flag of the Artsakh Armenians, the official flag of the breakaway republic, is a horizontal tricolor of red, blue, and orange with a white, step triangle on the fly.

*PEOPLE:* The Artsakh Armenians form a part of the ancient Armenian nation, which forms a separate branch of the Caucasian peoples. The most easterly of the traditional Armenian groups, the Artsakh Armenians speak a dialect of Armenian, the only surviving example of the Thraco-Phrygian group of the Indo-European languages. The majority of the Artsakh Armenians adhere to the independent Armenian Orthodox religion, with a small minority, called Khemsils, who practice a form of Sunni Islam.

*THE NATION:* According to Armenian legends, Noah's Ark landed on Mount

Ararat, the symbol of Armenian nationhood, and the Armenians claim descent from Noah through Haik and call their homeland Haikakan. Known to the world as a separate people since very ancient times, the Armenian nation was the first to adopt Christianity as the national religion in A.D. 303, their independent church established in 491. Sovereign Armenian states, with varying borders and always prey to stronger neighbors, have existed for only short periods during their long history.

Conquered by the Ottoman Turks in the fifteenth century, the Persian conquest of the eastern Armenian territories in 1639 effectively partitioned the ancient nation. Suffering persecution and discrimination under Muslim rule, the Armenians welcomed the advance of the Christian Russians into the Transcaucasus. In 1813 the Russians took the region known as Artsakh or Karabakh from the Persians.

Artsakh formed part of Russian Armenia, where the Armenian national movement was founded in 1840. Demands for the unification of the Armenian lands under Russian, Persian, and Turkish rule fueled the national movement in the nineteenth century. In Turkey, Armenian nationalism sparked stern countermeasures, including massacres and deportations that began in the 1890s and continued up to World War I.

Divided Armenia became a battleground when war began in 1914, the vast majority of the Armenians supporting Christian Russia. In Artsakh the Azeri Muslim minority openly favored Muslim Turkey, with frequent clashes and violence between the two peoples. Thousands of refugees, fleeing renewed massacres and deportation in Ottoman territory during the war, settled in the mountainous area away from the front lines.

Revolution in Russia in 1917 led to the independence of the Transcaucasian states of Armenia and Azerbaidzhan. Attempts at a federation to include Armenia, Azerbaidzhan, and Georgia failed due to the bitter rivalries between Armenia and Azerbaidzhan, including rival claims to the Karabakh region. In 1920–1921 pressure on the Transcaucasian republics increased from both the new Soviet government in the north and the nationalist Turkish government in the south. In March 1921 the Soviet Red Army took control of the eastern half of the Republic of Armenia while Turkey tightened its grip on the western portion.

A treaty between Turkey and the Soviet Union in 1921 settled their new international borders and separated Artsakh from Soviet Armenia as a separate national region. In 1923 Stalin arbitrarily placed Artsakh, called Nagorno-Karabakh or Mountain Karabakh, under the control of Soviet Azerbaidzhan over the adamant opposition of the Armenian peoples in Armenia and Artsakh. To justify its control over the region, the Azeri government cited evidence that an Azeri khanate had occupied the region for millennium prior to the Russian takeover in 1813.

Decades of Soviet rule tended to blunt the antagonism between the Armenians and Azeris, but in the more relaxed atmosphere of the 1980s the Artsakh Armenians began to call for reunification with Armenia and an end to the Azeri domination of their homeland. In early 1988 mass demonstrations erupted in Artsakh and Armenia in support of demands for the transfer of the enclave to Armenian control. In February 1988 the Soviet government refused to consider a transfer of sovereignty but responded with proposals for economic and political development schemes in the enclave. Unsatisfied, on 12 July 1988, the parliament of Nagorno-Karabakh voted to secede from Azerbaidzhan, a move denounced by both the Azeri and Soviet governments.

Ethnic tensions escalated rapidly and in November 1988 turned deadly when interethnic clashes left nineteen dead in the first open ethnic conflict in the Soviet Union since the end of strict Soviet control. In early 1989 the Soviet government changed the status of the enclave and placed it under direct rule from Moscow, a move that satisfied neither side, and after several months Nagorno-Karabakh returned to Azeri control as fighting intensified in the region.

The Azeri military subjected Stepanakert to months of bombardment in 1991 but failed to defeat the local militia, augmented by volunteers from Armenia. By late 1991 the Artsakh Armenians had taken control of the enclave, and in December the last of the former Soviet troops withdrew. On 25 December 1991 a referendum showed overwhelming support for independence from Azerbaidzhan, and on 31 December 1991 the enclave's leaders declared Artsakh an independent republic. Ideally, the Artsakh Armenians would like to unite with Armenia but chose independence as the less politically charged alternative.

The war between the Artsakh Armenians, aided by the Republic of Armenia, and the Azeris has continued sporadically since 1988. In 1993 Armenian and Artsakh forces overran the Azeri territories that divided the enclave from Armenia, driving over 600,000 Azeri refugees from the area and taking control of the important land corridors that connect the beleaguered enclave to its only source of aid and supplies in Armenia.

*SELECTED BIBLIOGRAPHY:*

Khorenats'i, Moses. *History of the Armenians.* 1978.

Lang, David Marshall. *The Armenians.* 1988.

Libardian, Gerald J., ed. *Armenia at the Crossroads.* 1991.

Walker, Christopher. *Armenia: The Survival of a Nation.* 1990.

# ASHANTILAND

*CAPITAL: Kumasi*

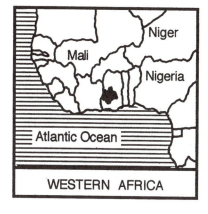

WESTERN AFRICA

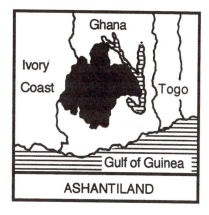

ASHANTILAND

*POPULATION:* (95e) 4,285,000 : 2,822,000 Ashanti, 917,000 Brong, and 137,000 Ahafo in Ghana. MAJOR NATIONAL GROUPS: (95e) Ashanti 65%, Brong 21%, Ahafo 3%, other Ghanaian. MAJOR LANGUAGES: Ashanti, Brong, English. MAJOR RELIGIONS: (95e) Christian 62%, animist 26%, Sunni Muslim 2%. MAJOR CITIES: (95e) Kumasi 416,000 (781,000), Obuasi 96,000, Tafo 85,000, Sunyani 73,000, Bekwai 48,000, Wenchi 39,000, Berekum 35,000.

*GEOGRAPHY:* AREA: 24,690 sq.mi.-63,963 sq.km. LOCATION: Ashantiland lies in West Africa, occupying the Kwahu Plateau west of Lake Volta in west-central Ghana. POLITICAL STATUS: Ashantiland, the area claimed by nationalists, forms the Ghanaian regions of Ashanti, Brong-Ahafo, and a small part of the Northern Region. Ashantiland is traditionally divided into sixteen Ashanti states and ten Brong states.

*FLAG:* The Ashanti flag, the flag of the national movement, is a horizontal tricolor of red, yellow, and green bearing a single white, five-pointed star on the upper hoist.

*PEOPLE:* The three peoples of the Ashanti nation, the Ashanti, Brong, and Ahafo, are closely related Bantu peoples of the Akan subgroup. Divided into numerous matriarchal clans that cut across tribal lines, the three peoples speak similar Twi or Agni-Ashanti languages of the Kwa group of Niger-Congo languages. The Twi languages, like the Chinese dialects, are tonal languages. A majority of the region's inhabitants are Christian, mostly Protestant, with minorities of Muslims, mostly in the north, and animists, who adhere to traditional beliefs.

*THE NATION:* The ancestors of the Akan peoples, thought to have migrated to the region from the east before the thirteenth century, established a number of small states or chiefdomships in the region. The foundation of the Ashanti nation is attributed to Osei Tutu, of the Oyoko clan, who established his capital at Kumasi in 1695. According to Ashanti legend, Osei Tutu plucked a golden stool from the sky, the sacred stool believed to be the abode of the Ashanti soul and the symbol of Ashanti glory. Another legend has the stool rising from a lake near Kumasi.

Two years after Osei Tutu established himself at Kumasi, in 1697, he formed several of the small neighboring states into a loose confederation under his leadership as the paramount chief of the Ashanti, the Ashantene. The confederation, its members and tributary states ruled by subkings, the Omahenes, steadily expanded over the next century to become one of West Africa's most powerful empires. In the late eighteenth century the confederation ruled an area of over 100,000 square miles and boasted a population of between 3 and 5 million.

Rich on gold and slaves, a highly sophisticated Ashanti administration collected taxes, made censuses, ordered commercial life, conscripted armies, and supported a constitution and courts of law. In order to provide a source of workers and revenue, Ashanti parties raided neighboring peoples for slaves, particularly the coastal states of the Fanti people, their traditional enemies.

The powerful empire, expanding its borders south in 1806–7, finally conquered the coastal Fanti states, the conquest bringing the Ashanti into conflict with the British, who had already established a foothold on the coast. Coveting the Ashanti's legendary mountains of gold, and seeing the powerful Ashanti as a major threat to their domination of the Gold Coast, the British authorities prodded the Ashanti into open conflict. Having miscalculated, the British were inconclusively defeated in the first Anglo-Ashanti war of 1824–31. Skirmishing continued over the next four decades and culminated in a second war in 1873–74. A British force, under General Wolseley, finally defeated the Ashanti and occupied Kumasi, which was looted and burned.

Weakened by a devastating civil war from 1883 to 1888, the Ashanti were decisively beaten in the third Anglo-Ashanti war in 1893–94. Outraged by a British proclamation claiming the confederation as a protectorate, the Ashanti refused to surrender to the British authorities, thus provoking a fourth war in 1895–96. The defeated Ashantene Prempeh I, his family, and many senior officials were exiled, and the fabulous royal treasury was shipped to London. The only treasure missing from the looted goods, the Ashantene's sacred stool, remained hidden from the invaders.

Sir Frederick Hodgson, the governor of the Gold Coast, while on a tour of the defeated confederation in 1899, demanded the golden stool for his seat. The outraged Ashanti rose in revolt rather than comply and until 1901 held off a superior British force.

Politically mobilized after World War I, the Ashanti began to demand separation from the Fanti-dominated Gold Coast and a separate administration for Ashantiland. In 1935, responding to continued agitation and threats of violence, the British authorities resurrected the Ashanti Confederation and installed a nephew of Prempeh I as the new Ashantene. However, over Ashanti protests, the confederation was formally joined to the Gold Coast colony in 1946.

Ashanti nationalists mobilized in 1954 as the British began to move the colony toward self-government. Rejecting the unitary state dominated by their ancient Fanti enemies, the nationalists demanded separation from the Gold Coast. Kwame Nkrumah, advocating a centralized state, won the 1956 elections and demanded immediate independence for the entire Cold Coast colony. Ashanti leaders pressed the British for separation, and the Ashanti secessionist crisis of 1956–57 forced the postponement of the scheduled grant of independence to the Gold Coast.

The Ashanti leaders, after long negotiations, finally accepted a compromise. The Ashanti settled for autonomy and a separate regional assembly within a federal Ghana, the first African colony to win independence, on 6 March 1957. Later in the year violent demonstrations broke out in Kumasi and other Ashanti cities following the arrest of the Ashanti leaders, the closure of the Ashanti assembly, and the banning of regional political parties. A wave of antigovernment terrorist attacks shook the new Ghanian state as the Ashanti pressed for secession.

The Nkrumah government firmly crushed the Ashanti rebellion and in 1964 established a one-party dictatorship notable only for squandering Ashantiland's enormous wealth and ultimately bankrupting Ghana. The overthrow of Nkrumah, in 1966, inspired an Ashanti national revival. Fueled by growing disputes over the Brong states and the disposition of revenues from Ashantiland's important cocoa crop, Ashanti nationalism gained widespread support. In September 1977, amid a growing crisis, the government decreed the death penalty for persons advocating secession from Ghana.

Ashanti nationalism, suppressed under successive military governments, is again a potent force in the region as Ghana slowly moves toward multiparty democracy. The heirs of one of Africa's most advanced political systems, the Ashanti claim that their historical right to separate nationhood is as strong as any in Africa.

*SELECTED BIBLIOGRAPHY:*
Davidson, Basil. *The Search for Africa.* 1994.
Fairchild, Shiela. *Peoples and Nations of Africa.* 1988.
Lystad, R. A. *The Ashanti.* 1958.
Morrison, Minion K. *Ethnicity and Political Integration: The Case of Ashanti, Ghana.* 1982.
Smith, Edwin W. *Golden Stool: Some Aspects of Conflict of Cultures in Modern Africa.* 1969.

# ASSAM

**Asom**

*CAPITAL: Dispur*

SOUTH ASIA

ASSAM

*POPULATION:* (95e) 23,418,000 : 18,750,000 Assamese in India. MAJOR NATIONAL GROUPS: (95e) Assamese 63%, Bengali 20%, tribal peoples 5%, other Indian. MAJOR LANGUAGES: Assamese, Bengali, English, tribal languages. MAJOR RELIGIONS: (95e) Hindu 70%, Sunni Islam 24%, Christian 1.5%, animist. MAJOR CITIES: (95e) Gawahati (Gauhati) 375,000 (640,000), Dibrugarh 155,000, Silchar 121,000, Nagaon (Nowgong) 133,000, Tinsukia 95,000, Dhubri 72,000 (93,000), Tezpur 68,000, Johrat 58,000 (134,000), Dispur 55,000, Lumding 55,000, Sibsagar 50,000, Digboi 50,000.

*GEOGRAPHY:* AREA: 30,318 sq.mi.-78,544 sq.km. LOCATION: Assam occupies the valley of the Brahmaputra River and the surrounding hill regions in northeastern India, bordering Bangladesh on the west, Bhutan on the northwest, and the Indian states of Meghalaya* on the southwest, Arunchal Pradesh on the northeast, and Nagaland,* Manipur (Meithei Laipak*), and Mizoram* on the east. POLITICAL STATUS: Assam, Asom in the Assamese language, forms a state of the Republic of India.

*FLAG:* The Assamese national flag, the flag of the national movement, is a red field with two Assamese knives, in white, crossed in the center.

*PEOPLE:* The Assamese are a people of mixed origins, descendants of early Aryan peoples with later admixtures of Thai and Tibeto-Burman peoples. The Assamese language, of the Indo-Aryan group of languages, is spoken by several distinct ethnic groups. The majority of the Assamese are Hindu, with a substantial Muslim minority in the south. The large Bengali population is mostly

Muslim, and the tribal peoples who inhabit the hill districts either are Christian or adhere to traditional beliefs. The physical diversity of the Assamese nation has resulted from a long history of invasion and conquest.

*THE NATION:* Aryan invaders, originally from the Iranian Plateau far to the west, occupied the valley of the Brahmaputra River about 1200 B.C., pushing the earlier inhabitants into the less accessible mountain areas. Isolated from the mainstream of Indian civilization until the first century A.D., ancient Assam's culture developed independently and incorporated influences from neighboring peoples, particularly the Tibetans to the north.

A Thai people, the Ahom, conquered the Brahmaputra Valley in 1229, part of the great expansion of the Thais. Gradually absorbed by the Aryan Assamese, the Ahom had disappeared as a separate people by the seventeenth century, although their influence on the language and culture of the region remains.

The Assamese kingdom, often at war with the neighboring Muslim Bengalis to the south, finally turned to the new power in the region, the British, for protection from their many enemies. Burman invaders, repulsed in 1822 with British military aid, returned later to conquer the kingdom, a major cause of the first Anglo-Burmese war of 1824–26. Taken from the defeated Burmans, Assam was added to the British province of Bengal. Assam remained part of British Bengal until the authorities created a separate autonomous province in 1937.

Assam's oil fields became an important resource in British India and were the object of an unsuccessful Japanese offensive during World War II. Japanese promises and inducements failed to attract the Assamese to their cause, but did open the discussion of autonomy and spurred the growth of Assamese nationalism.

The postwar partition of British India into predominantly Hindu India and Muslim Pakistan created a chaotic situation in Assam as refugees streamed across the newly established international borders that divided the region. Assam's Muslim majority region of Sylet went to the new Pakistani state, forming part of the eastern half of the Muslim republic, which later seceded as the Republic of Bangladesh.

The state's numerous minorities, dissatisfied with Assamese domination of the state government following Indian independence in 1947, demanded separation, greatly reducing Assamese territory as Nagaland, Mizoram, Meghalaya, and Arunchal Pradesh were removed to separate administrations during the 1960s and 1970s. The Assamese majority in the truncated state, affected by the loss of what they considered traditional Assamese territory, demanded greater political autonomy and control of their national wealth, which includes India's only important source of petroleum.

Illegal Muslim immigrants, fleeing poverty in East Pakistan, poured into the state in the 1970s, aggravating ethnic and religious tensions. The illegals, perceived as a threat to Assamese culture and ethnic identity, provoked a strong Assamese nationalist backlash.

In 1981, amid growing violence, the state government was dissolved and direct rule from New Delhi was imposed. Many of the Assamese political leaders were imprisoned. New state elections were called, but the Indian government, fearing a nationalist victory, allowed the millions of illegal immigrants to vote in the election in February 1983. The vote, boycotted by the Assamese, established a pro-Indian state government. A new state election, in 1985, was won by an Assamese nationalist party supported by anti-immigrant and militant student groups.

The demands for separation from Assam by the Bodo tribal minority in the 1980s strengthened the Assamese nationalists' determination not to surrender any more Assamese territory. Ethnic clashes between Assamese and Bodo, in the late 1980s, reached the levels of violence of the Assamese-Bengali confrontations.

Support for separatism has grown dramatically among the politicized Assamese. In 1990 a militant nationalist organization, the United Liberation Front of Assam (ULFA), launched a violent secessionist campaign, supported by nationalist factions within the state government. In November 1990 the Indian federal government dissolved the state government as separatist sentiment took hold in areas and among classes previously little affected. The Indian military made widespread use of the sweeping powers given it by the government to combat the separatists. In the 1990s nationalist sentiment and the ethnic and separatist violence in Assam have assumed the proportions of a major threat to India's fragile ethnic and religious cohesion.

*SELECTED BIBLIOGRAPHY:*

Bose, M. L. *Social History of Assam.* 1989.

Chandra, Bipan. *Communalism in Modern India.* 1984.

Das, B. M. *The Peoples of Assam.* 1987.

Datta, P. S. *Ethnic Movements in Poly-Cultural Assam.* 1990.

# ASSYRIA

*CAPITAL: Mosul (Al-Mawsil)*

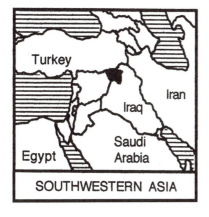

SOUTHWESTERN ASIA

ASSYRIA

*POPULATION:* (95e) 2,415,000 : 1,470,000 Assyrians in Iraq and Syria and another 350,000 in other Middle Eastern states and Turkey. The Assyrian Diaspora numbers over 2 million. MAJOR NATIONAL GROUPS: (95e) Kurd 40%, Assyrian 35%, Arab 20%. MAJOR LANGUAGES: Kurdish, Assyrian (New-Syriac), Arabic. MAJOR RELIGIONS: Sunni Muslim, Christian (Chaldean, Nestorian, Jacobite, Melchite, Syrian Catholic). MAJOR CITIES: (95e) IRAQ: Mosul (Al-Mawsil) 750,000, Aski Mosul (Tall Afar) 100,000, Sinjar 50,000. SYRIA: Qamishliye (Al-Qamishli) 150,000, Haseke (Al-Hasakah) 110,000, Amuda 45,000.

*GEOGRAPHY:* AREA: 23,558 sq.mi.-61,032 sq.km. LOCATION: Assyria occupies an upland region in the Jebel Sinjar Mountains of Kurdistan* just south of the Turkish border in northwestern Iraq and northeastern Syria, with most of the area lying between the Tigris and Euphrades Rivers. POLITICAL STATUS: Assyria has no official status; the area claimed by nationalists forms the province of Ninawa in Iraq and the province of Haseke in Syria.

*FLAG:* The Assyrian flag, the flag of the national movement, is a white field bearing wavy blue, white, and red stripes from the corners to the center and is charged with a centered blue four-pointed star around a yellow disc, outlined in white. OTHER FLAG(S): The flag of the Muslim Assyrian minority is a vertical tricolor of violet, yellow and green, bearing a white crescent moon and five-pointed star on the upper hoist.

*PEOPLE:* The Assyrians are a Christian people, the adherents of a bewildering variety of Christian sects, united by their minority status and the alienation of Muslim domination. The largest sects are the Chaldeans, accounting for over two-thirds of the Assyrian population, and the Nestorians, about a fifth of the total. The Assyrian language, also called Neo-Syriac, is Semitic in origin, having evolved from ancient Aramaic, the language of Christ. An Assyrian literary language developed in the 1840s on the basis of the Urmiye alphabet, the same twenty-two letters as Hebrew. A small minority of the Assyrians, around 1%, has converted to Islam but remains Assyrian in culture and language. The Assyrian Diaspora counts large populations in the United States, Canada, South America, South Africa, and Europe.

*THE NATION:* Christianity spread, from its roots in Palestine and Syria, throughout the Roman Empire by the third century A.D. The young religion, rent by controversies and schisms, began to divide into opposing sects in the first centuries of its rapid expansion.

Nestorius, the patriarch of Constantinople, in the year 428 objected to the term ''Mother of God,'' thus opening a 200-year controversy within the church. The followers of Nestorius organized themselves as a separate sect in Syria in 435 but, to escape persecution by church authorities, dispersed to Mesopotamia, Persia, and Asia. Nestorian refugees spread their doctrine as far east as India and China. The Church of Antioch, popularly called the Jacobites, established by Jacob Baradeaus in the sixth century, grew under the patronage of the Byzantine empress Theodora.

The opposition of the Syriac Christian sects to rule by the Orthodox Christian Byzantines weakened the empire's response to the sudden threat from the Arabian lands to the south. Arab Muslims, fired by missionary zeal, defeated the Byzantines in 634–36. Forced conversion to Islam, accompanied by terrible massacres, decimated the Christian population of the Middle East. The survivors lived as despised minorities among the Muslim majority, subject to special restrictions and taxes.

Invading Mongols overran the Middle East in 1258, and once again the Christians suffered massacres and dispersal. The devastated Christian population, just beginning to recover from the Mongol massacres, again faced eradication from Tamerlane's marauders in the fourteenth century. The Christians survived in small, dispersed groups in remote areas. The remnants of the Nestorians, sheltering in the mountains of Kurdistan, were the first to be called Assyrian Christians.

Jesuit missionaries, followed by Orthodox and eventually Protestant denominations, made converts in the region, but only among the already Christian populations, leading to a proliferation of sects and rites. The Chaldeans, while retaining most of the Nestorian rites and practices, accepted the authority of Rome in the sixteenth century. The Jacobites who formed a union with Rome are the Syrian Catholics, and the Arabic-speaking Orthodox reunited with Rome are the Melchites.

The various Christian sects began to unite after the Turkish conquest of the

Middle East in 1638. Denied the benefits of citizenship and excluded from many aspects of life in the Ottoman Empire, the Christians also suffered periodic persecutions. The mutually antagonistic sects began to unite and to put aside old grievances to reaffirm their common heritage as Christians, aliens, and infidels in the Muslim world.

The Christian populations, again numerous by 1900, lived primarily in the rural areas of the Ottoman Empire, the only large urban populations at Mosul in Mesopotamia and Antioch in Syria, the ecclesiastical seats of several of the sects. In the early twentieth century a cultural and national revival that had begun a half century before rapidly spread through the Christian communities. The Assyrian revival finally united the disparate peoples and sects as a nation. The ancient dialects gave way to a modern literary language with the appearance of an Assyrian dictionary that updated the language's usage and syntax.

An Assyrian national movement, growing out of the cultural revival, led to a widespread revolt against Turkish rule in 1908. Thousands of Assyrians died in savage reprisals and massacres of noncombatants. When world war began six years later, the Assyrians again rebelled, assured by the Allies that their support of the ''Christian'' powers would bring them an independent homeland at war's end. For their support of Turkey's enemies, the Assyrians, like the Christian Armenians, suffered horrible massacres, persecution, and expulsions. By the time the war ended in 1918, over half the pre-war Assyrian population had perished.

The surviving Assyrians, expecting the Allies to keep their promises, sent a delegation to the 1919 Paris Peace Conference. The representatives of the Assyrian-Chaldean nation put forward a claim to the Mosul District of Mesopotamia and Jhezeira District of Syria. Ignored by their former allies, the 250,000 surviving Assyrians in the region came under attack from Turks, Kurds, and Arabs, all claiming the same territories for their new states. The Assyrians in Turkey were driven out at gunpoint into refugee camps in British Iraq. Thousands of Assyrian refugees fled abroad, with only those in the Jhezeira District controlled by France given a measure of autonomy.

The Mosul Commission, appointed by the League of Nations to investigate the plight of the Assyrian refugees in 1924, recommended that they be settled in the Mosul District with a large measure of autonomy. Both Turkey and Iraq, with rival claims to Mosul, rejected the commission's recommendations. Although their claim to a homeland failed, the Assyrian claim to Mosul delayed the settlement of the territorial dispute until 1925, when the commission awarded the district to Iraq, with Great Britain responsible for minority rights for twenty-five years.

Years of dreadful suppression followed the Allied betrayal. Destitute and dependent on the hospitality of hostile Muslim governments, the Assyrians survived only through the support of the far-flung exile community, the Assyrian Diaspora.

Nationalists in the United States, insisting that only an independent Assyria would assure the ultimate survival of their beleaguered nation, formed the Bet Nahrain Democratic Party (BNDP) in 1976, with its stated aim the creation of an Assyrian state in their ancient homeland. The International Confederation of the Assyrian Nation, founded in 1977, organized a provisional Assyrian government.

The third largest ethnic-religious group in Iraq, the Assyrians formed an alliance with an old enemy, the Kurds, during the uprisings in northern Iraq in the 1960s and 1970s. In 1988 over 2,000 Assyrians died when the Iraqi military, also shelling Kurdish villages, bombarded five Assyrian villages with chemical weapons.

The Assyrians in Iraq suffered renewed persecutions during and after the 1991 Gulf War. Many Assyrians joined the Kurdish uprising that followed Iraq's defeat, and over 190,000 fled into the mountains with the Kurds when the rebellion collapsed.

The precarious existence of the Assyrians continues in several Middle Eastern countries where they remain suspect. The Assyrians, like their Kurdish allies, fear that without their own state they will eventually disappear as a nation.

*SELECTED BIBLIOGRAPHY:*

Attwater, Donald. *The Christian Churches of the East.* 1947–48.

Forman, Charles W. *Christianity in the Non-Western World.* 1967.

Hourani, Albert H. *Minorities in the Arab World.* 1947.

Joseph, John. *The Nestorians and Their Muslim Neighbors.* 1961.

Vine, Aubrey R. *The Nestorian Churches.* 1979.

# AZAWAD

**Azaouad; Eastern Sahara**

*CAPITAL: Timbuktu (Tombouctou)*

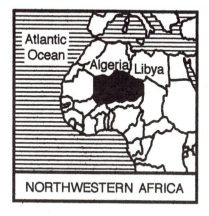

NORTHWESTERN AFRICA

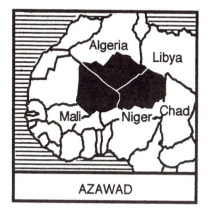

AZAWAD

*POPULATION:* (95e) 1,935,000 : 1,400,000 Tuaregs in Mali, Niger, and Algeria. MAJOR NATIONAL GROUPS: (95e) Tuareg 68%, other Malian, Nigerien, Algerian. MAJOR LANGUAGES: Tamachek (Tamahaq), Arabic, Songhai, Fulani, Djerma, French. MAJOR RELIGIONS: Sunni Muslim, animist. MAJOR CITIES: (95e) MALI: Timbuktu (Tombouctou) 60,000, Gao 40,000, Tessalit 20,000. NIGER: Tahoua 72,000, Arlit 38,000, Agades (Agadez) 33,000, Akouta 26,000. ALGERIA: Tamoust (Tamanrasset) 25,000.

*GEOGRAPHY:* AREA: 485,668 sq.mi.-1,258,207 sq.km. LOCATION: Azawad, also called Eastern Sahara, occupies the vast southern reaches of the Sahara Desert in northern Mali and Niger and southern Algeria. The region includes the Aïr and Ahaggar Mountains and the fertile Sahelian plains along the Niger River and in the Tilemai Valley. POLITICAL STATUS: Azawad has no official status; the area claimed by nationalists includes the provinces of Tombouctou and Gao in Mali, the department of Agadez and the northern districts of Tahoua in Niger, and all or part of the Algerian departments of Tamanrasset, Adrar, and Ouargla. Some nationalist organizations also claim parts of Mauritania and Libya.

*FLAG:* The Azawad flag, the flag of the Tuareg nationalist movement, is a white field bearing a centered, blue crescent moon and five-pointed star.

*PEOPLE:* The Tuareg are a Berber people, descendants of the Zenaga Berbers, a Caucasian people with later black African and Arabic admixtures. Tuareg society is divided into three distinct classes: the nobles; the Heratin, agriculturists and artisans; and the descendants of former slaves. Unlike most Muslim communities, the Tuareg are a matriarchal people, the unveiled women enjoying freedom and respect. The Tuareg men wear the veils, and their traditional clothing, including veils and indigo turbans, gives them the name the Blue Men of the Sahara. The seven major Tuareg tribes are the Kel Ahaggar and Kel Ajjer of southern Algeria, the Kel Adrar of northern Mali, the Kel Aïr of northern Niger, the Kel Geres of the plains, the Allemmeden Kel Dennek in the east, and the Aullemmeden Kel Atatam in the west. In spite of their dispersal over a very large geographical area, all of the Tuareg tribes speak closely related dialects of Tamachek, a Berber language with its own script called Tifinagh, the only Berber language to have retained its own alphabet.

*THE NATION:* Tuareg legends place their origins on a large island in the Atlantic Ocean. According to the legends, when their island home disappeared, the only survivors were traders stranded in the port cities of North Africa, the survivors becoming the ancestors of the Tuareg nation. The Zenaga Berbers, a settled farming people in North Africa, were pushed or fled into the southern desert during the Arab invasion of North Africa in the eighth century. Retaining their Berber language and culture, the refugees adapted to a nomadic existence in the vast reaches of the arid Sahara.

The Tuaregs migrated south during the eleventh century and occupied the fertile valleys on the desert's southern edge, where they erected several Tuareg states. Converted to Islam, the states amassed great wealth as the southern terminals of the caravan routes that crossed the Sahara and linked the Muslim Tuaregs to Muslim North Africa. The cities of Agades, Gao, and Timbuktu, the Tuareg's spiritual capital, became noted centers of Muslim culture and learning, instrumental in the spread of Islam through much of Central Africa.

The Tuareg states gradually fell to the expanding medieval empires of Songhai, Ghana, and Mali. These empires, in turn, were destroyed by invading Moroccans in 1591. Several small Tuareg states, notably Agades and Gao, established following the Moroccan withdrawal, recovered control of the trans-Saharan trade routes. In the late eighteenth century a Tuareg confederation dominated a large empire in the grasslands of the southern Sahara, its mounted warriors habitually raiding the settled black African tribes for slaves to ship north along the caravan routes to North Africa.

Lying far from Africa's coasts, the Tuareg homeland escaped European attention until the late nineteenth century. In 1890 the French proclaimed a protectorate in Aïr and the southern Tuareg states, but French troops attempting to enter Tuareg territory in 1898 met fierce resistance. Their lands eventually divided among several French colonies, the Tuaregs were finally subdued by a French military expedition in 1906.

The Tuaregs, with German backing and encouragement, launched a rebellion in 1916 and remained a threat to the European colonies until defeated by a combined French and British force in 1919. Unable to militarily suppress the Tuareg tribes, the French authorities formed an alliance with Tuareg leaders in 1923. In return for Tuareg aid in policing the black African tribes as part of

France's colonial army, the Tuaregs enjoyed extensive autonomy in their own territories.

The Negro peoples, quicker to accept French culture and education, began to dominate the colonial administration and to lead the drive for independence from France. Fearing domination by their former slaves, the Tuareg demanded the creation of an autonomous state in the northern districts of French West Africa and southern Algeria in 1959. Ignored by the French authorities, the Tuareg territories remained part of Mali and Niger, independent in 1960, and Algeria, which won its independence in 1962.

The newly independent states, ruled by one-party governments, mostly excluded Tuareg participation, which aggravated ethnic tensions. Open rebellion erupted in 1963 and was not completely crushed until the governments of Mali, Niger, and Algeria joined forces two years later. Government attempts to force the nomadic Tuareg to settle provoked renewed resistance in many areas in the 1960s and 1970s. Drought and famine devastated the Tuareg lands, particularly severe in 1973–74, 1977–78, and 1985. Their herds gone, many of the starving nomads moved into refugee camps or the squalid slums of the larger cities.

Tuareg leaders, claiming that only they can inhabit the semiarid lands of the Sahara without destroying them, in 1989 cited the numerous ecological disasters and their historic claims to the region to support their demands for peaceful secession and the establishment of an independent state, Azawad. In May 1990 atrocities by government troops in northern Niger provoked a widespread rebellion, which soon spread to the Tuareg districts of northern Mali. The Tuareg rebellion, despite numerous cease-fires and attempts at negotiations, continues as a major threat to the integrity of the postcolonial states, while a negotiated settlement recedes even further with each violent confrontation.

*SELECTED BIBLIOGRAPHY:*

Asiwaju, A. I. *Partitioned Africans: Ethnic Relations across Africa's International Boundaries, 1884–1984.* 1985.
Bodington, Nicolas. *The Awakening Sahara.* 1981.
Briggs, L. Cabot. *The Tribes of the Sahara.* 1960.
Martinez, R. *Among the Tuareg.* 1986.
Porch, Douglas. *The Conquest of the Sahara.* 1986.

# AZORES

Açores

CAPITAL: Ponta Delgada

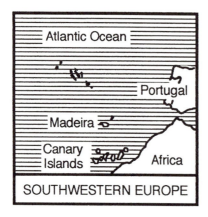

SOUTHWESTERN EUROPE

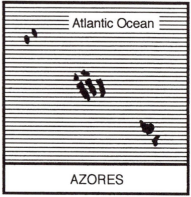

AZORES

POPULATION: (95e) 232,000 : 300,000 Azoreans in Portugal. MAJOR NA-
TIONAL GROUPS: (95e) Azorean 96%, other Portuguese. MAJOR LAN-
GUAGE: Portuguese (Azorean dialect). MAJOR RELIGION: Roman Catholic.
MAJOR CITIES: (95e) Ponta Delgada 82,000 (93,000), Angra do Heroísmo
42,000, Horta 16,000.

GEOGRAPHY: AREA: 902 sq.mi.-2,336 sq.km. LOCATION: The Azores lie
in the eastern Atlantic Ocean 750 miles west of the Portuguese mainland. The
nine major islands of the archipelago are geographically divided into three
groups: northwest, central, and eastern. POLITICAL STATUS: The Azores form
an autonomous region of the Republic of Portugal.

FLAG: The Azorean national flag, the official flag of the islands, is a vertical
bicolor, the third nearest the hoist dark blue, the remainder white. Overlaying
the color division is a golden hawk, açor in Portuguese, its spread wings surmounted by nine gold stars arranged in an arc, wing to wing. OTHER FLAG(S):
The same blue and white flag, but with the açor's wings spread downward
around nine stars as a map of the islands, is the flag of the largest nationalist
organization, the Front for the Liberation of the Azores (FLA).

PEOPLE: The Azoreans are descended from fifteenth-century colonists from
Europe, mostly Portuguese and Flemish. The Azorean language, the language
of daily life, is a dialect of Portuguese that incorporates borrowings from Flemish, English, and African languages, and nationalists claim it constitutes a separate Romance language. Large Azorean immigrant populations live in the

United States, Canada, and Brazil, and emigration to mainland Europe continues, as the poor economy offers few opportunities to young Azoreans.

*THE NATION:* The actual date of the discovery of the islands is lost in history, but their existence was known in Europe as early as the fourteenth century, since the islands appear on a map drawn in 1351. The uninhabited islands, rediscovered by the Portuguese in 1427, received colonists from Portugal beginning in 1445. For centuries the archipelago was called the Flemish Islands, stemming from the gift of the island of Faial to Isabela of Burgundy in 1466. Her Flemish subjects, dispatched to establish farming communities on Faial, later spread to all of the islands.

The remote islands, used as a place of exile, later developed as important stops on the sea routes between Europe and the New World. The first Azoreans emigrated during the colonial period, the forerunners of an exodus that continued for centuries.

Administered as a colonial possession until the 1930s, the islands remained neglected, overcrowded, and underdeveloped. High unemployment and the pressure of a rapidly growing population escalated the need for the Azoreans' traditional escape, emigration. Immigrant communities, retaining strong emotional ties to their island homeland, were the first to develop a sense of Azorean national awareness.

A military and economic agreement, signed in 1951, established joint American and Portuguese military facilities in the islands. The agreement, renewed many times since, financially benefits the Portuguese government but has conveyed few advantages to the Azoreans. Resentment of the continued colonialism kindled the first stirrings of national sentiment within the islands.

The devoutly Catholic and conservative Azoreans, alarmed by the revolution that installed a leftist government in Lisbon in 1974, quickly organized to resist the new government's nationalization of banks, industries, farms, and fisheries. Nationalists mobilized the population against the revolutionary excesses of the leftist Portuguese government.

The government's announced intention, to free the last of Portugal's colonial empire, incited a rapid growth of support for the nationalists. Several nationalist organizations formed as separatist demonstrations rocked the islands. Considering their islands a colony, although officially they formed an integral part of the Portugese republic, Azorean nationalists prepared for independence from Portugal.

Disappointed at the Portugese government's refusal to grant the Azores the same right to self-determination as the African colonies, nationalists gained widespread popular support. In January 1976 the local government reported that a poll of islanders indicated that 45% favored immediate independence while 55% favored varying degrees of autonomy, fearing that premature independence would aggravate the island's chronic economic problems and its lack of trained administrators.

Popular support for independence declined following a grant of autonomy by a newly installed democratic Portuguese government in 1976. Rejecting independence, for now, the regional government negotiated new agreements bringing major development funds and a large share of the money earned from the island's American military bases.

Portugal's entry in the European Economic Community in 1986 and rising prosperity, although incomes are still only a third of community levels, animated a resurgent nationalist movement in the late 1980s. Disputes over the use of the Azorean flag and anthem, and the disposition of Azorean properties confiscated in 1975 have become major nationalist issues. In 1991 Azorean nationalist leaders claimed that 74% of the Azoreans favored independence within the context of a united, federal Europe. The nationalists often receive the backing of local government officials, as support for secession is a useful tool when the Azoreans wish to pressure Lisbon, even though advocating secession is a grave offense in Portugal.

*SELECTED BIBLIOGRAPHY:*

Bragança-Cunha, Vicente. *Revolutionary Portugal.* 1987.
Kayman, Martin. *Revolution and Counter-Revolution in Portugal.* 1979.
Rogers, Francis M. *Atlantic Islanders of the Azores and Madeiras.* 1979.

# BALUCHISTAN

**Baloochistan; Balochistan**

*CAPITAL: Kalat*

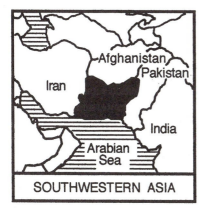

SOUTHWESTERN ASIA

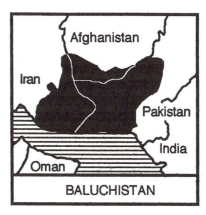

BALUCHISTAN

*POPULATION:* (95e) 6,325,000 : 5,395,000 Baluchis in Pakistan, another 1,750,000 in adjacent areas of Iran and Afghanistan. "Greater Baluchistan," 8,500,000. MAJOR NATIONAL GROUPS: (Pakistani Baluchistan 95e) Baluch 84%, Pushtu 11%, other Pakistani. MAJOR LANGUAGES: Baluchi, Brahui, Pushtu, English. MAJOR RELIGIONS: Sunni Muslim, Zikri Muslim, Shia Muslim. MAJOR CITIES: (95e) PAKISTAN: Kwatah (Quetta) 465,000, Sibi 75,000, Kalat 50,000. IRAN: Zahedan 340,000, Zabol 155,000, Fahrez 50,000. AFGHANISTAN: Zaranj 30,000.

*GEOGRAPHY:* AREA: Pakistani Baluchistan 133,117 sq.mi.-344,863 sq.km. "Greater Baluchistan," 241,049 sq.mi.-624,480 sq.km. LOCATION: Baluchistan, a generally arid region lying outside the monsoon zone, occupies a vast area in southwestern Pakistan, bordering the Pakistani provinces of Northwest Frontier (Pushtunistan*) and Punjab on the northwest and Sind* on the southeast, Afghanistan on the north, Iran on the west, and the Arabian Sea on the south. POLITICAL STATUS: Baluchistan forms a province of Pakistan. "Greater Baluchistan," as defined by many nationalist groups, also includes Iranian Baluchistan (the province of Baluchistan and Seistan) and Afghan Baluchistan (the regions of Seistan and Registan in the southern districts of the provinces of Nimruz, Helmand, and Kandahar).

*INDEPENDENCE DECLARED:* 15 August 1947; 20 June 1958.

*FLAG:* The Baluch national flag, the flag of the national movement, is a white field with a centered, five-pointed red star. OTHER FLAG(S): The traditional Baluch flag is a horizontal bicolor of red over green. The flag of Kalat is a red over green flag with a white, five-pointed star above a large white crescent moon, with its points extending into the red.

*PEOPLE:* The Baluchi nation is made up of two distinct but culturally and historically related peoples, the Baluch (Nharhui Baluch), the formerly nomadic descendants of Iranian tribes, and the Brahui (Brahui Baluch), the traditionally settled population descended from the region's pre-Aryan Dravidian inhabitants. The Baluch speak an Indo-Iranian language related to Farsi (Iranian); the Brahui also speak a Dravidian language related to the languages spoken in southern India. The majority of the Baluch adhere to the Sunni branch of Islam, with a Shia Muslim minority, mostly in Iran, and a Zikri Muslim group, numbering some 800,000, in Pakistani Baluchistan, followers of a sect founded in the fifteenth century.

*THE NATION:* Dravidian peoples, once dominant across the subcontinent, were mostly driven into southern India by the Aryan invasions that swept across the north between 1700 and 1200 B.C. The Dravidian population of the upland valleys in the arid northwest escaped the onslaught as the Aryans bypassed their homeland to move farther east, leaving only a few small, nomadic Aryan tribes in the region.

Muslim Arabs occupied the land in the seventh century, bringing the Islamic religion to the Brahui population. Baluch nomads, driven from their homeland on the Iranian Plateau by the invading Seljuk Turks, migrated to the region in the eleventh and twelfth centuries. The Brahui, with a long history of settled government, remained the dominant people with the region ruled by the powerful Brahui khans of Kalat from the seventeenth century.

First explored by Europeans in 1810, most of Baluchistan was occupied by the British during the first Anglo-Afghan war in 1839 and justified the occupation as preventing the Russians from gaining access to the Indian Ocean through the region. In 1846 the British authorities divided British Baluchistan into three distinct areas; the settled areas under direct British administration, the Khanate of Kalat, and the tribal zones governed through various Baluch chiefs. In 1877 the British established the northern area as the Protectorate of British Baluchistan. The southern districts, Kalat and the tribal states, remained semi-independent, tied to British India by treaties and resident British advisers. The frontiers between British and Persian territory, settled by agreements in 1895–96, left a substantial Baluch population under Persian rule.

Periodic uprisings continued into the twentieth century, most seriously in the British zone during World War I. In the 1930s nationalist groups in both British and Iranian Baluchistan put forward demands for autonomy and the unification of all Baluch populated territories. During the 1940s rapid population growth extended the Baluch ethnic frontiers into southwestern Afghanistan.

The British authorities, preparing the subcontinent for independence in 1947, partitioned British India into predominantly Hindu India and Muslim Pakistan. The numerous states and territories had to choose which state they preferred to join. British Baluchistan acceded to Muslim Pakistan, but the Baluchistan states, led by the khan of Kalat, refused to join either country. The khan, on 15 August 1947, one day after India and Pakistan became independent, proclaimed Baluchistan an independent state. In 1948, under intense pressure from the governments of Great Britain, Pakistan, Iran, and Afghanistan, the khan nullified the proclamation and acceded to Pakistan.

The province of Baluchistan, Pakistan's largest in area, was abolished, along with the other provinces, in 1958 and became part of a unitary Pakistani state. Rejecting Punjabi domination of the new state system, the khan of Kalat again declared Baluchistan independent of Pakistan on 20 June 1958, with the support of most of the tribal leaders. Pakistani troops soon overran the rebel state and deported the khan, but he was allowed to return as the spiritual leader of the Baluch nation following a resumption of the Baluch uprising in 1962.

The Pakistani government agreed to negotiations on Baluch autonomy in 1971, but, shaken by the secession of East Pakistan, now Bangladesh, the authorities ordered the arrest of the Baluch leaders when they arrived for the scheduled 1971 meeting. Suspecting Baluch intentions to follow Bangladesh into secession, the Pakistani authorities clamped down on the Baluch autonomist and nationalist organizations. In 1973 rebellion broke out in the province and soon spread to Iranian Baluchistan. Pakistani and Iranian military cooperation finally crushed the rebellion in 1977, leaving whole villages razed and over 10,000 Baluch dead. The revolt, which resumed in Iran following the 1979 revolution, was once again brutally crushed.

The Baluch tribal leaders, the *sadars*, are slowly losing influence to the younger, educated leaders who are determined to end the tribal system that they blame for past Baluch defeats. A strong sense of Baluch identity and a desire to unite in a united Baluch state reemerged with the end of the Cold War and the new global emphasis on nationalism and self-determination.

*SELECTED BIBLIOGRAPHY:*

Baloch, I. *The Problem of "Greater Baluchistan": A Study of Baluch Nationalism.* 1987.
Burki, Shahid J. *Pakistan: The Continuing Search for Nationhood.* 1985.
Harrison, Selig S. *In Afghanistan's Shadow: Baluch Nationalism and Soviet Temptations.* 1988.
Matheson, Sylvia A. *The Tigers of Baluchistan.* 1987.

# BAMILEKELAND

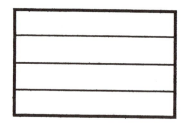

*CAPITAL: Bafoussam*

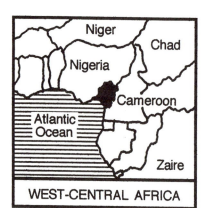

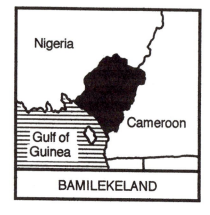

*POPULATION:* (95e) 5,383,000 : 3,800,000 Bamileke in Cameroon. MAJOR NATIONAL GROUPS: Bamileke 68%, Tikar 12%, Bamenda 11%, Bamoun, Bassa, other Cameroonian. MAJOR LANGUAGES: Bamileke, Tikar, French, English. MAJOR RELIGIONS: Protestant, Roman Catholic, animist, Sunni Muslim. MAJOR CITIES: (95e) Douala 1,367,000, Nkongsamba 213,000, Bafoussam 168,000, Bamenda 132,000, Foumban 124,000, Kumba 120,000, Nembe 73,000, Loum 63,000, Edéa 50,000, Buea 45,000.

*GEOGRAPHY:* AREA: 29,487 sq.mi.-76,392 sq.mi. LOCATION: Bamilekeland occupies a highland region in northwestern Cameroon, stretching from the lower Adamawa Mountains to Mount Cameroon just east of the international border with Nigeria, and south to the lowlands of the delta of the Sananga River. POLITICAL STATUS: Bamilekeland has no official status; the region claimed by nationalists forms the Cameroonian provinces of Nord-Ouest, Sud-Ouest, Ouest, and Littoral.

*FLAG:* The Bamileke national flag, the flag of the national movement, has four equal, horizontal stripes of green, yellow, red, and black.

*PEOPLE:* The Bamileke, the largest of Cameroon's numerous ethnic groups, are a Bantu people speaking a northwestern Bantu language of the Niger-Congo language group. Considered the most energetic and enterprising people in Cameroon, the prolific Bamileke have expanded rapidly during the twentieth century, occupying regions outside their traditional homeland, including the large city of Douala. The smaller highland tribes, especially the closely related Tikar and Bamenda, have long historic and cultural ties to the dominant Bamileke.

*THE NATION:* Thought to have originated farther to the north, the Bantu tribes moved into the highlands to escape Muslim invaders in the eleventh century. Over several centuries numerous small chiefdomships emerged, often warring among themselves. Some ninety of the small tribal states united in the fifteenth and sixteenth centuries to form a powerful confederation in the southern highlands. The confederation took the name Bamileke, the name of the largest member state. The confederation began to decline in the eighteenth century, its disintegration hastened by the secession of the Bamoun states.

British explorers, pushing inland from the slave ports, made contact with the confederation in the early nineteenth century. The European explorers were soon followed by Christian missionaries and merchant adventurers. Despite its considerable influence among the highland tribes in the region, Great Britain made no colonial claims.

In 1884 several chiefs signed a protectorate agreement with German explorer Gustov Nachtigal, laying the foundation for Germany's annexation of the confederation to its Kamerun colony. German rule, specifically, forced labor and the curtailment of the powers of the traditional chiefs, incited sporadic rebellions up to World War I. Taken by British troops from Nigeria in 1914, German Kamerun was partitioned between Britain and France. In 1922 the Allied powers established mandate governments under the auspices of the new League of Nations. The boundary between the two mandates, drawn without consideration for the region's traditional frontiers, partitioned the traditional Bamileke lands.

The expansion of the Bamileke into the lowlands, beginning in the 1920s, presented the British and French authorities with a major challenge, as the dynamic Bamileke soon controlled regional commerce on both sides of the international border and increasingly demanded the reunification of the lands populated by the Bamileke and related tribes. The two Cameroon mandates, under different administrative systems and using different languages, had little in common except the Bamileke-Tikar-Bamenda ethnic community and a shared past as a German colony.

Bamileke nationalism grew rapidly after World War II, with the first openly nationalistic organization, the Union Bamileke, formed in 1948. The continuing partition of Bamilekeland, reinforced by a United Nations decision to establish trust territories within the old mandate borders in 1946, spurred the rapid spread of nationalist sentiment. Strikes and demonstrations demanding a separate administration for a united Bamilekeland brought commercial life in the region to a halt in the late 1940s.

The British and French authorities met in Kumba in May 1949 and again in December 1951 to try to work out a program that would satisfy Bamileke demands, but the two sides failed to reach an agreement. In 1954 the British added their trust territory to Nigeria as a quasi-federal state with its own administration.

Planned independence for the French Cameroons, announced in 1958, provoked savage rioting and demands for immediate Bamileke independence. A Bamileke rebellion, joined by the Tikar and other smaller tribes, paralyzed western Cameroon. The separatists formed a government-in-exile in Guinea in 1960, led by the outlawed Union of Cameroonian Peoples (UPC), a nationalist, largely Bamileke political party vehemently opposed to domination by the northern Muslim tribes favored by the French administration. Undeterred by the continuing Bamileke rebellion, the French administration granted Cameroon independence in 1960, under a northern, Muslim-dominated government.

A February 1961 plebiscite gave the inhabitants of the British Cameroon a choice of joining independent Cameroon or neighboring Nigeria. In the north the vote favored Nigeria, but in the south the inhabitants voted overwhelmingly for the reunification of Bamilekeland within Cameroon. In 1962 the southern part of the British trust territory joined Cameroon as a separate state within a federal republic.

The Cameroonian government, with French military assistance, defeated the continuing Bamileke revolt in 1963. The five-year rebellion cost over 70,000 lives. Ethnic and religious tensions sparked a renewed rebellion in 1967. Bamileke rebels, called Maquisards, continued to fight government troops until they were finally eradicated in 1971.

Africa's turn toward democracy, following the end of the Cold War, has rekindled old tribal and regional tensions. Supposedly free elections, held in October 1992, polarized Cameroon and fueled a resurgent Bamileke national movement. The government responded by placing the Bamileke provinces under emergency military rule but failed to stem the resurgence of Bamileke national sentiment.

In early 1993 rumors that the English-speaking Bamilekeland was preparing to secede circulated amid a wave of strikes and disruptions that accompanied Bamileke demands for the return of a federal system and guarantees of language and minority rights. The national movement has greatly affected Cameroon's richest area, the English-speaking Bamilekeland, including the formerly French-speaking Douala area. Since 1992 the continuing confrontation has pitted French-speaking gendarmes against the English-speaking Bamileke, adding language to the volatile mix of ethnic tensions and economic problems. Once again Cameroon is faced with the old "Problemé Bamileke."

*SELECTED BIBLIOGRAPHY:*

Asiwaju, A. I. *Partitioned Africans: Ethnic Relations across Africa's International Borders, 1884–1984.* 1985.

Clavert, Albert F. *The Cameroons.* 1976.

Johnson, Willard R. *The Cameroon Federation: Political Integration in a Fragmentary Society.* 1970.

Sheperd, G. W. *The Politics of African Nationalism.* 1962.

# BANGSKA MORO

**Bang sa Moro**

*CAPITAL: Jolo*

SOUTHEASTERN ASIA

BANGSKA MORO

*POPULATION:* (95e) 12,932,000 : 5,950,000 Moros in the Philippines. MAJOR NATIONAL GROUPS: (95e) Moro 45%, other Filipino. MAJOR LANGUAGES: Moro-Magindanao, Visayan, Tagalog, English. MAJOR RELIGIONS: Roman Catholic, Sunni Muslim. MAJOR CITIES: (95e) Zamboanga 491,000, Cagayan de Oro 396,000, Iligan 281,000, Dadiangas (General Santos) 177,000, Cotabato 120,000, Gingoog 104,000, Basilan (Isabela) 98,000 (235,000), Pagadian 97,000 (134,000), Dipolog 85,000 (159,000), Jolo 76,000.

*GEOGRAPHY:* AREA: 19,622 sq.mi.-50,834 sq.km. LOCATION: Bangska Moro lies in the southern Philippine islands, comprising the western half of the large island of Mindanao and the islands lying to the west and south, including the major islands of Basilan, Tawitawi, Palawan, and the Sulu group just northwest of the Malaysian state of Sabah.* POLITICAL STATUS: Bangska Moro has no official status; the area claimed by nationalists forms thirteen Philippine provinces, including a small autonomous region called Muslim Mindanao.

*FLAG:* The Moro national flag, the flag of the Moro National Liberation Front (MNLF), is a red field bearing a centered white Moro sword with a yellow grip and a white, five-pointed star and crescent moon on the upper hoist. OTHER FLAG(S): The flag of the Mindanao Independence Movement (MIM) is a horizontal tricolor of red, white, and yellow, proportions 1:2:1, bearing a yellow crescent moon and five-pointed star centered.

*PEOPLE:* The Moros are a Malay people ethnically, religiously, and linguistically more closely related to the peoples of nearby Kalimantan (Borneo) than to the other Filipino peoples. Comprising thirteen tribal or cultural groups, the Moros speak Moro-Magindanao, a Malayo-Polynesian language with three major dialects: Tausug in the Zamboanga Peninsula region and the Sulu Islands, Magindanao in the Cotabato region of western Mindanao, and Maranao around Lake Lanao in northwestern Mindanao. The Muslim Moros are now outnumbered by Christian settlers in many areas of their traditional homeland.

*THE NATION:* The islands, inhabited by Malay peoples who originally migrated from the Asian mainland, often formed part of the early Indo-Malay empires centered in the Malay Archipelago to the south. Islam arrived in the islands during the great Muslim missionary era, spreading from Borneo through the Sulu Islands to Mindanao between the fourteenth and sixteenth centuries. By the end of the fifteenth century several Moro sultanates had extended Muslim rule to the central islands of the Philippine Archipelago.

European traders began to visit the Philippines in the early sixteenth century, the Spanish establishing the first permanent European settlement in 1565. The Spanish easily conquered the northern islands, but when they moved into the central islands, they came across the warlike Moros intent on extending Muslim rule to the north. Driven back to the southern islands by the better-armed Europeans, the Moros were checked, but not conquered. For the next two centuries Moro pirates harassed Spanish shipping and terrorized coastal settlements. Internecine warfare among the several sultanates continued, the Moros uniting only when the Spanish threatened their territories.

The Spanish colonial administration, in control of the entire Philippine Archipelago except for the southern islands, launched a military campaign against the Moros in 1850, but were beaten back. Sporadic clashes continued up to the Spanish-American War of 1897–98, which ended with the United States as the administrator of the Philippine islands.

American attempts to occupy the southern islands generated a widespread armed conflict, the Moro War of 1899–1905. American troops, led by General John Pershing, finally brought the islands under effective military control, ending over three centuries of Moro resistance to foreign domination. The Americans outlawed slavery and polygamy, established civil administration, and occasionally put down uprisings but generally left the Moros to their traditional way of life.

The Philippines, independent soon after World War II, settled on a policy of Christian colonization to dilute the Muslim majority in the south. Christian settlers, offered homesteads and generous government assistance, streamed into the area. As tensions and religious violence mounted during the 1960s, the Moros organized to resist the onslaught. Moro nationalists formed the Moro National Liberation Front (MNLF), its objective an independent Moro state in the traditionally Muslim regions of the southern Philippines.

The Moros, threatened by the continuing Christian immigration to their homeland, rebelled in 1972. With aid from many Muslim countries, the Moros attempted to drive the Philippine military and the colonists from their land. Heavy fighting over the next five years devastated the region and left over 60,000 dead and 250,000 refugees. In 1977 the government negotiated an agreement that provided for an autonomous region covering thirteen provinces, but the region's now majority Christian population rejected the plan.

A renewed Moro rebellion followed the rejection of the autonomy plan and continued sporadically until the Philippines' new democratic government began talks in 1986. A truncated autonomous region, including only the four provinces that still have Muslim majorities, was created in 1989. The resistance of the region's Christian majority continues to hamper government efforts to find a peaceful solution.

In late 1993 the government opened talks with the nationalist groups representing the Moros, but, in spite of the efforts of the Indonesian government to mediate, the talks again collapsed. With negotiations stalled in 1993–94 several organizations again turned to violence with a campaign of kidnappings, bombings, and confrontations with the Philippine troops stationed in the region. The seemingly intractable problem has made yet another Moro separatist war a very real possibility.

*SELECTED BIBLIOGRAPHY:*

Barrows, David P. *The History of the Philippines.* 1984.

Kessler, Richard J. *Rebellion and Repression in the Philippines.* 1989.

Von der Mehden, Fred. R. *Religion and Nationalism in Southeast Asia: Burma, Indonesia, and the Philippines.* 1989.

# BAROTSELAND

**Zambezia**

*CAPITAL: Mongu*

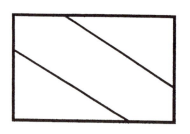

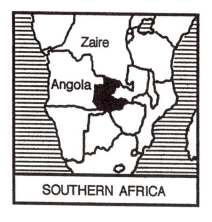

SOUTHERN AFRICA

BAROTSELAND

*POPULATION:* (95e) 1,765,000 : 1,445,000 Lozi (Barotse) in Zambia, and another 630,000 in adjacent areas of Namibia, Zimbabwe, Botswana, and Angola. MAJOR NATIONAL GROUPS: (95e) Lozi 74%, other Zambian. MAJOR LANGUAGES: Lozi (Luyana), English, Bemba. MAJOR RELIGIONS: Protestant, animist, Roman Catholic. MAJOR CITIES: (95e) Livingstone 122,000, Mongu 60,000, Solwezi 33,000, Zambezi 25,000, Batoka 15,000 (46,000), Lealui 15,000.

*GEOGRAPHY:* AREA: 130,273 sq.mi.-337,496 sq.km. LOCATION: Barotseland occupies the fertile floodplains of the Zambezi River in western Zambia, bordering Angola on the west, the Zairean province of Katanga\* on the north, and Zimbabwe, Botswana, and Namibia on the south. POLITICAL STATUS: Barotseland has no official status; the region forms the Western, Northwestern, and Southern provinces of Zambia.

*FLAG:* The Lozi national flag, the flag of the national movement, is a red field bearing a broad white, diagonal stripe from the upper hoist to the lower fly.

*PEOPLE:* The Lozi, called Barotse or Marotse by their neighbors, are a Bantu people thought to be the descendants of Lunda tribesmen from present eastern Zaire. The Lozi language, adopted in the nineteenth century, is related to the Sotho language spoken in South Africa and Lesotho far to the southeast. Divided into numerous clan groups, the Lozi are united by their language and their unique history. Formerly one of the wealthiest peoples in the region, the Lozi are now among the poorest in southern Africa.

*THE NATION:* Bantu peoples, thought to belong to the large Lunda tribe, conquered the Zambezi lowlands in the seventeenth century. Several of the small kingdoms established by the conquerors eventually united under a paramount king at Lealui. A highly advanced bureaucratic state, the Lozi kingdom expanded to eventually control over twenty-five subject states. The kingdom gradually developed the three major organs of a modern political community: a centralized authority, a well-defined administrative machinery, and established judicial institutions. The subject peoples did not enjoy the same privileges as the Lozi.

The Kalolo, a Sotho tribe from the southeast, displaced during the massive Zulu migrations, conquered the Lozi kingdom in the 1840s. The highland Kalolo, unused to the wet lowlands, were soon decimated by malaria, endemic along the Zambezi River. In 1864 the Lozi overthrew the weakened Kalolo administration and reestablished their kingdom. In spite of the short period of Kalolo domination, their Sotho language replaced the earlier Lozi tongue.

British explorer and missionary David Livingstone, visiting the kingdom in 1851, found a highly sophisticated and cultured state in control of a vast multitribal empire. In 1871 a British trader, George Westbuch, reached the kingdom and so impressed the Lozi king, the Litunga, with his guns that he was allowed to establish a trading post and later became a close adviser to the king. In the 1880s King Lewanika, realizing that with the arrival of the Europeans his kingdom would need powerful new allies, sent an appeal to the British authorities in Cape Town asking for Queen Victoria's protection.

The British South Africa Company, in 1889, established a protectorate in Barotseland, although wily King Lewanika signed away only the lands and mineral rights of the subject peoples. In 1891 the British and Portuguese agreed to delineate Barotseland's western border but were unable to agree on the territorial extent of Lozi influence. The king of Italy, asked to arbitrate the dispute, finally drew a straight line north to south. In 1903, over the protests of the Lozi that the transfer deprived them of over half their traditional lands, a vast area of western Barotseland became part of Portuguese Angola.

The Victoria Falls Treaty of 1900 gave the British the right to open the lands of the subject peoples to European settlement. Under British pressure Lewanika abolished slavery in the kingdom, devastating the agricultural base until the king devised schemes to grow and sell fruits and vegetables in the growing European city of Livingstone, founded in Barotse territory in 1905. In 1911 Barotseland was incorporated into the British colony of Northern Rhodesia with Livingstone as its administrative capital. Five years later Lewanika died, having retained at least the outward trappings of the monarchy.

Neglected by the colonial government that concentrated its attention on the lucrative copper mines in the east, the Lozi homeland formed a vast labor pool, with the proud tribesmen forced to seek work in the British mines and on farms far from their homeland. In the 1920s Lozi resentment sparked the first stirrings of nationalism and a campaign for Lozi self-government. Once the richest nation in the region, the Lozi became progressively poorer as development schemes favored the commercially important Copperbelt mining region, where many Lozi migrated in search of work. Ethnic tensions between the migrant Lozi and the region's dominant Bemba tribe fueled the growth of the Lozi national movement.

Separatist agitation peaked in the early 1960s as the British prepared Northern Rhodesia for independence. Fearing domination by the more numerous and sophisticated Bemba, the dominant tribe in the colony's heartland to the east, Lozi nationalists demanded separate independence, citing the kingdom's long and separate ties to Great Britain. The Lozi king, under British pressure, renounced the kingdom's special relationship with the British Crown, thus removing the last barrier to Zambian independence in October 1964.

The government of the new nation, renamed Zambia, having abolished all opposition, established a one-party state in 1972. The country, one of the richest in sub-Saharan Africa at independence, gradually became one of the poorest. Heavily subsidizing the Copperbelt and the urbanized east of the country, the government ignored Barotseland and its rich agricultural potential. The government's failure to develop an efficient road system to connect the regions effectively cut off the Barotse provinces from the Zambian heartland.

One-party rule in Zambia ended in November 1991. The new democratic government inherited a country suffering severe food shortages. The end of the copper boom fanned smoldering ethnic tensions. In December 1992 Lozi nationalists demanded the restoration of the monarchy, reversion to the name Barotseland, and a return to Barotseland's autonomous political status of 1964. The rapid growth of Lozi national sentiment has added to Zambia's instability. In March 1993 the new democratic government declared a state of emergency as economic and political difficulties multiplied. Increasing ethnic tensions between the Lozi and Bemba, since 1993, have been aggravated by the country's severe economic problems.

*SELECTED BIBLIOGRAPHY:*
Burdette, M. M. *Zambia: Between Two Worlds.* 1988.
Powdermaker, Hortense. *Copper Town: Changing Africa.* 1962.
Roberts, A. *A History of Zambia.* 1977.

# BASHKORTOSTAN

**Bashkurdistan; Bashkiria; Baškyrstan**

*CAPITAL: Ufa*

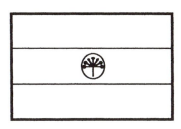

EASTERN EUROPE

BASHKORTOSTAN

*POPULATION:* (95e) 4,068,000 : 2,310,000 Bashkir (Bashkort) in Russia. "Greater Bashkortostan," 6,334,000. MAJOR NATIONAL GROUPS: (95e) Bashkortostan: Russian 36%, Bashkir 26%, Tatar 22%, Chavash 4%, Mishar 3%, Mari 3%. MAJOR LANGUAGES: Russian, Tatar, Bashkir, Chavash, Mari. MAJOR RELIGIONS: Sunni Muslim, Russian Orthodox. MAJOR CITIES: (95e) BASHKORTOSTAN: Ufa 1,202,000 (1,280,000), Sterlitamak 270,000 (305,000), Salavat 166,000 (263,000), Oktybrskiy 121,000, Neftekamsk 114,000 (191,000), Beloretsk 77,000, Ishimbay 74,000. ORENBURG: Orenburg 573,000 (621,000), Orsk 296,000 (430,000), Novotroitsk 116,000, Buzulak 85,000, Buguruslan 53,000, Mednogorsk 47,000 (140,000).

*GEOGRAPHY:* AREA: 55,443 sq.mi.-143,635 sq.km. "Greater Bashkortostan," 107,806 sq.mi-279,290 sq.km. LOCATION: Bashkortostan lies in eastern European Russia, occupying a plateau region just west of the Ural Mountains. Heavily forested in the east and in the foothills of the Urals, Bashkortostan's western districts form part of the important Ural industrial region. POLITICAL STATUS: Bashkortostan forms a member state of the Russian Federation. "Greater Bashkortostan," the region claimed by nationalists, also includes Russia's Orenburg Oblast.

*INDEPENDENCE DECLARED:* 29 November 1917.

*FLAG:* The Bashkir national flag, the official flag of the republic, is a horizontal tricolor of pale blue, white, and green bearing a centered gold circle surrounding a seven-petaled *kurai*, a reed that grows only in Bashkortostan.

*PEOPLE:* The Bashkir, who call themselves Bashkort, are a people of mixed

Finnic, Turkic, and Mongol ancestry. Traditionally, the Bashkir comprise seven clans in the area of "Greater Bashkortostan": the Kipchak, Yurmat, Myng, Usergan, Katai, Tabin, and Burzyan. The Bashkir language, a Turko-Tatar language closely related to Tatar, is the primary national language; however, with over half of the Bashkir population living outside the republic, most are bilingual, with only a third speaking just Bashkir. The Bashkirs are a Sunni Muslim people, as is the large Tatar minority living in the northwest of the republic. The large Slav population is mainly concentrated in the cities and the industrial areas in the west.

*THE NATION:* Nomadic herders in the southern Ural Mountains, in the first records that mention the Bashkirs, in the ninth and tenth centuries, list them as a people under the nominal rule of the Volga Bulgar state of the Chavash. Slavic monks, venturing into the pagan lands to the east, converted the Bashkirs to Christianity, traditionally in the year A.D. 922. By the eleventh century most of the Bashkirs had abandoned Christianity for the Islamic religion brought north by traders from Central Asia.

The Golden Horde, Mongol and Turkic warriors of the Mongol's vast empire, overran the region in the thirteenth century. The Bashkir lands later came under the rule of the Tatar Khanate of Kazan, established as Mongol power declined in the fourteenth century. A long series of wars with the growing Russian state ended with the khanate's conquest in 1557. The conquered Bashkir lands, settled by Slavic colonists and controlled by a string of Russian forts, formed the new frontier districts of the expanding Russian Empire.

In 1708 the Muslim Bashkirs rebelled and attacked the 3,000 Cossack and Russian settlements on their traditional lands. The Bashkir revolt quickly spread to the other subject peoples of the Volga River basin, thus threatening Russian rule in the east until enough troops arrived to defeat the rebels in 1711. Bashkir rebellions became so frequent that, in the late eighteenth century, smiths were forbidden to practice their trade to prevent the fabrication of weapons. To counter the endemic Bashkir revolts, the government established Cossak military colonies in the southern Bashkir lands. The Cossack colonists took the name of an important military fort, calling themselves the Orenburg Cossacks.

The abolition of serfdom in 1861 brought a massive influx of freed serfs seeking land. The migration, seen as a threat to the Bashkirs' survival, fanned the growth of Bashkir nationalism in the late nineteenth century. The Bashkirs again rebelled when news of the 1905 Russian Revolution reached the area. Nationalists demanded the return of 5.4 million acres of stolen land, while more radical groups attacked Russian settlements and estates and assassinated tsarist officials, including the governor-general of Ufa, before the Orenburg Cossacks quelled the revolt.

Largely untouched by World War I, the nationalists rapidly organized as revolution swept the empire in February 1917. In July the Bashkir leaders convened a national congress at Orenburg, which adopted an interim program favoring autonomy and the expulsion of Slav colonists from the traditional Bashkir lands in Ufa and Orenburg provinces. The threat posed by the Bolshevik coup, in October 1917, forced the reluctant Bashkirs into an alliance with their old enemies, the Orenburg Cossacks.

The revolution having failed to secure their lost lands, the Bashkir Revolutionary Committee (Bashrevkom) declared their homeland independent of the collapsing empire on 29 November 1917, claiming as national territory the traditional Bashkir lands in the provinces of Ufa and Orenburg. The claim to Orenburg ended the uneasy alliance with the Orenburg Cossacks, who fought and defeated the Bashkirs for control of the southern province. In February 1918 Bolshevik forces overran the new republic.

An alliance with the anti-Bolshevik forces, the Whites, including the Orenburg Cossacks, soon broke down over the White opposition to Bashkir nationalism. Spurned by the Whites, the Bashkirs accepted a Bolshevik promise of independence within a Soviet federation of sovereign states and went over to the Reds in March 1918.

Treated as a conquered peopled and denied the promised independence, the Bashkirs turned on their new allies. The Red Army, following its victory over the Whites in 1920, concentrated troops against the Bashkirs. The starving rebels finally surrendered in early 1922. The northern part of their traditional lands, called Little Bashkiria, the province of Ufa, became the first autonomous republic within the Soviet Russian Federation in March 1922.

Suppressed for over fifty years, a Bashkir cultural revival began in the late 1970s, spurred by a renewal of interest in their Islamic religion. The growing cultural movement coincided with the liberalization of Soviet society in the late 1980s, stimulating a resurgence of dormant Bashkir nationalism.

Bashkir pressure on the local Soviet government won significant cultural and linguistic concessions and, in 1990, a declaration of state sovereignty. In the wake of the disintegration of the Soviet Union, demands for independence gained public support in the republic. Negotiations with the new Russian government yielded new economic policies and more local control over the republic's oil reserves.

In November 1991 the republican government reversed previous policy and announced its aim of eventual independence and in February 1992 changed the official name of the republic to Bashkortostan. In early 1993 Bashkir nationalists renewed their old claims to Greater Bashkortostan, including Orenburg Oblast, which would give Bashkortostan, and the other republics in the Volga River basin an outlet and a land border with the Republic of Kazakhstan on the south.

*SELECTED BIBLIOGRAPHY:*

D'Encausse, Helene C. *Nationalities and the Bolshevik State, 1917–1930.* 1991.
Din, Shams. *Perestroika and the Nationalities Quest in the USSR.* 1991.
Hasler, Joan. *The Making of the Soviet Union.* 1989.

# BAVARIA

Bayern

*CAPITAL: Munich (München)*

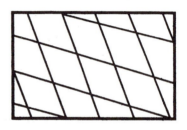

WEST-CENTRAL EUROPE

BAVARIA

*POPULATION:* (95e) 11,342,000 : 10,515,000 Bavarians in Germany. MAJOR NATIONAL GROUPS: (95e) Bavarian 85%, other German 13%. MAJOR LANGUAGE: German (Bavarian dialect). MAJOR RELIGIONS: (95e) Roman Catholic 70%, Protestant 26%. MAJOR CITIES: (95e) Munich (München) 1,224,00 (2,035,000), Nuremberg (Nürnberg) 443,000 (1,041,000), Augsburg 243,000 (435,000), Würzburg 126,000 (225,000), Regensburg 119,000 (224,000), Erlangen 97,000, Fürth 96,000, Ingolstadt 95,000 (153,000), Bayreuth 73,000 (98,000), Bamberg 67,000 (122,000), Aschaffenburg 58,000 (148,000), Landshut 58,000 (106,000), Kempten 55,000 (75,000), Rosenheim 54,000 (113,000), Schweinfurt 48,000 (118,000).

*GEOGRAPHY:* AREA: 27,332 sq.mi.-70,808 sq.km. LOCATION: Bavaria occupies a mountainous region, traversed by the Danube River and its tributaries, in the Bavarian Alps in southern Germany. POLITICAL STATUS: Bavaria forms a state of the Federal Republic of Germany.

*INDEPENDENCE DECLARED:* 22 November 1918.

*FLAG:* The Bavarian national flag, the official state flag, is a lozenge pattern of pale blue and white.

*PEOPLE:* The Bavarians are a German people comprising three distinct groups that reflect the regional distribution of the early Germanic tribes: the Bavarians in the south, the Swabians in the west, and the Franconians in the north. The Bavarian language, a dialect of High German, is more closely related to the German dialects spoken in neighboring Austria and Switzerland than to the standard German spoken throughout Germany. The Bavarians are the most nationalistic of the German peoples, their national pride based on over a thousand years of separate history. The majority of the Bavarians are Roman Catholic, with a Protestant minority, mostly in Franconia in the north.

*THE NATION:* Germanic tribes crossed the Danube River, for centuries the northern boundary of Roman rule, as Roman power declined in the fourth and fifth centuries A.D. Bavaria, named for the Bavarii tribe, formed a region tributary to the Franks in the sixth century and in 788 came under the rule of Charlemagne's empire. Converted to Christianity in the eighth century, Bavaria developed as one of the five stem duchies of the Holy Roman Empire and one of the most powerful of the German states.

Under Saxon rule in the twelfth century, the Bavarian Österreich (East Mark) separated in 1156 to become a distinct duchy, called Austria in English. In 1180 the Saxon lands were further divided by Frederick Barbarossa, who gave Bavaria to the house of Wittelsbach. The Bavarian state, traditionally allied to neighboring Austria, became the most powerful of the southern German states.

With Bavaria allied to France in the early nineteenth century, Napoleon awarded Bavaria additional territories in Swabia and Franconia and in 1806 raised the Bavarian ruler, Maximillian I, to the rank of king. The Bavarian king later deserted Napoleon and participated in the Congress of Vienna as the head of an allied nation. The congress awarded Bavaria additional territory.

Politically and culturally closer to Vienna than to Berlin, Bavaria joined Austria to fight the hated Prussians in 1866 and, with defeat, paid a large indemnity and joined the Prussian-dominated German Empire in 1871, effectively ending Bavaria's independence. Pan-German nationalism, fostered throughout the empire, spread to Bavaria, but without replacing Bavarian national sentiment. Bavarian nationalists remained adamantly opposed to the domination of the empire by Protestant Prussia.

Bavarian armies fought for the empire as war engulfed Europe in 1914 and shared Germany's defeat in November 1918. As revolution swept Germany, revolutionaries deposed the Bavarian king and declared the kingdom a republic. By mid-November the major functions of government had come under the control of the socialists, led by Kurt Eisner, who declared Bavaria independent of Germany on 22 November 1918.

Eisner, viewed as the one man produced by Germany's revolution who compared with his Russian counterparts, was assassinated by an embittered monarchist while on his way to open parliament on 19 February 1919. Without Eisner's leadership, the socialist government faltered, its weakness a pretext for a Communist coup. The Communists, inspired by Soviet Russia, declared the Soviet Republic of Bavaria on 7 April 1919. German troops, called in by the deposed socialists, invaded the state and defeated the Communists in May. A new Bavarian government, firmly under the control of Pan-German nationalists, joined the recently inaugurated German federation.

Bavarian nationalism, anti-Semitic and anti-Prussian, proved fertile ground for radical and reactionary political movements. In November 1923 monarchist groups attempted to seize the government, intent on secession and the restoration of the kingdom. A small, radical political group, the Nationalist Socialist Party, called Nazis, preempted the planned coup and attempted its own takeover of the Bavarian government. For his part in the failed coup, the group's leader, Adolph Hitler, received a five-year prison sentence. In the Bavarian prison he wrote *Mein Kampf*, his plan for world domination.

The Nazis, with their only strong support in Bavaria's Protestant north, after taking control of the German government in 1933, dispatched elite troops to take control of Bavaria on the pretext that the state authorities had proved unable to maintain order and supported Bavarian separatism. A Catholic separatist plot, discovered in 1934, gave the Nazis a reason to ruthlessly eliminate all remaining Bavarian opposition.

Initially enthusiastic in 1939, Bavarian support for the war declined rapidly as Allied bombers reduced many cities to rubble. A resurgent nationalist movement attempted to win Allied support for separate independence in 1945 but ultimately settled for major autonomy within a reconstituted federal Germany. The poorest of the states in 1949, Bavaria experienced an economic miracle when industries relocated from Communist East Germany. By 1972 Bavaria had become one of the federation's richest states.

European integration and German reunification, in 1990, rekindled Bavarian nationalism. Nationalists compare Bavaria's inclusion in united Europe, as part of Germany, to the still-controversial accession of the state to Bismarck's Germany in 1871. For many Bavarian nationalists, the German government has become an unwanted tier of government above Bavaria's cherished autonomy. Nationalists continue to press for greater direct Bavarian participation in united Europe, while an increasingly vocal minority argues for the ''European Option,'' Bavarian independence within a European federation.

*SELECTED BIBLIOGRAPHY:*
Schultz, Hagen, ed. *Nation-Building in Central Europe.* 1987.
Shlaes, Amity. *Germany: The Empire Within.* 1991.
Werner, George S. *Bavaria in the German Confederation 1820–1848.* 1977.

# BENIN

**Great Benin; Bendel; Edoland; Midwest Nigeria**

*CAPITAL: Benin City*

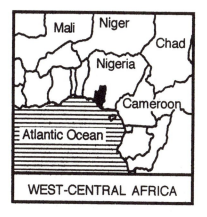

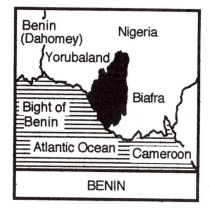

*POPULATION:* (95e) 4,899,000: 3,500,000 Edo in Nigeria (2,000,000 Edo, 1,200,000 Urhobo, 300,000 Bini). MAJOR NATIONAL GROUPS: (95e) Edo (including Urhobo and Bini) 63%, Itsekiri, Ibo, Ijaw, other Nigerian. MAJOR LANGUAGES: Edo, Jehiri, Ibo, Ijo, English. MAJOR RELIGIONS: Protestant, Roman Catholic, animist. MAJOR CITIES: (95e) Benin City 228,000, Sapele 138,000, Warri 127,000, Uromi 80,000, Asaba 72,000, Igarra 69,000, Ugwashi-Uku 55,000, Forcados 50,000, Burutu 35,000.

*GEOGRAPHY:* AREA: 15,361 sq.mi.-39,795 sq.km. LOCATION: Benin lies in southwestern Nigeria, occupying an upland savanna sloping down to the forest zone and the delta of the Niger River on the Bight of Benin. POLITICAL STATUS: Benin has no official status; the region forms Edo and Delta states of the Federal Republic of Nigeria.

*INDEPENDENCE DECLARED:* 18 August 1967.

*FLAG:* The Edo national flag, the flag of the national movement, is a black field, with a broad green, horizontal stripe at the bottom, bearing a yellow rising sun with eleven rays centered.

*PEOPLE:* The Edo are a Bantu people, the descendants of one of Africa's most sophisticated precolonial kingdoms. The Edo nation includes the Edo proper and two subgroups, the Urhobo (Sobo) south of Benin City and the Bini around the capital city, all three divisions speaking dialects of the same language of the Kwa group of Niger-Congo languages. The Edo form the largest of the six ethnic-linguistic groups that inhabit the territory formerly included in the territory of the Edo's Kingdom of Benin.

*THE NATION:* Early records mention Benin as a well-established state by around A.D. 1000. According to Edo legends, the first Edo empire declined, and the elders sent a delegation to Ife in Yorubaland* to find a prince to rule Benin. The second empire, thought to have been established between 1390 and 1440, developed as one of the most advanced states in Africa.

The Portuguese established contact with the kingdom in 1485. Ruled by a king, called the *oba*, and a council of state, the Uzama, Benin dazzled the Europeans with its wealth, art, and sophistication. However one facet of Benin's advanced culture profoundly shocked the visitors, human sacrifice, an important religious and political ritual.

Benin reached its greatest territorial extent between 1816 and 1848, controlling lands from the Niger River to west of present Lagos, a vast empire that included a number of states inhabited by non-Edo tribes. In the 1850s the empire began to disintegrate as the Itsekiri and other subject peoples broke away to establish relations with the rising power in the region, the British.

The lucrative slave trade, mostly involving the subject coastal peoples, attracted the Europeans and gradually resulted in the British taking control of the slave ports. In 1885 the British formally annexed the kingdom's coastal districts, leaving the heartland of the kingdom, the last part of present Nigeria, outside British rule. The Edo, in an effort to retain their independence, broke off all contact with the Europeans, but in 1892 the British succeeded in forcing the kingdom to outlaw slavery and human sacrifice and to accept protectorate status.

A peaceful British emissary, moving toward Benin City in 1896, so alarmed the Edo that they attacked and massacred the entire column. The British dispatched an expedition of 1,500 men to subdue the Edo rebels. When the column entered the deserted capital, Benin City, they found a treasure of magnificent artworks alongside the evidence of the human sacrifices the Edo had hoped would persuade the gods to help defeat the British invaders. The British looted and burned the city, with over 2,000 pieces of fabulous Benin art shipped to London. The British deported the captured king, his family, and advisers. In 1897 the British installed a new *oba* under close colonial administration scrutiny.

Direct British rule gave way to more indirect rule through the *obas* in 1914, but an administrative union of Benin and Yorubaland, opposed by the proud Edo, initiated the growth of modern Edo nationalism. In 1948 Edo students formed the first openly nationalist organization, the Edo National Union, the forerunner of the later Otu Edo, an organization dedicated to defending Edo interests against domination by the Yorubas.

The division of Nigeria into three autonomous regions in 1954 spurred the rapid growth of Edo nationalism in opposition to the inclusion of Benin in the Yoruba-dominated Western Region. Agitation for separation was complicated by the refusal of the non-Edo peoples of the region to support a resurgent Benin, and Edo refusal to consider a separate region without the non-Edo districts of the old Benin kingdom. The discovery of oil in the Niger delta gave Edo nationalism a strong economic base.

British preparations to grant independence to Nigeria strengthened the growing national movement. Serious agitation swept Benin in 1957–58 as demands for separate independence increased. In 1960 Nigeria became an independent federation of three regions. The new Nigerian government, acting on serious Edo threats to secede, in 1964 created a fourth region, the Midwest Region, encompassing the traditional Edo lands.

The federal government granted the region major autonomy in 1967 in an effort to undermine Edo nationalists' threats to take their petroleum wealth and to follow Biafra* into secession. Chaos ensued following the invasion of the region by Biafran forces on 10 August 1967. Mutineers, led by Major-General Okonkwo, an ethnic Ibo from eastern Benin, seized Benin City and on 18 August 1967 declared Benin independent of both Nigeria and Biafra. Invading federal troops ended the secession on 20 September 1967.

The only region not divided and redivided in response to ethnic and religious pressures following the end of the Biafran war, the Edo lands remained intact. However, in 1975 the Edo were forced to accept a new name for their state, Bendel, as the Republic of Dahomey, with no historic connection to Benin, had usurped their ancient name. Nigeria's recognition of Dahomey's name change fueled a resurgence of Edo nationalism already mobilizing in opposition to the continuing domination of Nigeria by the northern Muslim peoples.

Serious antigovernment rioting swept the region in 1989, fed by demands for greater autonomy and a fairer share of their oil wealth. In August 1991, in an attempt to undermine resurgent Edo nationalism, the government created a new state, called Delta, in the south, the first change to the status of the Edo lands since 1964. Most Edo national organizations, in September 1993, joined in denouncing Nigeria's new military government. Rising tensions, opposition to the Muslim northerners who dominate the military government, and closer ties to Yorubaland resulted from the annulation of the 1993 elections and the imposition of yet another Muslim-dominated military government in Nigeria.

*SELECTED BIBLIOGRAPHY:*

Asiegbu, J. U. *Nigeria and Its British Invaders.* 1984.

Coleman, James S. *Nigeria: Background to Nationalism.* 1971.

Igiehon, Noser. *To Build a Nigerian Nation.* 1987.

Irukwu, J. O. *Nigeria at the Crossroads.* 1983.

# BIAFRA

**Eastern Nigeria; Iboland**

*CAPITAL: Enugu*

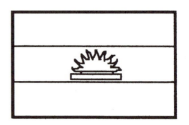

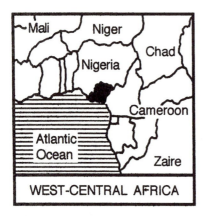

WEST-CENTRAL AFRICA

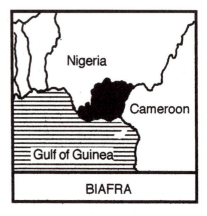

BIAFRA

*POPULATION:* (95e) 24,193,000 : 21,450,000 Ibos in Nigeria. MAJOR NATIONAL GROUPS: (95e) Ibo 65%, Ibibio 15%, Ijaw 9%, other Nigerian. MAJOR LANGUAGES: Ibo, Efik, Ijo, English. MAJOR RELIGIONS: Protestant, animist, Roman Catholic. MAJOR CITIES: (95e) Port Harcourt 324,000 (445,000), Onitsha 336,000 (422,000), Enugu 281,000, Aba 260,000, Calabar 168,000, Akwa 126,000, Owerri 122,000, Ikot Ekpene 110,000, Uyo 105,000, Abakaliki 104,000, Oron 95,000, Nnewi 76,000 (131,000).

*GEOGRAPHY:* AREA: 29,659 sq.mi.-76,838 sq.km. LOCATION: Biafra lies in southeastern Nigeria between the Niger River and the Cameroon border, a region of upland savanna with an extensive forest zone in the south, and the lowlands of the Niger River delta, which forms part of the coastline on the Bight of Benin, formerly the Bight of Biafra. POLITICAL STATUS: Biafra has no official status; the former republic now forms the Nigerian states of Abia, Akwa Ibom, Anambra, Cross River, Enugu, Imo, and Rivers.

*INDEPENDENCE DECLARED:* 30 May 1967.

*FLAG:* The Ibo national flag, the flag of the former republic, is a horizontal tricolor of red, black, and green bearing a gold bar surmounted by a rising gold sun with eleven rays centered.

*PEOPLE:* The Ibo, also called Igbo, are Nigeria's third largest ethnic group, a Bantu people speaking a Niger-Congo language. Known for their energy and industry, the Ibos are often called the ''Scots'' of Nigeria, a tribute to their business sense and willingness to live outside their homeland for commercial purposes. The largest of the non-Ibo ethnic groups are the Ibibio in the southeastern region of Calabar* and the Ijaw in the Niger River delta. The majority of the Ibos are Christian, most belonging to Protestant sects.

*THE NATION:* Divided into over 200 autonomous tribes, the Ibo never developed a central authority like that of neighboring peoples. Cultural influences, particularly from the sophisticated Kingdom of Benin* to the west, shaped Ibo customs and art, but, unified only by language and traditions, the numerous autonomous tribes remained subject to raid by slavers from the Muslim north and the coastal tribes trading with the Europeans.

Europeans, pushing inland from the slave ports, made direct contact with the Ibo tribes in the seventeenth century. One tribe, the Aro, developed a vast commercial trade network with the Europeans and eventually engaged in the lucrative slave trade, preying on the related tribes in the densely populated region.

Christian missionaries, arriving in the early nineteenth century, found the Ibo particularly receptive to both Christianity and the educational opportunities offered by mission schools. By the 1830s Christianity had gained a foothold and over the next decades spread throughout the region known as Iboland.

The Ibo homeland came under British rule in 1884, and a year later the authorities consolidated the territory as the Oil Rivers Protectorate, administered by the British Royal Niger Company. Enthusiastically adopting European culture and education, the Ibos quickly overtook the formerly more advanced coastal peoples. Population pressure and a lack of opportunity pushed many educated Ibos to seek administrative and commercial positions in other parts of British Nigeria. Substantial Ibo communities grew up in the coastal regions and in the Muslim north.

The dynamic Ibos, in the 1920s and 1930s, began to abandon clan and tribal divisions and to think of themselves as one people. The name Ibo came to symbolize the unity of the many related tribes. In the 1940s the Ibo became politically active, even though Ibo nationalism had no historical tradition. In 1944 the first Ibo nationalist organization, the Ibo Federal Union, formed to promote Ibo interests in multiethnic Nigeria.

Three regional governments, created by the British authorities in 1953, were dominated by Nigeria's three largest ethnic groups: the Ibo in the east, the Yoruba in the west, and the Hausa and Fulani in the north. Ethnic and regional rivalries among the three regions increased dramatically following Nigerian independence in 1960.

Oil production, begun in the Ibo's Eastern Region in 1958, fueled rapid economic growth and bolstered Ibo nationalism and confidence. Resentment of the dominant position of the more populous Muslim Northern Region and the extravagant use of the East's oil revenues for northern development projects finally erupted in an Ibo rebellion in 1966. Ibo military officers staged a bloody coup and replaced the Muslim-dominated Nigerian government with a new administration under an Ibo president.

The northern Muslims, in July 1966, launched a countercoup and installed a northern Christian, considered a neutral in the regional rivalries, as the new president. Before he could act, serious anti-Ibo rioting spread across the Northern Region, leaving tens of thousands of Ibos dead and wounded. Fleeing the massacres, over a million Ibos fled south to the safety of the Ibo homeland. Mistrust frustrated efforts at a political compromise. Following a futile attempt to win autonomy, Odumegwu Ojukwu, the Ibo leader, declared the Eastern Region independent on 30 May 1967. The new republic took its name from the body of water known as the Bight of Biafra, the part of the Atlantic Ocean that bordered the new state.

Federal troops invaded the breakaway state in June 1967, but, in spite of the overwhelming odds against them, the Biafrans fought on through 1968 and 1969. Starvation struck the helpless civilian population, and hundreds of thousands died of hunger. The Biafran government, pressed into a tiny fraction of its former territory, finally surrendered in 1970, ending the most savage war in African history and the first major televised conflict.

The Nigerian regions, officially divided into twelve states in 1967, were further divided in 1976 in an effort to dilute continuing ethnic nationalism. The civil war, which completed the consolidation of the Ibo nation, has become a component of Ibo nationalism, nourished by the legends and memories of the war of independence.

Regional nationalism, exacerbated by the rapid growth of Muslim fundamentalism in northern Nigeria, took on strong religious overtones in the 1980s. Serious ethnic and religious conflicts again threaten to tear Nigeria apart. The continuing Muslim-dominated military government, renewed in 1993 following the annulment of presidential elections, has provided resurgent Ibo nationalism with a cause, to free the mostly Christian Ibo from decades of Muslim rule.

*SELECTED BIBLIOGRAPHY:*

Coleman, James S. *Nigeria: Background to Nationalism.* 1971.
Gold, Herbert. *Biafra Goodbye.* 1970.
Nafziger, E. Wayne. *The Economics of Instability: The Nigerian-Biafran War.* 1982.
Okpaku, Joseph, ed. *Nigeria, Dilemma of Nationhood: An African Analysis of the Biafran Crisis.* 1970.

# BIOKO

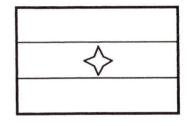

**Eri; Fernando Póo**

*CAPITAL: Malobo*

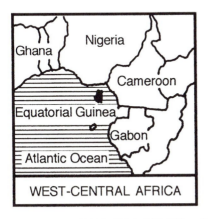

WEST-CENTRAL AFRICA

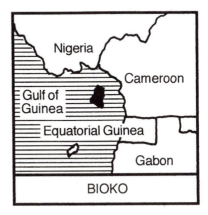

BIOKO

*POPULATION:* (95e) 101,000 : 62,000 Bubi in Equatorial Guinea. MAJOR NATIONAL GROUPS: (95e) Bubi 60%, Fernandinos 15%, Fang 12%, Ibo 9%. MAJOR LANGUAGES: Bubi, Spanish, Fang, Ibo, English. MAJOR RELIGIONS: (95e) Roman Catholic 78%, Protestant 10%, animist. MAJOR CITIES: (95e) Malobo 42,000, Luba 21,000.

*GEOGRAPHY:* AREA: 779 sq.mi.-2,017 sq.km. LOCATION: Bioko lies in the Atlantic Ocean off the coast of west-central Africa, an island in the Gulf of Guinea sixty miles west of Cameroon and some one hundred miles northwest of mainland Equatorial Guinea. The island is made up of two volcanic mountains connected by a long, fertile valley. POLITICAL STATUS: Bioko, called Eri by the Bubi, forms two provinces, North and South Bioko, of the Republic of Equatorial Guinea.

*FLAG:* The Bubi national flag, the traditional flag of the nation, is a horizontal tricolor of pale blue, white, and green bearing a centered black, four-pointed star. OTHER FLAG(S): The same tricolor flag of pale blue, white, and green is the flag of the Bubi national movement, except that the black star has five points.

*PEOPLE:* The Bubi are a Bantu people thought to have developed as a separate people from small groups and refugees arriving on the island from the African mainland. Speaking a northwestern Bantu language of the Niger-Congo language group, the Bubi have retained their language and culture, even though they have often been under the control of stronger mainland tribes. Smaller groups include the Fernandinos, descendants of freed slaves settled on the island in the nineteenth century; the Fang, part of Equatorial Guinea's most numerous tribe; and the Ibo, a tribe that predominates in the nearby Nigerian mainland.

*THE NATION:* The island, inhabited since prehistoric times, has received sporadic migrations of peoples from mainland Africa. The island's ancient inhabitants, representing several linguistic and cultural groups, gradually coalesced as a separate people. Relatively isolated from the influences of the mainland, the Bubi people developed many customs and cultural traits unique in Africa.

Encountered by Portuguese explorer Fernando Póo in 1471, the island served as a center of the growing Portuguese slave trade. In 1778 Portugal ceded the island to Spain as part of a series of agreements that settled colonial boundaries in South America. Almost totally ignored by the Spanish authorities, the island experienced its only contacts with the outside world with occasional Spanish ships from the South American colonies.

The colonial administration, seeing little commercial value in the island, allowed the British to take over the local administration in 1827. The island, a base for the ships involved in the suppression of the slave trade, the British established a mission at the site of Malobo in 1829 as a center for colonization by freed slaves. Between 1829 and 1843 the British landed the slaves taken from captured slave ships on the island, where they eventually came to be called Fernandinos. Returned to Spanish control in 1843, the island became a separate colony in 1858 and united with the mainland colony of Rio Muni in 1885.

The Spanish authorities began the systematic exploitation of the island only in 1926. The island's rich volcanic soil favored plantation agriculture, but the native Bubi resisted Spanish attempts to use them as plantation labor, the resistance movement the forerunner of the later national movement. To overcome the resulting labor shortage, the authorities imported thousands of Ibo workers from nearby British Nigeria.

The decolonization of Africa, begun with the independence of Ghana in 1957, exacerbated the ethnic tensions between the more prosperous Bubi and the Fang, the colony's largest ethnic group. In 1958 Bubi nationalists organized demonstrations to support demands for separation from the mainland area of Rio Muni and autonomy for the island as part of the Spanish state. Pressured by the growing popularity of the nationalists, the Spanish authorities granted autonomy to the island in 1963.

The Republic of Equatorial Guinea became independent in 1968 under a federal system that guaranteed the island's autonomy and reserved a third of the seats in the federal parliament for representatives of the Bubi tribe. In 1969 severe rioting swept the new country over the perceived advantages enjoyed by the Bubi minority. Continuing political and economic turmoil allowed the state's first president, mainlander Masie Nguema Biyogo, to take control and to proclaim himself president-for-life in 1972. Over the next year he established a harsh one-party dictatorship that effectively ended all Bubi autonomy.

Masie's eleven-year reign was one of postcolonial Africa's most brutal. The country's 7,000 Europeans fled, and in 1976 the Nigerian government evacuated over 45,000 Nigerian citizens. The Bubi tribe of the richer island province, seen as a potential threat to his hold on power, lost an estimated third of its population to the president's reign of terror. In 1979 Theodoro Obiang Nguema, Masie's nephew, deposed his uncle and took control of the state.

In 1985 Obiang, like his uncle before him, set up a one-party dictatorship. Pressed by aid donors and pro-democracy groups, presidential elections were held in 1988, which Obiang, as the only candidate, won with 99.98% of the vote.

Bubi nationalist organizations, mostly in exile in Spain, in 1989 stepped up demands for independence. Citing continuing human rights abuses and the rising interethnic violence, the nationalists claimed that the mainland Fang were colonizing and destroying the island. At independence in 1968, Fernando Póo was one of the richest areas of sub-Saharan Africa, but in the 1990s the island is one of Africa's poorest areas. The island receives 70% of its meager income from international aid, and much of that is stolen by corrupt government officials before it reaches the island's coffers.

Pressured by the international community and the principal aid donors, the government has begun to introduce some of the trappings of democracy. In April 1991 President Obiang announced the formation of other political parties and in October 1992 legalized a selected number of opposition groups. Bubi nationalist organizations calling for autonomy or independence remain illegal and persecuted, most of their leaders remaining in exile.

In spite of the small concessions to democracy, Equatorial Guinea, in practice, remains a dictatorial, unitary, one-party state dominated by the Mongomo clan of the Fang tribe, the clan of Macias and Obiang. The government continues to refuse to even discuss the limited cultural and economic autonomy advocated by the most moderate of the Bubi nationalists while a younger generation, less willing to compromise, takes over the leadership of the Bubi nationalist movement.

*SELECTED BIBLIOGRAPHY:*
Baule, E. *Equatorian Guinea: The Bubi Aspirations to Self-Government.* 1980.
Chamberlain, Muriel. *Decolonization: The Fall of European Empires.* 1985.
Fegley, R. *Equatorial Guinea.* 1991.
Liniger-Goumaz, Max. *Equatorial Guinea.* 1980.

# BRITTANY

### Breizh; Bretagne

*CAPITAL: Roazhon (Rennes)*

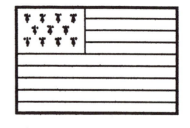

WESTERN EUROPE

BRITTANY

*POPULATION:* (95e) 3,894,000 : 2,820,000 Bretons in France. MAJOR NA-TIONAL GROUPS: (95e) Breton 72%, other French. MAJOR LANGUAGES: French, Breton. MAJOR RELIGIONS: Roman Catholic, Protestant. MAJOR CITIES: (95e) BRITTANY: Brest 151,000 (215,000), Roazhon (Rennes) 114,000 (309,000), Kemper (Quimper) 66,000, An Oriant (Lorient) 58,000 (120,000), Sant Malo (Saint-Malo) 50,000 (65,000), Sant Brieg (Saint-Brieuc) 46,000 (91,000), Givened (Vannes) 37,000 (54,000), Felger (Fougères) 33,000. PAYS DE LA LOIRE: Naoned (Nantes) 228,000 (472,000), Sant Nazaer (Saint-Nazaire) 72,000 (147,000), Raezez (Rezé) 43,000.

*GEOGRAPHY:* AREA: 13,643 sq.mi.-35,344 sq.km. LOCATION: Brittany occupies a large peninsula in the Atlantic Ocean, between the English Channel on the north and the Bay of Biscay on the south. Most of the region lies north of the Loire River in northwestern France. Brittany is traditionally divided into two distinct areas: Amor, the coastal regions, and Argoat, the hinterland. PO-LITICAL STATUS: Brittany, historically comprising five departments, is now divided between two French regions. The departments of Aodou-an-Hanternoz (Côtes-du-Nord), Penn-ar-Bed (Finistère), Il-ha-Givilun (Ille-et-Vilaine), and Ar Mor-Bihan (Morbihan) make up the region of Brittany. The department of Liger Atlantee (Loire-Atlantique) is included in the region of Pays de la Loire.

*FLAG:* The Breton national flag has nine horizontal stripes of black and white charged with a white canton on the upper hoist bearing eight black ermines.

*PEOPLE:* The Bretons are a Celtic people, the only Celtic-speaking nation in continental Europe. The Breton language belongs to the Brythonic branch of

the Celtic group of Indo-European languages. The French language is now the
first language of the region, although Breton, predominant in the western departments, is rapidly being reestablished as Brittany's national language. The
Bretons, with an extraordinary wealth of folklore and music, are said to be as
dreamy and passionate as the Irish, as whimsical as the Welsh, yet as tough and
energetic as the Scots.

*THE NATION:* The Celtic peoples of Britannia, subjugated by the Romans
in the first century B.C., became an urbanized, and later a Christian, population.
The gradual decline of Roman power, leading to the abandonment of Britannia
and the withdrawal of the Roman garrisons in A.D. 410, left the island open to
invasion. Angles, Saxons, and Jutes, Germanic peoples from Northern Europe,
overran the island, driving the Celts into the western peninsulas, Cornwall* and
Wales,* and eventually across the narrow channel to the peninsula called Ar-
morica. Celtic refugees arrived in such numbers in the fifth and sixth centuries
that the peninsula became known as Little Britannia, Britannia Minor, or Brittany.

The Bretons successfully defended their peninsula against the Germanic
Franks from the sixth to the ninth centuries and later repulsed incursions from
neighboring Normandy* and Anjou. In the twelfth century France and England
contested control of Brittany, and the two kingdoms backed rival claimants to
the ducal title during the War of the Breton Succession, which devastated the
peninsula from 1341 to 1365.

Anne of Brittany, heiress to the duchy in the fifteenth century, was wooed
by most of Europe until her marriage to Charles VIII of France in 1491, the
basis of later French claims to the duchy. In 1532 the French kingdom took
control of Brittany, ending Brittany's golden age and over five centuries of
independence. The duchy, annexed outright in 1589, became a French province,
one of the last territories incorporated into the French kingdom.

Brittany retained considerable autonomy, with its own parliament at Rennes
from 1590 to the French Revolution in 1789. An early center of revolutionary
activity, the Bretons soon turned against the revolutionary excesses, antireligious
doctrines, and the centralization of all political power in Paris. In 1793 the
Vendeé uprising spread to most of Brittany, the immediate causes of the uprising
the banning of religion and the introduction of universal conscription. The uprising, called the War of the Vendeé, continued sporadically until the rebels
were decisively routed in 1796. One of the rebel leaders, General Cadonal,
executed in 1804 on Napoleon's orders, is considered the first martyr to Breton
nationalism.

The Bretons, having lost all administrative and cultural autonomy, mobilized
to protect their culture and language. The first Breton dictionary, published in
1821, led to a proliferation of poetry, novels, and history written in the Breton
language. In 1829 the first pro-autonomy organization formed, the Association
Breton. Fired by the cultural revival and the nationalism of their Celtic cousins,
the Irish, the Bretons began to espouse nationalism in the 1870s, the movement

starting a reversal of the assimilation pursued by successive French governments.

The first avowedly separatist group formed in 1911, but, despite German overtures when war began three years later, the Bretons remained loyal to France during World War I. Another Breton national hero is France Laurent, a young soldier executed during the war for not obeying an order given in French, a language he did not understand.

Breton nationalism grew dramatically during the turmoil and economic depression of the 1930s. The Germans, during the World War II occupation of France, attempted to use Breton national sentiment by placing the region under separate administration and allowing broad cultural and linguistic rights. In spite of the German concessions, Nazi doctrine held little attraction for the majority of the conservative, devoutly Catholic Bretons.

The postwar suppression of the Breton language and culture provoked a Breton revival in the 1950s, with a parallel growth of nationalism over the next decade. Numerous cultural, nationalist, and separatist groups emerged, the most militant employing violence and terrorism to press their cause of Breton independence.

The decentralization of the French government, beginning in 1981, returned some powers to local authorities, but the creation of regions loosely based on the historic provinces gave rise to yet another nationalist grievance. The Nantes region, historically an integral part of Brittany, became part of a neighboring region, its separation loudly denounced by Bretons.

Resurgent nationalism, supported by a network of flourishing cultural language schools, cultural centers, and the Breton media, remains a potent force in the region. The Bretons, having won the struggle to save their nation from extinction, now focus on finding a place for Brittany within united Europe.

*SELECTED BIBLIOGRAPHY:*

Brustein, William. *The Social Origins of Political Regionalism: France 1849–1981.* 1982.

Delarue, Marie. *Brittany.* 1990.

Dutton, Ralph. *Normandy and Brittany.* 1953.

Gallioui, Patrick, and Michael Jones. *The Bretons.* 1991.

# BUGANDA

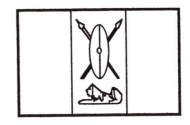

CAPITAL: *Kampala*

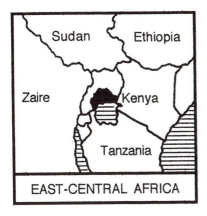

EAST-CENTRAL AFRICA

BUGANDA

*POPULATION:* (95e) 6,269,000 : 4,350,000 Baganda in Uganda. MAJOR NATIONAL GROUPS: (95e) Baganda (Ganda) 60%, Basoga (Soga) 20%, Banyoro (Nyoro) 6%, other Ugandan. MAJOR LANGUAGES: Luganda, Lusoga, Swahili, English. MAJOR RELIGIONS: Protestant, Roman Catholic, animist, Sunni Muslim. MAJOR CITIES: (95e) Kampala 517,000 (774,000), Jinja 188,000, Bugembe 116,000, Masaka 67,000, Mpigi 50,000, Entebbe 38,000.

*GEOGRAPHY:* AREA: 25,631 sq.mi.-66,401 sq.km. LOCATION: Buganda lies in East Africa, occupying the northern and western shores of Lake Victoria in southeastern Uganda. Buganda borders Kenya on the east, the Bunyoro* and Toro* regions of Uganda on the northwest, and the region of Ankole* on the west. POLITICAL STATUS: Buganda forms the Ugandan provinces of North and South Buganda, Central, and Basoga. The kingdom was partially restored in 1993.

*INDEPENDENCE DECLARED:* 31 December 1960.

*FLAG:* The Buganda flag, the flag of the former kingdom, is a blue field with a narrow, vertical white stripe centered, bearing a gold reclining lion surmounted by a gold shield and crossed gold spears.

*PEOPLE:* The Baganda, popularly called Ganda, are a Bantu people who have existed as a distinct nation for nearly a thousand years. In the Ganda's Bantu language, Baganda refers to the people or nation, Luganda the language, and Buganda the state. The Basoga (Soga), a closely related Bantu people, inhabit the region east of the Nile River, and a Banyoro (Nyoro) minority lives in the northwest. A majority of the Ganda, about 80%, belong to various Christian sects, with small animist and Sunni Muslim minorities.

*THE NATION:* Bantu peoples, thought to have settled the region west of Lake Victoria in the tenth century, united in the fourteenth century under the first Ganda king, Kintu. The kingdom, one of the most advanced in the lakes region of East Africa, fell to migrating Nilotic peoples in the sixteenth and seventeenth centuries, the tall warrior peoples eventually absorbed by the more sophisticated Bantu.

The kingdom came under the domination of the powerful neighboring kingdom of Bunyoro in the seventeenth century, beginning a long rivalry for power in the lakes region. Reestablished under hereditary kings in the late eighteenth century, by 1800 Buganda had regained its former glory as one of the most sophisticated states in precolonial Africa.

The Ganda established contact with the coastal Arabs in 1844, a lucrative trade developing in slaves and ivory. The first Europeans visited the kingdom in 1862, amazed to find a cultured, developed state evolving from a feudal monarchy to a modern, bureaucratic administration.

English Protestant missionaries arrived in Buganda in 1877, followed by French Catholics two years later. Ganda Christian converts rapidly became a political force in the kingdom, their power rivaled only by the important Muslim minority. A Muslim uprising, in 1888, provided the British with a pretext to intervene in Buganda. In 1893 the British proclaimed the kingdom a protectorate.

The British and their Christian Ganda allies subdued Buganda's ancient rival, Bunyoro, and imposed nominal British rule on the neighboring kingdoms. The Ganda king, called the Kabaka, for his assistance to the British authorities, received a tract of land taken from defeated Bunyoro, setting off the ''Lost Counties'' dispute that plagued the region for decades.

British policy in the 1920s and 1930s greatly reduced the power of the king and spawned the first stirrings of Ganda nationalism. Threats to the rights of their beloved Kabaka and resentment of British moves to integrate proud Buganda into a random collection of cultures in the Uganda protectorate incited periodic demonstrations and rioting, particularly serious in 1949.

A tentative British plan for a federation of Uganda and White-ruled Kenya in 1953 prompted the Ganda king to demand a timetable for separate Bugandan independence. The British authorities, alarmed by the strength of Ganda national sentiment, deposed the British-educated Kabaka, affectionately called King Freddie, in November 1953. Two years later the king returned from exile, but British permission for his return stipulated that he not oppose Buganda remaining part of Uganda.

Preparations for Ugandan independence provoked a resurgence of Ganda nationalism in 1960, incited by fears of domination by Uganda's non-Bantu northern tribes. Nationalists of the Kabaka Yekka (King Only) Party proclaimed the kingdom independent on 31 December 1960. The British authorities immediately dispatched the colonial army, drawn mostly from the northern tribes, to occupy Kampala and to force the Ganda to accept federal status within a united Uganda. In 1962 Uganda became an independent republic.

The first independent Ugandan government of Milton Obote, controlled by the northern tribes, abolished the autonomy of Buganda and the other Bantu kingdoms in 1966, setting off serious rioting in Kampala. The government accused the Kabaka of promoting secession and sent troops, led by a young northerner named Idi Amin Dada, to storm Twokobe Palace. King Freddie left the country for exile in Europe. In 1967 the Ugandan government abolished the kingdoms, and in 1969 the Kabaka, the thirty-seventh of his line, died in lonely exile.

Idi Amin, with initially widespread support in Buganda, overthrew the hated Obote regime in 1971. A northern Muslim, Amin soon proved to be more brutal than the deposed Obote. Whimsical dictatorial rule gave way to the systematic persecution of the Bantu peoples, Christians, regional leaders, the wealthy, and all suspected or imagined opposition. Massacres, torture, and atrocities became the norm as the former "Pearl of East Africa" collapsed into terror and devastation.

Invading Tanzanians and exiled Ugandans finally overthrew Amin in 1979. After several attempts to form a new government, Milton Obote again gained power in spite of the vehement opposition of the Ganda and the Bantu south. A Bantu guerrilla army gained support in the southern provinces and in 1986 drove Obote into exile and installed Uganda's first Bantu-dominated government.

The return of relative peace and freedom allowed Ganda nationalism to reemerge, with demands for the restoration of the kingdom. The Ganda demands, initially rejected by the government on the grounds that restoration would threaten the stability and integrity of Uganda, gained popular support in the 1990s. In July 1993 the government restored some autonomy to Buganda and allowed Prince Ronald Mutesa to take the throne of the restored monarchy as the new Kabaka of Buganda.

The restoration of the kingdom has encouraged the growth of Ganda nationalism with many groups pushing to win real power for the kabaka, under a federal constitution. The government, in December 1994, responded to the rapid growth of Ganda nationalism by ordering the authorities to shut down meetings and rallies called by the nationalists and federalists that they claim threatens Uganda's unity and national integrity.

*SELECTED BIBLIOGRAPHY:*

Ingham, Kenneth. *The Making of Modern Uganda.* 1958.
Karugire, Samuel R. *A Political History of Uganda.* 1980.
Kiwanuka, S. *History of Buganda: From the Foundation of the Kingdom to 1900.* 1972.
Sathyamurthy, T. V. *The Political Development of Uganda 1900–1986.* 1986.

# BUNYORO

**Bunyoro-Kitara**

*CAPITAL: Hoima*

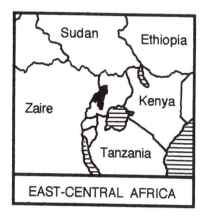

*POPULATION:* (95e) 2,424,000 : 2,550,000 Banyoro (Nyoro) in Uganda. MAJOR NATIONAL GROUPS: (95e) Banyoro (Nyoro) 91%, other Ugandan. MAJOR LANGUAGES: Lunyoro, Swahili, English. MAJOR RELIGIONS: Protestant, Roman Catholic, Sunni Muslim. MAJOR CITIES: (95e) Hoima 38,000, Mubende 30,000, Masindi 25,000, Biso-Butiaba 20,000.

*GEOGRAPHY:* AREA: 6,419 sq.mi.-16,629 sq.km. LOCATION: Bunyoro lies in western Uganda, a broad plain just east of Lake Albert between the Victoria Nile and Kafo Rivers. Bunyoro borders Zaire on the west and the Ugandan regions of Toro* and Buganda* on the south and southeast. POLITI-CAL STATUS: Bunyoro forms a district of the Western Province of Uganda. Nationalists claim the territory of the former kingdom, including the Mubende district of neighboring Buganda. The government allowed the partial restoration of the kingdom in 1993.

*FLAG:* The Bunyoro flag, the flag of the former kingdom, is a white field crossed by two serrated blue lines and charged with a red canton on the upper hoist bearing a white drum surmounted by crossed swords.

*PEOPLE:* The Banyoro, popularly called Nyoro, comprise three historical divisions: the Bito, descendants of sixteenth-century Nilotic invaders; the Huma, Hamitic herdsmen settled in the region in the Middle Ages; and the Bairu (Iru), Bantu agriculturists. All three Nyoro peoples speak Lunyoro, the language of the original Bantu inhabitants. A sense of nationhood and shared destiny has been forged only since Ugandan independence in 1962. Until the 1960s the three groups remained separate and intergroup marriage was forbidden in the kingdom. The majority of the Nyoro are Christian, primarily Protestant, with an important Muslim minority concentrated in the north.

*THE NATION:* Bantu peoples settled the fertile lands around Lake Albert between A.D. 1000 and 1100 and gradually united as a tribe under a paramount king. The Bairu (Iru), skilled farmers, developed a structured, pacific society overseen by a feudal hierarchy.

Hamitic migrants, the Huma (Hima), thought to have originated in present Ethiopia, conquered the kingdom and established themselves as a pastoral aristocracy. In the early sixteenth century a tall Nilotic people, the Bito Luo, replaced the Huma as the kingdom's dominant people. The conquerors reestablished the kingdom under the Bito dynasty. The Luo adopted the culture and language of the more advanced Bairu, relegated by the Nilotic aristocrats to a serflike condition and forbidden to own cattle, the new measure of wealth in the kingdom.

The state, called Bunyoro-Kitara and ruled by a king, the *omukama*, dominated a large area of the lakes region in the sixteenth and seventeenth centuries, but invasions and civil wars eventually divided the territory into a number of rival kingdoms. One of these kingdoms, Buganda, gradually assumed the position of the premier kingdom and expanded at Bunyoro's expense. In the 1840s the southern region of the kingdom seceded to become the separate kingdom called Toro. The succession of an adroit king, Kabarega, to the throne in the mid-nineteenth century restored Bunyoro power, and the kingdom engaged rival Buganda in a long series of wars in the second half of the century.

British influence, established in Buganda in 1888, made Bunyoro a center of resistance to the Europeans and their Baganda allies. In 1894 a suspected Belgian advance from the west provided the British and Baganda with a pretext for war. Defeated by the combined force, the king could not resist the incorporation of his kingdom into British Uganda in 1896. A Nyoro uprising, in 1899, ended with the exile of Omukama Kabarega to the British Seychelles, an island group in the Indian Ocean.

The British authorities allowed Kabarega to return to Bunyoro in 1900 but forced him to sign the Buganda Agreement, giving all Nyoro lands south of the Kafo River to Britain's ally and Bunyoro's ancient enemy, Buganda. The "Lost Counties" territorial dispute continues to the present, as the two counties taken by Buganda include Bunyoro's ancient center, Mubende, and the traditional burial site of Bunyoro's *omukamas*.

The "Lost Counties" controversy initiated the growth of modern Nyoro nationalism, the movement beginning as an anti-British popular movement. The Nyoro saw the British as the powerful protectors of their ancient enemies in Buganda. In 1921 Nyoro nationalists formed a political group called Mubende-Banyoro, which quickly became the kingdom's most popular political party, with demands for the return of the "Lost Counties" and secession from British Uganda. The British treated the kingdom as conquered territory until 1933, when the king finally signed a protectorate agreement.

The territorial dispute between Bunyoro and Buganda acquired renewed importance as Britain prepared Uganda for independence. In 1961 the *omukama* refused to attend a constitutional conference until the British authorities resolved the conflict. The Baganda refused to negotiate, setting off a serious crisis as Bunyoro moved toward secession and prepared for war. British mediation produced an agreement to hold a plebiscite in the disputed area, finally allowing Uganda to achieve independence in 1962. The Kingdom of Bunyoro reluctantly agreed to accept autonomy and a semifederal status within Uganda.

In 1964 the inhabitants of the "Lost Counties" voted to return the territory to Bunyoro. The conflict again became a crisis when Buganda refused to accept the results of the plebiscite. Nyoro soldiers gathered in Hoima and prepared for war, but the dispute quickly lost importance as even more serious threats appeared to menace the kingdoms. The Ugandan government, dominated by non-Bantu northern tribes, instituted laws to curtail the kingdoms' autonomy. In 1966 the government abrogated the autonomy statutes and in 1967 abolished the kingdoms as administrative units.

Nyoro nationalists enthusiastically supported the overthrow of the hated government in 1971 by a young army colonel, Idi Amin Dada. Amin's new government, a brutal dictatorship dominated by Amin's small northern Muslim tribe, soon lost all support in Bunyoro. In 1972 Nyoro leaders, sickened by the excesses of the Amin regime, called for Bunyoro secession, but the movement lost momentum as Amin's henchmen systematically eliminated the leaders.

The infamous Amin regime, finally overthrown in 1979, gave way to a series of weak, unstable Ugandan governments. A large resistance movement formed among the southern Bantu peoples of the former kingdoms and after years of fighting took control of Uganda in 1986 and created the country's first Bantu-dominated government.

Relative peace and democracy permitted the rebirth of Nyoro nationalism based on demands for the restoration of the kingdom. A more radical minority advocates the secession of Bunyoro from Uganda, arguing that the kingdom's inclusion in the multiethnic state has brought it only terror, death, and destruction. In July 1993 the government allowed the partial restoration of the kingdom and the enthronement of a new *omukama*. In September 1993 nationalists demanded the restoration of the kingdom's traditional boundaries, including the Mubende area of Buganda, the "Lost Counties."

*SELECTED BIBLIOGRAPHY:*
Bwengye, Francis A. *The Agony of Uganda: From Idi Amin to Obote.* 1986.
Ingham, Kenneth. *The Making of Modern Uganda.* 1983.
Nyakatura, V. W. *Anatomy of an African Kingdom: A History of Bunyoro-Kitara.* 1973.
Sathyamurthy, T. V. *The Political Development of Uganda 1900–1986.* 1986.

# BURYATIA

**Buryat Ulus; Buryat Mongolia**

*CAPITAL: Ulan Ude*

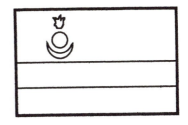

*POPULATION:* (95e) 1,302,000 : 455,000 Buryats in Russia. MAJOR NA-
TIONAL GROUPS: (95e) Russian 69%, Buryat 28%, Evenki, Tuvan. MAJOR
LANGUAGES: Russian, Buryat. MAJOR RELIGIONS: Russian Orthodox (including Old Believers), Buddhist (Lamaism). MAJOR CITIES: (95e) Ulan-Ude
385,000 (420,000), Kamensk 43,000 (60,000), Zakamensk 33,000, Gusinozersk
30,000, Kyakhta 25,000, Ust-Ordün 18,000, Agn 16,000.

*GEOGRAPHY:* AREA: 151,467 sq.mi.-392,402 sq.km. LOCATION: Bury-
atia lies in the southeastern Russian Federation, a region of mountains, steppe,
and fertile valleys around huge Lake Baikal, which represents 20% of the
world's freshwater reserves. Buryatia borders Mongolia on the south and the
Russian republic of Tuva (Tannu Tuva*) on the west. POLITICAL STATUS:
Buryatia forms the Buryat Republic, a member state of the Russian Federation.
Nationalists also claim the Ust-Ordün Buryatia autonomous region of Irkutsk
Oblast and Agün Buryatia autonomous region of Chita Oblast.

*INDEPENDENCE DECLARED:* 11 February 1919.

*FLAG:* The Buryat national flag, the official flag of the republic, is a horizontal tricolor of blue, white, and yellow, proportions 2:1:1, charged with a
yellow ideogram, the Soyonbo, on the upper hoist, consisting of a yellow flame
above a yellow sun and crescent moon. OTHER FLAG(S): The flag of Ust-
Ordün Buryatia is a tan field with two purple stripes at the bottom. The flag of
Agün Buryatia is a yellow field with two green stripes at the bottom.

*PEOPLE:* The Buryat are a Mongol people of disputed origins, physically
resembling the Mongols but displaying Turkic and Evenki physical and cultural

traits. The Buryat language forms a separate branch of the Mongolian languages of the East Altaic language groups. A majority of the Buryat are Buddhist, practicing the Tibetan form, Lamaism, with a small Orthodox minority, and a smaller group, in remote areas, who have retained the shamanistic beliefs that once dominated the region. Many of the Russians in the region are Raskolniki, Old Believers, who fled European Russia in the eighteenth century and mostly live among the Buryats in rural areas. The remainder of the Slav population is concentrated in the cities and the industrial towns around the lake.

*THE NATION:* The Buryat origins can be traced back to small Karluk Turkic tribes in the region east of Lake Baikal, tribes loosely controlled by China until A.D. 754. Absorbed by successive waves of Mongol migrations from the south, the last of the Turkic tribes disappeared with the conquest of the region by the Mongols of Genghis Khan in 1205. Known as a separate Mongol people from 1207, the Buryats formed part of the great Mongol Empire until the fourteenth century. In the sixteenth century the last remains of Mongol power in the area ended with the creation of an independent confederation of Buryat tribes.

Cossacks, the forerunners of Russian expansion, began to penetrate the region around Lake Baikal in the late sixteenth century. The Russians gradually took control of the region with the last of the Buryat tribes brought under European rule around 1700. Treaties signed by Russia and Manchu China in 1689 and 1727 established definite boundaries and effectively cut off Buryat contact with the Mongol peoples to the south. In 1742 the imperial Russian government recognized Buddhism as an official religion.

A violent schism within the Orthodox Church in European Russia at the end of the seventeenth century created a minority, called Raskolniki or Old Believers, who suffered severe persecutions. Many of the Raskolniki fled east to the new frontier districts around Lake Baikal to settle among the peaceful Buryats.

The Russian authorities allotted tribal territories to each of the four major Buryat tribes: the Khori in the east, the Ekhirit and Bulagar west of Lake Baikal, and the Khongodor in the south. The remainder of the former Buryat lands were opened to colonization. Over the next century Russian colonists occupied the tribal lands, forcing the tribes west of Lake Baikal to abandon their lands and to migrate to the Selenga and Barguzin Valleys east of the lake in the eighteenth century. In the early nineteenth century the Khori lost their lands and moved south to the Aga Steppe region.

The Tibetan form of Buddhism, called Lamaism, spread through the Buryat tribes in the nineteenth century, the gentle doctrine quickly replacing their earlier shamanistic belief in all but the most remote areas. Although they shared religion, culture, and language, the Buryats remained a disunited and backward tribal people in the rural areas of Russia's Transbaikal region. The completion of the Trans-Siberian Railroad in 1891 brought a massive influx of Russian peasants and finally united the Buryats in opposition to the discriminatory Russian land laws. Serious Buryat revolts erupted in the region in 1903 and 1905.

Virtually untouched by World War I until the onset of the Russian Revolution in February 1917, the Buryats became effectively independent as the tsarist civil government collapsed. Putting aside their remaining tribal differences, the Buryats united to drive all Russian officials from the region. A Buryat congress, held at Irkutsk in April 1917, voted for independence and for closer ties to Mongolia. Ironically, the Buryat Buddhist monks were the first to divest the monasteries of their extensive holdings, distributing the lands to Buryat peasants in an attempt to return the religion to a more traditional form.

A Japanese intervention force, sent to keep eastern Siberia from falling to Bolshevik control, occupied Buryatia in early 1918. Encouraged by the Japanese, who envisaged a reconstituted Mongol federation under Japanese influence, the Buryats formed a national government and sent delegates to a pan-Mongol conference that endorsed a Buryat demand for the expulsion of all Slavs east of Lake Baikal. Threatened by the spreading Russian civil war, Buryat leaders declared Buryatia independent on 11 February 1919 and set about creating a state administered according to Buddhist teachings.

The victorious Bolsheviks overran the state in 1920 and added Buryatia to the Far Eastern Republic, a Communist-dominated state incorporated into the Soviet Union in 1922. A Buryat autonomous region, created in January 1922, was upgraded to the status of an autonomous republic within the Russian Federation in 1923.

The Soviet suppression of all religions led to the closure of all but a few temples and monasteries during the 1920s, the closures arousing strong Buryat resistance. In 1929 the Buryats rebelled against Communist rule. Quickly crushed by the Red Army, over 35,000 Buryats died, including thousands of monks massacred on Stalin's orders. Accused of acting as Japanese agents, the remaining Buryats west of Lake Baikal were expelled. In 1937 Stalin arbitrarily separated two areas from Buryatia and reclassified the Ust-Ordün and Argün Buryats as separate nationalities.

A minority in their homeland since World War II, the Buryat national movement, suppressed for over fifty years, resurfaced with the liberalization of Soviet life in the late 1980s. The severe polluting of the Buryat's sacred Lake Baikal has become a rallying point for the growing national movement. The resurgence of the Buryat's Buddhist religion, closely identified with Buryat culture, has led the Buryat national revival, with the reopened temples and monasteries serving as centers of Buryat culture and national sentiment.

*SELECTED BIBLIOGRAPHY:*
Moses, Larry W. *The Political Role of Mongol Buddhism.* 1977.
Pushkarev, Sergei. *Self-Government and Freedom in Russia.* 1988.
Ulam, Adam B. *Stalin.* 1989.

# CABINDA

**Kabinda**

*CAPITAL: Cabinda*

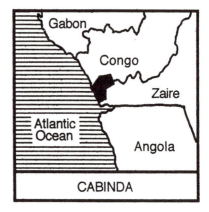

*POPULATION:* (95e) 160,000 : 145,000 Cabindans in Angola. MAJOR NATIONAL GROUPS: (95e) Cabindan (Bakongo, Mayumbe, Fiote) 91%, other Angolan. MAJOR LANGUAGES: Kikongo, Portuguese, French. MAJOR RELIGIONS: Roman Catholic, animist. MAJOR CITIES: (95e) Cabinda 45,000, Landana 12,000, Dinge 5,000.

*GEOGRAPHY:* AREA: 2,794 sq.mi.-7,238 sq.km. LOCATION: Cabinda lies on Africa's west coast, an enclave separated from the rest of Angola by a strip of Zairean territory, the only Angolan province north of the Zaire River. POLITICAL STATUS: Cabinda forms a province of Angola.

*INDEPENDENCE DECLARED:* 1 August 1975.

*FLAG:* The Cabindan national flag, adopted in 1975, is a horizontal tricolor of pale blue, yellow, and red bearing a centered white, five-pointed star backed by an inverted green triangle encircled by a brown ring. OTHER FLAG(S): The national flag bears the same colors as the flag of the largest nationalist organization, the Front for the Liberation of the Enclave of Cabinda (FLEC), a yellow field charged with a centered disc bearing a stylized scene of green earth, brown mountains, pale blue sky, and a red sun and rays.

*PEOPLE:* The Cabindans, who see themselves as a separate nation, are a Bantu people belonging to the tribes that make up the large Bakongo group of Musikongo* in parts of Angola, Zaire, and Congo. Kikongo, the Bakongo language, is the first language of the enclave, although Portuguese and French, the official language in the adjacent areas of Zaire and Congo, are widely spoken.

The Cabindan majority are Roman Catholic, with a minority retaining traditional tribal beliefs.

*THE NATION:* The Bakongo tribes, thought to have migrated from north-eastern Africa, settled the vast basin of the Zaire River before A.D. 1100. A powerful Bakongo kingdom, Kongo, united the tribes south of the Congo (Zaire) River in the thirteenth century and from there gradually expanded to control a number of tributary states north of the river.

Portuguese explorers established contact with the Kongo kingdom in 1493, the beginning of the colonial expansion into the huge Congo River basin. Eventually divided among Portugal, Belgium, and France, the old Kongo kingdom saw its ordered life rapidly disappear under the impact of colonial rule and the accompanying slave trade. The three European powers in 1884 demarcated and formalized the colonial boundaries. Portugal ceded part of its territory north of the Congo River to give the Belgian Congo an outlet to the Atlantic Ocean. The new colonial frontiers left the enclave of Portuguese Congo separated from Portuguese Angola by twenty-five miles of Belgian territory.

The enclave, administered as a separate colony from 1886, was the most neglected in Portuguese Africa, known principally for poverty and forced labor. A Bakongo revolt in northern Angola in 1914 spread to the unhappy Bakongo inhabitants of the enclave, where the revolt continued until 1917. The revolt united the Cabinda clans and planted the seeds of the later Cabindan national movement.

Administratively joined to Angola and renamed for its principal town in 1956, the enclave became the scene of serious agitation. Fearing domination by the large Angolan tribes, the Cabindans agitated for a resumption of separate status, the agitation gradually evolving a nationalist, anticolonial mass movement. The Cabindans rebuffed overtures from Angola's rival nationalist organizations in the early 1960s. In 1963 nationalists formed the Cabinda Liberation Front (FLC) and demanded separate independence for the enclave.

Oil, discovered in 1966, greatly increased the economic importance of Cabinda and gave the nationalists a firm economic base. Despite a growing separatist war in the enclave, oil production began in 1968 and expanded dramatically over the next decade.

The Portuguese government, drained by long and costly colonial wars, was overthrown in a popular revolution in 1974. A new leftist regime, determined to rid Portugal of its colonial burden, moved to grant independence to the remaining possessions within two years. The Cabindans' petition for separate independence aroused fierce opposition from Angola's three rival nationalist organizations. The three agreed on very few points, but one of those points was that Cabinda and its oil wealth belonged to Angola.

The premature departure of the Portuguese administration left behind a three-way civil war in Angola but created an opportunity for the Cabindan nationalists. On 1 August 1975 Cabinda leaders declared the enclave independent. The

American firm pumping Cabinda's oil, with its eye on future revenues, remained carefully neutral.

Angolan Marxists, aided by Soviet weapons and Cuban troops, gained control of most of Angola and dispatched troops to end Cabinda's secession and to secure its oil reserves. In spite of its continuing Marxist rhetoric, the new Angolan government, hampered by a lack of expertise, did not nationalize Cabinda's oil production, thus creating a very curious anomaly—an oil installation in a Communist country run by America's Gulf Oil Company and protected by Cuban troops against attacks by Cabindan separatists armed by Zaire, an American ally.

The Cabindans remain among the poorest people in Angola, even though their province produces some 80% of Angola's export earnings. In 1985, in a bid to undermine the nationalists' support, the Angolan government announced that 1% of Cabinda's oil revenues would be used for development projects in the enclave. Cabindan nationalists denounced the move as hypocritical since the oil belongs to Cabinda and the Cabindans. The oil reserves, which would give the citizens of an independent Cabinda incomes comparable to the oil-rich Middle East, are cited by nationalists who claim that an independent Cabinda would be economically viable.

The end of the Cold War, fought by proxy armies in Angola, ended most outside political and military support for the combatants. Pressed by their former sponsors, the Angolans moved to end the civil war, but, following negotiations and even elections, the war resumed. As part of the proposed democratic constitution for Angola, the Cabindans would have been granted autonomy in exchange for abandoning their goal of full independence.

In December 1991 five Cabindan factions met in Lisbon in an effort to end divisions and to foster closer coordination in the fight for independence. The following September 1992 a large majority of Cabinda's eligible voters honored a nationalist boycott of Angola's first free election. The election was later invalidated by the renewal of war in Angola in October.

Sporadic separatist violence continues in the province, and nationalist leaders continue to press for a referendum on separate independence; however, most Cabindans have been careful not to provoke the level of violence evident in the rest of the country. As Angola tears itself apart, the Cabindans, who want no part of the fighting, can only wait.

*SELECTED BIBLIOGRAPHY:*

Duffy, James. *Portuguese Africa.* 1959.

Martin, Phyllis. *Historical Dictionary of Angola.* 1980.

Okuma, Thomas J. *Angola in Ferment: The Background and Prospects of Angolan Nationalism.* 1974.

Wolfers, Michael, and Jane Bergerol. *Angola in the Frontline.* 1983.

# CALABAR

**Kalabar**

*CAPITAL:* Calabar

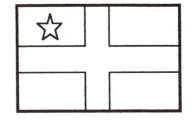

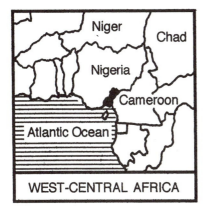

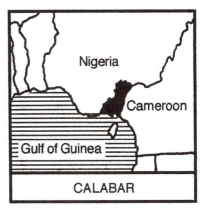

*POPULATION:* (95e) 4,820,000 : 5,200,000 Kalabari in Nigeria; another 900,000 live in adjacent areas of Cameroon. MAJOR NATIONAL GROUPS: (95e) Kalabari (Ibibio-Efik) 73%, Ibo 9%, Ekoi 5%, Cross Rivers tribes 5%, other Nigerian. MAJOR LANGUAGES: Efik, Ibo, Ekoi, English. MAJOR RELIGIONS: Protestant, Roman Catholic, animist. MAJOR CITIES: (95e) Calabar 168,000, Ikot Ekpene 110,000, Uyo 105,000, Oron 95,000, Ugep 82,000, Opopo 68,000 (100,000), Ikom 54,000, Ogoja 50,000.

*GEOGRAPHY:* AREA: 14,060 sq.mi.-36,424 sq.km. LOCATION: Calabar lies in southeastern Nigeria just west of the Cameroon border, a densely populated region that rises from the delta of the Cross River to the Oban Hills and a spur of the Adamawa Mountains in the north. POLITICAL STATUS: Calabar has no official status; the region claimed by nationalists forms the Nigerian states of Akwa Ibom and Cross River.

*FLAG:* The Kalabari flag, the flag of the national movement, is a horizontal bicolor of red over green divided by a centered yellow cross and bearing a five-pointed star on the upper hoist.

*PEOPLE:* The origins of the Kalabari remain disputed, but as they are generally shorter than neighboring peoples, theories suggest that they represent a pre-Bantu or a mixed Pygmy and Bantu people. The Kalabari comprise two main divisions, the majority Ibibio and the Efik, numbering 252,000 around the city of Calabar. The Kalabari language, often called Efik, the dialect that forms the literary language, is a non-Bantu language of the Benue-Niger language group. The majority of the Kalabari belong to various Protestant sects, the largest sect the nationalistic Brotherhood of the Cross and the Star.

*THE NATION:* The Kalabari, believed to have inhabited a much larger area prior to the Bantu migrations, settled in the coastal areas on the Gulf of Guinea in the fifteenth century. The newcomers, called Ibibio, founded a number of city-states along the coast, the most important the cities of Calabar, Bonny, Okrika, and Owome.

The Ibibio were among the first people in the region to come into contact with the Europeans. Visited by Portuguese expeditions in 1472–73, the city-states eventually established trading relations with several European countries. The original trade in local products soon gave way to the lucrative slave trade. Calabar, the most important port on the West African coast in the seventeenth century, formed the center of a great commercial empire based on powerful trading houses. The various Ibibio city-states formed a loose political and mercantile union similar to the Hanseatic League of Northern Europe.

A dispute over a royal ax led to the division of the Ibibio tribe in the eighteenth century. The Efik clan, living around the city of Calabar, separated from the Ibibio and established the Ekpe Society, which assumed control of Calabar. After the tribal division, the Ibibio continued to provide the manpower for the powerful Efik Calabar state before the European takeover of the region.

The Kalabari, raiding the interior Ibo and Ekoi tribes for captives to sell to the Europeans, passionately opposed the United Kingdom's abolition of slavery in 1807; however, lax enforcement until 1875 assured continued prosperity. Calabar, superseded by Lagos as the region's major slave market in the nineteenth century, turned to palm oil products for export.

The Kalabari homeland, included in the British Oil Rivers Protectorate in 1884, remained the most advanced region of British Nigeria. The first to establish relations with the Europeans, the Kalabari gained an advantage in education and dominated local governments and commercial enterprises in areas outside Calabar. The Efik language became the medium of instruction in the colony's early schools and the first into which the Europeans translated the Bible. The first secondary school in Nigeria opened at Calabar under the guidance of Scottish missionaries in 1895.

The better-educated Kalabari developed a feeling of superiority toward the peoples they formerly raided for slaves, particularly the Ibos, who began to migrate to Calabar in the early 1900s. Tensions between the Kalabari and Ibos erupted in violence in 1929, the rioting quickly taking on serious anti-British overtones. Colonial troops fired on a crowd at Opopo, killing thirty-two and wounding many more. The incident is considered the origin of the modern Kalabari national movement.

Kalabari nationalists formed the Ibibio State Union in 1944 to press for restrictions on Ibo immigration to their traditional lands and for the creation of a separate Calabar region within Nigeria. The growing domination of southeast Nigeria by the more numerous Ibo again set off riots in 1949 and fueled Kalabari demands for separation.

Granted independence in 1960, Nigeria formed a federation of three regions, each dominated by one of Nigeria's three largest tribes. Calabar, forming part of the Eastern Region, came under the control of the Ibos, who inherited the commercial and bureaucratic structure in the region. Kalabari agitation for separation increased as Nigeria's tribal tensions worsened in the first years after independence. In 1965 the largest of the Kalabari nationalist organizations began a campaign for separation, not just from the Eastern Region but from increasingly chaotic Nigeria.

The Nigerian government, amid rising tribal tensions, adopted a new constitution in 1967 that divided the three regions into twelve ethnic states. A new South-Eastern State, created for the Kalabari, provided a positive focus for loyalty to the federal government when, three days later, the Ibo proclaimed the Republic of Biafra* and withdrew the entire Eastern Region from the Nigerian federation.

The Kalabari rejected Ibo rule and generally refused to support the secession. When Calabar fell to federal troops in March 1968, the Kalabari were dismayed at the attitude of the government troops. The occupation army treated Ibo and non-Ibo alike, not caring that the Kalabari had supported the federal cause from the beginning. Resentment flared into violence, but the disorders lasted only a short time before the federal troops intervened.

The Kalabari national movement, dormant for nearly two decades, resurfaced in the late 1980s, fanned into life by renewed tribal tensions and the frequent conflicts between Nigeria's Christian and Muslim peoples. The once-proud Kalabari now live in shacks without electricity while surrounded by the filthy and polluting oil industry. Increasingly bitter, the Kalabari, the former ''Hanseatics'' of Africa, still dream of their past glory. Nationalists assert that Calabar's national wealth, in the form of abundant oil, their separate language and culture, and their long history, provides both the economic and spiritual resources for the creation of a viable, independent Kalabari state.

*SELECTED BIBLIOGRAPHY:*

Asiegbu, J. U. *Nigeria and Its British Invaders.* 1984.

Irukwu, J. O. *Nigeria at the Crossroads.* 1983.

Martin, Susan M. *Palm Oil and Protest: An Economic History of the Ngwa Region, Southeastern Nigeria 1800–1980.* 1988.

Nafziger, E. Wayne. *The Economics of Instability: The Nigerian-Biafran War.* 1982.

# CANARY ISLANDS

**Islas Canarias**

*CAPITAL: Santa Cruz de Tenerife*

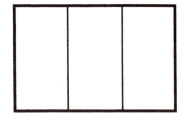

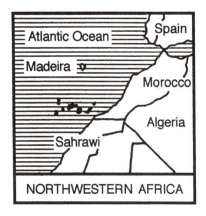

NORTHWESTERN AFRICA

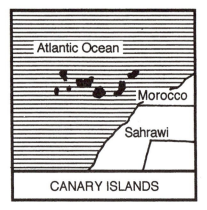

CANARY ISLANDS

*POPULATION:* (95e) 1,643,000 : 1,755,000 Canarians in Spain. MAJOR NATIONAL GROUPS: (95e) Canarian 90%, other Spanish. MAJOR LANGUAGE: Spanish (Canarian dialect). MAJOR RELIGION: Roman Catholic. MAJOR CITIES: (95e) Las Palmas de Gran Canaria 481,000 (565,000), Santa Cruz de Tenerife 310,000 (453,000), La Laguna 136,000, Telde 96,000, Puerto de La Cruz 78,000, La Orotava 52,000 (171,000), Arrecife 37,000, Arucas 36,000, Santa Cruz de La Palma 33,000.

*GEOGRAPHY:* AREA: 2,808 sq.mi.-7,274 sq.km. LOCATION: The Canary Islands, a volcanic archipelago of thirteen islands, lie off the west coast of North Africa, 823 miles southwest of the Spanish mainland. POLITICAL STATUS: The Canary Islands form an autonomous region of the Kingdom of Spain.

*FLAG:* The Canarian national flag, the official flag of the autonomous region, is a vertical tricolor of white, pale blue, and yellow. OTHER FLAG(S): The same white, pale blue, and yellow flag, with the addition of seven green stars on the center stripe, is the flag of the largest nationalist organization, the Movement for the Autonomy and Independence of the Canary Archipelago (MAIAC).

*PEOPLE:* The Canarians, mostly descendants of colonists from southern Spain, exhibit a high incidence of fair hair and eyes, considered a holdover from the islands' original Berber inhabitants. Isolated from the Spanish mainland, the islanders developed a distinctive culture, including a separate Spanish dialect called Canario. The Canarians, considered the most conservative of the Spanish peoples, are overwhelmingly Roman Catholic.

*THE NATION:* The islands, known to the ancient world, got their name from the fierce dogs found there by the ancients, *canis* in the Latin language. Fair Berbers from North Africa, the Guanche, believed to have arrived in the islands with Phoenician colonists from ancient Carthage, regressed to a tribal existence when contact with the mainland ceased following the Roman destruction of Carthage in 146 B.C.

Forgotten as Europe entered the Dark Ages, the islands were rediscovered and claimed by the Portuguese in 1341. Three years later a papal bull awarded the islands to the Spanish kingdom of Castile. A French adventurer, Jean de Betencourt, conquered the islands in 1402–4 and proclaimed himself king.

The object of a Portuguese expedition in 1425, the islands were again confirmed as Castilian territory by papal decree in 1479. Colonists from Andalusia, newly reconquered from the Moors, settled the islands. The Berber Guanches, either assimilated or exterminated, soon disappeared completely from the islands.

An important station on the sea routes to the New World, the islands often suffered attacks by pirates preying on Spanish shipping. Sir Francis Drake attacked the Canarian ports in 1595, and, before they could fully recover, Dutch pirates ravaged the towns in 1599. From the seventeenth century, the islanders supplied wine in exchange for fish brought by New England sailors, a trade that sustained the islands following the establishment of more direct sea routes and the independence of most of Spain's American empire.

Neglected by the Spanish government, the islanders obtained incomes only from locally produced wine until grape blight ruined the vineyards in 1853. Sugarcane then replaced wine as the island's economic mainstay. Unable to rely on government aid, the Canarian culture and way of life developed a strong tradition of self-sufficiency little affected by the trends and influences of the Spanish mainland.

Canarian agitation for an end to the islands' colonial status stimulated the first stirrings of modern Canarian nationalism. Formally incorporated into the Spanish state in 1927, the government divided the islands into two separate provinces ruled directly from Madrid. Provincial status, a disappointment to the islanders, did little to alleviate the problems created by centuries of neglect and underdevelopment.

Francisco Franco, sent to the islands as captain-general in 1932, greatly resented his posting to the remote province, virtual exile for an ambitious officer. Franco's indignation influenced his later decision to lead the Spanish fascists in revolt and civil war in the 1930s.

The Canarians, virtually unaffected by the civil war that swept mainland Spain from 1936 to 1939, began to think of themselves as separate, an idea that fueled the growth of the national movement in the 1950s. Tourism, beginning at the same time, brought much-needed income and development and gradually ended the island's insularity.

Nationalist groups, organized with the support of the radical North African states during the 1960s, gained widespread support for the advocacy of independence from Franco's dictatorial Spain. The largest of the groups, the Movement for the Autonomy and Independence of the Canary Archipelago (MAIAC), won recognition as a legitimate African liberation movement from the Organization of African Unity (OAU) in 1968. Considered by the OAU an African territory still under foreign rule, many African states and organizations championed the decolonization and independence of the islands.

A separatist bombing at Las Palmas Airport on Grand Canary Island on 27 March 1977 forced a Pan American 747, en route from Los Angeles and New York, to divert to the overcrowded Los Rodeos Airport on Tenerife. A runway collision between the American jet and a Dutch 747 resulted in the deaths of 583 people, the worst disaster in aviation history. The disaster horrified the Canarians and caused a dramatic loss of support for the separatists.

Democracy returned to Spain at Franco's death in 1975, allowing the formation of regional, even openly nationalist political parties. Granted autonomy in 1983, the islands have experienced a rapid development of territorial identity and a resurgence of national sentiment as the memories of the 1977 disaster faded.

Spain's entry into the European Economic Community in 1986 raised new issues as the islanders feel they suffer for decisions made far away in Brussels, while their concerns must be channeled through an often unsympathetic national government in Madrid. Nationalists, with increasing support, advocate independence and bilateral ties to both Spain and the European federation.

The Canarians, still referring to the mainland Spanish as Goths, experienced a resurgence of culture and national pride during the 1980s and have become increasingly more assertive in protecting their culture, dialect, and environment. In a further move to reclaim a separate Canarian culture, the regional parliament in April 1991 outlawed bullfights, the cruel and cherished symbol of mainland Spanish culture.

*SELECTED BIBLIOGRAPHY:*

Lancaster, Thomas D. *Politics and Change in Spain.* 1985.

Ossuma y Saviñon, Manuel. *The Guanches.* 1978.

Stone, Olivia M. *Tenerife and Its Six Satellites, or The Canary Islands Past and Present.* 1976.

Yeoward, W. *Canary Islands.* 1981.

# CARPATHO-UKRAINE

Ruthenia; Transcarpathia;
Subcarpathian Ruthenia; Zakarapattia

*CAPITAL: Uzhorod (Uzhgorod)*

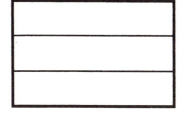

EAST-CENTRAL EUROPE

CARPATHO-UKRAINE

*POPULATION:* (95e) 1,272,000 : 1,505,000 Ruthenes (Carpatho-Rusyns) in Ukraine and another 330,000 in Slovakia and 100,000, called Lemkians, in Poland. Ruthene nationalists claim a national population of some 5 million in Central and Eastern Europe. MAJOR NATIONAL GROUPS: (95e) Ruthene (Carpatho-Rusyn) 69%, Hungarian 14%, Ukrainian 9%, Slovak 8%, Romanian, Russian, German. MAJOR LANGUAGES: Ukrainian (Ruthene dialect), Hungarian, Slovak. MAJOR RELIGIONS: Ruthene Uniate, Roman Catholic, Reformed Protestant, Orthodox. MAJOR CITIES: (95e) Uzhorod (Uzhgorod) 129,000 (155,000), Makaciv (Mukachevo) 102,000 (124,000), Berehove (Beregovo) 39,000 (52,000), Chust (Khust) 31,000, Vinogradiv (Vinogradov) 28,000, Rakhiv (Rakhov) 23,000.

*GEOGRAPHY:* AREA: 4,942 sq.mi.-12,803 sq.km. LOCATION: Carpatho-Ukraine, historically called Ruthenia, lies in southwestern Ukraine, occupying part of the Carpathian Mountains with long, fertile valleys leading into Slovakia. POLITICAL STATUS: Carpatho-Ukraine has no official status; the region forms the Transcarpathian Oblast of the Republic of Ukraine.

*INDEPENDENCE DECLARED:* 2 March 1939.

*FLAG:* The Ruthene national flag, the flag of the national movement, is a horizontal tricolor of pale blue, yellow, and green.

*PEOPLE:* The Ruthenes, calling themselves Carpatho-Rusyn, are descended from Slavic migrants and earlier Ruthene tribes of unknown origin. The name Rusyn, an early designation for all Slavs, persisted in the isolated valleys of the Carpathians. A long tradition of not mixing with neighboring peoples has safeguarded the unique Ruthene culture and dialect and the separate Ruthene Uniate Church, closely identified with Ruthene culture and national sentiment. The Ruthenes see themselves as a separate Ukrainian people, and national sentiment has grown rapidly since Ukrainian independence in 1991.

*THE NATION:* Slavic migrants settled among the earlier Ruthene tribes in the high valleys of the Carpathian Mountains in the eighth century. The Ruthenes' Carpathian homeland, in the tenth and eleventh centuries, formed part of Kievan Rus, the first great Slav state.

The Magyars of Hungary conquered Ruthenia in the eleventh century, with the Carpathians becoming a battleground for rival Hungarian and Polish states. Annexed by Hungary in 1382, the non-Slav Magyar cultural influences further distanced the Ruthene culture from the other Slav cultures to the east. The Byzantine rite Uniate Church of the Western Ukraine accepted the authority of Rome in 1586, and several bishops of the Ruthene population in northeastern Hungary organized the separate Ruthene Uniate Church in 1646.

The Ruthenes, without the territorial recognition accorded the other minority peoples of the Austrian Empire in the eighteenth century, remained divided among several counties in northeastern Hungary, the Presov region of Hungarian Slovakia, and the adjoining areas of Austrian Galicia. The majority, denied all cultural rights and under intense assimilation pressures, lived as illiterate peasants held in near-feudal conditions on large Hungarian estates. Without a clear ethnic identity, most identified with their church, around which Ruthene life revolved.

Initiated by a small, church-educated elite, a national and cultural revival spread through the Ruthene lands in the late nineteenth century. The growing self-awareness highlighted the misery of the Ruthenes' daily life. To escape grinding poverty, cultural repression, and pressure on their exploited lands, the Ruthenes turned to emigration. Thousands left, mostly for the Americas, mass emigration beginning in the 1880s and continuing until the outbreak of World War I blocked the immigrant routes.

One of Europe's poorest and most backward peoples, the Ruthenes refused to support the Hungarian war effort. Ruthene youths habitually fled conscription or deserted to the Allies when the opportunity arose. Nationalist sentiment grew rapidly during the First World War, developing as an anti-Hungarian mass movement. In May 1917 Ruthene leaders demanded the creation of a separate Ruthene state within the Austro-Hungarian Empire, their appeals obstructed by vehement Hungarian opposition.

The nationalists mobilized as revolution overtook the defeated empire in November 1918. A Ruthene provisional government sent a delegation to the 1919 Paris Peace Conference to demand recognition under Point Ten of U.S. president Wilson's Fourteen Points, self-determination for the peoples of the Austro-Hungarian Empire. Ruthenian independence, emphatically opposed by the region's large Hungarian minority, was finally put aside when the Ruthene leader, Gregory Zsatkovich, accepted an alternative proposed by the Allies, the status of a trust territory, with major autonomy, within the newly formed Czecho-Slovak state.

Zsatkovich, named the Ruthene autonomous state's first governor, resigned in 1920 to protest the abrogation of the autonomy agreement. Czechoslovakia's highly centralized government took control of most administrative functions and placed ethnic Czechs in most Ruthene government positions. The Czech government, threatened by Hungary and Germany in 1938, sought to bind the Ruthenes' loyalty by finally granting the long-promised autonomy.

The dismemberment of Czechoslovakia by the fascist powers gave the Ruthenes an opportunity. The nationalists mobilized to expel all Czech officials and to form a government under Augustin Voloshin. On 2 March 1939 the state, called Carpatho-Ukraine, declared its independence. The Ruthene government collapsed following an invasion by Hungarian troops on 14 March, and two days later Hungary annexed the region.

Soviet troops occupied Ruthenia in 1944, near the end of World War II, and under intense pressure the Czech government ceded the province to the Soviet Ukraine in 1945. The Ruthenes suffered decades of religious, cultural, and political oppression under Soviet rule. A national revival, begun as an underground movement in the 1970s, emerged as a powerful force with the Soviet liberalization in the late 1980s.

The disintegration of the Soviet Union in 1991 left the region within an independent Ukrainian state. In spite of initial enthusiasm for Ukrainian independence, in the referendum held in December 1991 the ballot used in the region contained a separate question about Ruthene autonomy. As Ukraine's economy faltered, and tensions increased, the nationalists, particularly among the Hungarian minority, gained support with demands for autonomy, federal status, and even open debate on separation. In 1992 the first openly separatist political organization was formed by nationalists advocating secession from Ukraine.

The Ukrainian government agreed to grant cultural autonomy to the Hungarians, but as chaos in independent Ukraine increases, all of the region's inhabitants increasingly look west to Budapest, not east to Kiev. Economic and political chaos in Ukraine has weakened the region's ties to Kiev and has forced the Ruthenes to establish a separate economic region, with its own rules and trade links. For a growing number of Ruthenes, separation means not only the cultural survival but the economic survival of their homeland.

*SELECTED BIBLIOGRAPHY:*

Busek, Vratislav, and Nicolas Spulber, eds. *Czechoslovakia.* 1957.

Hrushevsky, Michaelo. *The Historical Evolution of the Ukrainian Problem.* 1980.

Magocsi, Paul R. *The Shaping of a National Identity: Subcarpathian Rus' 1848–1948.* 1978.

Nemec, F., and V. Moudry. *The Soviet Seizure of Subcarpathian Ruthenia.* 1980.

# CASAMANCE

*CAPITAL: Ziguinchor*

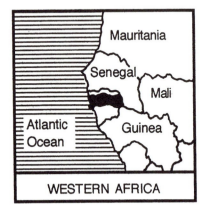

WESTERN AFRICA

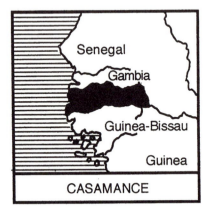

CASAMANCE

*POPULATION:* (95e) 1,365,000 : 975,000 Casamançais (800,000 Diola and 175,000 Bainouk) in Senegal. MAJOR NATIONAL GROUPS: (95e) Diola 57%, Mande 23%, Bainouk 12%, Fulani 5%. MAJOR LANGUAGES: Diola, Mande, Bainouk, Fulakunda, Wolof, French. MAJOR RELIGIONS: Sunni Muslim, Christian, animist. MAJOR CITIES: (95e) Ziguinchor 115,000, Kolda 48,000, Diouloulou 31,000, Bignona 25,000, Tobor 20,000.

*GEOGRAPHY:* AREA: 10,943 sq.mi.-28,349 sq.km. LOCATION: Casamance occupies the basin of the Casamance River on the west coast of Africa in southwestern Senegal. The region is geographically separated from the rest of Senegal except for a land corridor in the east. Casamance borders Gambia on the north, Guinea-Bissau on the south, and the Atlantic Ocean on the west. POLITICAL STATUS: Casamance, a province of Senegal until 1984, now forms the regions of Ziguinchor (Lower Casamance) and Kolda (Upper Casamance).

*FLAG:* The Casamance flag, the flag of the national movement, is a white field bearing a large green, five-pointed star centered.

*PEOPLE:* The Casamançais or Casamancians comprise two closely related peoples: the Diola in the coastal region and the Bainouk farther inland. The Diola and Bainouk have inhabited the Casamance region for over a thousand years, according to their legends and traditions. The two peoples speak closely related languages of the Niger-Congo language group and form a majority in the traditional region of Bas-Casamance (Lower Casamance) and a large minority in Haute-Casamance (Upper Casamance), where the Mande and Fulani populations are concentrated. The majority of the Diola and Bainouk are Muslim, with important Christian and animist minorities.

*THE NATION:* For centuries Diola kings ruled Casamance, often under the loose authority of Serer or Wolof states to the north. Mostly rice farmers in the lush valley of the Casamance River, the Diola inhabited small towns and villages, each with a paramount chief. Isolated from the north, the Diola never developed the strong caste system prevalent among the other peoples of Senegal.

Portuguese navigators, the first Europeans to visit the region in the fifteenth century, established trade relations with local Diola chiefs and eventually constructed a permanent trading station at the mouth of the Casamance River. The Portuguese, from their colony of Guinea just to the south, remained the Diola's main European contact for several centuries.

British claims and the creation of the colony of Gambia just to the north prompted French interest in the Casamance region. From 1854 the French gradually increased their influence over the region and in 1866 annexed Casamance. Although the other European powers recognized the French claim in 1870, the French generally ignored the isolated region. In 1888, to preclude incursions from neighboring European colonies, the French authorities in Senegal dispatched a force to occupy Ziguinchor, the Diola capital.

Islam spread to the Diola and Bainouk only after the European occupation, coming to the Casamance lowlands with traders and migrants from the Mande and Fulani peoples of Upper Casamance. Partly motivated by religion, anti-French disturbances broke out in 1899 and continued sporadically for several years. Nationalists point to the early twentieth-century disturbances as the beginning of the Casamance national movement.

Isolated from the rest of Senegal and with the natural trade and transportation routes blocked by British Gambia, the Casamance remained neglected and underdeveloped. Created a district of French Senegal only in 1920, it continued to exist in relative isolation until the British finally allowed direct access across Gambia in 1947.

The diverse peoples of Casamance, impelled by common interests, began to unite in the early 1950s. The first nationalist organization, the Casamance Autonomy Movement (MAC), led by Aleck Seck, formed to press for autonomy and a separate administration within French West Africa. In 1959 the MAC formed the nucleus of a Casamance-based political party, the Parti de Regroupment Africain-Senegal, known as PRA-Senegal. The party openly opposed the centralizing policies of the Wolof-dominated Senegalese government and demanded a separate Casamance state within a federal Senegal. Following Senegalese independence in 1960, the party was banned as secessionist and forced underground.

The nationalist movement resurfaced in the 1980s, led by the Movement of Democratic Forces of the Casamance (MFDC), with the aim of separating Casamance from Senegal. Severe nationalist rioting in December 1983 provoked the Senegalese government to abolish Casamance and to divide the region into two new regions: Ziguinchor with a Diola and Bainouk majority and Kolda with a Mande majority. The division, denounced by nationalists as a government ploy to undermine the historic ties and the regional identity of the peoples of the Casamance, failed to end the growing separatist sentiment in the region.

The Casamance nationalists, spurred by the discovery of oil in the region, launched an armed separatist campaign in 1990. Mass demonstrations in favor of immediate independence rocked Ziguinchor and other Casamancian cities. Government troops, given wide powers to combat the threat, retaliated with a brutal suppression that pushed even the more moderate Casamance leaders into closer cooperation with the growing separatist movement. A cease-fire, signed in May 1991, broke down after seven months, and the conflict resumed. By mid-1994 some 30,000 people had been displaced by the escalating violence.

The Senegalese authorities have consistently denied the nationalists' assertion that documents from the colonial era indicate that France favored separate independence for Casamance. In December 1993 the French government, asked by Senegal to submit a historical arbitration, issued a judgment that Casamance had not existed as an autonomous territory prior to the colonial period and that independence for the region had been neither demanded nor considered at the time of decolonization. The arbitration, dismissed by the nationalists as meaningless, has been used by the Senegalese government to justify the harsh methods employed by the military in the region.

*SELECTED BIBLIOGRAPHY:*
Colvin, Lucie G. *Historical Dictionary of Senegal.* 1981.
Crowder, Michael. *Senegal.* 1962.
Ingham, Kenneth. *Politics in Modern Africa: The Uneven Tribal Dimension.* 1990.
Manning, Patrick. *Francofone Sub-Saharan Africa, 1880–1985.* 1988.

# CATALONIA

Catalunya; Cataluña; Països Catalans

*CAPITAL: Barcelona*

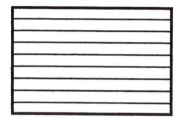

SOUTHWESTERN EUROPE

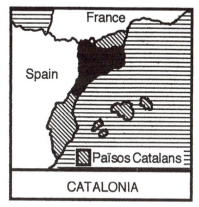

CATALONIA

*POPULATION:* (95e) Catalonia 6,284,000 : 10,230,000 Catalans (including Valencians and Mallorquins) in Spain and France. "Greater Catalonia," called Països Catalans, has a total population of 11,226,000. MAJOR NATIONAL GROUPS: (95e) Catalonia: Catalan 76%, other Spanish. MAJOR LANGUAGES: Catalan, Spanish (Castilian). MAJOR RELIGIONS: Roman Catholic, Protestant. MAJOR CITIES: (95e) CATALONIA: Barcelona 1,642,000 (4,425,000), Sabadell 183,000 (245,000), Terrasa (Tarrasa) 164,000 (218,000), Mataró 106,000 (175,000), Tarragona 105,000 (156,000), Lleida (Lerida) 105,000 (134,000), Reus 85,000 (115,000), Girona (Gerona) 69,000 (124,000). VALENCIA: Valencia 890,000 (1,882,000), Alacant (Alicante) 258,000 (304,000), Elx (Elche) 165,000 (221,000), Castelló (Castellon) 141,000 (170,000), Oriola (Orihuela) 80,000, Alcoi (Alcoy) 73,000 (110,000), Elda 64,000 (116,000). BALEARIC ISLANDS: Ciutat de Mallorca (Palma de Majorca) 331,000 (412,000). ROUSILLON (CATALUNYA NORD): Perpinyà (Perpignan) 122,000 (155,000).

*GEOGRAPHY:* AREA: 12,239 sq.mi.-31,940 sq.km. Països Catalans 24,839 sq.mi-64,348 sq.km. LOCATION: Catalonia lies on the Mediterranean sea in northeastern Spain just south of the Pyrenees Mountains, which form the international border with France. The Països Catalans also include North Catalonia (Rousillon) in southern France, Valencia, lying on the Mediterranean just south of Catalonia, and the Balearic Islands off the Catalan coast. POLITICAL STATUS: Catalonia forms an autonomous region of Spain. Països Catalans, the territory claimed by many nationalists, also includes the Spanish autonomous regions of Valencia and the Balearic Islands and the French department of Pyr-énées Orientales.

*INDEPENDENCE DECLARED:* 4 October 1934.

*FLAG:* The Catalan national flag, the official flag of the regions of Catalonia and French Catalonia and, with minor variations, of Valencia and the Balearic Islands, has nine yellow and red horizontal stripes. OTHER FLAG(S): The traditional yellow and red flag, with the addition of a yellow triangle bearing a five-pointed red star, or a blue triangle bearing a white star, at the hoist, is the flag of the Catalan nationalist movement.

*PEOPLE:* The Catalans are a Romance people, a mixture of early Pyreneean and Mediterranean strains speaking a Romance language with four major dialects: Oriental in eastern Catalonia and Rousillon (French Catalonia), Occidental in western Catalonia, Valencian in Valencia, and Mallorquin in the Balearic Islands. The language, related to the language of neighboring Occitania,* more closely reflects its Latin roots than most modern Romance languages. Catalan culture, famous for art and architecture, has its roots in the Catalan Renaissance of the Middle Ages, not in the mixture of Gothic and Moorish influences that prevails in Spain.

*THE NATION:* Originally inhabited by ancient Iberian tribes, Greeks colonized the Mediterranean coast around 600 B.C., followed by the Carthaginians some three centuries later. Absorbed by the Roman Empire in 218 B.C., the inhabitants adopted Latin culture and speech. The region flourished until overrun by Germanic Goths in the fifth century A.D. The Goths called the region Gothalonia, later changed to Catalonia.

Muslim Moors, extending their empire to the north, conquered Catalonia in 711 but lost the northern districts to Charlemagne in 795. While the county was independent in the ninth century, a merger by marriage united the county with the kingdom of Aragon in 1132, although the Catalans retained their own laws and autonomous government. The expanding kingdom conquered Valencia and the Balearic Islands from the Moors in the thirteenth century and expanded its ties to the eastern Mediterranean, competing with the republics of Genoa and Pisa for control of Mediterranean trade. From 1230 to the fifteenth century a Catalan trading empire stretched as far east as the Balkan Peninsula, and the wealth it generated financed a golden age accompanied by a great flowering of medieval Catalan arts and culture.

Aragonese attempts to curtail Catalonia's autonomous rights incited a Catalan rebellion and civil war in the kingdom in 1460–72. The war's devastation marked the beginning of a long decline, which accelerated following the unification of the kingdoms of Aragon and Castile in 1479. The 1659 Treaty of the Pyrenees, which ended one of the intermittent Franco-Spanish wars, established the northern boundary of Spanish territory in the Pyrenees Mountains and confirmed French rule of the northern districts of Catalonia.

The Generalitat, the Catalan parliament, met for the first time in 1705 to coordinate a Catalan rebellion intended to win Catalan independence. Reconquered in 1714, the government abolished all of the Catalans' special rights and all vestiges of self-rule. In 1716 the Spanish government banned the Catalan language and attempted to eradicate Catalan culture in the Spanish domains. Many Catalans emigrated to Spain's American colonies.

The suppressed culture and language began to revive with the spread of education and publishing in the 1830s, the revival leading to a resurgence of nationalism. A Catalan rebellion in 1842 provoked renewed government efforts to stamp out the Catalan culture. The Catalan cultural revival resumed in the 1870s and over the next decades produced some of Europe's greatest artists, architects, and writers.

Periodic attempts to break free of the Spanish state incited serious nationalist disturbances in 1909, 1923, and 1929, countered by the reimposition of political restrictions and frequently a prohibition on the use of the Catalan language. The Generalitat, suppressed for over two centuries, again convened in 1931 following the establishment of a more sympathetic republican government in Madrid. Granted autonomy, the Catalans demanded additional powers as disarray and instability in the Spanish state increased. Amid a severe government crisis, the Catalan leaders declared Catalonia independent of Spain on 4 October 1934, but government troops quickly ended the secession and routed the Catalan rebels.

In 1936 a new leftist government in Madrid restored Catalonia's autonomy, and to preserve their independence, the Catalans mostly sided with the Loyalists against Franco's fascist forces during the civil war that devastated Spain from 1936 to 1939. Aided by Germany and Italy, the fascists conquered Catalonia in early 1939 and executed the Catalan president and officials of the Generalitat as over 200,000 Catalans fled into exile. The Franco government banned all manifestations of Catalan culture, including severe penalties for publishing or teaching in the Catalan language.

Rapid industrial growth, particularly along the Mediterranean coast, in the 1950s and 1960s, drew in a massive influx of peasant immigrants from Spain's backward south. Dubbed "Franco's Legions" by the Catalans, the immigrants served the Spanish government in two ways, by providing a low-cost industrial workforce and by spreading the traditional Spanish culture approved by Franco.

Franco's death in 1975, followed by the rapid democratization of Spain, allowed the Catalan culture to resurface. Promoted by a proliferation of autonomist, nationalist, and separatist organizations, the Catalan culture and language quickly revived and replaced the Castilian language and culture the Franco regime had attempted to impose on Catalonia.

Granted autonomy in 1980, the Catalans elected a government dominated by moderate nationalists determined to win maximum independence within Spain. Following Spain's entry into the European Community in 1986, Catalan nationalism has focused on independence within a united Europe and the reunification of the Catalan regions in Spain and France. In 1988 the Catalan language, spoken by more Europeans than were many official state languages, became an official language of the European Community.

Nationalist leaders claim that Catalonia, Spain's richest and most advanced region, is now more closely linked to the rest of Europe than to the rest of Spain. As the member states of the European Union draw closer economically and politically the hold of the Spanish government over Catalonia is weakening. In February 1994 negotiations between Catalan leaders and members of the Spanish government centered on the Catalan's desire to take up the status the region enjoyed before 1714, independence under the Spanish king, but not subject to the Spanish government.

*SELECTED BIBLIOGRAPHY:*

Chaytor, Henry J. *History of Aragon and Catalonia.* 1969.
Shiels, Frederick L. *Ethnic Separatism and World Politics.* 1984.
Wigram, E. *Northern Spain.* 1976.
Woodward, Kathryn A. *Double Talk: Bilingualism and the Politics of Ethnicity in Catalonia.* 1989.

# CHAMPA

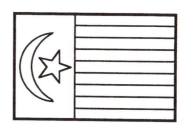

*CAPITAL: Dalat*

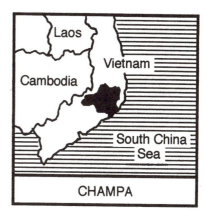

*POPULATION:* (95e) 660,000 : 220,000 Chams in Vietnam and another 95,000 in Cambodia. MAJOR NATIONAL GROUPS: (95e) Cham 33%, Vietnamese 30%, Moi, Khmer Krom, Muong, Man, Meo. MAJOR LANGUAGES: Vietnamese, Cham, French, English. MAJOR RELIGIONS: Sunni Muslim, Brahmanism, Roman Catholic, Cao Dai, Hoa Hao, Buddhist, animist. MAJOR CITIES: (95e) Dalat 184,000, Baoloc 50,000, Phanrang 40,000.

*GEOGRAPHY:* AREA: 3,691 sq.mi.-9,562 sq.km. LOCATION: Champa occupies a forested plateau, the Nui Lang Blan, just south of Lake Krong Ana, and a lowland coastal strip on the South China Sea in southern Vietnam. POLITICAL STATUS: Champa has no official status; the region claimed by nationalists forms the highland districts of the Vietnamese provinces of Dac Lac, Lam Dong, and Phu Khanh, including the coastal Mui Dinh district south of Camranh.

*INDEPENDENCE DECLARED:* 19 February 1964.

*FLAG:* The Cham national flag, the flag of the former republic, has nine red and white horizontal stripes with a broad, pale blue vertical stripe at the hoist bearing a large white crescent moon and five-pointed white star.

*PEOPLE:* The Chams, the descendants of the people of ancient Champa, are a Malay people speaking a Mon-Khmer language with two major divisions: the coastal dialects of Roglai and Cham and the plateau dialects of Rhadé, Jarai, and Bih. The Chams, culturally, ethnically, and religiously distinct from their neighbors, are mostly Sunni Muslims, with a large minority practicing Brahmanism, a religion derived from the Hindu religion of ancient Champa. In addition to a large Vietnamese population, mostly belonging to the Roman Catholic, Cao Dai, and Hoa Hao religious minorities, the region's inhabitants include ethnic Cambodians, called Khmer Krom, and several highland tribal peoples, collectively called Montagnards.

*THE NATION:* Ancient Champa, a distinct civilization influenced by contacts with Hindu India, emerged as a separate kingdom in the second century A.D. The kingdom expanded to eventually control most of present south and central Vietnam. The sophisticated Cham civilization left behind magnificent and durable architecture, temples and public buildings as smooth as sandstone but constructed without mortar, as the bricks were baked after they were in place, a construction process now lost.

The expansion of the coastal Cham kingdom brought it into conflict with the powerful Khmers in the south and the Viet in the north. From the tenth century Champa fought a long series of indecisive wars with the Viet and Khmer states and with China. The Cham defeat of the Khmers and the sack of the Khmer capital, Angkor, in 1177 marked Champa's apex as a military power. Conquered by invading Mongols in 1262, Champa declined rapidly, its flourishing agriculture devastated and its magnificent cities in ruins.

The Cham state slowly recovered and again came into conflict with Dai Viet, the Vietnamese state that had expanded at Champa's expense since the tenth century. Decisively defeated by the Viet in 1471–72, the kingdom lost all of its territory north of Danang. Cham refugees fled south to the remaining Cham lands around Dalat, Nhatrang, and Camranh. One group of refugees, settled in the Khmer kingdom of Cambodia, adopted the Islamic religion brought north by Malay traders. The new religion gradually spread to Champa, where it displaced the earlier Hindu religion as the predominant religious sect.

The Vietnamese, continuing to press Champa from the north, varied the methods of conquest, sometimes marrying into the Cham aristocracy, other times launching offensives spearheaded by assault troops of orphans raised by the state. In the seventeenth century a mighty Viet army pushed south into Champa and conquered all but a highland region around Dalat. The last Cham king fled into exile with the Viet conquest of Dalat in 1822. The Viet victory ended seventeen centuries of separate Cham existence. Horrible massacres in the 1830s decimated the remaining Cham population, with only a few pockets of refugees surviving in the highlands and along the Gulf of Thailand.

The French established a colonial administration in Vietnam and Cambodia in the mid-nineteenth century, the powerful Europeans welcomed by the Cham survivors as protection against the hated Vietnamese. The Chams, the most loyal allies of the French administration, provided many recruits for the colonial army and administration and, through contacts with other French colonies, gradually established ties to other Muslim peoples.

The Chams' renewed ties to the outside world began a process of national revival. Looking back on several periods of their history when conquered Champa regained its sovereignty under Cham princes, national leaders began to press for an independent Cham state under French protection. In 1946 the French administration created an autonomous region in the highlands centered on the Cham metropolis, Dalat.

The French defeat by Vietnamese nationalists in 1954, followed by a French withdrawal and the eventual partition of Vietnam, left the Chams without protection. Cham nationalists mobilized the population and formed the United Liberation Front of Highland Champa (FLHPC) to work for an independent Cham state. Their appeals to the United Nations in 1962–64 ignored, the nationalist leaders, on 19 February 1964, declared Champa independent of Vietnam. In 1965 government troops suppressed the Cham government and ended the Cham bid for independence. In 1968 the head of the underground Cham government, Y-Bham-Huol, after nearly four years in hiding, was escorted to the Cambodian border and expelled. He and his followers joined the Cambodian Chams of the Cham National Liberation Movement (MNLC).

The vehemently anti-Communist Chams suffered for their beliefs during the civil wars in Vietnam and Cambodia that ended with Communist victories in 1975. A Cham rebellion against the victorious Khmer Rouge in Cambodia ended with thousands massacred and the entire Cham population targeted for eradication. By the time the murderous Khmer Rouge had been driven from power in 1979, over a tenth of the Cham population of Cambodia had perished. Fearing a Khmer Rouge return to power in Cambodia, thousands migrated illegally to the Cham heartland in southern Vietnam.

Cham nationalist groups, with the support of several wealthy Muslim countries, organized in the 1970s and 1980s to resist Vietnamese government plans to ease lowland population pressure by encouraging settlement in the minority-populated highlands. Allied to the Montagnards and Khmer Krom and later joined by Vietnamese dissidents and religious minorities, the Chams encouraged a coalition of nationalist and anti-Communist groups to form the United Front for the Struggle of Oppressed Races (FULRO), the only sizable resistance movement in Vietnam. Vietnamese government countermeasures, apart from military offensives, include the elimination of the official position of the Mufti, the Cham religious leader, and prohibition of the Muslim pilgrimage to Mecca, measures that have reinforced the Muslim Cham's determination to win their freedom.

*SELECTED BIBLIOGRAPHY:*

Buttinger, Joseph. *The Smaller Dragon: A Political History of Vietnam.* 1958.
Chandler, David P. *A History of Cambodia.* 1983.
Maspero, Georges. *The Kingdom of Champa.* 1949.
Slavin, Morris. *The Making of an Insurrection.* 1986.

# CHAVASHIA

Chävash Jen; Chuvashia; Chavashistan

*CAPITAL: Cheboksary*

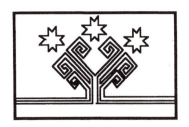

EASTERN EUROPE

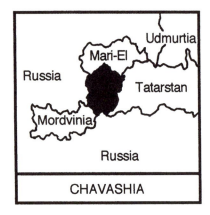

CHAVASHIA

*POPULATION:* (95e) 1,372,000 : 2,255,000 Chavash (Chuvash) in Russia. MAJOR NATIONAL GROUPS: (95e) Chavash (Chuvash) 71%, Russian 24%, Tatar 3%, Mordvin 2%. MAJOR LANGUAGES: Chavash, Russian, Tatar. MAJOR RELIGIONS: Russian Orthodox, Sunni Muslim. MAJOR CITIES: (95e) Cheboksary 487,000 (690,000), Novocheboksarsk 125,000, Alatyr 72,000 (111,000), Kanash 61,000, Shumerlya 51,000.

*GEOGRAPHY:* AREA: 7,066 sq.mi.-18,305 sq.km. LOCATION: Chavashia occupies the flat plains of the upland Chuvash Plateau, a wooded steppe in the western Volga River basin of eastern European Russia. POLITICAL STATUS: Chavashia forms a member state of the Russian Federation.

*FLAG:* The Chavash flag, the official flag of the republic, is a yellow field with a narrow crimson stripe on the bottom and bears a stylized "Tree of Life" and three stylized crimson suns in the center.

*PEOPLE:* The Chavash, called Chuvash by the Russians, are the descendants of the medieval Bulgar people, with later admixtures of Turkic and Finnic strains. The Chavash language, though of basic Turkic structure, is not considered to belong to any of the four Turkic language groups but forms a separate Bulgaric branch of the West Altaic language group. The mostly Orthodox Chavash comprise two major divisions, which correspond to the major dialects: Anatri (Lower Chavash) and Viryal (Upper Chavash). Even though more than half the Chavash live outside the republic, they have proved less susceptible to assimilation than many larger national groups and have preserved their unique culture intact.

*THE NATION:* A people known as the Black Bulgars began to occupy the vast basin of the Volga River in the eighth century. Converted to Islam in the tenth century, the Black Bulgars created an extensive, early medieval state that eventually controlled many neighboring Finnic and Turkic peoples. The flourishing state, conquered by the Mongols in 1236, never recovered, and the Black Bulgars later came under the rule of the Tatar Khanate of Kazan, a successor state established as Mongol power declined.

Russian Orthodox monks, venturing into the unknown east in the fourteenth century, converted the majority of the Chavash to Christianity by 1500. Following the Russian conquest of Kazan in 1552, the Chavash came under direct Russian rule. Russian attempts to assimilate the Chavash undermined the common bond of the Orthodox religion. Famine and political chaos in Moscow provoked the Chavash, and allied to the neighboring Mari and Mordvin, they attempted to throw off Russian rule in 1601–3. Savage reprisals against the entire population accompanied the defeat of the rebels.

An impoverished minority dominated by Russian landlords, the Chavash stubbornly clung to their language and culture. Serfdom, prevalent in most of Russia, failed in the region as the Chavash traditionally located their villages in remote ravines to elude tsarist officials. Chavash resistance to Russian rule manifested itself in periodic disturbances, crop damage, illegal timber cutting, and the looting of Russian property. Disturbances escalated with an influx of Russian peasants freed from serfdom in the provinces to the west in 1861.

Backward and illiterate, at least half of the Chavash rose during the 1905 Russian Revolution, attacking Slavic colonies, burning estates, and skirmishing with troops sent to restore order. Chavash guerrillas from hidden villages continued to harass the authorities for over two years, until finally routed out of hiding in 1907. Up to World War I, the Chavash remained primarily agricultural, with little development of the potentially important timber industry.

Chavashia, far from the front lines, felt little of the immediate effects of World War I until conscription of minorities began in 1916. When revolution overtook the conflict in February 1917, most of the Chavash soldiers deserted and returned home, bringing with them new ideas, including a new national sentiment that rapidly took root in the region.

The Chavash leaders convened a national congress to take over as civil government collapsed. The congress sent delegates to a conference of all the non-Russian peoples of the Volga-Ural region convened in late 1917 to discuss the Bolshevik coup and the future of the nations in the region. A majority of the Chavash supported inclusion in an independent regional federation of states; a minority favored a separate Chavash state or a federation only with the Orthodox Mari and Mordvin.

Bolshevik troops overran Chavashia in February 1918 before they had had a chance to decide their own future. Devastated by heavy fighting between 1918 and 1920, the Chavash homeland witnessed some of the largest battles of the Russian civil war. In June 1920 the victorious Soviets created a Chuvash autonomous region. In 1925 the region's status changed to that of an autonomous republic within the Soviet Russian Federation.

The Chavash, constituting over 80% of their republic's population in 1965, experienced a modest cultural revival over the next decade, partly in response to increased Slavic immigration to the republic. The cultural revival reinforced the Chavash resistance to the government's assimilation pressures in the 1960s and 1970s. The revival took on nationalist overtones following the introduction of liberal reforms in the late 1980s, and became openly nationalist with the disintegration of the Soviet Union in 1991.

Nationalist and cultural groups belonging to Tavas, a popular front organization, have pressed for the de-Russification of their language, the adoption of the Latin alphabet, and the creation of a Chavash university. Growing nationalist sentiment forced the local government to declare the republic's sovereignty and to change the name from the Russian to the Chavash version. In late 1991 the Chavash government unilaterally proclaimed the upgrading of the republic's status to that of a republic within the newly democratic Russian Federation.

Chavash nationalism focuses on the consolidation of their traditional lands and the incorporation of all Chavash populated territories in one state. The old idea of an independent Chavashia within a federation of Volga states has gained support since 1991.

*SELECTED BIBLIOGRAPHY:*

D'Encausse, Helene C. *The Great Challenge: Nationalities and the Bolshevik State, 1917–1930.* 1991.

Pushkarev, Sergei. *Self-Government and Freedom in Russia.* 1988.

Rywkin, Michael. *Russian Colonial Expansion to 1917.* 1988.

Smal-Stocki, Roman. *The Captive Nations: Nationalism of the Non-Russian Nations and Peoples of the Soviet Union.* 1960.

# CHECHENIA

### Nokhchyïchuo; Chechnya

*CAPITAL: Grozni (Grozny)*

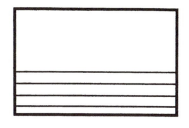

*POPULATION:* (All population figures are estimates for 1994, prior to the outbreak of fighting in the region.) (94e) 1,079,000 : 1,020,000 Chechens in Russia. MAJOR NATIONAL GROUPS: (94e) Chechen 71%, Russian 20%, Ossetian 2%, Ingush 1%, Ukrainian, Dagestani. MAJOR LANGUAGES: Chechen, Russian. MAJOR RELIGIONS: (94e) Sunni Muslim 75%, Russian Orthodox. MAJOR CITIES: (94e) Grozni (Grozny) 411,000 (490,000), Gudermes 54,000, Argun 38,000, Sali 30,000, Ursus-Martan 24,000.

*GEOGRAPHY:* AREA: 6,210 sq.mi.-16,088 sq.km. LOCATION: Chechenia occupies the northern slopes of the middle Caucasus Mountains and extends into the flood plain of the Terek River in southern European Russia. POLITICAL STATUS: Chechenia's status remains undecided; it officially forms a member state of the Russian Federation.

*INDEPENDENCE DECLARED:* 2 December 1917; 2 November 1991.

*FLAG:* The Chechen national flag, the official flag of the breakaway republic, is a green field with three horizontal stripes of white, red, and white on the lower half.

*PEOPLE:* The Chechens, who call themselves Nakh or Nakchuo, are a Caucasian nation comprising 128 clans. The Chechen language, a dialect of Vienakh, the northeastern branch of the Caucasian languages, developed as a literary language in the nineteenth century. The Chechens are mostly Sunni Muslims, adhering to the Shafi rite. The Chechens have retained an extremely high birthrate despite the urbanization of 40% of the Chechen population.

*THE NATION:* The Chechens, thought to be descended from ancient Scythian

tribes, have lived in the Ciscaucasia region since before 600 B.C. Their homeland, straddling the main invasion route between Europe and Asia, knew many
invaders, the Caucasian tribes evolving a warrior tradition necessary to hold
their lands against numerous would-be conquerors. Influenced by the Romans
and later the Byzantines, most of the fierce mountain tribes had adopted Christianity by A.D. 1000.

The Mongols conquered the region in 1241, laying waste the Chechen lowlands. Withdrawing to mountain strongholds, the Chechens fought the invaders
for over fifty years, finally throwing off Mongol rule in 1300. Over the next
centuries the Chechens resisted Persian and Turkish attempts to dominate the
region. In the seventeenth century the Chechens, while continuing to resist foreign domination, adopted the Turks' Islamic religion.

Slavic Cossacks, the spearhead of Russian expansion, began to explore the
region in the sixteenth century and in 1598 reached the Terek River in Chechen
territory. Slowly extending their influence as Persian and Turkish power declined, the Russians finally pushed south in the late eighteenth century. The
Russians met the fiercest resistance to their conquest of the Caucasus from the
Chechens. Grozni, founded in 1818 as a frontier fort, established a Russian
foothold in the center of Chechen territory.

The most ardent opponents of Russian rule, the Chechens, under their political
and religious leader, Shamyl, fought an effective guerrilla war against the Russians from 1834 to 1859. Tens of thousands of Muslim warriors died in the final
Russian conquest of the region. The surviving Chechens, driven from their fertile
lowlands along the Terek River, lived in abject poverty in the Caucasus Mountains. Hatred of the Slavs, particularly the Terek Cossacks settled on their confiscated lands, provoked repeated revolts, especially severe in 1863, 1867, and 1877.

Openly sympathetic to Muslim Turkey during World War I, the Chechens
rejoiced as revolution spread across Russia in February 1917. Believing the
revolution would redress old injustices and return their lost lands, the Chechen
leaders sent petitions to the new government detailing their grievances. Ignored
by Russia's beleaguered provisional government, the Chechens mobilized and
launched an offensive against the Terek Cossack settlements on their traditional
lands. In September 1917 a Chechen government took control of the local government and expelled all Slavic officials.

The Bolshevik coup in October 1917 ended Chechen attempts to win autonomy within Russia. Alarmed by the antireligious Bolshevik proclamations, the
Chechen formed an alliance with their old enemies, the Terek Cossacks, but the
ongoing territorial dispute quickly ended the alliance. Proclaiming a holy war,
the Muslim warriors drove the Cossacks from Grozni and declared Chechenia
independent on 2 December 1917 and established a theocratic democracy headed
by the Chechen emir, Sheikh Ilzum Hadji.

The Caucasus region, the scene of some of the heaviest fighting of the Russian
civil war, finally fell to the victorious Soviets in 1919. Communist attempts to
impose direct rule and to suppress the Islamic religion provoked serious revolts

in 1920, 1927, and 1939–40. A World War II German drive on the Caucasus oil fields reached the border of the rebellious region in 1942. The Nazi advance prompted a renewed Chechen revolt as many joined the Nazis' anti-Communist campaign.

Accused of treason by Stalin, the entire Chechen nation, including the families of soldiers in the Red Army, faced punishment. Driven from their homes at gunpoint and loaded on cattle cars, the Chechens suffered a brutal deportation to Central Asia. Officially rehabilitated and allowed to return to the Caucasus in 1957, the surviving Chechens arrived back in their homeland to find their homes occupied by Slavs and all traces of their culture eradicated. In 1958 severe Chechen rioting paralyzed the region, forcing the Soviet authorities to act on the Chechen grievances. Given some rights, the Chechen and the neighboring Ingush were joined in a joint autonomous republic.

Considered the most anti-Soviet of the subject peoples, the Chechen overthrew the local government soon after the disintegration of the Soviet state in August 1991. A new national government, led by General Dzhokhar Dudayev, declared Chechenia independent on 2 November 1991. The breakaway state soon gained a reputation as a center for the organized crime spreading throughout Russia.

In August 1994 opposition forces, with Russian government support, attempted to overthrow Dudayev. In mid-August Dudayev ordered a general mobilization to combat the Chechen opposition and its Russian backers. In September fighting between the Chechen government forces and the Russian-backed opposition broke out and in November spread across the republic.

The Russian government, determined to end Chechenia's self-proclaimed independence, sent troops into the republic in December 1994. The troops, expecting to easily overcome the poorly equipped Chechen fighters, met fierce resistance and became bogged down in a growing guerilla war after driving the Chechen forces from the capital and the main cities in months of heavy fighting, Over 200,000 civilians fled the fighting, mostly to the neighboring republics of Ingushetia* and Dagestan.* The Chechens, the most implacable enemies of nineteenth century Russian expansion have again become the major threat to the continued Russian domination of the non-Russian peoples of the Russian Federation.

*SELECTED BIBLIOGRAPHY:*
Adams, Arthur. *Stalin and His Times.* 1986.
Colton, Timothy, and Robert Levgold. *After the Soviet Union.* 1992.
Wixman, Ronald. *The Peoples of the U.S.S.R. An Ethnographic Handbook.* 1984.

# CHUKOTKA

**Chukotsky; Chukchi**

*CAPITAL: Anadyr*

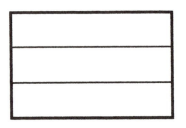

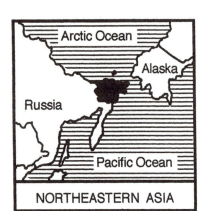

NORTHEASTERN ASIA

CHUKOTKA

*POPULATION:* (95e) 164,000 : 36,000 Chukot (Chukchi) in Russia. MAJOR NATIONAL GROUPS: (95e) Russian 68%, Chukot (Chukchi) 22%, Lamut 4%, Yakut 2%, Evenki, Koryak, Inuit. MAJOR LANGUAGES: Russian, Chukot, Even (Lamut). MAJOR RELIGIONS: Russian Orthodox, animist (shamanism). MAJOR CITIES: (95e) Anadyr 14,000, Provideniya 5,000.

*GEOGRAPHY:* AREA: 284,752 sq.mi.-737,700 sq.km. LOCATION: Chukotka lies in extreme northeastern Russia, a huge region partly above the Arctic Circle. Mountainous and with a long coastline on the Chukchi, Siberian, and Bering Seas, the peninsula region in the northeast is less than fifty miles from Alaska across the Bering Strait. POLITICAL STATUS: Chukotka's status is in dispute. Officially it forms an autonomous region of the Russian Federation, as the declaration by the regional legislature unilaterally upgrading Chukotka to republic status within the Russian Federation has not been recognized.

*INDEPENDENCE DECLARED:* 28 October 1921.

*FLAG:* The Chukot national flag, the flag of the self-proclaimed republic, is a horizontal tricolor of white, cranberry red, and blue.

*PEOPLE:* The Chukot, also called Chukchi or Chukchee, are a Paleo-Asiatic people ethnically related to the Native American peoples. The Chukot language, a Paleo-Asiatic language of the East Siberian group of the Hyperborean or Luorawetlan language group, is the largest of the isolated language group that also includes the languages of the related Koryak and Kamchatchdal peoples to the south. Traditionally, the Chukots are divided into two groups based on traditional occupations: the reindeer herders of the plains and mountains of the interior and the fishing people of the coasts. The related peoples include Lamuts in the southwest, Evenki in the southeast, Koryaks in the southwest, Yakuts in the west, and Inuit in the coastal regions of the northeast. Slavs, many the descendants of political exiles shipped to the region during the Stalinist era, now outnumber the native Chukot population, although the number of Slavs returning to Europe has increased rapidly in the 1990s.

THE NATION: In prehistoric times the Chukot Peninsula formed the western extension of a land bridge that once connected Asia and North America. Beginning some 30,000 years ago, small bands of nomadic hunters began to migrate across the land bridge, following the mammoths and other large quarry. Clan groups eventually settled on the western end of the bridge, the ancestors of the Chukots, Lamut, Inuit, and other native people. Well adapted to the harsh climatic conditions, the seasons, the reindeer herds, and the availability of food regulated traditional Chukot life.

Russian expansion, led by Cossack explorers and soldiers, reached the Pacific Ocean in 1640. Nine years later the Russians established Anadyr, called Novo-Mariinsk, as a fort and trading post on traditional Chukot land. Nominal Russian rule consisted of collecting an annual fur tax while leaving the native peoples to their traditional way of life. Between 1763 and 1800 Russia formally annexed the Chukot territories.

Orthodox missionaries in the nineteenth century introduced a system of education. Although usually limited to the sons of chiefs, the missionary education established a core of educated, modernizing leaders. Aided and often studied by educated political exiles sent to the remote region from European Russia, Chukot leaders began to demand the redress of past injustices. In the wake of the 1905 Russian Revolution, the Chukot movement focused on land and cultural rights.

Virtually untouched by World War I, which engulfed European Russia from 1914, the Chukots were dismayed by the news of the revolution that overthrew the empire. Slow to react, the Chukots began to organize only when the civil government collapsed. The Chukots, pushed aside as rival Russian factions sought to win control of the strategic region, remained unsure of what to do as the Russian civil war spread to even the most remote corners of the disintegrating empire. In 1920 the victorious Reds expelled the last of the White forces and established Soviet rule in the region.

Outraged by clumsy Soviet attempts to collectivize their reindeer herds, small groups organized to resist, and in early 1921 violence broke out. Allied to other anti-Soviet peoples and groups, Chukot nationalists routed the small Soviet force at Anadyr and on 28 October 1921 declared Chukotka independent of Soviet Russia. The nationalists sought Japanese and American aid and recognition, but without success.

A Soviet military force invaded the breakaway state, and on 21 October 1922 independent Chukotka ceased to exist, the Chukot nationalist leadership imprisoned or dead. As part of the Soviet nationalities programs, the authorities authorized a Chukchi national area in 1930, but all power remained with the Soviet bureaucracy that later oversaw the vast chain of slave labor camps established in the wilderness in the 1950s. In 1957 the Soviet authorities drove the Chukots off the tundra and into communal farms, their reindeer-hide tents, *urangas*, exchanged for prefabricated Soviet housing.

The reforms introduced by Mikhail Gorbychev in the late 1980s stirred dormant Chukot nationalism. In early 1990 the first openly nationalist organization formed. Supported by the resurgent national movement and the regional parliament, the area's governor, Alexander Nazorov, unilaterally declared the upgrading of the region's political status in October 1990. Chukotka's self-declared status as a member republic of the Russian Federation has not received official recognition.

The disintegration of the Soviet Union in August 1991 fueled the rapid growth of nationalism in the region. In late 1991 the republican government sent a delegation to Moscow to seek recognition of Chukotka's status as a republic of the revamped Russian Federation. Rebuffed by the ministries and bureaucrats in Moscow, the delegation returned home. In December 1992 the Chukot parliament proclaimed the republic independent of the provincial government of Magadan, the oblast it has formed part of since 1953. In order to finance the republic's autonomy, the Chukot government imposed a 10% tax on the production of gold.

The end of the Soviet command economy has doomed many of the subsidized industries and mines that originally drew the Russians from Europe with high wages and free housing. The uneconomic industries have virtually collapsed, and many of the Russians are returning to European Russia. The Chukots forced to work in the industries are beginning to return to their traditional way of life, herding reindeer on the tundra.

Looking across the Bering Strait, the new Chukot government has established close political and economic ties to Alaska. Increasingly ignoring edicts and laws issued in faraway Moscow, the nationalist Chukot government is entering into a number of joint commercial ventures with Alaskan companies and is seeking financial backing for oil exploration. Optimistic about the region's future, the government is even participating in a feasibility study for a rail tunnel under the Bering Strait that would connect Chukotka and its mineral wealth and natural resources to the huge consumer markets of the United States.

*SELECTED BIBLIOGRAPHY:*

Mandel, William. *The Soviet Far East.* 1944.

Segal, Gerald. *The Soviet Union and the Pacific.* 1990.

Wood, Alan, and R. A. French. *The Development of Siberia's Peoples and Resources.* 1989.

Yevtushenko, Yevgeny. *Divided Twins: Alaska and Siberia.* 1988.

# CIRCASSIA

Adygeny; Kerberdï; Cherkesiya; North
Caucasia

*CAPITAL: Cherkessk*

SOUTHEASTERN EUROPE

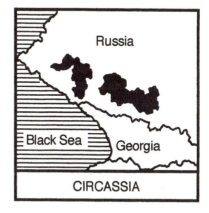

CIRCASSIA

*POPULATION:* (95e) 1,385,000 : 575,000 Circassians (373,000 Kabardin, 126,000 Adyge, 76,000 Cherkess) in Russia. MAJOR NATIONAL GROUPS: (95e) Circassian 37%, Cossack 21%, Russian 17%, Ukrainian 5%, Abaza 2%. MAJOR LANGUAGES: Russian, Circassian. MAJOR RELIGIONS: Russian Orthodox, Sunni Muslim. MAJOR CITIES: (95e) ADYGEI: Maikop 165,000, Kamennomostskiy 21,000. KABARDA: Nalchik 255,000 (282,000), Prokhaldny 59,000 (100,000), Mayskiy 42,000, Baksan 32,000, Nartkala 28,000. CHERKESS: Cherkessk 128,000.

*GEOGRAPHY:* AREA: 8,757 sq.mi.-22,686 sq.km. LOCATION: Circassia lies in the foothills of the western Caucasus Mountains in southern European Russia, occupying the valleys of the Kuban and Terek Rivers. Two of the three Circassian regions lie in the mountainous region, the third, Adyge lies in the lowlands and is separated by the Slav-populated Laba region. POLITICAL STATUS: Circassia has no official status. The region claimed by nationalists comprises three regions: Kabarda and Cherkessia, which form, with Karachai-Balkaria,* two republics of the Russian Federation; and the Adyge Republic, which forms an enclave within the Kuban.*

*INDEPENDENCE DECLARED:* 11 May 1918.

*FLAG:* The Circassian national flag, the flag of the national movement, is a horizontal bicolor of red over green bearing three crossed, yellow arrows surmounted by three yellow stars centered. OTHER FLAG(S): The flag of the Adyge is a green field bearing three crossed, yellow arrows surmounted by three yellow stars under an arc of nine yellow stars. The flag of the Cherkess is a yellow field with the same arrows and stars as the Adyge flag, but in red. The flag of the Kabardin, based on the independence flag of 1918, has seven green and white stripes with a light blue canton on the upper hoist bearing four yellow stars in the form of a diamond.

*PEOPLE:* The Circassians are a Northern Caucasian people comprising three divisions: the Kabardin in the east, the Cherkess in the center, and the Adyge (Adygei) in the west. The Kabardin speak Upper Circassian, and the Cherkess and Adyge speak Lower Circassian, both Kiakh languages of the Abkhazo-Adygheian group of Caucasian languages. Overwhelmingly and fervently Sunni Muslim, the Circassians adhere to the Shafi rite. Russians, including a large Cossack population, form the majority in all Circassian areas except Kabarda.

*THE NATION:* Known to the ancient Greeks as Zyukhoy, the Circassians probably settled the region of the North Caucasus before the sixth century B.C. Possibly the earliest representative of the Caucasian peoples, the Circassians populated a wide area north of the Caucasus Mountains that figured prominently in the legends of ancient Greece. The handsome Circassians, valued as slaves, developed a warrior society as protection against the region's frequent invaders and raids by slavers.

Greek monks introduced Christianity to the warlike tribes in the sixth century A.D. A common Christian religion facilitated the Circassian's establishment of ties to the Byzantines to the south and to opening trade routes to the early Slav state, Kievan Rus, in the north. By the late ninth century, regular trade and diplomatic ties existed with the Slavs.

Weakened by the Mongol conquest of 1241–42, the tribes came under the rule of Christian Georgia by the end of the thirteenth century. To escape Georgian rule, the Kabardin tribes migrated west to settle in the foothills of the central Caucasus Mountains. Kabardin princes, from the fifteenth to the seventeenth centuries, dominated much of the North Caucasus as tributaries of the Turkish Ottoman Empire. The majority of the Circassian tribes, influenced by the Turks, adopted the Islamic religion in the seventeenth century.

Russians, extending their frontiers south, proclaimed Kabarda a protectorate in 1557, but Russian expansion in the region, contested by the Ottoman Turks, led to a series of wars that continued sporadically for centuries. In 1774 the Russians finally established their authority, which prompted fierce Circassian resistance over the next decades. In 1864 the Russians, after years of fighting, triumphed over the Circassian warriors. Some 400,000 Circassians, rejecting Christian domination, fled or were expelled to Turkish territory. Only the Kabardin nobility, noted for wealth and extravagance, integrated into tsarist society.

Slavic migration to the region, spurred by the discovery of oil at Maikop in 1900, resulted in the formation of an urbanized, industrial proletariat. Relegated to a marginal existence in the rural areas, the Circassians proved an enduring problem for the Russian military and civil authorities.

Openly sympathetic to the Muslim Turks when war began in 1914, the Circassians enthusiastically welcomed the news that revolution had overthrown the hated tsarist government in February 1917. Circassian appeals to the new government for religious freedom, political autonomy, and the reunification of the Circassian lands received no response. Responding to calls for Muslim solidarity, the Circassians sent delegates to an all-Muslim conference in September 1917, seeking Muslim support for their demands.

Vehemently opposed to the antireligious stance of the new Bolshevik government, installed after a coup in October 1917, the Muslims organized an autonomous state called North Caucasia. Threatened by both the Bolsheviks and the anti-Bolshevik White forces, the Muslim leaders declared North Caucasia independent of Russia on 11 May 1918.

Overrun by the White forces of General Deniken in January 1919, the separatist leaders fled, and the republic collapsed. Violent White opposition to Muslim separatism prompted many Circassians to join the Reds, believing the Soviet promise of independence in a federation of Soviet states. The Red Army drove the last of the White forces from the region in January 1920. Under Soviet rule the region formed part of a new, autonomous Mountain Republic with the Soviet Russian Federation; however, ethnic tensions among the member regions led to the breakup of the republic after only twenty months.

Soviet repression, particularly of religion, provoked serious revolts in 1929 and 1937. Thinking to capitalize on the Circassians' grievances, the Nazi Germans, after taking the area during the Caucasus campaign of 1942, offered an alliance and promoted anti-Communist solidarity. The Circassian view that the Germans represented just another in a long series of invaders spared them the brutal deportations suffered by neighboring Muslim peoples following the return of the Soviet authorities.

Ethnic tensions, suppressed for decades, emerged with the easing of Soviet restraints in the late 1980s. The three Circassian peoples, separated under tsarist and Soviet rule, demanded unification and the dissolution of the hybrid territories that the Cherkess and Kabardin had been forced to share with the Turkic Karachai and Balkar peoples for most of this century. Demands for a separate Circassian republic within the Russian Federation accelerated with the disintegration of the Soviet state in August 1991.

Nationalist sentiment and growing conflicts between the Circassians and the Turkic peoples led to the partition of the parliament of Kabardino-Balkar into its constituent parts in February 1992. Demonstrators in Cherkessk demanded the withdrawal of the Cherkess from the parliament they share with the Karachai. In March 1992 the local republican governments signed a new federal treaty regulating relations with Moscow, but Circassian nationalists continue to demand a separate federal republic, reunification of the Circassian lands, and redress for past injustices.

The three Circassian peoples, joined to the other Muslim Caucasian peoples in traditional alliances and historic associations, in late 1994, condemned the

Russian military attack on the separatist government in Chechenia.\* The Russian advance, mirroring that of the nineteenth century, has raised nationalist and anti-Russian sentiment in the Circassian regions.

*SELECTED BIBLIOGRAPHY:*

Diuk, Nadia, and Adrian Karatnycky. *The Hidden Nations: The People Challenge the Soviet Union.* 1990.

Hasler, Joan. *The Making of the Soviet Union.* 1989.

Pushkarev, Sergei. *Self-Government and Freedom in Russia.* 1988.

Wixman, Ronald. *The Peoples of the U.S.S.R. An Ethnographic Handbook.* 1984.

# CORNWALL

**Kernow; Cornwall and the Isles of Scilly**

*CAPITAL: Truro*

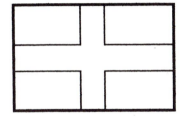

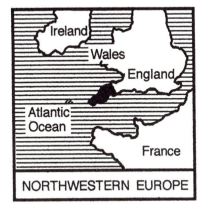

NORTHWESTERN EUROPE

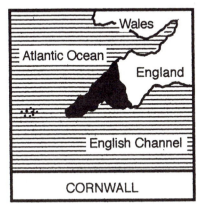

CORNWALL

*POPULATION:* (95e) 497,000 : 591,000 Cornish in the United Kingdom. MAJOR NATIONAL GROUPS: (95e) Cornish 89%, other British. MAJOR LANGUAGES: English, Kernewek (Cornish). MAJOR RELIGIONS: Methodist, Anglican. MAJOR CITIES: (95e) Cambronn (Camborne-Redruth) 50,000, Sant Austell (Saint Austell with Fowley) 39,000, Penzance 21,000, Falmouth 19,000 (30,000), Truro 14,000, Bodmin 13,000.

*GEOGRAPHY:* AREA: 1,369 sq.mi.-3,546 sq.km. LOCATION: Cornwall occupies a peninsula some seventy-five miles long, west of the Tamar River in southeastern England. The peninsula, marked by a rocky, indented coast, is England's only area of subtropical vegetation. Cornwall includes the Isles of Scilly, 140 small islands in the Atlantic Ocean west of Land's End. POLITICAL STATUS: Cornwall forms a county of England and a separate hereditary duchy, the title held by the heir to the British throne.

*FLAG:* The Cornish national flag, the flag of the national movement, is a black field charged with a centered white cross, the cross of St. Pirin, Cornwall's patron saint. OTHER FLAG(S): The official flag of the duchy of Cornwall is a black field bearing fifteen yellow discs, called bezants, arranged in an inverted triangle.

*PEOPLE:* The Cornish are a Celtic people, the descendants of the pre-Roman Celtic population of the British Isles. The Cornish culture, which has survived in the isolation of their peninsula, is closely tied to the traditional Cornish occupation, tin mining. The working of the mines in the region goes back for over thirty-five centuries. The Cornish language, Kernewek, belongs to the Brythonic branch of the Celtic languages and has recently been revived after near extinction. The majority of the Cornish belong to the Protestant Methodist faith, which has become closely identified with the Cornish culture.

*THE NATION:* The Brythonic Celts migrated to the island of Britain from the European mainland in the first century B.C. Conquered by the Romans in the first century A.D. the Celts assimilated into Roman life, becoming an urban, sophisticated population comfortable with the multiethnic Roman Empire. As Roman power declined in the fifth century and the Roman garrison withdrew, local squabbles further weakened the island's defenses. Germanic peoples from Northern Europe invaded the island, and many of the Romanized Celts fled, leaving the eastern districts to the newcomers, the Angles, Saxons, and Jutes.

Many of the refugees settled the western peninsulas, the present Cornwall and Wales,* and even crossed the narrow channel to settle the peninsula later called Little Britannia or Brittany.* The southern peninsula in Britain, called Corn, the old Celtic word for horn, referred to the horn-shaped peninsula and came to signify the Celts on the horn or Cornwall. In the eighth century Celtic Dumonia (Devon) collapsed, leaving the peninsula isolated beyond the Tamar River. Cornwall became closely associated with the Arthurian legend, the mass of popular medieval lore that originated with the tales of a Celtic warrior who fought twelve victorious battles against the Saxon invaders.

The region's tin mines, known to the ancient Greeks and Phoenicians, sustained Cornwall's independence until its conquest by Saxon king Athelstan in 936. In recognition of its separate character and history, Cornwall became a separate duchy in 1337, an appendage of the royal heir in England.

The Cornish fiercely resisted assimilation, although English gradually replaced Cornish as the language of daily life in the seventeenth century. Fervently Roman Catholic, the Cornish marched to protect their Catholicism in the sixteenth century but two centuries later abandoned the Roman faith to embrace the Wesleyan teachings. The Cornish converted en masse to the new Protestant Methodist sect.

Scorned as backward peasants and punished for speaking their Celtic language, the Cornish struck back the only way they could: they turned to the ancient Cornish traditions of piracy and smuggling. Cornish ''wreckers'' lured English ships onto the rocky coast, then legally salvaged the cargoes. The practice became so widespread that the Cornish coast came to be called the graveyard of ships.

Tin mining, closely tied to Cornish culture and the mainstay of the local economy, collapsed in 1866. Over 7,000 destitute Cornish families emigrated, mostly to Canada, the United States, Australia, and New Zealand. Between 1860 and 1900 over a tenth of the population left the region. The unprofitable mines continued as the only important source of income until the worldwide depression of the 1930s ended even the minimum of mining activity in Cornwall.

Demand for tin during World War II allowed the reopening of many of the mines, bringing a modest economic upturn that continued as Britain's access to colonial resources disappeared after the war. In the 1960s tourism replaced mining as Cornwall's economic mainstay. The visitors, drawn to Cornwall's subtropical climate and unique culture, are called *emmets* by the locals, a Cornish word for the insects they resemble as they swarm across the Cornish peninsula.

Cornish nationalism, spurred by increased inter-Celtic contact since the early 1960s, focused on the Cornish language, whose last native speaker died in 1777. A renewed interest in their language beginning in the 1920s prompted a revival of the Cornish culture. The successful revival of Kernewek and the revitalization of the traditional Cornish culture fueled the growth of Cornish nationalism in the 1960s and 1970s. Nationalists demanded the same status within the United Kingdom accorded the other Celtic nations, Wales and Scotland.* So successful was the national revival that, in the late 1980s, Kernewek, the Cornish language, became the fastest growing of all the Celtic languages.

Great Britain's entry into the European Economic Community opened a nationalist debate on Cornwall's future, the subject given added urgency by the closing of the last of Cornwall's 600 mines in 1990. The Cornish consider the closing of the last mine not only an economic disaster but a cultural disaster. Economic and cultural grievances have added to the rising Cornish nationalism, the more militant asserting that the European Union begins beyond the Tamar River until the Cornish are recognized as a separate European people with their own state under their St. Pirin flag.

*SELECTED BIBLIOGRAPHY:*

Ellis, Peter B. *The Celtic Revolution.* 1988.
Henwood, George. *Cornwall's Mines and Miners.* 1981.
Naoll, Cyril. *Cornish Seines and Seiners.* 1981.
Rees, A. D., and Brinley Rees. *Celtic Heritage.* 1961.

# CORSICA

**Corsu; Corce; Corse**

*CAPITAL: Corti (Corte)*

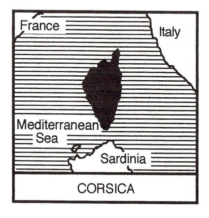

*POPULATION:* (95e) 238,000 : 390,000 Corsicans in France. MAJOR NATIONAL GROUPS: (95e) Corsican 55%, Italian 5%, other French. MAJOR LANGUAGES: Corsican, French, Italian. MAJOR RELIGIONS: Roman Catholic, Protestant. MAJOR CITIES: (95e) Aiacciu (Ajaccio) 59,000, Bastia 54,000 (71,000), Corti (Corte) 15,000.

*GEOGRAPHY:* AREA: 3,386 sq.mi.-8,772 sq.km. LOCATION: Corsica lies in the Mediterranean Sea between the Italian mainland on the north and the Italian island of Sardinia* on the south. Corsica is a mountainous island 114 miles long and is mostly covered in thick undergrowth called *maquis.* POLITICAL STATUS: Corsica, divided into two departments, Upper Corsica and South Corsica, forms a region of the French republic.

*FLAG:* The Corsican national flag, the flag of the national movement, is a white field bearing a centered black Moor's head in profile.

*PEOPLE:* The Corsicans are a Romance people, their Latin heritage modified by the influences brought to the island by its many conquerors. Related to the mainland Italians and to the Sards of Sardinia, the Corsicans speak a Tuscan dialect of Italian with an admixture of French. The Corsican nationalists claim the language is a separate Romance language. The islanders are known for the vendettas, the bitter, prolonged feuds that, until recent decades, were passed down from one generation to the next.

*THE NATION:* Originally settled by Etruscans, the mysterious pre-Roman people of northern Italy, the island has a long history of domination by various

Mediterranean empires. Phoenicians held the island, followed by their offspring, the Carthaginians, and from the third century B.C., the Romans.

Latinized under Roman rule, the islanders remained part of the Roman Empire until the fifth century A.D. when the collapse of Roman power left the island virtually defenseless. Devastated by the Germanic Vandals who crossed from the mainland, the island briefly returned to Roman rule in the guise of the Byzantines in A.D. 534. The Byzantines soon lost the island to the invading Goths, and eventually it came under the control of the Germanic Franks. Threatened by the Muslim Saracens in the eighth century, the Franks ceded the island to the Holy See. Pope Gregory VII in 1047 gave the island to the maritime republic of Pisa. In the fourteenth century Pisa's rival in the Mediterranean, Genoa, conquered the island.

Harsh and repressive, the Genoese Bank of San Gregorio administered the island on a strictly commercial basis, its rule inciting disturbances and sporadic rebellions. In 1729 the unhappy Corsicans launched a decades-long rebellion, after 1755 led by Pasquale Paoli, whose military successes achieved virtual independence for the island. Paoli created a Corsican government and opened a university to train the administrators needed by the new state. Unable to defeat the rebellion, Genoa sold the island to France in 1768, just in time for Corsica's most famous son, Napoleon Bonaparte, to be born a French citizen.

The French colonial administration dissolved all Corsican institutions and in 1770 forcibly closed the Corsican university. The Corsicans rebelled against the French after the 1789 French Revolution and in 1793 drove the last French officials from the island. The rebel leaders requested British assistance and in 1794 organized a plebiscite that confirmed Corsican appeals for union with Great Britain. Recovered by Napoleon's troops in 1796, the island fell to the British in 1814 during the Napoleonic Wars, but, despite Corsican protests, the 1815 Congress of Vienna returned the island to France.

Banditry, blood feuds, and attacks on French authorities continued to disrupt the island's administration, the *maquis* providing refuge for bandits and dissidents as it had for centuries. Neglected and underdeveloped, the island's inhabitants found it necessary to leave for the French mainland to find work. Resentment of this forced emigration coalesced national sentiment on the island in the 1920s. The first autonomist organization formed in 1927.

Italians occupied the island after the fall of France in 1940 and initiated a program to Italianize the islanders. A Corsican uprising in 1943, aided by Free French forces, drove the Italians from the island. The triumphant Corsicans, preparing for independence, felt gravely disappointed by the reimposition of French rule. Despair spurred a massive postwar exodus to the mainland, finally forcing the French authorities to accelerate the island's development, mainly in tourism.

Modern Corsican nationalism emerged from a failed insurrection in 1958 during the French colonial war in Algeria, partly provoked by the settlement on the island of colonists and loyal Algerians, some 17,000 between 1958 and 1963.

Numerous nationalist groups formed over the next two decades. Several nationalist groups turned to violence, mostly directed at tourist installations owned by foreigners, including the French.

The majority of the Corsican nationalists demand, as a minimum, autonomy, education in the Corsican language, the teaching of specifically Corsican history, and the reopening of the Corsican university closed by the French in 1770. More radical groups, after nearly four decades of opposition to French rule, demand nothing less than independence. A 1991 poll of the islanders resulted in overwhelming support for some form of autonomy, with a third favoring immediate independence from France.

*SELECTED BIBLIOGRAPHY:*
Chiari, Joseph. *Corsica, Columbus's Isle.* 1960.
Thrasher, Peter A. *Pasquale Paoli: An Enlightened Hero, 1725–1807.* 1970.
Wagner, Geoffrey. *Elegy to Corsica.* 1970.
Wilson, Stephen. *Feuding, Conflict and Banditry in 19th Century Corsica.* 1988.

# CRIMEA

**Krym; Krim**

*CAPITAL: Akmechet (Simferopol)*

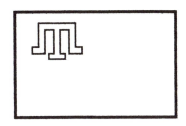

SOUTHEASTERN EUROPE

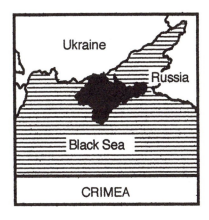

CRIMEA

*POPULATION:* (95e) 2,649,000 : 265,000 Crimean Tatars in Ukraine and another 310,000 in Russia, Kazakhstan, and Uzbekistan. MAJOR NATIONAL GROUPS: (95e) Russian 63%, Ukrainian 24%, Crimean Tatar 10%, Greek 2%, German 1%. MAJOR LANGUAGES: Russian, Ukrainian, Crimean Tatar. MAJOR RELIGIONS: Orthodox, Sunni Islam, Jewish, Roman Catholic. MAJOR CITIES: (95e) Akhtiar (Sevastopol) 401,000 (492,000), Akmechet (Simferopol) 379,000 (403,000), Cherzeti (Kerch) 190,000, Guesleve (Yevpatoria) 118,000 (189,000), Kefe (Feodosiya) 92,000 (110,000), Yalta 91,000 (175,000), Dhhankoi (Dzhankoy) 58,000, Saki 45,000, Bakchisarai (Bakhchysarai) 23,000.

*GEOGRAPHY:* AREA: 23,427 sq.mi.-60,693 sq.km. LOCATION: The Crimea lies in southern Ukraine, a large, subtropical peninsula jutting into the Black Sea and connected to the mainland by the narrow Isthmus of Perekop. POLITICAL STATUS: Officially, the Crimea forms an autonomous republic in Ukraine; however, the region's future is disputed by the Ukrainian government, the peninsula's Russian majority, and the returning Crimean Tatars.

*INDEPENDENCE DECLARED:* 10 December 1917; 16 May 1918; 5 May 1992.

*FLAG:* The Crimean Tatar national flag, the flag of the national movement, is a light blue field bearing the *tarak tamga*, a yellow device resembling a scale, on the upper hoist. OTHER FLAG(S): The flag of the Crimean Russian nationalists is a white field bearing a narrow, horizontal blue stripe at the top and a narrow red stripe on the bottom.

*PEOPLE:* The Crimean Tatars, the indigenous nation of Crimea, are a Turkic people belonging to the southern branch of the Turkic peoples, the Orguz. The Crimean Tatars comprise three distinct divisions united by culture and history: the Tatars, the descendants of the peninsula's original inhabitants; the Krymchaks, numbering some 60,000, formerly the inhabitants of the adjacent mainland; and the Karaites, numbering about 30,000, who speak a distinctive dialect and practice an archaic form of Judaism. Of the over 100 ethnic and national groups represented in Crimea, the Russians are the largest and now form a majority of the total population.

*THE NATION:* The peninsula, colonized by the ancient Greeks, knew many conquerors and has been settled by many different peoples in the course of its history, the basis of its multinational character. Scythians, Greeks, Romans, Genoese, and many other peoples conquered and settled the peninsula, accounting for its diverse population. The Byzantines ruled the multiethnic Crimea when the Turkic and Mongol hordes overran the region in 1239. Turkic tribes settled the peninsula and, following the disintegration of the Mongol-Turkic Golden Horde, erected a separate Tatar khanate in 1475.

The khanate, although eventually becoming tributary to the Turk's Ottoman Empire, expanded to control much of southern Russia, Ukraine, and eastern Poland. The Tatars established trading links to most of the Mediterranean and beyond through the contacts and ties of the large Genoese and Greek populations of their southern port cities. In the early eighteenth century the related Krymchaks settled the adjoining mainland region known as Tauria.

The khanate, rich on trade, developed a brilliant and sophisticated civilization even as its outer provinces fell to the expanding Russian Empire. In 1736 invading Russians conquered all except the Tatar heartland, the Crimean Peninsula and mainland Tauria. The Russian empress, Catherine the Great, forced the Ottoman Empire to recognize the independence of the khanate, thus opening the way for the Russian conquest of the remaining territories in 1792–93 without risking war with the still-powerful Turks.

Approximately 1 million Tatars fled the Russian onslaught to refuge in Turkish territory, leaving large parts of the newly annexed region virtually depopulated. Government-sponsored settlement brought an influx of Slavs to settle the mainland area. The remaining Tatars, mostly in Crimea, accused of collaborating with the Turks during the Crimean War of 1853–56, suffered another great population decline as the authorities deported some 100,000 to Russia's interior provinces, and over twice that number fled to Ottoman territory before the authorities stopped all emigration in 1862. By 1897 the devastated Tatar nation accounted for only 34% of the population of Taurida province, the Crimean Peninsula and mainland Tauria.

The opening of a Tatar press in 1883 stimulated a Tatar cultural revival and the growth of Tatar nationalism. Suppressed in 1891, many nationalists fled to Turkey. In 1909 Tatar students in Constantinople formed Vatan, a nationalist organization dedicated to the creation of an independent Crimean Tatar state. Openly favoring the Turks during World War I, the nationalists mobilized. By the time revolution swept Russia in February 1917, Vatan had underground cells in most Tatar towns and villages.

A Tatar congress, convened in September 1917, rejected the Bolshevik coup in October. Threatened by local Bolsheviks, nationalist leaders declared Taurida independent on 10 December 1917. Fighting soon broke out between Tatar nationalists and the pro-Bolshevik soldiers and sailors who took control of Sevastopol, and in January 1918 the poorly equipped Tatars suffered defeat.

In March 1918 German troops took control of the region, and the Tatar leaders emerged from hiding to organize an independent state on the Crimean Peninsula. On 16 May 1918 they declared the Crimean Democratic Republic independent of both the Russian factions, as civil war swept across the disintegrating Russian Empire. Defeated by the Soviet Red Army in 1919, the Tatars of the peninsula were allowed the status of a full union republic, a member state of the new Soviet Union.

Occupied by German forces in 1941, the Tatars attempted to protect their Jewish Karaite minority while collaborating the least of all the Soviet peoples in the zones under Nazi occupation, including the ethnic Russians. However, in May 1944, Stalin accused the entire Tatar nation of treason, and some 200,000 suffered a brutal deportation east in sealed cattle cars. The Tatars claim that 110,000 died as a result of the deportation, which they denounce as genocide. The Soviet authorities made a gift of the peninsula to the Ukrainian Soviet Socialist Republic on the 300th anniversary of Ukraine's union with Russia in 1954.

The deported Tatars, not rehabilitated with the other nations deported by Stalin in 1956–57, launched a campaign to win official recognition of their right to return to their homeland. The Tatars staged demonstrations and protests and attempted to bring the issue before the United Nations and other international organizations. Delegations sent to the Kremlin to present their case to successive Soviet leaders were simply ignored or imprisoned.

A Soviet government commission appointed in 1987 finally addressed the issue. By 1989 over 150,000 had returned to the Crimea. The liberalizing of Soviet society in the late 1980s allowed the nationalist movement to organize. On 28 June 1991 a Crimean Tatar congress proclaimed their historic right to the peninsula as the "national territory of the Crimean Tatar nation."

The disintegration of the Soviet Union, resulting in the establishment of an independent Ukrainian state, opened a bitter conflict over the fate of the region. Russian claims to the Crimea, particularly to the large former Soviet naval fleet at Sevastopol, quickly strained relations between the two states. Both the Ukrainian and Russian governments attempted to use the Crimean Tatars in the dispute while carefully avoiding the issue of the Tatars' ancient claim to the peninsula.

The peninsula's Russian majority, with the tacit approval of the Russian government, organized to oppose continued Ukrainian control of the peninsula. On 5 May 1992 the Russian Crimean leaders proclaimed the Crimea independent of Ukraine but, just five days later, under intense Ukrainian pressure, rescinded the declaration. The Crimean Tatars supported Ukrainian claims to the region as the less objectional alternative.

The returning Crimean Tatars, numbering over 250,000 by 1993, found themselves relegated to marginal lands or the shantytowns around their former capital and other cities. The harsh condition of the lives of the returnees has given new impetus to the national movement. In July 1993 a number of nationalist organizations joined to demand the resurrection of the independent Crimean Tatar state and reiterated the Tatar claim to the entire peninsula, a claim that Crimean Tatar nationalist leaders point out predates either the Russian or Ukrainian claims on the region.

*SELECTED BIBLIOGRAPHY:*

Adams, Arthur E. *Stalin and His Times.* 1986.
Colton, Timothy, and Robert Levgold, eds. *After the Soviet Union.* 1992.
Fisher, Alan W. *The Crimean Tatars.* 1978.
Gibbs, Peter. *Crimean Blunder.* 1960.

# DAGESTAN

### Daghestan

*CAPITAL: Makhachkala*

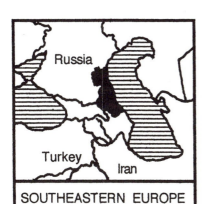

SOUTHEASTERN EUROPE

DAGESTAN

*POPULATION:* (95e) 1,926,000 : 2,050,000 Dagestanis in Russia (511,000 Avar, 418,000 Lezgin, 332,000 Dargin, 306,000 Kumyk, 100,000 Lak, 89,000 Tabasaran, 70,000 Ajai, 65,000 Nogai, 17,000 Rutul, 15,000 Agul, 15,000 Tsakhur). MAJOR NATIONAL GROUPS: (95e) Dagestani 85%, Russian 9%, Azeri 4%. MAJOR LANGUAGES: Bolmat's, Russian, Lezgin, Dargin, Kumyk, Azeri. MAJOR RELIGIONS: Sunni Muslim, Shia Muslim, Russian Orthodox. MAJOR CITIES: (95e) Makhachkala 345,000 (431,000), Derbent 95,000 (120,000), Khasavyur 83,000 (141,000), Temir-Khan-Shura (Buynaksk) 66,000, Kaspiysk 59,000, Kizlyurt 50,000, Kizylar 46,000, Izerbash 35,000.

*GEOGRAPHY:* AREA: 7,496 sq.mi.-19,421 sq.km. LOCATION: Dagestan lies in the North Caucasus region of southern European Russia, an area of sandy plains along the Caspian Sea rising to the eastern Caucasus Mountains in the south and southwest. POLITICAL STATUS: Dagestan forms a member state of the Russian Federation.

*INDEPENDENCE DECLARED:* 20 October 1917.

*FLAG:* The Dagestani national flag, the flag of the national movement, is a green field bearing a centered white crescent moon and three small, white, four-pointed stars. OTHER FLAG(S): The official flag of the republic is a tan field bearing two light blue, horizontal stripes across the bottom.

*PEOPLE:* Dagestan, meaning Land of the Mountains, is inhabited by a be-wildering variety of peoples representing thirty-one separate ethnic groups. The majority Caucasian peoples include the Avar, Lezgin, Dargin, Lak, Ajai, Tabasaran, Agul, Tsakhur, and several smaller groups. The Turkic peoples are the Kumyk and Nogai in the north and the Azeri in the south. Almost as many languages are spoken as there are ethnic groups, some dialects used by only a few hundred people. The Avar language, comprising thirteen related dialects called Bolmat's, has become the lingua franca and is understood by most of the Dagestani peoples. United by history and their common resistance to Russian conquest and rule, the Dagestanis also have a strong religious bond, the majority adhering to the Shafi rite of Sunni Islam.

*THE NATION:* For thousands of years invaders from Europe and Asia have crossed or conquered the Caucasus, with each valley becoming home to a distinctive ethnic group. Influenced by Sarmathians, Romans, Persians, and Khazars, the tribes never united but remained separate, often warring among themselves. Each tribe retained its own language, culture, and gods. Conquered by invading Arabs in A.D. 728, the mountain tribes converted to the Arabs' unifying religious and social system, Islam. A flourishing Muslim civilization developed, centered on Derbent, a major political and cultural center of the Muslim Empire known as the Caliphate.

The Mongol hordes devastated the lowlands in the early thirteenth century, forcing most of the tribes to withdraw to traditional mountain strongholds. Persians extended their rule to the coastal lowlands in the fourteenth century, beginning a long rivalry between the Persian and Turkish empires that eventually facilitated the Russian conquest of the Caucasus. In 1723 the Russians took control of the plains of northern Dagestan, and a weakened Persia ceded the rugged, mountainous south in 1813.

The Dagestanis fiercely resisted Christian Russian rule. Stirred to religious and nationalist fervor, they followed their *iman*, the political and religious leader known as Shamyl, in a long holy war against the Russians. Effective guerrilla tactics in the high mountains halted the Russian advance for over two decades. Thousands died in the final Russian conquest of the region in 1859–60. The last of the fierce Dagestani warriors did not submit to Russian rule until 1877.

Openly supportive of the Muslim Turks when war began in 1914, the Dagestanis celebrated the news that revolution had broken out in Russia in February 1917. Effectively independent as civil administration collapsed, a Muslim conference elected Mullah Gotinsky as their political and religious leader in May 1917. The Bolshevik takeover of the Russian government in October 1917 created chaos in the region as local Bolsheviks attempted to take power. The Muslim peoples joined with the Terek Cossacks to declare an independent Terek-Dagestan republic on 20 October 1917, but the new state, undermined by ethnic, religious, and territorial disputes, collapsed in December 1917.

The Muslim peoples formed a separate republic in March 1918 and attempted a cooperative defense as the Russian civil war spread south. The anti-Bolshevik forces, the Whites, took control of the region in January 1919, but forced conscription of Muslims incited strong resistance. Promised autonomy, the

Dagestanis went over to the Reds. The last of the Whites withdrew in January 1920.

The Dagestani leaders, disappointed at their treatment by the Soviet authorities, demanded the promised autonomy. Rebuffed by the Soviets, the Dagestanis rebelled and held out until finally subdued in May 1921, at a cost of over 5,000 Soviet casualties. A hypothetically autonomous Dagestani republic, created in early 1921, joined the new Soviet Russian Federation. Soviet rule brought decades of religious and cultural suppression.

A religious and cultural revival in the 1970s, spread through the thousands of illegal, underground mosques, marked a renewed Dagestani resistance to official Soviet atheism. By 1980 an estimated half of Dagestan's male population belonged to illicit Muslim brotherhoods called *tariqat*.

In the more relaxed atmosphere of the late 1980s religious and nationalist sentiment emerged as powerful forces in the republic. The rapid religious revival forced the Soviet authorities in April 1990 to authorize charter flights to those Muslims wishing to make the pilgrimage to Mecca. The Soviet authorities had formerly restricted the sacred pilgrimage to just twenty Dagestanis each year.

The attempted Soviet coup and the rapid disintegration of the Soviet Union in August 1991 gave new impetus to the Dagestani national revival. A Dagestani majority in the local parliament in November 1991 unilaterally declared the republic a full member republic of the Russian Federation, while adopting a measure that indirectly endorsed the eventual independence of the republic. Since 1991 one of the most difficult tasks of the national movement has become the region's national unity. The Dagestani federation mirrors the Russian Federation, with many national groups seeking separate autonomous states.

The Russian military assault on neighboring Chechenia* in December 1994 stirred nationalist and anti-Russian sentiment in the region, particularly among the Chechen's traditional allies, the Avars. Fighting broke out between Dagestanis and government troops crossing their territory enroute to Chechenia and raised Russian fears that Dagestan could pose the next nationalist crisis in the fragile Russian Federation.

*SELECTED BIBLIOGRAPHY:*
Bennigsen, Alexandre, and Marie Broxup. *The Islamic Threat to the Soviet Union.* 1983.
Gleason, Gregory. *Federalism and Nationalism: The Struggle for Republican Rights in the USSR.* 1990.
Minorsky, Vladimir. *Studies in Caucasian History.* 1953.
Wixman, Ronald. *The Peoples of the U.S.S.R. An Ethnographic Handbook.* 1984.

# DARFUR

**Dar Fur**

*CAPITAL: Tendely (El-Fasher)*

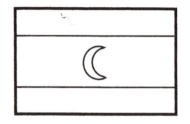

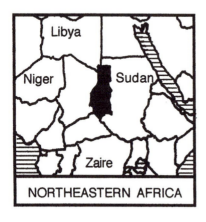

NORTHEASTERN AFRICA

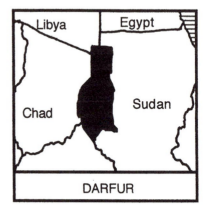

DARFUR

*POPULATION:* (95e) 4,453,000 : 3,200,000 Fur in Sudan. MAJOR NA-
TIONAL GROUPS: (95e) Fur 67%, Bagarra Arab 6%, Masalit 4%, Daju 2%,
Berti 2%, other Sudanese. MAJOR LANGUAGES: Fur, Arabic, Masalit. MA-
JOR RELIGIONS: Sunni Muslim, animist. MAJOR CITIES: (95e) Tendely (El-
Fasher) 170,000, Nyala 133,000, Geneina (El-Gunaynah) 90,000, Zalingei
62,000, Adda (Ad-Duayn) 52,000, Hilla (Al-Hillah) 34,000, Kutum 25,000.

*GEOGRAPHY:* AREA: 191,650 sq.mi.-496,502 sq.km. LOCATION: Darfur
occupies a high, flat plateau and part of the Libyan Desert in northwestern
Sudan, bordering on the Chadian region of North Chad* on the west, the Central
African Republic on the southeast, Libya on the northwest, and the Sudanese
region of Southern Sudan* on the south. POLITICAL STATUS: Darfur forms
a region of the Republic of Sudan, comprising two provinces.

*FLAG:* The Fur national flag, the flag of the national movement, is a horizontal tricolor of green, red, and black, proportions 1:2:1, bearing a centered
white crescent moon.

*PEOPLE:* The Fur, of mixed black African, Berber, and Arab background,
are generally dark-skinned, although physically more closely resembling the
Berbers and Arabs. The Fur language, not related to neighboring dialects, is
considered a separate, isolated language group. The Arabic-speaking Bagarra
inhabit parts of the center and south, and the Masalit, Daju, and Berti, speaking
related Nilo-Saharan languages, inhabit the Dar Masalit region in the west. The
majority religion, Sunni Islam, has incorporated many pre-Islamic and Christian
customs. In the more remote areas traditional beliefs are still followed.

*THE NATION:* Scholars know little of the region's early history, although ancient Egyptian records mention an organized state trading copper ore and slaves for Egypt's spices, cloth, and luxuries. Berbers, driven from North Africa by invading Arabs in the seventh and eighth centuries, settled in the region in large numbers. Early Christian kingdoms rose in the area between the tenth and thirteenth centuries but were later destroyed by Muslim invaders from North Chad.

A small Fur kingdom, established after the demise of the Christian states in the thirteenth century, became the most powerful of the region's Muslim kingdoms. In 1596 Suleiman Solong consolidated the rival tribes and established his family as the rulers, the Keira dynasty. The Bagarra, pastoral Arab nomads, moved into the kingdom over the next century, their presence tolerated for the annual tribute they paid the Fur sultan.

The sultan, often threatened by the Turks through their tributaries, the Egyptians, sent an emissary to congratulate Napoleon on his conquest of Cairo in 1798. Napoleon responded with a demand for 2,000 African slaves, prompting the sultan to break off relations and to abandon hopes of a French military alliance. The desert area just north of the sultanate came under Turko-Egyptian rule in 1821, bringing the threat ever closer. For over fifty years the sultanate resisted but finally fell to invading Egyptian troops in 1874.

Opposition to Egyptian rule united the area's diverse peoples in support of a Bagarra Arab religious leader known as the Mahdi. A holy war against the Egyptians and their British allies drove the foreigners from Sudan in 1883. The Mahdi established a theocratic dictatorship, but, weakened by a disastrous famine in 1889–91, his state fell to the Anglo-Egyptian forces of Lord Kitchener in 1898.

Ali Dinar, a member of Darfur's deposed Keira dynasty, reclaimed the throne in 1899. He rapidly consolidated his authority and managed to retain Darfur's independence as the only region of present Sudan not included in Anglo-Egyptian Sudan. The sultan, threatened by the British in the east and the French in the west, declared his allegiance to the Ottoman Empire when war began in 1914. Two years later Ali Dinar died fighting an invading British force. His kingdom, annexed to Anglo-Egyptian Sudan, was the last independent Muslim state in Africa to fall to European rule.

The Fur, with long ties to the peoples to the west, had little in common with Sudan's predominant Arab population. The resulting ethnic tensions initiated decades of ethnic tensions and attempts to restore Fur sovereignty. After World War I, many educated Fur made a point of mastering Arabic in the hope of making their way in the world in which they found themselves. Their lack of success against Arab intolerance and discrimination led to the formation of a popular regionalist movement and demands for federal status in the soon-to-be-independent Sudan. Fur separatism emerged as a force in 1956, following Sudanese independence and the creation of an Arab-dominated unitary state.

The national movement, forced underground in 1966, continued to have substantial support as relations between the Fur and the Arab-dominated government worsened. Antigovernment rioting in 1980 forced the government to grant limited autonomy and a regional assembly. The introduction of Sharia, strict Muslim laws contrary to many of the Fur's ancient religious practices, exacerbated the tensions already heightened by bureaucratic attempts to curtail Fur autonomy.

A new Sudanese government, installed by a coup in 1988 and dominated by radical groups, including Islamic fundamentalists, initiated a campaign to subdue the non-Arab peoples in western and southern Sudan. Arab militias, the Popular Defense Forces, armed by the government and dispatched to Darfur to enforce new language and religious laws, reportedly used indiscriminate violence and participated in the massacres of Fur villagers.

A Fur rebel movement, with arms from neighboring Libya, has operated in Darfur since 1987, raising government fears of a second front in the country's long civil war in the south. Government bans on trade unions, professional associations, political parties, and most Fur newspapers remain in effect. Strict censorship has almost completely stifled news of continuing unrest in the region. Visitors, particularly foreigners, need a special certificate from the government before they are allowed to enter Darfur. Fur leaders accuse the Sudanese government of attempting genocide, withholding much-needed international famine aid while using the vicious Arab militias to terrorize the starving Fur into submission.

*SELECTED BIBLIOGRAPHY:*
Duncan, J.S.R. *The Sudan's Path to Independence.* 1957.
O'Fahey, F. S. *State and Society in Dar Fur.* 1980.
Rienner, Lynne. *Sudan, 1898–1989: The Unstable State.* 1990.
Woodward, Peter. *Sudan since Nimeiri.* 1988.

# DHOFAR

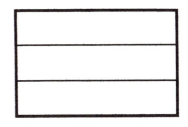

**Dhufar; Zhufar; Dofar**

*CAPITAL: Salala (Salalah)*

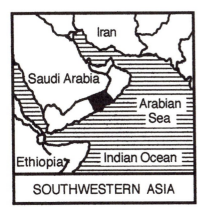

SOUTHWESTERN ASIA

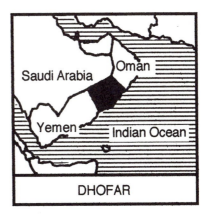

DHOFAR

*POPULATION:* (95e) 243,000 : 220,000 Dhofari (including Mahra and Qarra) in Oman. MAJOR NATIONAL GROUPS: (95e) Dhofari 88%, other Omani. MAJOR LANGUAGES: Dhofari, Arabic, Mahra, Qarra. MAJOR RELIGIONS: Sunni Muslim, Ibadi Muslim. MAJOR CITIES: (95e) Salala (Salalah) 57,000, Raysut 30,00, Mirbah (Murbah) 20,000.

*GEOGRAPHY:* AREA: 35,116 sq.mi.-90,976 sq.km. LOCATION: Dhofar lies on the eastern coast of the Arabian Peninsula in southern Oman. Geographically a large territory, the only inhabitable part is a 160-mile crescent between the sea and the high mountains. The only part of the peninsula to receive the rains of the southwestern monsoon, Dhofar's lush central district is separated from the rest of Oman by a formidable 400-mile stretch of desert. POLITICAL STATUS: Dhofar has no official status; the region forms the Southern Province of the Sultanate of Oman.

*FLAG:* The Dhofari national flag, the flag of the national movement, is a horizontal tricolor of red, white, and black. OTHER FLAG(S): The same tricolor, with the addition of the organization's name in black script centered on the white, is the flag of the Popular Front for the Liberation of Oman and Dhofar (PFLOD), the region's largest national group.

*PEOPLE:* The Dhofari are a Semitic people, the descendants of non-Arabic Semitic peoples and early Persian settlers, with a distinctive language that mixes elements of both Arabic and Farsi (Iranian). The Dhofari are not culturally or historically related to the Omanis, and, unlike the Omanis, who mostly adhere to the Ibadi sect of Islam, the majority of the Dhofari follow the Sunni rite. In the Qarra Mountains live the related Mahra and Qarra peoples, who speak their own pre-Arabic Semitic languages and practice a form of Islam that incorporates many pagan traditions and beliefs. In the coastal region there has been an infusion of African blood, but in the highlands and the mountains the inhabitants are pure Semites.

*THE NATION:* Ancient Semitic peoples, drawn to the luxuriant grazing lands, settled the region over 2,000 years ago. The Semites developed a Persian-influenced civilization in the coastal areas, a cultural island surrounded by desert and accessible only by ocean. In biblical times Dhofar was known as the Land of Frankincense. The trade in the aromatic gum resin, burned as incense throughout the ancient world, controlled by a single tribe, brought great wealth to ancient Dhofar. The rare resin, by tradition, was presented to the Christ child by one of the eastern kings who followed the star to Bethlehem.

The Dhofari, converted to Islam in the first rapid expansion of Islamic missionary zeal in the seventh century, remained under the nominal rule of the Muslim Caliphate for several centuries. The Islamic religion, as practiced in the isolated region, retained many of the beliefs and traditions of the earlier pagan religion.

The first Europeans visited Dhofar in the early sixteenth century. The Portuguese quickly gained control of the coastal towns that became ports on the trade routes to the East. The Dhofari expelled the Portuguese in 1650 and erected an independent sultanate that thrived on the trade routes among Persia, India, and Africa.

In 1877 the sultanate fell to the Omanis, invaders from across the northern desert. Neglected by the Omani sultanate, Dhofar rapidly lost its earlier prosperity and became a backward retreat for wealthy Omanis fleeing the desert heat in the north. The Dhofari, suffering religious and cultural discrimination, rebelled several times in the 1880s and 1890s.

Underdeveloped, backward, and poor, the region gradually became a political and economic dependency of the British authorities in neighboring Hadramaut. In 1939 the British, with Omani government agreement, installed a garrison in Salalah that stayed until the end of World War II.

Oppressive Omani rule, particularly after the discovery of oil in the 1950s, sparked a brief rebellion in 1957. Under the rule of Sultan Said bin Taimur, who imprisoned his son, the present Sultan of Oman, in Salalah, all newspapers, flashlights, and umbrellas were banned. Royal decrees prohibited dancing, smoking, photography, books, music, sunglasses, and trousers for men or women. In 1960 Dhofar province boasted only one elementary school.

In the early 1960s bands of rebels formed in the mountains and in 1963 formed the Dhofar Liberation Front (DLF), which led a Dhofari rebellion against Omani rule. In 1971 the DLF joined with other non-Communist groups to form the Popular Front for the Liberation of Oman and the Arab Gulf (FLOAG), which fought both government troops and the Marxist Popular Front for the Liberation of the Occupied Arab Gulf (PFLOAG). The Dhofari rebellion, sparked by the whimsical and oppressive rule of the Omani sultan, exacerbated religious tensions between the Sunni Dhofari and the Ibadi Omanis.

Armed and trained by the Marxist government of South Yemen,* the Marxist PFLOAG took control of Dhofar and surrounded Salalah in 1970. The Marxists quickly imposed a harsh regime, eliminating the nationalists and the anti-Communist Dhofari, outlawing the practice of Islam, and executing people for praying. The Marxist success prompted the British to engineer a coup that ended the despotic rule of Oman's old sultan and to replace him with his son. A combination of coercion and enticement persuaded many Dhofari rebel groups to negotiate, particularly the anti-Communist groups. The Omanis, aided by Britain, Jordan, and Iran, finally crushed the Dhofari Marxists in 1975.

Oil revenues from wells along the Dhofar-Oman border increased dramatically in the 1970s, bringing increasing prosperity to Dhofar. The new sultan, in an effort to redress the neglect and abuses of his father, increased development and proclaimed a general amnesty. Many Dhofari returned to their homes between 1978 and 1989, although sporadic rebellion continued. In the 1980s radical regimes in South Yemen and Iran supported Dhofari rebel groups. The growth of Muslim fundamentalism in the 1980s and 1990s fanned renewed tensions between the Ibadi and Sunni Muslims.

The government reforms have muted support for separatism but have not ended the Dhofari demands for political, cultural, and economic autonomy. Fearful of Dhofari unrest, the government severely restricts access to the region. Dhofaris now control tribal and town councils, but the real political power rests with the Wali, the governor appointed by the Oman government.

*SELECTED BIBLIOGRAPHY:*

Allen, Calvin. *Oman, the Modernization of the Sultanate.* 1986.

Anthony, John D. *Historical and Cultural Dictionary of the Sultanate of Oman and the Emirates of Eastern Arabia.* 1976.

Risso, Patricia. *Oman and Muscat: An Early Modern History.* 1986.

Sanger, Richard H. *The Arabian Peninsula.* 1954.

# DINETAH

### Dine Bikeyah

*CAPITAL: Window Rock*

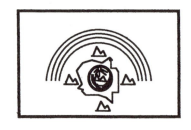

*POPULATION:* (95e) 192,000 : 220,000 Dine (Navajo) in the United States. MAJOR NATIONAL GROUPS: (95e) Dine (Navajo) 97%, Hopi 2%, other American. MAJOR LANGUAGES: Navajo, English, Hopi. MAJOR RELIGIONS: Native American Church, Roman Catholic, Protestant. MAJOR CITIES: (95e) Navajo 2,200, Window Rock 1,850 (5,000), Shiprock 1,250, Tuba City 1,000.

*GEOGRAPHY:* AREA: 26,862 sq.mi.-69,572 sq.km. LOCATION: Dinetah lies in the southwestern United States, a semiarid plateau region in northeastern Arizona and adjacent parts of New Mexico and Utah. POLITICAL STATUS: Dinetah forms a self-governing reserve within the United States, officially known as the Navajo Indian Reservation.

*FLAG:* The Dine flag, the official flag of the tribe, is a sand-colored field bearing an outline map of Dinetah with the tribal seal centered and surrounded by four mountains at each compass point and the entire design surmounted by a rainbow of blue, red, and yellow.

*PEOPLE:* The Dine, known as Navajo, the name given them by neighboring peoples, are a Native American people speaking an Athabascan language of the Nadene language group spoken in western Canada and Alaska. The Dine language remains the language of daily life, with about half of the Dine unable to speak English. Divided into fifty clans, the Dine are traditionally a matriarchal people. The majority belong to the Native American Church, which combines Christian and traditional beliefs.

*THE NATION:* Athabascan nomads, moving south from their origins in western Canada, moved into the high plateau region in the tenth century. Gradually splitting into several distinct groups, the most important of the tribal groups became the Dine, called Navajo, and the Apache. The Dine, adopting the agriculture, weaving, and sand painting of the settled Pueblo and Hopi peoples, had developed as a separate culture and nation by 1500.

The Dine, probably numbering no more than 9,000, controlled a vast territory when the Spanish, searching for the legendary cities of gold, reached the area in 1539. Unable to fully subdue the Dine warriors, the Spanish colonial authorities generally left them to their traditional way of life. Christian missions established across the region had a greater impact than the Spanish administration, especially the introduction of European farming methods and animals. Sheep, unknown to the Dine, profoundly changed their traditions as they adopted a seminomadic life based on large sheep herds.

The Dine lands, under nominal Mexican rule from 1821, formed part of the territories ceded to the United States in 1848. The Dine's historical resistance to outside rule led to clashes and quickly escalated to war with the U.S. military. In 1864 the U.S. Cavalry, led by Kit Carson, invaded Dinetah and destroyed everything in their path, including the Dine sheep herds. Captured Dine families, 8,500 men, women, and children, were forced to march from Fort Defiance, Arizona, to Fort Sumner, New Mexico, a distance of 350 miles. Those who survived the hardships of the trek were imprisoned in a squalid camp for four years before the authorities finally allowed them to return to Arizona in 1868.

A formal treaty, signed in 1868, recognized the Dine nation in exchange for the cession of huge tracts of land. The Dine retained a reserve territory of 3.5 million acres. The treaty, its terms soon abrogated, began a century of degradation, humiliation, and neglect.

Poor and uneducated, the Dine could only protest the actions of the Indian Agency, part of the U.S. Department of the Interior, which began to give out leases to oil and power companies in 1921. The leases, contravening existing laws, began the development of the enormous natural wealth of the Dine reservation lands, for which the Dine received nothing.

Granted U.S. citizenship in 1924, few of the Dine, uneducated and unable to read or speak English, were equipped to exercise their new rights. In the early 1930s concerted efforts began to end the Dine's long isolation. Between 1935 and 1940 an alphabet, devised for the Dine language, made the spoken dialect a literary language and greatly aided the spread of education in the 1940s and 1950s.

During World War II, 3,600 Dine served with the U.S. military, their language used as a battlefield code, one of the few never deciphered by Axis experts. After the war many veterans found work in the uranium mines operating on reservation lands. Not warned of the dangers or provided protection, the effects of uranium poisoning adversely affected an entire generation.

The Dine began to make progress in education in the 1960s. A young, educated, and more militant tribal leadership introduced Dine history and language to reservation schools, inaugurated radio in the Dine language, and founded the first college on a reservation run by a Native American people. Granted self-government on 25 July 1972, the Dine, for the first time in over a century, were free of outside control. On the basis of the mineral wealth of the autonomous reservation, the Dine became one of the world's wealthiest nations, but the wealth appeared only on paper. The reality of Navajo poverty, unemployment, and neglect remained unchanged.

The Navajo-Hopi Land Settlement Act, passed in 1974, clearly delineated reservation borders in the region but ignored the fact that the two peoples had shared the land since the sixteenth century. The land dispute, which envisioned the relocation of over 12,000 people, the largest forced relocation of an ethnic group since World War II, galvanized the Dine. Militants formed the Dine Bii Coalition (the Coalition for Dine Liberation) and in 1977 joined activists from other tribes to petition the United Nations for recognition as sovereign nations and for the admission of delegates to represent the red race, the only one of the five world races not represented.

Militants, often comparing their small nation to those of the former Soviet Union, in 1991 threatened to declare independence and to take the issue before the United Nations. The majority of the Dine would be satisfied if the U.S. government would simply honor the terms of the 1868 treaty and address unresolved Dine land claims. In November 1992 the government unveiled a plan to award lands just outside Dinetah to the Hopis, thus avoiding a confrontation with the growing Dine national movement.

*SELECTED BIBLIOGRAPHY:*

Bailey, Garrick. *History of the Navajos: The Reservation Years.* 1989.
Bailey, Lynn R. *If You Take My Sheep: The Evolution and Conflicts of Navajo Pastoralism 1630–1868.* 1980.
Goodman, James M. *The Navajo Atlas: Environments, Resources, People, and History of the Dine Bikeyah.* 1987.
Underhill, R. M. *The Navahos.* 1956.

# DNIESTRIA

Transdniestria; Podniestrskaya
Moldova; Transdniestr Moldova

*CAPITAL: Tiraspol (Tyraspil)*

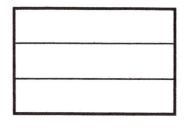

*POPULATION:* (95e) 624,000 : 1,260,000 Slavs in Moldova. MAJOR NA-
TIONAL GROUPS: (95e) Dniestrian Slav 54% (Russian 27%, Ukrainian 25%,
Bulgarian 2%), Moldovan 37%, Romanian, Gagauz, Jewish. MAJOR LAN-
GUAGES: Russian, Moldovan (Romanian), Ukrainian. MAJOR RELIGIONS:
Russian Orthodox, Romanian Orthodox, Jewish. MAJOR CITIES: (95e) Tiras-
pol (Tyraspil) 198,000, Rybnitsa (Rybnyca) 52,000, Dubossary 30,000.

*GEOGRAPHY:* AREA: 3,356 sq.mi.-8,694 sq.km. LOCATION: Dniestria occupies the lowlands on the east bank of the Dniestr River, a rich agricultural
and industrial area forming a long ribbon of land between the river and the
international border with Ukraine. POLITICAL STATUS: Dniestria forms an
autonomous republic within the Republic of Moldova.

*INDEPENDENCE DECLARED:* 2 September 1991.

*FLAG:* The Dniestrian national flag, the flag of the former Moldavian Soviet
Socialist Republic, has horizontal stripes of red, green, and red and is sometimes
charged with a yellow hammer and sickle surmounted by a red star, outlined in
yellow, on the upper hoist.

*PEOPLE:* The Dniestrians are Slavs, mostly Russian and Ukrainian, who
inhabit the region of Moldova east of the Dniestr River. The Dniestrians have
rejected Moldovan nationality and see themselves as a Russian people, even
though they are some 375 miles (600 kilometers) from the Russian border.
Although many moved to the region since 1940, the majority are the descendants
of the inhabitants of the Transdniestr region, which Stalin arbitrarily added to

the newly annexed Moldavia after World War II. The majority of the Dniestrians speak a Russian dialect with Ukrainian and Romanian admixtures.

*THE NATION:* The original inhabitants of the region, called Dacians by the Romans, came under Roman sway in the second century A.D. Overrun by Visigoths and Ostrogoths between 250 and 375, the Roman influence ended when the Roman authorities abandoned the colonies and withdrew to the territory south of the Danube in 270. Settled by Slav tribes during the great Slav migrations of the seventh century, the region formed part of the first Slav Empire, Kievan Rus, from the ninth to the eleventh centuries. Nomadic Cumans, a Turkic people, conquered the region and for almost two centuries carried on intermittent wars with the Byzantines, Kiev, and Hungary.

Devastated by the Mongols in 1242, the region slowly recovered under the rule of Stephen the Great, the creator of the first Moldavian principality in 1359. The Moldavian principality fell to the expanding Ottoman Empire of the Turks in 1513. Russia contested Turkish control from 1711 and finally annexed the region following the Russo-Turkish War of 1806–12. The newly annexed territory, with a Romanian-speaking majority, was subjected to intense Russification and opened to Slav colonization. Tiraspol, founded as a Russian fort in 1792, occupied the sight of a Moldavian village and became the metropolis for the expanding Slav population of the region.

In the nineteenth century the region, with its mixed population and growing industries, became the object of quarrels and propaganda by a number of political groups and the newly organized nationalists seeking to claim the area as Ukrainian, Moldavian, and Russian. During the 1905 Russian Revolution, serious disturbances broke out as rival groups fought running street battles and skirmished with Russian troops.

Devastated by nearly three years of war, Russia collapsed in revolution in February 1917, leaving the region and neighboring Ukraine and Bessarabia effectively independent. As chaos spread across the disintegrating empire, Moldavian and Ukrainian nationalists and Russian political organizations of every hue battled for control of the important industrial region. Following the October 1917 Bolshevik coup, nationalists in both Ukraine and Moldavia laid claim to the region.

Threatened by a Bolshevik advance, the Moldavians voted for union with Romania in April 1918 and continued to claim the lands on the right bank as part of united Romania. Romanian army units occupied the area in June 1918 and forcibly annexed the region to Romania. The Romanian military suppressed the vehement opposition of the Slav minority.

Menaced by the advancing Communist Red Army, the Romanian troops withdrew and stopped the Communist advance at the Dniestr River. The area, under Communist control, formed part of the autonomous Moldavian Autonomous Soviet Socialist Republic created within the Soviet Ukraine in 1924. The autonomous republic became a Soviet showpiece from which the authorities hoped to export Communism to neighboring Romanian Bessarabia. In 1930 the Soviet authorities moved the capital of the autonomous republic from Balta to Tiraspol on the Dniestr River.

The Soviet Red Army occupied neighboring Bessarabia in 1939 and formally annexed the region in 1940. Added to the Soviet Moldavia on the right bank of the Dniestr, an enlarged Moldavian republic became a constituent republic of the Soviet Union. The Slav majority of the Transdniestr region protested the union, citing the historical fact that the right bank of the river had never formed part of historic Bessarabia or Moldavia despite its large Moldavian minority.

Moldavian nationalism, suppressed for decades, grew dramatically in the more liberal atmosphere of the late 1980s, inciting mass demonstrations and demands for linguistic freedom. A nationalist government, elected in February 1990, endorsed a strict language law propagated in 1989 that outraged and alienated the republic's Slavs.

Led by Igor Smirnov, the Dniestrian Slavs demanded that Russian be reinstated as an official language and that the Slav majority regions on the east bank of the Dniestr become an autonomous province in Moldova or join Russia. In September 1990 the Dniestrian leaders unilaterally declared the region's autonomy and, backed by the Soviet Fourteenth Army, defied Moldova's nationalist government.

Moldavia, officially renamed Moldova, became an independent state following the disintegration of the Soviet Union in August 1991. The declaration of independence, on 27 August, was rejected by the Communist Dniestrian leadership. Demands for Dniestrian separation from Moldova escalated as even the non-Communist Slavs supported the Communist leaders who claimed to protect them from the Romanians. On 2 September 1991 the regional parliament declared the independence of the region as the Dniestr Moldavian Republic. In December 1991 armed conflict broke out, pitting the secessionists, backed by the Soviet Fourteenth Army, against the Moldovan army. By June 1992 over 700 had died and 50,000 people had fled the fighting.

On 21 July 1992, following a series of meetings with the participation of Moldova, Romania, Ukraine, Dniestria, and Russia, the region was accorded a special status within Moldova and granted the right to determine its own future should the Moldovans decide to merge with Romania. In late July Russian, Moldovan, and Dniestrian peacekeepers were deployed in the region. In January 1994 the Moldovan government accepted proposals for greater Dniestrian self-government within a Moldovan confederation. In March 1994 the Moldovan government rescinded the 1989 language law that began the alienation of Dniestria.

*SELECTED BIBLIOGRAPHY:*

Dima, Nicholas. *Bessarabia and Bukovina: The Soviet-Romanian Territorial Dispute.* 1982.

Jewsbury, George F. *The Russian Annexation of Bessarabia.* 1976.

Rowney, Don K., and G. Edward Orchard, eds. *Russian and Slavic History.* 1977.

# DON

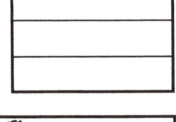

*CAPITAL: Novocherkassk*

SOUTHEASTERN EUROPE

DON

*POPULATION:* (95e) 4,552,000 : 2,250,000 Don Cossacks in Russia. MAJOR NATIONAL GROUPS: (95e) Don Cossack 47%, Russian 34%, Ukrainian 17%. MAJOR LANGUAGES: Russian, Ukrainian, Cossack. MAJOR RELIGIONS: Russian Orthodox, Ukrainian Orthodox. MAJOR CITIES: (95e) Rostov-na-Donau 1,044,000 (1,225,000), Taganrog 305,000 (329,000), Shakhty 225,000 (294,000), Volgodonsk 215,000 (318,000), Novocherkassk 191,000 (251,000), Novoshakhtinsk 110,000 (123,000), Bataysk 102,000, Azov 85,000 (104,000), Salsk 63,000 (111,000).

*GEOGRAPHY:* AREA: 38,919 sq.mi.-100,826 sq.km. LOCATION: The Don occupies the basin of the Don River in southern European Russia, a major agricultural region with a narrow outlet, the Gulf of Taganrog, on the Sea of Azov and the Black Sea. POLITICAL STATUS: The Don, formerly the Territory of the Don Cossacks, forms Rostov Oblast (province) of the Russian Federation.

*INDEPENDENCE DECLARED:* 10 January 1918.

*FLAG:* The Don Cossack national flag, the flag of the former republic, is a horizontal tricolor of blue, yellow, and red.

*PEOPLE:* The Don Cossacks, the largest of the Cossack peoples, are of Russian and "Eastern," probably Kalmyk, ancestry and evolved as a separate people in the sixteenth and seventeenth centuries. The Don Cossacks' claim to separate cultural and ethnic identity, not recognized by the Russian government, is based on their unique history, mode of life, geographic location, and language, a Cossack dialect of mixed Russian, Ukrainian, Kalmyk, and Tatar elements.

*THE NATION:* The fertile basin of the Don River has attracted migrants and conquerors since ancient times. Settled by nomadic Slavs around A.D. 880, the region formed a tributary state of Kievan Rus, the first great Slav Empire. In the early thirteenth century Mongols and Tatars of the Golden Horde overran the Don River area, and ethnic Tatars settled in the depopulated lowlands between 1241 and 1300.

The resurgent Slavs began to recover the area for the Russian Empire in the sixteenth century. To protect their expanding frontier, the Russian authorities founded Cossack (Free Warrior) settlements across the region. The Cossacks, living in autonomous communities under elected chiefs called atamans, were allowed to govern themselves in return for military service. The Don Cossacks pledged personal loyalty to the tsar in 1614 and received official recognition as a self-governing community in 1623.

The Don Cossacks fiercely resisted periodic attempts by the Russian bureaucracy to impose direct government control. Sporadic revolts against the government gradually eroded the Cossacks' privileges, and in 1708 they lost the right to elect their own atamans. The region, formally ceded to Russia by the Ottoman Empire in 1739, was organized as an autonomous military district, the Territory of the Don Cossacks, in 1790. A tsarist decree of 1835 established the Don Cossacks as a military caste with special privileges, their loyalty to the tsar ensured by special gendarme units garrisoned at Taganrog.

The Cossacks, better educated than most Russians, prospered on the proceeds from the rich farmlands. The Cossack communities held the land in common and rented parcels to Russian and Ukrainian peasants. An influx of freed serfs and urban workers to the expanding industrial cities in the 1860s impelled the Don leaders to establish a modern civil government. To centralize the administration of the territory, the Don Cossacks founded a new capital at Novocherkassk in 1865.

The Cossacks, after three centuries of guarding Russia's now-secure frontiers, became a mobile military force used within the country. From 1886 the Don Cossacks were dispatched to crush rebellions in other parts of the vast empire, the feared ''fist'' of the tsar.

Elite Don Cossack military units, sent to the front in 1914 and decimated in heavy fighting, greatly resented their new duties as they were pulled back to police an increasingly restive civilian population. Freed of their oath of loyalty by the overthrow of the tsar in February 1917, the Don Cossacks formed a military government under their own ataman, the first to be elected since 1708. The Don, virtually independent as Russia collapsed, remained calm and peaceful, the peace overseen by the the the Don Cossack military units.

The Bolshevik government in Petrograd, after taking power in October 1917, proclaimed the expropriation of the extensive Cossack lands. In December 1917 the Don Cossacks declared war on the new Bolshevik government. The region's leaders, refusing to recognize Russia's new government, on 10 January 1918 declared the independence of the Republic of the Don.

Allied to the anti-Bolshevik White forces as civil war spread across Russia, the Don Cossacks represented one of the White's most powerful military units, but strains soon appeared over the White's vehement opposition to the secession of any part of holy Russia. A Don Cossack delegation, sent to the 1919 Paris Peace Conference, failed to win recognition of the republic or to sway the Allies' support of the White position on secession.

Close to victory in October and November of 1919, the White offensive began to falter and finally to collapse. Refugees flooded into the republic, bringing turmoil, disease, and hunger. Its frantic appeals to the Allies ignored, the beleaguered Don Cossack state finally fell to the advancing Red Army in late 1920.

The Soviet authorities, determined to end the Cossack threat to their control, ended all traditional Cossack privileges, prohibited military training, and banned the use of the Cossack language and forbade all references to Cossack culture or history. The Don Cossack population, decimated by war and purges, suffered further losses to the famine that accompanied the forced collectivization of the Don Cossack lands in 1932–33.

The Nazis, following the invasion of their Soviet ally in 1941, proclaimed the Cossacks descendants of Germanic Ostrogoths and not subhuman Slavs, therefore acceptable allies. Thousands of Don Cossacks joined the Nazi's anti-Communist campaign, often facing Cossack soldiers in the Red Army in battle. Some 40,000 Cossacks, including 11,000 women and children, surrendered to the Allies in Austria. The Allies ignored their pleas and forcibly repatriated them to face Stalin's wrath.

A national and cultural revival that sprang from an aborted uprising in 1962 has grown dramatically since the late 1980s. Discarding bureaucratic neckties for the traditional Don Cossack uniforms, the Don Cossacks are resurrecting their long-banned heritage. A Don Cossack national movement, with its roots in the prerevolutionary autonomous state, has demanded recognition of the Don Cossacks as a separate people and creation of a separate Don Cossack republic within the Russian Federation. More militant groups view republican status as the first step to the restoration of the independent republic.

*SELECTED BIBLIOGRAPHY:*

Glaskow, Wasili G. *History of the Cossacks.* 1968.
McNeal, Robert H. *Tsar and Cossack: Eighteen Fifty-Five to Nineteen Fourteen.* 1987.
Shott, Paul. *Geography and Cultural Portrait of the Volga-Don Region.* 1986.

# EASTERN MONGOLIA

## Khingan; Mongoll Zizhiqu

*CAPITAL: Ulan Hot (Horqin Youyi Qiahqi)*

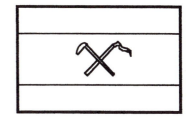

EASTERN ASIA

EASTERN MONGOLIA

*POPULATION:* (95e) 5,845,000 : 2,100,000 Eastern Mongols in China. MAJOR NATIONAL GROUPS: (95e) Chinese 62%, Eastern Mongol (Daghur, Solon, Oronchon, smaller groups) 35%. MAJOR LANGUAGES: Chinese, Mongol. MAJOR RELIGIONS: Buddhist, Taoist, Lamaism. MAJOR CITIES: (95e) Gegen Sume (Baicheng) 210,000, Ulan Hata (Chifeng) 165,000, Suquit Haka 150,000, Ulan Hot (Horqin Youyi Qiahqi) 145,000, Tungliao (Tongliao) 120,000, Taor (Taoan) 115,000, Khailar (Hailaerh) 115,000, Mergen (Nunjiang) 110,000, Zalantun (Butha Qi) 105,000, Manchouli (Manzhouli) 85,000, Oronchon (Oroqen) 70,000, Ergun (Ergun Youqi) 65,000, Dolonur (Duolan) 55,000, Solon (Suolan) 50,000, Khingan (Ksingan) 50,000.

*GEOGRAPHY:* AREA: 164,235 sq.mi.-425,479 sq.km. LOCATION: Eastern Mongolia lies in northeastern China, a region of fertile farmlands in the south and extensive grazing lands around the Greater Khingan Mountains in the north. POLITICAL STATUS: Eastern Mongolia has no official status; the region forms the northeastern districts of the Inner Mongolian Autonomous Region and the northwestern part of the province of Jilin in the People's Republic of China.

*INDEPENDENCE DECLARED:* 15 December 1928; 15 January 1946.

*FLAG:* The Eastern Mongol flag, the flag of the former republic, has horizontal stripes of red, pale blue, and red, the middle stripe twice the width of the red stripes, and charged with a white quirt and pick crossed in the center.

*PEOPLE:* The Eastern Mongols are a Mongol people, the eastern branch of the Mongols. Divided into tribal groups, the largest the Daghur, Solon, and

Oronchon, the Eastern Mongols are the descendants of the Mongols of the eastern leagues or principalities, more influenced by the Manchu and Tungus peoples than are the Mongol peoples to the west. While a minority still follow the ancient way of life as nomadic herders, the majority of the Eastern Mongols now live in the industrial towns and cities. The majority religion of the Eastern Mongols is a form of Tibetan Buddhism called Lamaism.

*THE NATION:* Nomadic tribes, often warring among themselves and raiding the Manchu and Chinese lands to the east and south, evolved six distinct principalities or leagues in the region: Khingan, Hulunbuir, Nonnimuren, Cherim, Chaota, and Jostu. The leagues, conquered by Genghis Khan in the twelfth century, were absorbed into the huge Mongol Empire, which eventually stretched across most of the known world.

The Eastern Mongol leagues fell to the Manchus in 1635. Retaining their own princes and religious leaders, the leagues formed part of Outer China following the Manchu conquest of the Chinese Empire in 1644. To ensure loyalty to the Manchu dynasty, immigration to the region by ethnic Chinese was restricted, and the Eastern Mongol leagues promised that they could reclaim their independence should there be a change of dynasty in China.

To relieve severe overcrowding, the Manchu administration opened the Mongol borderlands to Chinese immigration in 1878. Thousands of Chinese moved to the region, most settling in the more fertile southeast. The continuing immigration gradually pushed the native Mongols off the best lands and encroached on their grazing lands, causing serious ethnic clashes and sporadic revolts. In 1904 fears that the Chinese were determined to occupy all of the remaining league lands sparked violent rioting and attacks on immigration offices and Manchu officials.

Eastern Mongolia, ruled directly by the Manchus and not subject to the Chinese administration of Inner China, was the scene of grave disturbances during the Chinese Revolution in 1911. The overthrow of the Manchu dynasty, viewed by the Eastern Mongols as a change of dynasty, animated demands for independence under the terms of the 1635 Manchu agreement. Ignored by China's new republican government, the Eastern Mongol princes announced their intention to secede in 1913. Republican troops subdued the region, and the authorities placed it, stripped of all its former autonomy, under the control of the provincial government of Manchuria.*

Japanese influence in Manchuria increased in the 1920s during a period of turbulence and chaos in China. On 15 December 1928 the leaders of the Solon League declared the principality independent of China, but Chinese troops moved in to crush the movement. In 1931 the Japanese took effective control of the province and in 1932 supported a Manchu nationalist declaration of independence. First called Eastern Mongol by the Japanese, the Mongol tribes of western Manchuria were organized by the authorities into separate divisions of Manchuria's new army. Thousands of Eastern Mongols, trained by the Japanese to fight with modern weapons, gained practical fighting experience during World War II.

The Soviet Red Army occupied Manchuria in August 1945, accompanied by military units of the Mongolian People's Republic. Eastern Mongol nationalists, aided by the Mongol soldiers, formed a national army of 250,000, made up of the units from the former Manchurian army. In November 1945 Stalin ordered the Soviet and Mongol military units to withdraw in deference to the Chinese Communists, but before the Communists could reach the region, the Eastern Mongol leaders declared the region independent on 15 January 1946.

The nationalists rejected overtures from both the Chinese Communists and their civil war enemies, the Chinese Nationalists, and set about erecting an independent Eastern Mongolia. The new state, reorganized into six provinces corresponding to the former leagues, came under increasing pressure by the escalating Chinese civil war, and the Eastern Mongol military units skirmished with both Communist and Nationalist Chinese troops.

The Eastern Mongol government, its attempt to win allies in Mongolia blocked by Stalin, tried to win a promise of autonomy within China, but both Chinese factions rebuffed the proposal. Finally defeated by the Chinese Communists under Lin Piao in May 1947, the Eastern Mongol government was forcibly dissolved, and the region was added to the Communist-controlled Inner Mongolia.

Severe nationalist disturbances, provoked by government-sponsored immigration to the region, swept the Eastern Mongol districts during the Cultural Revolution in the late 1960s. The authorities responded by splitting the region from Inner Mongolia and dividing it among three Chinese provinces in 1969. Reduced to minority status by massive immigration, the Eastern Mongols began to assimilate, slowing losing their unique culture and history. In 1979 a less strident Chinese leadership rejoined Eastern Mongolia to Inner Mongolia, therefore restoring some cultural autonomy to the Mongol population.

The overthrow of Communism in the Soviet Union and Mongolia has stimulated a cultural resurgence and a parallel growth of nationalism in the region that has begun to reverse decades of assimilation. The rediscovery of their separate history has excited demands for the resurrection of the leagues and the medieval Mongol federation. Modern Eastern Mongol nationalists are determined to return to the traditional values and culture that over five decades of Communist rule nearly destroyed.

*SELECTED BIBLIOGRAPHY:*

Collier, Mac. *China in Disintegration, 1912–1949.* 1977.

Lattimore, Owen. *The Mongols of Manchuria.* 1969.

Schwartz, Henry G. *The Minorities of Northern China.* 1984.

Tang, Peter S. *Russian and Soviet Policy in Manchuria and Outer Mongolia 1911–1931.* 1979.

# EAST TIMOR

**Timur l'Este; Loro Sae**

*CAPITAL: Dili*

SOUTHEASTERN ASIA

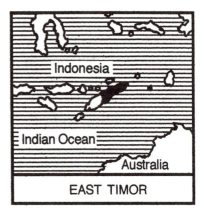

EAST TIMOR

*POPULATION:* (95e) 808,000 : 630,000 East Timorese in Indonesia. MAJOR NATIONAL GROUPS: (95e) East Timorese 78%, other Indonesian. MAJOR LANGUAGES: Tatum, Portuguese, Bahasa Indonesia. MAJOR RELIGIONS: Roman Catholic 68%, Sunni Muslim. MAJOR CITIES: (95e) Dili 143,000, Manatuto 15,000.

*GEOGRAPHY:* AREA: 5,762 sq.mi.-14,927 sq.km. LOCATION: East Timor occupies the eastern half of the island of Timor in the Timor Sea in eastern Indonesia. The region includes the enclave of Ocussi in western Timor and several smaller islands. POLITICAL STATUS: East Timor forms the province of Loro Sae in Indonesia.

*INDEPENDENCE DECLARED:* 28 November 1975.

*FLAG:* The East Timorese national flag, adopted in 1975, is a red field with a black triangle, outlined in yellow, at the hoist bearing a white, five-pointed star. OTHER FLAG(S): The flag of the major nationalist organization, the Revolutionary Front of Independent East Timor (FRETILIN) has horizontal stripes of red, yellow, and red with a vertical black stripe at the hoist bearing a white, five-pointed star.

*PEOPLE:* The East Timorese, of mixed Papuan, Malay, and European ancestry, speak Tatum (Tetum), a West Indonesian language with several major dialects and a marked Portuguese admixture. The majority of the East Timorese are Roman Catholics, converted over centuries of Portuguese rule. Non-Timorese and Muslim Timorese from the western half of the island have settled in East Timor since 1975 and now account for over 20% of the total population of the region.

*THE NATION:* Malays, coming from the islands to the west, colonized the island in the thirteenth century, driving the original inhabitants, small Papuan tribes, into the mountainous interior. The more advanced Malays settled the coastal areas but eventually spread into the interior and gradually absorbed the Papuans into their small tribal groups.

Visited by Portuguese and Dutch explorers in the early fifteenth century, the island of Timor came under Portuguese rule in 1586. The Dutch seized the western half of the island in 1618 and finally defeated the rival Portuguese for control of the East Indies in 1641, leaving Portuguese Timor the only Portuguese territory in the region.

Portuguese missionaries exerted tremendous influence in the isolated colony, and the Catholic religion became firmly established before Islam spread to the region. A neglected appendage of Portuguese India until 1844 and later administered from Portuguese Macao, the colony received few European settlers. Made a separate colony in 1896, the border with Dutch Timor was finally delimited, the actual frontier decided by the religion of the inhabitants, with the areas populated by Roman Catholics included in Portuguese Timor. The development of the colony, the smallest and poorest of the Portuguese Empire, began only after a serious Timorese rebellion against the colonial administration in 1910–12.

Indonesia, the former Dutch East Indies, gained independence in 1949 and immediately began to call for the decolonization of Portuguese East Timor, but with little support among the East Timorese. In 1951 the Portuguese government upgraded the colony's status to that of an overseas territory, and over the next two decades development accelerated, giving the East Timorese a higher standard of living than the inhabitants of neighboring Indonesian regions.

A leftist revolutionary government, installed in Lisbon in 1974, moved to free the remaining overseas possessions. Anticipating the end of colonial rule, political parties formed in East Timor: the Revolutionary Front of Independent East Timor (FRETILIN), favoring immediate independence, the Timor Democratic Union (UDT), advocating self-government and continued ties to Portugal, and a small, pro-Indonesian group, Apodeti. In July 1975 elections for local councils, FRETILIN took 55% of the vote, and UDT received 45%, while Apodeti's calls for union with Indonesia failed completely.

Apodeti activists attempted a coup in August 1975, setting off a civil war in the territory. FRETILIN, with the support of the Catholic majority, defeated the Indonesian-backed rebels and on 28 November 1975 declared East Timor independent. The Indonesian government, refusing to accept the declaration or the defeat of its faction, launched an invasion of the new state nine days later. Over 50,000 East Timorese died in the first two months of the Indonesian invasion.

The United Nations, in April 1976, called on Indonesia to withdraw and to allow a referendum on independence. Ignoring the resolution, the Indonesian government annexed the territory in July and embarked upon a brutal campaign to crush the widespread resistance. Up to 200,000 East Timorese perished over the next four years, about a third of the 1975 population.

International criticism pushed the Indonesian government to curtail the worst of the military excesses against the civilian population in 1984, although a campaign to defeat the FRETILIN insurrection continued. In November 1991 Indonesian troops fired on a funeral procession of a nationalist killed in previous clashes. Officially, some fifty mourners died, while nationalist reports claimed the number of dead and missing surpassed 180. The massacre marked a renewed international campaign, led by Portugal, to persuade the Indonesian government to allow the referendum called for in the 1976 United Nations resolution.

Stung by international calls for a termination of development aid and an impartial investigation of the harsh conditions in the province, the Indonesian government, for the first time, disciplined the military officers responsible for the massacre. While the East Timor situation retained world attention, the continuing repression eased somewhat.

Indonesian troops, in November 1992, captured Xanana Gusmao, the leader of the FRETILIN rebels, bringing renewed international demands for a fair trial and for investigations into Indonesia's administration of East Timor. The FRETILIN rebels continue to harass Indonesian military control from mountain strongholds.

In July 1994 demonstrators in Dili demanding religious freedom clashed with police seeking to break up the march. In August the Indonesian government banned all protest marches or demonstrations in the province in an effort to keep the region under tight control and out of the news in order to blunt increasingly strident criticism in the world press.

The November 1994 Pacific nations economic meeting, held in Jakarta, set off a new round of Timorese demonstrations and pleas to the heads of governments attending the meeting. Pro-independence demonstrations and violent confrontations continued into 1995. In spite of the efforts and repression of the Indonesian government, the East Timorese have once again brought the question of East Timor to the world's attention.

*SELECTED BIBLIOGRAPHY:*

Budiardjo, Carmel, and Liem Long. *The War against East Timor.* 1984.
Hawthorne, Daniel. *Islands of the East Indies.* 1977.
Marcel, Roger. *Timor.* 1989.
Retboll, Torben. *East Timor, Indonesia and the Western Democracies.* 1988.

# EAST TURKESTAN

Uigharstan; Uigherstan; Sinkiang;
Xinjiang-Uijgur

*CAPITAL: Urumchi (Urumqi)*

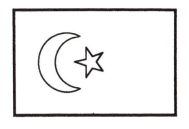

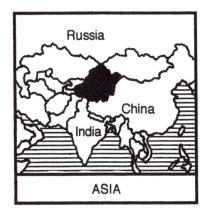

*POPULATION:* (95e) 16,320,000 : 7,950,000 Uighur in China, and another 250,000 in adjacent areas of Kazakhstan and Kyrgyzstan. MAJOR NATIONAL GROUPS: (95e) Uighur 48%, Han Chinese 35%, Kazakh 7%, Kyrgyz (Kirghiz) 3.5%, Mongol 2.5%, Tajik (Tadzhik) 2%, Uzbek 1%, Hui 1%. MAJOR LAN-GUAGES: Vigus (Uighur), Chinese, Kazakh, Kyrgyz, Mongol. MAJOR RE-LIGIONS: (95e) Sunni Muslim 68%, Buddhist, Taoist. MAJOR CITIES: (95e) Urumchi (Urumqi) 1,205,000, Kuldja (Yining) 348,000, Kashgar (Koshih) 245,000, Kitai (Kuchengtze) 211,000, Karamai (Kelamayi) 176,000, Yarkand (Schache) 168,000, Aqsu (Aksu) 133,000, Khotan (Hetien) 125,000, Kumul (Hami) 118,000, Turfan (Tulufan) 115,000, Kuytun (Wusu) 100,000, Keriya (Yutien) 80,000, Kargalik (Yecheng) 78,000, Chingil (Qinghe) 75,000.

*GEOGRAPHY:* AREA: 635,829 sq.mi.-1,647,225 sq.km. LOCATION: East Turkestan occupies a high, flat tableland, surrounded on three sides by mountains, in northwestern China. POLITICAL STATUS: East Turkestan has no official status; the region forms the Xinjiang-Uijgur Autonomous Region of the People's Republic of China.

*INDEPENDENCE DECLARED:* 23 January 1934; 31 January 1945.

*FLAG:* The East Turkestani national flag, the flag of the national movement, is a blue field charged with a large white crescent moon and five-pointed star near the hoist. OTHER FLAG(S): The flag of the majority of the nationalist movements is a white field bearing a small, blue crescent moon and five-pointed star centered above the Shahada, in blue Arabic script, reading "There is no God but God, Mohammed is the Prophet of God."

*PEOPLE:* The Uighur, called Wai Wuer by the Chinese, are the descendants of the Dzungars (Left Hand), the left wing of the hordes of the medieval Mongol Empire. The Uighur are the most numerous of the forty different national groups that inhabit the region. Their language, Vigus or New Uighur, is a Turkic language of the East Turkic language groups and is spoken in several regional dialects. The Uighurs are a Sunni Muslim people, as are the related Kazakh, Kyrzyz, Tajik, and Uzbek minorities. The large Han Chinese population, mostly settled in the area since 1949, formed nearly half the total population in the 1970s. In the 1980s the very high Muslim birthrate and a continuing exodus back to the Chinese heartland again made the Uighur the largest national group and reestablished a Muslim majority.

*THE NATION:* This vast plauteau possibly the human race's earliest home, the Turkic and Chinese peoples have contested control of it for thousands of years. The ancient Turkic cities, important stops on the Silk Road, the caravan routes that linked China and the Mediterranean, have known many conquerors. The Turkic Uighurs conquered the region in the early eighth century, only to fall to the expanding Mongols in 729–35. Militarily absorbed, the Uighurs formed the left wing of the Mongol-Turkic hordes that eventually conquered most of the known world.

Islam, introduced by tenth-century Arab invaders, spread rapidly along the Silk Road. Numerous small states, founded in the fourteenth century, gained fame as opulent centers of Muslim learning and tolerance. The cities, centers of world trade, boasted large populations of disparate ethnic and religious groups.

China's Manchu rulers dispatched a huge army that overran the region in a swift campaign in 1756–59, effectively ending the celebrated ethnic and religious tolerance. Interethnic conflicts and sporadic rebellions constantly threatened Chinese rule of the region. Great Britain held all of India with just 30,000 troops while China, in 1825, required a garrison of over 100,000 to control the region's rebellious Muslim tribes.

A widespread Muslim rebellion in 1864–66, encouraged by Russian and British agents, loosened China's hold on Sinkiang. Russian troops occupied Kuldja and the Ili Valley in 1871, and the British supported Uighur efforts to create a separate state centered on Kashgar. The Chinese reconquest, in 1876–78, marked by savage reprisals, drove thousands of refugees to seek shelter in neighboring Russian territory. The Kuldja region, returned to China in 1881, was added to the other regions and subject states to form a single province called Sinkiang, the New Territories.

The Muslims again rebelled as news reached the region of the overthrow of the Manchu dynasty in 1911, beginning several decades of instability and turbulence. In 1931 the Uighurs rebelled and drove all Chinese officials from Sinkiang. Aided and encouraged by the Soviet Union, on 23 January 1934 the rebels declared East Turkestan independent of China. Undermined by Soviet duplicity, the new state fell to the returning Chinese troops.

Weakened by civil war and a growing war with Japan, China's control weakened in the late 1930s. A renewed Muslim revolt, in 1936–37, culminated in the virtual collapse of Chinese control in the early years of World War II. In June 1943 the Kazakhs rebelled in the north, soon joined by the Uighurs and other Muslim peoples. In 1944 the Mongols joined the revolt. The rebels took the last Chinese garrison, Kuldja, in January 1945 and on 31 January 1945 declared the independence of the Republic of East Turkestan under a government led by Ali Khan Türe.

The Soviet government, fearing the effects on Soviet Turkestan, pressured the new government to negotiate with the Nationalist Chinese government of Chiang Kai-shek. After eight months of talks, the rebels agreed to accept political autonomy and to disarm. The Nationalist authorities, as soon as the rebels had laid down their arms, began brutal retribution. The Nationalist betrayal eventually cost Chiang Kai-shek a major defeat in the ongoing civil war with the Communists. The entire region went over to the Red Chinese without a fight in late 1949.

Communist rule, consolidated in 1949, proved as harsh as that of the earlier Nationalists. To dilute the region's Muslim majority, the government sponsored mass colonization. Only 3% Chinese in 1950, the percentage grew to nearly 50% in 1975. Targeted for forced assimilation during the Chinese Cultural Revolution, 1966–76, Chinese cadres destroyed thousands of mosques and shrines and paraded learned religious and cultural leaders through the streets with pigs' heads, anathema to Muslims, dangling around their necks.

The excesses of the Cultural Revolution gave way to a more relaxed Communist administration, and in 1981 the region's four major non-Chinese languages regained official status. A limited number of mosques and some religious schools reopened, but the momentous changes already under way across the Soviet border had begun to spread to the region. Nationalism, spurred by the changes taking hold in neighboring Soviet republics, grew rapidly in the 1980s and culminated in an abortive insurrection in April 1990. Supported by the newly independent Turkestan states on its western border, the East Turkestani national movement has become a potent force in the region.

In early March 1993 Uighur nationalists took their message and their plea for independence to the United Nations but received little open support. The majority of the nationalists look to the anticipated collapse of Chinese Communism as their best hope and next opportunity.

*SELECTED BIBLIOGRAPHY:*

Coyle, Dominick J. *Minorities in Revolt.* 1982.

Dreyer, June. *China's Forty Millions.* 1976.

Orleans, Leo A. *Every Fifth Child: The Population of China.* 1972.

Whiting, Allen, and Sheng Shih-Ts'Ai. *Sinkiang: Pawn or Pivot. 1958.*

# EUZKADI

Euskadi; Pais Vasco; Pays Basque;
Euskal Herria

*CAPITAL: Gasteiz (Vitoria)*

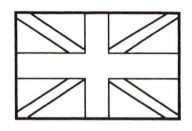

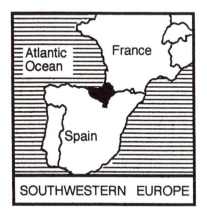

SOUTHWESTERN EUROPE

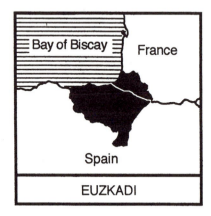

EUZKADI

*POPULATION:* (95e) 3,247,000 : 2,335,000 Basques in Spain and France, and another 500,000 in the Americas. MAJOR NATIONAL GROUPS: (95e) Basque (Eskauldunak) 71%, other Spanish, other French. MAJOR LANGUAGES: Spanish, Basque (Euzkarra), French. MAJOR RELIGIONS: Roman Catholic, Protestant. MAJOR CITIES: (95e) SPAIN: EUZKADI (PAIS VASCO): Bilbo (Bilbao) 362,000 (1,058,000), Gasteiz (Vitoria) 208,000, Donostia (San Sebastian) 189,000 (305,000), Barakaldo (Baracaldo) 121,000, Irun 56,000 (111,000), Errenteria (Renteria) 54,000, Gernika (Guernica) 21,000. NAFARROA (NAVARRA): Iruñea (Pamplona) 177,000 (240,000), Tudera (Tudela) 37,000. FRANCE: IPARRALDE (PAYS BASQUE): Baiona (Bayonne) 41,000 (146,000), Miarritz (Biarritz) 28,000, Angelu (Anglet) 26,000.

*GEOGRAPHY:* AREA: 8,097 sq.mi.-20,975 sq.km. LOCATION: Euzkadi lies in southwestern France, straddling the Franco-Spanish border on the Bay of Biscay at the western end of the Pyrenees Mountains. POLITICAL STATUS: Euzkadi forms the Euzkadi (Pais Vasco) and Nafarroa (Navarra) regions of Spain and the Benaparroa (Basse-Navarre), Lapourdi (Labourd), and Zuberos (Soule) districts of Pyrénées-Atlantiques Department of France.

*INDEPENDENCE DECLARED:* 14 June 1931.

*FLAG:* The Basque national flag, the official flag of the Pais Vasco in Spain, is a red field bearing a centered white cross backed by a green saltire.

*PEOPLE:* The Basques, of unknown origin, are thought to be Europe's oldest surviving ethnic group, with even the Basque blood type differing from that of other Europeans. The Basque language, Euzkarra, is the sole surviving example of the languages that preceded the spread of the Indo-European languages. Subgroups include the mainly Spanish-speaking Navarese in the east and the French-speaking Gascons and Bearnese in the north. The majority of the Basques are devoutly Roman Catholic, with a small Protestant minority, mostly in France.

*THE NATION:* The Basques, thought to predate the ancient Celts, were first mentioned as a people in Roman chronicles as a nation difficult to subdue, even though the region remained under nominal Roman rule until the fifth century A.D. During the barbarian invasions that followed the Roman collapse, Germanic Vandals and Visigoths passed through the Basque lands, destroying the last vestiges of Roman authority but failing to conquer the Basque strongholds in the Pyrenees Mountains.

Called Vascones, the Basques of Navarre expanded to the north of the Pyrenees in the sixth century and gave their name to the duchy of Gascony established in A.D. 601. Germanic Franks overran Gascony and Navarre in the eighth century while the Basques in the west successfully resisted the invasion. In 824 the western Basques returned to expel the Franks from the area south of the mountains, where they erected the kingdom of Navarre. Muslim Moors attacked the kingdom in the early tenth century and burned the capital, Pamplona, but by 937 the Basques had taken the offensive and later played a prominent role in the Christian reconquest of northern Spain.

The Spanish kingdom of Castile conquered the western Basque provinces between 1200 and 1390, and, with the conquest of Navarre in 1512, the Basques lost their last independent territory. Granted special rights, the Fueros, the Basques enjoyed broad autonomy in the Spanish kingdom. The northern Basques, incorporated in the French kingdom in 1601, enjoyed a similar status until the French Revolution in 1789. The border between France and Spain, established in the Pyrenees and confirmed by a 1659 treaty, has remained unchanged.

Passionate resistance to attempts by the highly centralized Spanish and French governments to abrogate their ancient rights stimulated the growth of Basque nationalism in the 1850s and 1860s. A national and cultural revival accelerated in the late nineteenth century, reversing centuries of assimilation and bringing the first demands for Basque reunification and self-determination. Emigration to escape poverty and cultural suppression became common, particularly to the Americas.

Turmoil in the Spanish state in the 1920s and 1930s strengthened the national movement. In 1931, as virtual civil war paralyzed the Spanish government, the Basques of the three western provinces voted for secession. The Republic of Euzkadi, declared independent on 14 June 1931, was rapidly suppressed by Spanish troops. Granted autonomy by a new leftist government in 1936, at the outbreak of the Spanish civil war, the Basques supported the government against the fascist rebels and their German and Italian allies.

The town of Guernica, the site of the sacred oak tree, the symbol of Basque liberty, was destroyed by Nazi bombers in 1937. The destruction of the Basques' spiritual capital, commemorated by a famous painting by Pablo Picasso, marked the end of Basque autonomy and the imposition of harsh fascist rule. Thousands fled to France as the victorious fascists banned the Basque language, suppressed the culture, and instituted a policy of forced assimilation into Castilian Spanish culture.

Industrialized by the Franco regime, eager to exploit its natural resources, by the early 1950s the Basque provinces had attained a standard of living comparable to that of the Benelux countries. Rapid economic development attracted thousands of migrants from Spain's backward south, their presence abetting the government's efforts to stamp out the Basque language and culture. In 1952 a nationalist group, Euzkadi ta Azkatazuna (Basque Homeland and Liberty), known by its initials ETA, launched a resistance campaign. In 1968, joined by their counterparts in French Euzkadi, ETA turned to violence and terrorism.

The Spanish dictatorship ended with Franco's death in 1975, and Spain rapidly democratized under a restored Bourbon monarchy. The Basque language, after decades of suppression, spoken by only 20% of Spain's Basques as compared with 60% in France, experienced a dramatic resurgence as part of the Basques' cultural renaissance. The Basque provinces received a grant of autonomy in 1980, and a moderate nationalist regional government took control with 70% support in local elections. Navarre, Navarra in Spanish, granted separate autonomous status, has strengthened ties to Euzkadi since 1988.

Vowing to settle for nothing less than full independence, ETA and its allies in France continue their campaign of terror. Since 1984 the Spanish and French governments have cooperated closely in a concerted antiterrorist crusade. Horrified by indiscriminate violence, the vast majority of the Basques have rejected violence and support moderate nationalist parties seeking greater independence within united Europe. In 1993 moderate nationalists put forward a plan for greater autonomy, closer official ties between Spanish and French Basques, and separate representation within the European Union.

*SELECTED BIBLIOGRAPHY:*

Clark, Robert P. *The Basque Insurgents: ETA 1952–1980.* 1984.
Heiberg, Marianne. *The Making of the Basque Nation.* 1989.
Payne, Stanley G. *Basque Nationalism.* 1975.
Wigram, E. *Northern Spain.* 1976.

# FAEROE ISLANDS

**Föröyar; Faeröerne**

*CAPITAL:* Thorshavn

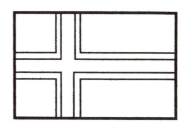

NORTHWESTERN EUROPE

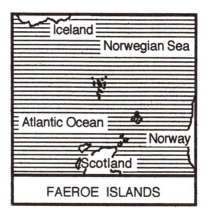

FAEROE ISLANDS

*POPULATION:* (95e) 46,000 : 53,000 Faeroese in Denmark. MAJOR NATIONAL GROUPS: (95e) Faeroese 95%, Danish 5%. MAJOR LANGUAGES: Faeroese, Danish. MAJOR RELIGION: Lutheran. MAJOR CITIES: (95e) Thorshavn 17,000, Klaksvik 9,000.

*GEOGRAPHY:* AREA: 540 sq.mi.-1,398 sq.km. LOCATION: The Faeroe Islands, an archipelago of twenty-one islands, seventeen inhabited, lie in the Atlantic Ocean 250 miles north of Scotland.* POLITICAL STATUS: The Faeroe Islands form an autonomous state within the Kingdom of Denmark.

*INDEPENDENCE DECLARED:* 18 September 1946.

*FLAG:* The Faeroese flag, the official flag of the autonomous state, is a white field bearing a red Scandinavian cross outlined in pale blue.

*PEOPLE:* The Faeroese are a separate Scandinavian nation, the descendants of early Viking colonists and the original Celtic inhabitants, speaking a separate Scandinavian language based on the Old Norse brought to the islands by the Vikings. Fishing, closely tied to Faeroese culture and history, accounts for 95% of the islands' economy, as only 6% of the land is suitable for agriculture. The Faeroese are overwhelmingly Lutheran and remain one of the more religious of the Scandinavian peoples.

*THE NATION:* The islands, inhabited in ancient times by Celts from mainland Europe, were colonized by Norwegian Vikings between the eighth and tenth centuries. In 1035 the islands became part of the Norwegian kingdom. Devastated by the plague that swept Europe in the fourteenth century, the kingdom's government augmented the surviving population with renewed immigration from the mainland. With Norway the islands passed to Danish rule in 1386. Under Danish rule the isolated Faeroese retained their language and culture; however, they accepted the Lutheran doctrine brought to the islands by Danish reformers in 1540.

The inhabitants of the remote islands, ignored by the Danish government, developed a strong tradition of self-reliance. Sparsely populated and underdeveloped, the islands became almost wholly dependent on fishing. In the eighteenth century the islanders discovered a new use for their large fishing fleet. The islands became a notorious center for smuggling goods between the British Isles and Scandinavia.

The Swedish kingdom took control of Norway in 1814, but the Faeroes, long considered part of Norway, remained under Danish rule. Between 1814 and 1856 all island trade came under the control of a Danish royal monopoly, which the islanders circumvented by returning to their traditional smuggling activities.

The Danish language, the only official language of government and education, replaced Faeroese as the first language in the nineteenth century. The decline of the Faeroese language became a major issue of the Faeroese cultural revival of the 1880s. The development of a distinct alphabet, based on that of the Icelanders to the northwest, spurred the development of an extensive Faeroese literature. Faeroese nationalism, growing out of the cultural revival, led to demands for political autonomy. In 1912, as a concession to growing Faeroese nationalism, the Faeroese language was made the second official language.

Faeroese self-awareness, a renewed appreciation of their unique culture and history, advanced rapidly during World War I. In the first decade after the war the Faeroese experienced a rapid population growth, but for the first time the islanders rejected emigration to the Danish mainland and began to colonize the formerly uninhabited islands of the group.

The British occupied the Faeroes following the fall of Denmark to the Nazis in 1940. Allowed to govern themselves, the islanders provided three-quarters of the fish consumed in Britain during the war. The effort cost the Faeroese over a third of their fishing fleet.

Pro-independence sentiment grew rapidly with the end of the war. Nationalists pressed for the islands to follow Iceland, which had declared its independence of Denmark in 1944. Following a plebiscite, the Faeroese parliament, the Lagting, declared the islands independent on 18 September 1946. The Danish authorities moved quickly to dissolve the Lagting and to nullify the declaration. Faced with continuing separatist sentiment, the Danish government granted extensive autonomy in 1948. The Faeroese took over all aspects of the island's administration except for defense and foreign relations.

The modernizing of the fishing fleet in the 1950s and 1960s raised the standard of living to mainland levels. The prosperous Faeroese, their language firmly established as the predominant language, became increasingly confident and assertive. Nationalist demands brought separate Faeroese representation in Scandinavian economic and cultural councils.

Denmark's entry in the European Economic Community in 1973 increased competition by the fishing fleets of the other member states. Threats to their one important industry, and therefore their unique culture, reopened the autonomy-versus-independence debate.

The massive overextension of the fishing fleet in the 1980s led to an industry collapse in 1992. Accompanied by a severe recession and high unemployment, the failure of the fishing industry affected the island's autonomous financial institutions. Falling marine stocks and fish prices brought economic hardship to the prosperous islands. In January 1993, for the second time in months, the Faeroese government faced the prospect of compromising its independence by accepting a loan from the Danish government.

The economic crisis has left many Faeroese angry with fishing quotas and austerity measures imposed by the European Union and the Danish government. The revitalized national movement has again begun to call for independence. The Faeroese are already recognized as a separate Scandinavian people, and the nationalists are determined to win official recognition as a separate, independent European people.

*SELECTED BIBLIOGRAPHY:*

Annandale, Nelson. *The Faeroes and Iceland: Studies in Island Life.* 1905.

Levine, Charlotte. *Danish Dependencies.* 1989.

Williamson, Kenneth. *The Atlantic Islands.* 1952.

Young, G.V.C. *Isle of Man and the Faeroe Islands: Two Similar Countries.* 1981.

# FAR EAST

**Dalni Vostochny**

*CAPITAL: Vladivostok*

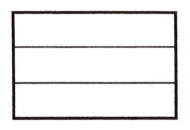

NORTHEASTERN ASIA

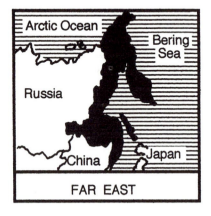

FAR EAST

*POPULATION:* (95e) 8,080,000 : 7,100,000 Far Eastern Slavs in Russia. MAJOR NATIONAL GROUPS: (95e) Far Eastern Slavs (Far Easterners) 84%, Korean 6%, German 2%, Evenki, Chukot, other Russian. MAJOR LANGUAGES: Russian (Far Eastern dialects), Ukrainian, Korean, German. MAJOR RELIGIONS: Russian Orthodox, Buddhist, Jewish. MAJOR CITIES: (95e) Vladivostok 670,000 (884,000), Khabarovsk 638,000 (692,000), Komsomolsk-na-Amure 352,000 (400,000), Petropavlovsk-Kamchatskiy 289,000, Blagoveshchensk 227,000 (246,000), Nakhodka 223,000, Yuzno-Sakhalinsk 180,000 (225,000), Ussuriysk 177,000, Magadan 169,000, Birobidzhan 90,000 (121,000), Svobodnyy 81,000 (102,000), Belogorsk 80,000 (113,000), Artem 78,000 (134,000), Suchan (Partizansk) 65,000 (110,000).

*GEOGRAPHY:* AREA: 1,842,969 sq.mi.-4,774,531 sq.km. LOCATION: The Far East occupies the Pacific Coast area of eastern Russia, a vast region stretching from the Arctic Circle to the border with China. At the closest point, in the Sea of Okhotsk, only three miles separate the Far East from Japan. POLITICAL STATUS: The Far East forms an economic region of the Russian Federation comprising the Primorski and Khabarovsk territories and the oblasts (provinces) of Amur, Kamchatka, Magadan, and Sakhalin. The region includes the autonomous areas of Chukotka,* Koryakia,* and the Jewish Autonomous Region.

*INDEPENDENCE DECLARED:* 23 May 1918; 6 April 1920.

*FLAG:* The Far Eastern flag, the flag of the national movement, is a horizontal tricolor of dark blue, white, and red. OTHER FLAG(S): The flag of Yidishtim

Yehudit, the Jewish Autonomous Region, is a horizontal tricolor of pale blue, white, and yellow.

*PEOPLE:* The Far Easterners are ethnic Slavs, descendants of Ukrainian and Russian settlers, Cossacks, and Slavic groups deported from European Russia since the seventeenth century. Thousands of miles and many time zones east of the Slavic heartland, the Far Easterners developed a unique frontier culture and distinctive dialects that incorporate Russian, Ukrainian, and borrowings from the region's indigenous peoples. Non-Slav Far Eastern peoples include the large Korean minority and smaller numbers of Evenki, Chukot, Koryak, and Germans, the descendants of World War II deportees.

*THE NATION:* The region, under nominal Chinese rule for centuries, remained a remote, tribal region sparsely populated by small tribal peoples. Penetrated by Slav explorers and traders in the 1640s, the Russians soon challenged China's claim to it. The Russians eventually abandoned a string of Cossack forts to Manchu China under the terms of the Treaty of Nerchinsk in 1689. The treaty confirmed Chinese sovereignty and defined the border between the two empires, the treaty the first between the Chinese Empire and a European power.

The Slavic traders and Cossacks, the vanguard of Russian expansion, returned to the region in large numbers in the late eighteenth century. Following the Russian seizure of some western districts, a weakened China ceded the region north of the Amur River to Russia in 1858. Two years later Russia forced China to cede the maritime region on the Pacific Ocean, and in 1875 Russian rule extended to Sakhalin Island.

Political prisoners and criminals, deported to the region's many penal colonies and labor camps, became the first settlers in many districts. Their legacy of antigovernment sentiments and revolutionary ideas became part of the Far Eastern culture. The completion of the Trans-Siberian Railroad in 1892 brought thousands of immigrants from Europe, particularly from the Ukraine.

Military conscription, introduced with the beginning of war in 1914, provoked widespread resentment as the Far Easterners generally viewed the distant conflict as Europe's war. Returning soldiers and tsarist exiles formed revolutionary organizations and enthusiastically supported the revolution of February 1917. The Social Revolutionary Party, the region's largest, took control of the collapsing civil administration and declared the Far East an autonomous state in May 1917 but was unable to enforce its authority across the region as other groups formed rival governments in several of the provinces.

The Bolshevik coup in October 1917 inspired local Bolsheviks to attempt to take power. The Bolsheviks fielded a well-armed militia against the more moderate political groups supported by anti-Bolshevik General Semenov and 3,000 Cossacks. Pressed by the Bolsheviks, the Far East government appealed for Japanese assistance in February 1918. Aided by 12,000 Japanese troops, the Far Easterners routed the Bolsheviks.

The Japanese, seeking a buffer between their Korean colony and the Bolsheviks, spread out across the region and sent soldiers to guard the vital railroad. With Japanese support, General Semenov declared the independence of the Far Eastern Republic on 23 May 1918.

Various international military forces intervened as the Russian civil war spread into the region, eventually numbering 72,000 Japanese, 7,000 Americans, 6,400 British, 4,400 Canadians, and smaller contingents of French and Italians. The American troops, holding the eastern end of the Trans-Siberian Railroad at Vladivostok, evacuated the Czech Legion, thousands of Czech and Slovak prisoners of war who had fought their way across revolutionary Russia in order to return to their homes in Europe.

The interventionist forces, except for the Japanese troops, all withdrew following the defeat of the local Bolsheviks in late 1918. Bolstered by troops sent from Europe, the Bolsheviks regrouped and formed a rival Far East Republic, which they declared independent on 6 April 1920. The newly formed Soviet Union recognized the Communist Far East as a sovereign state and the only legitimate government of the region. Gaining strength, the Communists took Khabarovsk in February 1922 and occupied Vladivostok when the Japanese withdrew in October 1922. Most of the defeated anti-Communist forces fled to Chinese territory. On 19 November 1922 the Communists dissolved the Far East Republic and accepted annexation by the Soviet Union.

Following the Soviet annexation, the Ukrainians, a majority in many districts, convoked a congress that voted for independence. The Ukrainians attempted to create an independent Ukrainian Far Eastern state or Green Ukraine in the Amur, Maritime, and Sakhalin provinces where they formed a majority.

The Soviet Union, having retained an armed neutrality with Japan during World War II, sent its troops into Japanese territory in August 1945. The occupied territories, southern Sakhalin Island and the Kurile Islands, became part of the Far East region.

The region was a dumping ground for political exiles and deportees during Stalin's decades of dictatorship; the exiles, many well educated and often anti-Communist, added to the region's distinct character in the 1950s and 1960s. A natural orientation to the booming Pacific countries, thwarted by the control of all economic activity by bureaucrats and ministries in faraway Moscow, increased Far Eastern resentment. Enmity to the growing number of temporary workers sent to the region from European Russia and attracted by the ''long ruble,'' the extra wages they received as hardship pay for working in the region, initiated the dramatic growth of modern Far Eastern nationalism in the 1980s.

The liberalization of Soviet society under Mikhail Gorbychev in the late 1980s allowed the Far Easterners to discuss and articulate the region's many economic problems. The subsequent disintegration of the Soviet Union has exacerbated the problems as the Far Easterners seek to join their homeland to the fast growing Pacific region. Spurred by economic grievances, nationalists in the region began to call for the resurrection of the independent Far Eastern Republic of 1918. In June 1993 the leaders of the Primorski Kray (Maritime Territory), which includes Vladivostok, unilaterally declared the province a member re-public in the Russian Federation. The declaration sparked off official debates in regional parliaments of the other provinces on reconstituting a separate republic in the entire Far East.

The last untapped region in the Northern Hemisphere, the resource-rich region needs to trade its minerals and timber for the manufactured goods readily avail-able in nearby countries but must still route every transaction through the ap-propriate ministry in Moscow. Nationalists point to the fact that, economically, little has changed and that the Far East, in order to develop and prosper, must take its place as an independent Pacific Rim country.

*SELECTED BIBLIOGRAPHY:*

Bradley, John. *Allied Intervention in Russia: Nineteen Seventeen to Nineteen Twenty.* 1984.

Hauner, Milan. *What Is Asia to Us? Russia's Asian Heartland Yesterday and Today.* 1990.

Mandel, William. *The Soviet Far East.* 1944.

Segal, Gerald. *The Soviet Union and the Pacific.* 1990.

Stephen, John J. *The Russian Far East.* 1994.

# FLANDERS

**Vlanderen; Vlaanderen; Flandre**

*CAPITAL: Brussel (Brussels)*

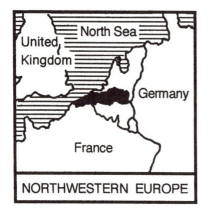

NORTHWESTERN EUROPE

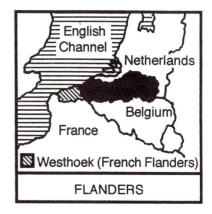

FLANDERS

*POPULATION:* (95e) 7,758,000 : 5,770,000 Flemish in Belgium and another 370,000 in Westhoek (French Flanders). MAJOR NATIONAL GROUPS: (95e) Flemish (Vlaams) 74%, other Belgian, other French. MAJOR LANGUAGES: Flemish, French. MAJOR RELIGIONS: Roman Catholic, Protestant. MAJOR CITIES: (95e) BRUSSELS REGION: Brussel (Brussels) 952,000 (2,401,000). FLANDERS REGION: Antwerpen (Antwerp) 461,000 (1,115,000), Gent (Ghent) 230,000 (524,000), Brugge 117,000 (229,000), Leuven 85,000 (174,000), Sint-Niklaas 84,000, Aalst 78,000 (103,000), Mechelen 77,000 (124,000), Kortrijk 73,000 (204,000), Oostend 67,000 (124,000), Hasselt 66,000 (Hasselt-Genk 306,000), Genk 62,000, Koeselare 52,000 (94,000), Geel 33,000 (95,000). FRENCH FLANDERS (WESTHOEK): Dunkirk (Dunquerque) 71,000 (208,000).

*GEOGRAPHY:* AREA: 5,216 sq.mi.-13,512 sq.km. LOCATION: Flanders occupies a broad, flat plain in northern Belgium, bordering the North Sea on the west, the Netherlands on the north, France on the southwest, and the Belgian region of Wallonia* on the south. POLITICAL STATUS: Flanders forms an autonomous region of Belgium. Nationalists also claim the Brussels metropolitan area, which forms an enclave within Flanders but constitutes a separate autonomous region, and French Flanders, Westhoek in Flemish, which forms the northwestern districts of the French region of Nord-Pas-de-Calais.

*INDEPENDENCE DECLARED:* 11 November 1917.

*FLAG:* The Flemish national flag, the official flag of the autonomous region, is a yellow field bearing the Black Lion of Flanders centered.

*PEOPLE:* The Flemish, also called Flemings, are a Germanic people closely related to the Dutch. The Flemish language, belonging to the West Germanic language group, in its spoken form diverged from Dutch in the sixteenth century but remains nearly identical in its written form. The language, long suppressed in favor of French, is the focal point of modern Flemish nationalism. The heirs of the Flemish Renaissance, the Flemish culture is one of the richest in Europe. Until the mid-twentieth century the Flemish majority remained rural; only since World War II has a large Flemish urban population developed.

*THE NATION:* Ancient Flanders, part of the Roman province of Belgica, named for the Celtic Belgae tribe conquered by the Romans in 57 B.C., became thoroughly Latinized in culture and language. The area was invaded by Salic Franks in the fourth century A.D., and the Germanic conquerors drove the Latins south to a line approximating the present linguistic division of Belgium.

The empire established by the Franks reached its apex under Charles the Great, better known as Charlemagne, and began to decline at his death in 814 and was divided by three heirs in 843. Flanders, included in the western French kingdom, became a separate fief in 862. The County of Flanders, with its capital at Lille, enjoyed virtual independence and at its greatest extent controlled Flanders, Westhoek, Artois, and part of Picardy.

The textile industry, introduced in the tenth century, made Flanders one of Europe's most prosperous regions and supported a great flowering of Flemish art and culture. In conjunction with the northern Italian cities, the French-speaking Flemish cities led the European Renaissance, a movement little affecting the rural Flemish-speaking peasantry.

In 1500, then the richest and most populous area of Europe, Flanders came under the rule of the Austrian Hapsburgs and in 1555 passed to the Spanish Hapsburgs and became part of the Spanish Netherlands. The religious differences between the southern and northern provinces led to a split. The Roman Catholic south remained under Spanish rule when the Protestant Dutch rebelled and won their independence in 1579. The expanding French kingdom took control of western Flanders between 1668 and 1678.

The military forces of revolutionary France occupied Flanders in 1792 and annexed the province in 1801. At the conclusion of the Napoleonic Wars, in 1815, the Low Countries reunited in the Kingdom of the Netherlands. Rejecting the domination of the kingdom by the Protestant Dutch, the southern provinces in Flanders and Wallonia rebelled in 1830 and formed the separate Kingdom of Belgium.

The new state, politically and economically dominated by the French-speaking Walloons, adopted French as the official language, which effectively barred Flemish speakers from most government positions. Flemish resentment stimulated a cultural and linguistic revival. The first works published in modern Flemish appeared in 1837. The revival spread to the Flemish minority in France, and the first cultural organization in Westhoek formed in 1852.

A strong sense of Flemish grievance grew throughout the nineteenth century.

Although Flemish became an official language in 1898, the dissatisfied Flemish leaders demanded full cultural and linguistic equality with the Walloons in 1900.

German troops overran the area in 1914, and the occupation authorities, to win Flemish support, granted the linguistic and cultural rights long denied by the Belgian government. A faction of the Flemish national movement formed a Council of Flanders in February 1917 and, with German encouragement, declared Flanders independent of Belgium on 11 November 1917. The republic collapsed with the German surrender in 1918, and its leaders faced charges of treason when the Belgian government returned.

Flemish extremist groups, many from the first Flemish university opened at Ghent in 1930, emerged during the turbulent interwar period. Some of the groups, drawn to the Nazi propaganda promoting the unity of Europe's Germanic peoples, collaborated following the German occupation in May 1940, some even joining Nazi fighting units.

The postwar reconstruction of Europe greatly increased the economic importance of the Flemish port cities. By the early 1960s Flanders had surpassed Wallonia as Belgium's economically predominant region. Material prosperity prompted demands for cultural and linguistic equality. Mass rallies erupted across Flanders in 1961–62. In November 1962 the government adopted Flemish as the sole official language of the Flemish provinces. Universities, banks, political parties, and other institutions split along linguistic lines.

The Egmont Pact, adopted in 1977, created autonomous governments in Flanders and Wallonia and later in bilingual Brussels. Demand for even greater devolution of government powers, agreed to in February 1993, has created a federation and has left the Belgian government responsible for little more than finance, foreign policy, and defense. When these powers are surrendered to a united European federation, Belgium will effectively cease to exist except as a geographic area. In 1994 nationalists launched a new campaign to win Flemish control of Brussels, called by the nationalists the Jerusalem of the Flemish national movement.

*SELECTED BIBLIOGRAPHY:*

Clough, S. B. *History of the Flemish Movement in Belgium.* 1930.
Esman, Milton. *Ethnic Conflict in the Western World.* 1977.
Fitzmaurice, John. *The Politics of Belgium: Crisis and Compromise in a Plural Society.* 1983.
Hermans, T. J. *The Flemish Movement: A Documentary History 1780–1980.* 1991.

# FRIESLAND

**Fryslân; Frisia; Vriesland**

*CAPITAL: Ljouwert (Leeuwarden)*

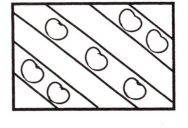

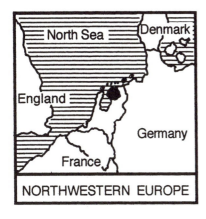

NORTHWESTERN EUROPE

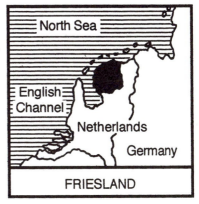

FRIESLAND

*POPULATION:* (95e) 611,000 : 650,000 Frisians in the Netherlands and another 160,000 in Germany and Denmark. MAJOR NATIONAL GROUPS: (95e) Frisian 89%, other Dutch. MAJOR LANGUAGES: Frisian, Dutch. MAJOR RELIGIONS: (95e) Dutch Reformed Church 85%, Mennonite 5%, Roman Catholic. MAJOR CITIES: (95e) Ljouwert (Leeuwarden) 86,000 (151,000), Drachten 47,000, It Fean (Heerenveen) 42,000 (60,000), Snits (Sneek) 32,000 (46,000), Burgum (Bergum) 30,000, Harns (Harlingen) 16,000 (41,000).

*GEOGRAPHY:* AREA: 1,646 sq.mi.-4,264 sq.km. LOCATION: Friesland lies in the northern Netherlands, a region of flat plains and polders, lands reclaimed from the North Sea between A.D. 1200 and 1600. The province includes a string of offshore islands along the northern coast, the West Frisian Islands. POLITICAL STATUS: Friesland forms a province of the Kingdom of the Netherlands.

*FLAG:* The Frisian flag, the official flag of the province is a blue field divided by three white, diagonal stripes charged with seven red devices representing water lilies. OTHER FLAG(S): The flag of the East Frisians in Germany is a horizontal tricolor of black, red, and pale blue. The flag of the North Frisians in Denmark is a yellow field bearing a blue Scandinavian cross outlined in red.

*PEOPLE:* The Frisians are a Germanic people speaking a language of the Anglo-Frisian branch of the West Germanic languages, the closest of the continental Germanic languages to English, particularly close to the northern English dialects, Lallans in Scotland* and Northumbrian in Northumbria.* The Frisians once controlled the whole of the North Sea coast, and isolated Frisian minorities still live in the East Friesland region and the East Frisian Islands of Germany and the North Friesland region and the North Frisian Islands of Denmark.

*THE NATION:* Migrating Germanic tribes settled the shores of the North Sea following the breakup of Celtic Europe. The Frisians eventually controlled the coastal region from present Bremen to Brugge. In the first century B.C. the Frisians stopped the northward advance of Roman power. The fierce Frisian warriors became the scourge of the settled peoples on the borders of the Roman Empire in the first centuries of the Christian Era.

Germanic Angles and Saxons moved into the region in the fifth century, establishing strong linguistic and cultural ties to the Frisians before they eventually moved on to cross the channel and conquer England. The Frisians defeated attempts by other Germanic peoples to conquer their territories in the sixth and seventh centuries.

The Salic Franks partially subdued the Frisians in the eighth century and gradually brought the Frisian lands under Frankish control during Charlemagne's reign. Friesland formed the northern portion of the middle kingdom, Lotharingia, at the division of the empire by Charlemagne's heirs in 843. The region passed to the eastern kingdom of Louis the German in 870 and ultimately became a fief of Holland. Subject to Viking raids between the eighth and tenth centuries, the Frisians reverted to their earlier warrior culture, striking fear into their more settled neighbors.

Friesland, along with the Low Countries, passed to the Spanish Hapsburgs and was finally pacified by Spanish troops in 1523. The Frisians joined the United Provinces in 1579, an alliance of the northern Protestant provinces opposed to Catholic Spanish rule. In 1581 the seven northern provinces of the Low Countries formed an independent Dutch kingdom. Friesland retained considerable autonomy, with a separate Frisian stadholder appointed by the Frisian people until 1748, when the Frisian stadholder, William of Orange, became the stadholder of all the Dutch provinces.

Separated from the other provinces by the waters of the Zuider Zee, the isolated Frisians retained their language and culture, which the Frisian parliament jealously guarded. In February 1782 the parliament of Friesland became one of the first official organs of a foreign government to extend recognition to the fledgling United States.

The Dutch language gradually replaced Frisian as the language of government and education in the nineteenth century and became the first language of the growing urban areas. A Frisian national revival, beginning in the 1880s, transformed the Frisian language into a modern literary language and slowly reversed the Frisian assimilation into Dutch culture. Friesland's relative isolation ended with the construction of dikes and a highway linking the peninsula to the Dutch heartland, giving new impetus to the efforts of Frisian cultural and national groups to protect their language and culture.

Intensely loyal to the House of Orange, the Frisians have not developed the militant nationalism of many smaller European nations. Following minor nationalist disturbances in the 1960s and 1970s, the Dutch government moved to defuse rising nationalism by granting broad linguistic and cultural autonomy, with the Frisian language accepted in the local courts, administration, and the Frisian parliament. The use of the Frisian language in radio and television broadcasting increased dramatically. In 1981, with government approval, the teaching of Frisian became obligatory in the province's 600 schools.

The unification of Europe has stimulated some sentiment for independence within a united Europe, but the majority are satisfied with the status quo. The relations between the Frisian minority and the Dutch government, considered the best of its kind in Europe, have attracted attention from other small nations within Europe and beyond. Free of the tensions and quarrels that preoccupy other small European national groups, the Frisian culture has flourished, and nationalist organizations turn their attention to other issues, such as the environment and threats to the Frisian coast and the wildlife of the Frisian tidal flats.

*SELECTED BIBLIOGRAPHY:*

Landheer, Bart. *The Netherlands in a Changing World.* 1947.

Mahood, Cynthia. *Frisian and Free: Study of an Ethnic Minority in the Netherlands.* 1989.

Snyder, Louis L. *Global Mini-Nationalisms: Autonomy or Independence.* 1982.

Tash, Robert C. *Dutch Pluralism: A Model in Tolerance for Developing Countries.* 1990.

# FRIULIA

**Friuli; Friûl**

*CAPITAL: Udin (Udine)*

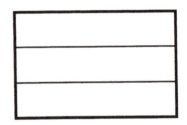

SOUTH-CENTRAL EUROPE

FRIULIA

*POPULATION:* (95e) 1,055,000 : 760,000 Friuli in Italy and another 700,000 in other parts of the world, mostly in the Americas. MAJOR NATIONAL GROUPS: (95e) Friuli 71%, Slovene 11%, Sauri 1%, other Italian. MAJOR LANGUAGES: Furlan, Italian, Zeglian. MAJOR RELIGION: Roman Catholic. MAJOR CITIES: (95e) FRIULIA: Udin (Udine) 96,000 (147,000), Pordenon (Pordenone) 56,000 (90,000), Gurizze (Gorizia) 45,000 (77,000), Monfalcon (Monfalcone) 31,000 (50,000), Codroip (Codroipo) 21,000. VENETO: Puartgruar (Portogruaro) 27,000.

*GEOGRAPHY:* AREA: 3,190 sq.mi.-8,264 sq.km. LOCATION: Friulia occupies a mountainous region in the Carnic Alps and the Julian Alps and the lowlands bordering the Adriatic Sea in northeastern Italy. POLITICAL STATUS: Friulia has no official status; the region forms the Gorizia, Pordenone, and Udine provinces of the Italian region of Friuli-Venezia Giulia and the Portogruaro district of Venezia province of the region of Veneto.*

*FLAG:* The Friuli national flag, the flag of the national movement, has three horizontal stripes of blue, yellow, and blue. OTHER FLAG(S): The traditional Friuli flag is a blue field charged with the Friuli national symbol, a yellow eagle with red beak and claws.

*PEOPLE:* The Friuli are an ancient people thought to predate the Romans. Related to the Romansh people of Grischun* in Switzerland and the Ladins of Ladinia* in northern Italy, the Friuli speak a similar Rhaeto-Romanic language, called Furlan, considerably influenced by the Venetian dialect of Italian. The

Friuli consider the large emigrant population, the Fôgalâr, numbering some 700,000, as an integral part of the nation. A Slovene minority, in the eastern districts, speaks a dialect called Zeglian, a mixture of Slovene and Furlan. A small, related Rhaeto-Romanic people, the Sauri, live in the mountainous north.

*THE NATION:* The Friuli, believed to have inhabited the area north of the Adriatic Sea before the rise of the Etruscans and Romans, originally formed part of the Celtic peoples. Roman rule, established in the coastal plain, extended to all of Friulia in the first century B.C. The Roman culture and language, over centuries, replaced the Celtic language and culture of the region.

Germanic Longobards (Lombards) conquered Friulia in 568, following the collapse of Roman power. Under Lombard rule, Friulia formed a separate duchy, and in 801, called the March of Friuli, the region came under the rule of Charlemagne's Frankish Empire.

In the Middle Ages the Friuli free cities formed a protective league, the union greatly aiding the perpetuation of the separate Friuli language and culture, which flourished during the Renaissance. Divided into two small states, Gorizia in the east and Friulia in the west, more powerful neighboring states gradually absorbed the Friuli lands. In 1420 Venice took Friulia, and in 1500 Gorizia passed to the Austrian Hapsburgs. Reunited under Austrian rule in 1797, Friulia was once again partitioned when western Friulia became part of the new Italian kingdom in 1866.

Subjected to intense government pressure to adopt the Italian language and culture during the nineteenth century, the Friuli mobilized to resist. Friuli opposition to assimilation inspired a national revival in the late nineteenth century. The growth of nationalism led to demands for autonomy within the Italian kingdom, and the unrest spread to the Friuli population of the Austrian crownland of Görz and Gradisca, with its mixed population of Friuli, Slovene, and Austrian inhabitants.

Italy remained neutral when war began in Europe in 1914 but, with Allied inducements, joined the conflict in 1915. Heavy fighting devastated the Friuli districts that formed the fluctuating front lines. Italy lost over 600,000 soldiers before taking Gorizia and eastern Friulia. The Italian government, with Allied approval, annexed the captured regions in 1919 and incorporated them into the province of Friuli-Venezia, which also included Trieste,* Istria,* and a number of enclaves on the Yugoslav coast.

The Italian fascists of Benito Mussolini took control of the Italian government in 1922. The fascist doctrine stressed Italian nationalism and a uniform Italian culture and language. The Friuli minority, their language outlawed, under intense official pressure Italianized all family names and place-names and abandoned the ancient customs and traditions not approved by the authorities. As repression increased, many Friuli fled to sanctuary among the related Romansh people of Grischun* in southeastern Switzerland.

Their homeland again devastated during World War II battles between Italian and Yugoslav forces, the Friuli faced even greater danger from the postwar territorial claims to their region. Communist Yugoslavia laid claim to eastern Friulia, with its large Slovene minority, while Italy claimed Istria, with its Italian and Friuli minorities. A 1947 agreement partitioned the region, with all of eastern Friulia, except Gorizia, assigned to Yugoslavia and the Free Territory of Trieste, with a mixed population, created in the southeast.

The competing national claims to their homeland inspired the growth of modern Friuli nationalism. Demands for autonomy grew after 1954 and the incorporation of the province of Trieste, with its large Italian-speaking population, into the largely Friuli-speaking region to form the new region of Friuli-Venezia Giulia. Protests against Friulia's inclusion in the ''hybrid region'' fueled the spread of national sentiment. In 1963 the Italian government granted the region limited autonomy in recognition of its distinct culture and language.

Dissatisfied with limited autonomy and cultural rights, nationalists formed the Moviment Friül (Friuli Movement) in 1966 as a pressure group to win real political autonomy for Friulia. Affected by the nationalism sweeping all of northern Italy in the late 1980s, the movement became increasingly nationalistic, and a large faction became openly separatist.

In concert with other northern Italian peoples, the Friuli increasingly look to a united Europe as their salvation. Disgusted with Italy's corruption and the huge, inefficient administration, nationalists point to the organized crime that plagues the Italian state and has recently moved into Friulia. Mafia-related crimes in the region increased 300% in 1990–91 alone. The inequities of the bloated Italian bureaucracy infuriate even the most moderate Friuli, who cite examples such as the fifteen men employed to shunt goods wagons at the Udine rail center, while 15,000 do the same work in the southern city of Reggio Calabria.

The independence of Slovenia, on Friulia's eastern border, and the dramatic increase of regional and national movements across northern Italy have fueled Friuli demands for greater independence and recognition as a separate European people. In 1992 over 100,000 Friuli signed a petition calling for separation from Friuli-Venezia Giulia and the creation of a separate Friuli region. In local elections, in June 1992, Friuli nationalists, supported by the Northern League, a grouping of northern Italian regional and national organizations, became the largest political order in the Friuli region.

*SELECTED BIBLIOGRAPHY:*
Cunsolo, Ronald S. *Italian Nationalism from Its Origins to World War II.* 1990.
Facaros, Dane, and Michael Pauls. *Northeast Italy.* 1990.
Grindrod, Muriel. *The Rebuilding of Italy.* 1955.
Smith, Denis M. *The Making of Italy 1796–1870.* 1988.

# GAGAUZIA

### Gagauz Khalki

*CAPITAL: Komrat (Comrat)*

SOUTHEASTERN EUROPE

GAGAUZIA

*POPULATION:* (95e) 244,000 : 179,000 Gagauz in Moldova and another 35,000 in adjacent areas of Ukraine. MAJOR NATIONAL GROUPS: (95e) Gagauz 71%, Moldovan 20%, Russian 7%, Ukrainian 2%. MAJOR LANGUAGES: Gagauz, Russian, Romanian. MAJOR RELIGIONS: Russian Orthodox, Moldovan (Romanian) Orthodox. MAJOR CITIES: (95e) Kagul (Cagul) 45,000, Komrat (Comrat) 35,000, Chadyr-Lunga 27,000, Tarakliya 18,000.

*GEOGRAPHY:* AREA: 1,320 sq.mi.-3,419 sq.km. LOCATION: Gagauzia occupies the valleys of the Prut and Jalpug Rivers south of the Roman fortification called Upper Trajan's Wall in southeastern Moldova. Gagauzia borders Romania on the west and Ukraine on the east. POLITICAL STATUS: Gagauzia forms an autonomous republic comprising the districts of Chadyr-Lunga, Cagul, Canguz, Comrat, Tarakliya, Vulkanechti, and Yagara of the Republic of Moldova.

*INDEPENDENCE DECLARED:* 19 January 1906.

*FLAG:* The Gagauz national flag, the flag of the national movement, is a light blue field bearing a centered yellow disc charged with a black wolf's head.

*PEOPLE:* The Gagauz are a people thought to be of Bulgarian or unknown origin, although culturally and linguistically the Gagauz are a Turkic people. Their language is a Turkish dialect with substantial Russian and Romanian borrowings. Wine production, the major economic activity, is closely tied to the Gagauz culture, which revolves around the yearly growing and production periods. The small nation, divided in 1945 when the eastern district of their territory was transferred to Ukraine, has developed a strong sense of its separate identity. The Gagauz, unlike the Muslim Turks, are overwhelmingly Orthodox Christian.

*THE NATION:* The ancestors of the Gagauz, a tribe called the Kay-Ka'us, formed a small state in the Dobruja region of northeastern Bulgaria in 1296, with its capital at Karvuna (Kavarna). In the thirteenth century the Kay-Ka'us converted to the Orthodox Christianity brought to their state by Bulgarian monks. Conquered by the Ottoman Turks in 1398, the people, called Gagauz by the Turks, adopted the Turkish language and culture but refused to abandon Christianity for the Turks' Islamic religion.

The Gagauz, over the next centuries, lived as a despised minority, persecuted by the Turks for their refusal to accept Islam and by the neighboring Bulgars for their Turkish speech. In the eighteenth century the Gagauz fled a concerted Turkish attempt to force their conversion to Islam. The refugees moved north in small groups. The first Gagauz arrived in the contested region of Bessarabia in 1750. The region, ceded to Russia by Turkey in 1812, was opened to immigration in an effort to dilute the Romanian majority. The remainder of the Gagauz refugees settled in Russian Bessarabia between 1812 and 1846.

The small nation, reunited in its new homeland, experienced a dramatic revival of its culture and religion. A nationalist movement developed as tsarist rule became progressively onerous, with intense pressure on the Orthodox Gagauz to assimilate. Although the small Christian nation had always looked on the Christian Russians as protectors, in 1848 the Gagauz rebelled. Cossacks, sent against the rebels, ended the rebellion with great brutality.

Serious disturbances broke out during the 1905 Russian Revolution but gradually quieted after concessions and promises of increased rights. In December 1905, their authority restored, the local tsarist authorities moved to punish the disturbances, setting off a widespread Gagauz uprising. The rebels drove all tsarist officials from the region and formed a provisional government. On 19 January 1906 the Gagauz leaders declared an independent Gagauz republic. A Gagauz militia resisted attacks by Cossacks and Russian police for two weeks but finally succumbed. Continuing discontent and reprisals meted out by the returning tsarist officials fueled a renewed rebellion in March and April 1907.

The Gagauz homeland, with Bessarabia, passed to Romanian rule after the Russian Revolution, only to revert to Soviet domination in 1940 and to come under renewed Romanian rule from 1941 to the Soviet reconquest near the end of World War II, in 1944. The Gagauz, too weak to resist but refusing to assimilate to either Russian or Romanian culture, withdrew into isolation, preferring to tend their prosperous vineyards and farms while leaving the painful issue of politics to others.

A cultural revival, begun in 1982 by a few young intellectuals, rapidly took on nationalist overtones in 1988 in response to edicts issued by the increasingly nationalistic authorities of Soviet Moldavia. Already obliged to learn Russian, the Gagauz rejected a 1989 language law that would oblige them to learn yet another language, Moldavian (Romanian). The language issue provoked a torrent of grievances and fueled the growth of the national movement.

A national congress in May 1989 demanded autonomy for the seven Gagauz districts. Ignored by the Moldavian authorities, the Gagauz leaders unilaterally declared the region an autonomous republic in November. In October the Moldavian authorities, during the October 1990 elections, moved to disband the Gagauz government and to retake control of the Gagauz districts, setting off a severe nationalist crisis in the region. The Gagauz nationalists, successful in the local elections, proclaimed Gagauz independent of Moldavia, but not of the Soviet Union, on 11 August 1990.

Soviet Moldavia, renamed the Republic of Moldova, became independent following the collapse of the Soviet Union in August 1991. The Moldovan authorities attempted to end the Gagauz secession and to bring the region under the authority of the new republican government. Fearing the ethnic violence that had broken out in a number of former Soviet republics the Gagauz accepted a March 1992 offer of autonomy within Moldova, but with the stipulation that should Moldova decide to reunite with neighboring Romania, Gagauzia would be allowed to secede peacefully.

The Gagauz nationalists carefully monitor the events taking place in Moldova that will affect the future of their nation. In January 1993 the Moldovan parliament narrowly rejected a proposal to hold a nationwide referendum on reunification with Romania. In elections, held in early 1994, the Moldovan nationalists won greater support than those favoring Romania, which aided relations between the Gagauz and the Moldovan government. In May 1994 Moldova's draft constitution provided for a special legal status and for broad powers of self-government for the Gagauz republic.

*SELECTED BIBLIOGRAPHY:*

Colton, Timothy, and Robert Levgold, eds. *After the Soviet Union.* 1992.

Dima, Nicholas. *Bessarabia and Bukovina: The Soviet-Romanian Territorial Dispute.* 1982.

Dins, Shams. *Perestroika and the Nationalities Quest in the USSR.* 1991.

Jewsbury, George F. *The Russian Annexation of Bessarabia.* 1976.

# GALICIA

**Galiza**

*CAPITAL: Santiago de Compostela*

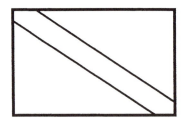

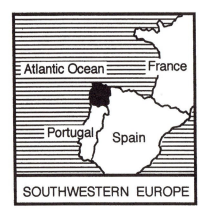

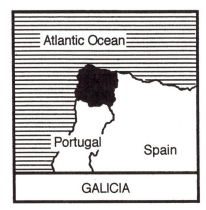

*POPULATION:* (95e) 2,953,000 : 3,434,000 Galicians in Spain. MAJOR NATIONAL GROUPS: (95e) Galician (Galego) 94%, Portuguese 2%, other Spanish. MAJOR LANGUAGES: Galician (Galego), Spanish, Portuguese. MAJOR RELIGION: Roman Catholic. MAJOR CITIES: (95e) Vigo 296,000 (353,000), A Coruña (La Coruña) 264,000 (283,000), Narón (El Ferrol) 89,000 (140,000), Ourense (Orense) 88,000 (102,000), Lugo 87,000 (99,000), Santiago de Compostela 82,000 (125,000), Pontevedra 30,000 (78,000).

*GEOGRAPHY:* AREA: 11,256 sq.mi.-29,160 sq.km. LOCATION: Galicia occupies the mountainous northwestern corner of the Iberian Peninsula, just north of Portugal. The region has a rugged coastline on the Atlantic Ocean on the west and on the Bay of Biscay on the north. POLITICAL STATUS: Galicia forms an autonomous region of the Kingdom of Spain.

*FLAG:* The Galician national flag, the official flag of the region, is a white field crossed by a diagonal stripe of pale blue, upper hoist to lower fly. OTHER FLAG(S): The Galician national flag, with the addition of a centered, five-pointed red star, is the banner of the Galician national movement. n

*PEOPLE:* Named for the Celtic Gallaeci, the Galicians are the descendants of early Celts and later Germanic Visigoths and are the only Iberian people not of Latin origin. The Galician language is a Romance language more closely related to Portuguese than to Castilian Spanish and is spoken in four major dialects corresponding to the region's four provinces. The Galicians have retained much of their Celtic heritage, including bagpipes and a high incidence of fair hair and light eyes. Most Galicians are Roman Catholics, and their capital,

Santiago de Compostela, is one of the great Catholic pilgrimage centers of Europe.

*THE NATION:* The Celtic Gallaeci, conquered by the Romans in the first century A.D., mostly adopted the Romans' Latin language and culture. Germanic Suevi overran the Latinized region with the decline of Roman power and established a separate Suevi kingdom in A.D. 411. The Suevi kingdom fell to the invading Visigoths in 585, and a substantial Germanic population eventually settled in the region.

The Gothic kingdom fell to the Muslim Moors in 711–12. Many Goths took refuge in the mountains, where they formed the Christian kingdom of Asturias and eventually led the reconquest of Galicia from the Moors. The areas reclaimed from the Moors united with the kingdom of Leon in 866, Leon, in turn, uniting with the kingdom of Castile, newly liberated from Moorish rule, in 1037.

A unique medieval culture developed in Galicia, uniting Celtic, Germanic, Latin, and Iberian elements. The Galician language, originally a dialect of Portuguese, diverged in the fourteenth century to become the foremost literary language of the Iberian Peninsula. The devoutly Roman Catholic Galicians, the caretakers of the important medieval shrine of St. James at Santiago de Compostela, maintained contact with all of Europe through a constant stream of religious pilgrims visiting the shrine.

Opposition to the centralizing tendencies of the Castilian kingdom prodded the Galicians to follow the Portuguese in an attempt to leave the Spanish kingdom in 1640. Crushed by Castilian troops, the Galicians embarked on a long cultural and economic decline. By the eighteenth century the Galician language had degenerated to a peasant dialect, and the upper classes had adopted Castilian speech and culture. The Galician tradition of splitting lands among heirs resulted in a backward, fragmented agriculture that forced many to emigrate, mostly to South America.

The region's severe economic problems, mostly blamed on the highly centralized government in Madrid, provoked widespread resentment, and a movement to revive the Galician culture and nation in the 1880s and 1890s. In 1931 the Galicians demanded autonomy from Spain's new republican government, and in 1932 they established a Galician parliament and pressed for greater linguistic autonomy. Serious nationalist demonstrations rocked the region between 1932 and 1936, the nationalist resurgence overtaken by the outbreak of the Spanish civil war.

The leader of the rebel fascist forces, Francisco Franco, born in El Ferrol, looked to his native Galicia for support, but the majority of his countrymen joined the antifascist forces. Following Franco's 1939 victory, the Galicians suffered punishments, their culture suppressed and edicts issued forbidding the speaking, teaching, or publishing of the Galician language. Only one book was published in the Galician language between 1936 and 1945.

The Galician culture and language began to revive in the 1950s, despite the official restrictions. Publishing began tentatively with poetry, and later publications included fiction, the sciences, philosophy, and economics. The post-war revival increased friction with the Franco authorities and spurred the growth of Galician nationalism. Openly nationalist organizations in the 1960s gained support in the region, which had benefited little from the modernization of Spain.

In early 1975 nationalist sentiment exploded with an outbreak of violence and demonstrations. Nationalist organizations called for immediate independence. In August 1975 the elderly Franco unleashed a reign of terror accompanied by mass arrests, unexplained deaths and disappearances, and widespread torture. Franco's death in November 1975 brought an end to the terror as liberated Spain rapidly embraced democracy under a restored Borbon monarchy.

Granted autonomy in 1980, Galicia experienced a dramatic cultural and na-tional revival, and in the late 1980s 90% of the Galician population spoke the Galician language. Growing ties to other Celtic nations in France and the United Kingdom have resulted in cultural exchanges and strong support for the Gali-cians' campaign to win greater freedom. Small, militant nationalist groups turned to violence in 1988, even though the majority of the conservative Galicians support the more moderate nationalist policies that they hope will eventually establish their small nation within a united, democratic Europe.

*SELECTED BIBLIOGRAPHY:*

Coyle, Dominick J. *Minorities in Revolt.* 1982.

Lancaster, Thomas D. *Politics and Change in Spain.* 1985.

Way, Ruth, and Margaret Simmons. *A Geography of Spain and Portugal.* 1962.

Wilgram, E. *Northern Spain.* 1976.

# GERALIA

**Pampas; Southern Brazil**

*CAPITAL: Porto Alegre*

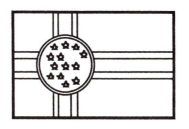

*POPULATION:* (95e) 25,396,000 : 22,500,000 Geralians in Brazil. MAJOR NATIONAL GROUPS: (95e) Geralian 87%, other Brazilian. MAJOR LANGUAGES: Portuguese, Italian, Spanish, German, Japanese. MAJOR RELIGIONS: Roman Catholic, Protestant, Jewish. MAJOR CITIES: (95e) Porto Alegre 1,516,000 (3,556,000), Curitiba 1,423,000 (2,344,000), Londrina 436,000, Pelotas 354,000, Santa Maria 334,000, Caxias do Sul 331,000, Canoas 327,000, Joinville 281,000 (409,000), Rio Grande 237,000, Ponta Grossa 222,000, Maringa 216,000, Passo Fundo 210,000, Florianopolis 175,000 (316,000), Sao Leopoldo 188,000, Bagé 186,000, Nova Hamburgo 179,000, Blumenau 174,000, Cascavel 131,000, Lajes 126,000, Uruguaiana 109,000 (188,000), Paranaguà 107,000, Itajai 106,000, Apucarana 88,000 (172,000), Santa Ana do Livramento 73,000 (140,000), Tubaro 75,000 (123,000), Arapongas 64,000 (138,000).

*GEOGRAPHY:* AREA: 223,059 sq.mi.-577,873 sq.km. LOCATION: Geralia occupies the flat plains called the pampas in southern Brazil. The region, bounded by the coastal mountains, the Serra do Mar and the Serra Geral, borders the Atlantic Ocean on the east, Uruguay on the south, and Argentina on the west. POLITICAL STATUS: Geralia has no official status; the region forms the Southern Region of Brazil, comprising the states of Parana, Santa Catarina, and Rio Grande do Sul.

*INDEPENDENCE DECLARED:* 8 September 1892.

*FLAG:* The Geralian national flag, the flag of the national movement, is a red field bearing a black cross, outlined in yellow, behind a blue disc, outlined in yellow, charged with thirteen small, white, five-pointed stars.

*PEOPLE:* The Geralians, also known as Gauchos after the legendary cowboys of the pampas, are mostly the descendants of nineteenth- and early twentieth-century immigrants. The Geralians, unique in Brazil, have retained a basically European culture and their original languages, widely used as second languages. The European-influenced Geralian culture has not assimilated into the Brazilian culture, with its roots in the north of the country. The Geralian population has expanded in this century without losing population at the center, an unusual phenomenon in Latin America. Largely middle-class and urbanized, the average Geralian's standard of living and way of life are remarkably similar to those in Europe and North America. The majority are Roman Catholic, with an important Protestant minority and smaller Jewish and Buddhist minorities.

*THE NATION:* The original inhabitants, small Tupi-Guarani tribes, had virtually disappeared under the impact of colonization by the seventeenth century. European settlers, moving south from the Portuguese colonies and north from the Spanish colonies, began to settle the grasslands, the pampas, in the late seventeenth century. Organized in a captaincy, the equivalent of a feudal principality, Portugal's rival in the New World, Spain, recognized the Geralian colonies as Portuguese territory in 1790.

Small numbers of European immigrants, Italians, Germans, Portuguese, and Spanish, settled the coastal districts in the early nineteenth century. Rejecting Brazil's prevalent slavery and plantation agriculture, the immigrants settled on small family farms in the European manner. Gradually expanding into the virgin lands of the pampas, the immigrants created farms, towns, and cities remarkably similar to those left behind in their European homelands. Feeling little affinity with the culturally and economically separate north, the Geralians attempted to take the pampas provinces out of Brazil in 1835, setting off an ultimately unsuccessful ten-year war.

European immigration to the region accelerated after the revolutionary upheavals that swept Europe in 1848, becoming a flood after 1870. Immigrants poured into the Geralian region of Brazil from every country in Europe, Japan, and Lebanon. By 1900 over 5 million immigrants had settled in the three southern states, including 1 million Italians and over 400,000 Germans.

The centralization of Brazilian government in the 1880s ended the traditional autonomy of the states and provoked widespread resistance in the southern states. In 1892 the Gauchos of Rio Grande do Sul rebelled, and the rebel leaders declared the state independent of Brazil on 8 September 1892. As the other southern states moved toward secession, federal troops invaded. The rebels finally surrendered in 1894.

Rebellion again spread across the southern states in 1930. In what was called the Great Southern Revolt, the rebels followed the governor of Rio Grande do Sul, Getulio Vargas, who finally overthrew the Brazilian government and installed himself as Brazil's new president. His authoritarian rule incited a renewed revolt in the three southern states that continued sporadically until 1937.

The Geralians began to expand outward from the original settlements after

World War II, but without losing population at the center, a demographic rarity in Latin America. New interior settlements included Maringa, founded in 1947, which had grown into a city of over 50,000 inhabitants by 1960 and by 1990 had become a metropolis of over 200,000, with wide boulevards and soaring skyscrapers.

Decades of dictatorship and government mismanagement pushed the three Geralian states to establish close economic and political cooperation in the 1960s. An influx of landless peasants from Brazil's poor and backward northeast kindled a strong Geralian reaction. A cultural revival, emphasizing the region's unique history, spawned the growth of nationalist and anti-immigrant groups. The more radical of the groups advocated restrictions on internal immigration and even the forced repatriation of the poor, culturally distinct migrants.

Brazil's return to democracy in 1985, greeted with tremendous enthusiasm, has disappointed the Geralians. Hope soon gave way to despair as Brazil's severe economic and social problems continue to multiply. The dream of an advanced, prosperous twenty-first century Brazil, the one dream shared by all Brazilians, has rapidly disappeared.

In the southern states the dream has largely given way to strong regionalist sentiment and a growing separatist movement. Citing neighboring Uruguay, historically and ethnically similar, and with the continent's highest gross national income, achieved without Geralia's impressive resources, the nationalists in 1990 advanced a plan for an independent Republic of the Pampas. A poll of the inhabitants of the Geralian states in December 1991 showed overwhelming support for some form of economic and political autonomy. Two-fifths of those polled favored complete independence.

The dramatic decline in the region's living standards that has accompanied Brazil's grave economic problems and hyperinflation is destroying the social order that lasted only as long as hope for a united Brazil's future was sustainable. The nationalists, dismissed as a fringe group just a decade ago, gain support with each new Brazilian crisis.

*SELECTED BIBLIOGRAPHY:*
Bruce, J. *Brazil and the Brazilians.* 1976.
Lubbock, John. *Notes on Rio de Janeiro and the Southern Parts of Brazil.* 1976.
Saunders, John V. *Modern Brazil: New Patterns and Development.* 1971.

# GIBRALTAR

Calpe

*CAPITAL: Gibraltar (Calpe)*

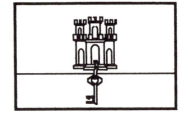

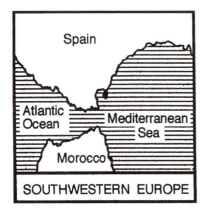

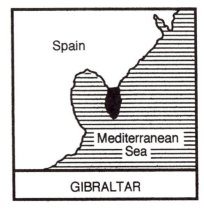

*POPULATION:* (95e) 29,500 : 35,000 Gibraltarians in Gibraltar and the United Kingdom. MAJOR NATIONAL GROUPS: (95e) Gibraltarian 68.5%, other British, Spanish, Moroccan. MAJOR LANGUAGES: English, Spanish. MAJOR RELIGIONS: (95e) Roman Catholic 75%, Protestant 8%, Sunni Muslim 6%, Jewish 2%. MAJOR CITY: (95e) Gibraltar (Calpe) 29,500.

*GEOGRAPHY:* AREA: 2.3 sq.mi.-6 sq.km. LOCATION: Gibraltar lies in southwestern Europe, a peninsula 2.5 miles long surrounding the Rock of Gibraltar, an enclave on Spain's southern coast at the western entrance to the Mediterranean Sea. POLITICAL STATUS: Gibraltar is a self-governing British colony.

*FLAG:* The Gibraltarian flag is a horizontal bicolor of white over red, proportions two by one, charged with the red, three-towered castle of Gibraltar, from which is suspended a golden key.

*PEOPLE:* The Gibraltarians are a European people of mixed Italian, Maltese, British, Spanish, and Portuguese background, the ethnic divisions blurred by extensive intermarriage. The majority speak English, along with a variant of Andalusian Spanish called Yanito. National self-awareness, a recent phenomenon, is based on Gibraltar's unique history and culture, a blend of British and Mediterranean traditions. The majority of the Gibraltarians are Roman Catholic, with important Protestant, Muslim, and Jewish minorities.

*THE NATION:* The two promontories at the eastern end of the Strait of Gibraltar, the Rock of Gibraltar and Jebel Musa at Ceuta in Africa, known in ancient times as the Pillars of Hercules, were long believed to mark the edge of the world. The peninsula, guarding the entrance to the Mediterranean and the short-est route from North Africa to Europe, has attracted conquerors since boats first ventured into the Mediterranean Sea.

Gibraltar's name is derived from Jebel-al-Tarik, the Mountain of Tarik, named for the Moorish leader who crossed from Africa to capture southern Spain in 711. Fortified by the Moors, Gibraltar served as the southern defense of the opulent Muslim state of Al-Andalus, later called Andalusia by the Spaniards.

The Spanish, during the Christian reconquest of Spain, took the citadel in 1462. Taken by British and Dutch troops participating in the War of the Spanish Succession in 1704, the peninsula was confirmed a British possession in 1713. A heavily fortified British naval base, Gibraltar was several times besieged by Spanish forces.

Designated a Crown colony in 1830, the impregnable fortress, Britain's major Mediterranean military base, developed a flourishing trade that attracted immi-grants from Italy, Malta, and other parts of Mediterranean Europe. Numerous caverns and galleries, extending two to three miles in length and of sufficient width for vehicles, were cut through solid rock, providing sheltered communi-cations from one part of the garrison to another. The citadel and naval base protected Allied shipping during both world wars.

Spain sought to regain control of the peninsula, considered an integral part of the Spanish state, after World War II. Despite Spain's protests that the move contravened the 1713 Treaty of Utrecht, Britain granted autonomy to Gibraltar in 1964, giving the Gibraltarians their own elected government and control of the colony's booming economy. The British government refused to cede the colony to Spain against the wishes of the inhabitants. In 1967 the authorities agreed to a referendum, but only 44 out of the 12,762 voters chose Spain and the Franco dictatorship.

A new constitution, in 1969, created a Gibraltarian legislature with substantial powers. In retaliation the Spanish government closed the border and forbade Spanish citizens to cross to jobs in the colony. As the colony was almost wholly dependent on the Spanish mainland for food, the blockade forced the British authorities to mount an extensive program to provision the colony by sea and air. The blockade hardened the inhabitant's attitude to Spanish claims.

Spain's return to democracy in 1975 decreased tensions, and the border re-opened to foot traffic in 1983 and to vehicles in 1985. Following Spain's entry into the European Economic Community in 1986, the Spanish government again raised the question of sovereignty. In 1988 the Gibraltarians again voted to retain their ties to the United Kingdom.

Rising prosperity, based on banking and trade, has given the colony's inhab-itants new confidence. The results of an August 1991 poll showed a majority desire to be known as Gibraltarians, a separate European people. For the first time the poll showed majority support for independence, with support for re-taining ties to Britain at 47%, down from 62% in 1988. In late 1991 the British government confirmed Gibraltar's right to independence, the only hindrance being Spain's continuing territorial claims to the Rock.

*SELECTED BIBLIOGRAPHY:*

Jackson, William G. *The Rock of the Gibraltarians.* 1988.

Lutz, William. *Gibraltar.* 1987.

Shields, Graham J. *Gibraltar.* 1987.

# GILAN

**Ghilan; Guilan**

*CAPITAL: Resht (Rasht)*

SOUTHWESTERN ASIA

GILAN

*POPULATION:* (95e) 4,619,000 : 3,500,000 Gilaki in Iran. MAJOR NA-
TIONAL GROUPS: (95e) Gilaki 74%, Azeri 10%, Kurd 6%, Mazandarani 5%,
Tatar 2%, other Iranian. MAJOR LANGUAGES: Gilaki, Farsi, Azeri, Kurdish.
MAJOR RELIGIONS: Shia Muslim, Sunni Muslim. MAJOR CITIES: (95e)
Resht (Rasht) 418,000 (773,000), Zenjan (Zanjan) 339,000, Enzeli (Bandar e-
Anzali) 143,000, Lahijan 105,000, Astara 84,000 (145,000), Abhar 79,000, Lan-
garud 75,000, Rud Sar 63,000, Hashtpar 50,000.

*GEOGRAPHY:* AREA: 14,115 sq.mi.-36,567 sq.km. LOCATION: Gilan lies
on the south shore of the Caspian Sea in northwestern Iran, a heavily forested
plateau separated from the coastal plains by the Elburz and Talish mountain
ranges. POLITICAL STATUS: Gilan forms a province of the Islamic Republic
of Iran, including the Zanjan Governorate in the southwest.

*INDEPENDENCE DECLARED:* 20 May 1920.

*FLAG:* The Gilaki national flag, the flag of the largest national organization,
the Hizb-i Jangali (Jungle Party), is a green field bearing a white crescent moon
and six-pointed star on the upper hoist.

*PEOPLE:* The Gilaki are an Iranian people of mixed Caucasian, Turkic, and
Persian background, speaking a West Iranian language of the Indo-Iranian language group that shows a marked Turkic admixture. Gilaki culture, incorporating Iranian and Turkic elements, includes a distinctive cuisine, literature, and
architecture. The majority of the Gilaki are Shia Muslims, the official sect of
Iran, with a large Sunni Muslim minority. Non-Gilaki populations include the

Azeris and Kurds, mostly in the Zanjan region, Iranians and Tatars in the urban areas, and Mazandaranis in the east.

*THE NATION:* Nomadic Caucasian tribes, as early as 1500 B.C., migrated south to settle the fertile plains and marshlands along the Caspian Sea. By the sixth century B.C. the region formed a satrapy (province) of the ancient Persian Empire. Conquered by the Greeks of Alexander the Great in 334–331 B.C., the region later formed part of the Greek province of Media Atrophene. In the second century B.C. the Persians reconquered the Caspian region.

Included in the Muslim Empire, the Caliphate, following the Arab conquest of A.D. 641, the majority of the Gilaki converted to the new religion. From the tenth century Gilan formed part of the newly established linguistic frontier between the Turkic and Iranian peoples. After conquest by Turkic peoples, the Gilaki culture and language absorbed many Turkic borrowings from the region's Turkic rulers. Devastated by the Mongols in the thirteenth century and by the forces of Tamerlane a century later, Gilan had declined to a poor, backward region when the Persians regained control of the Caspian provinces in 1592.

English traders, moving south from Russia, reached Gilan in the late sixteenth century and opened trade routes to the west. Russian explorers and Cossacks, spearheading the Russian expansion into the Turkish and Persian lands, soon followed. Cossacks overran Gilan in 1636 and caused considerable damage before withdrawing. In 1722 the Russians took Gilan from Persia and held the region for ten years, finally returning the region to Persia in exchange for territorial concessions in the Caucasus.

Silk production, introduced in the Middle Ages, flourished in the nineteenth century and accounted for most of Persia's silk exports. Influenced by British and Russian silk traders, Gilan began to modernize in the 1880s and 1890s. Over the next decades the region advanced more rapidly than the rest of decadent, feudal Persia.

Opposition to the excesses and neglect of the Persian monarchy erupted in open rebellion in 1905. Led by discontented farmers, the Gilaki formed guerrilla groups called Jangli, the rebels known as Jangali (Men of the Jungle) for the dense forests that gave them refuge. A British-Russian agreement signed in 1907 divided the weak Persian state into spheres of influence. In 1909 Russian troops crushed the Gilaki rebellion, which reformed as an anti-Russian movement in 1912. In 1917, with their country collapsing in revolution, the Russian troops withdrew from Gilan.

The Gilaki rebels, called the ''Robin Hoods of the Caspian Marshes'' for their generosity to the poor, demanded autonomy and assistance to farmers from the returning Persian administration in 1918. Their appeals rebuffed, the Gilaki resumed the rebellion. Rebels later clashed with British troops landed to counter a growing Soviet threat to the region in 1920.

The rebellion, joined by Azeris, Kurds, and Armenians, spread across Persia's northwestern provinces. A Soviet force in May 1920 invaded the region in support of the rebels, and with Soviet military assistance the Gilaki rebels dislodged the British from their base at Enzeli on 19 May. The next day the Gilaki leader, Kuchek Khan, declared the independence of the Persian Soviet Socialist Republic of Gilan. A separatist government of northern Communists and Gilaki rebels began to redistribute lands traditionally held by absentee Persian landlords, religious bodies, the Persian state, and the Crown.

A 1921 revolution in Tehran installed a new Persian dynasty, the Pahlevi. Faced with a large rebel force preparing to march on Tehran, the Iranian government hastily granted generous oil concessions to the new Soviet state in exchange for the withdrawal of the Red Army from Gilan and the northwest. Imperial troops then invaded the breakaway state in December 1921. The head of the captured Gilaki leader, Kuchek Khan, was displayed in Tehran to prove to all that the long Jangali rebellion had finally ended.

Rapid post–World War II modernization transformed Gilan, economic advances financed by the growth of tourism to the plush Caspian Sea resorts. Greater prosperity incited new appeals for regional autonomy and resulted in a brutal crackdown by the feared secret police in 1975. Most Gilaki supported the revolution that overthrew the hated monarchy in 1979. Soon disappointed by the installation of an even more repressive Islamic government, the Gilaki rebelled. With widespread support, particularly among Gilan's modern, liberated women, the Jangli were revived to fight the new government. The Gilaki rebellion ended with mass executions and the imposition of a dictatorship of strict Islamic law.

Terrorized by officious government gangs for over a decade, Gilaki national sentiment revived after the government's poor response to a severe earthquake that devastated the region in June 1990. Gilaki nationalism, still an underground movement, drew new support following the breakup of the Soviet Union in 1991 and the establishment of new national states where oppressed provinces had formerly existed.

*SELECTED BIBLIOGRAPHY:*

Cottam, Richard W. *Nationalism in Iran: Updated through 1978.* 1979.
Lenczowski, George. *Russia and the West in Iran 1918–1948: A Study in Big Power Rivalry.* 1968.
Sivan, Emmanud. *Radical Islam.* 1987.
Tapper, Richard, ed. *The Conflict of Tribe and State in Iran and Afghanistan.* 1983.

# GORKHALAND

Gurkhaland

*CAPITAL: Darjeeling*

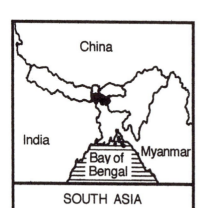

*POPULATION:* (95e) 5,935,000 : 6,345,000 Gorkhas in India. MAJOR NATIONAL GROUPS: (95e) Gorkha (Gurkha) 82%, other Indian. MAJOR LANGUAGES: Gorkhali (Khas), Bengali, English. MAJOR RELIGIONS: Hindu, Buddhist. MAJOR CITIES: (95e) Siliguri 182,000, Cooch Behar 101,000 (122,000), Jalpaiguri 87,000 (158,000), Darjeeling 82,000, Alipur Duar 77,000 (123,000), Kalimpong 64,000, Dhupgari 58,000, Dinhata 50,000.

*GEOGRAPHY:* AREA: 4,888 sq.mi.-12,663 sq.km. LOCATION: Gorkhaland occupies a highland region in northeastern India that is connected to the Indian heartland by a narrow, twelve-mile corridor between Nepal and Bangladesh. POLITICAL STATUS: Gorkhaland forms a semiautonomous region with its own government, the Darjeeling Hill Development Council, comprising the districts of Darjeeling, Jalpaiguri, and Cooch Behar of India's West Bengal State.

*FLAG:* The Gorkha national flag, the flag of the national movement, is a green field with four narrow, horizontal yellow stripes at the bottom and bearing a yellow *kukri*, a Gorkha knife, on the fly and three yellow, five-pointed stars on the hoist.

*PEOPLE:* The Gorkhas, popularly called Gurkhas, are the descendants of Magar and Gurung immigrants from western Nepal. The ethnic term Gurkha, first used by the British, is now applied to all of the Gorkhali-speaking peoples in northeastern India. The language, a Rajastani dialect of the West Indic group of Indo-Aryan languages, incorporates many borrowings from the Tibeto-Burman languages of the region's original Buddhist inhabitants. There is a continuing controversy over whether the name Gorkha or Gurkha is an ethnic or a political designation.

*THE NATION:* Rajput warriors, driven from western India, conquered the small Nepalese state of Gurkha in the sixteenth century. Over the next two centuries they extended their rule over much of present Nepal, and in 1791 they invaded Tibet.* Raiding south into British territory, the fierce Gurkha warriors threatened Britain's hold on the Himalayan foothills.

The British authorities sent an expedition against the raiders, provoking the Gurkha War of 1814–16. The ferocity of the Gurkhas greatly impressed the British officers, whose forces were mauled in two separate campaigns. In 1815 the British overran many of the Gurkha hill forts, and the next year the Gurkha defenders sued for peace. The war established a strong British influence in Nepal and the Himalayas. In 1816 the British military formed the first Gurkha units within the colonial Indian army.

The British forced Sikkim* to cede the Darjeeling region in 1835 and to cede further territories in the foothills in 1849. The town of Darjeeling, in the cool highlands, soon became a favorite resort of the British colonials of Calcutta and the humid lowlands. Encouraged by the colonial administration, migrants from western Nepal settled in the uplands to work in the important British tea industry. The British called the Nepalese migrants Gurkhas, no matter their ethnic or cultural origins.

The Gurkha military units served with distinction in many parts of India although their use by the British provoked ethnic animosities that continue to the present. When the First World War began in 1914, the British shipped thousands of Gurkha troops to the European theater. Over 20,000 Gurkhas died in the campaigns in France, Gallipoli, Suez, and Mesopotamia. British military pay and pensions became the prime source of income for the Gurkha peoples of Nepal and northeastern India. In India the peoples called Gurkha by the British began to call themselves Gorkha and slowly began to unite as a separate people.

Independent India, from 1947, also recruited Gurkha units, mainly from the large immigrant population that moved into northern West Bengal State in the 1950s and 1960s. Despite their loyal service to the British and Indian armies, ethnic tensions grew in the northeast between the Gorkhas and the ethnic Bengalis, called Kala Log (Black Folk) in the Gorkhali language. Responding to Bengali demands, the Indian government moved to restrict further immigration from Nepal in the 1970s.

The expulsion of some 10,000 ethnic Gorkhas from the state of Meghalaya* during an anti-immigrant campaign in 1986 sparked a Gorkha rebellion that rapidly spread across northern West Bengal. The rebels formed the Gorkha National Liberation Front (GNLF) under an ex-soldier, Subash Ghising, and demanded the creation of a separate Gorkha state within India. Their demands punctuated by strikes and mass demonstrations in the summer of 1986, the Gorkhas' attitudes polarized following a number of deaths in violent clashes with Bengali police. Over 80,000 Gorkha tea plantation workers refused to harvest the valuable crop as the separatist violence spread.

The appeals and petitions for separation from West Bengal ignored or rejected, Gorkha nationalists began to advocate the creation of a "Greater Gorkhaland" to encompass the Gorkha-populated areas of West Bengal, Sikkim,* Bhutan, and Assam,* a sovereign state independent of both India and Nepal. Claiming the support of over 40,000 ex-soldiers, the Gorkhas threatened to escalate the conflict if attacks by Bengalis continued.

Indian troops, dispatched by the federal government, occupied the tea plantations in 1987 and moved on to the main separatist centers in Darjeeling and Kalimpong over the objections of the Communist-dominated West Bengal government. The rebels accepted an offer of negotiations, and an autonomy agreement, reached in July 1988, provided for a semiautonomous hill council to take over the local administration from the West Bengali authorities. Elections to the new body, won by the GNLF, split the nationalist movement. The more militant groups threatened a terrorist campaign in support of full independence.

The increasingly authoritarian West Bengal government, stifling dissent with violence and the confiscation of the property of the offenders, inadvertently rekindled the separatist movement in 1990. The Gorkha majority renewed its demands for separation from West Bengal while a vocal minority again called for independence. In return for dropping territorial claims to western Assam,* the militants reportedly are receiving arms and training from the Assamese separatists.

The nationalists, increasingly militant, called a boycott of district elections in August 1993. Only 20% of those eligible voted in the elections, so the nationalists see the Communist-dominated district councils as illegal. The nationalists have refused to consider new elections until their demands for separation and autonomy are met. The Gorkha nationalists have become yet another ethnic threat to India's control of the turbulent northeastern states.

SELECTED BIBLIOGRAPHY:

Farwell, Byron. *Gurkhas.* 1990.
Karotempral, S., ed. *The Tribes of Northeast India.* 1984.
Tuker, F.I.S. *Gorkha.* 1957.
Vajpeyi, Dhirendra, and Yogenda Malik, eds. *Religious and Ethnic Minorities in South Asia.* 1990.

# GRISCHUN

**Graubünden; Grisons; Rhaetia**

*CAPITAL: Cuera (Chur)*

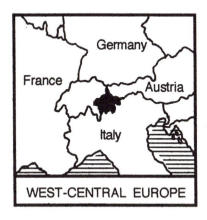

WEST-CENTRAL EUROPE

GRISCHUN

*POPULATION:* (95e) 168,000 : 71,000 Romansh (Grischa) in Switzerland. MAJOR NATIONAL GROUPS: (95e) Romansh (Grischa) 39%, German Swiss 37%, Italian Swiss 22%. MAJOR LANGUAGES: German, Romansh, Italian. MAJOR RELIGIONS: (95e) Protestant 64%, Roman Catholic 35%. MAJOR CITIES: (95e) Cuera (Chur) 33,000 (52,000), Davos 12,000, San Murezzan (Saint-Moritz) 7,000 (16,000).

*GEOGRAPHY:* AREA: 2,745 sq.mi.-7,111 sq.km. LOCATION: Grischun lies in the Rhaetian and Leopontine Alps in southeastern Switzerland and includes the famed Engadin Valley. POLITICAL STATUS: Grischun, called Graubünden in German and Grisons in French, forms an autonomous canton of the Swiss Confederation.

*FLAG:* The Romansh national flag, the official flag of the canton, is a square banner divided horizontally, the lower half bearing a black mountain goat on white; the upper half, divided vertically, has blue and gold squares on the upper fly and black and white vertical stripes on the upper hoist.

*PEOPLE:* The Romansh, calling themselves Grischa, are a Rhaeto-Romanic people, the descendants of Latinized alpine tribes. The Romansh language, of the Rhaeto-Romanic branch of the Romance languages, is spoken in three major dialects, which can be traced back to the original Latin brought to the region by the Romans. A conservative alpine people, the Romansh have preserved their unique culture in the high mountain valleys. The majority of the Romansh are Protestant, as are many of the canton's non-Romansh inhabitants.

*THE NATION:* Populated during the ancient Celtic expansion, the Celtic Suanetes dominated the high alpine valleys when Rome annexed the region in 15 B.C. Incorporated into the Roman province of Rhaetia, the region had practically no importance except for the Roman military control of the high mountain passes.

The Latinized Romansh fought to preserve their Latin language, laws, and culture against the Germanic tribes that invaded the crumbling Roman Empire in the fifth century. Overrun by Ostrogoths in A.D. 493 and by the Franks in 537, the region eventually came under the authority of the Frankish kingdom, the forerunner of the Holy Roman Empire.

The bishops of Chur, after 1170 the prince-bishops, dominated the province from the ninth century, having allied themselves to the rising power of the Hapsburgs. The power of the prince-bishops was checked and gradually reduced by leagues of free communes and feudal lords that formed between 1367 and 1436. The leagues, allied to the Swiss Confederation, made Grischun a regional military power. In 1512 the leagues conquered the Valtellina region from Milan and ruled the region, richer and more populous than their alpine homeland, as a subject territory.

The majority of the population of the leagues accepted the Protestant Reformation in 1524–26, but their Catholic subjects in the Valtellina staunchly resisted it. In 1620, during the Thirty Years' War, the Valtellina Catholics rose and massacred their Protestant masters, the ensuing conflict eventually drawing in most of the European powers. Restored to league rule in 1639, the Valtellina remained a subject territory until its incorporation into the French-dominated Cisalpine Republic by Napoleon in 1797. Two years later Grischun, more popularly known by its German name, Graubünden or Gray League, was forced to join Napoleon's Helvetic Republic. In 1803 Grischun joined the restored Swiss Confederation, with German and Italian, but not Romansh, as official cantonal languages.

Mass emigration, mainly to the Americas during the drought and depression after 1815, greatly reduced the number of German speakers in the canton, giving the native Romansh more access to local authority. The bitter controversy in the early nineteenth century over Switzerland's political system emphasized religious and cultural differences and marked the beginning of a particular Romansh nationalism. The conflict, settled in the nearly bloodless civil war of 1847–48, resulted in a new Swiss constitution that guaranteed cantonal autonomy in a loose confederal political system.

Protected by Switzerland's armed neutrality during World War I, the Romansh launched a peaceful campaign to end their domination by the German-speaking population and to win equal linguistic and cultural rights. The campaign, led by an active and persistent national movement, continued for over two decades. In 1937 the Swiss government finally accepted the Romansh language as one of the confederation's four official languages. Added protection for Romansh group, linguistic, and cultural rights became part of the constitution.

Their national identity protected by cantonal autonomy and guaranteed by the Swiss constitution, few Romansh felt culturally or linguistically threatened in multinational and multireligious Switzerland. The small national movement received little support and remained on the fringes of political life until the late 1980s and the growing debate over Switzerland's relations with a uniting Europe.

The growth of pro-European sentiment in the canton paralleled the emergence of a new awareness of their right to recognition as a separate European people. In May 1992 the Swiss government formally applied for membership in the European Community, a move widely supported in Grischun. In December 1992 the Romansh, like the other non-German Swiss, voted for closer ties with the European Community, but the vote, due to the opposition in the German-speaking cantons, was narrowly defeated.

A future within a united Europe has animated the long-dormant Romansh national movement. The movement's leaders stress that the national movement is a pro-European movement and is not directed against the confederation that has sheltered the Romansh for nearly two centuries. The growing pro-European faction of the national movement foresees Romansh sovereignty transferred from the Swiss Confederation to a united and secure federal Europe that would protect the independence of one of Europe's smallest but most ancient of nations.

SELECTED BIBLIOGRAPHY:

Irving, R.L.G. *The Swiss Alps.* 1962.
Lundman, B. J. *Nations and Peoples of Europe.* 1984.
Mayer, K. B. *The Population of Switzerland.* 1982.
Snyder, Louis L. *Global Mini-Nationalisms: Autonomy or Independence.* 1982.

# GUADELOUPE

*CAPITAL: Basse-Terre*

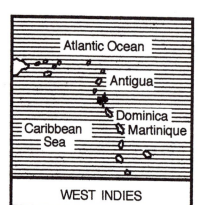

WEST INDIES

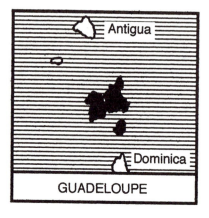

GUADELOUPE

*POPULATION:* (95e) 395,000 : 380,000 Guadeloupean (Guadeloupéine) in Guadeloupe and France. MAJOR NATIONAL GROUPS: (95e) Guadeloupean 89%, French 8%, Chinese, Indian. MAJOR LANGUAGES: Creole, French. MAJOR RELIGIONS: Roman Catholic, Protestant, animist. MAJOR CITIES: (95e) Les Abymes 65,000, Pointe-à-Pitre 26,000 (140,000), Gosier 21,000, Capesterre 20,000, Saint-Martin 19,000, Basse-Terre 14,000 (33,000).

*GEOGRAPHY:* AREA: 687 sq.mi.-1,779 sq.km. LOCATION: Guadeloupe, actually two islands divided by a narrow channel, Grande-Terre and Basse-Terre, forms part of the Leeward Islands in the Caribbean Sea between the island states of Antigua and Barbuda on the north and Dominica on the south. Guadeloupe includes the island dependencies of Marie Galante, Les Saintes, St. Barthelemy, and the French half of the island of St. Martin. POLITICAL STATUS: Guadeloupe, with its dependencies, forms an overseas department of the French republic.

*FLAG:* The Guadeloupean national flag, the flag of the nationalist coalition, the Popular Union for the Liberation of Guadeloupe (UPLG), is a red field with narrow green and white stripes at the top and bottom and bearing a large, five-pointed yellow star on the hoist. OTHER FLAG(S): The flag of the rival group, the People's Movement for an Independent Guadeloupe (MPGI), has four horizontal stripes of green and red with a black triangle at the hoist bearing broken yellow chains.

*PEOPLE:* The Guadeloupeans are mostly descended from African slaves imported to work the French plantations in the seventeenth to nineteenth centuries. A Creole minority of mixed African and European ancestry forms an economic elite and freely mixes with the French population, both the continental French, called Metros, and the French born on the island. The population of the dependencies is mixed, mostly the descendants of Breton and Norman settlers on Marie Galante and Les Saintes and the smaller islands except St. Martin, which has a Creole majority. The language of daily life is a French patois called Creole. The majority of the islanders are Roman Catholic, their religion often mixed with beliefs brought from Africa.

*THE NATION:* Christopher Columbus discovered the island in 1493 and named it for the monastery of Santa Maria de Guadelupe. Due to the resistance of the inhabitants, fierce Arawaks, the Spanish authorities ignored the island for over a century and abandoned attempts to colonize Guadelupe in 1604. A French colony, founded in 1635, survived, and the French laid claim to the entire island, their claim contested by the English from the neighboring islands. Sweden, participating in the European scramble for colonies, sent settlers to St. Barthelemy, and the Dutch, Danes, and other Europeans fought for island territories.

The prosperity of the French islands, particularly Guadeloupe, required imported labor as the native peoples disappeared under the impact of colonization. Norman and Breton farmers settled the smaller islands and farmed small plots in the European manner, but Guadeloupe developed a plantation economy and an aristocratic planter society dependent on slaves imported from Africa to work the vast sugar plantations.

The revolution in France in 1789 arrived in Guadeloupe in 1794. Revolutionaries set up a guillotine in the center of Pointe-à-Pitre, and a reign of terror virtually eliminated the island's plantation aristocracy, leaving a population of a few poor whites and thousands of freed black slaves. Occupied by the British during the Napoleonic Wars that followed the revolution, the islands returned to French rule in 1816. Economically devastated by the revolution and its aftermath, the colony became a neglected outpost of the French Empire.

The freed slaves adopted many aspects of French culture, but their native languages so changed the spoken French that a new dialect, called Creole, developed as the language of daily life. African influences also changed the religious practices as traditional beliefs became part of Christian services. The majority of the islanders remained poor subsistence farmers generally ignored by the French colonial administration that controlled all aspects of the island's daily life and the economy.

France, liberated from Nazi occupation during world War II, moved to end the colonial status of its Caribbean islands. In 1946 Guadeloupe became a department of the French republic, theoretically equal to the departments of metropolitan France, however the reality of island life remained the same: poverty, unemployment, and subsistence farming.

In the late 1950s educated Guadeloupeans began to mobilize as the neighboring British islands moved toward independence. Several nationalist organizations emerged to denounce French rule as disguised colonialism and to demand independence. In 1968 serious rioting and pro-independence violence rocked the island and led to mass arrests and the suppression of all nationalist activity.

To curb the growth of national sentiment, the government stressed a common French citizenship and dramatically increased economic subsidies. The economic aid eventually gave the islanders one of the highest standard of living in the Caribbean, but nationalist violence escalated, with attacks on French authority extending to Paris and the French heartland. Guadeloupean nationalists admit that French citizenship and departmental status greatly benefited the islands; however, unrelieved poverty and unemployment continue to fuel nationalism. The socialist victory in French elections in 1981 gave the island's government some additional autonomy under a new socialist program of government decentralization.

Numerous nationalist organizations, supported by the black majority, the Creoles, and the poorer whites, increasingly turned to violence during the 1980s. In 1984 the French government rushed gendarmes to the islands to quell serious separatist violence. In 1987 separatist leaders established a National Council of the Guadeloupean Resistance (CNRG), which organized a provisional government of a future Republic of Guadeloupe.

The nationalists enjoy widespread support in Guadeloupe, but nationalism is tempered by the knowledge that an end to the generous French government subsidies would bring tremendous economic hardships. The benefits of French departmental status may be too much to sacrifice for the majority of the Guadeloupeans, but that has not stopped the nationalists from disrupting the region, including a general strike called in coordination with nationalists in Martinique* and Guiana* in January 1994 to protest French government policies in the Antilles-Guiana region.

*SELECTED BIBLIOGRAPHY:*

Barry, Tom. *The Other Side of Paradise: Foreign Control in the Caribbean.* 1985.
Knight, Franklin W. *The Caribbean: The Genesis of a Fragmented Nationalism.* 1990.
Langley, Winston E. *The Troubled and Troubling Caribbean.* 1989.
Naipaul, V. S. *The Middle Passage: Impressions of Five Societies—British, French and Dutch—In the West Indies and South America.* 1981.

# GUIANA

**Guyane; French Guiana**

*CAPITAL: Cayenne*

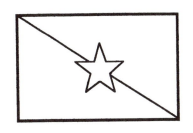

*POPULATION:* (95e) 134,000 : 145,000 Guianans in Guiana and France. MAJOR NATIONAL GROUPS: (95e) Creole 43%, Chinese 14%, Metros and French 11%, Amerindian 10%, Haitian 8%, Lebanese, Indian. MAJOR LANGUAGES: Creole, French. MAJOR RELIGIONS: Roman Catholic, Protestant, Buddhist, animist. MAJOR CITIES: (95e) Cayenne 45,000 (86,000), Kourou 17,000, Saint-Laurent du Maroni 16,000.

*GEOGRAPHY:* AREA: 35,135 sq.mi.-91,023 sq.km. LOCATION: Guiana lies on the northeastern Caribbean coast of South America. The region is mostly dense jungle with a fertile coastal strip where the majority of the population is concentrated. Guiana borders Suriname on the west and Brazil on the south and east. POLITICAL STATUS: Guiana forms the Department of French Guiana, an overseas department of the French republic.

*FLAG:* The Guianan national flag, the flag of the national movement, is a diagonal bicolor of yellow over green, divided upper hoist to lower fly, and bearing a large red, five-pointed star centered.

*PEOPLE:* The Guianan population, of mixed origins, includes the majority Creoles, descendants of slaves imported from Africa; a large Chinese minority; Europeans, many the descendants of prisoners released from the former prison colonies, French administrators, police, and military known as Metros; and smaller minorities of Amerindian, Haitian, and various Asian groups. The language of daily life, spoken by 90% of the population, is Creole, a French patois incorporating borrowings from African and Amerindian languages. Many religions are represented in Guiana, but the majority are Christian, with important Buddhist and Protestant minorities and some smaller groups, particularly the Amerindians, that continue to adhere to traditional religious beliefs.

*THE NATION:* Sparsely inhabited by Amerindian peoples, mostly living in the jungle interior, the region became one of the last in South America to know European colonization. Amerigo Vespucci sailed along the coast in 1499, but Europeans avoided the region until the French landed at the site of present Cayenne and claimed the territory for France in 1604. The native Amerindian people wiped out the first group of colonists who had established themselves at Cayenne in 1643, but the French reestablished the colony in 1664. Captured by the Dutch in 1676, the region returned to French control but remained largely unexplored and underpopulated. During the eighteenth century the French authorities made several unsuccessful attempts to establish settlements in the territory.

In the years after the French Revolution of 1789, the remote colony became a place of exile, the first penal colony created in 1834. Despite the discovery of gold in 1853, further settlement from Europe was deterred by the establishment of more penal colonies in 1854. The region became France's largest penal colony, with seven separate prison areas, the most notorious the penal colony known as Devil's Island. Thousands of criminals peopled the vast penal colonies following the enlargement of the system in the 1880s.

The colony, controlled by continental French administrators and police, grew slowly, its population augmented by freed slaves and released prisoners. French criminal law dictated that prisoners sentenced to eight years or more must remain in Guiana after their release. The last prisoners arrived from France in 1937 as the government began to phase out the penal colony system. In 1946 Guiana became an overseas department, and in 1951 the last of the colonies, Devil's Island, closed forever. In the 1960s the French government constructed a space research center at Kourou, the center and its related activities becoming the mainstay of the departmental economy other than the generous government subsidies.

Autonomist sentiment spread in the mid-1970s. Nationalists demanded a loosening of the tight control of the department by the administrators and police sent from metropolitan France. Ordinary Guianans began to criticize the French sent out from France, the beneficiaries of hardship pay during their term of duty in Guiana. The continental French, called Metros to distinguish them from those born in Guiana, dominated all local government and virtually all economic activity.

The newly organized political parties reflected the dispute over the control of local government. Diverse organizations represented pro-French unionists, autonomists, pro-independence nationalists, and later nationalist groups employing violence and terrorism. During the late 1970s and the 1980s the South American countries pressed France to decolonize the territory, the last European possession on the South American continent.

The French space center, considerably enlarged in the 1980s, has become a question of pride for the French government and its attempts to compete with the other major powers. The center, increasingly discussed and used as a European space center, has become a major source of income with other countries, industries, and government departments paying for rocket launches to take their experiments and equipment into space.

Nationalist groups, led by the more radical leaders, threatened the French space center at Kourou, and in 1983 and 1987 the government dispatched reinforcements to the region to quell separatist violence. Growing racism in France, including attacks on non-European Guianans, has increased support for nationalism, but the French budget subsidies and the income from the space center may be too much to give up.

*SELECTED BIBLIOGRAPHY:*

Barry, Tom. *The Other Side of Paradise: Foreign Control in the Caribbean.* 1985.
Chamberlain, Muriel. *Decolonization: The Fall of the European Empires.* 1985.
Naipaul, V. S. *The Middle Passage: Impressions of Five Societies—British, French and Dutch—In the West Indies and South America.* 1981.

# HAIDA GWAII

### Haada Gwaii; Haida Nation

*CAPITAL: Skidgate*

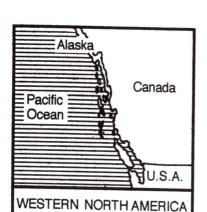

**WESTERN NORTH AMERICA**

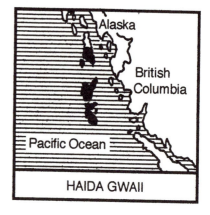

**HAIDA GWAII**

*POPULATION:* (95e) 8,000 : 9,000 Haida in Canada and the United States. MAJOR NATIONAL GROUPS: (95e) Haida 88%, other Canadian, other American. MAJOR LANGUAGES: English, Haida. MAJOR RELIGIONS: Protestant, Roman Catholic, animist. MAJOR CITIES: (95e) CANADA: Skidgate 1,000 (Skidgate–Queen Charlotte 2,000), Masset 1,500. UNITED STATES: Craig 1,500, Hydaburg 1,000.

*GEOGRAPHY:* AREA: 5,093 sq.mi.-13,194 sq.km. LOCATION: Haida Gwaii lies in northwestern North America, occupying the Queen Charlotte Islands in Canada and the southern district of Prince of Wales Island in Alaska. Due to the island's isolation from the mainland plants and animals not found elsewhere have survived. POLITICAL STATUS: Haida Gwaii has ho official status pending the resolution of outstanding land and sovereignty claims in Canada and the United States.

*FLAG:* The Haida national flag is a red field bearing the national symbol centered, a two-headed white bird, surrounded by a white oval of traditional Haida design.

*PEOPLE:* The Haida are a Native American people speaking an isolated language, the only representative of the Skittagetan language family of the Nadene language group. Although the people are physically and culturally related to the Tlingit and Tsimshian peoples of the mainland, the isolation of the Haida's island homeland has helped to preserve the unique Haida culture, including customs and traditions that have disappeared elsewhere. The ancient tradition of the potlatch continues as an important part of Haida culture.

*THE NATION:* The islands off the coast of North America, settled at least four thousand years ago by migrants crossing the ancient land bridge from Asia, formed the center of a sophisticated culture. Thickly wooded and with a temperate climate and heavy rainfall, the islands supported a large population, with the abundant salmon as the staple food. Skilled artisans, the Haida erected elaborately carved totems and built cedar plank canoes, some measuring up to seventy feet in length. According to legend the Haida occupied the islands off the coast for over 10,000 years before the arrival of the Europeans. A fiercely territorial people, the Haida in their carved war canoes defended their islands, the warriors engaging in the cannibalistic rituals associated with war in the region. Haida warriors, in huge war canoes, raided as far south as present California.

The Haida evolved a highly stratified society of chiefs, nobles, commoners, and slaves. The public disposal of personal wealth, the potlatch was a winter ceremony characterized by the giving of gifts, usually copper plates and elaborate goat-hair blankets. The ceremony brought the giver of the gifts great communal respect. Custom demanded that an offered gift be acknowledged by an even larger or more valuable gift. The potlatch formed a basic feature of the highly evolved Haida culture.

The most skilled maritime boat builders, the Haida traveled great distances up and down the coast. In the early seventeenth century a group of Haida warriors drove the Tlingit from the island to the north of the home islands. A group of colonists settled the southern part of the large island, calling themselves Kaigani. The streams of the new land were too small for the traditional salmon harvest, forcing the northern Haida to take to the sea in search of halibut and cod.

The Haida constructed some of the largest gabled houses in Mesoamerica, with many measuring sixty feet by one hundred feet. Haida society was organized in households in which dozens of extended families lived in the large cedar houses. The Haida never pursued whales as did neighboring peoples, but relied on the candlefish for cooking and lamp oil.

Russian exploration of the region farther north prompted the Spanish to send an expedition, under Juan Pérez Hernández, from Mexico up the coast in 1775. Over the next decade other Europeans visited the islands to marvel at the sophisticated society and to trade for the valuable furs. An Englishman, George Vancouver, surveyed the coast in detail from 1792 to 1794. The Russians, from their headquarters at Sitka, extended their authority south to Haida Gwaii in 1802, setting off an intense European rivalry for control of the region.

In 1821 the Russians laid claim to the entire region south to the fifty-first parallel. A compromise in 1824 set the boundary at 54°40' north latitude, the present boundary between Alaska and British Columbia. The compromise partitioned Haida Gwaii, the largest area, under British administration, which experienced a more lenient rule than the harsh authority exercised by the Russians over the Haida of Prince of Wales Island.

In 1780 the Haida population numbered around 10,000. Although not greatly affected by European influences until the arrival of fur traders and hunters in the early nineteenth century, the diseases, alien relationships, and alcohol introduced to the region by the Europeans decimated the tribe. In the north the brutal Russian colonial rule further devastated the Haida. A century later only 2,000 to 2,500 had survived the small nation's contact with the outside world. Missionaries set up stations and schools in the 1870s, gaining considerable influence over the remaining Haida and aiding the beginning of a cultural and national revival.

The long Haida decline began to reverse after World War II. Employment in the factories established for the processing and canning of the region's rich fishing harvest stabilized the economic base of the islands. In the 1950s the Haida began to press the pending land claims in both Canada and the United States. The campaign to win control of their ancient islands stimulated demands for tribal sovereignty and promoted closer ties to other Native American peoples and groups in Alaska and British Columbia.

In 1991 a judge in British Columbia ruled that aboriginal title to lands in the province had been extinguished by the simple fact of colonial rule. The ruling stimulated new demands for a compromise with the provincial government over the pending land claims and tribal sovereignty.

The border between the United States and Canada is in dispute. Canada recognizes the 1903 boundary at 54°40' known as the AB Line, the Alaska–British Columbia Line. The United States contends that the boundary lies some twenty-five miles south, equidistant from Canada's Graham Island and Prince of Wales Island, the prize the rich fishing grounds of the strait called the Dixon Entrance.

The destruction wrought by mining, whaling, and timber companies has outraged Haida who seek control over the development of their rich natural resources. The Haida claims to sovereignty include the control and management of the natural resources of the region, including the region under dispute. They refuse to recognize the boundary between Alaska and British Columbia and continue to press their ancient right to the land and the sea, rights, that if recognized by the various governments, would make the dispute over the exact placement of the international border that divides the Haida Nation merely an academic point.

*SELECTED BIBLIOGRAPHY:*

Harrison, Charles. *Ancient Warriors of the North Pacific.* 1925.
Jenness, Diamond. *Indians of Canada.* 1967.
Miller, Polly. *Lost Heritage of Alaska.* 1967.
Page, Dance H. *Heritage of the North American Indian People.* 1982.

# HASAVA

**Nenets-Dolgan**

*CAPITAL: Salekhard*

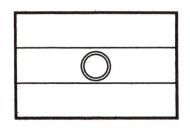

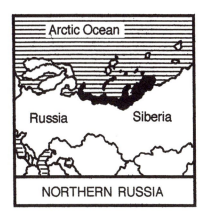

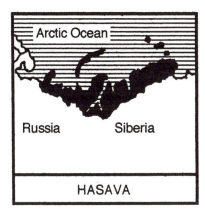

*POPULATION:* (95e) 161,000 : 54,000 Hasavans (38,000 Nenets [Nentsy], 7,000 Dolgan, 3,000 Yenets [Entsy Yenentsy], 2,000 Nganasan) in Russia. MAJOR NATIONAL GROUPS: (95e) Russian 42%, Hasavan 32%, Ukrainian 13%, Komi 5%, Evenki, Yakut, Khanty. MAJOR LANGUAGES: Russian, Nenen, Dolgan, Yenen. MAJOR RELIGIONS: Russian Orthodox, animist. MAJOR CITIES: (95e) NENETS: Naryan-Mar 21,000, Amderma 6,000. YAMALO-NENETS: Salekhard 24,000, Yamburg 7,000. TAIMYR (DOLGANO-NENETS): Dudinka 21,000, Nason 5,000.

*GEOGRAPHY:* AREA: 434,272 sq.mi.-1,125,057 sq.km. LOCATION: Hasava lies in northern Russia, an enormous region occupying the tundra, taiga, and permafrost regions just north of the tree line. Lying almost entirely within the Arctic Circle, the region stretches from the Kanin Peninsula in northeastern European Russia to the Taimyr Peninsula in north-central Siberia* and includes a number of large islands in the Kara and Laptev seas of the Arctic Ocean. POLITICAL STATUS: Hasava has no official status; the region claimed by nationalists forms the Nenets Autonomous Region and the northern districts of the Yamalo-Nenets and Taimyr (Dolgano-Nenets) autonomous regions of the Russian Federation.

*FLAG:* The Nenets national flag, the flag of the national movement, has three horizontal stripes of blue, white, blue and is charged with two concentric red rings centered. OTHER FLAG(S): The Dolgan flag has three horizontal stripes of white, pale green, and white bearing a broad vertical, red stripe at the hoist.

*PEOPLE:* The Hasava nation includes several distinct groups united by history, way of life, and intermarriage. The Nenets, the largest national group, formerly called Samoyeds, and the smaller related groups, the Yenets and Nganasan, speak Samoyedic (North Ural) languages of the Uralic language group. The Samoyed peoples are traditionally reindeer herders. The Dolgan, in the Taimyr Peninsula region, originally a Tungus people, have been influenced by long contact with the neighboring Yakuts of Sakha Omuk.* The majority of the Hasavans are Orthodox Christians, but with a substantial number adhering to traditional beliefs. The large Slav population, mostly concentrated in the towns and the oil and gas fields, now outnumber the native peoples in the Arctic region.

*THE NATION:* For uncounted centuries the Nenets and the related tribes herded reindeer across the vast reaches of the Arctic, moving their herds to the seasonal grazing lands in the tundra and taiga lands north of the tree line. European chronicles first mentioned the northern reindeer herders in the eleventh century. At the end of the fifteenth century some of the western tribes became tributary to the duchy of Moscow. Between 1552 and 1596 the majority of the Nenets and Yenets, called Nentsy and Entsy by the Russians, came under direct Russian rule. The tribes trapped the valuable fur animals in order to pay the annual taxes and tributes demanded by Moscow.

Protected by the Ural Mountains, the tribes of the Yamal Peninsula remained free of Russian domination until the early seventeenth century. The tribes of the Taimyr Peninsula and the Yenisei Valley came under Russian rule in the late seventeenth century. Small in numbers and spread across vast territories, the Hasavan tribes found themselves nearly powerless to resist the determined capitalists of prerevolutionary Russia.

Russian encroachments incited a widespread rebellion in the late seventeenth century. The tribal warriors initially triumphed, but gradually they were forced to retreat. By the beginning of the eighteenth century most of the tribes had become tributary to Russia. In the nineteenth century a Dolgan leader, Vauli, organized resistance to Russian imperialism and has become a Hasavan national hero and the inspiration of the modern national movement.

The Russians called the tribes Samoyeds, a word denoting cannibal. The tribes traditionally ate raw meat, particularly at ceremonies, but even though the Hasavans feasted on raw flesh, they never slaughtered more of their reindeer than immediate needs required. The reindeer herds, closely tied to the Hasavans' traditional way of life and even their ancient religious beliefs, provided the nomadic tribes with food, shelter, and clothing.

The arrival of the Communists, after the Russian civil war of 1918–20, saw the implementation of the Soviet plan to create a modern socialist society in the region. The plan involved the confiscation of all ''surplus wealth'' from the Hasavan tribes. Their reindeer herds were taken away, and the authorities allowed each herder to retain just four animals. Each band's hunters were also relieved of any furs they had stored. As an average band needed at least 250 reindeer just to survive, thousands of Hasavans perished of hunger.

The consolidation of Soviet power included theoretical autonomy for non-Russian national groups. When the Soviet authorities began to exploit the Hasavan lands, they organized nominally autonomous regions for the Nenets in 1929 and for the Yamalo-Nenets and Dolgano-Nenets in 1930.

Stalin's collectivization in the late 1920s forced the surviving nomads to work for the state and to move to permanent settlements chosen by local Soviet bureaucrats. Those who opposed the settlements faced forced collectivization, and by the 1950s most of the nomadic tribes had submitted. The Soviet authorities outlawed their nomadic lifestyle, and the Hasavans' only source of income became the huge Soviet enterprises that invaded the region from the 1950s onward. Even those who found employment received payments three or four times less than the so-called "incomers."

The discovery of huge oil and natural gas reserves in the 1960s brought a renewed influx of "incomers." Communist development plans devastated the fragile Hasavan homeland. Treated as a classic colony to be exploited, some 20 million hectares of land were destroyed by careless mining and drilling between 1979 and 1989 alone.

The era of liberalization, in the late 1980s, allowed the first Hasavan attempts to organize resistance to the despoliation of their lands. A nascent national movement organized the first protests against the suffering caused by decades of Communism and collectivization, which had resulted in the uncontrolled destruction of the fragile environment and even the dumping of radioactive waste in the Kara Sea and along the coast of Novaya Zemlya Island.

The governments of the three autonomous regions, dominated by ethnic Russians, in the autumn of 1990 declared the regions autonomous states. A taste of real autonomy only whetted the Hasavan appetite for more. Following the collapse of the Soviet Union in August 1991, the Hasavans refused to recognize the authority of the regional governments and began to organize in the Hasava majority regions in the far north.

In March 1993 the leaders of the Yamalo-Nenets struggled to take control of their national wealth from the bureaucrats, setting off a well-organized effort to regain control of their homelands across the Nenets regions. In the east the Nenets and Dolgans fought for the Great Arctic Reserve, finally designated a safe environment area in the Taimyr Peninsula in July 1993. The northern peoples share a sense of outrage at the abuses they have suffered and feel that only by regaining their right to self-determination will they reestablish their identity and begin to rebuild their Arctic homeland.

*SELECTED BIBLIOGRAPHY:*

Lied, Jonas. *Siberian Arctic.* 1960.

Rywkin, Michael. *Russian Colonial Expansion to 1917.* 1988.

Wixman, Ronald. *The Peoples of the U.S.S.R. An Ethnographic Handbook.* 1984.

Wood, Alan, and R. A. French. *The Development of Siberia's Peoples and Resources.* 1989.

# HAUDENOSAUNEE

## Iroquois Confederation

*CAPITAL: Onondaga*

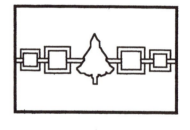

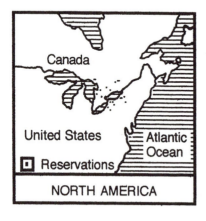

NORTH AMERICA

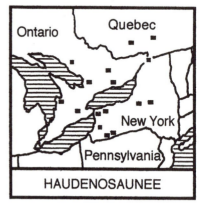

HAUDENOSAUNEE

*POPULATION:* (95e) 64,000 : 175,000 Iroquois in the United States and Canada. MAJOR NATIONAL GROUP: (95e) Iroquois (Mohawk, Oneida, Onondaga, Cayuga, Seneca, Tuscarora). MAJOR LANGUAGES: Iroquoian languages, English. MAJOR RELIGIONS: Longhouse religion, Roman Catholic, Protestant. MAJOR CITIES: (95e) UNITED STATES: Salamanca 6,500, Onondaga 1,200, Hogansburg 1,000. CANADA: Six Nations 2,000.

*GEOGRAPHY:* AREA: 509 sq.mi.-1,318 sq.km. (Land claims involving thousands of square miles of territory in the United States and Canada remain unsettled.) LOCATION: Haudenosaunee lies in eastern North America, currently forming scattered reserved lands in the state of New York in the United States and in the Canadian provinces of Ontario and Quebec. POLITICAL STATUS: Haudenosaunee has no official status, even though the Iroquois consider their confederacy a sovereign nation that predates both the United States and Canada. Pending the resolution of sovereignty and land claims, the confederacy is confined to sixteen reservations in the United States and Canada.

*FLAG:* The Haudenosaunee flag, the official flag of the confederacy, is a pale blue field bearing a centered white tree, the Tree of Peace, flanked by two white chain links on either side, symbolizing sacred wampum. OTHER FLAG(S): The Mohawk national flag is a red field with a Mohawk brave in profile against a yellow sun with twelve rays.

*PEOPLE:* The Iroquois, calling themselves and their nation Haudenosaunee or People of the Longhouse, are a Native American people comprising six sovereign nations: Mohawk, Oneida, Onondaga, Cayuga, Seneca, and Tuscarora. The six nations are united by historical, clan, and family ties that cut across tribal lines. The Iroquois are mostly bilingual, speaking English and distinct, but related, languages of the Iroquoian group of the Hokan-Siouan languages. Traditional Haudenosaunee culture remains matriarchal. The majority of the Iroquois belong to their own Longhouse religion, a Quaker-influenced belief that spread through the nations in the nineteenth century.

*THE NATION:* Small tribes in the eastern woodlands of the land they called Great Turtle Island began to cultivate corn, squash, and other vegetables some 1,000 years ago. Agriculture allowed a new form of society with large, fortified towns, sophisticated artisans, and a stratified caste system. The tribes, often warring among themselves, united sometime between 1350 and 1600, although many historians claim that the tribes achieved unification over a thousand years before the accepted dates.

The Peacemaker, the author of confederation, gathered together five warring tribes and planted a white pine, the Tree of Peace, under which tribal leaders buried their weapons of war. The Peacemaker's original instructions form the basis of the oral constitution still honored by the Haudenosaunee nation. The confederacy, the most sophisticated and powerful north of central Mexico, extended its political sway over a huge area from eastern Canada south to the Carolinas.

The French first came across the confederacy in the St. Lawrence River and the eastern Great Lakes regions. The French called the confederated tribes Iroquois, probably a corruption of a native epithet. Iroquoian animosity to the French traditionally dates from the participation of Samuel de Champlain in Huron attacks on Iroquois towns in the seventeenth century. The confederacy, strengthened by the adhesion of a sixth member, the Tuscarora, in 1722, played a vital role in the British victory that ended the French and Indian War in 1763.

The American Revolution nearly destroyed the confederacy. Four of the member nations ultimately joined their traditional British allies, while the Oneida and Tuscarora mostly aided the Americans. During the terrible privations at Valley Forge in the winter of 1777–78, Oneida chief Shenendore brought 3,000 bushels of white corn and even provided a teacher to show the starving Americans how to prepare the food.

General George Washington in 1779 sent an expedition to strike at the heart of the confederacy, Onondaga. The Americans destroyed towns, orchards, and crops. Their passing completely changed the face of the Iroquois nation. Following the British surrender at Yorktown in 1781 many Iroquois joined the Loyalists moving north to British Canada.

Benjamin Franklin is thought to have modeled parts of the new American Constitution on that of the confederacy, which outlined a voluntary association of sovereign nations. In spite of their contribution to American independence, the Iroquois found themselves excluded from American life. In 1794 the Treaty of Fort Stanwix forever guaranteed Iroquois control of much of present New

York State. The treaty, soon abrogated by American settlers and an unsympathetic government, became the first of 371 treaties signed with the Native American nations and subsequently ignored.

The tribes gradually lost their traditional lands and were forced into ever-dwindling reservations on both sides of the border. The nations, mostly supporting peace with their powerful white neighbors, adopted a pacific religion, the Longhouse religion, in the early nineteenth century. Begun among the Senecas and believed to have its roots in Quaker ideals, the religion spread rapidly through the scattered remnants of the confederacy.

Increased education in the 1920s and 1930s renewed an appreciation of their unique history and culture. By the early 1950s the revival of the Iroquoian languages and traditions had greatly affected the young. A growing demand for Native American rights and for redress of past injustices merged with the liberation philosophy of the 1960s to produce Red Power. The militancy of the period marked the beginning of the modern national movement and the end of the patient acceptance of abuses and neglect.

Young lawyers took over the leadership of the nationalist movement in the 1970s and pressed the U.S. and Canadian governments to negotiate the Iroquois land claims, some filed as early as 1946–51 but still pending resolution. Taking the position that the Iroquois confederacy is a sovereign nation that predates the United States and Canada, tribal lawyers filed numerous court cases attempting to force the governments to honor the treaties signed between sovereign political entities.

Iroquois representatives in 1977 presented a petition to the United Nations seeking that body's recognition of Iroquois sovereignty. Passports issued by the authorities of the Haudenosaunee government have been honored by dozens of countries and are used by Iroquois runners monitoring the situation of indigenous peoples in other areas of the Americas.

Disappointed by government responses to the Iroquois attempts to gain redress by legal means, young militants have begun to fight for their remaining lands, sparking violent conflicts with state and provincial authorities. The settlement of outstanding land claims is seen as the first step to the recognition of Haudenosaunee as a sovereign nation.

*SELECTED BIBLIOGRAPHY:*

Brundin, Judith. *The Native Peoples of the Northeast Woodlands: An Education Resource Publication.* 1990.

Conners, Dennis. *Onondaga: Portrait of a Native People.* 1986.

Hauptman, Lawrence. *The Iroquois Struggle for Survival: World War II to Red Power.* 1986.

Versluis, Arthur. *The Elements of Native American Traditions.* 1993.

# HAUSA

**Hausaland; Hausa Bakwai; Northern Nigeria**

*CAPITAL: Kaduna*

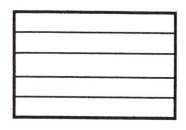

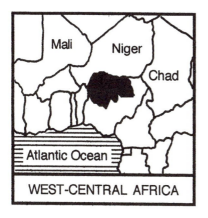

WEST-CENTRAL AFRICA

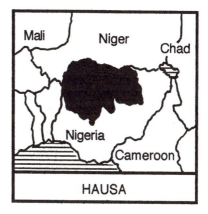

HAUSA

*POPULATION:* (95e) 31,840,000 : 22,500,000 Hausa and 7,500,000 Fulani in Nigeria. MAJOR NATIONAL GROUPS: (95e) Hausa 70%, Fulani 21%, Nupe 4%, other Nigerian. MAJOR LANGUAGES: Hausa, Fulani, Nupe, English. MAJOR RELIGIONS: Sunni Muslim, Christian, animist. MAJOR CITIES: (95e) Kano 1,547,000 (2,425,000), Zaria 498,000, Kaduna 376,000 (590,000), Katsina 320,000, Sokoto 249,000, Mina 205,000, Kumo 174,000, Abuja 165,000, Gusau 122,000, Deba 128,000, Bida 124,000, Gombe 126,000, Bauchi 125,000, Birin Kebbi 118,000, Kaura Namoda 116,000, Jega 110,000, Azare 103,000, Gumel 100,000.

*GEOGRAPHY:* AREA: 51,803 sq.mi.-134,204 sq.km. LOCATION: Hausa occupies an upland plateau, drained by the Niger River and its tributaries, in Northern Nigeria. Hausa borders Niger on the north and northwest, Benin on the west and the Nigerian regions of Kanowra* on the east, and Yorubaland* on the south. POLITICAL STATUS: Hausa has no official status; the region defined as Hausa or Hausaland forms the Nigerian states of Bauchi, Jigawa, Kaduna, Katsina, Kano, Sokoto, Kebbi, Niger, and the Federal Capital Territory.

*FLAG:* The Hausa national flag, the flag adopted by nationalists in 1966, has five horizontal stripes of red, yellow, indigo blue, green, and khaki beige.

*PEOPLE:* The Hausa and Fulani are closely related Muslim Hamitic peoples speaking languages of the Niger-Congo language group. The Hausa language is the lingua franca in much of West Africa, spoken or understood by over 40 million people. Ethnically, it is now difficult to distinguish between the Hausa and the originally lighter-skinned Fulani, as extensive mixing has blurred the ethnic, cultural, and linguistic differences between the two Muslim peoples. Overwhelmingly Sunni Muslim, there remains a Hausa minority, the Muguzawa, who have retained their traditional pre-Islamic beliefs. The Muslim Nupe in the southwest are the largest of the region's numerous ethnic minorities.

*THE NATION:* The Hausa, according to oral tradition, migrated from the northwest in ancient times. Settling along the northern tributaries of the Niger River, they developed an advanced civilization with a strong urban tradition, unusual in sub-Saharan Africa. The Hausa city-states united between the eleventh and thirteenth centuries to form Hausa Bakwai, a confederation of seven states: Kano, Zaria, Katsina, Davra, Rano, Gobir, and Biran.

The Hausa cities, the southern terminus of the Saharan caravan routes, carried on an extensive trade with North Africa. Arab traders coming south with the caravans introduced Islam to the region. A Muslim prohibition against enslaving fellow Muslims facilitated the rapid spread of the religion. The majority of the Hausa clans had embraced the new religion by the fifteenth century. Muslim slavers, often employed by the Hausa emirs, raided the pagan tribes to the south, sending thousands of captives north along the trade routes.

Fulani nomads from the northwest began to move into the region in the seventeenth century. Refusing to pay tribute to the local emirs, the nomads moved west and in 1801 took control of the leading Hausa state, Sokoto. The Fulani gradually adopted the Hausa culture, and intermarriage became common.

The British, after decades of controlling the southern coastal regions, began to establish relations with the Hausa-Fulani emirs in the mid-nineteenth century. In 1885 the Sarduana of Sokoto, the spiritual and temporal leader of the region, signed a treaty with the British. The treaty marked the beginning of the British penetration of Hausaland. In 1903 the British authorities took direct control of the Muslim states and in 1906 defeated a Hausa-Fulani attempt to expel the Europeans.

The British admired the Muslims and preferred to control the region indirectly by retaining the traditional administrative structures. Christian missionaries, forbidden to enter the North, concentrated their efforts among the southern pagans, and missionary education gave the southern tribes a definite advantage over the northern Muslims. Educated Christians from southern Nigeria, more familiar with European ways, moved north in large numbers to fill administrative and clerical positions spurned by the proud Muslims. Feudal and traditional, education received little attention, with only 251 students attending secondary schools in northern Nigeria in 1947.

The Hausa-Fulani leaders belatedly realized that the northern region had fallen behind the western and eastern regions of the Christian south. In 1949 the Muslims launched their own political party, the Northern People's Congress. The postwar political mobilization is considered the beginning of modern Hausa-Fulani nationalism. In the 1950s the Muslims made an effort to catch up with the South, but, already decades behind, the disparity incited a growing resentment and provoked increasingly violent incidents. The Hausa-Fulani leaders, claiming that the British favored the southern regions, threatened secession in 1953.

Nigeria's three regions, each dominated by rival tribes, joined a political confederation in 1954 and won full independence from the United Kingdom in 1960. The new Nigerian government, dominated by the numerically predominant Hausa-Fulani, incited strong opposition in the Christian south. In 1966 a coup by southern officers overthrew the government, and a new regime, dominated by the southeastern Ibo tribe, took control. Rioting swept the north, with violent attacks on southerners, especially Ibos, leaving hundreds dead.

Vehemently opposed to domination by a tribe once taken as slaves, the Hausa-Fulani leaders prepared a plan, code-named *araba* (Secession Day). The northern leaders planned to reassert Muslim control of Nigeria or, alternatively, to proclaim the secession of a republic of Hausa. Before the chosen day, 29 July 1966, a new Nigerian government, headed by a northern Christian, considered a neutral in the regional conflicts, proposed a compromise acceptable to the Hausa-Fulani leaders, a loose confederation of the Nigerian regions.

In September 1966, before the compromise took affect, rioting again spread across the north, the rioters joined by Muslim soldiers. Over 30,000 Ibos died in the riots, and a million fled back to their homeland in the eastern region. The Hausa-Fulani leadership evacuated all northern civil servants and military personnel from the federal capital at Lagos and prepared to declare the north independent of Nigeria. The proclamation, overtaken by the Ibo declaration of the secession of the east as the Republic of Biafra,* was put aside as the Muslims regained their predominance in the government and military, which finally defeated the Ibo secession after a three-year war in 1970.

Muslim fundamentalism rekindled Hausa-Fulani nationalism in the 1980s, the new militancy setting off periodic ethnic and religious clashes. The Hausa-Fulani's weakening hold on Nigeria has fueled the growth of nationalism since 1990. International pressure to restore democracy after decades of Muslim-dominated military governments has inserted new strains into the relationships between Nigeria's Christian south and Muslim north. The volatile mix of religion and ethnic tensions, exacerbated by political segmentation, has renewed the nationalisms that nearly tore Nigeria apart three decades ago.

*SELECTED BIBLIOGRAPHY:*
Asiegbu, J. U. *Nigeria and Its British Invaders.* 1984.
Coleman, James S. *Nigeria: Background to Nationalism.* 1971.
Kirk-Greene, A. H. *The Hausa Emirates.* 1972.
Shaw, Timothy, and Julius D. Ihonubere. *Nigeria: The Illusions of Power.* 1982.

# HAWAII

Hawai'i

*CAPITAL: Honolulu*

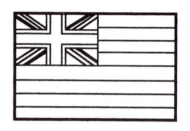

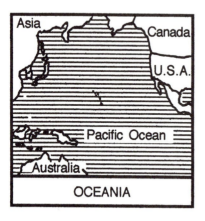

OCEANIA

HAWAII

*POPULATION:* (95e) 1,210,000 : 350,000 Hawaiians and part-Hawaiians in the United States. MAJOR NATIONAL GROUPS: (95e) Caucasian 24%, Japanese 23%, Hawaiian and part-Hawaiian 20%, Filipino 11%, Chinese 5%, Samoan and other Pacific Islanders 3%. MAJOR LANGUAGES: English, pidgin, Hawaiian, Japanese. MAJOR RELIGIONS: Protestant, Roman Catholic, Buddhist. MAJOR CITIES: (95e) Honolulu 365,000 (873,000), Kaneohe 39,000, Hilo 38,000 (66,000), Kailua 37,000 (Kailua-Kaneohe 129,000), Kahalui 18,000 (33,000).

*GEOGRAPHY:* AREA: 6,471 sq.mi.-16,764 sq.km. LOCATION: Hawaii, the Hawaiian Islands, lies in the south-central Pacific Ocean just south of the Tropic of Cancer. The archipelago, eight major islands and numerous smaller islands, is dominated by the island of Oahu, with the majority of the population and Hawaii's only large city. POLITICAL STATUS: Hawaii forms a state of the United States.

*INDEPENDENCE DECLARED:* 4 July 1894.

*FLAG:* The Hawaiian flag, the official flag of the state, has eight horizontal stripes of white, red, blue, white, red, blue, white, and red and is charged with a canton on the upper hoist bearing the British Union Jack. OTHER FLAG(S): The flag of the national movement is a dark blue field bearing a constellation of nine white, fifteen-pointed stars.

*PEOPLE:* The Hawaiians and the part-Hawaiians who identify with Hawaiian culture and history are now the third largest ethnic group in the islands and the state's least advantaged. A Polynesian people, the Hawaiians speak a Polynesian language of the Malayo-Polynesian language group. Nationalists claim that those of pure Hawaiian blood account for 10% of the total population of the islands. The majority of the Hawaiians are trilingual, speaking their own Polynesian language and English plus a mixed dialect understood by 60% of the state population, pidgin. Over forty ethnic groups are represented in the islands.

*THE NATION:* Hawaiian tradition places the arrival of Polynesian colonists from Samoa sometime between the fifth and ninth centuries. The settlers slowly spread through the uninhabited islands of the chain. A later wave of colonists reached the islands between the twelfth and fifteenth centuries. Separate kingdoms, established on each of the major islands, carried on sporadic interisland wars.

Captain James Cook, leading a British expedition, came across the islands in 1778 and christened them the Sandwich Islands. British attempts to explore their find met with fierce resistance from the islands' kings, and Cook himself died in a skirmish in 1779. The introduction of European firearms dramatically increased the destructiveness of the internecine wars, further decimating a population ravaged by European diseases.

King Kamehameha I, called the Great, the ruler of the largest of the islands, finally conquered the neighboring islands and established a unified kingdom in 1810. The king welcomed American and European traders and whalers, learning from them and encouraging the introduction of technology.

American missionaries arrived in the islands in the 1830s and 1840s. Soon engaging in trade, the missionaries laid the foundations of the islands' most important family fortunes. Plantation agriculture drew in Japanese, Portuguese, Filipino, and Chinese labor. The foreign population soon outnumbered the native Hawaiians.

Influenced by native advisers, King Kamehameha II established a constitutional monarchy in 1840. Two years later the kingdom received recognition as a sovereign state from the United States and the major European powers. In 1848 the king abolished the feudal landholding system, allowing investment and economic exploitation.

The Americans' growing commercial and political influence in the kingdom, opposed by King Kalakaua, prompted demands for his abdication in 1889. His more amenable sister, Lydia Liliuokalani, became queen amid rising American demands for constitutional reform. The American residents, on 14 July 1893, staged a coup and deposed the queen. The coup leaders, supported by the American ambassador to the kingdom, requested annexation by the United States. A commission sent from Washington reported that the majority of the islanders opposed annexation, and the commissioners refused the appeal.

The provisional Hawaiian government, dominated by American planters, on 4 July 1894 declared the islands independent as the Republic of Hawaii. The declaration set off a Hawaiian revolt, and the deposed queen traveled to Washington seeking aid from an unsympathetic American government. In 1897 the new republic signed a treaty with the United States that laid the groundwork for the formal transfer of sovereignty on 12 August 1898.

The ethnic Hawaiian population, estimated to number around 300,000 in 1778, dropped to about 70,000 in 1853 and by 1910 numbered only some 40,000 including the growing number of part-Hawaiians. The poorest segment of the population, the former rulers of the islands, retained only small subsistence plots. Just forty individuals, the majority the descendants of early missionaries, held 97% of the land.

The territorial government applied for statehood in 1937. The federal government denied the application on the grounds that the ethnically mixed population made statehood impossible. The islands remained an exotic outpost until the surprise attack on Pearl Harbor in December 1941. Hawaii's importance as a military base became crucial to the war in the Pacific. An influx of mainlanders during and after the war greatly changed the ethnic composition. On 21 August 1959 Hawaii became a state. Commercial jet service, inaugurated the same year, quickly made mass tourism the mainstay of the island economy.

The Hawaiians, with incomes some 15% lower than the state average, experienced a cultural revival in the 1960s and 1970s, a reculturation highlighting their unique history, language, and traditions. Younger, more militant Hawaiians began to demand cultural rights and economic equality, including compensation for 1.4 million acres of land stolen from the Hawaiians over the last century. In response a Bureau of Hawaiian Affairs came into being in 1976, but in 1983 the U.S. Congress rejected government responsibility for the seized lands. The decision provoked a dramatic growth of Hawaiian nationalism.

The land issue remains central to the national movement. In Hawaiian tradition the land is sacred, the state's unbridled growth, environmental destruction, and growing pollution considered blasphemy. In 1988 the nationalists rejected an offer of aid from Libya's dictator, but in 1991 they asserted that the Hawaiians are citizens of a sovereign nation, subverted and annexed illegally by the United States. Support is growing for the creation of a "Hawaiian Nation" similar to the other Native American nations. The move would give the Hawaiians some legal protection and rights in their fight for self-determination.

*SELECTED BIBLIOGRAPHY:*
Blacman, William. *The Making of Hawaii.* 1985.
Davidson, Donald. *Regionalism and Nationalism in the United States.* 1990.
Dudley, Michael Kioni, and Keoni Kealohe Agard. *A Hawaiian Nation II: A Call for Hawaiian Sovereignty.* 1991.
Fuchs, Lawrence H. *Hawaii Pono: A Social History.* 1961.
McDermott, John F. *Peoples and Cultures of Hawaii: A Psychocultural Profile.* 1980.

# HEJAZ

## Hijaz

*CAPITAL: Mecca (Makkah)*

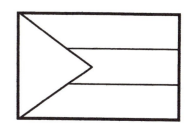

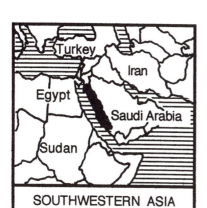

SOUTHWESTERN ASIA

HEJAZ

*POPULATION:* (95e) 4,694,000 : 3,950,000 Hejazis in Saudi Arabia. MAJOR NATIONAL GROUPS: (95e) Hejazi 82%, other Saudi Arabian. MAJOR LANGUAGE: Arabic (Hejazi dialect). MAJOR RELIGIONS: Sunni Muslim, Wahabi Muslim. MAJOR CITIES: (95e) Jidda (Jeddah) 1,495,000, Mecca (Makkah) 664,000, Taif (At-Ta'if) 463,000, Medina (Al-Medinah) 375,000, Yenbo (Yanbu' al-Bahr) 175,000, Tabuk (Tebuk) 172,000, Rabigh 85,000, Lith (Al-Lith) 70,000, Qadhima (Al-Qadimah) 55,000, Ashaira (Ashayrah) 50,000.

*GEOGRAPHY:* AREA: 149,961 sq.mi.-388,500 sq.km. LOCATION: Hejaz lies in southwestern Saudi Arabia, mostly an arid, mountainous plateau, but with several large, fertile oases and a narrow coastal plain on the Red Sea suitable for farming. POLITICAL STATUS: Hejaz has no official status; the region forms the Western Province of Saudi Arabia, comprising the districts of Madinah, Makkah, and Tebuk.

*INDEPENDENCE DECLARED:* 27 June 1916.

*FLAG:* The Hejazi flag, the flag of the former kingdom, is a horizontal tricolor of black, white, and green bearing a red triangle at the hoist. The colors of the flag of Hejaz, the first independent Arab state in modern times, became the colors of Arab liberation and appear on the flags of many Arab countries.

*PEOPLE:* The Hejazi, the only nontribal people in Saudi Arabia, are an Arab people with substantial admixtures of nonpeninsular Arabs and non-Arab Muslims, the result of centuries of Muslim pilgrimages to the holy cities of Mecca and Medina. One of the most urbanized societies in the Arab world, the Hejazis have assimilated many cultural and linguistic influences brought to the region by religious pilgrims. The majority of the Hejazi nation adheres to the Sunni branch of Islam, a more tolerant sect than the puritanical Wahabi rite, the official branch of Islam in the Saudi kingdom.

*THE NATION:* Nomadic Semitic tribes began to settle the region in ancient times. An urbanized culture developed along the coast and the inland oasis with the growth of trade. The city of Mecca early acquired importance as a center of commerce and a place of worship for the region's multitude of pagan sects. At the time of Mohammed's birth in A.D. 570, the region had a mixed population of urbanized pagan tribes, Judaized Arabs, Christians, and Zoroastrian merchants.

Mohammed, at age forty, experienced a revelation of his destiny as the Arab prophet. Mohammed's teachings gathered a small group of followers but met fierce resistance from the pagan majority. In 622 Mohammed and his followers fled to Medina to escape a pagan plot to murder him. Mohammed's flight, the Hegira, marked the beginning of the Muslim era. By the time of his death in 632, all of Hejaz had come under Muslim rule. The Hejazi people, united by Mohammed, formed the core of the vast Muslim empire that eventually controlled much of the known world.

Hejaz declined following the transfer of the center of Muslim power, the Caliphate, to Damascus in 661, even though Mecca and Medina remained pilgrimage centers for the Muslim faithful. In 762 the Caliphate moved from Damascus to Baghdad, even farther from its roots in Hejaz. The Muslim Empire disintegrated rapidly, splitting into a number of antagonistic territories, after the Persian conquest of Baghdad in 1258.

Hejaz came under the rule of the Egyptian Mamelukes but remained the spiritual focus of the divided Muslim world. Absorbed by the expanding Ottoman Empire of the Turks, imperial authority in the region rested with the sherif of Mecca, the protector of the holy cities and the chief of the powerful Hashemite clan of Hejaz.

Wahabi Muslims, a puritanical sect from the harsh interior Nejd Desert, began to raid the cities and oasis of Hejaz in the early nineteenth century. On the pretext that the Muslim holy cities must be protected, the Turks brought Hejaz under direct Ottoman administration in 1845. The sherif of Mecca retained only his religious office as the caretaker of the holy cities.

Arab nationalism emerged in the late nineteenth century, based on the demands for the creation of a separate Arab state within the multiethnic Ottoman Empire. In 1908, amid rising Arab opposition to Turkish rule, Husein ibn Ali succeeded to the position of sherif of Mecca. With the outbreak of war in 1914, British agents, especially T. E. Lawrence, urged Husein to lead the Hejazi in revolt against the Turks. The British promised to support the creation of an Arab state from the Arab lands of the Ottoman Empire at the end of the war.

The Arab revolt, supported by British gold, began on 5 June 1916. On 27 June 1916 Husein declared the independence of the Hashemite Kingdom of

Hejaz, with himself as king. In September 1918 the Hejazis defeated the Turks in the region, but, contrary to earlier promises of Arab unity, the United Kingdom and France took control of Palestine, Syria, and other Arab territories of the defeated Ottoman Empire.

Hejaz participated in the 1919 Paris Peace Conference as an Allied nation; however, Husein's representative, his son Emir Faisal, accused the British of duplicity on their promises of a united Arab state and refused to sign the Versailles Treaty. In retaliation the British withdrew their military support of the kingdom just as tensions began to mount between Hejaz and Nejd, the realm of Ibn Saud, the leader of the desert Wahabi sect.

Ibn Saud led his tribal warriors to victory over the neighboring state of Jebel Shammar in 1921, thus bringing the Wahabis within striking distance of the Hejazi heartland. In 1924, after three years of skirmishing, the Wahabis invaded the kingdom. The last Hashemite strongholds, the holy cities, fell to Ibn Saud in 1926. The puritanical Wahabis, long opposed to the Haj, the annual Muslim pilgrimage to Mecca and Medina, as a blasphemous rite, quickly revised their religious views to accommodate the revenue brought to their expanded state by the hundreds of thousands of religious pilgrims.

The United Kingdom recognized the Saudi control of Hejaz in 1927. To compensate their former Hashemite allies, they installed Husein's sons as rulers of the British-administered Iraq and Trans-Jordan. Formally incorporated into the kingdom of Saudi Arabia in 1932, Hejaz retained some autonomy until the centralization of the Saudi kingdom in 1952.

Hejazi nationalism began to reemerge in the 1970s, spurred by growing radical fundamentalism and tensions between the Sunni and Wahabi sects. The Hejazi belief that the oil-rich Saudis cared more for their overseas investments than for the well-being of Hejaz spurred the growth of regional and national sentiment. A peaceful and orderly annual Haj, viewed by the Hejazis as a continuing test of Saudi legitimacy, began to unravel with attacks on Mecca's Great Mosque by fundamentalists in 1979 and the violence that has marred the annual pilgrimage since 1987.

The traditional Saudi practice of stifling dissidence with generous bounties is a custom the Saudi government can no longer afford. The era of Saudi opulence is over. Water shortages and power outages, increasingly common, have increased Hejazi resentment of the 10,000 royals who control the kingdom's commerce and administration amid massive abuses and royal privilege.

*SELECTED BIBLIOGRAPHY:*
Sivan, Emmanud. *Radical Islam.* 1987.
Zeine, N. *Arab-Turkish Relations and the Emergence of Arab Nationalism.* 1981.
Zwemer, Samuel M. *Arabia: The Cradle of Islam, Studies in the Geography, People and Politics of the Peninsula.* 1980.

# HO'AIDO

**Kurile Islands; Kuril Islands; Chishima Rettō**

*CAPITAL: Shana (Kurilsk)*

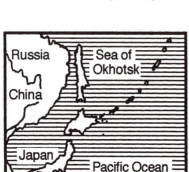

NORTHEASTERN ASIA

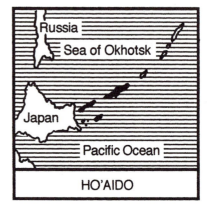

HO'AIDO

*POPULATION:* (95e) 11,000 : 37,000 Ainu in Japan and Russia. MAJOR NATIONAL GROUPS: (95e) Russian 80%, Ainu 18%, Japanese 1%. MAJOR LANGUAGES: Russian, Ainu, Japanese. MAJOR RELIGIONS: Russian Orthodox, Buddhist, animist. MAJOR CITIES: (95e) Shana (Kurilsk) 1,500, Kunashir (Yuzhno-Kurilsk) 1,000.

*GEOGRAPHY:* AREA: 3,637 sq.mi.-9,422 sq.km. LOCATION: Ho'aido, the ancient name of the Ainu homeland and applied by nationalists to the Kurile Islands, lies in the Okhotsk Sea just northeast of the Japanese island of Hokkaido. The islands are of volcanic origin and retain numerous active volcanoes and hot springs, considered sacred by the original Ainu inhabitants. POLITICAL STATUS: The status of the islands remains in question. Officially, they form part of Sakhalin Oblast of the Russian Federation; however, Japan has claimed the islands since 1945, and in 1991 Ainu nationalists laid claim to the islands as part of the historic Ainu homeland.

*FLAG:* The Ainu flag, the flag of the national movement, is a pale purple field with the white and red Ainu national symbol on the upper hoist.

*PEOPLE:* The Ainu, which means simply "people" in the Ainu language, are the descendants of the original inhabitants of the Japanese islands. Physically short and stocky, they are thought to be more closely related to the Caucasians than to the Japanese or other Oriental peoples and have round eyes and wavy, brunette hair. Their language is an isolated language group possibly related to the language of the inhabitants of Okinawa* south of the Japanese main islands. The majority of the Ainu retain their traditional beliefs, an animistic cult centered on a sacred bear. Every year a captive bear is sacrificed at the annual Ainu winter festival. The Ainu nationalists claim a national population of some 37,000, including 17,000 Ainu and 7,000 part-Ainu in Japan and 13,000 in Russia.

*THE NATION:* The Ainu, of unknown origin but believed to constitute a branch of the Caucasian peoples, inhabited the northern Japanese islands, the Kurile Islands, and the southern part of Sakhalin for millennia. According to Ainu tradition their ancestors populated the islands some 3,000–4,000 years ago. Although known as a warrior people, the Ainu developed their culture and religion in harmony with nature. Holding their lands in common, various nomadic bands lived by hunting, fishing, and gathering.

The Japanese began to colonize the Ainu lands in northern Honshu in the late Kamakura Era in the thirteenth and fourteenth centuries. The Ainu retreated north in front of the expansion of the more advanced Japanese. Sporadic warfare with the Japanese decimated the Ainu population, and they were finally subdued by the early sixteenth century. The Japanese moved across the Tsugaru Strait and began to colonize the southwest of the island they called Hokkaido, soon after subduing the Ainu. Commercial development of the newly conquered lands during the Edo Era, from 1603, included the suppression of the Ainu population. In 1669 the Ainu national hero, Shakushian, led the Ainu against the Japanese invaders, only to once again suffer defeat. A century later, in 1789, another national hero, Kunashiri Menashi, led the Ainu in a final battle against harsh Japanese domination.

Until about 1800, the Ainu outnumbered the Japanese inhabitants of the most northerly of the principal Japanese islands. Up to the 1868 Meiji Restoration the government officially classed the Ainu as "foreign" and treated them as illegal foreigners living in the empire. After the restoration, a plan for government-sponsored Japanese emigration formed an integral part of the strategy for exploiting Hokkaido's rich natural resources.

In 1870 the government recognized the Ainu as Japanese and forced them to take up settled agriculture on communal lands, an activity total alien to the Ainu tradition. An American, Horace Capron, inadvertently contributed to the decline of the Ainu by introducing scientific farming methods that greatly accelerated Japanese colonization of Ainu territory, including the Kurile Islands off Hokkaido's northwest coast. In 1877 all Ainu communal lands were nationalized, and the Ainu language and traditions were forbidden. The government ordered that all Ainu names must be changed to recognizable Japanese names.

In 1885, when the Japanese population of Hokkaido had reached nearly 300,000 the Japanese government granted the island a separate provincial administration, which completely ignored the welfare or the rights of the Ainu minority. The Law for the Protection of the Primitive Peoples of Hokkaido in 1899 described the Ainu as an inferior race and assigned them to reservations set up on Hokkaido's least productive lands. The Ainu began to assimilate as the only means to survive.

The Ainu, since the turn of the century, have increasingly adopted the Japanese language and culture and attempted to hide their origins. The homogeneous Japanese, extremely intolerant of minorities, subjected the Ainu to many forms of discrimination.

In the late 1980s a new nationalism took hold of the remaining Ainu population, spurred by renewed contacts between the Ainu of Japan and their kin in the collapsing Soviet Union. The Japanese government, in the wake of the disintegration of the Soviet Union in 1991, began to press its claim to the Kurile Islands. The controversy over the disposition of the islands, part of the original Ainu patrimony, stimulated the growth of Ainu nationalism. Although fewer than 20,000 Japanese citizens claim Ainu identity, nationalists assert that several hundred thousand Japanese are of Ainu ancestry. In 1984 nationalists demanded a new statute to replace the racist aboriginal law of 1899, under which they are still governed, but their petitions and pleas made no impression on the Japanese government.

The nationalists mobilized the Ainu population in one of the most remarkable revivals since the end of the Cold War. In 1991 the Ainu nationalist organization, Untari, formally laid claim to the Kurile Islands and cited the chronicles of Dutch navigator Martin de Vries, who wrote of the island's Ainu inhabitants in 1634. The nationalists demanded ''exclusive possession'' of two or three of the smaller islands as a first step toward establishing a sovereign Ainu state. The Ainu claim that their right to sovereignty over the islands predated either the Japanese or Russian claims by several millennia. The Japanese claim to have controlled the Kuriles since the seventeenth century. The Russians claim that the Ainu of the Kuriles paid taxes to the Russian Empire in the form of furs in the same century.

The Kurile Islands have been disputed by Japan and Russia since 1875, when the Russians gave the islands to Japan in exchange for northern Sakhalin. At the end of World War II, in September 1945, the Soviet Union ignored its armed neutrality with Japan and occupied the islands. Two years later the Soviet government annexed the islands outright. The Japanese and some of the Ainu inhabitants of the islands left for nearby Hokkaido.

The Japanese government refuses to recognize the Ainu claim and pushes for the return of the islands to Japanese sovereignty, even though polls show that the Japanese people do not care about the islands and do not see them as an important issue. For the Ainu, the claim to the islands is a very important issue; a sovereign state in the islands would assure their survival as a separate nation.

*SELECTED BIBLIOGRAPHY:*

Fallows, James. *Looking at the Sun.* 1994.
Groot, G. J. *The Prehistory of Japan.* 1951.
Munro, N. G. *Ainu, Creed and Culture.* 1963.
Partal, Vicent. *The Ainu Law of 1899.* 1992.

# HONSAWATOI

**Mon; Hamsavati; Sheldrake Country**

*CAPITAL: Thaton*

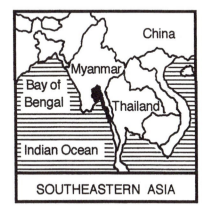

SOUTHEASTERN ASIA

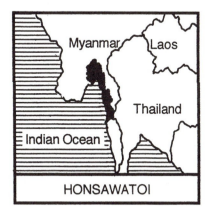

HONSAWATOI

*POPULATION:* (95e) 3,614,000 : 2,300,000 Mons in Myanmar, another 900,000 in adjacent areas of Thailand. MAJOR NATIONAL GROUPS: (95e) Mon (Taliang) 62%, Karen 15%, other Burmese. MAJOR LANGUAGES: Burmese, Mon, Karen. MAJOR RELIGIONS: Buddhism, Sunni Muslim, Christian. MAJOR CITIES: MON STATE: (95e) Moulmein (Mawlamyiang) 278,000 (375,000), Thaton 184,000, Kyaikkam 95,000 (177,000), Mudon 90,000, Martaban 65,000, Kyaikto 56,000, Ye 50,000. PEGU DIVISION: Pegu (Bago) 224,000, Nyaunglebin 46,000 (85,000), Shwegyin 40,000.

*GEOGRAPHY:* AREA: 9,572 sq.mi.-24,798 sq.km. LOCATION: Honsawatoi lies in southern Myanmar occupying the flat coastal plains east of the Gulf of Martaban and the lowlands of the Sittang River basin. POLITICAL STATUS: Honsawatoi has no official status; the region claimed by nationalists forms Mon State and the Pegu District of Pegu Division of Myanmar.

*FLAG:* The Mon national flag, the flag of the national movement, is a red field bearing a centered yellow sheldrake in flight and is charged with a pale blue, five-pointed star on the upper hoist.

*PEOPLE:* The Mons are a Mon-Khmer people related to the Khmers of Cambodia. Called Taliang by the Burmans, the Mons speak a Mon-Khmer language that is related to Cambodian Khmer and the languages of some of the smaller national groups in northeastern Myanmar, but not to the languages spoken by the Burmans or neighboring peoples. The language, with its own script, an alphabet of thirty-five letters, has an extensive literature revered in Asia much as Greek or Roman literature is regarded in Europe. The majority of the Mons live outside the designated Mon state, mostly in neighboring Pegu Division.

*THE NATION:* The Mon originated in the upper Mekong River region of present China. In the third century B.C. the Mon-Khmer peoples migrated south, the Khmer following the river into present Cambodia while the Mon veered southward to occupy the delta of the Irrawaddy River. According to Mon legend, a sacred sheldrake carried the Buddha across the Gulf of Martaban. The ancient Mons adopted the sheldrake as their national symbol.

The Mons developed a highly sophisticated civilization with a strong literary tradition and an extensive classical literature. Influenced by maritime contacts with ancient India, the Mon kingdom evolved the most advanced and wealthy society in Southeast Asia. Neighboring peoples called the kingdom the Golden Land. By the sixth century A.D. the Mon kingdom extended to the basin of the Chao Phraya River in present Thailand. A new capital, Pegu, founded in 573, grew into one of the largest and wealthiest cities in ancient Asia.

Burmans, a warrior people from eastern Tibet,* began to penetrate the kingdom in the tenth century. They eventually moved south in large-enough numbers to overwhelm the Mon kingdom in 1044. The victorious Burmans adopted much of the advanced Mon culture as their own. The Mons reestablished their kingdom following the Burman defeat by invading Mongols in 1287. Called Hamsavati, meaning Sheldrake Country, the Mon kingdom entered a second golden age in the fourteenth and fifteenth centuries.

Resurgent Burmans overran the kingdom in the 1530s and established their new capital at Pegu, the capital of the defeated Mons. In 1740 the Mons' great national hero, Binnya Dala, led a twelve-year rebellion against harsh Burman rule. In 1752 the victorious Dala re-created the Mon kingdom and formed an alliance with the French forces in the region. In spite of some European assistance, the kingdom fell to the returning Burmans in 1757. Pegu and the other Mon cities were sacked and burned. Horrible massacres of the populations ended the Mon threat to Burman domination for the next two centuries.

The Mon heartland came under British rule after the first Anglo-Burmese War in 1826, the remainder in 1852. Preferring British authority to that of the hated Burmans, the Mon became one of the most loyal of the region's peoples. Many Mons entered the local colonial administration and the colonial military forces.

The ethnic Burmans, having absorbed the ancient Mon culture, in the late nineteenth century asserted that there had never been a separate Mon nation, only an early branch of the Burmans. The outraged Mons, claiming that they created what is now called the golden age of Burma, began to reassert their separate culture and identity. Violent ethnic conflicts broke out in the 1920s as the Mons relentlessly pressed their national and cultural revival.

Loyal to the British during World War II, the Mons petitioned for a separate state as Burma moved to independence after the war. Ignored by the British in their haste to leave Burma, the Mons unsuccessfully sought negotiations with the Burman authorities. In 1948 Mon nationalists formed the Mon National Defense Organization (MNDO) and allied with insurgent Karens despite overlapping territorial claims. Fighting during the 1950s sent a wave of Mon refugees into Thailand to join the Mons, who had fled previous wars with the Burmans in the sixteenth, eighteenth, and nineteenth centuries. Defeated by the Burmese military in 1958, the Mons suffered renewed oppression, particularly after the military took control of Burma in 1962. The Mon rebellion resumed in the late 1960s, often in alliance with other ethnic insurgent groups in Burma.

The aim of the resurgent Mon nationalism was no longer autonomy but an independent Mon state. Mon nationalists claimed a large part of Burma as traditional Mon territory. The more radical groups claimed the Burmese divisions of Rangoon, Irrawaddy, and Pegu and the states of Mon, Karen, and Kayah. The moderate majority set the limits of the territorial claims at the Mon heartland in Mon State and southern Pegu Division. The nationalists called their proposed state Honsawatoi, Sheldrake Country, the modern version of the name of their ancient kingdom. In pursuit of their aim, the Mons joined with several other national groups fighting the Burmese military government to replace the hated Burmese state with a federation of independent states.

Widespread Mon support for the democracy movement in Burma in 1988–90, with its promise of independence within a democratic federation, turned to despair as the government loosed its soldiers on peaceful demonstrators and refused to relinquish power to a freely elected civilian government. The Mon insurgency resumed in 1989 and escalated rapidly in response to the excesses of the brutal military regime. Thousands fled to Thailand to escape the indiscriminate attacks on civilian targets in 1992.

The Myanmar military government declared a unilateral cease-fire in 1992 in an effort to draw the Mons into negotiations. The Mon leadership, skeptical of government intentions, refused to accept the stated terms. In late 1994 the government broke its own cease-fire and began a new offensive against the Mon nationalist forces.

*SELECTED BIBLIOGRAPHY:*
Aung-Thwin, Michael. *The Origins of Modern Burma.* 1985.
Cady, J. F. *A History of Modern Burma.* 1958.
Lintner, Bertil. *Land of Jade: A Journey through Insurgent Burma.* 1990.
Smith, Martin. *Burma: Insurgency and the Politics of Ethnicity.* 1988.

# INGRIA

**Inkeri; Ingriya; North Ingermanland**

*CAPITAL: Kirjasalo (Kirilloskoye)*

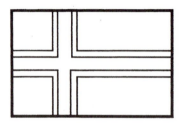

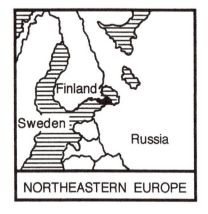

NORTHEASTERN EUROPE

INGRIA

*POPULATION:* (95e) 173,000 : 85,000 Ingrians in Russia and another 20,000 in Estonia and 250,000 in Finland. MAJOR NATIONAL GROUPS: (95e) Russian 49%, Ingrian (Inkeri) 47%, Finn 3%. MAJOR LANGUAGES: Russian, Ingrian (Inger), Finnish. MAJOR RELIGIONS: Lutheran, Russian Orthodox. MAJOR CITIES: (95e) Terÿoki (Zelenogorsk) 31,000, Kirjasalo (Kirilloskoye) 10,000, Toksovo (Sosnovo) 8,000.

*GEOGRAPHY:* AREA: 1,546 sq.mi.-4,005 sq.km. LOCATION: Ingria lies in northwestern Russia, a flat plain between Lake Ladoga and the Gulf of Finland, just north of St. Petersburg. POLITICAL STATUS: Ingria has had no official status; the region forms a nonpolitical district of St. Petersburg Oblast of the Russian Federation.

*INDEPENDENCE DECLARED:* 23 January 1920.

*FLAG:* The Ingrian national flag, the flag of the former republic, is a yellow field charged with a blue Scandinavian cross outlined in red.

*PEOPLE:* The Ingrians or Ingers, who call themselves and their homeland Inkeri, are a Finnic people, the remnant of a much larger pre–World War II Ingrian population. The Ingrians are related to the Finns and to the Estonians, the other Finnic peoples who live on the shores of the Gulf of Finland, and speak a separate language of the Finno-Ugric language group closely related to Finnish. Estimates of the total Ingrian population in the region, including the Izhor on the south shore of the Gulf of Finland, vary greatly, as many have registered as ethnic Russians since the Second World War. Official figures for 1989 included 70,000 Ingrians in St. Petersburg Oblast (formerly Leningrad),

18,000 in Karelia,* and only a few hundred Izhor. Nationalists claim an Ingrian population in the region of over 200,000 and another 400,000 outside Russia, mostly in Finland. The majority of the Ingrians and Finns are Protestant Lutherans, with an Orthodox minority.

*THE NATION:* Populated during the migration of the Finnic tribes from the Volga River basin in the eighth century, the region around the Gulf of Finland became home to the Inkeri or Inger tribe. Christianized in the thirteenth century, the Ingrians settled as farmers and fishermen in the flatlands around the gulf. Under the rule of the Slav Republic of Great Novgorod from the thirteenth century until the late fifteenth century, the Ingrians prospered on trade routes that crossed their homeland between Scandinavia and the Slav lands.

Russians, Swedes, and Teutonic Knights contested the control of Ingria following the overthrow of Novgorod by the Russians in 1478. Conquered by the Swedes under Gustavus II in 1617, the Ingrians adopted many Swedish cultural traits and accepted the Swedes' Protestant Lutheran religion.

The major Swedish fort on the Neva River fell to the Russian forces of Peter I in 1702. The next year Peter, called the Great, began to lay out a new city on the site, St. Petersburg, Russia's new window on the West. The construction of Russia's new capital brought a massive influx of Slav workers, the city's expansion slowly pushing the native Ingrians west along the north and south shores of the gulf. In 1721 Sweden formally ceded Ingria to permanent Russian rule. Despite the loss of many of their ancient lands, the Ingrians prospered, supplying the growing capital with timber, grains, and vegetables.

The government policy that stressed the assimilation of minorities succeeded in the expanding urban area but met strong resistance among the large rural Ingrian population. Influenced by the neighboring Finns and Estonians, a cultural revival began to take hold in the 1880s. The revival spawned a modest national movement that gained support following the disturbances and violence of the 1905 revolution.

The Ingrians, weary after three years of war and the increasing hardships and hunger, welcomed the revolution that spread outward from Petrograd (St. Petersburg) in February 1917. Numbering some half million, the Ingrians in the district petitioned the new democratic government for autonomy within a new democratic Russia. More militant nationalists proposed the creation of an independent Ingria around the Gulf of Finland, linking Finland and Estonia, and with Petrograd given autonomous status within the state.

Promised autonomy by the Bolsheviks who took power in Petrograd in October 1917, the nationalists soon faced harsh suppression as the Soviets consolidated their power. The Ingrians rebelled and took control of the territory between the new Finnish border, Lake Ladoga, the northern shore of the Gulf of Finland, and the outskirts of Petrograd. Hard-pressed by the demands of the escalating Russian civil war, the Soviet authorities were unable to spare troops to deal with the Ingrian rebels until late 1919. Threatened by units of the Red Army, the Ingrians leaders declared the independence of Ingria, sometimes called North Ingermanland, on 23 January 1920 and issued frantic appeals to newly independent Finland.

The Finns, in the final months of war with the Soviets in the north, could not respond to the appeals. But in late 1920 they negotiated Finnish control of western Ingria as part of the peace treaty with the new Soviet Union. The Ingrians left under Soviet rule surrendered to the Red Army in 1921.

The Soviet government, as part of its nationalities program, created a national district for the remaining 115,000 Ingrians in 1928. Accused of anti-Soviet sentiment as relations with neighboring Finland worsened in the late 1930s, the entire Ingrian leadership was purged in 1937, and all Ingrian books were ordered burned. In 1938 the Soviet authorities dissolved the Ingrian national district.

The Soviet government in 1939 demanded that Finland cede western Ingria and western Karelia, including Finland's fourth largest city, Viipuri. Forced to give up the territories following a brief war, the defiant Finns joined the German assault on the Soviet Union two years later. Finnish troops liberated Ingria in June and July 1941, but the Finns refused to join the German siege of Leningrad, claiming that theirs was a separate war.

In 1944 the majority of the Ingrians joined the flood of refugees fleeing the advancing Red Army. Thousands of Ingrians, unable to escape, faced deportation and labor camps in 1944–45. In 1947 all Ingrian autonomy ended, and the region became part of Leningrad Oblast. In the 1950s over 16,000 Ingrians were forcibly resettled in Soviet Estonia. Their homes on the south shore of the gulf were occupied by ethnic Russians for security reasons.

The liberalization of Soviet society, beginning in 1987, allowed the first Ingrian contacts with Finland and the large Ingrian exile population since 1944. Language schools, opened with Finnish aid, and thousands of books donated by sympathetic Finnish citizens have begun to reverse decades of forced isolation and assimilation.

An Ingrian congress, held in Tallinn, Estonia, in April 1990, and a second congress convened at Zelenogorsk following the collapse of the Soviet Union in September 1991 endorsed the Ingrians' right to self-determination and closer ties to Finland. In November 1992 the Ingrians demanded official recognition of their suffering over seven decades of Soviet domination.

*SELECTED BIBLIOGRAPHY:*

Allison, Roy. *Finland's Relation with the Soviet Union 1944–84.* 1985.

Hall, Wendy. *Green Gold and Granite.* 1953.

Wixman, Ronald. *The Peoples of the U.S.S.R. An Ethnographic Handbook.* 1984.

Wuorinen, John H. *Finland and World War II, 1939–44.* 1983.

# INGUSHETIA

**Galgai; Ingushia; Ingushya**

*CAPITAL: Nazran*

SOUTHEASTERN EUROPE

INGUSHETIA

*POPULATION:* (95e) 328,000 : 287,000. MAJOR NATIONAL GROUPS: (95e) Ingush 80%, Chechen 9%, Russian 6%, Osset 4%. MAJOR LANGUAGES: Ingush, Chechen, Russian. MAJOR RELIGIONS: Sunni Muslim, Russian Orthodox. MAJOR CITIES: (95e) Malgobek 46,000, Nazran 35,000, Muzici 10,000.

*GEOGRAPHY:* AREA: 1,242 sq.mi.-3,218 sq.km. LOCATION: Ingushetia lies in the Northern Caucasus, occupying the slopes and northern foothills of the Caucasus Mountains between Chechenia* and Ossetia* in southern European Russia. POLITICAL STATUS: Ingushetia forms a member state of the Russian Federation.

*FLAG:* The Ingush national flag, the official flag of the republic, is a white field with narrow green, horizontal stripes at the top and bottom, charged with the Ingush national symbol centered, a purple circle with three extensions or points.

*PEOPLE:* The Ingush are a Caucasian people closely related to the neighboring Chechen, and speak a dialect that, with Chechen, makes up the northeastern or Vienakh group of Caucasian languages. The Ingush dialect became a literary language only in 1923. Both the Ingush and Chechen call themselves the Nakh or Natakhchuo, although in recent decades the Ingush have increasingly asserted their own identity. In the past many scholars and linguists referred to the Ingush as Western Chechens. The majority of the Ingush are Sunni Muslims, mostly of the Shafi rite.

*THE NATION:* The Ingush claim descent from the region's early Scythian tribes and have inhabited the North Caucasus region from about 600 B.C. The Caucasus Mountains, an often-used invasion route between Asia and Europe, became the only refuge for the early tribal peoples who sheltered in the high, inaccessible valleys. The tribes early developed a warrior society in response to the region's many invaders. Influenced by the Roman culture in the lands to the south, the tribes adopted the Christian religion in the sixth century, but without giving up their warlike culture and traditions.

In the fifteenth century Persians and Turks fought for predominance in the strategic region. In the seventeenth century the Ingush, driven into the mountains by the thirteenth century Mongol invasion, returned to settle their ancestral lands along the Terek River, where they formed close cultural and military ties to the neighboring Chechens. For centuries the Ingush were not distinguished from the larger Chechen population. Under the influence of the Ottoman Turks, the Ingush accepted the Islamic religion late in the seventeenth century.

Increasing Russian interest in the potentially rich area sent Cossack explorers and soldiers to the North Caucasus in the sixteenth century. The Cossacks constructed a string of forts as they moved south. In 1784 Vladikavkaz was founded as a fort on the edge of Ingush territory, beginning the Russian expansion in the region.

The Ingush rose to drive the invaders from their territory in 1818 but failed to take the Cossack forts. Joining the region's other Muslim peoples, the Ingush participated in a great holy war against the Russians from 1847 to 1860. After seventy years of sporadic warfare, the Russians finally pushed into the mountain strongholds in 1859, often slaughtering entire populations. Some three-fourths of the Ingush people perished in the war, and the survivors were driven into the mountains. The government granted their confiscated lands along the Terek River to the Cossack hordes, the colonists taking the name the Terek Cossacks.

Frequent rebellions and grinding poverty devastated the Ingush culture. By the turn of the century most of the Ingush lived as poor herders in the high valleys, close to the strongholds the Russian military dared not enter.

The Ingush enthusiastically supported their fellow Muslims, the Turks, when war began in 1914. With the overthrow of the hated tsarist regime in February 1917, the Ingush believed that, at last, old wrongs would be righted. Their petitions and pleas ignored, the Ingush swept out of their mountains to attack the lowland Cossack and Russian settlements.

In September 1917 Ingush delegates participated in the newly created autonomous government of North Caucasia, and the Ingush warriors declared *gazava*, holy war, on the Terek Cossacks. The Bolshevik coup in October 1917 forced the Muslims into an uneasy anti-Bolshevik alliance with the Cossacks, but the alliance soon ended in violent confrontations. In December 1917 the Ingush captured Vladikavkaz but were again driven from the lowlands in the confused fighting and shifting alliances of 1918. On 11 May 1918 the Muslims of the region declared the independence of the Republic of North Caucasia.

The Ingush transferred their capital to Nazran after the Cossacks, aided by the anti-Bolshevik Whites, retook Vladikavkaz in August 1918. Believing the Soviet promise of independence in the Soviet Federation, the Ingush and Chechens went over to the Reds. With the aid of the Bolshevik forces, the Ingush captured and looted Vladikavkaz in November.

In January 1920, despite earlier promises, the Soviets attempted to incorporate the Ingush and Chechen lands into their new Soviet state. The Muslims turned on their Red allies but were finally defeated in a vicious two-month war. In 1924 the authorities set up a separate Ingush region, which united with Chechenia to form an autonomous republic ten years later. In 1937 the Ingush joined a mass Muslim uprising in the region but again suffered defeat and reprisals.

An enduring hatred of the Russians pushed many Ingush to support the German invasion of the region during World War II. Stalin accused the entire Ingush nation of treason. In January 1944 Soviet soldiers herded the Ingush into Nazran and forced them onto cattle cars for deportation to the east. The dissolved Ingush national region was divided, part given over to the neighboring republic, North Ossetia.

In 1957 the deported Caucasian peoples received an official rehabilitation, allowing them to return to their homes in the officially designated Ingush homeland. Rioting broke out in the region in 1958 as Russians and Ossetians refused to vacate the properties they had taken in 1944. The bitter return sparked the beginning of the modern national movement.

The collapse of the Soviet Union in 1991 fueled a dramatic growth of Ingush nationalism and stimulated demands for the return of the Ingush region in North Ossetia. The neighboring Chechens declared their independence of Russia, but the Ingush refused all Chechen overtures. In January 1992 Ingushetia officially separated from Chechenia, and on 4 June 1992 the Russian parliament approved the creation of a separate Ingush republic.

Rising demands for the return of the territory transferred to Ossetia in 1944 became the primary nationalist issue. In October 1992 fighting broke out in the disputed region. In November Ossetians, aided by Russian troops, drove 60,000 Ingush into squalid refugee camps in Ingushetia and left over 300 dead. The involvement of the government troops ended the Ingush support for the Moscow government. In July 1993 the Ingush parliament voted to hold a referendum on the republic's ties to the Russian Federation, and in early 1994, on the fiftieth anniversary of their deportation, nationalists confirmed support for the eventual independence of the Ingush nation.

*SELECTED BIBLIOGRAPHY:*
Minorsky, Vladimir. *Studies in Caucasian History.* 1953.
Nekrich, Alexander. *The Punished Peoples.* 1978.
Rywkin, Michael. *Russian Colonial Expansion to 1917.* 1988.

# ISTRIA

**Istra**

*CAPITAL: Pulj (Pula)*

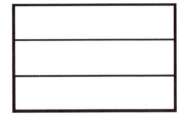

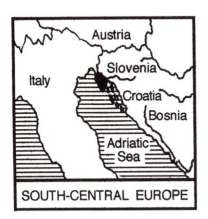

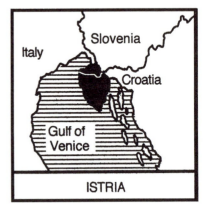

*POPULATION:* (95e) 378,000 : 412,000 Istrians in Croatia and Slovenia. MAJOR NATIONAL GROUPS: (95e) Istrian 91% (Croat 65%, Slovene 11%, Italian 8%, Morlakh 5%, Friuli 2%), other Croat, other Slovene. MAJOR LANGUAGES: Croat, Slovene, Italian, Furlan. MAJOR RELIGIONS: Roman Catholic 92%, Sunni Muslim 4%, Protestant 1%. MAJOR CITIES: (95e) CROATIA: Pulj (Pula/Pola) 67,000 (85,000), Opatija (Abbazia) 32,000, Rovinj (Rovigno) 12,000, Pazin (Pisino) 10,000. SLOVENIA: Koper (Capodistria) 24,000, Pirin (Pirino) 9,000 (16,000).

*GEOGRAPHY:* AREA: 1,545 sq.mi.-4,005 sq.km. LOCATION: Istria occupies a heavily wooded peninsula projecting into the Adriatic Sea between the gulfs of Trieste and Rijeka just south of the Karst Plateau in southwestern Slovenia and northwestern Croatia. POLITICAL STATUS: Istria has no official status; the region forms the Istria district of Croatia and the Koper district of Slovenia.

*FLAG:* The Istrian national flag, the traditional flag of the region and the flag of the national movement, is a horizontal tricolor of red, yellow, and blue.

*PEOPLE:* The Istrians, who refer to themselves as an Istro-Romanic people, are a Slav people with a unique culture that has developed over centuries of mixed Slav, Germanic, and Latin elements. The Istrians, inhabiting a region that has long been a crossroads of cultures and languages, have a strong sense of their separate identity, which embraces the three main Istrian groups, the Croats, the Slovenes, and the Italians, along with smaller numbers of Friuli and the mostly Muslim Morlakh. Extensive intermarriage has added to the development of a separate Istrian identity. All of the Istrian peoples have lived together in relative peace for centuries.

*THE NATION:* The peninsula's original inhabitants, Illyrian tribes, came under Roman rule in 177 B.C. and over centuries adopted the Latin culture. Roman towns, complete with elegant buildings, villas, theaters, and public arenas, dotted the lush landscape. In the fifth century Huns and Visigoths destroyed the last Roman strongholds before the Byzantines could extend their authority to the region. Migrating Slav tribes settled the peninsula and accepted nominal Byzantine rule in the sixth century. The settlers soon adopted much of the Latin culture that still dominated the peninsula and the surrounding regions.

The territory of the peninsula was divided among several neighboring states following the collapse of Byzantine rule in the eighth century. By the fifteenth century, after centuries of division and changing borders, Austria and Venice had absorbed the majority of the peninsular territories. The northern part, under Hapsburg rule, formed a separate crownland of the Austrian Empire. The southern districts remained under Venetian rule until they, too, passed to Austria under the terms of the Treaty of Campoformio in 1797.

Under Austrian rule the peninsula formed part of a region of mixed Italian, South Slav, and Austrian population. The Istrians, after centuries of foreign rule, gradually realized that they had more in common with their neighbors than with populations outside their peninsula.

In the late nineteenth century the large Italian-speaking population became the subject of irredentist claims by the newly united Italian kingdom, and a movement to unite the peninsula with Italy gained support. In 1915, to entice Italy into the war, the Allies promised Istria and other Italian-speaking Austrian territories to Italy. However, with Austria's defeat, a strong movement for separate Istrian independence won widespread support in 1918–19.

The prospect of dividing the peoples that had coexisted for centuries stimulated the national movement. In October 1918 the regional parliament at Trieste* voted to erect an autonomous Republic of Venezia-Giulia under the protection of the new League of Nations, an Italo-Croat-Slovene state to include Trieste and its territory, the Julian region, and the Istrian peninsula.

The fate of the peninsula remained unsettled until 1920, when the entire region came under Italian administration. The area's economic and political importance declined rapidly under Italian rule, particularly following the fascist takeover of Italy in 1922. Increasingly nationalistic, the fascists instituted programs designed to homogenize the many regional cultures and to eradicate the non-Italian influences. In 1926 the government banned the Slav languages and many of the South Slav traditions. The Italianization of the peninsula included government-sponsored immigration from Italy's poor and backward south. The growing tensions between the peninsula's Italians and Slavs paralleled the similar tensions between the Istrian Italians and the culturally and dialectically different newcomers.

The outbreak of World War II exacerbated the peninsula's simmering ethnic and regional tensions. Pro-fascist, Istrian nationalist, and Yugoslav-supported pro-Communists clashed with rival groups and the Italian army.

In the spring of 1945 Tito's Yugoslav partisans occupied the peninsula. Thousands of Istrians, both Italian and Slav, real or imagined fascists, anti-Communists, and Istrian nationalists opposed to Yugoslav rule were rounded up and executed. In an orgy of revenge, the partisans tossed the bodies of men, women, and children from the Istrian cliffs into the Adriatic Sea. The Yugoslav Communist authorities expelled over 300,000 Italian Istrians between 1945 and 1951.

Yugoslavia received most of Istria in the postwar territorial transfers in 1946; however, part of the peninsula, due to the ongoing territorial dispute, became part of the newly created Free City of Trieste in 1947. In 1954 the state of Trieste was divided by Italy and Yugoslavia. The city of Trieste and its environs became part of Italy, and the southern zone went to Yugoslavia, divided between the Yugoslav republics of Slovenia and Croatia. Istrian opposition to the division delayed the ratification of the Treaty of Osimo until 1975.

The breakup of the Yugoslav state in 1991 again divided Istria, this time between the independent republics of Slovenia and Croatia. The new Croatian government, under a resolute nationalist administration, began to limit local government autonomy and passed new laws that threatened Istrian culture. With excellent interethnic relations in the peninsula, the Croat Istrians rejected the virulent nationalism emanating from Zagreb and began to campaign for closer ties to the neighboring Istrian Slovenes and the Italians.

In 1990, even before the disintegration of Yugoslavia, the Istrians had formed the Istrian Democratic Diet (Dieta Democratica Istriana, DDI), a trilingual, tri-ethnic forum that advocated autonomy for the peninsula. Nationalists proposed a plan for a transnational autonomy of two sovereign provinces, one in Croatia with its capital at Pula, the other in Slovenia with its capital at Koper.

The Croatian Istrians in February 1993 firmly rejected Croatia's aggressive nationalism. The Istrian party, the DDI, won 72% of the vote, as opposed to the Croat national party's 16%. The DDI won on a platform of liberal tolerance and a multiethnic region away from the chaos and violence of the former Yugoslavia.

A border dispute between Slovenia and Croatia over the Istrian Bay of Pirin is fueling Istrian nationalism and demands for a separate transborder Istrian region. However, Slovenia and Croatia are united in their opposition to the Istrian national movement.

*SELECTED BIBLIOGRAPHY:*

Eterovich, Francis, and Christopher Spalatin. *Croatia: Land, People, and Culture.* 1970.
Macan, Tripimir. *A Short History of Croatia.* 1992.
Novak, Bogan C. *Trieste Nineteen Forty-One to Nineteen Fifty-Four: The Ethnic Politics and Ideological Struggle.* 1970.

# JEBEL ED DRUZE

### Jabal ad Duruz; Druzistan

*CAPITAL: Sweida (Es Suweida)*

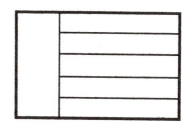

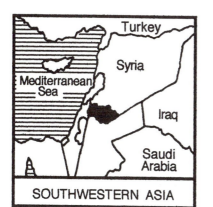

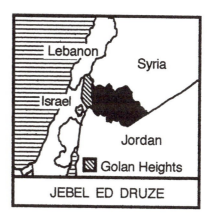

*POPULATION:* (95e) 967,000 : 875,000 Druze in Syria and another 250,000 in adjacent areas of Lebanon, 77,000 in northern Israel, and 15,000 in the Golan Heights. MAJOR NATIONAL GROUPS: (95e) Druze (Druse/Duruz) 88%, other Syrian. MAJOR LANGUAGES: Arabic (Druze dialect), French. MAJOR RELIGIONS: Druze, Sunni Muslim. MAJOR CITIES: (95e) Sweida (Es Suweida) 131,000, Dera (Dar'a) 106,000, Nava (Nawá) 40,000, Busra (Busrá ash-Sham) 38,000, Izra (Mahattat Izra') 35,000, Kunietra (Al-Qunaytirah) 10,000.

*GEOGRAPHY:* AREA: 4,328 sq.mi.-11,212 sq.km. LOCATION: Jebel ed Druze lies in southern Syria, occupying the mountainous Hawran region bordering Jordan on the south, Israel on the west, and Lebanon on the northwest. POLITICAL STATUS: Jebel ed Druze has no official status, the region forms the Syrian provinces of Es Suweida, Dar'a, and Al-Qunaytirah. Israel annexed the western districts of the latter two, called the Golan Heights, in 1981.

*FLAG:* The Druze national flag, the flag of the national movement, has five horizontal stripes of green, red, yellow, pale blue, and white, with a vertical white stripe at the hoist. OTHER FLAG(S): The flag of the Druze in Lebanon has four horizontal stripes of red, yellow, pale blue, and white and bears a green triangle at the hoist. The flag of the Druze in Israel has horizontal stripes of green, red, yellow, pale blue, and white and is charged with a white Star of David on the upper hoist.

*PEOPLE:* The ethnic origins of the Druze are unknown. According to Druze legend, the high incidence of tall, fair, and light-eyed Druze results from the mixture of ancient nomads and the Greek soldiers of Alexander the Great. The Druze speak a dialect of Arabic that retains many pre-Arabic influences and forms. The Druze religion, a secretive sect that combines Muslim, Christian, and pagan traditions, prohibits intermarriage or religious conversion and is an integral part of the Druze culture. Druze society encompasses two distinct groups, the Eqal (the Knowers), accounting for 10% of the population and privy to the secrets of the Druze religious rituals, and the Juhal (the Ignorant), the majority excluded from the secrets and the leadership of their religion. A large Druze population inhabits the mountains between Beirut and the Syrian border in Lebanon, and smaller minorities live in sixteen Druze towns in Israel's Galilee region and in the Israeli-occupied Golan Heights.

*THE NATION:* Druze legends trace their origins to an ancient nomadic people, the Auranites, the origin of the name of their mountainous region, Hauran or Hawran. The pagan Auranites, influenced by Jewish and later Greek religious traditions, converted to Christianity under Roman rule in the second century A.D. The Christianity they practiced retained a number of pre-Christian traditions and rituals.

Muslim Arabs invaded the Auranite homeland in the seventh century. The conquerors forcibly converted the inhabitants to their Islamic religion, but many of the Auranite converts secretly continued to adhere to their pre-Islamic traditions. The blend of the Islamic and pre-Islamic traditions formalized as the Druze religion in the tenth century.

The Druze rejection of Mohammed as the ultimate prophet and the Koran as the revealed word earned them the enmity of their Muslim neighbors. Considered non-Muslim infidels, they suffered discrimination and persecution by the Sunni Muslim majority. The despised Druze finally withdrew to the mountain strongholds in the Hawran and the Lebanon Mountains, where they evolved a clannish, closed society.

Druze warriors fiercely resisted the sixteenth-century Turkish conquest of their homeland and the renewed persecution that followed their defeat by the Ottoman troops. In 1860 the Druze rebelled and attacked both the Turks and the Maronite Christian population of the lowlands. A French expedition, sent to protect the Christians in the Turkish province in 1861, defeated the Druze and drove thousands into the isolated plateaus of the Hawran.

In the Hawran the refugees built a new capital, Sweida, a Druze fortress city ruled by the powerful Al-Atash clan. The Druze warriors, heartened by a religious belief that those who fall in battle are instantly reborn, successfully resisted Turkish attempts to reimpose their rule on Dera, the main town of the Hawran, or Sweida, the new Druze capital.

Druze attacks on Christians, renewed in the 1890s, provoked a French reaction, with French troops sent to occupy the Druze homeland. The French administration allowed the Druze considerable autonomy under a sultan of the Al-Atash clan. In 1914, when war broke out in Europe, the French attempted to impose direct rule, provoking a Druze uprising that was not fully subdued until after the war had ended, and more French troops became available for active duty against the Druze rebels.

In 1920 the French incorporated the Hawran into the League of Nations mandate in the former Turkish provinces of Syria. The mandate authorities created an autonomous Druze state, called Jebel ed Druze, in 1921 as one of the Levant States. French attempts to replace the Al-Atash ruler with a French governor incited serious revolts in 1925–27, 1937, and 1939. After the French surrender to the Axis in 1940, the Levant States came under the control of the Vichy French government, a Nazi ally.

Allied troops, mostly British and Free French, liberated the Levant States in 1941. The Free French granted independence to Syria but retained the separate French-protected states in Jebel ed Druze and Latakia.* In 1942 the Syrian republic incorporated Jebel ed Druze over strong Druze opposition to domination by their ancient Sunni Muslim enemies. In 1944 the Syrian government, in a conciliatory gesture, guaranteed Druze cultural and religious rights.

Druze opposition to Syria's military government erupted in revolts in 1949 and 1954. Defeated by the Syrian military, the Druze lost all their former autonomous rights. With few economic opportunities Syria's non-Sunni Muslim minorities joined the military in large numbers in the 1960s. Dominated by the minorities, the military purged the officer corps in 1964–65 and replaced most of the Sunni Muslims with Alawites and Druze. Following the Syrian defeat in the 1967 war with Israel, a power struggle developed within the military, with most Druze officers eliminated in 1969. The expulsion of the Druze and the smaller minorities from the military left Syria under the effective control of an Alawite military clique.

The Druze, having enthusiastically embraced militant Arab nationalism to deflect Sunni Muslim hatred, have seen the value of their support decline rapidly with the end of the Cold War and the splintering of Arab unity. Druze nationalism has gradually superseded the former pan-Arab nationalism the Druze had embraced after World War II. The resurgent Druze nationalism has grown with the renewed ties and contacts with the Druze minorities in Lebanon and Israel.

Israel's good relations with its Druze minority have facilitated contacts between the Druze national leadership and the Israeli government. The very real possibility of fragmented and coup-prone Syria's splintering along ethnic and religious lines has become an important element in Druze calculations. Good relations with their powerful southern neighbor, Israel, could be vital to the future of the Druze nation.

*SELECTED BIBLIOGRAPHY:*
Antoun, Richard T. *Syria: Society, Culture and Polity.* 1991.
Betts, Robert B. *The Druze.* 1988.
Ziadeh, N.A. *Syria and Lebanon.* 1957.

# JHARKHAND

### Forest Land; Jungle Country

*CAPITAL: Ranchi*

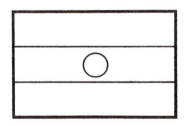

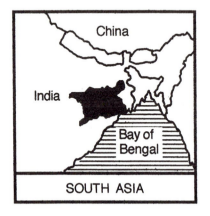

SOUTH ASIA

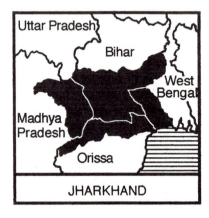

JHARKHAND

*POPULATION:* (95e) 36,250,000 : 14,500,000 Adivasi in the Chota Nagpur region of India. MAJOR NATIONAL GROUPS: (95e) Indian 60% (Bihari, Orissan, Bengali), Adivasi 40% (Santal, Munda, Oraoan, Ho, Kilda, Bhumy, Koura, smaller groups). MAJOR LANGUAGES: Bihari, Oriya, Santali, Munda, Hindi, Kurukh (Oraoan), English. MAJOR RELIGIONS: Hindu, animist, Christian. MAJOR CITIES: (95e) BIHAR: Ranchi 844,000 (953,000), Jamshedpur 548,000 (942,000), Dhanbad 145,000 (1,016,000), Hazaribagh 143,000, Daltonganj 113,000, Jaridih 59,000 (128,000). WEST BENGAL: Kharagpur 180,000 (420,000), Bankura 126,000, Midnapore 122,000, Purulia 110,000, Bankura 100,000. ORISSA: Raurkela 230,000 (419,000), Sambalpur 128,000 (190,000). MADHYA PRADESH: Raigarh 105,000, Ambikapur 50,000.

*GEOGRAPHY:* AREA: 61,590 sq.mi.-159,560 sq.km. LOCATION: Jharkhand occupies the heavily forested Chota Nagpur Plateau and the lowlands on the Bay of Bengal east of the Hooghly River in northeastern India. POLITICAL STATUS: Jharkhand, which translates as Forest Land or Jungle Country, has no official status; the region claimed by Jharkhand nationalists forms a number of administrative districts of the northeastern Indian states of Bihar, Orissa, Madhya Pradesh, and West Bengal.

*FLAG:* The Jharkhand flag, the flag of the national movement, has three horizontal stripes of green, white, and green and bears a red disc centered on the white stripe. OTHER FLAG(S): The flag of the largest of the national groups, the Jharkhand Mukti Morcha, is a green field bearing a centered white rooster.

*PEOPLE:* The Adivasi (Original Settlers), as they call themselves, are the surviving remnants of the region's pre-Aryan inhabitants. Relegated to the lowest rungs of India's rigid caste system, the twenty Adivasi tribes are included in the so-called Scheduled Tribes. The Adivasi tribes encompass the pre-Dravidian holdovers from ancient India, some 5 million Santal, 2 million Munda, and smaller groups speaking Munda languages of the Austro-Asiatic language group, and the Dravidian peoples, the 2 million Oraoan, 1 million Ho, half million Kolha, and smaller groups speaking Dravidian languages, the pre-Aryan languages now mostly confined to southern India. Although they represent different ethnic communities and languages, the Adivasi stress pan-tribal unity and claim that, with their allies among the Hindu Scheduled Castes and the other oppressed groups, 80% of the population supports the Jharkhand movement. The Chota Nagpur Adivasi are over half Christian, with large Hindu, Muslim, and animist minorities.

*THE NATION:* The Munda peoples, believed to have originated in central or southeastern Asia, inhabited large tracts of northern India prior to the ancient Dravidian settlement of the region. The Munda tribes, pushed into the less accessible highland jungles, adopted many Dravidian traditions while retaining their ancient pre-Dravidian languages and cultures.

Aryan invaders from the Iranian Plateau overran northern India between 1700 and 1200 B.C. The fair, warlike Aryans drove the darker Dravidians into southern India except for small groups of Dravidian refugees who fled into the jungled Chota Nagpur Plateau to escape the onslaught. Under successive Aryan kingdoms and empires, the lowlanders ignored and avoided the region. The autonomous Munda and Dravidian tribes retained their own chiefs and rulers under only nominal Aryan rule.

Muslims conquered the region in the twelfth century, and in 1497 the region's small Muslim states came under the rule of the powerful Sultanate of Delhi. The tribal peoples, despised and persecuted by the Hindu majority, enjoyed greater rights under the more tolerant Muslims. Some of the tribal peoples embraced Islam as an escape from the harsh and rigid Hindu caste system.

The plateau came under British rule in 1765 and formed part of the British province of Bengal. Christian missionaries arrived in the area in the early nineteenth century. The missionaries won many converts with their message of equality and tolerance. An educated minority, the product of the mission schools, gradually took over the leadership of the tribes. The last Adivasi uprising, a reaction to Hindu encroachment on tribal lands in the 1890s, was led by Birsa, a missionary-educated Christian.

Generally ignored until the discovery of rich mineral deposits around the turn of the century, the region suddenly took on great economic importance. In 1908 the government restricted the Adivasi tribes to allotted reserve lands. The rapid industrialization brought a large influx of Hindu industrial workers. The major industrial center, Jamshedpur, developed around the steel mills built on traditional Santali land between 1907 and 1911. The poorest segment of the population, the Adivasi moved to the new industrial cities in large numbers in the 1920s and 1930s. The urbanized tribals mostly adopted Christianity to escape the violence and discrimination of the Hindu caste system.

Relegated to the least desirable lands and jobs, the Adivasi began to organize after World War I. In 1938 nationalists founded the Jharkhand Party to press for pan-tribal unity and autonomy. In 1947, as Indian independence neared, militants demanded that the British grant separate independence to Jharkhand as a Christian majority area outside Hindu India and Muslim Pakistan, but they found little sympathy among the British authorities.

India's independence constitution included provisions for the protection of minority peoples and their lands, but, in practice, high-caste Hindus controlled large areas, and the Adivasi became virtual serfs on land that should have been theirs. Adivasi activists mobilized the tribes in the 1960s, demanding autonomy and the creation of a separate state of Jharkhand. The autonomy movement, gaining wide support in the tribal belt, broke down the remaining tribal barriers. Opposition to the autonomy movement by "civilized" Hindus sparked violent ethnic and religious confrontations in 1968–69.

Adivasi literacy rates are very high for rural India. The legacy of early mission schools and the Adivasi willingness to educate both boys and girls, unusual in India, have produced a highly motivated and aware national leadership. Even though they suffer caste and racial discrimination more aggressive and violent than South Africa's former apartheid, until the early 1990s Adivasi nationalists conducted a peaceful, reasoned, and articulate campaign to win equal rights for their people. Their moderate demands had little impact.

Younger, more militant nationalists, claiming that the Adivasi condition has steadily worsened since Indian independence in 1947, have formed militias to protect defenseless Adivasi against the continuing atrocities perpetrated with impunity by high caste Hindus. The movement has adopted environmental issues as national issues in one of the world's most polluted regions. Their grievances mostly ignored by state and federal authorities, the young Adivasi moving into leadership positions have begun to call for their followers to emulate the Sikhs of Khalistan* or the Muslims of Kashmir* in fighting for their rights and the self-determination of an Adivasi homeland in Jharkhand.

*SELECTED BIBLIOGRAPHY:*

Chanra, B. *Nationalism and Colonialism in Modern India.* 1979.
Churye, G. S. *Caste and Race in India.* 1986.
Singh, K. S. *Tribal Movements in India.* 1982.
———. *The Tribal Situation in India.* 1986.

# KABYLIA

**Kabylie**

*CAPITAL: Tizi-Uzu (Tizi-Ouzou)*

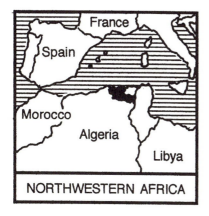

NORTHWESTERN AFRICA

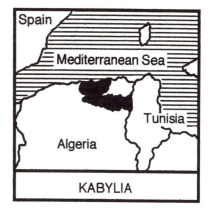

KABYLIA

*POPULATION:* (95e) 5,774,000 : 4,130,000 Kabyles in Algeria. MAJOR NATIONAL GROUPS: (95e) Kabyle 68%, other Algerian. MAJOR LANGUAGES: Kabyle, Arabic, French. MAJOR RELIGIONS: Sunni Muslim, Roman Catholic, Ibadi Muslim. MAJOR CITIES: (95e) Stif (Setif) 302,000, Tizi-Uzu (Tizi-Ouzou) 246,000, Bougee (Bejaïa) 216,000, Batna 203,000, Bordj Bou Arreridj 90,000, Djidjelli (Jijel) 86,000, Tbessa (Tebessa) 85,000, Eulma (El-Eulma) 80,000, Kenchia 76,000, Bordj Menael 60,000, Aïn Beda 60,000, Delles 52,000.

*GEOGRAPHY:* AREA: 24,333 sq.mi.-63,039 sq.mi. LOCATION: Kabylia lies in northeastern Algeria, occupying a coastal plain east of Algiers and the mountainous regions of the Hodna and Aurs Mountains east to the Tunisian border. The Kabyle heartland on the Mediterranean Sea is divided into Great Kabylia and Little Kabylia by the Sahel-Soumman Valley. POLITICAL STATUS: Kabylia has no official status; the region claimed by nationalists forms the Algerian departments of Batna, Bejaïa, Jijel, Oum-el-Bouaghi, Setif, Tebessa, and Tizi-Ouzou.

*FLAG:* The Kabyle national flag, the flag of the national movement, is a horizontal tricolor of pale blue, green, and white.

*PEOPLE:* The Kabyles are a Berber people more closely related to the peoples of Europe than to the Semitic Arabs. The Kabyles claim descent from the area's ancient inhabitants and call themselves Amazigh (Free Men). Often fair and light-eyed, the Kabyles have retained a distinctive culture that allows unveiled women great respect and social stature. Most Kabyles are trilingual, speaking their own Hamitic language along with Arabic and French and the Kabyle university at Tizi-Ouzou is the only university in Algeria to teach in the French language. The majority of the Kabyles are Sunni Muslims, with important Roman Catholic and Ibadi Muslim minorities.

THE NATION: Peoples related to the early Europeans inhabited North Africa by 3000 B.C., their fair coloring attributed to Celtic migrants from Europe. Ancient Berber states, Numidia and Mauritania, flourished in the fertile region, their civilizations influenced by Phoenician and later Carthaginian culture. Numidia, approximately coextensive with modern northern Algeria, was drawn into the conflict between Rome and Carthage. Its two great tribes divided over their support of the opposing empires. A Roman province from 46 B.C., the region became one of the Roman Empire's major agricultural regions.

In the fifth century, incursions by Saharan tribes and an invasion by Germanic Vandals from Europe effectively destroyed Roman civilization in the region. The wanton destruction of the Vandals is recalled by the word coined to describe their actions, "vandalism." Taken by the Byzantines of the Eastern Roman Empire in the sixth century, most of the Berber inhabitants welcomed Byzantine protection, but Roman civilization failed to revive.

Muslim Arab invaders overran North Africa in the seventh century and suffered one of their rare military defeats at the hands of the Kabyles in A.D. 703. Unable to subdue the fierce Berbers, the Arabs formed alliances with individual Kabyle chiefs. The religion they failed to impose by force gradually spread to the Kabyle lands over the next centuries. In the eleventh century the Kabyles created a powerful state centered on Bougee (Bejaïa) that ultimately fell to Arab rule in the thirteenth century.

The Turks of the Ottoman Empire took Algiers in 1518 but left the Kabyles to rule themselves in return for oaths of loyalty and an annual tribute. In 1705 the Kabyles repudiated Turkish rule and sent their annual tribute to a closer threat, the bey of Algiers, the ruler of one of the nominally independent Muslim states notorious for piracy and the enslavement of Christian captives. The object of an American expedition in 1815 and a British bombardment in 1816, the state finally ceased preying on Mediterranean shipping. The French, claiming that the piracy continued, occupied Algiers in 1830 and rapidly extended their authority to the Algerian lowlands.

A French expedition moved into Kabylia in 1833. The force met the fiercest resistance they were to encounter in all of North Africa, and the Kabyles continued to resist until 1850. Sporadic Kabyle revolts culminated in a widespread uprising in 1871. The French reconquest of Kabylia left massive destruction in its wake. To punish the rebels, the French authorities confiscated 1 million acres of prime land, most parceled out to arriving French colonists. A renewed Kabyle rebellion again met defeat in 1899, but the French required an army of 80,000 to subdue the rebels.

The loss of productive farmlands forced thousands of Kabyles to leave their densely populated homeland to search for work in Algiers or the French mainland. The increasing economic competition fanned the historic enmity between the Arabs and Berbers. Anti-Arab rioting spread through Kabylia in 1934, and only French intervention averted civil war.

The Kabyles of Setif, during the victory in Europe celebrations in May 1945, rebelled against the French authorities. The rebellion rapidly spread across Kabylia. Crushed with unprecedented French savagery, the Kabyles later turned the same brutality against the French during the war of liberation. Harboring an intense hatred of the French, the Kabyles put aside old enmities to form an anti-French alliance with the Arab majority.

The Algerian war of independence, spreading from its cradle in Kabylia in 1954, is now considered one of the most brutal conflicts in recent history. The "Kabyle Smile," the gaping wound of a slit throat, became the hallmark of the nationalist forces. Promised autonomy in free Algeria, the Kabyles paid a very high price, losing 10% of their population before Algeria finally won its independence in 1962. Refused the promised autonomy the Kabyles rebelled in September 1963, the last rebel forces routed two years later. Betrayed by the country they had done so much to win, the Kabyles lost even the cultural and linguistic rights they had enjoyed under French rule.

Devastated by over two decades of socialist experimentation, Algeria exploded in 1988. Belatedly introducing reforms, the military-backed government found itself under intense pressure by Islamic fundamentalists. In December 1990 the government adopted a law that makes Arabic the only official language after 1997, with substantial penalties for the users of Berber languages or French. Over 100,000 Kabyles marched in defense of their linguistic rights. In spite of some government concessions, fundamentalist violence has increased dramatically, most often targeting Europeans, Christians, and Berbers.

The Kabyles no longer look for justice in an Algeria that many Kabyles feel is finished. The Kabyles' minimum involvement with the military or the Islamic fundamentalists has maintained Kabylia as the calmest and least violent region of Algeria, partly due to the increasing mobilization of nationalist self-defense forces. The nationalists are gaining widespread support with their calls for separation from the disintegrating Algerian state. In August 1994 the U.S. State Department issued a confidential paper that outlined the possibility that Kabylia, where the majority oppose Muslim fundamentalism, will obtain independence while the remainder of Algeria accommodates an Islamic government.

*SELECTED BIBLIOGRAPHY:*

Bourdieu, P. *Outline of a Theory of Practice.* 1977.
Esposito, John. *Islamic Threat.* 1993.
Hostetler, Marian. *Fear in Algeria.* 1979.
Lustick, Ian. *State-Building Failure in British Ireland and French Algeria.* 1985.

# KACHINLAND

**Kachin**

*CAPITAL: Myitkyana*

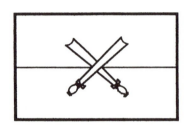

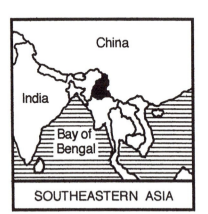

*POPULATION:* (95e) 1,334,000 : 2,410,000 Kachins in Myanmar and another 200,000 in adjacent areas of China and 125,000 in India. "Greater Kachinland" 2,518,000. MAJOR NATIONAL GROUPS: (95e) Kachin 88%, Shan 6%, other Burmese. MAJOR LANGUAGES: Kachin, Burman, Shan, English. MAJOR RELIGIONS: animist, Christian, Buddhist. MAJOR CITIES: (95e) KACHIN STATE: Bhamo 53,000, Myitkyana 44,000 (92,000), Mogaung 38,000, Mohnyin 24,000. SHAN STATE: Namtu 33,000. SAGAING DIVISION: Katha 46,000, Kanbalu 25,000. MANDALAY DIVISION: Mogok 44,000.

*GEOGRAPHY:* AREA: 34,397 sq.mi.-89,111 sq.km. "Greater Kachinland" 61,213 sq.mi.-158,582 sq.km. LOCATION: Kachinland lies in northern Myanmar, a mountainous area in the Himalayan foothills around the basin of the upper Irrawaddy River. Kachinland borders China on the east and north, the Indian states of Arunchal Pradesh, Nagaland,* and Manipur (Meithei Laipak*) on the west, and the Sagaing Division and Shan State of Myanmar on the south. POLITICAL STATUS: Kachinland forms Kachin State of Myanmar. The region claimed by nationalists, "Greater Kachinland," also includes the northern districts of Sagaing and Mandalay divisions and the Namtu region of Shan State in Myanmar.

*FLAG:* The Kachin national flag, the flag of the national movement, is a horizontal bicolor of red over green bearing two white Kachin swords crossed in the center.

*PEOPLE:* The Kachins are a tribal people encompassing a number of distinct groups related by language and culture. The largest of the groups, the Jingpaw, called Jingpo in China, are considered the only true Kachins and inhabit an area larger than the territory officially designated as Kachin State. Of the numerous Tibeto-Burman dialects in use, that of the Jingpaw is the most widely distributed. Never under Indian or Chinese cultural influence, the Kachins have not developed the caste distinctions of neighboring peoples. Most of the Kachin tribes have retained their traditional religious beliefs, although there is a large Christian, mostly Baptist, minority. Smaller ethnic groups in the region include the large Shan minority in the areas bordering Shanland* in the south and the tribal peoples of the mountains: Palaung, Lisu, Maru, Azi, Lashi, and Rawang.

*THE NATION:* Migrations of small tribal groups moved south from the eastern Tibetan Plateau to settle the region, probably in the eighth century A.D. The numerous tribes, never united under a central authority, often warred among themselves and cooperated only when faced with an outside threat. Invaded by the Shans, a Thai people, in the thirteenth century, the Kachins retreated to mountain strongholds and later in the same century successfully repulsed the invading Mongol hordes.

Ethnic Burmans, the dominant people in the Irrawaddy basin to the south, moved into the Kachin tribal lands in the seventeenth and eighteenth centuries. Fierce Kachin resistance limited Burman rule to the river lowlands. The Chinese, while pacifying the tribal peoples of Yunnan, sent an army to occupy the Kachin region in 1766. To the dismay of the imperial government, the army withdrew in disorder under ferocious Kachin attacks in 1770. China retained control of only a small eastern Kachin region.

The British, seen as natural allies against the Burmans and Chinese, took control of the lowlands of Upper Burma in 1886. The tribal peoples on the northern frontier, never part of the Burmese kingdom, signed separate treaties with the British authorities. The British eventually organized the Kachin territory as a British protected region.

The British authorities, in the protectorate called the Kachin Hill Tracts, closed the area to immigration by the lowland Burmans and gave the various tribes considerable autonomy. The last of the tribes submitted to British rule in 1935. In the east the international border with China remained porous, and Kachins on both sides ignored the frontier. The British-imposed peace allowed the creation of Christian missions. The Kachins began to advance rapidly, led by a Christian minority educated in the mission schools.

The Kachins remained loyal to their British allies during World War II. Guerrilla bands, trained by British and American officers, parachuted into the region following the Japanese occupation in 1942, wreaked havoc with Japanese communications, and terrified the Japanese patrols. The guerrillas, the nucleus of a future Kachin army, gained fame for their valor and tenacity in fighting the Japanese.

Immediately after the war, the British authorities began preparations for Burmese independence. Convinced that the small protectorates lacked the resources to become viable independent states, the British urged the creation of a Burmese federation. After long negotiations the Kachins agreed to join the federation, but with a guaranteed right, after ten years, of secession, under British protection, if they decided to leave Burma.

The Burmese government, soon after independence in January 1948, abrogated the autonomy agreement and incorporated large tracts of Kachin land into the neighboring provinces. The government then created a truncated Kachin State with only semiautonomous status. The outraged Kachins rebelled and overran much of northern Burma. In March 1949 the victorious Kachins captured Burma's second city, Mandalay. The British, exhausted from World War II, refused to intervene in spite of earlier assurances to the Kachins.

The Burmese army counterattacked and drove the Kachins back to their mountains in 1950. Several Kachin factions formed an alliance with the Burmese Communists, facilitating the arrival of arms and aid through the Jingpo minority on the Chinese side of the border. The Chinese government, in the early 1950s, supported the creation of an independent Kachinland. Other factions, opposed to the Communist alliance, turned to the lucrative opium trade to finance the ongoing separatist war. In 1958 the Chinese closed the border and cut all aid.

In 1958, ten years after Burmese independence, the Kachins formally notified the government of their intention to secede under the 1948 independence agreement. The government ignored the Kachins until 1962. Armed with helicopters and sophisticated weapons provided by the United States to fight the drug trade, the Burmese military launched a widespread offensive. The government soldiers, badly mauled, retreated to a few fortified military garrisons, leaving the Kachins in effective control of the countryside.

Moderate Kachin leaders, initially favoring an independent Kachinland with a federation of states that would replace Myanmar's brutal military government, mostly joined the separatists following the crushing of the Burmese democracy movement in 1988–90. The Kachins defeated renewed government offensives in 1989 and 1991 and in early 1992 stopped the largest offensive against them in three decades. Approached by government leaders seeking negotiations in late 1992, the Kachins agreed to a cease-fire, but the armed standoff in the region continues.

*SELECTED BIBLIOGRAPHY:*

Leach, E. E. *Political Systems of Highland Burma: A Study of Kachin Social Structure.* 1986.
Lintner, Bertil. *Land of Jade: A Journey through Insurgent Burma.* 1990.
Silverstein, Joseph, ed. *Independent Burma at Forty Years.* 1989.
Smith, Martin. *Burma, Insurgency and the Politics of Ethnicity.* 1988.

# KADERIA

### Chittagong Hill Tracts

*CAPITAL: Rangamati*

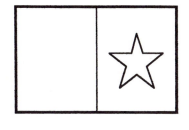

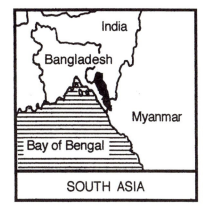

SOUTH ASIA

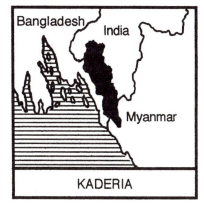

KADERIA

*POPULATION:* (95e) 1,265,000 : 750,000 Kaderis (Tribals) in Bangladesh. MAJOR NATIONAL GROUPS: (95e) Kaderi 59% (Chakma, Mogh, Tippera, Mro, Bawm, smaller groups), Bengali 40%. MAJOR LANGUAGES: Chakma-Mogh, Bengali, Tippera (Tripuri), Mro, English. MAJOR RELIGIONS: Buddhist, Sunni Muslim, Christian, Hindu. MAJOR CITIES: (95e) Kaptai 72,000, Rangamati 45,000, Ramgarh 37,000, Barkal 20,000.

*GEOGRAPHY:* AREA: 5,157 sq.mi.-13,361 sq.km. LOCATION: Kaderia occupies a highland region of parallel mountain ranges and long, fertile valleys in southeastern Bangladesh. POLITICAL STATUS: Kaderia forms the Chittagong Hill Tracts and the Bandaran District of the Chittagong Division of Bangladesh.

*FLAG:* The Kaderi national flag, the flag of the national movement, is a vertical bicolor of red and white bearing a large yellow, five-pointed star centered on the white stripe on the fly.

*PEOPLE:* The Kaderi, called Tribals by the Bengalis, belong to sixteen distinct tribes that have intermingled over the centuries. The largest of the tribes, the Chakma, nearly all Buddhists, are of mixed, unknown origin and have absorbed more Bengali cultural influences than the smaller tribes. The related Mogh, with a Buddhist majority, are thought to be of Thai origin. The mainly Hindu Tippera (Tripuri) are part of the larger population concentrated in adjacent India. The Mro or Moorang, majority Buddhist with a substantial animist minority, are considered the region's original inhabitants. The Bawm are the largest Christian group in the region. The other tribes, numerically quite small, are closely allied to the larger tribes. The Muslim Bengali population, migrants from the lowlands, has grown rapidly in recent decades.

*THE NATION:* The mountain valleys, inhabited since ancient times, became the refuge of numerous small tribal groups seeking protection in the forested isolation. The Chakma and Mogh moved into the highlands in the thirteenth century, pushing the earlier tribes into the mountainous jungles. Settled in the fertile valley, the newcomers called themselves the Khyungtha (Children of the River) and called the dispossessed tribes the Thongtha (Children of the Hills).

The remote area came under nominal Bengali rule in 1666, but, to secure their rule, the Bengalis had to fight their way into the hills, valley by valley. Constantly harassed by tribal warriors, the Bengalis finally ceded the troublesome region to Great Britain in 1760. The British officials, rather than engage in a long and arduous campaign to subdue the tribes, established treaty relations with the tribal leaders. The treaties, in effect, created a tribal preserve called the Chittagong Hill Tracts.

European missionaries arrived in the hills in the 1840s and 1850s. The Christians achieved some success with the smaller pagan groups, but only mission education found favor with the Buddhist and Hindu tribes. An educated minority, the product of the mission schools, gradually brought an end to the endemic tribal feuds and fostered closer relations among the diverse tribal peoples.

The British, responding to tribal appeals, formally designated the region a tribal reserve and prohibited further Bengali settlement in 1900. Continued illegal migration from the overcrowded lowlands provoked serious ethnic clashes and tribal protests over the next decades. In 1935 the authorities declared the region a totally excluded area, with entry for any reason forbidden without specific permission from the local British officials.

Tribal leaders, influenced by the Indian national movement in the late 1930s, organized a campaign to win separate independence for the tribal peoples. Nationalists based their claims on the ethnic, linguistic, and religious differences of the tribal peoples. A council of tribal chiefs formally appealed to the British authorities to prepare the region for independence under British protection. To ensure tribal loyalty during the World War II Japanese advance, local British officials promised separation should India become independent.

The violent postwar partition of British India into separate Indian and Pakistani states altered British attitudes to independence for minority areas. In 1947 the British joined the Chittagong Hill Tract to Muslim Pakistan. The tribes united in rebellion but could not hold the areas they captured against the advancing Pakistani troops. To forestall renewed violence, the Pakistani government applied the former British policy. In 1948 the government granted limited autonomy and prohibited Bengali settlement in the region.

The Pakistani government, in violation of the autonomy statute, took direct control of the district in 1955 and lifted all immigration restrictions. Funded by well-intentioned international aid agencies, thousands of Bengali Muslims migrated to the area from the densely populated lowlands. The Bengali secession from Pakistan in 1971 obscured the increasing violence between the Bengali migrants and the Kaderi tribes. To relieve severe land pressure, the new Bangladeshi government also encouraged lowland Bengalis to colonize the underpopulated hill tracts.

The Kaderi tribes organized guerrilla groups to fight the invasion. In 1975 tribal leaders demanded secession and the establishment of a sovereign state, to be called Kaderia or the Confederacy of Chittagong. Government attempts to negotiate a solution having failed, the military won broad powers to combat the rebellion. Brutal reprisals and attacks on undefended villages by Bengali settlers sent a wave of refugees fleeing into India.

Moderate tribal leaders, including the Chakma king, formerly favoring dialogue, joined the separatists following the passage of new laws in 1987–88 that made the Bengali language compulsory in education and local administration and imposed Sharia, strict Muslim civil law. Tribal leaders denounced the government for its failure to protect the Kaderi tribes as attacks by Bengali settlers escalated in 1989–90. Massive Bengali immigration, protected by 40,000 government troops, has provoked charges of virtual genocide by the beleaguered tribal peoples and many international human rights groups. ep   Pressed by international opinion, the Bangladeshi government opened negotiations with the rebel leaders in October 1992. Once again the talks collapsed over Kaderi demands for the expulsion of Bengali settlers from their lands. The renewed rebellion, drawing willing recruits from the estimated 60,000 refugees in camps in India, has become a war of independence rather than a fight for rights. After decades of increasing Bengali immigration to their homeland, even the most moderate of the Kaderi leaders admit that their fight is no longer for tribal rights, but for the survival of the Kaderi peoples.

*SELECTED BIBLIOGRAPHY:*

Ali, Asghan. *Ethnic Conflicts in South Asia.* 1987.

Mey, Wolfgang. *Genocide in the Chittagong Hill Tracts.* 1987.

Spate, O.H.K. *India and Pakistan: A General and Regional Geography.* 1954.

Vajpeyi, Dhirendra, and Yogenda Malik, eds. *Religious and Ethnic Minorities in South Asia.* 1990.

# KALAALLIT-NUNAAT

**Kalatdlit-Nunat; Greenland; Grønland**

*CAPITAL: Nuuk (Godthåb)*

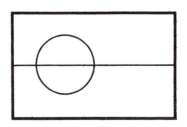

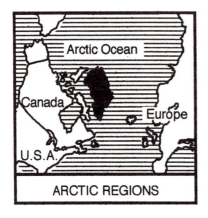

ARCTIC REGIONS

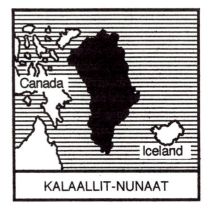

KALAALLIT-NUNAAT

*POPULATION:* (95e) 56,000 : 42,000 Greenlanders in Denmark. MAJOR NATIONAL GROUPS: (95e) Greenlander 75%, Dane 13%, Inuit 12%. MAJOR LANGUAGES: Greenlandic, Danish, Inuit. MAJOR RELIGIONS: Lutheran, animist. MAJOR CITIES: (95e) Nuuk (Godthåb) 14,000, Sisimuit (Holsteinsborg) 7,000, Qaqortoq (Julianhåb) 5,000.

*GEOGRAPHY:* AREA: 453,999 sq.mi.-1,176,163 sq.km. LOCATION: Kalaallit-Nunaat, considered part of the North American continent, is the world's largest island, with most of its territory lying above the Arctic Circle northeast of Canada's Nunavut* region. POLITICAL STATUS: Kalaallit-Nunaat forms an autonomous dependency of the Danish Crown.

*FLAG:* The Greenlander flag, the official flag of the autonomous state, is a horizontal bicolor of white over red charged with a large bicolor disc, red over white, offset toward the hoist.

*PEOPLE:* The Greenlanders, of mixed Inuit (Eskimo) and European background, speak a language of Inuit origin with substantial Danish and Norwegian admixtures. Some 90% of the population inhabits the ice-free coastal regions in the south. In the center and north of the island, the icy wastes are home to the seminomadic Inuit. The large Danish minority is concentrated in the capital and the other important towns.

*THE NATION:* About 3000 B.C. a Greek sailor, Pytheas of Massila, brought back stories of a great northern land six days sail north of Britain. The story of Pytheas marked the first mention of the island in European chronicles and the first reported contact by Europeans. Called Thule or Ultima Thule, the Farthest

Land, by the Romans, knowledge of the island gradually faded into myth and legend.

Norse Vikings, led by Eric the Red, rediscovered the island in A.D. 982. In an effort to make the island more attractive to potential colonists, Eric named the frozen land Greenland. The Vikings established settlements on the narrow coastal plains in the south where agriculture was possible. The number of Viking settlers grew to some 10,000 by the twelfth century. The Vikings reported the first contacts with the Inuit in the thirteenth century, the forerunners of the Inuit migration across the polar lands.

The Norwegian kingdom gained control of the colony in 1261 and ruled the island through a separate Greenland assembly. In 1380 the Danes took over the island's administration but did not attempt further colonization.

Sometime in the fourteenth century the weather grew colder, and the colonists disappeared. The fate of the Scandinavian colonists is still not fully known. Theories claim that they returned to Europe, joined the Inuit, succumbed to plague or Inuit attacks, or simply died out as agriculture collapsed.

Norway, then ruled by Denmark, began to resettle the island in 1721, however the European influence remained slight. In 1815 Denmark lost Norway to Sweden but retained Greenland through an oversight at the Congress of Vienna. Underpopulated and economically unimportant, the island remained a forgotten outpost, ignored by the Danish government.

The United States established military bases on the island during World War II and at the end of the war offered to purchase Greenland from Denmark. The Danes refused but allowed the maintenance of American military bases as part of a mutual defense treaty.

The island's status changed to that of a Danish county in 1953. The benefits of the Danish welfare system that followed helped to eradicate the tuberculosis and other European diseases that had ravaged the population. Immigration from Denmark increased during the 1950s and 1960s, the influx generating an extensive ethnic mixing and intermarriage.

The Greenlanders, dependent on the products of the land and sea, actively opposed foreign investment and the development of the Arctic oil deposits. The opposition formed the first nationalist group, Suimut, in 1977. Fearing that the unchecked development threatened their culture and way of life, the nationalists mobilized. In 1979, 70% of the Greenlanders voted for home rule. In 1982 they voted to withdraw their autonomous state from the European Economic Community, the first and, so far, only territory to do so.

The island's three major political parties have developed different views of the future. Suimut works for eventual independence. Atassut, with the support of the Danish minority, is pro-European. Ataqatiqiit favors independence from Denmark as the first step to the establishment of a transpolar Inuit state uniting all Inuit peoples. In March 1991 the Greenlanders rejected a move to review their membership in the European Community. The defeat of the pro-European faction moved the island a step closer to eventual independence.

*SELECTED BIBLIOGRAPHY:*

Jones, Gwyn. *The Norse Atlantic Saga: Being the Norse Voyages of Discovery and Settlement to Iceland, Greenland and America.* 1986.

Malaurie, Jean. *The Last Kings of Thule.* 1985.

Steltzer, Ulli. *Inuit: The North in Transition.* 1985.

# KALMYKIA

**Khal'mg Tangch**

*CAPITAL: Elista (Stepnoi)*

SOUTHEASTERN EUROPE

KALMYKIA

*POPULATION:* (95e) 332,000 : 210,000 Kalmyks in Russia. MAJOR NATIONAL GROUPS: (95e) Kalmyk (Kalmuck) 53%, Russian 36%, Kazakh 6%, Dagestani 3%. MAJOR LANGUAGES: Russian, Kalmyk, Kazakh. MAJOR RELIGIONS: Buddhist (Lamaism), Russian Orthodox, Sunni Islam. MAJOR CITIES: (95e) Elista (Stepnoi) 97,000, Lagan (Kaspiyskiy) 52,000, Ulan-Kholl 20,000, Yaskul 19,000, Tsagan-Aman 17,000.

*GEOGRAPHY:* AREA: 29,305 sq.mi.-75,919 sq.km. LOCATION: Kalmykia lies in southern European Russia, a region of plains and barren steppe south of the Volga River and west of the Caspian Sea. POLITICAL STATUS: Kalmykia forms a member state of the Russian Federation.

*INDEPENDENCE DECLARED:* 12 June 1918.

*FLAG:* The Kalmyk national flag, the official flag of the republic, is a yellow field with a narrow, pale blue stripe at the top and a narrow, pink stripe on the bottom and is charged with the Kalmyk national symbol centered, two concentric pink circles around a yellow disc bearing the Kalmyk talisman in pink above stylized pink waves.

*PEOPLE:* The Kalmyk, also called Kalmuck, are a branch of the Oirot people of Altai-Khakassia* on the Mongol border. The descendants of Mongol nomads, the Kalmyks are the only large Buddhist nation in Europe. The Kalmyk speak a western Mongol language and adhere to the Tibetan branch of Buddhism, Lamaism, although traces of their pre-Buddhist shamanism are still evident. Over a third of the Kalmyks speak only their own language, but the majority are effectively bilingual, also speaking the Russian language. The

large Slav population is mostly concentrated in Elista and the other towns of
the region.

*THE NATION:* A branch of the Oirot Mongols left their homeland in the
Altai Mountains of Central Asia in 1636, fleeing the disintegration of the Mongol Empire. The last Asian people to penetrate Europe, the refugees settled the
steppe lands of the lower Volga River, lands newly acquired by the expanding
Russian Empire.

The Mongols established an independent khanate, a confederation of tribes
ruled by *noyons* (princes) under the ultimate authority of the khan. In 1646 the
confederation signed a treaty of allegiance to the Russian tsar, Peter I, who
charged them with guarding Russia's new eastern frontier. In the eighteenth
century the Mongols adopted the Lamaism brought to the region by missionary
monks from Mongolia. As the Kalmyk were adherents of Tibetan Lamaism, the
Dalai Lama in distant Tibet,* the spiritual leader of their religion, appointed the
confederation's khans.

Catherine II, called the Great, in the winter of 1773 put aside the 1646 allegiance treaty and attempted to impose direct Russian rule. Refusing to submit
to Christian domination, the Mongols east of the Volga River suddenly uprooted
and undertook a harrowing journey to return to their original homeland over
2,000 miles to the east. Of the 300,000 that departed, only a third survived the
passage. The majority succumbed to cold, heat, hunger, and attacks by Muslim
tribes. The Volga River did not freeze in the winter of 1773, trapping the Mongol bands on the west bank. Unable to cross the raging river, some 60,000 stayed
behind. Called Kalmyk from the Turkic word for remnant, the Mongols left
behind accepted nominal Russian rule.

The Kalmyks took on many of the military attributes of the Cossacks while
retaining their own culture and social structure. Kalmyk society was dominated
by the White Bone, the *noyons* and aristocracy. The majority of the Kalmyk
population formed the Black Bone, the commoners. In return for military service, the Kalmyks enjoyed broad powers of self-government, from 1803 overseen
by a Guardian of the Kalmyk People appointed by the Russian monarch.

Numbering over 200,000 when war began in 1914, the small nation's warriors
formed elite military units sent to the front. Released from their oath of loyalty
by the overthrow of the tsar in February 1917, the Kalmyk soldiers returned
home. A Kalmyk congress, convened in March, authorized the formation of a
national army from the returning military units and renewed an old alliance with
the Cossacks of the Don.* In the wake of the Bolshevik coup in October 1917
the Kalmyks rebelled as Russia collapsed in chaos.

The Kalmyk congress, dominated by the White Bone, voted for secession.
On 12 June 1918 the congress declared Kalmykia independent. Devastated by
heavy fighting during the Russian civil war, thousands of Kalmyks died in battle
or of hunger and disease. The Red Army occupied Kalmykia in 1920. The
Communists eliminated the White Bone aristocrats and nationalized the Kalmyk
herds. The last Kalmyk guerrilla bands fought on until 1926.

The anti-Communist and fervently Buddhist Kalmyks, their monasteries and temples destroyed during the Stalinist purges, mostly welcomed the German invaders who reached Kalmykia in 1942. Promoted as German allies, many Kalmyks joined the German's anti-Communist crusade. Émigré Prince N. Tundutov, the Kalmyk leader during the Russian civil war, arrived in Elista as head of a new Kalmyk government. The authorities allowed the reopening of shrines and monasteries. A Kalmyk army, the Kalmyk Banner Organization, fought as German allies, often against Kalmyks fighting with the Red Army.

Defeated at nearby Stalingrad, the Germans withdrew from the region, and the Red Army returned in February 1943. Stalin accused the entire Kalmyk nation of treason and ordered deportation. Often with only minutes' notice, the Kalmyk population, including the families of soldiers in the Red Army, was herded into closed cattle cars and shipped east. Thousands perished from hunger and thirst on the twenty-two-day journey. Dumped at rail sidings in the Siberian wastes, many more died of disease, exposure, and malnutrition. By 1950 over half the prewar Kalmyk population of 140,000 had perished.

Officially rehabilitated in 1956, the survivors gradually made their way back to the North Caucasus. In 1958 their homeland again became an autonomous republic, but under strict surveillance and with a large ethnic Russian presence to ensure stability.

The Gorbychev reforms, introduced in 1987, fueled a Kalmyk religious revival. Lapel pens of the Dalai Lama rapidly replaced the omnipresent hammer and sickle. Inspired by the new freedoms, Kalmyk nationalism became a popular movement in the republic. In August 1990 the first Khural (congress) since World War II convened in Elista and included delegates from the White Bone exile community. The congress adopted a nationalist platform endorsing the Kalmyk right to self-determination.

The collapse of the Soviet Union in August 1991 provoked a strong nationalist reaction. In February 1992 the Kalmyks changed the name of the republic to Khal'mg Tangch and unilaterally upgraded the republic's legal status within the Russian Federation. In April 1992 a young Kalmyk millionaire, Kirsan Ilyumzhinov, won the republican presidential elections with a vow to convert Kalmykia into a neutral, Buddhist state.

*SELECTED BIBLIOGRAPHY:*

Antonov-Dvseyenko, Anton. *The Time of Stalin.* 1983.

McAuley, Alistair, ed. *Soviet Federalism, Nationalism and Economic Decentralization.* 1991.

Nekrich, Alexander. *The Punished Peoples.* 1978.

# KANAKI

Nouvelle-Calédonie; New Caledonia;
Kanaky; Kanakia

*CAPITAL: Noumea (Nouméa)*

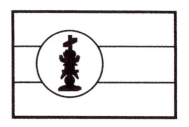

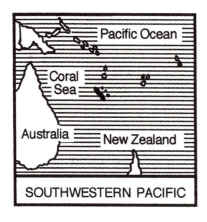

SOUTHWESTERN PACIFIC

KANAKI

*POPULATION:* (95e) 159,000 : 69,000 Kanaks in New Caledonia. MAJOR NATIONAL GROUPS: (95e) Kanak 43%, French 35%, Wallasian 8%, Tahitian 4%, Javanese, Vietnamese, Chinese. MAJOR LANGUAGES: French, Kanak. MAJOR RELIGIONS: Roman Catholic, Protestant. MAJOR CITIES: (95e) Noumea (Nouméa) 66,000 (106,000), Bourail 9,000.

*GEOGRAPHY:* AREA: 7,367 sq.mi.-19,085 sq.km. LOCATION: Kanaki lies in the southwestern Pacific Ocean 750 miles northeast of Australia. The archipelago comprises the main cigar-shaped island of New Caledonia, the Loyalty Islands, the Isle of Pines, and several smaller islands. POLITICAL STATUS: Kanaki forms the French overseas territory of New Caledonia. The territory is made up of three provinces, two of which constitute an autonomous Kanak region.

*FLAG:* The Kanak national flag, the flag of the national movement, is a horizontal tricolor of blue, red, and green charged with a large yellow disc bearing a stylized black ridge-beam spire common to local architecture.

*PEOPLE:* The Kanak, or Kanaka, are a Melanesian people of mixed Melanesian and Polynesian background that form part of the large Melanesian population of the Pacific islands known as Melanesia. The Kanak speak a western Melanesian of the Melanesian branch of the Malayo-Polynesian language group. The majority also speak French, the language of government and of the large European minority. The Kanak islanders, mostly Roman Catholics, make up the largest segment of the island's multiethnic population, which also includes Caldoche (island-born French), Metros (continental French), and smaller minorities from other French or former French possessions in the Pacific.

*THE NATION:* The islands, settled by early Melanesian migrants from the Papuan islands to the south and by later Polynesians migrating from the east, evolved a segmented tribal society. Numerous small tribes, each with its own dialect and culture, jealously maintained tribal territories and often warred among themselves.

East of the sea routes taken by early European explorers, the islands remained unknown to the Europeans until 1774. British captain James Cook called the mountainous main island New Caledonia, the poetic name for Scotland,* and named the entire group the Loyalty Islands. Although visited by various European expeditions between 1792 and 1840, the islands remained virtually unknown, exploration or colonization discouraged by the fierce Kanak.

A French military expedition finally subdued the tribes in 1853, and France formally annexed the islands in 1864. The French authorities established an important naval base at Nouméa and designated the entire archipelago a penal colony. New Caledonia's isolation allowed a penal system considerably less harsh than similar establishments in Guiana* in South America. In 1894 the French disbanded the penal colony, the prisoners either returned to France or released to settle in the islands.

The Kanak population, unsuited to plantation agriculture, was generally ignored by the French authorities, which imported workers from other French colonies. By 1900 the non-Kanak population had grown to form a quarter of the total. The discovery of rich nickel deposits brought an influx of workers from France and reinforced the European domination of the islands. Nouméa grew rapidly, and the large European minority enjoyed fine restaurants, clubs, theaters, and branches of famous Paris shops. The Kanak, excluded from the colony's political and economic life, retained their traditional village society. The colony's two largest population groups lived distinctly separate lives.

Kanak resentment of French privilege swelled in the 1950s as related Melanesian peoples moved toward independence in Fiji, Vanuatu, and other islands. Nationalist groups began to demand Kanak autonomy and redress for a century of neglect. Embarrassed by Kanak poverty, many of the Caldoche French supported the Kanak demands. The interests of the powerful Société Nickel prevailed, and the demands were ignored, economic concerns taking precedence over Kanak appeals for equality. In 1958 the voters of the islands, mostly French, approved a proposal to remain a French territory.

Island politics polarized in the 1970s. Pro-independence, pro-autonomy, and pro-French groups campaigned for Kanak support. In 1978 rioting swept the main island, the most serious disturbances in the colony's history. Nationalists, supported by the mostly Caldoche local government council, demanded immediate independence. The authorities dismissed the regional government and sent troops to restore order. The French Socialists, with vague promises of autonomy, won 60% of the Kanak vote in 1981, but government inaction in the months that followed rekindled militant Kanak nationalism.

Pro-independence Kanak and Caldoche parties won a majority in the territorial assembly in 1982. The assembly voted to set a date for independence, choosing 24 September 1983, exactly 130 years after the French occupation. In July 1983 serious violence between pro-independence and pro-French groups spread across the main island. The French authorities seized on the violence as a pretext for not granting independence on the designated day.

New elections for an autonomous regional government, boycotted by nationalists in 1984, returned a pro-French faction to power. Serious disturbances again broke out across the main island, forcing many settlers to abandon outlying farms and towns for the relative safety of Nouméa. The swift actions of the French police and military, augmented by reserves from Europe, narrowly averted civil war.

Separatist violence once again erupted in April 1988 after two years of relative calm. Gun battles between Kanak separatists and the French police spread even to the suburbs of Nouméa. Kanak leaders, rejecting the escalating conflict, agreed to negotiate and finally accepted a compromise. The Kanak gained greater participation in the regional government, autonomy for the two Kanak majority provinces, and a massive aid package designed to raise the Melanesian standard of living to the European level. A referendum on independence is scheduled for 1998, ten years after the signing of the accord.

The compromise ended the separatist violence and avoided a civil war that would probably have ended with the partition of the territory. Kanak leaders are carefully monitoring the French promise to raise Kanak living standards to the level of opulent Nouméa, a daunting task even without the opposition of the majority of the French settler population.

*SELECTED BIBLIOGRAPHY:*
Spencer, Michael. *New Caledonia in Crisis.* 1988.
————, ed. *New Caledonia: Issues in Nationalism and Dependency.* 1988.
Theroux, Paul. *The Happy Isles of Oceania.* 1992.
Whiteman, Darrel L. *Melanesians and Missionaries.* 1990.

# KANOWRA

**Kanem-Bornu; Borno**

*CAPITAL: Maiduguri*

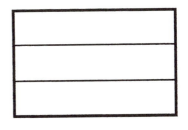

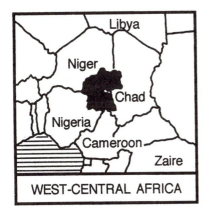

WEST-CENTRAL AFRICA

KANOWRA

*POPULATION:* (95e) 6,594,000 : 4,600,000 Kanuri (Kanowri) in Nigeria and another 3,750,000 in adjacent areas of Niger, Chad, and Cameroon. "Greater Kanowra" 9,500,000. MAJOR NATIONAL GROUPS: (95e) BORNU (NIGERIAN KANOWRA): Kanuri 69%, Fulani 11%, Hausa 6%, Margi 3%, Shuwa Arab 3%, other Nigerian. MAJOR LANGUAGES: Kanuri (Kanowri), Fulah, Hausa, Arabic, English. MAJOR RELIGIONS: Sunni Muslim, animist, Christian. MAJOR CITIES: (95e) NIGERIA: Maiduguri 330,000, Nguru 138,000, Potiskum 80,000, Gashua 45,000, Giedam 25,000. CHAD: Moussoro 30,000, Mao 25,000, Bol 20,000. NIGER: Diffa 40,000, Gouré 20,000. CAMEROON: Maroua 124,000, Kaélé 30,000, Mora 25,000.

*GEOGRAPHY:* AREA: 46,636 sq.mi.-120,818 sq.km. "Greater Kanowra" 205,529 sq.mi.-532,460 sq.km. LOCATION: Kanowra occupies the vast Biu Plateau of northeastern Nigeria, a semiarid tableland sloping down to the fertile lands around Lake Chad. POLITICAL STATUS: Kanowra has no official status; the region forms Borno and Yobe states of Nigeria. "Greater Kanowra," the territory claimed by pan-Kanuri nationalists, also includes the prefectures of Lac and Kanem in Chad, the southern districts of the departments of Diffa and Zinder in Niger, and the province of Extrème Nord in Cameroon.

*FLAG:* The Kanuri national flag, the flag of the national movement, is a horizontal tricolor of blue, yellow, and green, representing the sky, the land, and the water of Lake Chad.

*PEOPLE:* The Kanuri, calling themselves Kanowri, are called Kanembu in

Chad and Manga or Beri-Beri in Niger. Of mixed black African, Berber, and Arab background, the Kanuri are more closely related to the peoples of North Africa than to the inhabitants of the neighboring areas in Central Africa. The Kanuri speak a Nilo-Saharan language, unrelated to neighboring dialects and one of the few languages of sub-Saharan Africa to have developed a pre-colonial literary tradition. The Muslim Kanuri, divided among four African states, are united by culture, language, and over 1,000 years of shared history.

*THE NATION:* Pastoral Berbers, driven from North Africa by the Arab invasion, occupied the region around Lake Chad probably in the late seventh century. The Berbers later absorbed migrants from the area of the upper Nile River. A number of walled city-states existed east of the lake in the eighth century. According to Kanuri tradition, Sef, the son of Dhu Ifazan of Yemen, came to Kanem in the ninth century and united the various city-states. The dynasty he founded in Kanem took his name, the Sefwa dynasty.

Converted to Islam by Arab invaders in the eleventh century, Kanem became a center of Muslim learning and a diffusion center for the spread of Islam. Kanem eventually expanded to control all of the territory around Lake Chad. By tradition the region of Bornu, west of the lake, was bestowed on the Sefwa heir to rule during his apprenticeship. In 1386 Kanem fell to nomadic invaders, and the center of the state shifted west to Bornu. From Bornu the resurgent Kanuri, in time, reconquered Kanem and created a powerful empire known as Kanem-Bornu. At the height of its power, in the sixteenth and seventeenth centuries, the Sefwa dynasty of Kanem-Bornu ruled much of Central Africa.

Muslim Fulani, having conquered the states of Hausa* to the west, invaded the declining empire in 1809. The Kanuri successfully resisted the invasion, but two years later the empire collapsed because of a civil war begun by Kanembu warriors who had come to Bornu to fight the Fulani. In 1814 the Sefwa ruler regained control of Bornu and the western territories.

The empire was visited by a British expedition in 1823. Impressed by the sophisticated state the British established formal diplomatic relations with Kanem-Bornu in the 1830s.

Civil war again erupted in 1835 and culminated with the overthrow of the Sefwa dynasty in 1846. The sense of continuity so important to the Kanuri was not lost with the succession of a new dynasty; however, a series of weak rulers in the late nineteenth century seriously undermined the state.

The Kanuri, threatened by the "Napoleon of Africa," Rabeh Zobier, a Sudanese ex-slave turned conqueror, appealed to the European powers for assistance in 1890. While the Europeans negotiated for advantage, Rabeh advanced and destroyed the Kanuri capital, Kukawa, a city of 60,000 inhabitants. After consolidating his control of Kanem-Bornu, Rabeh founded a new capital at Dikwa in Bornu.

Rabeh's empire expanded into areas claimed by the European powers and finally met defeat at the hands of a combined European military force in 1900. In 1902 the European powers divided the empire's territories. The British took

Bornu and added it to British Nigeria, the French absorbed Kanem into French Equatorial Africa, and the Germans added most of the Dikwa region to their colony of Kamerun.

Bornu formed a part of the region of Northern Nigeria, a region dominated by the more numerous Hausa-Fulani peoples. The region became the center of growing Kanuri nationalism in the 1950s. Neglected by the regional government, Bornu remained an underdeveloped region, its economy the least developed and the literacy rate the lowest in all of Nigeria. Fearing domination by the Hausa-Fulani in a projected independent Nigeria, nationalists formed the Bornu Youth Movement (BYM) in 1954. Initial aims included separation from Nigeria's Northern Region, but more radical views included the reunification of the Kanuri-populated territories of the former Kanem-Bornu Empire.

Nigeria, granted independence in 1960, emerged as an unstable confederation of three regions with Bornu included in the Hausa-Fulani-dominated Northern Region. Kanuri nationalist agitation, only temporarily interrupted by the secession of Biafra* and the civil war of 1967–70, continued to dominate regional politics.

The Nigerian government attempted to satisfy the country's numerous ethnic groups by dividing the regions into ethnic states. A Kanuri state called Borno, created in 1976 only whetted nationalist appetites. In November 1976 mass demonstrations erupted, demanding immediate independence. Hundreds of armed men tried to force the new state government to establish a separatist Kanuri government. The uprising, crushed by Nigerian troops, was ultimately blamed on Kanuri from outside Nigeria, particularly the numerous Kanembu refugees from North Chad* who had fled Chad's ongoing civil war. Muslim fundamentalism spread through the region in the early 1980s with serious religious rioting in 1982–83. The disturbances, with nationalist overtones, continued sporadically until 1989.

The end of the Cold War, the reunification of Germany, and Africa's slow turn toward multiparty democracy fueled a resurgence of Kanuri nationalism in 1991–92. In March 1992 protests paralyzed Maiduguri over the Nigerian government's attempts to expel jailed Kanembu back to Chad, where they faced persecution. The protests marked the beginning of a new militancy and unity among the divided Kanuri, whose strong sense of identity has its roots in a thousand years of shared history, an identity that has not been diminished by partition or the imposition of artificial international borders.

*SELECTED BIBLIOGRAPHY:*

Asiwaju, A. I. *Partitioned Africans: Ethnic Relations across Africa's International Borders, 1884–1984.* 1985.

Benton, P. A. *Languages and People of Bornu.* 1968.

Cohen, Ronald. *The Kanuri of Borno.* 1987.

# KARACHAI-BALKARIA

Karachay-Malkar; Karachaistan and
Balkarstan

*CAPITAL: Mikoyan Shakhar*
*(Karachayevsk)*

SOUTHEASTERN EUROPE

KARACHAI-BALKARIA

*POPULATION:* (95e) 338,000 : 159,000 Karachai and 91,000 Balkars in Russia. MAJOR NATIONAL GROUPS: (95e) Karachai (Karachay) 46%, Russian (including Cossacks) 27%, Balkar 25%, Nogai, Circassian. MAJOR LANGUAGES: Karachai-Balkar, Russian. MAJOR RELIGIONS: Sunni Muslim, Russian Orthodox. MAJOR CITIES: (95e) KARACHAI: Mikoyan Shakhar (Karachayevsk) 33,000 (51,000), Novy Karachai 15,000, Zelenchuk (Zelenchukskaya) 12,000. BALKARIA: Tirni-Auds (Tyrnauz) 30,000, Verchnaya Balkariya 8,000.

*GEOGRAPHY:* AREA: 4,076 sq.mi.-10,559 sq.km. LOCATION: Karachai-Balkaria lies in southern European Russia, a rugged area in northern foothills of the western Caucasus Mountains traversed by the valleys of the upper Kuban and Baksan Rivers. POLITICAL STATUS: Karachai-Balkaria has no official status; the region forms the southern districts of the republics of Karachai-Circassia and Kabardino-Balkar, member states of the Russian Federation. The northern districts of the republics form part of the region known as Circassia.*

*INDEPENDENCE DECLARED:* 18 May 1918; 11 August 1942.

*FLAG:* The Karachai-Balkar national flag, the flag of the national movement, is a yellow field charged with a centered red circle enclosing a yellow disc bearing a red, five-pointed star. OTHER FLAG(S): The Karachai flag is a yellow field bearing a centered circle of eight small, red, five-pointed stars. The Balkar flag has three horizontal stripes of pale blue, white, and pale blue charged with a centered yellow disc, outlined in red, bearing a red, five-pointed star.

*PEOPLE:* The Karachai and Balkar constitute the two parts of a single nation, a people of mixed Turkic and Caucasian background speaking dialects of the same Turkic language of the Kipchak Turkic language group. The two peoples share the same language, culture, and history but have been divided by decades of Communist rule. The Karachai live in the west, concentrated in the valley of the upper Kuban River. The Balkar, who call themselves Malkar, inhabit the mountains and the valley of the Baksan River in the east. The two Muslim peoples have retained their religion and culture despite of decades of harsh Communist rule.

*THE NATION:* The Karachai-Balkar left Crimea* during political upheavals in the fourteenth century. Migrating south along the shore of the Black Sea, they mixed extensively with the native Circassian peoples. In the fifteenth century they finally settled the river valleys of the northern slopes of the Caucasus Mountains.

A tribal people, the Karachai-Balkar became vassals of the Kabardin Circassian princes in the sixteenth century. Over the next century Turkish influence in the region grew, and the tribes gradually adopted the Turks' Islamic religion. In 1733 the Turks annexed the tribal lands of the Karachai and Balkar and brought the tribes under direct Turkish rule.

Russians moved into the territory of the declining Ottoman Empire in the eighteenth century and reached Karachay in 1774. In 1829 the Russians succeeded in forcing the Turks to cede the Caucasian territories to the Russian Empire. Resistance to Christian rule erupted in a long and savage guerrilla war that continued until 1864. Thousands of Karachai-Balkar moved south to Turkish territory. Those who remained under Russian rule took up arms against the tsarist authorities at every opportunity.

The Muslim peoples of the empire, their loyalty suspect, were exempted from military duty when war began in 1914. Even though a majority of the Muslim peoples openly favored Muslim Turkey, the Russian government, desperate for manpower, began conscripting Muslims in 1916. The Muslim work units, sent to the front, came into contact with new revolutionary and nationalist ideas that took hold as Russia slipped into chaos.

The Karachai-Balkar conscripts deserted the front to return home after the revolution of February 1917. As civil government collapsed, a Karachai-Balkar national committee took control of the region. The national committee gave its support to Russia's new provisional government, which vaguely promised autonomy for Russia's minority peoples.

The Muslim peoples of the North Caucasus attempted to unite in a cooperative independence following the Bolshevik coup in October 1917 but faced tremendous problems of increasing disorder and pressure from rival political groups, including local Bolsheviks. Threatened by a Bolshevik attempt to take power, the Karachai-Balkar leaders declared their homeland independent of Russia on 18 May 1918. Vehemently opposed to the antireligious Bolsheviks, the tiny republic allied to the White forces fighting the Bolsheviks in the expanding Russian civil war.

The collapse of White resistance opened the way for the Red Army in August 1920. A detachment of the Ninth Soviet Army invaded Karachai-Balkaria in support of an uprising of local Communists. The victorious Soviets overthrew the separatist government of "bourgeois nationalist exploiters" and divided the territory. The Soviet authorities added Karachay to the territory of the Cherkess Circassians and incorporated Balkaria into a region that included the Kabardin Circassians.

Nazi Germany turned on its Soviet ally in June 1941, and a German offensive drove into the Caucasus in mid-1942. Welcomed by many of the Karachai and Balkar as liberators from hated Soviet rule, the Germans won thousands of recruits to their Turkish League, an anti-Communist military unit under Nazi command. Nationalists convened a national committee and formed a national government under Kadi Kairamukov. Supported by the Germans, the national committee declared Karachai-Balkaria independent on 11 August 1942.

The new government moved to restore the region's traditional social and religious structure, opening closed mosques and decollectivizing rural life. Horrified by German brutality, the republican government increasingly distanced itself from German sponsorship and attempted to create a neutral state allied to Turkey. By early 1943 over a dozen guerrilla bands had taken up arms against the German occupation force.

The Karachai-Balkar state collapsed with the Soviet reconquest in October 1943. Stalin accused the entire nation of treason and participation in Nazi atrocities, and in November 1943 the 75,000 Karachai were shipped east in closed cattle cars. In March 1944 the 46,000 Balkars followed. The Soviet guards dumped the deportees in the Central Asian wastes without provisions or shelter. Thousands died of exposure, hunger, and disease.

The survivors, officially rehabilitated in 1956, returned to their Caucasian homes to remain under close KGB security until the Soviet liberalization in the late 1980s. Renewed contact between the two peoples of the small nation, forbidden for over three decades, spurred a dramatic resurgence of Karachai-Balkar nationalism.

The Soviet collapse in August 1991 stimulated demands for separation from the hybrid regions they had been forced into under Communist rule. In 1992 the Karachai and Balkar unilaterally withdrew their territories from the joint republics, a move that the Russian authorities have not recognized. Demands for the official unification of the long-divided nation have so far been ignored by the Russian authorities, which has raised tensions in the region, one of the least assimilated areas of the North Caucasus.

*SELECTED BIBLIOGRAPHY:*

Adams, Arthur E. *Stalin and His Times.* 1986.
Akiner, Shirin. *Islamic Peoples of the Soviet Union.* 1986.
Nekrich, Alexander. *The Punished Peoples.* 1978.
Seton-Watson, Hugh. *Russian Empire, 1801–1917.* 1967.

# KARAKALPAKSTAN

Karakalpakistan; Kara-Kalpakstan;
Karakalpakia

*CAPITAL: Nukus*

CENTRAL ASIA

KARAKALPAKSTAN

*POPULATION:* (95e) 1,290,000 : 468,000 Karakalpaks (Tudzit) in Uzbekistan. MAJOR NATIONAL GROUPS: (95e) Karakalpak (Tudzit) 33%, Uzbek 30%, Kazakh 27%, Russian 5%, Turkmen 3%, Tatar 1%. MAJOR LANGUAGES: Karakalpak, Uzbek, Russian, Kazakh. MAJOR RELIGIONS: Sunni Muslim, Russian Orthodox. MAJOR CITIES: (95e) Nukus 190,000 (254,000), Urgench 136,000, Khodzheyli 61,000, Khiva 41,000 (106,000), Chimbai 26,000.

*GEOGRAPHY:* AREA: 63,938 sq.mi.-165,642 sq.km. LOCATION: Karakalpakstan lies in Central Asia, occupying parts of the Ust-Urt Plateau and the Kyzyl-Kum Desert and the basin of the Amu Darya River south of the Aral Sea in northwestern Uzbekistan. POLITICAL STATUS: Karakalpakstan forms an autonomous republic within the Republic of Uzbekistan.

*FLAG:* The Karakalpak national flag, the flag of the national movement, is a green field bearing a yellow *dzungara* (ceremonial vessel) surmounted by a yellow crescent moon, horns pointed down, above a yellow, five-pointed star.

*PEOPLE:* The Karakalpaks, also called Tudzit or Kara-Kalpak, meaning Black Caps, are a Central Asian people of mixed origins. They include in their ancestry Oghuz and Kipchak Turks, Mongols, and Iranians and developed as a separate people in the fifteenth century. The Karakalpaks are closely related to the neighboring Kazakhs, although they are more Turkic in apppearance than the Kazakhs. Their language, of the West Turkic (Kipchak) language group, is classed by some scholars as a dialect of Kazakh, although it developed as a separate literary language after the Russian Revolution. The status of women, more advanced in the region than in the rest of Uzbekistan, is considered one of the few positive legacies of the Communist era. Even though the Karakalpaks' sense of separate identity is well developed, their status as a Kazakh sub-group or a separate ethnic group is still debated.

*THE NATION:* The fertile lands around the Aral Sea, originally inhabited by Caucasian peoples, came under the domination of the Oghuz Turks from Mongolia in the seventh century. The Turkic invaders absorbed the settled Caucasians, and their Turkic language and culture supplanted the Caucasians' original culture. In the eighth century Arab invaders overran the region and converted the inhabitants to Islam. The Aral Sea area later fell to the Seljuk Turks and in the thirteenth century came under the rule of the great Mongol Empire.

The Karakalpaks, the Black Caps, according to their national tradition, split from the Mongol-Turkic Golden Horde to emerge as a separate people in the fifteenth century. Sixteenth-century chronicles mention the Karakalpaks as a pastoral, nomadic people in the valley of the Syr Darya River east of the Aral Sea, subjects of the emirate of Bukhara. Under pressure from the Kazakhs to the north, the Karakalpaks moved southwest to settle the region south of the Aral Sea between the sixteenth and eighteenth centuries, an area loosely controlled by the Uzbek khanate of Khiva.

Russian and Cossack explorers first came across the Karakalpaks in the seventeenth century while traveling through the Uzbek-dominated Central Asian states. The states repulsed early attempts to extend Russian rule to the region, however the Russians returned in force in the nineteenth century. Between 1865 and 1876 nearly all of Central Asia came under Russian control. The Russians annexed the western districts of Karakalpakstan outright in 1873, while the districts east of the Amu Darya River remained under the rule of the khanate of Khiva, a nominally independent Russian protectorate.

The Karakalpak nomads, except for the loss of favored grazing lands, felt little of the effect of Russian rule until World War I. In desperate need of manpower, the tsarist authorities began to conscript Central Asians into labor battalions in June 1916. Resistance to conscription provoked serious incidents and finally resulted in a widespread rebellion in August 1916. Fearing Russian reprisals, many Karakalpaks took shelter in the marshes in the Amu Darya delta. The Central Asian rebellion forced the tsarist government to withdraw badly needed troops from the front. Confrontations between the Muslim rebels and the Russian military units ended with the news of the Russian Revolution of February 1917.

The Karakalpak leaders, as civil government collapsed, attempted to establish the instruments of self-rule, but several rival governments established in Central Asia contested their control of the territory south of the Aral Sea. In 1918 the Russian civil war spread to Central Asia, bringing increased chaos and confusion. In spite of a valiant resistance to the antireligious Bolsheviks, the Karakalpak territory came under Soviet rule in 1920.

The Soviets dissolved the traditional state borders and divided Central Asia into ethnic states in 1924. A Karakalpak autonomous region, created in May 1925, became part of the Kazakh autonomous republic. In 1932 the authorities transferred the region to the Russian Federation and upgraded its status to that of an autonomous republic. Four years later the Soviets again transferred the small republic to the authority of the Uzbek Soviet Socialist Republic. The former nomads, in spite of the political confusion and the repression of their Muslim religion, made great strides in education and culture and developed a strong sense of their separate national identity.

The Soviet authorities developed the region as a major producer of cotton, to the exclusion of the traditional agricultural and pastoral products. The Amu Darya River, one of the major sources of regional water, was diverted for cotton irrigation in 1962. The river rapidly became heavily polluted with chemical fertilizers. With its main feeder rivers diverted, the Aral Sea began to shrink rapidly, an ecological disaster mostly hidden from the world until the reforms and liberalization introduced in the Soviet Union in 1987.

Karakalpak nationalists, with a strong environmental faction, began to organize in 1989. The revelations of the extent of the serious health problems caused by the massive use of chemical fertilizers in the cotton production over decades both shocked and galvanized the nationalists. The nationalists condemned the bureaucrats of the Uzbek government and demanded separation and the creation of an autonomous Karakalpak republic within the Soviet Union. In 1990 the Karakalpak government declared the republic a sovereign state.

Uzbekistan became an independent country with the disintegration of the Soviet Union in August 1991. The new Uzbek national government, dominated by ex-Communists turned Uzbek nationalists, moved to crush the Karakalpak national movement. In late 1991 serious ethnic violence erupted. Disputes over water and land rights became national issues. Rival factions developed within the national movement, some calling for a federal relationship with Uzbekistan, while the more radical faction advocated declaring independence before negotiating with neighboring states.

The Karakalpaks, although the smallest of the Central Asian peoples, have a sense of identity as strong as that of the larger nations. In January 1994, ignoring Uzbek government pressure, the Karakalpaks announced plans to introduce the Latin alphabet, which would give them access to Turkish newspapers and television and would help to end their dependence on the largesse of the Uzbek government.

*SELECTED BIBLIOGRAPHY:*
Bacon, Elizabeth E. *Central Asians under Russian Rule: A Study in Cultural Change.* 1980.
Hiro, Dilip. *Between Marx and Muhammad: The Changing Face of Central Asia.* 1994.
Thubron, Colin. *The Lost Heart of Asia.* 1994.
Wheeler, Geoffrey. *The Modern History of Soviet Central Asia.* 1975.

# KARELIA

**Karjala; Karlya; Carelia**

*CAPITAL: Petroskoi (Petrozavodsk)*

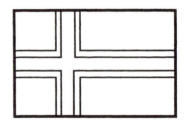

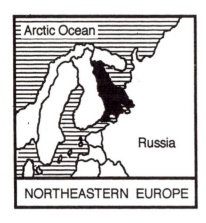

NORTHEASTERN EUROPE

KARELIA

*POPULATION:* (95e) 809,000 : 250,000 Karels in Russia and another 450,000 in Finland. "Greater Karelia" 1,470,000. MAJOR NATIONAL GROUPS: (95e) KARELIA: Russian 55%, Karel 26%, Belarussan 6%, Finn 6%, Ukrainian 2%, Vep 2%, Ingrian 2%. MAJOR LANGUAGES: Russian, Finnish, Karel. MAJOR RELIGIONS: Russian Orthodox, Lutheran. MAJOR CITIES: (95e) KARELIA: Petroskoi (Petrozavodsk) 289,000 (343,000), Kemi (Kem) 42,000, Sortavala (Serdobol) 41,000, Kontupokja (Kondopoga) 36,000, Kekehen (Segezha) 35,000 (70,000), Karhumaki (Medvezhyegorsk) 25,000. WESTERN KARELIA (ST. PETERSBURG OBLAST): Viipuri (Vyborg) 88,000 (117,000), Käkisalmi (Priozorsk) 29,000. NORTHERN KARELIA (MURMANSK OBLAST): Kaananlahti (Kandalaksha) 53,000, Kovdhen (Ze-lenoborskiy) 15,000.

*GEOGRAPHY:* AREA: 66,572 sq.mi.-172,466 sq.km. "Greater Karelia" 81,228 sq.mi.-210,435 sq.km. LOCATION: Karelia lies in northwestern European Russia, occupying the wooded Karelian Plateau between the White Sea and the Finnish border, a region of over 50,000 lakes. POLITICAL STATUS: Karelia forms a member state of the Russian Federation. "Greater Karelia," the region claimed by nationalists, also includes Western Karelia, transferred to Leningrad (St. Petersburg) Oblast in 1946, and Northern Karelia, transferred to Murmansk Oblast in 1938.

*INDEPENDENCE DECLARED:* 21 April 1921.

*FLAG:* The Karelian national flag, the flag of the national movement, is a

pale green field bearing a black Scandinavian cross outlined in red. OTHER
FLAG(S): The official flag of the republic is a horizontal tricolor of red, blue,
and green. The flag of the small Vep nation is a pale green field bearing a light
blue Scandinavian cross outlined in yellow.

*PEOPLE:* The Karels, a major branch of the Finnish peoples, speak a Finno-
Ugric language with three major dialects: Karjala, close to spoken Finnish, in
the north and central areas; Livvi, closer to Ingrian, in the southeast, and Lyddi,
closer to the language of the Finno-Ugric language of the related Vep minority,
Vepse, in the south and southwest. The Karels and Veps are mostly Orthodox
Christians, while the Finns and Ingrians, more numerous in the neighboring
region of Ingria,* are primarily Lutheran. The historic boundary between Karelia
and Finland reflected the religious division between the Orthodox Karels and
the Lutheran Finns. The large Russian population in the region, including many
descendants of exiles, has adopted Finnic cultural traits while retaining traditions
and customs that have disappeared elsewhere in Russia.

*THE NATION:* Nomadic Finnic tribes, originally from the Volga River basin
far to the east, settled the forested plateau in the eighth century during the great
tribal migrations that spread Finnish tribes across present Finland, Estonia, and
Ingria. Mentioned in the ninth century in European and Russian chronicles, the
Karel tribes lived in autonomous groups with few ties beyond the clan level.

The Swedes conquered the neighboring Finns in the twelfth and thirteenth
centuries and in the fifteenth century took control of western Karelia. The area
to the northeast, eastern Karelia, came under the rule of the Slavic Republic of
Great Novgorod, a commercial empire conquered by the expanding Russians in
1478. Freed from Slavic rule by the collapse of Novgorod, the Karels created
a flourishing medieval state in the north. The Karel's independence fostered a
great medieval flowering of Karel culture and folklore, including the creation
of the Kalevala, the great Finnish national epic. In 1617 the region fell to the
Swedes and became part of Swedish Finland.

At the conclusion of the Northern War in 1721, the Swedes ceded Eastern
Karelia to Russia. Western Karelia, along with Finland, came under Russian rule
in 1809, but the two Karelian regions remained divided by Russia's internal
political borders. Eastern Karelia, backward and underdeveloped, became known
chiefly as a place of exile for tsarist political prisoners and common criminals.
The Russian authorities generally ignored the local Karel population in the
largely rural region.

Influenced by the more advanced Finns, the Karels experienced a national
and cultural revival in the late nineteenth century. In 1899 the tsarist authorities
clamped down on the Karels and imposed new restrictions on education and
publishing in the Karel language. Nationalist literature, smuggled across the
border by Finnish nationalists, supported the growth of an underground nationalist movement.

Karel military units, deserting the front following the overthrow of the tsar
in February 1917, took control of Karelia as civil government collapsed. Protected by British troops landed to support the Whites, the Karel forces opposing

the Bolsheviks in the spreading Russian civil war. The Karel leaders declared their homeland an autonomous state in May 1919.

The White defeat and the withdrawal of the foreign troops left Karelia to the mercy of the Red Army in 1920. A Karel congress in March 1920 voted for independence, but occupation by the Red Army ended the movement. In early 1921 the Karels rebelled and drove the Soviets from the region. On 21 April 1921 the rebels proclaimed the independence of the Republic of Eastern Karelia (Itä Karjala) and created a democratic government that invited participation by the area's many national groups. The republic was reconquered by the Red Army in 1922, and the Soviets dissolved the republic and added Karelia to the new Russian Federation.

In late 1939 the Soviet government demanded the cession of Western Karelia from Finland as part of a plan to reunite the Karels under Soviet rule. The ensuing conflict, the Winter War, ended with Finnish defeat in 1940. The Soviets added conquered Western Karelia to Soviet Eastern Karelia to form the Karelo-Finnish Soviet Socialist Republic, which joined the Soviet Union as the twelfth constituent republic.

The Finns, unreconciled to the loss of Western Karelia, joined the German assault on the Soviet state in June 1941. The Finns liberated all of Karelia but, claiming that theirs was a separate conflict, refused to join further German offensives. Defeated in 1944, the Finnish troops withdrew, accompanied by over 400,000 Karels and Finns fleeing the Soviet advance. The Soviets again divided the Karel lands in 1945–46, transferring the western districts to Leningrad Oblast and returning Northern Karelia to Murmansk Oblast. On the grounds that the Karels formed only a minority in the republic, the Soviet government downgraded Karelia's status to an autonomous republic within the Russian Federation in 1956.

Contacts with the Finns and the large Karel exile population following the liberalization of the Soviet Union in the late 1980s spurred a rapid growth of national sentiment. Pressed by the multiethnic Karel national movement, the region's government became the first in the Soviet Union to declare sovereignty on 9 August 1990. The first Karel congress in seventy years, at Olonets on Lake Ladoga, endorsed the Soviet Finnish peoples right to self-rule.

The nationalist mobilization accelerated after the disintegration of the Soviet Union in August 1991. In February 1992 republican leaders warned Moscow that the demands for independence could spin out of control if the Russian government refused to grant greater autonomy. In November 1992 representatives of the Karels, Finns, and Veps demanded legal recognition as ''repressed nations'' that suffered disportionately during seventy years of Soviet Communist rule. Democracy in Russia has allowed the Karels to reestablish close cultural ties to neighboring Finland, which has begun to finance development in Karelia.

*SELECTED BIBLIOGRAPHY:*

Allison, Roy. *Finland's Relation with the Soviet Union 1944–84.* 1985.
Cohen, Yohanan. *Small Nations in Times of Crisis and Confrontation.* 1990.
Wuorinen, John H. *Finland and World War II, 1939–44.* 1983.

# KASHMIR

**Jammu and Kashmir**

*CAPITAL: Srinagar*

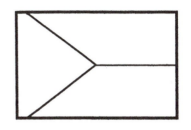

SOUTH-CENTRAL ASIA

KASHMIR

*POPULATION:* (95e) 10,218,000 : 7,150,000 Kashmiris in India and Pakistan. MAJOR NATIONAL GROUPS: (95e) Kashmiri 68%, Dogra 16%, Punchi, Balti, Ladakhi, Kohistani, Punjabi, Hunzakut, Burushaski. MAJOR LANGUAGES: Kashmiri, Urdu, Dogri, Pahari, English. MAJOR RELIGIONS: (95e) Sunni Muslim 78%, Hindu 16%, Sikh 2%, Buddhist 1.5%, Shia Muslim, Christian. MAJOR CITIES: (95e) INDIA (JAMMU AND KASHMIR): Srinagar 955,000 (1,204,000), Jammu 257,000, Anantnag 162,000, Baramula 71,000 (120,000), Sopur 62,000, Kathrea 55,000, Udhampur 45,000, Leh 40,000, Punch 36,000. PAKISTAN (AZAD KASHMIR): Muzaffarabad 57,000; (NORTHERN AREAS): Skardu 35,000, Gilgit 20,000.

*GEOGRAPHY:* AREA: 86,023 sq.mi.-222,857 sq.km. LOCATION: Kashmir occupies an extremely mountainous region in the western Himalayas and the Karakoram Range in northwestern India and northeastern Pakistan. The center of the region is the Vale of Kashmir, the basin of the Jhelum River. POLITICAL STATUS: Kashmir forms the Indian state of Jammu and Kashmir and Pakistani Kashmir, encompassing Azad (Free) Kashmir and the Northern Areas.

*FLAG:* The Kashmiri national flag, the flag of the national movement, is a horizontal bicolor of green over red with a white triangle at the hoist. OTHER FLAG(S): The flag of the largest of the nationalist organizations, the Jammu and Kashmir Liberation Front (JKLF), has three horizontal stripes of green, red, and green.

*PEOPLE:* The Kashmiris are an Aryan people, often tall and fair, speaking a language of the Dardic (Central Asian) branch of the Indo-Iranian languages that is written in the Persian script. Believed to have originated in Central Asia, the Kashmiri culture retains many ancient customs and traditions, brought to the region by the original settlers, that have combined with later Indian and Muslim influences. The majority of the Kashmiris are Sunni Muslims, as are most of the smaller national groups in the region. The only large religious minorities are the Shia Muslims, the Hindu Dogras of Jammu, and the Buddhists of Ladakh.*

THE NATION: The region, first mentioned in ancient chronicles as part of the Buddhist Mauryan state about 200 B.C., mostly converted to Hinduism under later rulers. Lying at the confluence of several ancient empires, the region knew many conquerors. The smaller ethnic groups survived only in the highly inaccessible mountain valleys. Aryan Muslim tribes, moving south from Central Asia, conquered Kashmir in the fourteenth century. Their Islamic religion rapidly spread across the area to most of Kashmir's earlier inhabitants.

A Muslim sultanate centered on the Vale of Kashmir controlled an extensive area until its conquest by the Mogul Empire in 1586. Reestablished at the collapse of the lowland Moguls in 1751, the Kashmiri state soon fell to invading Afghans. From 1756 the Kashmiris retained considerable autonomy under loose Afghan rule.

The Sikhs of Khalistan* conquered the region in 1819. For his services the Sikhs placed a Hindu Dogra, Gulab Singh, as the ruler of Jammu in 1820 while retaining the rest of Kashmir under direct Sikh control. Sikh incursions into British territory provoked war in 1846. The victorious British deposed the Sikh rulers and sold the conquered Kashmir area to Gulab Singh of Jammu, who had remained carefully neutral during the conflict. In 1885 the British installed a resident in Srinagar to oversee the relations between Kashmir and British India.

The rule of Gulab Singh's descendants, the Hindu rajas of Kashmir, became increasingly despotic in the early twentieth century. The growing Muslim discontent and resentment of their Hindu ruler finally erupted in open rebellion in 1931. Forced to make concessions, the raja legalized political parties and in 1934 conceded a legislative assembly. The Muslims, led by Muhammad Abdullah, called the "Lion of Kashmir," in 1939 formed the Kashmir National Conference. The formation of the political party is considered the inception of modern Kashmiri nationalism.

The British authorities at the end of World War II began preparations to grant independence to the two divisions of British India, Hindu-dominated India and Muslim Pakistan. Kashmir's Hindu raja, Hari Singh, imprisoned Muhammad Abdullah for leading a pro-Pakistani campaign but refused to accede his state to either India or Pakistan. Faced with a Muslim uprising, the raja released Abdullah, who kept Kashmir calm as violence and horrible massacres flared in many other areas during the political partition of British India.

An invasion of Muslim tribesmen from Pakistan and a pro-independence uprising within the state forced Hari Singh to flee to Delhi, where he signed a treaty of accession to India on 17 October 1947. Indian troops, airlifted into the

Vale of Kashmir, confronted the Muslim rebels and an invasion of Pakistani troops. A United Nations cease-fire in 1948 effectively partitioned Kashmir between India and Pakistan, but only as a temporary measure until a referendum could be organized to decide the state's future. In 1949 the Indian government rejected the plan for a referendum and organized Indian-occupied Kashmir as the Indian state of Jammu and Kashmir, the only Indian state with a Muslim majority.

Muhammad Abdullah, continuing to demand a referendum, spent years in prison for nationalist agitation. Released in 1964, Abdullah denounced India's authority as illegal. In response the Indian government replaced Kashmir's local administration with Indian civil servants. The tensions in the region sparked another inconclusive war with Pakistan in 1965, as a Pakistani invasion failed to win Kashmiri support for union with Pakistan. Fighting again erupted in 1971, with a new cease-fire line drawn across Kashmir in 1972.

Abdullah died in 1982, but his National Conference Party, led by his son Farooq, won state elections in 1983. Moves toward secession ended with the imposition of direct rule from New Delhi in 1984. The disbanding of the nationalist government marked a rapid upsurge of nationalist sentiment. In 1988 a widespread Muslim rebellion began in the state. The separatist organizations soon split into two rival camps, pro-independence and pro-Pakistan.

Pro-independence sentiment spread to Pakistani Kashmir. The mounting tensions in the region and Pakistani support of the pro-Pakistani Kashmiri groups brought India and Pakistan close to war in 1990. Attempts by nationalists in Pakistani Kashmir to march across the cease-fire line ended in violent confrontations with Pakistani troops in early 1992. The violence fueled a rise of pro-independence feeling in the Pakistani zone.

The Indian government, in an attempt to crush the rebellion, has given broad powers to the Indian military, powers that have led to widespread abuses and a brutal repression. The Indian excesses have alienated even moderate Kashmiris and have polarized Kashmiri opinion in favor of a united republic independent of both India and Pakistan.

*SELECTED BIBLIOGRAPHY:*
Korbel, Josef. *Danger in Kashmir.* 1954.
Lamb, A. *Kashmir: A Disputed Legacy, 1846–1990.* 1991.
Raina, Dina N. *Unhappy Kashmir: The Hidden Story.* 1990.
Singh, Raghubir. *Kashmir.* 1987.

# KATANGA

### Shaba

*CAPITAL: Lubumbashi*

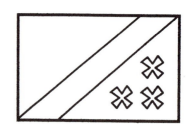

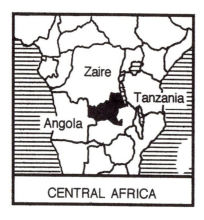

*POPULATION:* (95e) 6,128,000 : 4,530,000 Balunda (Lunda) in Zaire. MA-JOR NATIONAL GROUPS: (95e) Balunda 72%, Baluba 18%, Bayeke 6%, Batabwa 2%, other Zairean. MAJOR LANGUAGES: Lunda, Luba-Shaba, Bay-eke, French. MAJOR RELIGIONS: Roman Catholic, Protestant, animist. MA-JOR CITIES: (95e) Lubumbashi 862,000 (1,213,000), Kolwezi 323,000, Likasi 301,000 (382,000), Kamina 175,000, Kalemie 125,000, Manono 74,000, Kabolo 63,000, Moba 57,000 (111,000), Dilolo 52,000.

*GEOGRAPHY:* AREA: 191,878 sq.mi.-497,093 sq.km. LOCATION: Katanga occupies the fertile Shaba Plateau in southeastern Zaire, a forested area traversed by the Lomami and Lualaba Rivers, tributaries of the Zaire (Congo) River. POLITICAL STATUS: Katanga forms a province of the Republic of Zaire.

*INDEPENDENCE DECLARED:* 11 July 1960.

*FLAG:* The Katangan national flag, the flag of the former republic, is a di-agonal bicolor of red over white divided by a green stripe lower hoist to upper fly, charged with three red-brown crosses representing the old form of smelted copper on the white triangle at the lower fly.

*PEOPLE:* The Katangans are a Bantu people divided into a number of sep-arate tribes, the largest the Balunda or Lunda, with the allied Bayeke (Yeke) and Batabwa (Tabwa) in the south and the Baluba (Luba) minority in the north. All of the Katangan peoples speak Bantu languages of the Benue-Congo lan-guage group. The majority of the Katangans are Christian, mostly Roman Cath-olic, with an animist minority in the remote areas. Non-Katangans include the numerous Kasaians, primarily Baluba (Luba), immigrants from Kasai, and a small European minority, employed in mining and manufacturing, concentrated in the urban areas.

*THE NATION:* Little is known of the region's ancient history or of the early Bantu peoples, probably from present Uganda and Kenya, who settled the plateau. The first known records are of small states that formed in the area in the eleventh and twelfth centuries. In the sixteenth century a number of states united to form a powerful Lunda empire. Constant war with the rival Luba state, Murato Yanvo, blocked Lunda expansion to the north, but in the south the Lunda controlled vast territories in present Zaire, Zambia, and Angola. The empire, one of the most powerful in sub-Saharan Africa, drew its wealth from copper, the mines mostly worked by Swahili Muslims from Africa's east coast.

Continuous warfare, migrations, and internal disputes split the empire in the early nineteenth century, and numerous autonomous chiefdomships replaced the imperial authority. In the 1850s a local chief, M'siri, began to expand his territory by conquering neighboring tribes, including a chiefdomship called Katanga, whose name he took for his new kingdom.

A large tribal migration moving into his kingdom in the 1880s undermined M'siri's resistance to European encroachments. The turmoil caused by the migration gave the Belgians an opportunity to begin acquiring influence in the kingdom. On 31 December 1891 a European colonialist assassinated M'siri, and his kingdom rapidly disintegrated. The Belgians quickly took control of the kingdom, the last part of present Zaire to come under Belgian rule.

In 1910 the Belgians set up the Katanga Company to exploit the rich mineral deposits and simultaneously separated Katanga's colonial administration from the Belgian Congo, the basis of later Katangan separatism. Katanga won considerable autonomy from the Belgian Congo authorities in 1926. Katanga's large European population, supported by the powerful mining companies, organized a national movement in 1933 in support of an independent European settler state in the region. Industrialized in the early 1950s, the region flourished as one of sub-Saharan Africa's most advanced areas. The inhabitants, both European and African, enjoyed one of Africa's highest standards of living.

The Belgian Congo government, dominated by the mining companies, allowed no African participation in government until the municipal elections of 1957. The Belgian government, under international pressure, opened the elections to Africans and lifted a longstanding ban on political parties. Moise Tsombe, with a European cofounder, organized the Confederation of Tribal Associations of Katanga (CONAKAT), which quickly became the party of Katangan nationalism with the support of the southern tribes, the European minority, and the mining companies. In 1960 CONAKAT won control of the provincial assembly. The only large opposition group formed among the Luba tribe in the north.

Accompanied by widespread violence and chaos, the unprepared Belgian Congo gained independence on 30 June 1960. The new state rapidly disintegrated along tribal and regional lines. Supported by the Europeans and the majority southern tribes, Tsombe declared Katanga independent on 11 July 1960. Protected by its Belgian-officered and supplied army, Katanga remained calm as most of the Congo dissolved in civil war. For a time Katanga continued, the administration functioned, the mines produced, and its industries boomed. The only jarring note came from a growing Luba rebellion in the northern districts.

Katanga, with only 13% of the Congo's population, produced 60% of the export revenues, funds badly needed by the Congolese government. An appeal to the United Nations (UN), supported by other African states, received approval for the dispatch of UN troops. A UN attempt to disarm the Katangans failed and fighting broke out in the border areas. The UN troops invaded Katanga in December 1961. Katanga's former tranquillity collapsed into anarchy as fighting spread. Luba rebels launched a campaign of terror against the Lunda and Europeans in the southern cities. The terrorist campaign of murder, rape, and looting provoked a flood of terrified refugees.

Belgium and its Western allies, having installed a "reliable" man, Mobutu Sese Seko, as head of the Congolese government, forced an end to the Katangan secession in 1963. Lunda refugees in neighboring Angola formed the nationalist Congolese National Liberation Front (FLNC) in 1968 and twice invaded Katanga, rechristened Shaba by Mobutu, in 1977 and 1978.

President Mobutu, propped up by Western governments as a bulwark against Communism, systematically plundered the country. Shaba, which provided the bulk of Zaire's annual revenues, remained under the omnipresent control of the brutal state security forces.

The end of the Cold War also ended Mobutu's usefulness to the West. Widespread demands for democracy rocked the country in 1991–92, accompanied by looting and violence by unpaid government soldiers. Deprived of Western support, Mobutu's corrupt and ruthless regime faltered, and Zaire began to unravel amid widespread violence and ethnic conflicts.

In August 1992 the provincial governor of Shaba restored the forbidden name, Katanga, and announced his aim of eventual independence. The resurgence of nationalism in the region has been marked by a cruel anti-Kasaian campaign. Militant Lundas have driven tens of thousands of immigrant Kasaians from their homes, with covert government support. In December 1993 the Katangan government declared the political and economic autonomy of Katanga while the brutal "ethnic cleansing" of the Kasaians continued.

*SELECTED BIBLIOGRAPHY:*

Chamberlain, Muriel. *Decolonization: The Fall of European Empires.* 1985.

Gann, Lewis, and Peter J. Duignan. *Crisis in Zaire.* 1988.

Schuyler, Philippa. *Who Killed the Congo?* 1962.

Shepard, G. W. *The Politics of African Nationalism.* 1962.

# KAWTHOOLEI

**Kawthule; Karen**

*CAPITAL:* Toungoo

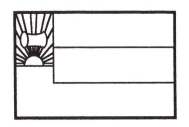

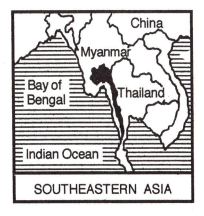

SOUTHEASTERN ASIA

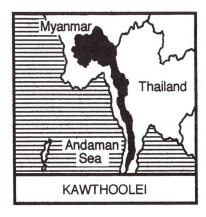

KAWTHOOLEI

*POPULATION:* (95e) 6,940,000 : 4,455,000 Karens in Myanmar and another 300,000 in adjacent areas of Thailand. MAJOR NATIONAL GROUPS: (95e) Burman 48%, Karen 44%, Shan 3%, Mon 2%. MAJOR LANGUAGES: Burmese, Karen, Shan. MAJOR RELIGIONS: Buddhist, animist, Christian. MAJOR CITIES: (95e) KAREN STATE: Paan 31,000. PEGU DIVISION: Toungoo 160,000, Prome (Py) 133,000, Pyu 74,000, Thonze 69,000, Paungde 53,000. TENASSERIM DIVISION: Thabaw 15,000.

*GEOGRAPHY:* AREA: 26,925 sq.mi.-69,753 sq.km. LOCATION: Kawthoolei, meaning Land of Flowers, lies in southeastern Myanmar, a lowland region in the Irrawaddy River basin and the mountainous areas to the east and southeast, just west of the international border with Thailand. POLITICAL STATUS: Kawthoolei has no official status; the region claimed by nationalists forms Karen State, Toungoo and Prome districts of Pegu Division, and the mountainous eastern strip of Tenasserim Division of the Union of Myanmar.

*INDEPENDENCE DECLARED:* 14 June 1949.

*FLAG:* The Kawthoolei flag, the flag of the national movement, is a horizontal tricolor of red, white, and blue bearing a vertical blue stripe at the hoist charged with a rising red sun surmounted by a golden Karen drum.

*PEOPLE:* The Karens are a people of mixed Thai, Chinese, and Malay ancestry encompassing three main divisions: the Sgaw in the hills and upper valleys of the east and southeast; the Bwe in the more remote mountain valleys; and the Pwo, the lowland Karens dispersed among other ethnic groups in the center and west. The Karen language, a Thai language of the Sino-Thai language group, is spoken in two major dialects, Pho in the lowlands and Sgaw in the mountains. The majority of the Karens adhere to traditional beliefs, with a large and important Christian minority, mostly Baptist. Nationalists claim a national population of over 8 million Karens in southeastern Myanmar.

*THE NATION:* According to Karen legend, they originated in an area north of ancient Babylon and passed through the Gobi Desert, called the River of Sand, some 4,500 years ago. The tradition claims that the Karens arrived in their present homeland from China in the fifth century B.C. An early Karen state, a federation of tribes called Thowanabonmi, flourished in the area until its destruction by invading Burmans in 1044. Abandoning the lowlands to the invaders, many of the Karen tribes retreated to strongholds in the mountains.

Constant war with Burmans forced the Karens to develop a strong military tradition. Fierce Karen warriors repulsed the Mongols in the thirteenth century and defeated Burman offensives in the sixteenth and seventeenth centuries. The passionately independent Karen tribes, fighting all invaders of their mountain homeland, retained a precarious freedom constantly threatened by Burman and Thai incursions.

The British conquest of Burma, beginning in 1826, eased Burman military pressure on the highland Karens. Tribal chiefs and elders, welcoming the British as valuable allies, signed military and political agreements and provided willing recruits to Britain's colonial army.

A Karen belief that their true religion would arrive with light-skinned strangers facilitated the establishment of European missions in their homeland. Mission schools introduced the tribes to modern education. The Karens became the first people in the region to evolve an educated, Christian leadership. Western ideas, particularly the ideas of culture and nation, stimulated the growth of national sentiment. The first Karen cultural organization formed in 1881, the forerunner of the later Karen separatist movement.

Outstanding soldiers, the Karens provided over half the recruits to the British colonial army in Burma in the 1930s. Increasingly used to contain a growing Burman nationalist movement, the ancient enmity between the two peoples deepened. In 1941 the Burmans, promised independence, supported the Japanese invasion. To counter the Japanese, the British ensured Karen loyalty with a parallel promise of eventual Karen independence. Less dependent on Karen support after the Burmans switched sides in 1944, the British began to support Burman demands for the inclusion of the non-Burman areas in an independent state.

A Karen delegation traveled to London in 1946 to discuss the details of the promised independence. Disappointed by the British support of a Burman state to include all of the British territories in the region, the Karens initially refused to discuss inclusion. Under intense British pressure they finally negotiated an agreement that provided for major autonomy within Burma and the right to secede if they wished, under British protection, after ten years.

Burma's first president, Aung San, died at the hands of opponents soon after independence in 1948. Burma's new leaders rejected the independence constitution and refused to grant Karen autonomy. Their appeals to the British government ignored, the Karen nationalists led a widespread revolt. Quickly overrunning most of south-central Burma, the rebel army laid siege to the Burmese capital, Rangoon. The Burmese leaders, U Nu and Nu Win, agreed to negotiations, but once in the city the entire Karen delegation was murdered.

The leaderless Karen rebellion began to collapse, and the rebels fell back under heavy attacks. The surviving Karen leaders, disavowing earlier demands for autonomy, declared the independence of the Republic of Kawthoolei on 14 June 1949. They created a new national capital at Toungoo, the center of lowland Karen culture. Overrun by advancing government troops in March 1950, the Karen nationalists once again retreated to their mountains.

A number of nationalist organizations emerged during the decades of insurgency since 1949, the proliferation reflecting the Karen's religious, political, and regional differences. The rebels, controlling a region with 75% of the world's remaining teak forests, have long depended on modest logging operations to finance the separatist war. Logging concessions sold to Thai officials by the Burmese military government have devastated the forests, and some of the Karen organizations have turned to the drug trade for revenue.

Myanmar's military government, considered one of the most brutal of the surviving dictatorships, launched the largest offensive against the Karens in over a decade in early 1992, but again faced with a stalemate decreed a unilateral cease-fire. The Karens, harboring many Burman opponents of the government, are seen as the greatest threat to the military regime and the key to the country's other ethnic insurgencies.

Lulled by the government cease-fire, in January 1994 several Karen groups announced their intention to open dialogue with the government. The decision opened a rift between the various Karen factions and revealed the continuing religious and regional divisions. In December 1994, disregarding its own cease-fire, the government sought to take advantage of the Karen rift by launching a strong offensive against the Karen mountain strongholds. The offensive reunited the Karen leadership and reopened the long separatist war. The Karen leaders denounced the Thai involvement as the Thai government, interested in lucrative ties to the military junta in Rangoon closed their border and cracked down on Karen nationalist and refugee organizations operating in Thailand.

*SELECTED BIBLIOGRAPHY:*

Lintner, Bertil. *Land of Jade: A Journey through Insurgent Burma.* 1990.

Smith, Martin. *Burma, Insurgency and the Politics of Ethnicity.* 1988.

Von der Mehden, Frederick R. *Religion and Nationalism in Southeast Asia: Burma, Indonesia, and the Philippines.* 1968.

# KAYAH

**Karenni**

*CAPITAL: Loikaw*

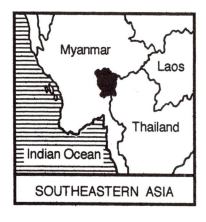

SOUTHEASTERN ASIA

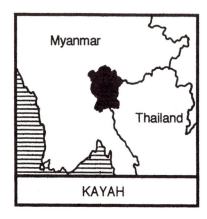

KAYAH

*POPULATION:* (95e) 335,000 : 540,000 Kayah in Myanmar and another 185,000 in adjacent areas of Thailand. MAJOR NATIONAL GROUPS: (95e) Kayah (Karenni) 84%, Shan 7%, Karen 5%, other Burmese. MAJOR LANGUAGES: Kayah-Li, Shan, Karen, Burmese. MAJOR RELIGIONS: animist, Christian, Buddhist. MAJOR CITIES: (95e) Loikaw 30,000, Bawlake 20,000.

*GEOGRAPHY:* AREA: 4,519 sq.mi.-11,707 sq.km. LOCATION: Kayah lies in eastern Myanmar, a highland region around the basin of the upper Salween River and its tributaries just north of the Thai border. POLITICAL STATUS: Kayah forms a state of the Union of Myanmar.

*FLAG:* The Kayah national flag, the flag of the national movement, is a horizontal tricolor of pale blue, white, and red bearing a white, five-pointed star on the upper hoist. OTHER FLAG(S): The flag of the largest national organization, the Karenni National Progressive Party (KNPP) and its military wing, the Karenni Revolutionary Army (KRA), is a horizontal tricolor of red, white, and pale blue bearing a centered disc representing the top of a Kayah frog drum.

*PEOPLE:* The Kayah, also called Karenni, Kayaw, or Red Karen, are an Asian people of Thai-Chinese background speaking a Thai language of the Sino-Thai language group. Less assimilated than the related Karens, the Kayah culture has been less influenced by the Burmans and has more Thai and Shan influences. The Kayah mostly retain their traditional religious beliefs, although in recent decades Christianity has gained many followers.

*THE NATION:* The Kayah arrived in their present homeland from southwestern China, traditionally in the fifth century B.C. Differentiated by the color of their cloaks, the Kayah or Red Karens slowly separated from the larger black Karen population to the south. Influenced by the neighboring Shan, a Thai people, the Kayah erected small, independent states ruled by princes and adopted many Shan cultural traits.

The Kayah retained close ties to the tribal Karens, and the two peoples often cooperated when threatened by invaders, especially the ongoing threat posed by the warlike Burmans, who conquered the lowlands in the eleventh century. In the thirteenth century the Kayah states became vassals of the Shans, who ruled most of Burma until their defeat by the resurgent Burmans in 1586.

The small principalities, protected by a long military tradition, maintained their independence against repeated Burman offensives in the sixteenth and seventeenth centuries and against a Thai incursion in the eighteenth century. The five Kayah states, later reduced to three, grew rich from the sale of precious stones from their mines.

Europeans, drawn by the state's fabulous gems, visited the region in the eighteenth century. Sustained contact with Europeans began with the British annexation of the lowlands in 1852. Never part of the Burman kingdom, the principalities established direct treaty relations with the British authorities and accepted British residents attached to the courts of the Kayah princes. An agreement signed on 21 June 1875 recognized Kayah independence under British protection and provided for full independence should the protectorate agreement be terminated.

The ethnic Burmans, allied with the invading Japanese, drove the British from Burma in 1942. Declared independent under Japanese protection, the new Burman state laid claim to the Kayah principalities. Their small states occupied by Burman and Japanese troops, many Kayah retreated to the mountains to form guerrilla groups, the nucleus of the later Kayah national army. The guerrillas, trained by Allied officers parachuted into the highland jungles, terrorized the Burman and Japanese units sent against them.

The British began to prepare Burma for independence at the end of the war and pressed the small British protectorates on the borders to join a proposed federation. The Kayah, expecting the British to honor the terms of the 1875 agreement, rejected the Burmese federation and notified the British of their wish for separate independence. The British authorities refused to honor the 1875 agreement; their refusal and the insistence that the Kayah join Burma provoked a Kayah uprising that spread following Burmese independence.

The Burmese government finally crushed the Kayah rebellion in 1950. Determined to separate the Kayah from the ongoing Karen insurgency to the south, the government granted the Kayah states semiautonomous status in 1952. Seven years later the authorities deposed the Kayah princes. The outraged Kayah resumed their rebellion in 1959 and renewed their traditional alliance with the Karen groups fighting the government.

Kayah support for the democracy movement that the government brutally crushed in 1990 reaffirmed Kayah determination to separate from Burma. The destruction of the democracy movement, with its possibility of democracy within a new federation that would replace the hated military junta, marked a new phase in the Kayah's fight for self-rule. The Burmese government's agreements with economic interests in neighboring Thailand to log Kayah's forests and exploit the region's mineral wealth alienated the more moderate Kayahs and have made negotiations more difficult.

The Kayah, claiming that they never agreed to inclusion in Burma, have fought for decades to secure the independence guaranteed by the 1875 agreement, which has not been nullified. The brutal military government of Burma, renamed Myanmar, has only reinforced the Kayah desire for separation, citing their abundant timber and mineral wealth as the economic base for viable independence. The Kayah leaders assert that the war is no longer just about freedom, but about the survival of the Kayah nation.

In December 1994, after a two-year lull, fighting again erupted in the region. The Kayah leaders, citing new border restrictions, accused the neighboring Thai government of backing the offensive by Myanmar's military junta in order to win lucrative logging and mining concessions in the Kayah's national territory.

*SELECTED BIBLIOGRAPHY:*
Lintner, Bertil. *Land of Jade: A Journey through Insurgent Burma.* 1990.
Nicholl, Charles. *Borderlines.* 1989.
Smith, Martin. *Burma, Insurgency and the Politics of Ethnicity.* 1988.
Von der Mehden, Frederick R. *Religion and Nationalism in Southeast Asia: Burma, Indonesia, and the Philippines.* 1968.

# KERALA

**Travancore-Cochin; Chera**

*CAPITAL: Tiru-Anantapuram (Trivandrum)*

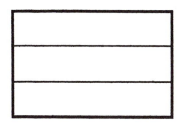

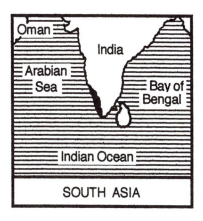

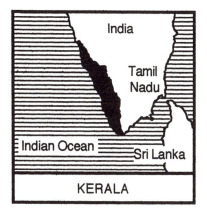

*POPULATION:* (95e) 30,576,000 : 34,500,000 Keralans in India. MAJOR NATIONAL GROUPS: (95e) Keralan 95%, other Indian. MAJOR LANGUAGES: Malayalam, English, Tamil, Kannarese, Talu. MAJOR RELIGIONS: (95e) Hindu 48%, Christian 31%, Sunni Muslim 20%, Jewish. MAJOR CITIES: (95e) Tiru-Anantapuram (Trivandrum) 646,000 (722,000), Kochi (Cochin) 576,000 (1,049,000), Kozikode (Calicut) 530,000 (728,000), Alappuzha (Aleppey) 248,000 (279,000), Kollam (Quilon) 201,000 (266,000), Palakkad (Palghat) 168,000 (245,000), Thalassery (Tellicherry) 149,000 (180,000), Trichur 92,000 (264,000), Kannanur (Cannanore) 90,000 (231,000), Kayangulam (Kayankulam) 84,000 (261,000), Badagara 83,000 (110,000).

*GEOGRAPHY:* AREA: 15,003 sq.mi.-38,867 sq.km. LOCATION: Kerala lies in southwestern India, a tropical coastal plain on the Indian Ocean rising to the Cardamon Hills on the border of Tamil Nadu* in the east. POLITICAL STATUS: Kerala forms a state of the Indian republic.

*INDEPENDENCE DECLARED:* 15 August 1947.

*FLAG:* The Keralan national flag, the traditional flag of the state, is a horizontal tricolor of red, yellow, and turquoise.

*PEOPLE:* The Keralans are a Dravidian people, the descendants of peoples driven into southern India by the ancient Aryan invasions of northern India. Keralan society embraces four major divisions: high-caste Hindu Nairs; low-caste Hindu Ezhavas; the Christians, further divided among several sects; and the Moplahs, Muslim Keralans of mixed Dravidian and Arab background. There is also a small, ancient Jewish community. All Keralan groups encompass castes and subcastes, including the Christian and Jewish communities. The Keralan language is a Dravidian language based on Old Tamil, from which it separated in the tenth century to develop as a separate literary language in the eleventh century. Kerala, only about half Hindu, has the largest Christian population and one of the largest Muslim populations in India.

*THE NATION:* Dravidian peoples, pushed south by the Aryan invasions of northern India between 1500 and 1200 B.C., established a number of small, independent states in the coastal plain along the Indian Ocean. Hindu culture, replacing the earlier Buddhism by 200 B.C., helped to unite the region's peoples. A powerful maritime kingdom, called Kerala and later Chera, emerged in the early Christian Era as the region's dominant power.

Kerala's trade ties, extending as far west as the Roman provinces of Arabia, brought new cultural and religious traditions to the kingdom. By the first century A.D., Keralan development had begun to diverge from the uniform Hindu Dravidian culture of south India. Traditionally, St. Thomas brought Christianity to the kingdom in the first century A.D. Jewish refugees established themselves in the kingdom in 69 A.D., and a Syrian Christian community had settled in Kerala by 325.

Conquered by the Tamils in the fourth century, the Keralans developed an intense hatred of the related Tamil conquerors that remains to the present. The Malayalam language, a dialect of ancient Tamil, began to diverge in the tenth century. The language, like the culture, absorbed influences from the many maritime peoples to visit the Keralan ports, particularly the Arabs, who settled the Malabar Coast, bringing with them their Islamic religion.

The region divided into a number of petty states before the first European, Portuguese explorer Vasco de Gama, rounded the Cape of Good Hope and reached the Malabar Coast in 1498. The Europeans recorded their amazement to find native Christians whose existence was unknown in Europe. Jewish refugees, expelled from Portugal in 1496, used the new sea routes to join the region's ancient Jewish community. In 1516 the Portuguese built the first European church in India to serve the growing number of traders. English, Dutch, and French expeditions followed the Portuguese, and an intense European rivalry developed for control of the lucrative Indian trade.

The descendants of the ancient Keralan kings united the petty states of southern Kerala in 1745. Two states, Travancore and Cochin, with close dynastic ties, established separate treaty relations with Great Britain in 1795. Staunch British allies, the two states provided troops to Britain's colonial army. In return, British troops supported the states' Hindu rulers by suppressing a Moplah Muslim uprising in 1921 and by controlling the ethnic and religious disturbances and the Communist agitation that plagued the states in the 1930s. Indian nationalism, gaining support prior to World War II in northern India, won few adherents in the region.

Local nationalism increased after the war, as India prepared for independence in the early months of 1947. The rulers of the Keralan states expressed their preference for association, but not incorporation, into the new Indian state. C. P. Ramaswani Aiyer, the prime minister of Travancore, announced the adoption of a new constitution and withdrew the state from all Indian political bodies. Keralan nationalists claimed that Travancore, with its considerable coastline and near monopoly on several important commodities, was better fitted for independence than any other in British India.

The governments of Travancore and Cochin rejected Indian overtures and threats and refused to accede to India. On 15 August 1947, the day India became independent, Aiyer proclaimed Travancore a sovereign state, while neighboring Cochin prepared to follow. The Indian government threatened reprisals, but Keralan appeals to the British brought only pressure to negotiate. Following protracted talks, the two states finally accepted guaranteed autonomy under their traditional rulers, with the Indian government responsible only for defense and foreign relations. Disturbances broke out at the news of the compromise, led by nationalists and Communists, but particularly affecting the Muslim Moplahs, who vehemently opposed inclusion in predominantly Hindu India.

In 1948, in spite of the earlier guarantees, the Indian government ended the states' autonomy and combined the two into a new state. In 1949 the maharajas, under pressure, renounced their political rights. As part of the government's 1956 reorganization, all the Malayalam-speaking regions of southwest India were united in a new state called Kerala.

Opposition to Indian rule coalesced around the Kerala Socialist Party (KSP), a Communist-dominated party that openly advocated secession from India. In 1957 the KSP won state elections and formed the world's first freely elected Communist government. In 1959 the federal authorities dissolved the government of ''Red Kerala'' and in 1962 passed a law making the advocation of secession a crime.

Keralan nationalism remains a strong force in the state, based on anti-Aryan and anti-Tamil traditions, with national sentiment particularly strong among the non-Hindus. The state, with India's highest literacy rate, best health care, and most extensive road system, has little in common with the rest of India. The neat and clean Keralan cities are remarkably free of the squalid slums and communal tensions that dominate most of India. In spite of a long flirtation with Communism, the collapse of the Soviet Union has brought changes to Kerala. Economics, not ideology, has become the prime national issue in the state.

*SELECTED BIBLIOGRAPHY:*

Bayly, Susan. *Saints, Goddesses and Kings: Muslims and Christians in South Indian Society 1700–1900.* 1990.

Chanra, B. *Nationalism and Colonialism in Modern India.* 1979.

Vajpeyi, Dhirendra, and Malik Yogenda, eds. *Religious and Ethnic Minorities in South India.* 1990.

# KHALISTAN

**Punjab; Punjabi Suba**

*CAPITAL: Amritsar*

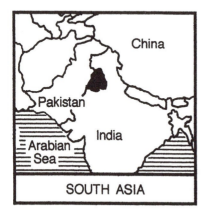

*POPULATION:* (95e) 22,445,000 : 17,500,000 Sikhs in India. MAJOR NATIONAL GROUPS: (95e) Sikh 62%, other Indian. MAJOR LANGUAGES: Punjabi, Hindi, English. MAJOR RELIGIONS: (95e) Sikh 62%, Hindu 35%, Sunni Muslim 2%, Christian. MAJOR CITIES: (95e) PUNJAB: Ludhiana 847,000 (1,109,000), Amritsar 807,000 (1,020,000), Jalandhar (Jullundur) 541,000 (678,000), Patiala 273,000 (347,000), Bhatinda 158,000, Pathankot 145,000, Hostiarpur 123,000, Abohar 116,000, Batala 116,000, Moga 109,000, Phagwara 107,000, Maler Kotla 100,000. CHANDIGARH: Chandigarh 528,000 (719,000).

*GEOGRAPHY:* AREA: 19,492 sq.mi.-50,497 sq.km. LOCATION: Khalistan lies in northeastern India, a flat plain traversed by several important rivers, the subcontinent's most fertile and productive agricultural lands. Khalistan borders Pakistan on the west and Kashmir* on the north. POLITICAL STATUS: Khalistan, meaning Land of the Pure, has no official status; the area claimed by nationalists forms the Indian state of Punjab and the territory of Chandigarh, currently the joint capital of Punjab and the neighboring state of Haryana.

*INDEPENDENCE DECLARED:* 30 April 1986.

*FLAG:* The Sikh national flag, the flag of the national movement, is a vertical bicolor of yellow and pale blue bearing two crossed black swords centered and backed by a black spear, its point enclosed in a black circle. OTHER FLAG(S): The traditional Sikh flag is an orange triangle bearing the black swords and spear.

*PEOPLE:* The Sikhs, a religious and military sect, are among the newest of India's national groups, the disciples of a religion founded in the fifteenth century. The Sikh religious beliefs, which prohibit tobacco and alcohol, command Sikh adherence to the Five Ks: Kesha, long, uncut hair wrapped in a turban; Kangla, a wooden or ivory comb; Kacha, military knee britches; Kara, a steel bracelet; Kirpan, the Sikh sword. The Sikh language, Punjabi, closely resembles Hindi but uses the Gurmukhi script, the alphabet of the Sikh's sacred texts.

*THE NATION:* The Sikh religion emerged in the fifteenth century as an attempt to reconcile hostile Hindus and Muslims. The religious and military sect, created by guru (teacher) Nanak, is based on a monotheistic creed, the fundamental identity of all religions, and the reality of God through religious exercises and meditation. The new sect, opposed to idolatry, religious ritual, the maintenance of a priesthood, and the caste system, rapidly gained adherents. In 1574 the faithful built a new capital city, Amritsar, around the spiritual center of their new religion, the Golden Temple.

Successive gurus codified the precepts of the religion. By the late seventeenth century the Sikhs had consolidated as a people and had begun to develop as a military power. Goviad Singh, in the 1690s, created a powerful military unit, the Khalsa, meaning the Pure, based on the Five Ks. The militarization of the Sikhs, hastened by a Muslim invasion in 1710, evolved as an anti-Muslim movement. In the late eighteenth century the Sikhs defeated the Muslims and conquered the Punjab. Over the next decade the Sikhs extended their empire to include much of northwestern India and Kashmir.

The Muslims declared holy war against the Sikhs in 1826. The Sikh victory over the Muslims in 1831 brought the Sikh warriors to the borders of British territory. Tensions on the border provoked the first Anglo-Sikh war in 1845. A second war, 1848–49, resulted in the British annexation of the Sikh heartland in the Punjab. Impressed by the Sikhs' military prowess, the British recruited Sikh soldiers for the colonial army. By the late nineteenth century the Sikh units formed the backbone of Britain's colonial forces in India.

Serious violence between Sikhs and Muslims, the majority in western Punjab, broke out with the beginning of World War I in 1914. Anti-Muslim sentiment pushed the Sikhs to embrace the growing Indian national movement, particularly the Sikh soldiers returning from military duty in Asia and Europe. In 1919 British general Dyer ordered soldiers to fire on a huge crowd of Sikh demonstrators in Amritsar. The massacre left over 400 dead and 1,200 wounded and galvanized Sikh opposition to continued British rule.

Sikh leaders after World War II began negotiations on the creation of a Sikh homeland separate from both India and Pakistan. The British authorities agreed to separate Sikh independence but, pressured by Indian leaders Nehru and Gandhi, reneged on the agreement and terminated the negotiations. Unable to move ahead with their plans for independence, the Sikhs, promised religious and cultural autonomy, acceded to India.

Over vehement Sikh protests, the authorities partitioned their homeland in the Punjab between India and Pakistan, setting off savage fighting in the region that left thousands dead in communal massacres. Approximately 2 million Sikhs fled Pakistani West Punjab, often in protected caravans miles long. The feeling that they had been duped by Indian leaders spread through the Sikh community soon after Indian independence in 1947, provoking a peaceful campaign for a separate Sikh state within India. In 1956 the government agreed to the creation of a linguistic state, but with a Punjabi-speaking Hindu majority. Following serious Sikh agitation the largely Hindu areas became separate states in 1966, leaving a truncated Punjab with a slight Sikh majority.

The energetic Sikhs, often beginning as refugees in 1947, achieved India's highest standard of living by the 1970s. Material prosperity gave the Sikhs new confidence and raised new demands for autonomy. An increasingly vocal minority began a campaign to win support for secession and the creation of an independent Sikh state.

Nationalist organizations proliferated as the national movement splintered between the groups advocating violence and the nonviolent factions. Amid growing separatist violence the Indian authorities imposed direct rule from New Delhi in October 1983. Five months later Indian police and troops attacked separatists sheltering in the Sikh's holiest shrine, the Golden Temple in Amritsar. Over 500 Sikh nationalists died in the assault.

The Sikh revenge, the assassination of India's prime minister, Indira Gandhi, on 31 October 1984, set off violent anti-Sikh rioting that left over 3,000 dead and thousands more homeless. Amid the continuing turmoil, nationalists declared the independence of Khalistan on 30 April 1986. The secession, crushed by security forces, set off a renewed and even more violent campaign to win independence.

The terrorist campaign by radical Sikh nationalists and the often brutal official reprisals had taken over 20,000 lives by 1992. A government attempt to hold state elections, boycotted by the nationalists and under the shadow of terrorist attacks, returned a new state government in 1992, but with the votes of less than 20% of the eligible voters. The ongoing crisis in the Punjab, India's breadbasket, remains one of the most serious nationalist threats to the fabric of multinational India.

*SELECTED BIBLIOGRAPHY:*

Basu, Aparna. *Imperialism, Nationalism and Regionalism in Canadian and Modern Indian History.* 1989.
Butani, D. H. *The Third Sikh War? Toward and Away from Khalistan.* 1986.
McLeod, W. H. *The Sikhs: History, Religion and Society.* 1989.
Singh, K. *The Sikhs Today: Their Religion, History, Culture and Customs.* 1976.

# KÖNIGSBERG

**Kaliningrad; East Prussia**

*CAPITAL: Königsberg (Kaliningrad)*

NORTHEASTERN EUROPE

KONIGSBERG

*POPULATION:* (95e) 1,092,000 : 975,000 Kaliningrad Slavs in Russia. MAJOR NATIONAL GROUPS: (95e) Kaliningrad Slav 85% (Russian, Ukrainian, Belorussan), German 6%, Lithuanian 5%, Polish 3%. MAJOR LANGUAGES: Russian, German. MAJOR RELIGIONS: Russian Orthodox, Roman Catholic, Protestant. MAJOR CITIES: (95e) Königsberg (Kaliningrad) 417,000 (499,000), Tilsit (Sovetsk) 50,000 (92,000), Insterburg (Chernyakhovsk) 35,000, Gumbinnen (Gusev) 28,000, Pillau (Baltiysk) 25,000, Ragnit (Neman) 24,000.

*GEOGRAPHY:* AREA: 5,830 sq.mi.-15,103 sq.km. LOCATION: Königsberg lies in northeastern Europe, an enclave of Russia nearly 500 miles west of the nearest Russian territory, between Poland on the south and Lithuania on the north and east. About half of the enclave's territory is under the direct control of the Russian military. POLITICAL STATUS: Königsberg has no official status; the enclave forms Kaliningrad Oblast, Russia's smallest province, although the provincial government has unilaterally declared the enclave a republic within the Russian Federation.

*FLAG:* The Königsberger national flag, the flag of the national movement, is a horizontal tricolor of green, white, and blue.

*PEOPLE:* The Kaliningrad Slavs, increasingly using the nationalist name Königsberger or Königsberg Slav, are Russia's newest group to claim separate national identity. Comprising the Russians, Ukrainians, and Belorussans settled in the region after 1945, the Slavs have begun to adopt the area's former German history and culture as their own. A unique German-Slav culture and identity are evolving from a fusion of the Russian present and the German past. The German minority, increased by the arrival of 20,000 ethnic Germans from Siberia* and Central Asia since 1990 and the return of over 40,000 from Germany, are mostly a remnant of the region's pre–World War II population.

*THE NATION:* The low, sandy area east of the Baltic Sea was the ancient home of the Borussi, a Baltic people related to the Lithuanians and Latvians to the north. Called Prussians by the Germanic peoples, the Baltic tribes fell to the onslaught of Teutonic knights in 1226. The crusading knights, theoretically on a mission to Christianize the pagan tribes, exterminated the native Prussians. The Prussian's lands, colonized and Germanized, retained only the name.

The city of Königsberg, founded in 1255, developed as a major trading center and a leading member of the Hanseatic League from 1340. The Order of the Teutonic Knights, expelled from lands taken by the Poles to the south, made Königsberg their seat in 1457. They retained control of the region called Prussia as vassals of the Polish kingdom. In 1525 Albert of Brandenburg secularized the Teutonic Order and took for himself the title duke of Prussia.

The German state of Brandenburg conquered Prussia from Poland in 1660. Frederick III, the elector of Brandenburg, in 1701 had himself crowned king of Prussia in Königsberg's famous gothic cathedral. Called East Prussia, the area formed a province of the kingdom of Prussia, a region of vast Junker estates and a stronghold of the Prussian landed and military aristocracy.

The eastern outpost of German power and a major naval base during World War II, East Prussia fell to the advancing Red Army in the autumn of 1944. The East Prussian capital, Königsberg, surrendered to the Soviets after months of siege. Its famous university and cathedral, the fourteenth-century castle, and most of the old city lay in ruins. The majority of the German population fled west. Forty thousand Germans who failed to escape were either executed or deported to make way for the settlement of displaced Slavs.

Königsberg and the surrounding territory, incorporated into the Soviet Union in 1945, received a new name to glorify the memory of Mikhail Kalinin, the Soviet Union's first president. The Sovietization of the region involved the re-naming of the region's German monuments, cities, and place-names, with all references to the German past forbidden. Thousands of ethnic Slavs, displaced during the war, settled in the province. The Soviets laid out a new capital, Kaliningrad, in the former residential suburbs of Königsberg. The province, closed to foreigners, functioned as a virtual fief of the powerful Soviet military bureaucracy.

The rapid changes overtaking the Soviet Union and its allies began to filter into the closed province following the overthrow of Communist governments in neighboring Poland and Lithuania. Younger Slavs, disillusioned with decades of joyless socialism, began to question the belief that the province was merely a substitute for homes lost during the war and that the region had no past prior to 1945.

Influenced by resurgent Polish and Lithuanian nationalism, numerous organizations formed in the region, the largest the Königsberg National Memorial

Association and the Russian-German Society. Determined to overcome official suppression, the nationalists began to rediscover and expose seven centuries of history that they feel is theirs by right of birth. Nationalists pressed for a reversion to the former names, heartened by a similar movement to regain the old name of Leningrad, St. Petersburg. The effort to rehabilitate the region's past rapidly replaced the meager Soviet culture of sad war memorials with a fledgling European nation that combines the past with the present.

The movement to reclaim the region's cultural heritage led to efforts to save the remains of the city's gothic cathedral, scheduled for demolition, and demands for the reopening of the university, originally founded in 1544. The university is famed for the tenure of Immanuel Kant, who has become a symbol of the new national movement. The Königsberg movement, a coalition of several national and cultural groups, rapidly gained support following the declaration of a special economic zone in late 1990 and the opening of the oblast to foreign visitors in March 1991.

The abortive Soviet coup in August 1991 and the subsequent breakup of the Soviet Union accelerated demands for radical change. Pressured by an increasingly critical public, the provincial parliament voted to oust the local Communist leadership and passed resolutions prohibiting the resettlement of Soviet troops returning from the former satellite countries.

The younger Slavs, calling themselves Königsbergers, pressed the local government to unilaterally declare the province a full republic within the Russian Federation. Republican status would give the region greater economic and cultural autonomy during an interim period of economic and political restructuring that the nationalists maintain must be completed before further political changes can be contemplated.

In 1994 the reconstruction of the medieval cathedral began, based on prewar photographs and records. The city's ancient Germanic crest, a mermaid blowing a trumpet, has been adopted as the region's official symbol in yet another step to recuperate Königsberg's lost heritage. In spite of fears that Poland and Lithuania could resurrect old claims on the region, the nationalists are pressing ahead with plans for the independence of the fourth Baltic state, the proposed Free City of Königsberg.

*SELECTED BIBLIOGRAPHY:*
Carsten, Francis L. *The Origins of Prussia.* 1982.
Christians, F. W. *Paths to Russia: From War to Peace.* 1991.
Clark, Alan. *The Russian-German Conflict, 1941–1945.* 1985.
Colton, Timothy, and Robert Levgold, eds. *After the Soviet Union.* 1992.

# KORYAKIA

Chav' Chüv

*CAPITAL: Palana*

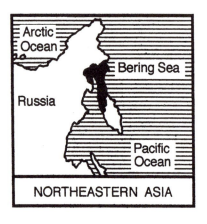

*POPULATION:* (95e) 46,000 : 11,000 Koryaks (Nymylany) and 3,000 Itel'-men (Kamchadals) in Russia. MAJOR NATIONAL GROUPS: (95e) Russian 50%, Koryak 20%, Even (Lamut) 17%, Itel'men 5%, Chukot 2%. MAJOR LANGUAGES: Russian, Koryak, Even. MAJOR RELIGIONS: Russian Orthodox, animist. MAJOR CITIES: (95e) KORYAKIA: Palana 8,000. KOVRAN: Kovran 4,000.

*GEOGRAPHY:* AREA: 117,953 sq.mi.- 305,577 sq.km. LOCATION: Koryakia lies in the sub-Arctic region of Russia's Far East,* a mountainous region around the Penzhina basin northeast of the Sea of Okhotsk. The region occupies a large mainland region south of Chukotka* and part of the large Kamchatka Peninsula. POLITICAL STATUS: Koryakia forms an autonomous region of the Russian Federation. The region claimed by nationalists, called Chav' Chüv in the Koryak language, also includes the Kovran district of Kamchatka Oblast.

*FLAG:* The Koryak national flag, the flag of the national movement, is a white field with a horizontal green stripe at the bottom and a large gold sun and twelve rays centered.

*PEOPLE:* The Koryaks and the closely related Itel'men of Kovran are a Paleo-Asiatic people divided into twelve clans or tribes, speaking a Paleo-Siberian language of the Luorawetlan language group, which also includes the closely related Itel'men language. The Koryaks and Itel'men are ethnically related to the Native American peoples of the American continents. The majority of the Koryaks are reindeer herders, while the Itel'men are fishermen, harvesting salmon from the huge region's rivers and coasts, these traditional occupations the criteria that divided the two closely related peoples. The Itel'men, concentrated around the town of Kovran, are now mostly employed in the town's fishcanning factories. The majority of the Koryaks are Orthodox Christians, with a minority that has retained traditional beliefs. The related Evens or Lamuts live in the northeast, and the Chukot minority inhabits the northern areas. The Slav population is mostly concentrated in the coastal towns.

*THE NATION:* In prehistoric times small nomadic groups migrated across the vast stretches of wilderness in eastern Siberia. In pursuit of game, many of the bands crossed the land bridge that connected the continents of Asia and North America some 30,000 years ago. The small bands on the Asian side, gradually pushed north by strong peoples, spread out across the harsh landscape, some to take up herding in the interior grazing lands, others to settle on the coasts, where fishing became the tribal mainstay.

Russian expansion, led by explorers and Cossack warriors, reached the Pacific Coast in 1640. By 1649 the majority of the Koryak tribes had come under Russian rule, and between 1697 and 1732 the Russians annexed the territories belonging to southern tribes and the Itel'men of the Kamchatka Peninsula.

Exploited for its valuable furs, the region was held under a Russian trade monopoly that forbade trading in the coastal settlements. The harsh Russian rule decimated the tribal peoples. Already devastated by European diseases, thousands perished in unprovoked massacres. Only a few thousand Koryaks and Itel'men survived the first half century of Russian rule.

The tribes slowly recovered in the nineteenth century, the long decline in population beginning to reverse. Exiled Russian intellectuals deported to the region studied the Koryak and Itel'men peoples, and amateur linguists began to devise a written form of their languages. Orthodox missionaries introduced a system of education for a few tribals that produced the first educated Koryaks and Itel'men able to deal with the tsarist authorities.

The disturbances of the 1905 Russian Revolution, with its calls for equality and the redress of the empire's past mistakes, awakened a sense of grievance in the Koryak peoples. Led by the educated minority, the Koryaks began to demand land rights, particularly the right to fish in the streams and rivers of their ancestral lands.

In 1920 the Soviet authorities took control of Koryakia, until that time virtually untouched by the world war and the revolution that had followed in Russia. The Soviets outlawed the nomadic lifestyle of the interior and collectivized the fishing communities along the Pacific Coast and the Gulf of Shelekhov east of Kamchatka. Collectivized in the late 1920s, the former nomads were forced by the authorities to work for the state and to settle in permanent villages chosen for them. The Soviet redistribution of wealth involved the confiscation of nearly all of the Koryaks' reindeer herds, resulting in severe suffering and hunger. Many of the former nomads and fishermen, without experience or training, were assigned to the coal mines in the north of the peninsula.

The Soviet authorities suppressed their traditional religion and eliminated the shamans. The officials sent from European Russia banned their languages and the traditions that conflicted with bureaucratic ideas of modern socialism. Alcohol abuse accompanied a sense of loss and the dreariness of Soviet life. By the 1930s alcohol had become a sort of money, traded and used for barter. Official attempts to curtail the sale of alcohol to the native peoples met with fierce resistance. Soviet priority in the region stressed production, not the well-being of the indigenous population. The Communist ideology devastated the Koryak social structures while Communist development plans devastated the Koryak's fragile homeland.

The liberalization of the late 1980s, begun under the presidency of Mikhail Gorbychev, gradually seeped into the region from the west. The ideas of renewal and openness began a period of Koryak reawakening. In 1990 the Koryaks joined with other small northern nations to form the Association of Northern Minorities, a coalition of nationalist and cultural groups dedicated to reclaiming the northern peoples' lands, cultures, and languages.

In February 1993 the Koryak leaders put forward a plan for an autonomous Koryak republic within the Russian Federation and unilaterally withdrew Koryakia from the authority of the provincial government of Kamchatka Oblast. The proposed republic would extend to the Kovran region of Kamchatka populated by the small, related Itel'men people.

The breakdown of the Soviet command economy has brought the state-subsidized industries and mining to a halt. Thousands of the Russians settled in the region since the 1950s have begun to leave. The end of the Soviet system is forcing the Koryaks and Itel'mens to rediscover their past. In order to survive, they are returning to the tundra and to their traditional way of life.

The small Koryak-Itel'men nationalist movement has gained support since the collapse of the Soviet Union in 1991 and has drawn support from the other small national groups and many of the Slavs, the descendants of tsarist and Soviet exiles. The national movement has denounced corruption and abuses by officials, and has given voice to the Koryaks and the related peoples to express their shared sense of outrage at the abuses they suffered under Communist rule. The national claims put forward by the nationalist movement are based on the sovereignty of the ancient tribes, sovereignty they claim was never surrendered to the Soviet Union or Russia.

*SELECTED BIBLIOGRAPHY:*

Lied, Jonas. *Siberian Arctic.* 1960.

Segal, Gerald. *The Soviet Union and the Pacific.* 1990.

Stephen, John J. *The Russian Far East.* 1994.

Wilson, Andrew, and Nina Bachkatov. *Russia Revised: An Alphabetical Key to the Soviet Collapse and the New Republics.* 1993.

# KOSOVO

Kosova

*CAPITAL: Pristina*

SOUTH-CENTRAL EUROPE

KOSOVO

*POPULATION:* (95e) 2,263,000 : 2,375,000 Kosovar Albanians in Yugoslavia. MAJOR NATIONAL GROUPS: (95e) Kosovar (Albanian) 90%, Serb 7%, Muslim 2%, Montenegrin 1%. MAJOR LANGUAGES: Albanian (Gheg), Serbian. MAJOR RELIGIONS: (95e) Sunni Muslim 72%, Serbian Orthodox, Roman Catholic. MAJOR CITIES: (95e) Pristina 128,000 (210,000), Prizren 59,000 (75,000), Kosovska Mitrovica 55,000 (78,000), Peć 54,000, Gnjilane 36,000.

*GEOGRAPHY:* AREA: 4,203 sq.mi.-10,888 sq.km. LOCATION: Kosovo occupies a mountainous, upland region in southwestern Yugoslavia. Kosovo borders Albania and Montenegro* on the west, the Sanjak* region of Serbia on the northwest, Serbia on the north and east, and Macedonia on the south. POLITICAL STATUS: Officially, Kosovo forms an autonomous province of the Yugoslav Republic of Serbia, but since 1989 the province has been occupied by the Yugoslav military and ruled directly by the Serbian government.

*INDEPENDENCE DECLARED:* 11 October 1991.

*FLAG:* The Kosovar national flag, the flag of the national movement, is a red field charged with the Albanian symbol, the Eagle of Scanderbeg, on the fly and bears a large red, five-pointed star, outlined in yellow, on the hoist that represents the Kosovar Albanians.

*PEOPLE:* The Kosovars are ethnic Albanians, their culture and language, a Gheg dialect of Albanian, influenced by centuries of contact with neighboring Slav peoples. The Kosovars are mostly peasant farmers, although a very high birthrate, possibly Europe's highest, has accelerated recent urbanization. The majority of the Kosovars are Sunni Muslim, with Orthodox and Roman Catholic minorities. The Serbs, the only large minority in Kosovo, are concentrated in the urban areas.

*THE NATION:* Ancient Illyrians, the ancestors of the Albanian peoples, populated the Balkan Peninsula as early as the second century B.C. Latinized under Roman rule, the province of Illyricum became known for its wealth and culture. Destroyed by invasions of Germanic Visigoths in A.D. 376 and 395, Illyria later came under the rule of the Byzantines of the Eastern Roman Empire and had a mixed population of Illyrians and Greeks when the first migrating Slav groups arrived in the region in the sixth century. The swell of Slav migration eventually pushed the Illyrian inhabitants into the mountainous southwest.

A Slavic state, the medieval Serbian Empire, emerged in the twelfth century and gradually extended its rule over much of the peninsula. In the fourteenth century the Serbs rallied the Christian peoples of the region to face the advancing Ottoman Turks. On 20 June 1389 a force of Serbs, Albanians, and Bosnians met the Turkish army on the elevated plain called Kosovo. The Christian defeat began five centuries of Muslim Turkish rule.

Conversion to Islam placed the Albanians in a more favored position in the empire and sparked an enmity with the Orthodox Serbs that continues to the present. The Albanians, landlords and administrators, held large estates worked by mainly Christian serfs. The sporadic Serb uprisings generally focused on the Albanian landlords and merchant class rather than their Turkish overlords.

The Turks granted Serbia considerable autonomy in 1829 but retained Kosovo under direct Turkish rule despite Serb claims to the region. In 1867 the Serbs secured the withdrawal of all Turkish troops from Serbia proper and in 1878 won full independence from the weakened Ottomans. At the conclusion of the first Balkan war in 1913, Serbia annexed Kosovo from defeated Turkey. The major European powers blocked Serb efforts to annex Albania, which became an independent state.

Serbia's historic claim to Kosovo, vehemently rejected by the Albanian majority, the Kosovars, is based on the Serbian assertion that Kosovo formed the heartland of medieval Serbia and that the Kosovars arrived in the region in the seventeenth and eighteenth centuries as lackeys of the Turks. The Kosovars claim descent from the ancient Illyrians and believe that their claim, as the original inhabitants, predates the Serbian claim.

In the aftermath of World War I, a united South Slav state, later called Yugoslavia, became a kingdom under Serbian political domination. The government, to dilute Kosovo's Albanian majority, settled thousands of ethnic Slavs, mostly Serbs, in the region between 1918 and 1940. Occupied by Italian troops during World War II, the Italians separated it from Serbia and added it to Italian Albania. Freed from Slav rule, many Kosovars joined attacks on the region's Serb settlers setting off violence and massacres that eventually claimed 50,000 lives, including the Kosovars, who died resisting Kosovo's reincorporation into Yugoslavia by the Communists in 1945–46.

Tito's postwar Yugoslav government added Kosovo to Serbia as an autonomous province, thus denying the Kosovars the cultural and linguistic rights granted Yugoslavia's other national groups. Neglected by the Serbian administration, the region stagnated. By 1960 the Kosovars had the highest birthrate but the lowest level of development in Yugoslavia.

Kosovo's burgeoning population, high unemployment, and abject poverty fueled a growing unrest and resistance to Serbian domination. In 1968 violent riots swept the province. The continuing disturbances provoked serious ethnic clashes. To defuse the rising tensions, Tito granted the province an autonomy statute broadly comparable to that of the Yugoslav republics in 1974. The formation of an autonomous Kosovar government prompted many ethnic Serbs to abandon the province. Charging ethnic harassment, some 65,000 had left by late 1975.

Kosovar nationalists, demanding full republic status, sent petitions to the federal government and led mass demonstrations. Riots, especially severe in 1976 and 1981, ended only after the Yugoslav military intervened in April 1981.

Renewed tensions, part of the increasing instability of the Yugoslav federation, provoked a Serbian nationalist backlash in March 1989. The Serb government dissolved the Kosovar legislature and passed constitutional changes that effectively ended the autonomy granted the province in 1974. Thousands of Kosovars lost their positions in local government, schools, and universities. A peaceful campaign for Kosovar rights began in late 1989.

The disintegration of Yugoslavia in June 1991 spurred Kosovar nationalist efforts to break Serbia's military hold on the province. In September 1991 a clandestine referendum on independence resulted in a 90% vote in favor. On 11 October 1991 the Kosovar leaders declared Kosovo independent of Yugoslavia. Only neighboring Albania has recognized the independence declaration.

Kosovo's national leaders, fearing an extension of Serbian ''ethnic cleansing'' to Kosovo, frantically attempt to put the issue on the international agenda. In September 1994 the Yugoslav government refused to discuss a Kosovar demand that a neutral third party be brought in to mediate the growing conflict. Many Kosovars, with the liberalization in Albania, have begun to contemplate some ties between Kosovo and Albania, effectively splitting the Kosovar national movement between pro-Albanian and pro-independence factions.

*SELECTED BIBLIOGRAPHY:*

Colletts Staff. *Relationship between Yugoslavia and Albania.* 1984.

Dragnich, Alexander N., and Slavko Todorovich. *The Saga of Kosovo: Focus on Serbian-Albanian Relationships.* 1985.

Juka, S. S. *Kosova: The Albanians in Yugoslavia in Light of Historical Documents.* 1984.

Kaplan, Robert D. *Balkan Ghosts.* 1993.

# KUBAN

**Krasnodar**

*CAPITAL: Ekaterinodar (Krasnodar)*

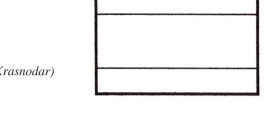

SOUTHEASTERN EUROPE

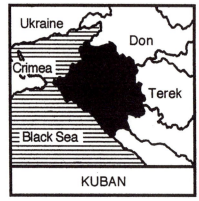

KUBAN

*POPULATION:* (95e) 5,367,000 : 1,730,000 Kuban Cossacks in Russia. MAJOR NATIONAL GROUPS: (95e) Russian 35%, Kuban Cossack 32%, Ukrainian 21%, Adygey 2.5%, Armenian, Greek. MAJOR LANGUAGES: Russian, Cossack, Ukrainian, Adygey (Circassian). MAJOR RELIGIONS: Russian Orthodox, Sunni Muslim. MAJOR CITIES: (95e) Ekaterinodar (Krasnodar) 637,000 (752,000), Sochi 340,000 (422,000), Novorossiysk 201,000 (228,000), Armavir 180,000, Maikop 165,000, Yeysk 81,000, Kropotkin 76,000 (103,000).

*GEOGRAPHY:* AREA: 32,278 sq.mi.-83,622 sq.km. LOCATION: Kuban occupies the Kuban Steppe and the valley of the Kuban River on the eastern shore of the Black Sea in southern European Russia just north of the Caucasus Mountains. Kuban borders the other so-called Cossack Provinces, Don* and Terek,* on the north and east. POLITICAL STATUS: Kuban has no official status; the region forms the Krasnodar Kray (territory), including the Adyge Republic, claimed by Circassian nationalists as part of Circassia, in the Russian Federation.

*INDEPENDENCE DECLARED:* 16 February 1918.

*FLAG:* The Kuban Cossack national flag, the flag of the former republic, is a tricolor of blue, raspberry red, and green, the red twice the width of the other stripes.

*PEOPLE:* The Kuban Cossacks are a Slavic people of mixed Russian, Ukrainian, and Circassian background traditionally divided into two groups: the Chermomortsy, descendants of Zaporozhye Cossacks and Ukrainian settlers concentrated in the lower reaches of the Kuban River; and Lineitsy (First Liners), descendants of Don Cossacks and Russian colonists in the middle and upper reaches of the Kuban basin. The Kuban Cossacks speak a Cossack dialect of mixed Russian and Ukrainian admixtures, although the dialect spoken in the upper Kuban basin has considerably less Ukrainian influence. The Cossack claims to separate national status are based on their history, way of life, and their culture and language.

*THE NATION:* An ancient region overrun by migrating Slavs around A.D. 880, the fertile steppe formed the southern limit of Slav settlement. Fierce Caucasian peoples blocked further Slav extension to the south. Nominally a part of the first great Slav state, Kievan Rus, the Kuban fell to the invading Golden Horde in 1241 and later formed part of the Tatar successor state, the Khanate of Crimea.*

Russians began to penetrate the area in 1774 and ultimately annexed the territory to the expanding Russian Empire in 1783. Zaporozhye Cossacks, defeated in an uprising in Ukraine in 1775, accepted tsarist inducements to return from exile in Turkish territory to settle the newly annexed lands between 1787 and 1792. Called Chermomortsy, the Black Sea People, they governed themselves in exchange for a vow of loyalty to the tsar and military service as the guardians of Russia's new southern frontier. Don Cossacks, from the Don River basin to the north, settled the interior of the territory in the 1830s and became known as Lineitsy, the First Liners. Collectively rechristened the Kuban Cossacks in 1860, the Kuban Horde formed the largest Cossack community in southern Russia.

Muslim Circassian peoples in the south, finally defeated in 1864, mostly fled or were expelled to Turkish territory. Their confiscated lands became Cossack lands, held in common by the villages and clans. Thousands of freed Russian and Ukrainian serfs migrated south following the abolition of serfdom in 1861. The Kuban Cossack communes absorbed many of the former serfs, while others settled on the Cossacks' communal lands as tenant farmers.

Personally loyal to the tsar, not to the Russian state, the Kuban Cossacks formed elite military units when war began in 1914. Sent to the front, the units suffered heavy casualties that fueled growing unrest. Their oath of loyalty invalidated by the overthrow of the tsar in February 1917, the Kuban Cossacks deserted the front in large numbers to return to their homeland to protect it from a threatened Turkish advance from the south.

Cossack leaders convened a parliament, the Rada, in March 1917, creating a Kuban military government to replace the local tsarist administration. On 17 July 1917 the Rada declared the Kuban a sovereign state within the new democratic Russia.

The Bolshevik coup in October 1917, followed by edicts confiscating all Cossack communal lands, fueled the rapid spread of Kuban nationalism. The Rada, dominated by the Chermomortsy, declared Kuban independent of Russia on 16 February 1918. The separatists faced strong resistance from many of the Lineitsy, committed to Russian unity, and the Ingorodnie, the Slavic tenant farmers won over by Bolshevik promises to redistribute the Cossack communal lands.

The new republic allied with the anti-Bolshevik White forces, but rifts soon developed over the Kuban Cossacks' insistence on a separate army and the Whites' vehement opposition to any division of Holy Russia. The base for General Deniken's Volunteer Army, the major White military force, the tensions between the Whites and Kuban separatists mounted. In the fall of 1919 Deniken arrested the Kuban's leaders and executed eleven before moving his headquarters out of the state he claimed was dominated by nationalists.

The White defeat in 1920 was followed by the rapid occupation of the Kuban by the Red Army and the formation of a Kuban-Black Sea Soviet Republic. Many of the Cossacks fled abroad or joined guerrilla bands that the Reds finally eradicated in 1924. The Soviet authorities revoked all traditional Cossack privileges, including military training. The authorities reclassified the Kuban Cossacks as ethnic Russians and banned their separate culture, dialect, and history.

The Nazi Germans, advancing on the Maikop oil fields in late 1942, decreed that the Cossacks descended from Germanic Ostrogoths, not subhuman Slavs, and therefore constituted acceptable allies. Thousands joined the German's anti-Communist crusade. At the end of the war some 40,000 Cossacks, with their families, surrendered to the Allies. However, at Stalin's insistence, the Allies forcibly repatriated the Cossacks to face Stalin's punishment.

A cultural revival in the 1960s began with the publication of the first Cossack dictionary and works on Kuban Cossack history and culture that exile groups smuggled into the Soviet Union. The revival raised demands for recognition as a separate ethnic and cultural group. The resurgence of their culture and traditions incited a parallel nationalist revival and Kuban Cossack nationalism emerged as a potent force following the liberalization of Soviet society in the late 1980s.

Kuban Cossack nationalists, with the support of the Ukrainian minority, are gaining support for demands that Kuban be granted republican status within the Russian Federation. More radical nationalists claim that their separate history and culture are the basis of a viable national state, while even more nationalistic groups advocate the creation of a greater Cossackia of some twenty million inhabitants to incorporate the traditionally Cossack lands between Kazakhstan, Ukraine, and the Caucasus Mountains. The growing divisions within the Kuban national movement have not blunted the power of the nationalism that emerged after seven decades of suppression.

*SELECTED BIBLIOGRAPHY:*
Cresson, William P. *The Cossacks: Their History and Country.* 1919.
Glaskow, Wasili G. *History of the Cossacks.* 1968.
McNeal, Robert H. *Tsar and Cossack: 1855–1914.* 1987.

# KURDISTAN

### Kurestan; Kordestan

*CAPITAL: Arbil (Irbil) is the capital of
the Kurdish autonomous area in
northern Iraq.*

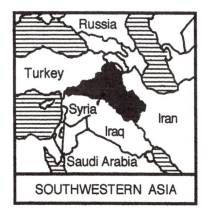

SOUTHWESTERN ASIA

KURDISTAN

*POPULATION:* (95e) 35,000,000 : 25,000,000 Kurds in Turkey, Iran, Iraq, Syria, and adjoining areas of Armenia and Azerbaidzhan. MAJOR NATIONAL GROUPS: (95e) Kurd 70%, Arab, Turk, Iranian, Azeri, Assyrian, Turkmen, Armenian. MAJOR LANGUAGES: Kurdish, Turkish, Arabic, Farsi (Iranian). MAJOR RELIGIONS: Sunni Muslim, Shia Muslim, Christian. MAJOR CITIES: (95e) TURKEY: Diyarbarkir 1,225,000, Gaziantep 671,000, Erzurum 337,000, Malaytya 311,000, Urfa 262,000, Elazig 229,000, Batman 145,000, Van 138,000, Erzincan 104,000, Adiyaman 102,000, Kars 100,000. IRAN: Bakhtaran 895,000, Rezaiyeh 407,000, Sanandaj 281,000, Saggez 157,000, Ilam 155,000, Khvoy 153,000, Mahabad 126,000, Eslamabad e-Gharb 125,000, Miandouab 100,000. IRAQ: Mosul 750,000, Karkuk (Kirkuk) 440,000, Arbil (Irbil) 420,000, Sulaimaniya 355,000, Dohuk 310,000, Qala Duz 160,000, Tall Afar 100,000, Kanaqin 100,000. SYRIA: Qamishliye 150,000, Haseke 110,000.

*GEOGRAPHY:* AREA: 224,540 sq.mi.-581,710 sq.km. LOCATION: Kurdistan occupies a mostly mountainous region of disputed extent in southeastern Turkey, northern Iraq, northwestern Iran, and northeastern Syria. POLITICAL STATUS: Kurdistan, with the exception of a small area in northern Iraq, has no official status; the region forms a number of administrative units of Turkey, Iran, Iraq, and Syria.

*INDEPENDENCE DECLARED:* 22 January 1946.

*FLAG:* The Kurdish national flag, recognized in all Kurdish areas, is a horizontal tricolor of green, white, and red bearing a centered, multirayed yellow sun. OTHER FLAG(S): The flag of the Kurds in Turkey is a red field with a centered yellow disc, outlined in green, bearing a five-pointed red star.

*PEOPLE:* The Kurds are a tribal, mountain people who trace their ancestry back to the Gutu of the ancient Assyrian Empire, the ancient Medes, and later admixtures of the region's many conquerors. Often fair and light-eyed, the Kurds exhibit a variety of physical types and regional variations. The fourth largest ethnic group in the Middle East, the Kurds make up the world's most numerous ethnic group that, with the exception of northern Iraq, has no legal form of self-government. The Kurds' division into numerous tribes, subtribes, and clans makes Kurdish unity difficult to achieve. The Kurdish language, a West Iranian dialect of the Indo-Iranian language group, is spoken in four major dialects, which are not always mutually intelligible; Manji and Zaza in Turkey, Gorani in Iran, and Sorani in Iraq and Syria. The Kurdish majority is Sunni Muslim, with Christian and Shia Muslim minorities.

*THE NATION:* The Kurds trace their history back more than 4,000 years to a people called the Gutu, who predate the ancient Indo-Aryan Medes. The Kurds claim that they have been fighting for independence since their ancestors rebelled and captured ancient Ninevah in 612 B.C. The event is now celebrated as the Kurdish new year, Nev Roz or Nevruz, on 21 March of each year, the most important holiday of the Kurdish year.

Ancient Kurdistan, most often under Persian rule during its early history, fell to invading Muslim Arabs in the seventh century. The Arab conquerors settled in the lowlands and pushed the native Kurds into the northern mountain regions. Converted to Islam, the region formed an important part of the Muslim Empire, the Caliphate. In the eleventh century Seljuk Turks overran most of Kurdistan, ending Arab domination. Briefly independent, Kurdistan produced one of Islam's greatest heroes, Saladin, called Salah ad-Din by the Arabs, who led the twelfth-century Muslim resistance to the Christian crusades.

The rival empires of the Ottoman Turks and the Persians contended for power in Kurdistan, most of which came under Ottoman rule following the decisive Persian defeat in 1514. The Ottoman victory marked the first formal partition of the Kurdish lands. The Kurds of the Ottoman Empire, ruled as a separate principality from the fifteenth century to the eighteenth century, enjoyed considerable autonomy as the guardians of the empire's eastern frontier.

The government of the decaying Ottoman empire centralized its administration in the nineteenth century and ended all minority self-rule. Resistance to direct Turkish rule sparked serious Kurdish revolts in 1826, 1834, 1853–55, and 1880. The sporadic revolts consolidated a national revival in the late nineteenth century, a period marked by Kurdish participation in horrible massacres of the empire's Christian minorities in Armenia and Assyria.*

The beginning of war in 1914 finally brought allies for the Kurds' continuing fight against the Turks. Promised independence, most of the tribes aided the Allies' war effort which ultimately defeated the Ottoman Empire in 1918. Encouraged by the Turkish defeat and U.S. president Wilson's call for the independence of the non-Turkish peoples of the empire, the Kurds sent a delegation to the 1919 Paris Peace Conference. The Allies incorporated a provision for an independent Kurdistan in the 1920 Treaty of Sèvres, a treaty that resurgent, nationalist Turkey refused to sign. A second treaty, the Treaty of Lausanne, signed by Turkey and the Allies in 1923, omitted the Kurds. Turkey, Iran, and the French and British administrations of Syria and Iraq partitioned Kurdistan over the opposition and pleas of the Kurdish inhabitants.

Betrayed by the Allies, the Kurds began to mobilize. Rioting erupted across Kurdistan, followed by rebellion in northern Iraq in 1922. The rebellion spread across the new international borders, provoking a harsh repression by the various governments and military incursions by the British military. Sporadic revolts continued in the 1920s and 1930s, but tribal divisions hampered unity and facilitated the ability of the different governments to deal with regional uprisings.

Soviet troops, soon after World War II began, occupied the northern provinces of neutral Iran to ensure their southern supply route. Encouraged by the Soviets, the Iranian Kurds declared their independence at Mahabad on 22 January 1946. Granted generous oil concessions by the Iranian government, the Soviets eventually withdrew, leaving their nationalist Kurd allies to face an Iranian invasion and years of brutal reprisals.

The pawn of regional politics, the Kurds' desire for a united, sovereign Kurdistan has motivated generations of Kurds but has brought them only horrible suffering, deportations, and massacres. Until 1991 the largest of the Kurdish populations, in Turkey, called Mountain Turks, were forbidden to use their language, and their very existence was officially denied.

In the wake of the Gulf War of 1991, the Kurds of northern Iraq created the first autonomous Kurdish state in modern history. Protected by foreign military units, the Kurds have created a government and held free elections. In February 1993 representatives of Turkey, Iran, and Syria met to discuss the threat posed by the increasingly independent Kurdish entity in northern Iraq and its powerful effect on their own Kurdish populations.

The Kurds claim that they have survived where other nations have disappeared into history. The Kurdish leaders, in spite of differing ideologies, tribal divisions, and a lack of support or aid, all agree on one goal, the self-determination of the Kurdish nation.

*SELECTED BIBLIOGRAPHY:*

Bunter, Michael M. *The Kurds in Turkey: A Political Dilemma.* 1990.

Kutschen, Chris. *The Kurdish National Movement.* 1988.

Laizer, Sheri. *Into Kurdistan: Frontiers under Fire.* 1990.

Olson, Robert. *The Emergence of Kurdish Nationalism and the Sheikh Said Rebellion 1880–1925.* 1989.

# KWAZULU-NATAL

**Natal**

*CAPITAL: Thekwini (Durban)*

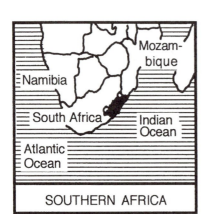

SOUTHERN AFRICA

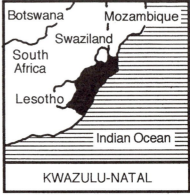

KWAZULU-NATAL

*POPULATION:* (95e) 8,784,000 : 8,225,000 Zulus in South Africa. MAJOR NATIONAL GROUPS: (95e) Zulu 71%, Indian 9%, white 8%, Xhosa 7%, colored 2%, Swazi 1%, other South African. MAJOR LANGUAGES: siZulu, English, siXhosa, Afrikaans. MAJOR RELIGIONS: Christian, animist, Hindu, Sunni Muslim. MAJOR CITIES: (95e) Thekwini (Durban) 638,000 (1,852,000), Umlazi 245,000, Mpulalanga (Hammersdale) 211,000, KwaMashu 188,000, Madadeni (Newcastle) 170,000, Hlaweni (Pietermaritzburg) 126,000 (276,000), Inanda 85,000, Empangeni (Richard's Bay) 62,000, Talana (Dundee) 37,000 (82,000), Ladysmith 34,000, Tendeka (Vryheid) 28,000, Ulundi 24,000, Eshowe 16,000.

*GEOGRAPHY:* AREA: 33,578 sq.mi.-86,989 sq.km. LOCATION: KwaZulu-Natal lies in eastern South Africa, a region of upland plains between the Drakensburg Mountains and the Indian Ocean. POLITICAL STATUS: KwaZulu-Natal forms a province of the Republic of South Africa.

*FLAG:* The Zulu national flag, the flag of the largest political organization, the Inkatha Freedom Party (IFP), has equal horizontal stripes of red, white, black, green, yellow, white, and red. OTHER FLAG(S): The flag of KwaZulu, the official flag of the homeland until April 1994, is a white field with three narrow, horizontal stripes of yellow, green, and black centered and bears a broad, vertical red stripe at the hoist charged with a Zulu shield.

*PEOPLE:* The Zulus, South Africa's largest national group, encompass over one hundred separate tribes united by culture, history, language, and loyalty to the paramount chief, the Zulu king. The Zulus speak dialects of an Nguni language of the Bantu language group, along with English, the major European language spoken in the province. The majority of the Zulu are Christians, with both the Roman Catholic Church and a variety of Protestant sects represented. Other large population groups in the province include Indians, both Hindu and Muslim, the whites, the majority English-speaking, a group of mixed race called colored, and a Xhosa minority in the south and Swazis in the north.

*THE NATION:* Migrating tribal groups, believed to originate in the Great Lakes region of Central Africa, entered the region from the north in successive waves to populate the plains east of the Drakensburg Mountains. Spreading across the region, the tribes established numerous small chiefdomships based on clan and family ties. One of the tribes, the Ama-Zulu, began to gain local power in 1799. The tribes, later called Zulu, expanded by incorporating or scattering neighboring tribes.

King Dingiswayo in 1807 initiated the unique Zulu military system of disciplined regiments called *impis*. In 1818 civil war erupted between rival Zulu factions. Chaka (Shaka), a protégé of Dingiswayo, eventually emerged as the victor. Chaka refined the Zulu military system, making the *impis* the nucleus of a formidable army. The Zulu *impis* attacked one tribe after another, either destroying or absorbing the conquered tribes into the expanding Zulu nation. Many tribes fled, pushing others before them, during the so-called Time of Troubles. Chaka, considered one of history's greatest military leaders, ruled a vast empire by 1826, but two years later he died, murdered by his brother, Dingaan.

Portuguese navigator Vasco da Gama sighted the coast on Christmas 1497, naming the land Terra Natalis. The first European settlers to arrive in the region, the English, shortened the name to Natal in 1824. Afrikaner Dutch emigrants moving north to escape British rule in the Cape of Good Hope pushed into the interior in 1836. The migrants met with fierce Zulu resistance to their passage. In 1838 the Zulus suffered a decisive defeat at the Battle of Blood River. The victorious Afrikaners created a new republic, Natalia, in the districts conquered from the Zulus. Conflicts between the Boers (Afrikaners) and the British in the region ended with the British annexation of Natalia in 1843 and the creation of a united Natal in the southern districts as a separate British colony in 1856.

A Zulu prince, Cetewayo, succeeded his father to the Zulu throne in 1872 and immediately initiated a program to rebuild Zulu military power. A border incident in 1878 provoked war with the British. On 12 January 1879 a large British column crossed into Zululand and on 27 January suffered the most devastating defeat of a colonial force in British military history, the Battle of Isandhlwana. British reinforcements, rushed to Zululand, defeated the *impis* at Ulundi on 4 July, the defeat effectively ending Zulu military power.

The British military occupation of Zululand set off a rebellion in 1882. The rebellion fizzled as civil war over the succession to the throne threatened as Cetewayo neared death. Cetewayo's demise in February 1882 left the British in effective control of Zululand, which the authorities proclaimed a protectorate in 1887. Following renewed rebellion in the protectorate in 1897, the British annexed Zululand to Natal. The Zulus rebelled one last time, the Bambata Rebellion, in 1906. Their traditional economy completely disrupted, desperation forced thousands of Zulus to seek work in the mines and factories of white South Africa in the 1920s and 1930s.

South Africa's apartheid system, the separation of the races, included the creation of self-governing homelands for the country's various tribes. A Zulu homeland, KwaZulu, its territory fragmented among parcels of land separated by 13,000 white farms, created in 1970, received self-government in 1977. Zulu resistance to apartheid coalesced around the Zulu royal family and Chief Mangosuthu Buthelezi, the KwaZulu head of government and the leader of the Zulu Inkatha national movement, later renamed the Inkatha Freedom Party (IFP).

Zulu relations with South Africa's largest antiapartheid group, the African National Congress (ANC), deteriorated after 1980 over ideological differences and growing ethnic violence between Zulus and Xhosas, the dominant tribe in the ANC. In 1982 Chief Buthelezi set up the Buthelezi Commission in an effort to regulate Natal's ethnic relations. After eight months of talks among Zulu, white, and Indian leaders, the conference reached a consensus on integrating KwaZulu and Natal in a self-governing multiethnic state. In spite of broad support for the proposal in Natal and KwaZulu and internationally, the South African government rejected the idea of multiethnic power sharing in November 1986.

Zulu nationalism grew rapidly as South Africa moved toward black majority rule. In January 1992 Chief Buthelezi raised the question of the secession of KwaZulu-Natal amid an expanding war that pitted his Inkatha Freedom Party against the followers of the ANC.

The end of South Africa's apartheid system and the emergence of a new multiethnic government mostly ended the severe ideological and ethnic violence that left thousands of Zulus and Xhosas dead, but not the Zulu demands for self-determination. In January 1994 the Zulu leaders demanded guarantees for the KwaZulu-Natal and the monarchy before agreeing to the province's participation in South African elections, and in February thousands demonstrated in Durban in support of Zulu independence. In March 1994 King Goodwill Zwelithini declared KwaZulu-Natal a sovereign state, and in April the homeland of KwaZulu was officially dissolved and merged into the new province of KwaZulu-Natal.

*SELECTED BIBLIOGRAPHY:*

Clammer, David. *Zulu War.* 1989.
Keppel-Jones, Arthur. *South Africa: A Short History.* 1962.
Morris, Donald R. *The Washing of the Spears: The Rise and Fall of Zulu Nationalism.*
    1986.
Reardon, M. *Zululand.* 1989.

# LADAKH

Ladak

*CAPITAL: Leh*

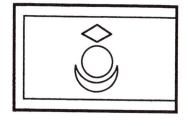

SOUTH-CENTRAL ASIA

LADAKH

*POPULATION:* (95e) 660,000 : 525,000 Ladakhis (including Baltis) in India and Pakistan. MAJOR NATIONAL GROUPS: (95e) Ladakhi (including Balti) 77%, Kashmiri 12%, other Indian, other Pakistani. MAJOR LANGUAGES: Balti, Ladakhi, Kashmiri. MAJOR RELIGIONS: (95e) Shia Muslim 54%, Buddhist (Tibetan Lamaism) 21%, Sunni Muslim 17%. MAJOR CITIES: (95e) INDIA: Leh 40,000, Kargil 20,000, Zaskar 15,000. PAKISTAN: Skardu 35,000.

*GEOGRAPHY:* AREA: 45,750 sq.mi.-118,524 sq.km. LOCATION: Ladakh occupies an extremely mountainous region at the confluence of the Indian, Pakistani, and Chinese borders in the Zaskar and Deosai Mountains and the Ladakh Range of the eastern Himalayas. POLITICAL STATUS: Ladakh forms the districts of Leh, Zaskar, and Kargil of the state of Jammu and Kashmir* in India, the Ladakh District of the Northern Areas of Pakistani Kashmir, and the Aksai Chin region, under Chinese control.

*FLAG:* The Ladakhi national flag, the flag of the national movement, is a green field bordered by narrow yellow stripes at the top, bottom, and hoist, bearing a centered white disc above a white crescent moon and surmounted by a white diamond representing a traditional Buddhist stupa.

*PEOPLE:* The Ladakhis are a people of Tibetan origin encompassing two major divisions: the Ladakhi, speaking a Tibetan dialect in the east, and the Balti or Balts, speaking a related dialect with more Indo-European admixture in the Kargil District of Indian Ladakh and the Baltistan region of Pakistani Ladakh. The Ladakhis are primarily Buddhists, practicing the Tibetan form, Vajrayana Lamaism. The Balts are mostly Shia Muslims with a Buddhist and Sunni Muslim minority. The region, often called Little Tibet, has a basically Tibetan culture with an admixture of Muslim customs and traditions in Baltistan.

*THE NATION:* The Ladakhis trace their history to Nya tri Tsampo, who ruled Ladakh in the third century B.C. Traditionally populated by migrants from western Tibet* in prehistoric times, Ladakh was often considered an outer province of Tibet. In 1531 the weakened Ladakhi kingdom lost its western districts to invading Kashmiris. The Ladakhis of the conquered area, called Balti or Balts by the Muslims, under Kashmiri rule mostly adopted the Islamic religion. A descendant of the Tibetan kings, Chovang Namgyal, conquered eastern Ladakh in 1533 and established the Namgyal dynasty in the kingdom.

In the seventeenth century a resurgent Ladakh defeated the Kashmiris and recovered the western region, Baltistan, but came under renewed pressure from Tibet. In 1644 the Ladakhi king appealed for assistance to the Mogul emperor in Delhi. The Moguls, exacting the price of making Ladakh a tributary kingdom, cleared the kingdom of Tibetan invaders in 1650 and defeated a second Tibetan invasion in 1683.

Invading Mongols defeated the Mogul troops in 1685 and overran the kingdom. In desperation the Ladakhis turned to their old enemies, the Kashmiris, for military aid. In the next decades, under a series of weak rulers, the Ladakhi kingdom gradually became a vassal state of Kashmir.

The kingdom, rich from the caravan trade among India, China, Tibet, and Central Asia, gradually threw off Kashmiri rule in the eighteenth century. In 1809, threatened by the expanding Sikhs, Tsepal Namgyal sought an alliance with the British, but his remote kingdom had little to offer the Europeans, and they rebuffed his appeal. The Dogras of Jammu, allies of the Sikhs, invaded Ladakh in 1834. Appeals to the Tibetans and British ignored, the kingdom finally surrendered in 1842. The Dogras deposed the royal family but allowed the Namgyal family to retain Stok Palace, where they remain to the present. As part of the Dogra state of Kashmir, the former kingdom eventually came under British rule in the nineteenth century.

An agreement between Great Britain and China in 1918 delimited Ladakh's formerly indefinite boundaries and for the first time established a firm frontier between Ladakh and Tibet. Despite the official boundaries, the Ladakhis and Tibetans continued to move freely back and forth, and the caravans continued to connect the high mountain valleys on both sides of the new border. Cut off by high mountain passes, closed from November through June, the Ladakhis retained their traditional culture, and the Buddhists, Shia, and Sunni Muslims continued living in harmony as they had for centuries.

The Ladakhis, after World War II, communicated their unwillingness to become part of either Hindu-dominated India or Muslim Pakistan to the British in 1946. Their wishes ignored, Ladakh remained part of the disputed state of Jammu and Kashmir when India and Pakistan gained independence in 1947. The first Indo-Pakistani war, ended by a United Nations cease-fire in January

1949, marked the first partition of Ladakh. India retained Ladakh, but the western districts, including Muslim Baltistan, came under Pakistani control.

China, following its conquest of Tibet in 1959, laid claim to all of Ladakh as a historic appendage of Tibet. In 1962 Chinese troops invaded Indian Ladakh from Tibet. The invasion formed part of an advance all along the frontier that provoked war with India. The Indian government rushed troops to the formerly ignored district. A cease-fire in the region left China in control of the strategically important, but mostly uninhabited, high desert area, the Aksai Chin. The Chinese takeover of Aksai Chin marked the second partition of Ladakh.

An Indian military force of over 40,000 remains in Ladakh to guard the sensitive Pakistani and Chinese frontiers. The military, often seen by Ladakhis as an occupation army, supported the Indian government's decision to introduce the Kashmiri and Punjabi languages to the region's schools. The Ladakhis have resisted assimilation and continue to look to their former royal family for guidance. In 1974 the Ladakhi king died and was succeeded by Queen Diskit Wangmo, who assumed the role of Ladakh's political leader.

In the late 1980s, influenced by the Chinese repression in Tibet and the dramatic rise of Kashmiri nationalism, the Ladakhis began to organize in both India and Pakistan. The Ladakhis and Balts, having lived in harmony for over a thousand years, began to demand reunification. The violence that broke out in Kashmir in 1988 accelerated the growth of Ladakhi nationalism, which focused, in India, on separation from Kashmir and the creation of a Ladakhi territory within India. In Pakistan the religious issue fueled Ladakhi nationalism as tensions increased between the mostly Sunni Muslims in the Northern Areas and Pakistani Kashmir and the Shia Muslim Balts. In August 1989 severe ethnic violence between Ladakhis and Kashmiris erupted in Indian Ladakh.

The Ladakhi national movement, in the wake of the Cold War, has evolved a separatist faction that claims the partition of Ladakh was the result of big power politics and has pressed for reunification as a first step to restoring Ladakh's sovereignty. In 1994 the non-Ladakhi Muslims of the western districts of the Northern Areas began a campaign to join Pakistan, a move that has galvanized Ladakhi national groups in the eastern Ladakh District. The ideal behind Ladakhi separatism is the creation of a neutral multiethnic, multireligious Ladakh, a zone of peace in one of the world's least peaceful regions.

*SELECTED BIBLIOGRAPHY:*
Barth, A. *Religions of India.* 1990.
Chandra, Bipan. *Communalism in Modern India.* 1984.
Naudou, Jean. *Buddhists of Kashmir.* 1980.
Rizvi, Janet. *Ladakh, Crossroads of High Asia.* 1990.

# LADINIA

**Patrje Ladine**

*CAPITAL: Cortina di Cadore (Cortina d'Ampezzo)*

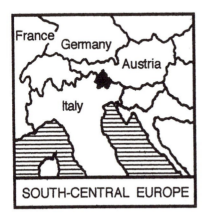

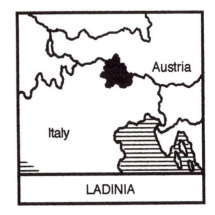

*POPULATION:* (95e) 56,000 : 31,000 Ladins in Italy. MAJOR NATIONAL GROUPS: (95e) Ladin 55%, Tryolean 35%, other Italian 10%. MAJOR LANGUAGES: Italian, Ladin, German. MAJOR RELIGIONS: Roman Catholic, Protestant. MAJOR CITIES: (95e) Cortina di Cadore (Cortina d'Ampezzo) 8,000 (14,000), Ortisei (San Ulricio) 3,000.

*GEOGRAPHY:* AREA: 920 sq.mi.-2,382 sq.km. LOCATION: Ladinia lies in the Dolomite Alps in northern Italy, occupying high alpine valleys between the Piave and Isarco Rivers just south of the Austrian border. POLITICAL STATUS: Ladinia has no official status; the region forms the Cadore district of Belluno Province and the Val Gardena district of Bolzano province of the Republic of Italy.

*FLAG:* The Ladin national flag, the flag of the national movement, is a horizontal tricolor of pale blue, white, and green.

*PEOPLE:* The Ladins are a Rhaeto-Romanic people who traditionally trace their origins to the ancient Celtic tribes Latinized under Roman rule. The Ladins speak a Rhaeto-Romanic language derived from ancient Latin that is spoken in three major dialects: Cadorino in the Cadore district and the valley of the Piave River; Atesino in the Val Gardena region; and Venetian-influenced Zoldino in the southern valleys. The Ladins are mostly Roman Catholics, with a small, but important, Protestant minority.

*THE NATION:* The Retic and Noric tribes, of Celtic origin, resisted Roman incursions for decades following Julius Caesar's military campaigns in the first century B.C. Their mountain homeland effectively divided Italy from Caesar's conquests in Germania and Gaul. Emperor Augustus, between 25 and 15 B.C., directed several military campaigns against the tribes. Finally pacified, the region became part of Roman Raetia, and the Alpine tribes gradually adopted the Romans' Latin culture and speech.

The collapse of Roman power left the region defenseless. Germanic tribes, Vandals and Lombards, invaded the region in the fifth and sixth centuries A.D. The Lombards and smaller tribes settled in the lowlands and spread into the mountains, displacing or absorbing all but a few of the Latinized Rhaetian population. Most of the region formed part of a Lombard county until the eighth century, when the expanding Frankish Empire took control of the Lombard territories. Under Germanic rule the Ladins formed a small minority overlooked in their isolated alpine valleys. In the eleventh century the western Ladin valleys came under the rule of the bishops of Brixen and Trent. In 1420 the Cadore and Zoldo regions in the east came under Venetian rule.

The Hapsburgs extended their influence into the area in the fourteenth century. In 1797 the Austrians took control of Venice, and the eastern Ladin valleys came under Austrian rule. Hapsburg rule was extended to the western Ladin valleys following the secularization of the bishoprics of Brixen and Trent in 1802. For centuries the Ladins lived under the cultural and linguistic domination of the neighboring Tyroleans and Venetians, their alpine culture taking on many borrowed traits and customs. In the multiethnic Hapsburg Empire, the Ladins formed one of many different ethnic groups, and pressure to assimilate eased. In 1866 the Austrians ceded the Veneto* to Italy, again partitioning the small Ladin nation.

The influence of the national awakening throughout the Austro-Hungarian Empire in the late nineteenth century sparked a renewed interest in the Ladins' own history, culture, and language. The cultural revival began to reverse centuries of assimilation, strengthened by the standardization of the language. The early Ladin national movement focused on the reunification of the divided Ladin territories in Italy and Austria.

Italy, promised the South Tyrol and other Austrian territories with substantial Italian-speaking populations by the Allies, entered World War I in 1915. The fighting between the Italians and Austrians swept through the Ladins' alpine valleys and settled down to a war of attrition on the line of defense, the Piave River, in 1917–18.

Tyrolean opposition to the Italian claims fueled a nationalist movement that had some support from the Ladins, even though unification under Italian rule became the theme of Italian propaganda directed at the nationalists. In October 1918 the Tyroleans convened an assembly of all of the region's peoples, which approved a plan for a federation of autonomous cantons based on the Swiss model. On 24 April 1919 the Tyroleans declared independence but were blocked by the Allies, and the Italian state annexed the region. In a conciliatory gesture, the Italian government made Italian, German, and Ladin the official languages of the annexed territory.

Italian guarantees of cultural and linguistic freedom lasted only until the fascists took power in Rome in 1922. The fascist authorities closed all Ladin cultural institutions, schools, and publications and forbade the use of the Ladin language. In 1926 the authorities decreed that all family names and place-names must conform to Italian guidelines.

The Ladins' brief administrative reunification, under German rule, between 1943 and the end of World War II, initiated the growth of modern Ladin nationalism. After the war the Ladins attempted to win Allied support for the creation of an independent state modeled on Liechtenstein and under the protection of the new United Nations. With the Allies occupied with the reconstruction of Europe, their appeals generated little enthusiasm. In the 1950s and 1960s, influenced by the Tyrolean nationalist movement, the Ladins pressed for linguistic, economic, and cultural autonomy in a united Ladin district within Italy.

Ladin nationalism experienced a resurgence in the 1980s as Europe began to unite in a proposed federation of independent states. The European ideal, theoretically able to accommodate an independent Ladinia that is economically integrated with the rest of the union, spurred the growth of nationalism since 1988. The Ladin nationalists claim that their movement is not separatist but works for the equality of their small nation with the other nations of a united Europe.

*SELECTED BIBLIOGRAPHY:*

Del Guerra, Roland, and Genoveva Gomez. *Language, Dialect, Nation, Ethnic Group.* 1986.

Kann, R. A. *Multinational Empire.* 1950.

Levy, Miriam. *Governance and Grievance: Hapsburg Policy and Italian Tyrol in the Eighteenth Century.* 1988.

# LAKOTA

**Lakota Nation; Paha Sapa**

*CAPITAL: Wounded Knee*

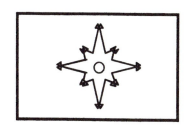

NORTH-CENTRAL U.S.A.

LAKOTA

*POPULATION:* (95e) 292,000 : 210,000 Lakota (Sioux) in the United States. MAJOR NATIONAL GROUPS: (95e) Lakota (Sioux) 35%, other American. MAJOR LANGUAGES: English, Lakota (Sioux). MAJOR RELIGIONS: Protestant, Roman Catholic. MAJOR CITIES: (95e) Rapid City 58,000 (88,000), Sturgis 6,000, Lead 4,000 (12,000), Deadwood 2,000.

*GEOGRAPHY:* AREA: 41,288 sq.mi.-106,963 sq.km. LOCATION: Lakota lies in the north-central United States, a region of flat plains and barren desert, the Badlands, rising to the Black Hills in the southeast. POLITICAL STATUS: Lakota has no official status; the region forms the territory that by treaty, guaranteed in perpetuity, belongs to the Lakota Nation in the state of South Dakota, mostly west of the Missouri River, in the central United States. The territory includes the remnants of the original territory left to the Lakota, the Rosebud, Pine Ridge, Lower Brule, Cheyenne River, Yankton, and Standing Rock Indian Reservations.

*FLAG:* The Lakota flag, the official flag of the Pine Ridge Reservation, is a red field charged with a centered red octagon surrounded by a yellow starlike device of eight points. OTHER FLAG(S): The flag of the Ogalala Sioux is a red field with a narrow blue border, except at the hoist, bearing a centered circle of eight stylized teepees.

*PEOPLE:* The Lakota, called Sioux by early French explorers, are a Native American people, the descendants of the nation that once controlled most of the Great Plains of the north-central United States and Canada. The nation comprises

seven tribes, called the Seven Council Fires: the Teton, Wahpekute, Mdewak-
anton, Wahpeton, Sisseston, Yankton, and Yanktonai. The tribes are also known
by the names given them by the early Europeans in the region: Brulé, Hunk-
papas, Miniconjou, Ogalala, Two Kettles, Sans Arc, and Blackfeet. The Lakota
speak a Siouan language of the Hokan-Siouan language group, although English
is the first language for the majority.

*THE NATION:* French Jesuit missionaries first encountered the Lakota peoples near Sault Sainte Marie in the early seventeenth century. The tribes, living
in small agricultural villages, probably numbered some 50,000 when the first
Europeans visited their lands. Called Sioux by the French, the tribes were divided into a northern group occupying the valleys of the Missouri River and its
tributaries and a southern group living in the upper Mississippi Valley. In the
late seventeenth century the Lakota migrated to the southwest to escape hostile
neighbors equipped with firearms by the Europeans. The tribes finally settled in
the Mille Lac region of present Minnesota.

The horse, introduced into the Southwest by the Spanish, appeared on the
Great Plains at the beginning of the eighteenth century and revolutionized the
life of the plains peoples. By the mid-eighteenth century the Lakota had abandoned agriculture and had moved out onto the flat, northern plains where they
evolved a mobile culture based on the hunting of buffalo. The Lakota tribes, in
the early nineteenth century, dominated a vast area of the Great Plains, their
spiritual center the Black Hills they occupied around 1775.

The U.S. government bought the northern plains as part of the vast territory
sold by France in 1803, the Louisiana Purchase. U.S. officials signed treaties
with the Lakota in 1815, 1825, and 1851, but each time the Americans ignored
the terms of the treaty. Distrust of American intentions and the steady advance
of the American frontier pushed the tribes westward. The wanton destruction of
the buffalo herds on which the Lakota depended provoked violence in 1856.
The Lakota, until 1861, attempted to remain at peace, roaming the plains in
winter and returning to the sacred Black Hills each spring to conduct religious
ceremonies and to summer in the cooler highlands.

The Lakota, under increasing pressure from land-hungry American settlers,
rose in 1862 and killed over 800 settlers and soldiers in Minnesota. The Lakota
uprising began a long war of resistance to the illegal colonization of their lands
and the slaughter of the buffalo herds. Trapped by the devastation of the once-
great herds and under increasing military pressure, the Lakota signed a new
treaty with the United States in 1868. Under the terms of the treaty the Lakota
retained some 20 million acres of land while turning over huge tracts to the
U.S. government. They agreed to move, before 1876, to the territory, mostly
west of the Missouri River, that would form the lands reserved in perpetuity for
the Lakota Nation.

An expedition into Lakota territory, led by General George Custer in 1874,
discovered gold in the sacred Black Hills. The resulting gold rush provoked war
as the Lakota sought to protect their sacred hills. General Custer and 200 soldiers

died at the Little Big Horn in June 1876. The Battle of the Little Big Horn became the last major Lakota victory in the long war to preserve their lands and way of life. Soon after the battle, the Lakota surrendered. In direct violation of the 1868 treaty, the victors seized the Black Hills and drove the Lakota into the barren Badlands to small reservations in the most arid parts of their former lands.

In 1890 a band of starving Lakota warriors fled the reservations and took refuge in the Badlands, followed by their families. Captured and brought to Wounded Knee, a scuffle broke out, and an army officer was wounded. Without warning soldiers opened fire and within minutes nearly 200 men, women, and children had died. The massacre at Wounded Knee ended the last major conflict of the so-called Sioux Wars.

Plagued by disease, alcohol, and unemployment, the small reserves became notorious for abject poverty and desolation. In 1920, when new laws allowed the tribes to sue for their rights, a small band of educated Lakota filed the first in a long series of court cases seeking to win the return of stolen lands through the justice system. In 1924 the U.S. government granted the Indian tribes U.S. citizenship, a right few Lakota were equipped to use.

Younger Lakota began to leave the reservations in the 1960s, seeking greater educational and employment opportunities. A growing number of the educated Lakota turned to activism and launched a campaign to open investigations into Lakota conditions and treatment. Lakota militancy centered on the 1868 treaty, with demands that the government honor its terms, beginning with the return of the sacred Black Hills. In the Lakota language the Black Hills are called *wamaka ognaka onakizin*, the Sanctuary of Everything That Is.

Hundreds of activists occupied Wounded Knee in 1973 and held out for seventy days. The siege ended with over 300 arrests, but also with promises to initiate talks on Lakota grievances. In 1980 the U.S. Supreme Court decided that the Lakota should be awarded $106 million for lands illegally taken but that the Black Hills would not be returned to Lakota control. The Lakota refused the offer, not only because of the Black Hills but because the money is only a fraction of the real worth of the stolen lands. In 1987 a bill introduced in the Senate would have reaffirmed the Lakota's 1868 boundaries but did not cover all of the lands agreed to in the 1868 Fort Laramie Treaty.

The Lakota reservations, virtually undeveloped enclaves with up to three-quarters of the inhabitants unemployed and income levels equal to the poor states in Africa and Asia, continue to fuel the Lakota national movement. Lawyers, not warriors, are now the heroes of the movement, fighting in the courts for the sovereign rights the Lakota never surrendered.

*SELECTED BIBLIOGRAPHY:*
Eagle, Tom C., and Ron Zeilinger. *Black Hills: Sacred Hills.* 1987.
Zeilinger, Ron. *Sacred Ground.* 1986.
Zimmerman, Bill. *Airlift to Wounded Knee.* 1976.

# LATAKIA

**Alawiya**

*CAPITAL: Latakia*

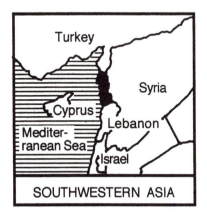

SOUTHWESTERN ASIA

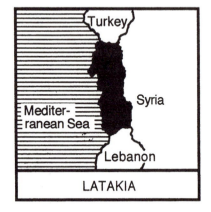

LATAKIA

*POPULATION:* (95e) 1,526,000 : 1,850,000 Alawites (Alawi) in Syria. MAJOR NATIONAL GROUPS: (95e) Alawite (Alawi) 73%, other Syrian. MAJOR LANGUAGES: Arabic, French. MAJOR RELIGIONS: Alawite 70%, Christian 14%, Sunni Muslim 12%, Ismaili Muslim 2%. MAJOR CITIES: (95e) Latakia (Al-Ladhiqiyah) 301,000 (340,000), Tartus 82,000 (100,000), Banias (Baniyas) 56,000, Jeble (Jablah) 44,000, Hamidia (Al-Hamidiyah) 24,000.

*GEOGRAPHY:* AREA: 2,433 sq.mi.-6,303 sq.km. LOCATION: Latakia occupies a wide coastal plain on the Mediterranean Sea backed by the Jebel and Nusayriyah Mountains in western Syria, between Turkey on the north and Lebanon on the south. POLITICAL STATUS: Latakia forms the provinces of Latakia and Tartus of the Syrian Arab Republic.

*INDEPENDENCE DECLARED:* 28 June 1939.

*FLAG:* The Alawite flag, the flag of the former republic, is a white field bearing a centered yellow sun with eleven rays and small red triangles at each corner.

*PEOPLE:* The Alawites or Alawi, also called Nusayri, trace their ancestry to the ancient Canaanites. Isolated by high mountains and avoiding intermarriage, the Alawites have survived for millennia and have retained distinct physical features. The Alawite nation comprises four ancient tribal confederations: Kalbiyah, Khaiyatin, Haddadin, and Matawirah. The Alawite religion, claimed by the Alawites as a sect of Shia Islam, is considered by most Muslims as a non-Muslim or heretical sect. The Alawite liturgy is believed to derive from early Christianity, including the observance of Christmas and the use of ceremonial wine. The Alawites also observe certain Iranian traditions such as Persian New

Year. Nearly half of the Alawites now live outside the coastal Alawite provinces, mostly in Damascus and other large Syrian cities in the interior.

*THE NATION:* The high incidence of fair hair and light eyes among the Alawites is attributed to the conquest of the Phoenician city-states by the Greeks of Alexander the Great in the third century B.C. Included in the Roman province of Syria from 64 B.C., the rural coastal tribes retained much of their original culture, even after adopting Christianity. Isolated by high mountains from the Syrian plains, the coastal peoples retained many historic traditions.

Muslim Arab invaders conquered the region in A.D. 635, forcibly converting the population to Islam. The Nusayri tribes of the Syrian coast publicly practiced the Islamic religion of the Muslim Empire, the Caliphate, while continuing to observe pre-Islamic practices in secret. The conflict over the succession to the Caliphate, begun at Mohammed's death in 632, eventually split the Muslim world. The Nusayri tribes, like the Shias or Shiites, favored Ali, Mohammed's nephew and son-in-law. The Alawites, unlike the Shias, deified Ali and incorporated his worship into their Muslim and pre-Muslim religious practices. The Nusayri came to be called the Aliwites or Alawites, the worshipers of Ali.

Persecuted for their beliefs, the Alawites welcomed the conquest of Latakia by the Christian crusaders in the eleventh century and prospered under Christian protection. Reconquered by Saladin in 1188, the region declined, and the Alawites again suffered persecution. Devastated by the Mongol invasion of 1260, the Alawites had only begun to recover when the Ottoman Turks took Latakia in 1516.

The Alawites, considered non-Muslim infidels, were allowed by the Turks to retain some autonomy under their own rulers, although subject to special taxes and restrictions and the continued persecution of the Sunni Muslim majority in the region. In the mid-nineteenth century the Turkish authorities abolished Alawite's autonomy and imposed harsher restrictions under the direct rule of Turkish governors. The Alawite national movement of the 1880s began as an anti-Turkish movement.

Allied agents secretly entered Latakia after war began in 1914. Promising an end to centuries of virtual slavery, the agents encouraged Alawite nationalism as a way to disrupt the Turkish administration of the region. When French troops occupied Latakia in 1917, the Alawites demanded the promised self-government. Disappointed by the French response, the Alawites rebelled in 1919 and launched attacks on French outposts and columns. The rebellion continued until reinforcements arrived from France in 1921.

Granted a League of Nations mandate in 1921, the French authorities divided Syria into several autonomous states, ostensibly to protect the minorities against the persecution of the Sunni Muslim majority. The Republic of the Alaouites, declared an autonomous state under French protection on 1 July 1922, formed a member state of the French-sponsored Syrian Federation. In 1924 the Alawite legislature voted for complete separation from Syria. Pressed by the non-Sunni minorities, the French dissolved the federation and created a unitary Syrian republic, without the minority dominated states of Latakia, Lebanon, and Jebel ed Druze.*

The Alawites, fearing the hated Sunni majority, became fervently pro-French and provided willing recruits to the French colonial army. After centuries of discrimination and persecution, the Alawites greatly benefited from French rule. The French authorities raised Alawite education, health care, and social services to the level enjoyed by Syria's Sunni majority.

A Franco-Syrian treaty in 1936 provided for a reunited Syrian state, soon dominated by the Sunnis. The Alawites rebelled against Sunni domination in 1939, quickly driving all Syrian officials from the province. On 28 June 1939 the rebels declared Latakia independent. The rebellion gave the French a pretext to intervene without violating the 1936 treaty. French troops landed, and the French resurrected the autonomous Alawite Republic of Latakia.

The French authorities, ignoring Alawite opposition, ceded Latakia to Syria in 1942 and in 1944 the last French troops withdrew. The Alawites again rebelled in 1946 and unsuccessfully attempted to gain French support for an independent Alawite state.

Thousands of Alawites joined the Syrian military in the 1950s, the only escape from grinding poverty. A despised minority, the Alawites sought acceptance by embracing militant pan-Arab nationalism. The socialist Baath Party, in power following a 1963 coup, offered equality in exchange for loyalty. The Alawites, dominant in the military officer corps and backed by the Baath Party, purged most non-Alawite officers between 1963 and 1969 and in 1970 led a coup that installed Alawite strongman Hafiz al-Assad.

The Moslem Brotherhood, based in the Sunni majority, mounted a serious challenge to the "heretical" Alawite regime in the 1970s. Sunni resistance to minority Alawite domination broke into open rebellion in the Sunni bastion of Hama in 1982. Crushed by the Alawite military, over 20,000 Sunnis died, and all Sunni opposition was forced underground.

Sunni resistance to Alawite rule resumed following Syria's loss of Soviet support in 1989. The frail health of Hafiz al-Assad, in the 1990s, has heartened the Sunni opposition. When Assad goes a struggle between Alawite chiefs is sure to ignite the Sunni opposition, representing 70% of the population. Until then, the minority Alawites remain in a precarious position as the hated ruling class in fragmented, coup-prone Syria.

*SELECTED BIBLIOGRAPHY:*

Antoun, Richard T. *Syria: Society, Culture and Polity.* 1991.
Longrigg, S.H. *Syria and Lebanon under French Mandate.* 1958.
Makiya, Kanen. *Cruelty and Silence.* 1993.
Sivan, Emmanud. *Radical Islam.* 1987.

# LOMBARDY

**Lombardia**

*CAPITAL: Milan (Milano)*

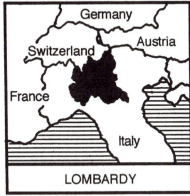

*POPULATION:* (95e) 8,957,000 : 8,145,000 Lombards in Italy. MAJOR NA-
TIONAL GROUPS: (95e) Lombard 77%, other Italian. MAJOR LANGUAGES:
Italian, Lombard, German. MAJOR RELIGIONS: Roman Catholic, Protestant.
MAJOR CITIES: (95e) Milan (Milano) 1,408,000 (4,754,000), Brescia 187,000
(381,000), Monza 128,000 (230,000), Bergamo 114,000 (404,000), Como
109,000 (216,000), Varese 106,000 (162,000), Pavia 90,000 (120,000), Cremona
85,000 (103,000), Vigevano 68,000 (140,000), Mantua (Mantova) 61,000
(179,000), Lecco 50,000 (89,000), Lodi 42,000 (57,000), Treviglio 26,000
(64,000).

*GEOGRAPHY:* AREA: 9,202 sq.mi.-23,839 sq.mi. LOCATION: Lombardy
occupies the broad Lombard Plain in the valley of the Po River, rising in the
north to a region of lakes and foothills and the high peaks of the Leopontine
Alps. POLITICAL STATUS: Lombardy forms a semiautonomous region of the
Italian Republic.

*FLAG:* The Lombard national flag, the flag of the national movement, is a
white field charged with a centered red cross.

*PEOPLE:* The Lombards are an Italian people descended from the region's
early Latin population and the later Germanic settlers. The Lombards speak
standard Italian but have also retained their own dialect, which incorporates
many words and forms based on French and German borrowings. The dialect,
claimed as a separate language by Lombard nationalists, is still spoken and
understood by the majority of the population. In 1990 only 36% of Lombardy's
population spoke standard Italian only. The Lombards' sense of identity and the

growth of national sentiment, dormant since the late nineteenth century, have again become a potent cultural force as part of the Lombard revival.

*THE NATION:* An ancient region, the fertile northern plains came under the rule of the Etruscans as early as 500 B.C. The Romans, extending their authority to the north, absorbed the Etruscan cities one by one in the third century B.C. Joined to the Roman province of Cisalpine Gaul, the northern cities developed as centers of Roman culture and art and continued to flourish for a time after the division of the empire in A.D. 395. The rapid decline of Roman power left the wealthy region nearly defenseless as the garrisons withdrew.

Germanic tribes invaded the Roman lands in the fifth century, the fertile plains and rich cities of the Po Valley overrun by Goths in 412 and Huns in 452. The Germanic Longobards (Lombards), who conquered the valley in 568, settled on the plains of the Po River. The invaders erected a small kingdom centered on Pavia and extended their rule to much of northern Italy. The newcomers gradually adopted the Latin language and culture of their Latinized subjects. Disunited under thirty-six dukes from 575 to 584, the Lombard nobility gathered to elect a new king to wear the Lombard Iron Crown and to unite the Lombard lands against the threats posed by the expanding Franks and the growing power of the papacy.

The leader of the Franks, Charlemagne, took control of Pavia and assumed the Iron Crown in the early ninth century. Following the breakup of his empire in 843, power in the region gradually passed from the feudal lords to the urban communes. The Lombard cities formed a defensive alliance in 1167, the Lombard League. In 1176 the Lombards defeated the forces of the Holy Roman Empire and forced the emperor to recognize their status as free cities in 1183. The northern Italian cities were mostly ruled by branches of the Sforza and Visconti families, patrons of Leonardo da Vinci, and the cultural revival of these Italian cities initiated the Renaissance, the great medieval flowering of European culture.

Family rivalries and wars between the city-states accelerated the rise of Milan and the loss of territories to Venice and other powers in the fifteenth and sixteenth centuries. The dominant Lombard power, the duchy of Milan, came under Spanish rule in 1535 and passed to the Austrian branch of the Hapsburgs in 1713. Taken from Austria by Napoleon in 1796, Lombardy returned to Austrian rule in 1815. The territorial exchanges and the imposition of differing laws, languages, and political systems sparked a Lombard national movement that culminated in widespread disturbances in 1848. The region formed part of the so-called Lombardo-Venetian Kingdom of the Austrian Empire until its liberation by French troops in 1859. In 1861 Lombardy joined the Risorgimento, the union of the numerous Italian states in a united Italian state, the Kingdom of Italy.

The numerous Italian peoples, united between 1861 and 1870, spoke dozens of regional dialects, many mutually unintelligible. The new Italian government chose a Tuscan dialect as a national language, a dialect spoken by only 10% of the population and written by just 1%. The adoption of a standard language failed to impose national unity on the diverse Italian peoples loyal to their regions, dialects, and cultures. The Lombard dialect, like many others, began to give way to standard Italian only with the arrival of radio broadcasts in the 1930s.

Lombard industrialization, accelerated after unification, evolved an urbanized, middle-class culture unlike the cultures of most of agrarian Italy. The fascist government in the 1920s and 1930s began to settle poor and culturally and linguistically distinct southern Italians in Lombardy to staff the booming factories. The Lombard industries, vitally important to Italy during World War II, suffered massive bombing and destruction.

Lombardy recovered quickly in the postwar era. The region became the center of the "Italian Miracle," the rapid industrial expansion of the 1950s. Millions of poor southerners from Italy's underdeveloped Mezzogiorno migrated north to the expanding Lombard industrial cities. The influx further strengthened standard Italian as a lingua franca used by southern workers and Lombard supervisors. Lombardy's postwar growth raised living standards to the equal of any region in Europe.

The unification of Europe, widely supported in Lombardy, began to raise questions and resentment in the 1970s. In 1978 Umberto Bossi published a tract advocating Lombard secession from Italy, the tract widely denounced as the work of a lunatic. Undeterred, Bossi organized the Lombard League in 1981. Anti-Rome and anti-immigrant, meaning both foreigners and the southern Italians, the league's nationalist message struck a cord in Lombardy, which pays more taxes to the Italian state than the entire region south of Rome.

Growing dissatisfaction with Rome's huge and hugely inefficient bureaucracy and with the Lombard taxes lavished on southern Italy only to line the pockets of corrupt officials and organized crime bosses, fueled the growth of Lombard nationalism. The movement raised the Lombard League's portion of the vote from only 8% in 1988 to 20% in 1989 and to between 37% and 46% in local elections since 1992.

Italy's ongoing corruption scandals, affecting hundreds of politicians and officials of the traditional political parties, have outraged many Lombards, who see themselves as Europeans first and Italians second. The pull of Europe, the idea of an independent Lombardy that is able to participate as an equal in a united Europe, continues to fuel the growth of nationalism and the growing support for the reversal of the Risorgimento that would make Italy once more just a geographical expression.

*SELECTED BIBLIOGRAPHY:*

Butler, William F. *Lombard Communes.* 1969.

Carello, Adrian N. *The Northern Question: Italy's Participation in the European Economic Community and the Mezzogiorno's Underdevelopment.* 1989.

Greenfield, Kent R. *Economics and Liberalism in the Risorgimento: A Study of Nationalism in Lombardy 1814–1848.* 1965.

# LUSATIA

Luzička Serbja; Sorbia; Lausitz

*CAPITAL: Budysin (Bautzen)*

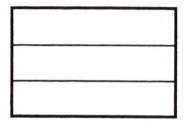

NORTH-CENTRAL EUROPE

LUSATIA

*POPULATION:* (95e) 1,280,000 : 600,000 Sorbs (Lusatians) in Germany and another 40,000 in adjacent areas of Poland. MAJOR NATIONAL GROUPS: (95e) German 55%, Sorb 45%. MAJOR LANGUAGES: German, Sorbian (Lusatian). MAJOR RELIGIONS: Lutheran, Roman Catholic. MAJOR CITIES: (95e) Khociebuz (Cottbus) 91,000 (120,000), Zgorzelec (Görlitz) 75,000 (121,000), Jarybodzin (Hoyerswerda) 60,000, Budysin (Bautzen) 53,000, Sitowir (Zittau) 43,000 (61,000), Gubin (Guben) 35,000 (51,000), Forst (Zasieki) 30,000 (45,000).

*GEOGRAPHY:* AREA: 4,933 sq.mi.-12,780 sq.km. LOCATION: Lusatia lies in southeastern Germany, a region of rolling hills and forests traversed by the basin of the Spree River, bordering Poland on the east and the Czech Republic on the south. POLITICAL STATUS: Lusatia has no official status; the historic region forms the districts of Bautzen, Görlitz, Kamenz, Niesky, and Zittau of the German state of Saxony* and Callau Cottbus, Forst, Guben, Hoyerswerda, and Weisswasser districts of Brandenburg state.

*INDEPENDENCE DECLARED:* 1 January 1919.

*FLAG:* The Sorb national flag, the flag of the national movement, is a horizontal tricolor of blue, red, and white.

*PEOPLE:* The Sorbs, also called Lusatians or Wends, refer to themselves as Srbi. They are a Western Slav people, the smallest of the Slav nations. The Sorb language, of the West Slavic language group, is spoken in two dialects: Upper Sorbian, resembling Czech, and Lower Sorbian, in its spoken form closer to Polish. The Sorbs have retained their traditional ties to the neighboring Poles and Czechs and have preserved their Slavic culture and traditions. However, a majority now speaks German, with only some 200,000 able to understand Sorbian and only 60,000 using the language as the language of daily life. The majority of the Sorbs are Lutheran, the only Slav nation with a Protestant majority, with a Roman Catholic minority concentrated in the border districts on the Polish border.

*THE NATION:* Western Slav tribes, the Milceni and Luzici, settled the region east of the river Elbe in the seventh and eighth centuries. In the ninth century Charlemagne's Franks checked the westward expansion of the tribes. Called Wends by the Germanic peoples, the Slavic tribes soon came into conflict with the Germans spreading to the east in the tenth century.

Saxons and Brandenburgers launched a crusade to Christianize the Wends in 1147. The Wends had already begun to adopt Christianity, so the crusade served German expansion rather than the propagation of the faith. The German onslaught drove many of the Slavs east across the Oder and Neisse Rivers. German nobles and merchants colonized the conquered lands and reduced the Wends to serfdom. The Germans relegated urban Slavs to restricted sections or to districts outside the city walls of their conquered towns and cities.

Seven Sorb cities in the southeast, free cities of the Holy Roman Empire, formed a defensive alliance in 1346, the Lusatian League. The cities preserved considerable independence from the surrounding German states and maintained the Sorb language and culture. The Czechs of Bohemia took control of Lusatia in 1368, temporarily easing the pressure to assimilate into German culture. Divided into two margravates, Upper and Lower Lusatia, in the fifteenth century, the Sorb lands were partitioned. The Saxon annexation of the margravates reunited the area under Saxon rule in 1635.

The majority of the Sorbs accepted the Lutheran Reformation in 1530, their conversion to Protestantism inciting cultural and national revival. A written form of the Sorbian language was devised in order to publish the New Testament in the language in 1548 and a Lutheran Catechism in 1574. In the Spree Forest and the highlands, the Sorbian language remained the first language of the Slav population, the isolated regions becoming bastions of the beleaguered language and culture. In the Germanized lowlands, German slowly gained prominence as the language of daily life.

Saxony, allied to Napoleonic France, lost Lower Lusatia to victorious Prussia in 1815. The Prussians instituted an intense Germanization policy in the region. The Sorbs of Upper Lusatia, under more lenient Saxon rule, published the first grammar in the Upper Sorbian dialect in 1830 and the first dictionary in 1840. Reunited in the German Empire in 1871, the Sorbs experienced a national revival with the first grammar in Lower Sorbian published in 1891. Resistance to forced assimilation sparked the growth of Sorb nationalism. The first openly nationalist organization, Macica Serbska, formed in the late nineteenth century.

The German parliament, in 1908, declared that German must be the spoken language of the empire and placed official restraints on the Sorb cultural and national revival. Domowina (Nation), formed in 1912, pressed for Sorb secession from the German Empire.

Conscripted to fight fellow Slavs in 1914, the Sorbs' opposition to German domination expanded rapidly. In November 1918, as defeated Germany collapsed in revolution, Sorb leaders declared the autonomy of Lusatia and dispatched a delegation to Berlin to negotiate the peaceful secession of Lusatia from Germany. Rebuffed by the German government, the Sorbs declared Lusatia independent of Germany on 1 January 1919.

A Sorb delegation traveled to the Paris Peace Conference in 1919 to seek recognition under U.S. president Wilson's call for the self-determination of Europe's minority peoples. Their appeals ignored, the Sorbs surrendered to invading German troops. In the postwar German reorganization, the states of Saxony and Prussia divided the Sorbs' homeland.

In 1920 only 170,000 used Sorbian as their first language, with over 600,000 able to speak both Sorb and German. The number of Sorbian speakers fell rapidly under the Germans' intense efforts to assimilate them. In 1929 the Sorbs won the right to use their language in education and religion, but the concessions fell far short of the cultural autonomy demanded by Domowina and other national organizations.

The Nazis, in control of Germany from 1933, persecuted the Sorbs as subhuman Slavs and banned the use of their language. In 1938 Domowina was suppressed, and its leaders were condemned to Nazi concentration camps. Finally liberated by the German defeat in 1945, the Sorbs again attempted to win Allied support for independence. In an exchange of territories, the Americans withdrew from the region and allowed the Soviets to occupy Saxony and Lusatia. The Soviet authorities quickly suppressed the Sorb national movement.

Sorb nationalism reemerged as Communism in East Germany collapsed in 1989. The nationalists dared to show their forbidden flag at a national rally in Bautzen for the first time since 1945. Nationalist demands for a separate Sorb state within united Germany were ignored in the rush to German reunification in October 1990.

Mass unemployment and economic hardships followed unification, giving rise to a wave of German intolerance of "foreigners," including the Sorbs, who do not fit the vision of a pure "Fatherland" propogated by the more radical German national organizations. Attacks on Sorbs and growing discrimination have fueled the national movement, which now focuses on formalizing their position as the first Slav nation in the European Union.

*SELECTED BIBLIOGRAPHY:*

Dvornik, Francis. *The Slavs.* 1956.

Lundman, B. J. *Races and Peoples of Europe.* 1984.

Neilsen, George R. *In Search of a Home: Nineteenth Century Wendish Immigration.* 1989.

Shlaes, Amity. *Germany: The Empire Within.* 1991.

# MADEIRA

**Madeira Islands**

*CAPITAL: Funchal*

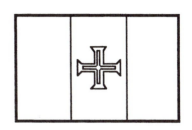

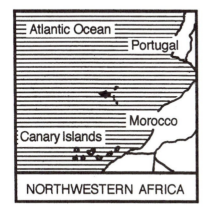

NORTHWESTERN AFRICA

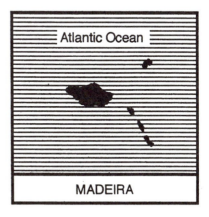

MADEIRA

*POPULATION:* (95e) 284,000 : 350,000 Madeirans in Portugal. MAJOR NA-TIONAL GROUPS: (95e) Madeiran 92%, other Portuguese. MAJOR LAN-GUAGE: Portuguese (Madeiran dialect). MAJOR RELIGION: Roman Catholic. MAJOR CITIES: (95e) Funchal 51,000 (146,000), Camara de Lobos 29,000, Machico 24,000 (39,000).

*GEOGRAPHY:* AREA: 314 sq.mi.-813 sq.km. LOCATION: Madeira, com-prising the large island of Madeira, the smaller island of Porto Santo, and two groups of barren islets, lies in the Atlantic Ocean 530 miles southwest of the Portuguese mainland and 360 miles west of Morocco. POLITICAL STATUS: Madeira forms an autonomous region of the Republic of Portugal.

*FLAG:* The Madeiran national flag, the official flag of the autonomous state, has three vertical stripes of blue, yellow, and blue with a centered cross of the Order of Christ, a square white cross outlined in red, in the center. OTHER FLAG(S): The same blue, yellow, and blue flag, but with five blue shields, each with five white *guinas* (roundels), in the form of a centered cross, is the flag of the largest nationalist organization, the Madeira Archipelago Liberation Front (FLAMA).

*PEOPLE:* The Madeirans are an island people mostly of Portuguese descent, but with admixtures of African slaves, Arabs, and Berbers. The Madeiran dialect of Portuguese has been influenced by Madeira's closeness to Africa and cen-turies of contacts with many different maritime peoples. Emigration, particularly in the twentieth century, has resulted in a large immigrant population, estimated to number over 1 million, primarily in South America and South Africa. The immigrants contribute to the Madeiran economy and are the most nationalistic and the most ardent supporters of the Madeiran national movement. An insular, conservative people, the Madeirans are overwhelmingly Roman Catholic.

*THE NATION:* The archipelago, known to the Romans as the Purple Islands, due to their habitual haze, was lost to all but legend with the coming of the Dark Ages to Europe. In 1420 a Portuguese navigator, Jaõ Goncalvo Zarco, sighted Porto Santo and claimed the uninhabited islands for Portugal. The name of the largest island, called Madeira, the Portuguese word for wood in reference to its extensive forest cover, became the name of the entire group.

Portuguese colonists established a settlement at Funchal in 1421, Portugal's first overseas colony. The introduction of sugarcane cultivation in 1452 transformed Madeira, as sugar is a crop that requires a large workforce. The islanders bought black African and Moorish slaves in the markets of nearby Morocco to work on the sugar and tropical fruit plantations. The Portuguese, without the strong racial prejudices common in other parts of Europe, freely mixed with the large slave population.

Madeira, lying on the sea routes among Europe, Africa, and the Americas, prospered in the sixteenth and seventeenth centuries. Madeirans, drawn by tales of riches, emigrated to the new Portuguese colonies, particularly Brazil. The emigrants began a tradition of leaving the islands in search of work or fortune that continued for centuries.

Occupied by the British during the Napoleonic Wars, 1801–14, a number of British families settled in the islands, most to engage in the lucrative wine trade. The production of the famous Madeira wine began when a shipment of red wine, sent to the East Indies, was returned unsold. On opening the cask the owner discovered that the heat of the warm hold had considerably enhanced the flavor. The production of the unique Madeira wine has involved heat since that time.

The islands neglected, overpopulated, and underdeveloped, thousands of Madeirans began to leave in the nineteenth century, some settling as far away as Hawaii, where they introduced the musical instrument called the ukulele. Tourism, particularly from Britain, brought some much needed-income in the early twentieth century, but the economic mainstays of tourism, sugar, wine, and lace making provided for only a fraction of the burgeoning population. By the early 1960s emigration reduced Madeira's population by an average of 2.5% to 3% a year.

A cultural revival, beginning in the 1960s, partly in response to the need to leave their beloved islands to find work, quickly evolved a strong nationalist faction following the leftist revolution in Portugal in 1974. Portugal's revolutionary government moved quickly to dismantle the costly remnants of the Portuguese Empire, granting independence to remaining overseas possessions. Nationalists, led by the Madeira Archipelago Liberation Front (FLAMA), created a provisional government in anticipation of independence. Disappointed by the government's refusal to grant independence to Madeira along with the other overseas possessions, thousands of Madeirans joined demonstrations demanding immediate independence.

Conditions in Lisbon stabilized under a new centrist government in 1975, and mass support for Madeiran separation waned over fears that the islands would suffer economically and lacked trained administrators. Although many nationalists agreed that premature independence might prove a disaster, the national organizations pressed for association status or other forms of independence. In 1976 the Madeirans accepted a government offer of broad economic and political autonomy, seen by the more radical nationalists as an interim step to the eventual independence of the islands.

Rising prosperity, accelerating after Portugal's entry into the European Economic Community in 1986, has given the Madeirans a new confidence. Madeira's membership in the European Community again raised the question of independence within a united Europe. Emigration, once a necessity, has reversed, and the population is again growing. Many Madeirans found work in the expanding financial and banking industries spawned by the islands' emergence as a major offshore European financial center, tax haven, and free port.

The national movement, with the support of the large immigrant Madeiran population, focuses on ending the state's semicolonial status. In October 1990 the president of the regional government met with nationalist leaders to discuss the independence issue and to forestall threatened separatist activities. Since then the autonomous government has moved closer to the nationalists, and their cooperation has benefited the island state. In September 1993, during a heated disputed with the Lisbon government, the governor, Social Democrat Alberto Joan Jardim, threatened to throw his government's support behind the separatists. In 1994 Portuguese intelligence officers spying on Madeiran leaders were exposed, further harming relations between the Madeiran and Portugese governments.

Portuguese law makes advocating secession a grave offense, and nationalist organizations are banned under the terms of the Portuguese constitution. In the islands the nationalists have begun to integrate into local politics. The Portuguese prohibitions on secession and nationalism have become irrelevant under the growing relationship between the nationalists and the autonomous Madeiran government.

*SELECTED BIBLIOGRAPHY:*

Bragança-Cunha, Vicente. *Revolutionary Portugal.* 1976.
Mailer, Phillip. *The Impossible Revolution.* 1977.
Rogers, Francis M. *Atlantic Islanders of the Azores and Madeiras.* 1979.

# MANCHURIA

**Tung-pei-sheng (Northeast Provinces)**

*CAPITAL: Chungchun*

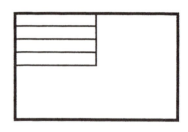

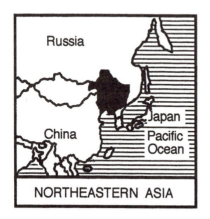

*POPULATION:* (95e) 95,135,000 : 10,630 Manchu in China. MAJOR NA-TIONAL GROUPS: (95e) Chinese 81%, Manchu 11%, Korean 2%, Hui 2%, Evenki, Mongol. MAJOR LANGUAGES: Chinese (northeastern dialects), Man-chu, Korean, Even, Mongol. MAJOR RELIGIONS: Buddhism, Taoism, Sunni Muslim. MAJOR CITIES: (95e) Mukden (Shengyang) 3,422,000 (5,630,000), Harbin 2,726,000, Lüda 1,597,000 (1,855,000), Changchun 1,539,000 (1,921,000), Fushun 1,358,000 (1,709,000), Qiqihar 995,000 (1,914,000), Jilin 943,000 (1,189,000), Benxi 879,000, Jixi 690,000 (878,000), Jinzhou 662,000, Fuxu 625,000, Mudanjiang 472,000 (655,000), Dandong 463,000 (881,000), Jia-musi 423,000, Hegang 390,000, Liaoyuan 357,000.

*GEOGRAPHY:* AREA: 309,498 sq.mi.-801,808 sq.km. LOCATION: Man-churia lies in northeastern China, occupying the vast Manchurian Plain east of the Great Khingan Range. Manchuria borders the Russian regions of Far East* on the north and northeast, Siberia* on the northwest, Korea on the southeast, and includes the Eastern Mongolia* region of Inner Mongolia on the west. POLITICAL STATUS: Manchuria has no official status; the region forms the Northeast Provinces, Heilongjiang, Jilin, and Liaoning, of the People's Republic of China.

*INDEPENDENCE DECLARED:* 8 February 1926; 18 February 1932.

*FLAG:* The Manchu flag, the flag of the former Manchurian state, is a dark gold field bearing a canton of four equal horizontal stripes of red, blue, white, and black.

*PEOPLE:* The Manchu, the original inhabitants of the region, are a robust,

Tungus people averaging some five inches taller than the majority Han Chinese. Calling themselves Niuchi, thought to mean simply ''people,'' the Manchu speak a Tungistic language of the East Altaic language group that has been written in its own script since the seventeenth century and was an official language in China until 1911. A majority of the Manchu, estimated at 99%, are now bilingual, also speaking the northeastern Chinese dialects or the official Mandarin language. In spite of decades of Communist egalitarianism, the Manchu tend to be more prosperous and better educated than the Han Chinese. The government of the People's Republic of China asserts that the Manchu do not now and never did exist as a separate people.

*THE NATION:* The Manchu, according to tradition, have inhabited the region since at least the third century B.C. Originally a nomadic people, the Manchu settled in permanent communities near the grazing lands. A warrior people, the Manchu successfully resisted sporadic Chinese attempts to conquer the region and in the twelfth century defeated the rising power of the Mongols. In the thirteenth century the Manchu swept into northern China, only to be driven back by the Mongol conquest of the Chinese Empire.

The Manchu created a powerful state about 1616 under Nurhatsi, known as Nurachu to the Chinese. In 1644 the Manchu invaded the weakened Chinese Empire and installed a Manchu dynasty in Beijing. The Manchu adopted many Chinese customs and cultural traits while retaining their own language and culture. Some Chinese customs, such as the Golden Lilies, the deformed feet so prized by the Chinese upper classes, never found favor with the Manchu. Intermarriage between the Manchu nobility and their Chinese subjects was strictly forbidden. Some 4 million Manchu formed an elite nobility, ruling an empire of more than 400 million Chinese.

Manchuria, the ancestral homeland, remained closed to non-Manchu settlement until severe population pressure forced the Manchu government to allow limited Chinese immigration in 1878. Even limited immigration soon reduced the Manchu to minority status in their homeland. Russian influence in the region, growing with construction of the Chinese-Eastern Railway, prompted the Manchu rulers to open Manchuria to unlimited immigration in 1896. In 1900 the immigrant ethnic Han Chinese formed 80% of Manchuria's population.

Russia established a virtual protectorate in Manchuria, as Manchu power waned in China. The Japanese, after defeating China in a brief war in 1895, also sought to assert their influence in the mineral-rich area, culminating in war with Russia in 1904–5. The victorious Japanese quickly consolidated their economic and political influence after 1905.

The long decline of Manchu power finally ended in revolution in 1911. The last Manchu emperor, the child Pu-Yi, was deposed, and a Chinese republic was proclaimed. The weak republican government soon lost control of many areas to local factions and warlords. Chang Tso-lin, named governor of Manchuria in 1918, created a virtually independent state supported by a strong military force drawn from the numerous White Russian refugees fleeing Russia. On 8 February

1926 Chang declared Manchuria independent of China, and in the ensuing war his forces drove republican troops back on Beijing.

The Japanese, taking advantage of the turmoil, persuaded Chang to give them responsibility for the important South Manchurian Railway. They used Chang's assent as a pretext to occupy key positions in the state and to grab power when Chang Tso-lin died in a mysterious bomb explosion in 1931. The League of Nations, drawn into the conflict, recommended an autonomous Manchurian state under nominal Chinese rule. Both the Japanese and the Manchurian nationalists rejected the recommendation.

Encouraged by the Japanese, the nationalists declared the independence of Manchukuo, the Manchu State, on 18 February 1932. The nationalists and their Japanese allies installed Pu-yi, the last Manchu emperor of China as the state's chief executive. The state was renamed Manchutikuo, the Manchu Empire, and in 1934 Pu-yi, the last Manchu ruler of China, assumed the Manchu throne as Emperor Kang Teh. In spite of the trappings of sovereignty, ultimate power rested with the Japanese advisers assigned to all high Manchu officials. In 1937 the state served as base for the Japanese invasion of China, and in 1941 Manchutikuo declared war on the United States and its allies.

The neighboring Soviet Union, despite its alliance with the United States and the United Kingdom, recognized Manchu independence in 1941 and retained an armed neutrality with both Manchutikuo and Japan until the end of the war in June 1945. Hastily declaring war on the two states the Soviet authorities sent an occupation force into Manchuria in July. The Soviet troops quickly removed as many of the huge industries established by the Japanese as possible. Other troops arrested Pu-yi, who was later turned over to the Soviet's allies, the Chinese Communists.

The Soviets supported the Chinese Communists in the Chinese civil war of 1945–49 and retained considerable influence in Manchuria. The Manchurian leader, Kao Kang, for his support of the Communists, became the head of an autonomous Manchurian state in 1949. Accused of attempting to resurrect Manchurian independence in 1954, the Communist leaders dismissed Kao Kang, and in 1955 he disappeared. Divided into three provinces, Manchuria disappeared from Chinese official maps. Ignoring the fact that the Manchu had ruled China from 1644 to 1911, the Communist authorities decreed that a separate Manchu people had never existed and forbade the use of the names Manchu and Manchuria and all references to over two centuries of Manchu domination in China.

Manchurian regionalism, supported by the majority Chinese and the minority peoples, again became a strong force in the 1980s, sparked by government policies that favored the development of the southeastern coastal provinces. The government neglected the Northeast Provinces, with their aging heavy industries and traditionally independently minded people, to concentrate economic development in the provinces near Hong Kong and Taiwan.

The relatively relaxed atmosphere of the period allowed the Manchu to emerge from decades of forced obscurity. In 1990, for the first time since the

Communist victory of 1949, the Manchu were counted as a minority people in the official census. The Manchu population of China, considerably higher than expected, officially numbered 9,821,000, a figure not adjusted for the unknown number of ethnic Manchu who have listed themselves as ethnic Han Chinese for decades to escape persecution. The memories of the grimmer aspects of the Japanese military occupation having faded, a wave of nostalgia swept the region in early 1989. The nostalgia and the emerging Manchu national movement were crushed, along with the pro-democracy movement in China in a vicious military campaign in June 1989.

The region in the 1990s has experienced the highest level of unrest since the Cultural Revolution of the 1960s. The unrest is propelled by falling incomes, lower than the dismal Chinese average and only a quarter of those in the privileged southeast. The overthrow of Communism and the disintegration of the Soviet Union have reverberated in Manchuria. In 1994 the three Northeast Provinces put forward a plan for economic independence, including direct access to the Sea of Japan through the delta of the Tumen River on the narrow frontier between Russia and Korea. The loosening of Communist control in China has allowed Manchuria to turn away from ideology and to emphasize economic and political ties with the countries that have shaped so much of its modern history, Japan and Russia.

*SELECTED BIBLIOGRAPHY:*

Collier, Mac. *China in Disintegration, 1912–1949.* 1977.

Lattimore, Owen. *The Inner Asian Frontiers of China.* 1951.

Lee, Chong-Sik. *Revolutionary Struggle in Manchuria: Chinese Communism and Soviet Interest, 1922–1945.* 1983.

Schwartz, Henry G. *The Minorities of Northern China: A Survey.* 1984.

# MANNIN

Ellan Mannin; Ellan Vannin; Isle of Man

*CAPITAL: Douglas*

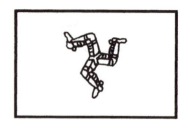

NORTHWESTERN EUROPE

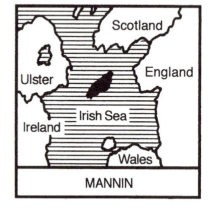

MANNIN

*POPULATION:* (95e) 72,000 : 80,000 Manx in the United Kingdom. MAJOR NATIONAL GROUPS: (95e) Manx 89%, other British. MAJOR LANGUAGES: English, Manx. MAJOR RELIGIONS: Methodist, Anglican, Roman Catholic. MAJOR CITIES: (95e) Douglas 22,000 (32,000), Onchan 9,000, Ramsey 7,000, Peel 5,000, Castletown 4,000 (8,000).

*GEOGRAPHY:* AREA: 227 sq.mi.-588 sq.km. LOCATION: Mannin lies in the Irish Sea, equidistant from Ireland, Scotland,* England, and Wales.* The island, thirty miles long and twelve miles wide, is ringed by high cliffs indented by numerous bays. POLITICAL STATUS: Mannin forms the self-governing state called the Isle of Man, a dependency of the British Crown.

*FLAG:* The Manx national flag, the official flag of the autonomous state, is a red field bearing three white legs, armored and spurred, detailed in gray and yellow.

*PEOPLE:* The Manx are a Celtic people, descendants of the island's early Celtic inhabitants, with later admixtures of Scandinavians, Scots, and Welsh. The Manx language, of the Goedelic branch of the Celtic languages, nearly extinct in the 1950s, has revived as part of the Manx cultural resurgence, although English remains the first language of the island. The culture, including many traits and traditions that have disappeared from the other Celtic cultures, has revived in the ultimate decades and is once again flourishing on the island. The Manx are mostly Protestant, the majority belonging to the Methodist sect.

*THE NATION:* Celtic peoples from the European mainland settled the island around 500 B.C. Ruled by a Welsh line of kings from the sixth to the ninth centuries, the island remained a Celtic kingdom while most of Celtic Britain fell to the Germanic Angles, Saxons, and Jutes. The island, a Celtic stronghold, was reinforced by refugees fleeing the Germanic invasion of the nearby mainland districts.

Scandinavian Vikings first raided the island in 798 and returned in 800 to overthrow the Celtic kingdom. Norse colonists settled on the island, a dependency of the Kingdom of Norway. Magnus, the Norwegian king, sold the island to Alexander III of Scotland in 1266. The Manx, unhappy under Scottish rule, placed their island under the protection of the English king, Edward I, in 1290. The island's mixture of Celtic and Scandinavian influences evolved a distinct culture by the fifteenth century, with traditions and customs quite unlike those of the neighbor islands.

The English king gave the island to the Stanley family in 1405. Later the earls of Derby and Salisbury, the Stanleys ruled Mannin for over three centuries. The island's economy revolved around smuggling among Ireland, Scotland, Wales, and England, and many Manx fortunes stemmed from the illegal trade. In an effort to stop the Manx smuggling of goods into England, the British Crown purchased the island in 1765. Granted self-government in 1828, the Crown formalized the relationship with the island in 1866. The Isle of Man would remain subject to the British monarch, but not the British parliament.

In the eighteenth and nineteenth centuries the English language gradually took over as the language of daily life. By 1871 only a quarter of the population could speak Manx. The island's mild climate, beautiful scenery, and unique culture attracted many visitors, the island becoming one of the premier resorts of Victorian Britain. The large number of visitors increased the use of English, and by 1900 only 5,000 could still speak their Celtic language. Opposition to the arrival of thousands of English tourists sparked periodic demands for independence, but no serious negotiations were undertaken as the authorities considered the island too small for viable nationhood.

After World War II, the island again prospered as a major British resort. Younger Manx, fearing that tourism guaranteed the extinction of their ancient culture, began a campaign to save the Manx culture and language. In 1961 only 165 people spoke the Manx language, the numbers beginning to grow as younger Manx took pride in learning and using the language. The Manx renewed ties and contacts with the other Celtic peoples of Europe, the annual festivals and congresses sustaining a growing cultural and national revival.

Britain's entry into the European Economic Community in 1973, accompanied by a separate agreement giving the island associate status, initiated a dramatic economic surge. Favorable tax and banking laws turned Mannin into a major offshore banking center and attracted numerous new residents from the British mainland. From 1980 the population grew rapidly, raising house prices to a level higher than those of London, far beyond the reach of the average Manx.

The invasion of newcomers sparked renewed Manx nationalism, accompanied by a campaign of arson against holiday homes owned by foreigners in 1989–90. Pressed by the nationalist agitation, the island's government passed laws restricting immigration from the mainland and giving special protection to the Manx culture and language. In 1992 the government introduced the Manx language in the school curriculum, and the nearly extinct Manx language began to revive dramatically.

The unification of Western Europe in the European Economic Community, now the European Union, has given Manx nationalism a new focus. The Manx nationalists now look to the union, theoretically able to accommodate smaller nations, not to Great Britain as their future. A nationalist campaign favors transferring the island's sovereignty from the British Crown to a similar relationship with the European Union.

*SELECTED BIBLIOGRAPHY:*

Ellis, Peter B. *The Celtic Revolution.* 1988.

Moore, A. W. *A History of the Isle of Man.* 1986.

Robinson, V., and D. McCarroll, eds. *The Isle of Man: Celebrating a Sense of Place.* 1990.

Young, G.V.C. *Isle of Man and the Faeroe Islands: Two Similar Countries.* 1981.

# MARI-EL

**Marii El**

*CAPITAL: Yoshar-Ola*

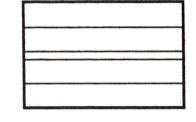

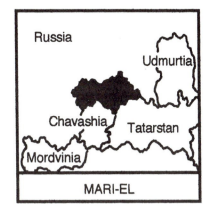

*POPULATION:* (95e) 770,000 : 765,000 Mari in Russia. MAJOR NA-
TIONAL GROUPS: (95e) Mari 48%, Russian 42%, Tatar 6%, Chavash 1%,
Udmurt 1%. MAJOR LANGUAGES: Russian, Mari (Chermis), Tatar. MAJOR
RELIGIONS: Russian Orthodox, animist, Sunni Muslim. MAJOR CITIES:
(95e) Yoshar-Ola 289,000 (320,000), Lopatino (Volzhsk) 68,000 (110,000),
Koznodemyanok 30,000, Suslonger 20,000.

*GEOGRAPHY:* AREA: 8,957 sq.mi.-23,204 sq.km. LOCATION: Mari-El occupies a level plain north of the Volga River in eastern European Russia, a
wooded region of numerous lakes and peat bogs bordering the Russian oblasts
of Nizhni Novgorod on the west and northwest, Vyatka on the north, the republics of Tatarstan* on the southwest, and Chavashia* on the south. POLITI-
CAL STATUS: Mari-El forms a member state of the Russian Federation.

*FLAG:* The Mari national flag, the official flag of the republic, is a horizontal
tricolor of pale blue, white, and red, the white twice the width of the other
stripes and bearing a narrow horizontal, purple stripe across the center.

*PEOPLE:* The Mari are a Finnic people, believed the region's earliest inhabitants, divided in two major groups: the Olyk or Volga Mari and the Kuryk or
Vetluga Mari in the northwest. Each group speaks a mutually unintelligible Mari
language of the Finno-Ugric language group. The Mari have sucessfully resisted
assimilation into Russian culture. Over 90% speak the Mari languages, with
only 65% able to speak Russian, even though over half the Mari live outside
the republic. The Mari are related to the Finns and the other Finnic peoples who

inhabit the region around the Gulf of Finland far to the west. The majority of the Mari adhere to a nationalistic animist sect called Kugu Sorta, with an Orthodox Christian minority concentrated among the Mari living in adjacent provinces and republics.

*THE NATION:* The Mari, traditionally the first inhabitants of the Volga River basin, the original home of the Finnic peoples, formed a seminomadic tribal people first mentioned in sixth-century records. The disunited Mari tribes never developed a state system but lived under the political control of stronger neighbors. In the eighth century the Turkic Khazars established a nominal authority in the Volga basin, and in the tenth century the Mari formed part of the Bulgar Chavash state destroyed by the Mongols in 1236. The Mari lands came under the rule of the Tatar Khanate of Kazan following the disintegration of the Mongol Empire in the fourteenth century.

Slavic Cossacks and Orthodox missionaries began to penetrate the Tatar khanate in the fifteenth century. Under the influence of the Slavs, a Mari minority converted to Orthodox Christianity. In 1522 the Russians, led by Ivan the Terrible, conquered Kazan and initiated the Slav colonization of the Volga River basin. The Mari, more blond and Nordic than the Russians, were subjected to a harsh colonial regime and relegated to virtual slavery on the vast estates of Russian landlords.

The Mari's resistance to Christianity resulted in severe persecution and intense assimilation pressures led by the Orthodox church. Official efforts to eradicate their languages and culture provoked several serious revolts in the seventeenth and eighteenth centuries. To divide Mari resistance, the tsarist authorities partitioned their lands among several Russian provinces and banned the Mari language and culture. Living in conditions of cruelty, ignorance, and poverty, the Mari clung to the traditional shamanistic beliefs that played a large part in the maintenance of their separate identity.

The Mari effort to preserve their animist beliefs stimulated a strong religious and nationalist resurgence, a mass anti-Russian movement, in the latter half of the nineteenth century. In the 1870s the various Mari religious beliefs were formalized as part of a nationalistic religious sect called Kugu Sorta, intensely anti-Russian and anti-Orthodox.

The population of the Mari lands, 90% illiterate, rose during the 1905 Russian Revolution to attack and burn Russian estates and settlements on their traditional lands. Following a number of skirmishes with government troops, the Mari rebels moved into the thick forests and former guerrilla bands called the Forest Brethren. The government troops sent against them finally overcame the last rebel bands in 1906.

Thousands of young Mari, conscripted during World War I, deserted and returned home with the outbreak of revolution in Russia in February 1917. The Mari soldiers formed the nucleus of a national army that formed to protect the Mari people as civil government collapsed and armed bands became common.

Freed from Russian domination, the Mari established the organs of self-rule that oversaw the setting up of hospitals and the organization of literacy classes and Mari language schools, Likeezes. In the summer of 1917 the Mari convened a national congress and voted in favor of a federation of non-Russian states in the Volga-Ural region and the expulsion of the region's Slav settlers. On 24 January 1918 the federation, the Idel-Ural Federation, made up of several Finnic and Turkic nations in the Volga basin, declared independence from Russia.

Bolshevik troops invaded the region in February 1918, rapidly overrunning Marii El, Mari Territory. In July 1918 the Mari rebelled against the excesses of the Red Army and the bureaucratic Soviets. Crushed by the Red soldiers, the authorities ordered the detention of the Mari's small, educated elite. Branded class enemies, all of the Mari's potential leaders were deported or liquidated.

In 1920 the Soviets created a nominally autonomous region for the surviving Mari. In 1920–21 thousands perished in the famine that followed the massive destruction of the civil war and the inept introduction of Communism. Over a third of the 1914 Mari population had died by the end of 1921. Under Soviet rule the Mari language was again allowed and became one of the official languages of the autonomous republic created in 1936. In spite of official Soviet suppression, the Mari made great strides in education and culture.

The small republic industrialized and urbanized during World War II. Whole factories and Slav populations transferred to the region from western Russia and by 1945 the Mari formed a minority in their homeland. Resentment of their minority status sparked a cultural reawakening in the 1960s. Younger Mari took a new interest in their history, their language, and their unique religion.

The revival, taking on nationalistic overtones in the 1970s, grew into a mass movement following the Gorbychev reforms that liberalized Soviet life after 1987. Unofficial nationalist organizations, organized in 1989, pressured the republican government to change the republic's name and to declare Marii El a sovereign state in October 1990, with three official languages: Lowland Mari, Highland Mari, and Russian. The republic's government unilaterally declared Mari-El a full republic within the reorganized Russian Federation following the disintegration of the Soviet Union in August 1991. Nationalists aim for independence within a Volga federation and are adamant that the Mari will not trade Soviet domination for renewed Russian domination.

*SELECTED BIBLIOGRAPHY:*
Hilderley, Jeri. *Mari.* 1990.
Kozlov, Viktor. *The Peoples of the Soviet Union.* 1988.
Pushkarev, Sergei. *Self-Government and Freedom in Russia.* 1988.

# MARTINIQUE

*Madiana*

*CAPITAL: Fort-de-France*

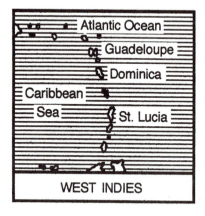

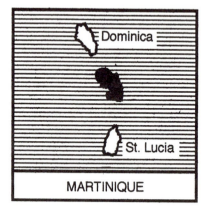

POPULATION: (95e) 357,000 : 365,000 Martinicans in Martinique and France. MAJOR NATIONAL GROUPS: (95e) Martinican (Creole 90%, French 5%, Indian, Chinese, Lebanese), other French. MAJOR LANGUAGES: Creole, French. MAJOR RELIGIONS: Roman Catholic, animist. MAJOR CITIES: (95e) Fort-de-France 103,000 (143,000), Sainte-Marie Trinité 33,000, La Lamentin 29,000, Schloecher 20,000, Le Francois 18,000.

GEOGRAPHY: AREA: 431 sq.mi.-1,116 sq.km. LOCATION: Martinique lies in the southern Caribbean Sea in the Windward Island group. The island, one of the most fertile in the Caribbean, is of volcanic origin and has several high, active volcanoes. The island is located between the island republics of Dominica on the north and St. Lucia on the south. POLITICAL STATUS: Martinique forms an overseas department of the French republic.

FLAG: The Martinican national flag, the flag of the national movement, is a red field bearing a stylized yellow tree near the hoist and has narrow horizontal black stripes at the top and bottom divided from the red by thin white stripes.

PEOPLE: The Martinicans or Martiniquans, called Martiniquais in French, are mostly the descendants of African slaves, with some European admixture called Creoles. The Martinican language and culture also reflect the mingled African and French influences. The French minority includes island-born Europeans called Békés and continental French, mostly administrators, military, and merchants, called Metros. The majority of the population is nominally Roman Catholic, the religion often mixed with traditions originally brought from Africa by the slaves imported between the seventeenth and nineteenth centuries.

*THE NATION:* The island, inhabited by a native tribal people, the Caribs, was called Madiana, the Island of Flowers. Christopher Columbus is credited with the European discovery of the island in 1502 and the establishment of Spain's territorial claim. Fierce Carib resistance to European incursions precluded Spanish settlement, and the Spanish government ignored the island for over a century.

A French expedition began the settlement of the island in 1635, the colonists rapidly eliminating the native Caribs. Sugarcane cultivation, introduced from Portuguese Brazil in 1654, required a large workforce to provide the necessary labor. The French imported thousands of black African slaves to work the sugar and tropical fruit plantations.

A French planter aristocracy dominated the island; its most famous representative, Josephine Rose Tascher de La Pagerie, gained fame as Napoleon's empress. Josephine was born in 1763 under British military occupation, during one of the intermittent Anglo-French wars for domination in the Caribbean Sea region.

Martinique's large slave population enjoyed a brief freedom following the French Revolution of 1789. A guillotine, erected in the center of the capital, Saint-Pierre, abruptly ended the domination of the planter aristocracy. During the wars that followed the revolution, the island changed hands several times before returning to permanent French rule in 1814. The French authorities abolished slavery in 1848, and thousands of freed slaves suddenly became freemen. The French planters imported low-paid East Indians and Chinese plantation workers to take the place of the freed slaves on the sugar plantations.

The Martinican capital, Saint-Pierre, became the center of French culture in the Caribbean, a sophisticated city nicknamed the "Paris of the West Indies." On 8 May 1902 the volcano above the city, Mount Peleé, erupted and buried the city. Over 40,000 people in the city and its surroundings perished. Fort-de-France, a town in the south away from the active volcanoes, was designated the new administrative center.

The colony, dominated by the Békés, the descendants of colonial families, and the Metros, continental French officials and businesspeople, flourished on the trade in sugar and tropical fruits in the early twentieth century. The European elite ignored the majority Creoles, relegated to menial jobs or subsistence farming until after World War II.

The island's status, upgraded in 1946 as an overseas department of the French republic, brought all of the rights of the metropolitan departments and just as little say in their local affairs. In spite of the continuing overcentralization of government in faraway Paris, the new status benefited the Martinican population materially, but rising prosperity incited demands for greater Martinican participation in the economic and political decisions that determined the island's future. In the 1950s and 1960s leftist political parties gained support among the majority Creoles. In 1965 antigovernment, pro-autonomy demonstrations turned to rioting, the beginning of the Martinican national movement.

A number of separatist, nationalist, and autonomist groups emerged in the 1970s and 1980s, some demanding immediate independence, others a gradual transition to eventual independence or to autonomy and continued ties to France. Pro-independence disturbances rocked the island, particularly in 1974 and 1980–81, and forced the French government to send reinforcements from France as a series of bomb attacks disrupted the island. The disturbances continued until 1988, when an uneasy calm settled on the island.

The French welfare state, extended to Martinique after World War II, has given the population one of the highest standards of living in the Caribbean. Pro-French groups point out that Martinique is part of France, not a colony, and vehemently oppose the loss of the generous French benefits and economic subsidies.

The Creole population, with a birthrate twice that of continental France, remains the base for the numerous nationalist organizations. With 50% of the population under twenty years of age, the Creoles suffer endemic unemployment and few economic opportunities and are forced to emigrate to find work. Nationalists assert that the Creoles' problems are associated with colonialism, as is the island's domination by the European minority.

The nationalists, in local elections since 1990, have made substantial gains and hold nearly half the seats in the local assembly, but the nationalist upsurge has not generated violence on the scale seen before 1988. Periodic calls for a referendum on independence are mostly ignored by both the French administration and rejected by the nationalists, who would likely lose a plebiscite on economic issues. The majority of the islanders would probably vote against complete independence and the loss of the lucrative French subsidies. The island, with virtually no natural resources and 80% of the economy devoted to sugar production, depends on the sugar and tourism, but mostly it depends on the French economic subsidies.

*SELECTED BIBLIOGRAPHY:*

Glasgow, Roy A., and Winston E. Langley. *The Troubled and Troubling Caribbean.* 1989.

Mills, William F. *Elections and Ethnicity in French Martinique: A Paradox in Paradise.* 1985.

Phillips, Fred. *Freedom in the Caribbean: A Study in Constitutional Change.* 1977.

# MASAILAND

**Maasailand**

*CAPITAL: Magadi*

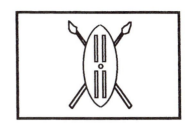

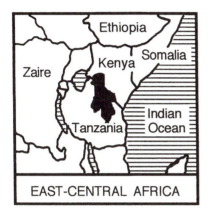

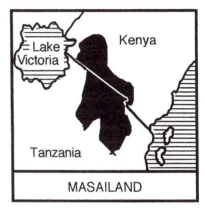

*POPULATION:* (95e) 1,845,000 : 870,000 Masai in Kenya and Tanzania. MAJOR NATIONAL GROUPS: (95e) Masai 45%, other Kenyan, other Tanzanian. MAJOR LANGUAGES: Masai, Swahili, Kikuyu, Chagga, Gogo, English. MAJOR RELIGIONS: animist, Protestant, Roman Catholic. MAJOR CITIES: (95e) KENYA: Nakuru 123,000, Ngong 38,000, Naivasha 36,000, Magadi 35,000, Narok 20,000. TANZANIA: Arusha 155,000, Makuyuni 25,000.

*GEOGRAPHY:* AREA: 40,391 sq.mi.-104,639 sq.km. LOCATION: Masailand is located in East Africa, a region of rolling grasslands in the highlands of the Masai Steppe and the Great Rift Valley in southern Kenya and northwestern Tanzania. POLITICAL STATUS: Masailand is a nonpolitical region forming the southern districts of the Kenyan province of Rift Valley and the Tanzanian province of Arusha.

*FLAG:* The Masai national flag, the flag of the national movement, is a red field bearing a centered white and black Masai shield over crossed white spears.

*PEOPLE:* The Masai are a tall Nilotic people, the most southerly of the Nilotes. Probably originally of Hamitic origin, the Masai speak a Paranilotic language of the Sudanic language group. A pastoral people, the Masai consider taking things from the earth as impure; however, a Masai minority has settled on permanent farms in recent decades. Most Masai still live in *manyattas*, villages fortified by walls of thorn bushes, and sustain themselves on a diet of milk and blood taken from their herds of longhorn cattle. The Masai have only recently begun to urbanize, mostly in small towns but also in the cities of Arusha, Nakuru, and Nairobi, just northeast of the Masai homeland in Kenya. The urbanized Masai live in the cities during the week, but on weekends most return to their villages in the countryside.

*THE NATION:* The creation of the world, according to Masai legend, began with God allocating the earth's resources to his various sons. The Masai claim direct descent from the son designated by God as the keeper of the world's cattle. Therefore all of the earth's cattle belong to the Masai, who inherited the right from their legendary ancestor, the son of God. For centuries the Masai warriors raided neighboring peoples to appropriate their cattle, held, in the eyes of the Masai, illegally and against God's will.

The Masai, originating far to the north, probably arrived with their herds in the area west of Mount Kilimanjaro in the mid-eighteenth century. The Masai continued to push south until checked by hostile tribes in the 1830s. Expanding across the grasslands, the Masai reached the coast south of Mombasa in 1859. Considered invincible by neighboring tribes, the Masai established their dominance over much of East Africa. At the height of their power, in the 1870s, the Masai controlled some 80,000 square miles of territory and raided as far west as Lake Victoria and east to the Indian Ocean.

Organized in a complex age-set system, young Masai trained to join the ranks of the warriors. Most of the Masai's power rested with a class of ritual rulers, sorcerer priests called Laibon, an important link between the member tribes and the loose Masai confederation. First visited by German missionaries in 1848–49, few Masai showed an interest in the new religion, which would deny their right to the world's cattle.

An epidemic of rinderpest swept the Masai herds in the 1880s, setting off wars with neighboring tribes that the Masai raided to replenish their cattle wealth. In the 1890s smallpox, inadvertently introduced by European visitors, decimated the Masai tribes, with up to 75% of the Masai population dying in the epidemic. Even during this time of troubles, the Masai maintained their domination over their huge territory.

The British, seeking to open trade routes to the kingdoms of the highland region around Lake Victoria, needed to pacify the Masai, whose territory straddled the trade routes and blocked British commerce. Weakened by the time of troubles, the Masai could not sustain a long war. Treating the Masai with caution and respect, the British authorities pacified them with diplomacy, and the fierce Masai accepted nominal British rule.

The boundaries between the British territories and German East Africa, fixed by negotiations between 1886 and 1890, included provisions for supposedly inalienable Masai land reserves in the Rift Valley, the highlands northwest of Nairobi, and the southern Masai Steppe. The European powers took direct control of the territories outside the reserves.

The British authorities in Kenya often viewed the Masai as a threat and their way of life worthless and destructive. Many officials believed that their lands must be divided into private farms and their migrations stopped. The authorities, ignoring the earlier agreements, moved the Masai into delimited grazing lands in 1911. The colonial government again reduced reserves in 1913. The reserve lands taken for European settlement became the so-called White Highlands, the heartland of the European settler community of colonial Kenya.

Their lands reduced to small, inadequate reserves, the disillusioned Masai began to reject modernization. In the 1920s Kikuyu tribesmen began to move into the Masai grazing lands to set up farms. Unable to interest the British officials in their problems, in the 1930s the Masai retreated into egocentric tribalism.

Rival tribes, particularly the numerous Kikuyu in Kenya, advanced more rapidly than the Masai and often filled administrative positions in the Masai districts. Disputes over land and water rights sparked the beginning of Masai nationalism in the 1950s. Nationalists formed the Masai United Front (MUF), a coalition of Masai organizations in both Kenya and Tanganyika. The nationalists demanded separate Masai independence as the British began the decolonization of the two territories in the late 1950s. Less educated and unfamiliar with politics, the Masai failed to sucessfully press their case for separation effectively.

Land disputes, especially in Kenya, escalated in the 1960s and 1970s. Rapid population growth put enormous pressure on the open Masai grazing lands by the settled farming tribes. The Kenyan government, determined to divide the Masai lands for food production, introduced an interim measure in 1968 in the form of group ranches. In Tanzania the socialist government appropriated and nationalized the Masai grazing lands, exacerbating the growing Masai alienation.

Younger, educated Masai moved into the leadership of the tribe in the 1980s as land pressure increased dramatically. Unsuccessful appeals to national governments to stop the encroachments of farming peoples and Somali herdsmen led to demands for the return of nationalized lands in Tanzania and the reunification of the Masai nation. Moves to introduce multiparty democracy have greatly increased ethnic and tribal rivalries in the region.

In 1991 serious ethnic violence broke out in Kenya's Rift Valley. The disputes over land and water rights in the region spread across the Masai districts in 1992–93. In 1994 the violence extended into the highlands above Nairobi, with violent confrontations between Masai and the Kikuyu living in Nakuru illegally. The Masai have increasingly turned to nationalism as the tribal and ethnic conflicts proliferate, seeking a united independent Masailand free of Kenya's tribal violence and Tanzania's economic woes.

*SELECTED BIBLIOGRAPHY:*
Amin, Mohamed, and Duncan Willetts. *Last of the Masai.* 1990.
Arnhem, Kaj. *The Masai and the State.* 1986.
Bechwith, Carol. *Masai.* 1990.
Bentsen, Cheryl. *Masai Days.* 1991.

# MATABELELAND

**Zambezia**

*CAPITAL: Bulawayo*

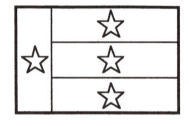

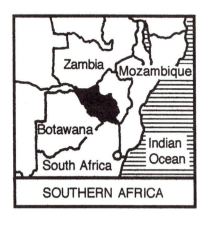

SOUTHERN AFRICA

MATABELELAND

*POPULATION:* (95e) 3,159,000 : 2,398,000 Ndebele in Zimbabwe. MAJOR NATIONAL GROUPS: (95e) Ndebele (Matabele) 81%, Kalanga 6%, European 2%, other Zimbabwean. MAJOR LANGUAGES: siNdebele, English, siKalanga. MAJOR RELIGIONS: Protestant, Roman Catholic, animist. MAJOR CITIES: (95e) Bulawayo 464,000 (1,078,000), Gweru 172,000, Hwange 78,000, Zvishavane 55,000, Shurugwi 35,000, Matapos 20,000.

*GEOGRAPHY:* AREA: 58,214 sq.mi.-150,813 sq.km. LOCATION: Matabeleland occupies the part of the southern African plains between the Zambezi and Limpopo Rivers in southwestern Zimbabwe, a region of rolling farm and grazing lands rising to the Matapos Hills near Bulawayo. POLITICAL STATUS: Matabeleland forms the Zimbabwean provinces of Matabeleland North and South and the Gweru district of Midlands Province.

*FLAG:* The Ndebele national flag, the flag of the former Zimbabwe African People's Union (ZAPU), is a horizontal tricolor of black, red, and green, each stripe charged with a centered, five-pointed star respectively red, green, and yellow, and with a broad yellow, vertical stripe at the hoist charged with a black, five-pointed star.

*PEOPLE:* The Ndebele, also Matabele, are a Nguni people related to the Zulu of KwaZulu-Natal* in South Africa. The descendants of nineteenth-century Zulu migrants and the area's original Bantu peoples, the Ndebele speak a Nguni language of the Bantu language group. Minorities in Matabeleland include the Kalanga, allied to the Ndebele for decades, and Europeans, descendants of the colonists who dominate the region's farming and commerce. The majority of the Ndebele are farmers and herders, with a large urbanized minority. Most Ndebele adhere to the various Christian sects, with traditional beliefs still followed in the more remote rural regions.

*THE NATION:* The formation of the Ndebele as a nation began with Mzilikazi, a Zulu military leader under the Zulu king, Chaka. In 1823 Mzilikazi gathered a large following as disputes erupted among Zulu factions. In 1827 he and his followers fled over the Drakensburg Mountains into the upland plains of Transvaal. Reinforced by other Zulu deserters, the tribe coalesced into a formidable power, raiding as far south as the Orange River, destroying or absorbing conquered tribes. Under attacks by Boers moving north from the Cape of Good Hope and by resurgent Zulus, the Ndebele moved north of the Limpopo River in 1837.

The highly sophisticated Ndebele military formations easily conquered the more numerous, pastoral Shona people. The conquerors established a large, highly centralized kingdom. The Ndebele ruled as the kingdom's pastoral aristocracy, with the more numerous Shona reduced to a serflike condition. The conquest of the Shona created an ethnic enmity that continues to color the relations between the two peoples to the present.

Courted by both the British and the Boers of the Transvaal, Lobengula, a descendant of Mzilikazi, finally signed a treaty with the British in 1880. The treaty gave Cecil Rhodes and the British South Africa Company exclusive rights over all minerals in Matabeleland in return for one hundred pounds a month, a thousand modern rifles, and a steamboat on the Zambezi River. Assured that no more than ten European miners would enter Ndebele territory, Lobengula was dismayed to learn that a column of 600 Europeans had crossed the frontier.

The British column constructed Fort Salisbury, present Harare, in the center of the lands of the subject Shona, the British presence effectively ending Ndebele domination in 1889. Rhodes' British South Africa Company offered 3,000-acre farms to lure European colonists, who boldly seized lands and cattle from the Ndebele and their former Shona serfs.

Lobengula vainly attempted to avoid armed conflict, but unscrupulous Europeans, believing that the kingdom contained massive gold deposits, provoked war in July 1893. The Ndebele warriors, joined by the Shona, attacked fortified British positions, only to be mowed down by the first machine gun ever used in battle. By November 1893, the famous Ndebele *impis*, military regiments, had mostly surrendered to the Europeans. In January 1894 the British troops occupied the Ndebele capital at Bulawayo.

Lobengula, a victim of naked European aggression, died in late January 1894, a hunted exile in the mountains. Following Lobengula's death, the kingdom collapsed, and the British took complete control of the region, offering parcels of confiscated land to European settlers. Ndebele nobles, artists, and warriors were reduced to selling their ostrich-feather headgear to curious Europeans on the streets of Bulawayo.

In 1923 the British authorities dissolved Matabeleland's separate colonial government and joined the province to Shonaland to form the colony of Southern Rhodesia. Increasingly restrictive race laws and resentment of European privilege erupted in a general strike and violence in 1948, the first violence in Bulawayo since 1896.

Joshua Nkomo, a young trade unionist, formed the first nationalist organization in Matabeleland in 1957. Nkomo's nationalists joined the Shona-dominated Zimbabwe African National Union (ZANU). Differences among the Ndebele and Shona leaders led to the Ndebele withdrawal from ZANU and the formation of the rival Zimbabwe African People's Union (ZAPU) as the focus of Ndebele nationalism in 1963.

Both nationalist groups established bases in neighboring states and launched attacks on white-ruled Rhodesia, unilaterally declared an independent republic in 1965. The long and vicious guerrilla war came to a negotiated end in 1980, and white Rhodesia became the new African state of Zimbabwe.

The new Zimbabwe government, dominated by the larger Shona tribe, rapidly alienated the Ndebele minority. The Ndebele claimed that they had sacrificed too much for Zimbabwe's independence only to fall under the rule of their former Shona serfs. Overriding Ndebele nationalist protests, Joshua Nkomo opted for peaceful unification and merged ZAPU into the Shona-dominated ZANU.

In 1981, amid rising tensions between the two peoples, Ndebele national leaders demanded autonomy for Matabeleland. The Zimbabwe government rejected autonomy as fighting broke out in Matabeleland between nationalists and Shona military units. Deserting Ndebele soldiers formed guerrilla groups as the fighting spread. In 1982 the Shona-dominated government accused the Ndebele of separatism and dismissed Nkomo and other Ndebele government officials. As Matabeleland moved toward secession, elite Shona battalions, trained in North Korea, unleashed a terror campaign against the Ndebele. Over 10,000 died before serious negotiations began in an effort to avert all-out civil war in 1988.

Talks between tribal leaders to end the violence stalled over the Shona leadership's insistence on a one-party state, just as many African states began to move toward multiparty democracy. In 1991 the Zimbabwe government, beset by growing unrest and economic problems, finally introduced a multiparty system and renounced its former socialist economics. The moves temporarily eased tensions, but in December 1993 many Ndebele leaders, including the governor of North Matabeleland, charged the increasingly authoritarian Zimbabwean government with ethnic discrimination and the unfair division of development funds amid an upsurge of Ndebele national sentiment.

*SELECTED BIBLIOGRAPHY:*

Astrow, Andre. *Zimbabwe: A Revolution That Lost Its Way?* 1983.
Herbst, Jeffrey. *State Politics in Zimbabwe.* 1990.
Weiss, Ruth. *Zimbabwe and the New Elite.* 1994.
Williams, R. H. *Matabeleland Problem: Confrontation in Zimbabwe.* 1983.

# MEGHALAYA

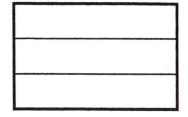

*CAPITAL: Yeddo (Shillong)*

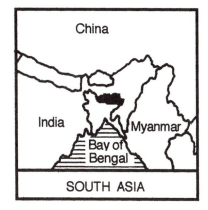

*POPULATION:* (95e) 1,779,000 : 1,490,000 Meghalayans in India (505,000 Khasi, 380,000 Jaintia Bodo, 375,000 Gharo, 80,000 Koch, 75,000 Rabna, smaller groups). MAJOR NATIONAL GROUPS: (95e) Meghalayan 87% (Khasi 28%, Jaintia [Bodo] 21%, Gharo 21%, Koch 4.5%, Rabna 4%, smaller groups), other Indian. MAJOR LANGUAGES: Khasi, Bodo, Gharo, English. MAJOR RELIGIONS: (95e) Christian 48%, animist 32%, Sunni Islam 10%, Hindu 10%. MAJOR CITIES: (95e) Yeddo (Shillong) 147,000 (258,000), Tura 58,000, Nongstoin 27,000, Jowai 24,000.

*GEOGRAPHY:* AREA: 8,706 sq.mi.-22,554 sq.km. LOCATION: Meghalaya lies in northeastern India, occupying a mountainous region south of the Assam Plain. Meghalaya's three geographical areas correspond to the major ethnic groups: the Gharo Hills in the west, the Khasi Hills in the center, and the Jaintia Hills in the east. Meghalaya borders Bangladesh on the west and south and the Indian state of Assam* on the north and east. POLITICAL STATUS: Meghalaya forms a state of the Republic of India.

*FLAG:* The Meghalayan flag, the flag of the national movement, is a horizontal tricolor of red, pale blue, and yellow.

*PEOPLE:* The Meghalayans are closely related, matriarchal tribal peoples comprising the Khasi, speaking a Mon-Khmer language and practicing a traditional religion called Seng Khasi, and the Gharo, Jaintia Bodo, Koch, Rabna, and smaller groups, who speak Bodo-Gharo languages of the Tibeto-Burman languages and are mostly Christian, mainly Baptist. Centuries of contact and intermingling have somewhat blurred tribal differences. The Bodo-Gharo peoples have mostly converted to Christianity, but the Khasi have retained their own animist religion, which teaches that God is everywhere and should not be represented in any special form or worshiped in special buildings.

*THE NATION:* The Meghalayan peoples, thought to have inhabited a much larger area in ancient times, retreated to the mountains to escape successive waves of invaders in the lowland plains. Protected in mountain strongholds, the Meghalayans developed elaborate and unique cultures and ways of living. In the western hills, the Gharo lived in numerous autonomous towns and villages. In the central and eastern hills, the Khasi and Jaintia evolved a system of small, independent states.

The tribal peoples, although at times tributary to various Indian empires, retained their independence during the period of state consolidation in northern India. Assamese kings asserted some influence in the hill states in the twelfth century. The Assamese hegemony was later challenged by Tibetans, Burmans, and Bengalis. In the late eighteenth century European missionaries braved headhunters and disease to bring their message to the tribes of the isolated hill tracts.

Overrun by invading Burmans in 1822, the region came under British rule following the first Anglo-Burman war in 1826. The hill tribes, under the nominal rule of the British government of Assam, retained considerable self-rule, with only occasional British incursions to settle disputes or to subdue periodic rebellions. The British effectively blocked immigration into the more abundant hill lands of the tribal peoples by the Bengalis of the overcrowded lowlands to the south.

Christian missionaries returned to the hill tracts in the early twentieth century, and many tribal people adopted the new religion to avoid absorption into India's rigid caste system, which relegates tribal peoples to the despised lower castes. Younger tribal leaders, educated in mission schools and better able to protect the interests of the tribes, moved into the tribal leadership positions in the 1930s and 1940s.

On the eve of Indian independence, in 1947, Khasi and Gharo leaders began a campaign for the separation of the hill tracts from Hindu-dominated Assam and the creation of a new tribal state in the region. Ignored in the chaos of partition and independence, a small part of the hill tracts became Pakistani territory while India retained control of the remainder as part of the state of Assam.

Conflicts and violence between the Hindu Assamese and the tribal peoples increased during the 1950s. Leaders of the five major tribes formed the Assam Hill Tribal Union (AHTU) to press for autonomy and separation from Assam. In 1960 the tribal leaders formed a coalition of nationalist and cultural groups in the All-Party Hill Leaders Conference and demanded the self-government and unification of the non-Indian regions of southwestern Assam. In late 1963 thousands of their kinsmen, fleeing Pakistani troops, crossed the Indian border and were allowed to stay. The Indian government, aware of the propaganda value, announced that the mostly Christian tribesmen preferred secular India to Muslim Pakistan.

The Indian government hoped that autonomy would preempt the increasing calls for armed rebellion. In 1969 the Indian government issued a decree that created an autonomous state within Assam called Meghalaya, the Abode of the Clouds. In 1972, following renewed demonstrations and pressure from tribal leaders, the government finally separated Meghalaya from Assam and made the tribal region a full state of the Indian union.

The new state government in 1974 demanded greater autonomous powers and restrictions on immigration of the lowland peoples to the tribal homeland. Tribal fears that they would be swamped by lowland immigrants incited a rapid expansion of nationalist sentiment in the 1980s. In 1986 over ten thousand illegals fled the state during nationalist demonstrations and anti-immigrant violence. In 1987 the Indian government restricted nontribals from running for office in the state but stopped short of meeting nationalist demands for a ban on settlement from outside the state.

A rebellion by the Bodo in neighboring districts of Assam in 1989 dramatically increased anti-Indian nationalism in Meghalaya. Ethnic violence in Assam left over 500 dead and thousands of refugees, most sheltering with their ethnic kin in Meghalaya.

The rise of Hindu militancy in the early 1990s further alarmed the tribal leaders and brought renewed demands for protection of their small nation. In October 1991, after serious nationalist disturbances, the Indian government suspended the state government and placed the state under direct president's rule from New Delhi. Meghalaya, with one of India's highest literacy rates, the result of over 200 years of missionary activity, has produced an articulate leadership determined to protect their small nation, even at the expense of India's national unity.

*SELECTED BIBLIOGRAPHY:*

Barth, A. *Religions in India.* 1990.

Karotempral, S., ed. *The Tribes of Northeast India.* 1984.

Singh, R. Suresh. *The Tribal Situation in India.* 1986.

Vajpeyi, Dhirendra, and Malik Yogenda, eds. *Religious and Ethnic Minorities in South Asia.* 1990.

# MEITHEI LAIPAK

**Manipur; Kuneipak**

*CAPITAL: Imphal*

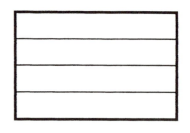

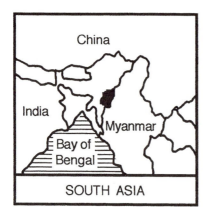

*POPULATION:* (95e) 1,938,000 : 1,250,000 Meithei (Manipuri) in India. MAJOR NATIONAL GROUPS: (95e) Meithei (Manipuri) 64%, tribal peoples (Kuki, Naga, Chin, Bodo) 31%, other Indian. MAJOR LANGUAGES: Meithei (Manipuri), Kuki-Chin, Naga, Bodo, English. MAJOR RELIGIONS: (95e) Hindu (Vishnaism) 67%, Christian 27%, animist, Sunni Muslim. MAJOR CITIES: (95e) Imphal 181,000, Bishenpur 42,000, Kangpokpi 25,000.

*GEOGRAPHY:* AREA: 8,628 sq.mi.-22,352 sq.km. LOCATION: Meithei Laipak occupies a huge valley 2,600 feet above sea level and surrounded by high mountains in northeastern India, bordering Nagaland* on the north, Assam* on the east, and Mizoram* on the south. POLITICAL STATUS: Meithei Laipak forms the state of Manipur in the Republic of India.

*FLAG:* The Meithei national flag, the flag of the national movement, has four equal, horizontal stripes of yellow, pale blue, red, and green. OTHER FLAG(S): The traditional Meithei flag is a red field bearing an elaborately coiled serpent, the Mani.

*PEOPLE:* The Meithei are of mixed background, descended from the valley's early tribal inhabitants and the later Kassey, a Thai people. The Meithei speak a language related to the Kuki-Chin languages of the state's tribal peoples, but with a considerable Aryan admixture. The dominant religion in the region is a form of Hinduism called Vishnaism, incorporating many pre-Hindu beliefs and practices. Nearly a third of the population, mostly in the hills and mountains around the valley, is made up of twenty-nine Christian and animist tribal groups, some assimilating into the Meithei culture. The state, in spite of its relative isolation, boasts one of India's highest literacy rates.

*THE NATION:* An enormous valley in the hills, the remains of a prehistoric lake, developed as the center of an early Hindu state with a highly sophisticated civilization. The valley culture incorporated influences from the original tribal peoples and the Aryans who reached the region during the Aryan invasions of northern India between 1500 and 1200 B.C. Named for the Mani of Ananta, the ancient serpent god of the valley, Manipur evolved into a powerful regional state, often controlling areas beyond the central valley.

The state, under the nominal rule of Tibet* from the eighth to the twelfth centuries A.D., fell to a Thai people, the Kassey or Moy, in the thirteenth century. The conquerors gradually adopted the language and culture of the valley. By the sixteenth century the Kassey had ceased to be culturally Thai and eventually were fully absorbed by the Meithei.

Manipur's power increased during a series of wars with neighboring Muslim and Buddhist peoples in the sixteenth century. The state expanded to control a large area of the surrounding hill districts. A Meithei army, led by Raja Gharib Newaz, the greatest of the Meithei national heroes, devastated Upper Burma, the homeland of their ancient Burman enemies, between 1715 and 1749. The resurgent Burmans, in turn, invaded Manipur in 1758, forcing the raja to seek British protection. In 1762 the raja signed a protectorate agreement and, with British aid, repulsed renewed Burman attacks in 1764 and 1822.

The British authorities added Manipur to British India and began to settle Christian Kubai Nagas in the valley to work in the lucrative citrus groves. The privileged position of the Christian minority incited Meithei resentment and mistreatment of the Christians and other tribals, the persecution of the tribals provoking sporadic rebellions.

The numerous Kuki tribesmen in the hill districts revolted in March 1891 and drove the British authorities from the state. The British flight prompted the Meithei to join the rebellion. In late April the reinforced British forces returned to execute the rebel leaders and to install a new raja under strict British supervision. The authorities placed the state under the administration of the British colonial government of Assam.

European missionaries introduced Christianity and Western education in the early twentieth century. The mission campaign, most successful among the pagan hill tribes, allowed all of the population to gain from mission education. A Meithei leadership, educated in the Christian schools, led a strong campaign for separate status as India moved toward independence after World War II.

The British, concerned that India, already partitioned into two states, might splinter, pressured the Meithei leaders to reach an accommodation with the new Indian government. On 15 August 1947, the day India gained its independence, the Manipuri government signed an interim agreement providing for Indian responsibility for the state's defense and foreign relations. Faced with large anti-Indian demonstrations and demands for full independence, the Indian government dispatched troops to dissolve the state administration on 15 October 1949. The government imposed direct rule from New Delhi and downgraded the state's status to that of a union territory.

Tanghul and Kubai Nagas, who had begun to assimilate into Meithei culture, launched a campaign to join northern Manipur to the newly created Nagaland state in 1963. The Naga revolt provoked a Meithei nationalist backlash. Mobilized against the Naga separatists, the campaign became openly nationalist, with Meithei and Kuki leaders demanding independence for a new country to be called Meithei Laipak. A violent secessionist war spread across Manipur in 1965. In a futile effort to undermine the nationalist movement, the Indian government granted statehood in 1972.

In the 1970s the growing numbers of Bengali and Nepalese immigrants entering the state became an explosive issue that provoked nationalist demands for their expulsion. Anti-immigrant violence in the state increased when several of the Kuki and Naga groups joined the Meithei separatists in attacks on the illegal migrants. In 1981 the Indian government suspended the state government and imposed direct rule from New Delhi. Four years later the authorities declared Manipur a disturbed area, allowing the Indian military broad powers to combat the separatist bands. In 1990 government troops launched a military campaign called Operation Bluebird in an effort to end the Meithei rebellion.

The Indian anti-insurgency methods, including mass arrests, torture, rape, and executions, alienated many moderates in the state, some joining the renewed rebellion in 1991. The violence in the once-peaceful valley, in the 1990s, has involved all of the population groups, either fighting the Indian military or fighting among themselves, raising fears that the separatist war could end with the partition of the ancient state among its various national groups.

Increasing violence between the northern Naga tribes, who seek to unite with a projected independent Nagaland, and the Kuki tribes who dispute their control of the districts, has overshadowed the Meithei nationalist activities. Naga attacks on Kuki villages, in an effort to drive the Kukis from the disputed districts have escalated since early 1994 and has forced the Kuki to reinforce their ties to the Meithei nationalist organizations. The violence has polarized the opposing nationalist forces and has converted Manipur to one of the least stable areas in India's turbulent northeastern region.

*SELECTED BIBLIOGRAPHY:*
Chanra, B. *Nationalism and Colonialism in Modern India.* 1979.
Hodson, T. C. *The Meitheis.* 1975.
Karotempral, S., ed. *The Tribes of Northeast India.* 1984.

# MESKHTEKISTAN

**Meskhtekia**

*CAPITAL: Akhaltsikhe*

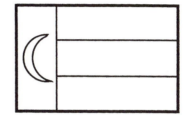

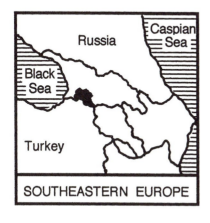

SOUTHEASTERN EUROPE

MESKHTEKISTAN

*POPULATION:* (95e) 335,000 : 265,000 Meskhtekians in Georgia and the former Soviet Union. MAJOR NATIONAL GROUPS: (95e) Georgian 83%, Ajar 10%, Meskhtekian 4%, Russian 1%. MAJOR LANGUAGES: Georgian, Russian, Meskhtekian. MAJOR RELIGIONS: Georgian Orthodox, Shia Muslim, Sunni Muslim, Russian Orthodox. MAJOR CITIES: (95e) Akhaltsikhe 33,000, Borzomi 22,000, Chulo 13,000.

*GEOGRAPHY:* AREA: 1,724 sq.mi.-4,465 sq.km. LOCATION: Meskhtekistan lies in southern Georgia, occupying a highland region in the Meskhtekian Range, including a part of the autonomous republic of Ajaristan,* just north of the Turkish border. POLITICAL STATUS: Meskhtekistan has no official status, the region claimed by nationalists forms several districts of the Republic of Georgia.

*FLAG:* The Meskhtekian national flag, the flag of the national movement, is a horizontal tricolor of white, red, and black bearing a vertical green stripe at the hoist charged with a white crescent moon.

*PEOPLE:* The Meskhtekians, one of the world's newest nations, are the remnants and descendants of various Muslim peoples deported from the Turkish border region of Georgia in 1944. Taking the collective name Meskhtekian, the small nation includes Georgian Muslims called Meskhi, Armenian Muslims called Khemsil, Shia Muslim Ajars, Kurds, and Karapapakh Turks. United by hardships, common experiences, and their Shia Muslim religion, the diverse peoples formed a separate nation in exile, including the development of a national language, a hybrid dialect combining the Laz dialect of Georgian and admixtures from several Turkish languages. Although a Shia Muslim nation, a minority adheres to the Sunni branch of Islam.

*THE NATION:* Known to the ancient Greeks who founded a number of cities on the coastal lowlands, the mountains east of the Black Sea have always been a refuge for peoples fleeing wars and invasions. In the early Christian Era the mountains came under nominal Roman rule and later formed part of the Georgian kingdom in the early ninth century and the Kingdom of Armenia from 846 to 1046.

The Turkish Ottoman Empire conquered the area in the fifteenth century and established the capital of Turkish Armenia at Akhaltsikhe in 1579, the chief town of a Turkish pashalik and a center of the Caucasian slave trade. By the seventeenth century the region's inhabitants, mostly ethnic Georgian and Armenian Christians, had converted to Islam and had adopted some elements of Turkish culture.

The Ottoman Turks ceded the region to the expanding Russian Empire in 1829, beginning decades of Russian efforts to force the small Muslim peoples of the Meskhtekian Range to revert to their earlier Christian religion. In spite of the common oppressor, the small groups remained separate, uniting only when threatened by Christian violence or attacks by the majority Sunni Muslim population. In 1905 serious unrest broke out among the Muslim peoples of the region. The Russians' brutal methods in crushing the disturbances reinforced the pro-Turkish sentiment shared by the diverse groups.

Their homeland formed part of the front line when war began in 1914. As the war dragged on, the Muslims suffered increasing persecution for their pro-Turkish sentiments. Briefly occupied by Turkish troops after the Russian Revolution in 1917, the Muslims again became the brunt of anti-Turkish Georgian nationalism when the region became part of the new Georgian republic in 1918.

Soviet rule, established in 1921, was especially harsh for the suspect Muslim peoples. During World War II, Turkey remained neutral, but Stalin still regarded Russia's ancient adversary as an enemy state. In 1943 and 1944 Stalin accused many of the small Muslim nations of the Caucasus of treason during the German invasion of the region in 1942. A number of the nations suffered brutal deportations to the wastes of Central Asia and Siberia.* Unknown to the West, the small Muslim peoples of the Meskhtekian highlands, far south of the German advance, also suffered deportation, probably for their strong anti-Soviet and pro-Turkish sentiments.

In 1944 over 130,000 Meskhtekian Muslims were driven from their homes and herded onto railcars. Many of the deportees died of hunger, thirst, and cold on the long journey east. Their Soviet guards dumped them at rail sidings across a vast region, often without food, water, or shelter. Meskhtekian soldiers fighting with the Red Army, over 4,000, began to return to their homes in the Meskhtekian hills in 1945, only to face arrest and deportation. The Meskhtekians claim that 50,000 of their people died as a direct result of the deportations and the deprivations suffered in exile.

The Meskhtekians, not included in the rehabilitation of the deported peoples in 1956, were forgotten in the Soviet Union and unknown in the West. The scattered groups began to establish contact in the early 1960s, and to coordinate petitions, appeals, and agitation for the right to return to their homes. Delegates from the dispersed Meskhtekian groups attended a congress in Tashkent, Uzbekistan, in 1964. The congress voted to form the Meskhtekian National Movement (MNM) and to send representatives to Moscow and Tbilisi to plead their case for the right to return to their homes.

Officially rehabilitated and restored to full rights as Soviet citizens in 1968, the Meskhtekians stepped up their campaign to win the right to return to their homeland. Their shared hardships and the long, bitter exile shaped a new nation from the diverse peoples. A lingua franca used for intergroup communication developed as a viable national language. Details of the Meskhtekian deportation began to leak out to the West in 1969, bringing some international support, particularly among Western human rights groups.

Released from KGB control in 1968, many Meskhtekians moved from their scattered settlements to the Fergana Valley in Uzbekistan, the site of the largest Meskhtekian exile community. The growing prosperity of the energetic exiles, who advanced more rapidly than their Uzbek neighbors, raised ethnic and religious tensions, which worsened with the Soviet liberalization of the late 1980s.

An Uzbek nationalist demonstration in June 1989 turned into a pogrom as the Sunni Muslim demonstrators turned on the Shia Muslim Meskhtekians. Enraged Uzbeks hunted the terrified exiles through a week of violence, rape, and murder. Over a hundred Meskhtekians died, and over 500 suffered wounds before the Soviet military evacuated them to guarded camps outside the Uzbek cities. Told they would be returned to their Georgian homeland within two weeks, the majority of the refugees still languish in the camps. Considered foreigners in newly independent Uzbekistan, now unwanted foreigners, they can obtain neither work nor housing.

The government of Georgia, also independent following the Soviet disintegration of 1991, under a radical Christian and nationalist administration refused to discuss the return of a troublesome Muslim minority. A more moderate Georgian government, installed in January 1992, has received Meskhtekian delegations but, beset by problems on every side, has not allowed the Meskhtekians to return home from their long exile.

*SELECTED BIBLIOGRAPHY:*
Adams, Arthur E. *Stalin and His Times.* 1986.
Allen, W. E. *A History of the Georgian People.* 1978.
Boyette, William. *Soviet Georgia.* 1988.

# MIZORAM

**Lushailand**

*CAPITAL: Aizawl*

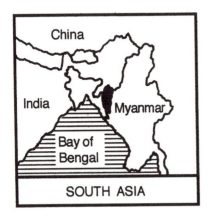

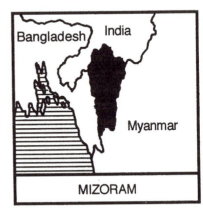

*POPULATION:* (95e) 721,000 : 950,000 Mizo in India. MAJOR NATIONAL GROUPS: (95e) Mizo (Lushai) 85%, other Indian. MAJOR LANGUAGES: Mizo, Assamese, Bengali, Lakheri, English. MAJOR RELIGIONS: (95e) Christian 86%, Hindu, Sunni Muslim. MAJOR CITIES: (95e) Aizawl 191,000, Kolosib 36,000, Lungleh 22,000.

*GEOGRAPHY:* AREA: 8,142 sq.mi.-21,093 sq.km. LOCATION: Mizoram occupies a rugged, mountainous region, formerly called the Lushai Hills, in northeastern India, bordering the Indian states of Assam* and Manipur (Meithei Laipak*) on the north, Tripura* on the northwest, the Zoram* region of Myanmar on the east, and the Kaderia* region of Bangladesh on the west. POLITICAL STATUS: Mizoram forms a state of the Republic of India.

*INDEPENDENCE DECLARED:* 6 July 1966.

*FLAG:* The Mizo national flag, the flag of the national movement, is a blue field charged with a red cross, offset toward the hoist and outlined in white.

*PEOPLE:* The Mizo, called Lushai by the Indians, are a tribal people speaking a Kuki-Chin language of the Tibeto-Burman language group. The descendants of early tribes pushed into the less accessible hills by successive invasions of the lowlands, the Mizo are closely related to the neighboring tribal peoples, the Chin (Zomi) people of Myanmar and the Kuki people of Manipur. The Mizo, divided into forty-nine subtribes, are mostly Christian and have a literacy rate of 46%, one of the highest in India, a result of early Christian missionary activity. The majority of the Mizo are Christian, mostly Baptist.

*THE NATION:* The origins of the Mizo can be traced to eastern Tibet.* Following the rivers south, the migrating tribes arrived in their present area in the eighth century A.D. Driven into the jungled hills by invasions of the lowlands, the Mizo divided into a number of small tribal states. The states, nominally under the rule of successive empires, absorbed cultural traits from the lowland Indian peoples and the region's many conquerors.

The Hindu Assamese of the Brahmaputra River valley to the north extended their influence into the hill tracts. The Assamese left the tribal peoples to their traditional way of life and ruled through the local chiefs. The Mizo retained their language, religion, and traditions, including head-hunting, an integral part of Mizo culture.

Burman invaders from the east conquered Assam in 1822, provoking war with the British. The defeated Burmans ceded Assam and the hill tracts, including the Mizo Hills, to British India in 1826. The new authorities attempted to stamp out head-hunting but, like the former Assamese rulers, generally left the Mizo to govern themselves. British troops entered the hills only to put down occasional revolts and to settle disputes.

European missionaries established stations in the Lushai Hills in the 1840s, converting a majority of the pagan Mizo and introducing modern education through their mission schools. Even though the leaders became nominally Christian, the Mizo warriors continued to raid neighboring peoples, and sporadic revolts plagued the British administration. The Christian leadership led a widespread revolt in 1891. The rebels drove the British soldiers from the hills but left the mission stations in peace. A British expedition reconquered the Lushai Hills in 1895, the soldiers surprised to find the missionaries safe and protected by Mizo warriors. The conversion of the Mizo majority to Christianity raised yet another barrier between the Mizo and India's Hindu majority.

After World War II, the British prepared to leave India. The Mizo acknowledged a tacit agreement that they formed a part of the British Empire but denied their inclusion in British India. The Mizo, loyal British allies during the war, petitioned the authorities for separate independence. The Mizo adamantly rejected inclusion in Hindu-dominated India or Muslim Pakistan. Ignored in the rush to independence, the Lushai Hills legally remained part of Assam at Indian independence in 1947. The Mizo rose as the British prepared to withdraw, determined to resist the imposition of Indian rule. With British military assistance, the Indians subdued the Mizo, and a large Indian contingent of troops and police remained in the region called the Lushai Hills.

Large numbers of Hindu refugees from neighboring East Pakistan settled in the region between the 1947 partition of British India and 1950. Religious conflicts between the Christian Mizo and the refugee Hindus exacerbated the Mizo's refusal to acknowledge Indian authority. Nationalists formed the Mizo National Front (MNF) in 1954 to work for autonomy and restrictions on immigrants to their territory. Famine, largely ignored by the Indian government, killed several hundred Mizo in 1959. The government's poor response fueled the growth of the Mizo's anti-Indian sentiment.

The Mizo leadership, tiring of futile efforts to win autonomy, called for secession and the creation of an independent Mizo state in 1965. Open rebellion broke out in 1966, with nationalist guerrillas skirmishing with Indian troops stationed on the sensitive Pakistani and Burmese borders. Rebel leaders declared the independence of Mizoram on 6 July 1966. Indian troops occupied key points in the district and drove the rebels into the jungled hills. Armed by Pakistan and China, the rebels launched a secessionist war from their mountain hideouts.

The Indian government belatedly made concessions. In 1972 the authorities separated the Lushai Hills from Assam and created a separate union territory of Mizoram. In 1976 the Mizo accepted an offer of autonomy but resumed the rebellion when a cease-fire broke down in 1979. In 1986, after two decades of insurgency, the rebel leader, Laldenga, opened negotiations with the Indian government. Under a new agreement Mizoram became a full state of the Indian union, with Laldenga its first chief minister.

The accommodation with the Indian government split the nationalist movement. More militant nationalists continued to demand independence for a "Greater Mizoram," including the Mizo-populated districts of the neighboring Indian states. Factional disputes and violence provoked a government response. In September 1988 the government dissolved the Mizoram state administration and imposed direct rule from New Delhi.

The dramatic growth of Hindu militancy, accompanied by the miltants' demands that the Indian government end its policy of coddling ethnic and religious minorities, alarmed even the most moderate Mizo leaders in the 1980s and 1990s. The new threat forced the Mizo to put aside their factional disputes and to cooperate more closely in their fight for an autonomous future for their small nation.

*SELECTED BIBLIOGRAPHY:*

Chanra, B. *Nationalism and Colonialism in Modern India.* 1979.

Karotempral, S., ed. *The Tribes of Northeast India.* 1984.

Singh, R. Suresh. *The Tribal Situation in India.* 1986.

Vajpeyi, Dhirendra, and Malik K. Yogenda, eds. *Religious and Ethnic Minority Policies in South Asia.* 1990.

# MONTENEGRO

### Crna Gora

*CAPITAL: Podgorica*

SOUTH-CENTRAL EUROPE

MONTENEGRO

*POPULATION:* (95e) 645,000 : 580,000 Montenegrins in Yugoslavia. MAJOR NATIONAL GROUPS: (95e) Montenegrin 69%, Muslim 13%, Albanian 7%, Serb 3%, other Yugoslav. MAJOR LANGUAGE: Serbian (Montenegrin dialect). MAJOR RELIGIONS: Montenegrin Orthodox, Serbian Orthodox, Sunni Muslim, Roman Catholic. MAJOR CITIES: (95e) Podgorica 90,000 (140,000), Niksic 36,000, Kotor 20,000, Ulcinj 18,000, Cetinje 13,000.

*GEOGRAPHY:* AREA: 5,332 sq.mi.-13,813 sq.km. LOCATION: Montenegro, called Black Mountain, Crna Gora in Serbian, occupies a rugged, mountainous region of the Balkan Peninsula with high, fertile valleys and a short coastline on the Adriatic Sea. POLITICAL STATUS: Montenegro forms a constituent republic of the Federal Republic of Yugoslavia.

*INDEPENDENCE DECLARED:* 13 July 1941.

*FLAG:* The Montenegrin national flag, the official flag of the republic, is a horizontal tricolor of red, blue, and white. OTHER FLAG(S): The flag of the nationalist movement, the former royal flag, is a red field with a narrow white border bearing a centered white cross charged with the Cyrillic letters *HI*.

*PEOPLE:* The Montenegrins are a South Slav people originally of Serb origin, but with a separate history since the fourteenth century. A clannish, warlike people, the Montenegrins developed a distinct culture and dialect in the isolation of their mountain homeland. Like the Serbs, the Montenegrins are Orthodox Christians. The Montenegrins speak a dialect of the Serbian branch of the Serbo-Croatian language that, like Serbian, is written in the Cyrillic alphabet. The Montenegrins are mostly Orthodox. In 1993 their Montenegrin Orthodox

Church, closely tied to their culture and history, separated from the Serbian Orthodox Church.

*THE NATION:* The highland region formed part of the Roman Empire, and, later, the Byzantine Empire before its occupation by Slavic tribes in the seventh and eighth centuries. Called Black Mountain by the Venetians, who controlled the coast on the Adriatic Sea, the highland tribes formed a small state in the mountains. In the twelfth century the region came under the rule of the expanding Serbian state. Known as the Zeta principality, Montenegro formed part of the medieval Serbian Empire in the early fourteenth century.

The Serbian Empire collapsed in 1355, leaving Zeta effectively independent. The expanding Ottoman Turks, taking advantage of the region's turmoil, extended their frontiers to the north. In 1389, at the Battle of Kossovo, the Turks defeated a combined Christian force that paved the way for over five centuries of Turkish domination of the southern Balkan Peninsula, except for tiny Montenegro, whose warriors defeated Turkish attempts to conquer the state and maintained a precarious independence in their high mountains.

The prince-bishop of Cetinje in 1515 became the ruler of the small state, his office combining both the secular and religious leadership of the Montenegrins. The hereditary titles traditionally passed from uncle to nephew within the Petrovich dynasty established in the sixteenth century. In 1702–3, under Prince-Bishop Danilo I, the Montenegrins massacred their countrymen who had adopted the Turk's Islamic religion, the "Montenegrin Vespers."

Threatened by a renewed Turkish advance, Danilo requested Russian aid in 1715. His tiny state became a traditional Russian ally in the Balkans, and, with Russian assistance, the Montenegrins defeated a Turkish invasion in 1796. Three years later the Ottoman Turks finally recognized the independence of Montenegro. The reigning prince-bishop made an annual pilgrimage to St. Petersburg to reaffirm the indispensable Russian alliance.

The tiny state, allied to resurgent Serbia, expanded with the addition of territories taken from the decaying Ottoman Empire between 1878 and 1913. In 1914 the Montenegrins joined the Serbs in their conflict with Austria, the conflict that spread to become World War I.

The Austrian occupation of Montenegro in 1915 strengthened the faction that favored the creation of a united South Slav state in the Balkan Peninsula. In 1917 Montenegrin delegates signed the Pact of Corfu, agreeing to merge the small kingdom into a South Slav federation at the end of the war, the pact vehemently opposed by the king and some clans. South Slav nationalists triumphed following the surrender of the Central Powers in November 1918. On 2 December 1918 the pan-Slav nationalists deposed the Petrovich dynasty and joined Montenegro to the new Kingdom of the Serbs, Croats, and Slovenes.

The surrender of Montenegrin sovereignty divided the clans, the crisis worsened by the takeover of their cherished autonomous church by the Serbian Orthodox hierarchy in 1920. A rebellion of the clans dissatisfied with the status of the former kingdom, little better than that of a Serb province, kept the area in turmoil until their defeat in 1921. The same year King Nicolas, who had done so much to modernize Montenegro, died in exile. Up to World War II, the Serbs claimed the Montenegrins as a branch of the Serb Nation.

A number of clans remained unreconciled to Serb domination and again rose as Yugoslavia collapsed under German and Italian attack in 1941. The clan leaders, on 13 July 1941, declared Montenegro an independent, neutral kingdom under the deposed Petrovich dynasty. Before the clan leaders could mobilize the kingdom, Italian troops occupied the state. The majority of the Montenegrins joined the royalist partisans fighting the fascists. The royalist partisans also fought against the rival Communist partisans led by Josep Broz Tito.

Montenegro, with the addition of territory on the Dalmatian coast, became a separate republic in Tito's Communist Yugoslav federation in 1946, the smallest and poorest of the six republics. The rapid development of mines, ports, and industries urbanized the rural Montenegrins, the urban population growing by 40% between 1948 and 1953.

Montenegrin nationalism, dormant since 1945, reemerged in 1966–67 as part of a campaign to resurrect their separate Orthodox church. The relative prosperity of the 1970s gave the Montenegrins a new confidence. In 1981, at Tito's death, nationalism again gained support as the republics of the Yugoslav federation began to take on greater autonomy.

The collapse of Communism in 1989 again divided the Montenegrin clans. In free elections in December 1990, the ex-Communists won, ending dissident clans' efforts to move Montenegro away from Serbian domination. In June 1991 the Yugoslav federation collapsed, and the ex-Communists in control of Serbia and Montenegro joined in opposing the breakaway republics and in creating a new Yugoslav federation of the two states.

Montenegrin dissatisfaction with Serb domination grew into a strong nationalist movement; however, in a March 1992 referendum 66% voted to remain in the truncated Yugoslav state. Since 1992 Montenegrin nationalists have regained support against misguided Serb nationalism that dragged Montenegro into war and the status of an international pariah. Increasingly strident Serb nationalists deny that the Montenegrins are a separate nation and call for Serbian annexation of the state, calls that have strengthened Montenegrin nationalists, who work for a declaration of neutrality in the continuing wars and secession from the rump Yugoslav state.

*SELECTED BIBLIOGRAPHY:*

Banac, Ivo. *The National Question in Yugoslavia: Origins, History, Politics.* 1984.
Hoptner, J. B. *Yugoslavia in Crisis, 1934–1941.* 1987.
Margas, Branka. *The Destruction of Yugoslavia.* 1993.
Phillips, John. *Yugoslav Story 1843–1983.* 1987.

# MORDVINIA

**Mordva; Mordovia**

*CAPITAL: Saransk*

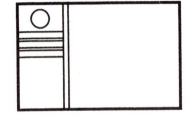

EASTERN EUROPE

MORDVINIA

*POPULATION:* (95e) 960,000 : 1,850,000 Mordvins in Russia. MAJOR NATIONAL GROUPS: (95e) Russian 52%, Mordvin 43%, Tatar 3%, Chavash 1%. MAJOR LANGUAGES: Russian, Mordvin, Tatar. MAJOR RELIGIONS: Russian Orthodox, Sunni Muslim. MAJOR CITIES: (95e) Saransk 368,000 (481,000), Ruzayevka 58,000, Ardatov 45,000 (60,000), Kovylkino 30,000, Timnikov 25,000.

*GEOGRAPHY:* AREA: 10,116 sq.mi.-26,207 sq.km. LOCATION: Mordvinia occupies the Volga uplands, the Oka-Don lowlands, and the wooded Mordvin Steppe in the Volga River basin of European Russia. POLITICAL STATUS: Mordvinia forms a member state of the Russian Federation.

*FLAG:* The Mordvin national flag, the official flag of the republic, is a red field bearing a broad, pale blue vertical stripe, divided from the red by a narrow white stripe, at the hoist charged with three narrow, horizontal orange stripes under an orange disc on the upper half.

*PEOPLE:* The Mordvins are a Finnic people, the descendants of the pre-Slav population of the Volga basin, speaking a Finno-Ugric language with two major dialects, Moksha and Erza, which constitute a separate branch of the Volga-Baltic language group. The majority of the Mordvins are Russian Orthodox. The Mordvin, often tall and Nordic, had been assimilating into Russian culture before the upheavals of the collapse of Communism and the nationalist reawakening since 1989. Nationalists claim a Mordvin ethnic population of over 2 million in Russia, including 120,000 Mordvins in Siberia.*

*THE NATION:* First mentioned as a separate people by the Gothic historian

Jordanes in the sixth century A.D., the seminomadic Mordvin tribes lived as tillers and herdsmen with ties to the Slavs. An early Mordvin state, between the Volga, Don, and Sura Rivers, became a dependency of the Bulgar Chavash state in the Volga basin in the late eighth century. The Russian princes of Ryazan and Nizhni Novgorod subjugated the Mordvin tribes in the early thirteenth century. In 1236 the Mordvin lands fell to the invading Mongols and Tatars of the Golden Horde.

Between 1392 and 1521 the majority of the Mordvin territories came under the rule of the Russian state expanding east from Moscow. Between the sixteenth and eighteenth centuries the pagan Mordvins, whose native religion revolved around ancestor worship, were forcibly converted to Orthodox Christianity. In the early seventeenth century the Mordvins joined the neighboring Chavash and Mari in a widespread revolt against Russian rule. The Russians finally crushed the rebellion in 1613, and thousands of Mordvins fled across the Urals to Siberia to escape reprisals and forced conversion to Christianity.

The Mordvins, occupying a large area of fertile lands west of the Volga River, were reduced into servitude on large Russian estates. The harsh Slav rule and serfdom provoked sporadic Mordvin rebellions. In 1641, to better control the tribes, the Russians constructed Saransk as a fort in the center of Mordvin territory. The Mordvins again rebelled in 1670, 1743–45, and 1773–75, but Russian rule only grew harsher with each uprising.

Russian colonization, accelerating with the freeing of the serfs in 1861, pushed the Mordvins into scattered ethnic pockets surrounded by Slavs. Mordvin assimilation into Russian culture accelerated even as nationalism began to affect the small, educated elite. During the revolutionary disturbances in 1905, the Mordvin rose, attacking Russian estates and settlements and skirmishing with Russian police and troops. The rebels retreated into the thick forests and continued to harass the authorities until 1907.

Mordvin nationalism grew rapidly after the outbreak of war in 1914. A coalition of nationalists and moderate Russian political parties took power in the region following the overthrow of the tsarist government in February 1917. A Mordvin congress sent delegates to a meeting of the region's non-Russian nations in Kazan. The majority of the Mordvins favored inclusion in a federation of states in the Volga-Ural region or in a smaller federation of the Christian peoples of Mordvinia, Mari-El,* and Chavashia.*

The Mordvin debate on the future of their homeland within a democratic Russia ended with the Bolshevik coup in October 1917. In November, before the Mordvins could organize effectively, Bolshevik forces took control of the region. Mordvin resistance ended after several weeks of fighting, and by December 1917 the Soviets had firmly established their control.

The Soviet authorities, in an effort to win Mordvin support, distributed the lands of the great Russian estates to individual farmers in 1918, just before the Russian civil war spilled into the region. Devastated by war, famine, and disease, over a third of the Mordvin population of 1914 had perished by 1921. The

Soviets, emerging victorious from the civil war, created a theoretically autonomous territory for the Mordvins in 1921, but the forced collectivization of the lands distributed to the Mordvins following the Bolshevik takeover in 1918 sparked renewed disturbances and violence in the region.

The Mordvins, despite the oppressive Soviet rule, made rapid advances in education and culture. A Mordvin literary language developed in the 1930s and aided the revival of the Mordvin culture after World War II.

The arbitrary borders of the Mordvin autonomous republic, created in 1934, left a majority of the Mordvin population outside the state in the neighboring Russian provinces. The majority, denied even the cultural autonomy allowed those within the autonomous republic, became the target of Soviet assimilation efforts. By 1970 only 78% of the total Mordvin population considered Mordvin their first language, and the number claiming Mordvin nationality continued to decline in the 1970s and 1980s.

The liberalization of Soviet society in the late 1980s started a slow reversal of decades of Mordvin assimilation. The collapse of Communism, followed by the disintegration of the Soviet Union in 1991, stimulated a Mordvin national and cultural revival. Nationalist organizations, organized among the scattered Mordvin population, began to press for the redrawing of the republic's borders to incorporate the Mordvin-populated districts of the neighboring provinces of Nizhni Novgorod, Simbirsk, and Penza.

In April 1993 the pro-reform president of the republic since 1991 was toppled by the conservative, Communist-dominated republican parliament in what amounted to a coup. The reformers, including the growing national movement, now constitute the major challenge to the neo-Communist republican government. Until the coup, supporters of full independence, within a Volga federation of states, made up only a small minority in the national movement. Since 1993 the nationalist majority's support for economic and political autonomy in Russia has come increasingly under pressure from the so far small, but growing, militant wing of the movement, which demands reunification of the Mordvin lands in a sovereign Mordvin state.

*SELECTED BIBLIOGRAPHY:*

Din, Shams. *Perestroika and the Nationalities Quest in the Soviet Union.* 1991.
Kozlov, Viktor. *The Peoples of the Soviet Union.* 1988.
Pushkarev, Sergei. *Self-Government and Freedom in Russia.* 1988.

# MOSQUITIA

**Moskitia; Mosquito Coast; Costa de Mosquitos**

*CAPITAL: Waspan*

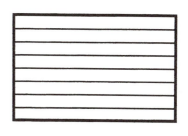

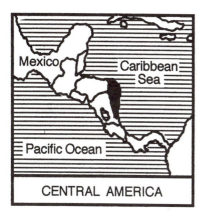

CENTRAL AMERICA

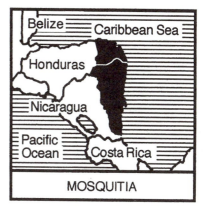

MOSQUITIA

*POPULATION:* (95e) 386,000 : 275,000 Moskitu in Nicaragua and Honduras, including the related groups, 6,000 Sumo and 1,000 Rama. MAJOR NATIONAL GROUPS: (95e) Moskitu (Mosquito) 68%, Creole 9%, other Nicaraguan, other Honduran. MAJOR LANGUAGES: Moskitu, English, Spanish. MAJOR RELIGIONS: (95e) Protestant 80% (Moravian 70%, Baptist 10%), Roman Catholic. MAJOR CITIES: (95e) NICARAGUA: Bluefields 35,000, Bragman's Bluff (Puerto Cabezas) 17,000, Waspan 10,000. HONDURAS: Tansin (Puerto Lempira) 2,000.

*GEOGRAPHY:* AREA: 29,236 sq.mi.-75,740 sq.km. LOCATION: Mosquitia lies in eastern Central America, a region of river lowlands and swamps some forty miles wide, from the San Juan River in southeast Nicaragua to the northeast coast of Honduras. POLITICAL STATUS: Mosquitia forms the Zelaya Special Zone in Nicaragua, and the small, northern portion forms the province of Gracias a Dios in Honduras.

*FLAG:* The Moskitu national flag, the flag of the national movement, has eight horizontal stripes of blue and white.

*PEOPLE:* The Moskitu are a Native American people with some admixtures of Jamaicans, Europeans, and escaped slaves. A minority, called Sambos, are of mixed Caribbean black and Native American background. The Moskitu speak a language of the Macro-Chibchan language group, which includes considerable borrowings from English and Spanish. English is the lingua franca of the multiethnic region and is spoken by the majority of the inhabitants. Minorities include Creoles, descendants of Jamaican blacks who speak a Caribbean-accented

English, Spanish-speaking immigrants from western Nicaragua and Honduras, and the smaller Native American peoples related to the Moskitu, the Sumo and Rama.

*THE NATION:* Chibchan migrants from present Colombia are believed to have settled the Caribbean lowlands, where they developed a lowland culture based on fishing and agriculture. They were sighted by Christopher Columbus on his fourth visit in 1502, but fierce Moskitu resistance precluded Spanish colonization. Some 500,000 people, members of related tribes west of the mountains in Nicaragua and Honduras, suffered enslavement and effectively disappeared as a separate people by the 1520s. Only the Moskitu and the related tribes successfully barred the colonization of their homeland.

Dutch pirates established bases on the coast in the early seventeenth century, preying on Spanish shipping from their settlement at Bleuwvelt, later called Bluefields. In 1630 English Puritans established a colony on Providence Island off the coast, the immigrants and the native people enjoying good relations. A chief's son, sent to England for education, returned to convert the Moskitu into unabashed Anglophiles. The Spanish destroyed the Providence Island colony in 1641, but many English remained on the coast, including numerous English buccaneers.

A slave ship floundered on the coast in the mid-seventeenth century. The Moskitu adopted the surviving slaves, the origins of the tribe's characteristic Afro-Indian appearance. Recruited to serve as proxies for English forces in the area, the Moskitu's position as an English ally was institutionalized in 1687 with the selection of the first Moskitu king. Moskitu warriors, armed by the English, plundered Spanish settlements and raided neighboring tribes for slaves to sell in Jamaica. In the eighteenth century the English imported Jamaican blacks to work the plantations and logging operations. The Jamaicans, later freed, became the basis of the region's Creole population.

Great Britain formally claimed the Mosquito Coast in 1740, but only in 1844 did a British agent arrive in the kingdom to formalize the protectorate agreement. German Moravian missionaries arrived in the kingdom in 1849, soon followed by Baptists and other sects. The Moskitu's conversion to Protestant beliefs and the introduction of education in the English language perpetuated the kingdom's separate character and culture as an English-speaking Caribbean nation.

Nicaragua and Honduras, independent of Spain in 1835, claimed the Caribbean coasts as national territory, with the support of the United States. Occupied by British troops in 1848, the Mosquito Coast became a point of contention between the United States and the United Kingdom. A British-American treaty, signed in 1850, eventually led to the cession of the northern part of the Mosquito Coast to Honduras in 1859 and the larger, southern district to Nicaragua in 1860. The Catholic, Spanish-speaking Central American states agreed to grant the regions political and religious autonomy and not to interfere in their internal affairs or to impose the Spanish language on the English-speaking inhabitants.

Nicaragua's president, José Santos Zelaya, in 1894 sent Nicaraguan troops to occupy the Mosquito Coast in violation of the 1860 agreement. The British in

Jamaica, citing the autonomy agreement, moved warships to the coast but later withdrew rather than confront the United States. The United States quoted the Monroe Doctrine, but interest in a possible canal route from the Caribbean to the Pacific dictated American support of Zelaya. The Mosquito Convention, adopted by Nicaragua in 1895, deposed the king, ended all Moskitu autonomy, and renamed the region for the Nicaraguan president, Zelaya.

The United States, indirectly in control of Nicaragua from the turn of the century, landed troops on the Atlantic coast in 1910, provoking fierce Moskitu resistance. With the aid of a Nicaraguan peasant army led by Augusto Cesar Sandino, the Moskitu expelled the Americans between 1928 and 1930. The Moskitu warriors were later defeated by the troops of dictator Anastasio Somoza, installed in Managua by the Americans in 1934.

Generally ignored by the Somoza regime, the region remained isolated and largely English-speaking. The Nicaraguans, called the Spanish by the Moskitu, maintained only a military presence in the main towns. The Moskitu continued to live their traditional way of life in numerous scattered villages.

The Moskitu took little part in the revolution that finally overthrew the Somoza regime and installed a leftist government in 1979. The revolutionaries, called Sandinistas after the peasant leader of the 1920s and 1930s, desperately needed the revenue from the Moskitu region's natural resources. The new government implemented a plan for the total integration of Mosquitia into the Sandinista state. The government organized the region's inhabitants in a self-help organization, Moskitu-Sumo-Rama Asla Tanaka, which means "working together." The organization was known by its initials MISURATA.

Accused of fomenting separatism in 1981, the leaders of MISURATA and 3,000 followers fled to Honduras, where they formed an alliance with the anti-Sandinista forces, the Contras, supported by the United States. The Moskitu leadership soon split over the question of autonomy or independence, the independence faction favoring the creation of Central America's second English-speaking state. Sandinista forces moved into the rebellious province, burning towns and villages and eventually driving 85,000 refugees from their homes. The Moskitu fought back, the first time in the twentieth century that a native people had taken up arms against a Latin American government. A change of government in Nicaragua in 1990 has not changed the Moskitu's desire for self-rule.

*SELECTED BIBLIOGRAPHY:*

Hamilton, Hamish. *Mosquito Coast.* 1981.
Naylor, Robert A. *Mosquito Shore and the Bay of Honduras, 1600–1914: A Case Study in British Informal Empire.* 1989.
Olson, James S. *Indians of Latin America: An Ethnohistorical Dictionary.* 1991.

# MOUNT LEBANON

Jabal Liban; Phoenicia

*CAPITAL:* East Beirut

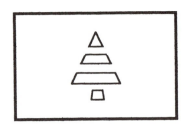

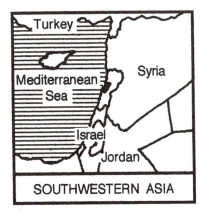

SOUTHWESTERN ASIA

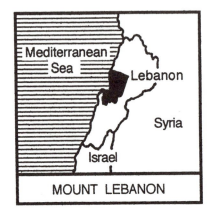

MOUNT LEBANON

*POPULATION:* (95e) 1,767,000 : 1,325,000 Christians in Lebanon. MAJOR NATIONAL GROUPS: (95e) Maronite 51%, Greek Orthodox 17%, Armenian 9%, other Lebanese. MAJOR LANGUAGES: Arabic (Lebanese dialect), French, Armenian, English. MAJOR RELIGIONS: Maronite, Greek Orthodox, Armenian Orthodox, Melchite, Protestant, Greek Catholic, Sunni Islam, Shia Islam. MAJOR CITIES: (95e) East Beirut 535,000 (800,000), Jounieh (Juniyah) 115,000 (180,000), Dbayeh 78,000, Antilas (Antilyas) 72,000, Halat 35,000, Jubail 30,000.

*GEOGRAPHY:* AREA: 1,321 sq.mi.-3,422 sq.km. LOCATION: Mount Lebanon lies in the Middle East, occupying part of Lebanon's Mediterranean coast, a roughly rectangular area that includes Christian East Beirut and the Christian enclave north and east of the city and west of the Lebanon Mountains. POLITICAL STATUS: Mount Lebanon, the region claimed by the Christian Lebanese, has no official status but forms the northern divisions (*cazas*) of the Jabal Liban region (Mount Lebanon) of Lebanon.

*FLAG:* The flag of the Lebanese Christians, the flag of the Christian national movement, is a white field with a stylized, centered green and brown cedar tree.

*PEOPLE:* The Lebanese Christians are a people of mixed background, mostly Arabic and European, the descendants of the region's many conquerors. The largest segment of the population, the Maronites, are the adherants of a Syrian Christian sect of the seventh century and claim ultimate descent from the ancient Phoenicians of the region. Smaller groups include the Greek Orthodox, Greek Catholics, Syrian Catholics, Melchites, and small Protestant groups. The large

Armenian population is concentrated in East Beirut. The Christians speak a dialect of Arabic, along with French, the former colonial language. The region's culture is basically European although before the unification of the Christians during the vicious civil war of the 1970s, greater cultural diversity existed among the various groups. A large Muslim minority, traditionally dispersed among the Christian peoples, has grown rapidly since the end of the civil war.

THE NATION: The ancient Canaanite peoples established a string of coastal city-states in the region and by 1250 B.C. had become the navigators and traders of the Mediterranean Sea. First called Phoenicians by the Greeks in the ninth century B.C., the wealthy city-states planted colonies around the Mediterranean and as far west as Spain. The region gained fame in the ancient world for the magnificent cedar trees of the Lebanon Mountains.

Successively under the rule of Babylon, Assyria, the Greeks, Selucids, Romans, and Byzantines, the region became a patchwork of differing cultures and languages. Considered part of ancient Syria, the region early came under Christian influence, and by the third century A.D. the majority of the population had become Christians.

In the seventh century the region split over the doctrinal dispute that swirled around Monotheletism. Many of the Christians of Syria broke with the established church and created the Maronite sect with its own hierarchy. Persecuted by the Byzantine authorities, the Maronites fled northern Syria to the relative safety of the coastal region west of the Lebanon Mountains. Living around the city of Berytus on the coast, the Maronites formed a distinct community under their own spiritual leader, the patriarch of Antioch.

Muslim Arab invaders conquered the region in 635, rapidly converting a majority of the region's population to Islam. The Maronites clung to their Christian sect. Tolerated as infidels and subject to special taxes and other indemnities, the Maronites were excluded from government and the professions and suffered periodic persecutions.

The Christian minority welcomed the Christian Crusaders from Europe in the eleventh and twelfth centuries. In 1110 the Maronite homeland became part of the Christian Kingdom of Jerusalem, the Europeans employing the local Christians to administer the region. Under Crusader influence, the Maronites again accepted the authority of Rome in the twelfth century. In 1291 the resurgent Muslims defeated the Crusaders. Technically a part of the Ottoman Empire, the Druze became the region's real rulers. The Maronites and the smaller Christian sects, in spite of official discrimination, prospered in trade and agriculture.

Rivalry between the Druzes and the Christians under Ottoman rule culminated in terrible massacres of the Maronites by the Druze in 1841 and 1860. The massacres of Christians prompted European intervention in the region, led by the French. In 1861 the Christian homeland became an autonomous region under a Christian governor.

The French, after the First World War, established a League of Nations mandate in the former Turkish province of Syria. Under pressure from the Maronites, the mandate authorities consolidated five districts into a Greater Lebanon, a region with a mixed population but a Maronite majority. In 1926 the French split Lebanon from Syria as a French protectorate. In 1941 the French proclaimed Lebanon, dominated by the Maronites, an independent state.

The establishment of Israel on Lebanon's southern border provoked strong Arab resentment. Under Muslim pressure Lebanon joined the Arab League and participated in the war against Israel in 1948. The Arab defeat divided the Lebanese population. The Maronites favored an independent course for Lebanon and stressed the state's strong ties to Europe. The growing Muslim population demanded close ties to the more radical Arab states.

The growing divisions within Lebanon continued to destabilize the state even as it became wealthy as a Middle Eastern tourist, trade, and financial center. The growing enmity between the Christians and Muslims finally erupted in a Syrian-backed Muslim revolt in 1958, leading to U.S. military intervention, but not to Christian concessions.

The Muslim population, growing more rapidly than the Christian, formed a majority in Lebanon by the early 1970s. Demands for greater Muslim political and economic participation in the Maronite-dominated state were exacerbated by the large, radicalized Palestinian refugee population. The tensions finally erupted in civil war in 1975. The war gave the world a new word, Lebanonization, the irreversible breakup of an existing state.

The division of Lebanon into militarized enclaves virtually destroyed the country and raised Maronite nationalist sentiment for secession of the Christian enclave, an undeclared ministate at war with its neighbors. Israeli and Syrian military intervention worsened the situation. In 1982 Christian militiamen massacred hundred of Palestinians in camps south of Beirut. Thousands of Christians fled abroad, mostly to Europe, as feudal warlords with private militias fought for control of land, resources, and power.

A peace plan approved in 1989 provided for power-sharing and the end of the former Christian domination. The plan divided the Christian heartland, with some groups in favor while others pushed for secession. The conflict provoked a two-year civil war within the Christian enclave that ended only with the intervention of Syrian troops in 1991. The ingrained sense of superiority, which has long influenced Christian conduct in Lebanon, is now a shattered ideal. Well aware of the fate of other Christian minorities in the Muslim world, the Christians of Lebanon have not discarded the nationalism that has aided the survival of the small nation under centuries of Muslim rule.

*SELECTED BIBLIOGRAPHY:*

Abraham, Antoine J. *Maronite-Druze Relations in Lebanon 1840–1860: A Prelude to Arab Nationalism.* 1982.

Bates, D. C., and A. Rassam. *Peoples and Cultures of the Middle East.* 1983.

Hourani, Albert H. *Minorities in the Arab World.* 1947.

Sivan, Emmanud. *Radical Islam.* 1987.

Ziadeh, N. A. *Syria and Lebanon.* 1957.

# MUSIKONGO

Musicongo; Kongo; Congo

*CAPITAL: Kinshasa*

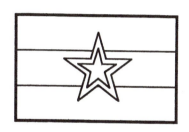

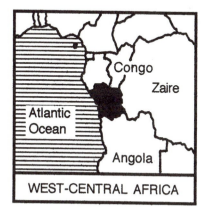

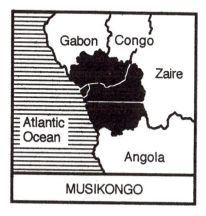

*POPULATION:* (95e) 11,440,000 : 8,000,000 Bakongo (Kongo) in Zaire, Angola, and Congo. MAJOR NATIONAL GROUPS: (95e) Bakongo (Kongo) 65%, Kituba, Batéké, M'Bochi, Bambala, Ovimbundu. MAJOR LANGUAGES: Kikongo, Kituba, Lingala, Kimbochi, Kimbala, French, Portuguese. MAJOR RELIGIONS: Roman Catholic, Protestant, animist. MAJOR CITIES: (95e) ZAIRE (CENTRAL CONGO): Kinshasa 4,591,000 (6,230,000), Bandundu 207,000, Matadi 204,000, Boma 156,000, Mbanza-Ngungu 116,000, Kisantu 52,000. ANGOLA (SOUTH KONGO): Uíge 121,000, Negage 64,000, Cabinda 45,000, Mbanza Kongo 45,000. CONGO (NORTH KONGO): Ntámo (Brazzaville) 730,000 (825,000), Kouilou (Pointe-Noire) 416,000, Loubomo 69,000.

*GEOGRAPHY:* AREA: 106,675 sq.mi.-276,360 sq.km. LOCATION: Musikongo lies in west-central Africa, occupying the basin of the lower Zaire (Congo) River in western Zaire, northern Angola, and southern Congo. POLITICAL STATUS: Musikongo has no official status; the area claimed by nationalists forms the Zairean regions of Bas-Zaire, Kinshasa, and western Bandundu, the Angolan provinces of Cabinda,* Uíge, and Zaire, and the Congolese regions of Bouenza, Brazzaville, Kouilou, Lékoumou, Niari, and Pool.

*FLAG:* The Bakongo (Kongo) national flag, the flag of the national movement, is a horizontal tricolor of red, white, and yellow bearing a white, five-pointed star, outlined in black, centered on the white stripe.

*PEOPLE:* The Bakongo, commonly called Kongo, are a Bantu people divided among twelve clans spread across parts of Zaire, Angola, and Congo. Historically a united people, the descendants of the medieval Kongo Empire, all of the clans speak dialects of Kikongo, a language of the Bantu group of the Niger-Congo languages. Large non-Kongo Bantu minorities inhabit the outlying districts or live in the large urban centers, particularly Kinshasa and Brazzaville, where the small European population is concentrated. The majority of the Kongo are Roman Catholic, with smaller Protestant and animist minorities.

*THE NATION:* Bantu peoples settled the region in successive waves, the migrants believed to originate in the highland lakes region to the northeast. The Bantus created a number of small, autonomous chiefdomships or states. In the thirteenth century a number of the states united under a paramount king, the Manikongo. The united Kongo state eventually expanded to incorporate twelve related clans or tribes living in six provinces south of the Congo River and three tributary states north of the river. The Kongo kingdom, based on tropical agriculture, evolved a sophisticated state system, an efficient bureaucracy, and an advanced culture.

The Kongo kingdom, visited by Portuguese explorer Diogo Cao in 1482, welcomed the strangers. In 1483 the reigning king, Nzinga Knuwu, sought the aid of the powerful newcomers against a rebellion, allowing missionaries, artisans, and soldiers to reside in his capital from 1491. By 1500 the Manikongo and most of his court had adopted Catholicism and regularly exchanged emissaries with Portugal and the Vatican. The pope consecrated history's first black bishop, a member of the Kongo royal family, in 1520.

The Portuguese, having established a foothold in the kingdom, turned to the slave trade. The impact of the trade spelled disaster for the Kongo kingdom and its formerly peaceful inhabitants. Raids on surrounding peoples for slaves to sell to the Europeans disrupted a wide area of the Congo basin. In 1665 Portuguese adventurers, believing stories of gold, invaded the declining kingdom, the invasion spreading chaos across a wide area.

The kingdom disintegrated into a number of small warring states, easy prey for the encroaching European powers. The colonial partition of the Kongo lands eventually gave Portugal the region south of the Congo River and the enclave of Cabinda to the north, the Belgians took the northern part of the kingdom with an outlet to the sea between Cabinda and Portuguese Angola, and the former tributary states to the north came under French control.

The Bakongo rebelled against European domination several times, the rebellions particularly serious in Portuguese Angola from the 1880s up to World War I. In 1921 a Bakongo prophet, Simon Kimbangu, began a religious-nationalist movement in the Belgian Congo that rapidly gained support in all three colonies. The Europeans ultimately arrested and exiled Kimbangu, but the cultural reawakening he started continued to grow, and the exiled prophet became a powerful symbol of Kongo irredentist nationalism.

Nationalists in the Belgian sector in the late 1940s formed the Association for the Maintenance, Unity, and Expansion of the Kikongo Language (ABAKO), a Kongo cultural organization that quickly became the major political force among the Belgian Bakongo. In 1954 ABAKO, led by Joseph Kasavubu, demanded autonomy for the Bakongo regions of the Belgian Congo. In 1958 ABAKO announced its support for the reconstitution of the old Kongo kingdom, Musikongo, within its historic borders. A speech by French president De Gaulle in Brazzaville in August 1958, in which he declared that whoever wants independence shall have it, fired Bakongo nationalism in all three colonies. Kasavubu and Fulbert Yolou, the first president of Congo, called for a reunited Musikongo state, but the European authorities in all three colonies vehemently rejected a resurgent Kongo state.

ABAKO leaders in June 1959 sent the Belgian government a detailed plan for an independent Republic of Central Kongo, including within its proposed limits mostly the Bakongo capital of Belgian Congo, Leopoldville (Kinshasa). The Belgians rejected the plan and instead granted hasty independence to the entire Belgian Congo in 1960. In the first Congolese elections, ABAKO won a sweeping victory in the Kongo-populated areas, and, due to the overall number of votes, Kasavubu became the first president of the rapidly disintegrating republic.

French Congo, also granted independence in 1960, became a republic dominated by the large Bakongo ethnic group. A coup in 1963 overthrew the Bakongo-dominated government and replaced it with a government dominated by non-Kongo northerners.

Nationalists in the Portuguese Congo in northern Angola founded the Front for the Liberation of Angola (FNLA) in 1955, and led a violent rebellion against the Portuguese in 1961, the beginning of the long colonial war in Angola. Nationalists from the three regions in 1961 petitioned the United Nations for the creation of a separate Kongo state as violence spread across the huge region, but without success.

The civil war in Congo, later renamed Zaire, the leftist takeover of Congo-Brazzaville, and the Bakongo defeat in the Angolan civil war in the 1970s, ended the initial postcolonial spurt of Kongo nationalism. Dominated by rival tribes or vicious dictatorships, the Kongo sought only to survive the upheavals and violence of the 1970s and 1980s.

The end of the Cold War and most of its echoes in the proxy wars in Africa, have allowed Kongo nationalism to reemerge since 1989–90. The continuing conflict in Angola, the dictatorship in Zaire, and domination by less advanced tribes in Congo have spurred a resurgence of Kongo nationalism in the 1990s. The former unity of the Kongo kingdom has become the focus for ethnic loyalty and the basis of the reawakening Kongo nationalism.

*SELECTED BIBLIOGRAPHY:*

Asiwaju, A.I. *Partitioned Africans: Ethnic Relations across Africa's International Borders, 1884–1984.* 1985.

Benden, Gerald J. *Angola under the Portuguese: The Myth and the Reality.* 1978.

Schuyler, Philippa. *Who Killed the Congo?* 1962.

Thornton, John. *The Kingdom of Kongo: Civil War and Transition 1641–1718.* 1983.

# NAGALAND

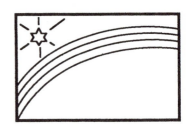

*CAPITAL: Kohima*

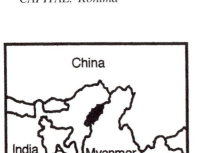

SOUTH ASIA

NAGALAND

*POPULATION:* (95e) 1,745,000 : 1,500,000 Nagas in India and Myanmar. MAJOR NATIONAL GROUPS: (95e) Naga 84%, other Indian, other Burmese. MAJOR LANGUAGES: MAJOR RELIGIONS: (95e) Christian 68%, animist 20%, Hinduism, Buddhism. MAJOR CITIES: (95e) INDIA: Kohima 88,000, Dimapur 65,000, Mokokchang 41,000, Tuensang 33,000, Ledo 12,000. MYAN-MAR: Nathkaw 20,000, Lahe 10,000.

*GEOGRAPHY:* AREA: 19,611 sq.mi.-50,805 sq.km. LOCATION: Nagaland occupies a highland region, formerly called the Naga Hills, in the Paktai Range in northeastern India and northwestern Myanmar. POLITICAL STATUS: Nagaland, the region claimed by nationalists, forms Nagaland State, the Ledo District of Arunchal Pradesh State, the Maram and Tamma districts of Manipur State in India, and the Naga Hills District of Sagaing Division of Myanmar.

*INDEPENDENCE DECLARED:* 14 August 1947.

*FLAG:* The Naga national flag, the flag of the national movement, is a light blue field with a curving rainbow of narrow red, yellow, and dark blue stripes from the lower hoist to the upper fly and bearing a white, six-pointed star on the upper hoist.

*PEOPLE:* The Nagas are an Indo-Chinese people thought to be distantly related to the Malay peoples of Southeast Asia. Divided into sixteen tribes, the Nagas speak several different dialects of a Tibeto-Burman language written in the Latin alphabet, a legacy of missionary education. The Naga culture, lacking the rigid caste and class divisions of neighboring peoples, is unique as men and women enjoy equal status. Naga nationalists claim a total national population of over 2 million, including, in addition to the Naga majority in Nagaland State, 190,000 in Manipur, 80,000 in Arunchal Pradesh, and 215,000, called Koryak, in Myanmar. The majority of the Nagas are Christians, primarily Baptist, with a large minority adhering to traditional beliefs and smaller minorities that have adopted the Hindu or Buddhist religions that dominate in India and Myanmar.

*THE NATION:* Thought to have moved south from China or Tibet,* the ancestors of the Nagas possibly originated in Southeast Asia. The Nagas occupied a much wider area than at present but gradually lost the lowlands to successive waves of invaders. The Naga tribes, concentrated in the high mountain valleys, developed a culture markedly distinct from neighboring peoples, including the important religious and cultural ritual of head-hunting.

The Naga tribes, often warring among themselves, never developed a state system. The autonomous tribes at times came under the nominal rule of the powerful Assam* or Manipur states. The earliest mention of the Nagas was recorded by Thai invaders from present Myanmar, a grudging praise of the fierce Naga resistance.

The British, after taking control of Assam in 1826, moved into the jungled mountains and made their first contact with the Naga tribes in 1832. The violent encounter prompted the British to withdraw and to ignore the tribes for nearly two decades. The decision to construct a road from Manipur to Burma required the subjugation of the fierce tribes blocking the route. In 1851 a British force burned Kohima and killed some 300 Nagas. ''Slaughter and withdraw'' became the British policy for dealing with the Naga tribes. Finally subdued in 1881, the Naga chiefs signed treaties with the British authorities that allowed the British to add their tribal lands to the British governments of Assam and Burma.

European and American missionaries converted a majority of the Nagas to Christianity and introduced modern education through a network of mission schools. A written form of the Naga language, devised by missionaries, began the process of molding the diverse tribes into a distinct nation.

Christian Naga leaders in 1929 demanded the unification of the several Naga districts of India and Burma under a separate administration and asked for a British promise of Naga independence should the British ever quit India. Outraged at the British lack of reply, several of the Naga tribes rebelled, the disturbances continuing up to World War II. In 1942 the Japanese invaded northeast India and sought to win dissident Nagas with promises of independence. The collaboration of some tribal leaders seriously divided the nascent national movement. The Naga National Council (NNC), formed during the war to promote Naga interests, in 1945 opened negotiations on separate independence.

Pressed by the British authorities to join India, the Nagas refused. On 14 August 1947 the Naga leaders declared Nagaland independent of India and Burma, one day before the date set for Indian independence. Unlike other territories, Nagaland was not specifically included in the Indian Independence Act of 1947; however, the new Indian government, without legal sanction, sent troops to occupy the breakaway state. The Nagas resisted until the hard-pressed

Naga leaders finally accepted inclusion in India as a district of Assam State in 1950.

Dissatisfied with the Indian administration, the Nagas organized a democratic plebiscite on 16 May 1951. The vote overwhelmingly favored reaffirming their earlier declaration of independence, but the Indian government refused to accept the plebiscite's result. In 1955 the Nagas rebelled. The rebels, armed only with bows and arrows, fought against the heavily armed Indian troops, but later with arms from China and Pakistan organized a national army of 40,000 soldiers. In 1956 the sixteen tribes set aside their historic differences to form a united provisional government, the Naga Federal Government (NFG).

The Indian authorities, unable to subdue the Nagas in their highland jungles, granted the Nagas autonomy within Assam in 1960. Following renewed disturbances, the government upgraded the region's status to full statehood in the Indian union in 1962. The new status failed to satisfy Naga demands for unification of all the Naga lands, and the rebellion continued. When Chinese troops invaded northeastern India in 1962, the Naga leaders offered to end the rebellion in return for Indian recognition of a democratic referendum on independence. Rebuffed, the Nagas resumed the rebellion in 1963. By 1985 over 100,000 people had died in the three decades of the Naga rebellion.

A campaign to win control of territory, beginning in 1992, has focused in driving rival tribes from disputed territory in Manipur and other areas claimed as Naga national lands in anticipation of a proposed referendum on reunification and independence. In 1994 violence escalated as Naga nationalists attacked Kuki villages in the northern districts of Manipur in a campaign to clear the region of non-Naga tribesmen. The Indian government, unable to quell the rising violence, in late 1994 placed several districts of Nagaland and neighboring states under emergency rule.

The Naga revolt, overshadowed by the separatist violence in other parts of India and Myanmar, continues to claim lives, mostly unarmed villagers and separatists killed by Indian or Burmese troops. Younger, educated Nagas, keen to preserve their culture and to eliminate the tribal and clan divisions that have seriously hampered the independence movement, are now moving into leadership positions.

*SELECTED BIBLIOGRAPHY:*

Ali, Asghan. *Ethnic Conflicts in South Asia.* 1987.

Chanra, B. *Nationalism and Colonialism in Modern India.* 1979.

IWGIA. *The Naga Nation and Its Struggle against Genocide.* 1991.

Karotempral, S., ed. *The Tribes of Northeast India.* 1984.

# NAN CHAO

**Nan Zhao; Nanzhao**

*CAPITAL: Nanning*

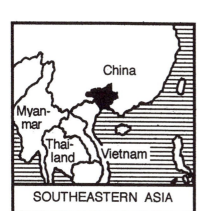

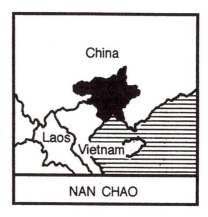

*POPULATION:* (95e) 23,925,000 : 17,105,000 Chuang (Zhuang), 7,923,000 Miao (Hmong), 2,681,000 Bouyei, 2,622,000 Dong, 2,316,000 Yao, 820,000 She, and 1,100,000 smaller Chao nationalities in China. MAJOR NATIONAL GROUPS: (95e) Chuang 68%, Chinese (Han, Hui, Chungkia) 20%, Miao (Hmong), Dong, Yao, Bouyei, She, smaller groups 12%, other Chinese. MAJOR LANGUAGES: Tai (Zhuang), Cantonese (Yue), Min, Hakka, Miao (Hmong), Dong (Tong), Yao (Mien), She. MAJOR RELIGIONS: Buddhist, Taoist, Sunni Muslim, animist. MAJOR CITIES: (95e) Nanning 1,208,000, Paise (Bose) 140,000, Hechi 105,000, Guixian 97,000, Ishan (Yishan) 77,000, Qinzhou 68,000, Pingxian 65,000, Tiangdong 50,000, Binyang 50,000.

*GEOGRAPHY:* AREA: 43,114 sq.mi.-111,695 sq.km. LOCATION: Nan Chao occupies a mountainous region in southeastern China, mostly consisting of upland grazing lands and fertile valleys just north of the international border with Vietnam. POLITICAL STATUS: Nan Chao has no official status; the region forms the territory of the former West Kwangsi Chuang Autonomous Area, the western half of the Guangxi Zhuang (Kwangsi Chuang) Autonomous Region of the People's Republic of China.

*INDEPENDENCE DECLARED:* 12 January 1927.

*FLAG:* The Nan Chao flag, the flag of the national movement, is a red field bearing a centered yellow, six-pointed star.

*PEOPLE:* The Nan Chao peoples form a compact non-Chinese population of over 32 million in the region. The largest of the Chao nations is the Chuang, spelled Zhuang in the Chinese Pinyin system, a Tai (Thai) people related to the Thai, Shan, and Lao peoples of Thailand, Myanmar, Laos, and northern Vietnam. China's largest ethnic minority, the Chuang and the related Tai groups, the Bouyei, Dong, and the smaller Sui, Mulan, Maonan, and Primni, mostly speak the Wu-ming dialect of northern Tai. The language, now accepted as the standard language of the region, uses the Latin alphabet with six additional letters. The language, the lingua franca of the mountainous region, is the second language of the non-Tai peoples, who speak Tibeto-Burman languages, the Miao or Hmong, the Yao, and the She. The Chungkia (Zhungkia) or Ikia, counted as ethnic Chinese, are the descendants of early Chinese settlers who now speak the Chuang's Tai language. The majority of the Nan Chao peoples are Buddhist or Taoist, with a large Chinese Muslim population related to the Hui of Ningsia* and a smaller animist minority in the more remote areas.

*THE NATION:* Tai peoples inhabited much of southern China before the establishment of the Chinese Empire in 221 B.C. Alone among the early peoples known to the Chinese, the Tai were not considered barbarians as they possessed a sophisticated state system and a developed culture. A powerful Tai state, Nan Chao, erected in the third century A.D., controlled a large territory in present southern China. The highly evolved Tai culture, including a refined system of writing and an illustrious literature, culturally influenced areas far beyond the state's borders.

Nan Chao gradually lost territory to the expanding Chinese Empire. The Chinese advance slowly pushed the Tai peoples into the more mountainous south and eventually into the lowland valleys of present Thailand, Myanmar, Laos, and Vietnam. China's Sung dynasty prepared the way for Chinese domination by defeating the Tai in the twelfth century, winning for China the rice lands of Kwangtung (Guangdong). Chinese migration to the conquered lands began the long process of assimilation of the lowland Tai. The Chuang trace their descent from the period of Chinese expansion, from coastal refugees and Tai mountain tribes.

Nan Chao survived in the mountains until its conquest by the Mongols of Kublai Khan in 1253. Marco Polo visited the state soon after the Mongol conquest. Under successive Chinese dynasties, the authorities encouraged Chinese migration to the region, leaving only the less productive lands and the mountain areas to the Chuang and other minority peoples. Mostly ignored by the imperial government, the minority peoples developed their own systems under local rulers. The Manchu, after their conquest of China in 1644, finally imposed direct imperial administration on the minority regions in 1650.

The Nan Chao area came under French influence in the nineteenth century. The French established a sphere of influence in the non-Chinese region following the Franco-Chinese war of 1884–85. Unhindered by the weak Manchu government, French missionaries introduced modern education and the Latin alphabet. The turbulence of the last years of the Manchu dynasty and the Chinese Revolution of 1911 gave the Chuang effective control of their homeland, under French political influence, between 1910 and 1916.

The feeble Chinese republican government, installed in 1911, exerted some influence in the southern border regions in 1916 but again lost effective control during the chaos that swept China after 1917. Badly treated by the Chinese republican troops during the government's brief control of the region in 1916–17, the Chuang and other minorities resisted the return of Chiang Kai-shek's Nationalist Chinese in 1926–27. On 12 January 1927 the rebel leaders declared the region independent of China and appealed to the French in neighboring Tonkin for support. Covertly aided by the French, who avoided direct involvement, the breakaway state resisted Nationalist attacks until 1929.

The region, controlled by local warlords, remained virtually independent during the Chinese civil war of the 1930s. An agreement reached in 1936 allowed the Nationalist Government to reassert its authority in the region. During World War II Nationalist forces and American military units garrisoned the strategic region. With their Allies present, the Nationalist Chinese were careful to suppress all signs of minority dissent.

The Chinese Communists, victorious in the civil war that resumed in 1945, drove the last Nationalist forces from the area in November 1949. Greeted as liberators, the Communists soon proved as harsh as the Nationalists. In 1950 the Chao peoples revolted with the covert aid of the French in neighboring Vietnam. Dubbed bandits, the Communist authorities executed thousands of minority rebels and civilians. In 1952, as part of its nationalities system, the Communists erected an autonomous region, only to dissolve it six years later amid charges of separatism. To prevent the minority peoples from consolidating in a viable nation, the Communist authorities split the large minority region among several provinces.

China's Cultural Revolution, beginning in 1966, led by the fanatical Red Guards, destroyed shrines, institutions, and monuments to force assimilation. The Communists, between 1958 and 1977, outlawed many traditions and cultural traits judged detrimental to development. A period of relative leniency in the 1980s ended with the crushing of the pro-democracy movement in 1989. The Chinese leaders, fearing that the disintegration of the Soviet Union would spread nationalist ideas to the minorities, imposed new restrictions.

The Chuang and the related peoples, despite over seven centuries of Chinese domination, retain a strong urge to unite in an independent state. Nationalists claim that they are a nation by all modern criteria: a long and separate history, separate language and culture, and a compact ethnic national area. Whether China splinters like the Soviet Union or not, many in Nan Chao have already begun to view the region as part of Southeast Asia.

*SELECTED BIBLIOGRAPHY:*

Coates, Austin. *China Races.* 1984.
Collier, Mac. *China in Disintegration, 1912–1949.* 1977.
Dreyer, June. *China's Forty Millions.* 1976.

# NEWFOUNDLAND

### Newfoundland and Labrador

*CAPITAL: St. John's*

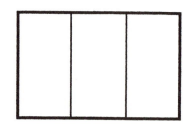

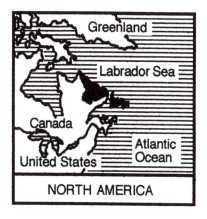

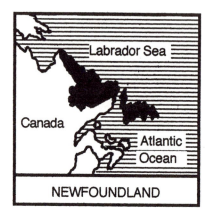

*POPULATION:* (95e) 586,000 : 590,000 Newfoundlanders (Newfies) in Canada. MAJOR NATONAL GROUPS: (95e) Newfoundlander (Newfie) 96%, other Canadian. MAJOR LANGUAGE: English (Newfie dialect). MAJOR RELIGIONS: (95e) Protestant 66%, Roman Catholic 32%. MAJOR CITIES: (95e) St. John's 81,000 (165,000), Corner Brook 26,000 (39,000), Labrador City 15,000, Gander 11,000, Grand Falls 9,000 (16,000).

*GEOGRAPHY:* AREA: 160,339 sq.mi.-415,385 sq.km. LOCATION: Newfoundland lies in eastern Canada, a large island in the Gulf of St. Lawrence separated from its mainland dependency, Labrador, by the Strait of Belle Isle. POLITICAL STATUS: Newfoundland, with Labrador, forms a province of Canada.

*FLAG:* The Newfie national flag, the flag of the national movement, is a vertical tricolor of pink, white, and pale green. OTHER FLAG(S): The flag of the autonomy movement in Labrador is a horizontal tricolor of white, green, and blue, proportions 2:1:2, bearing a green spruce bough on the upper hoist.

*PEOPLE:* The Newfoundlanders, popularly called Newfies, are a distinct North American people. Although the Newfies became Canadian citizens in 1949, they retain closer ties to the British Isles in accents, appearance, and family connections. The origins of the Newfies are 76% English and Scots, 18% Irish, and 2% French. The major occupation of the region, fishing, is not just a livelihood but the basis of the distinct Newfie culture, one of the unique regional cultures in North America. About half the population live in small fishing villages along the coasts. The Newfie language, a mixture of archaic West Country English and Erse (Gaelic), with borrowings from French and the Indian and Inuit languages, has developed over centuries to produce many words and constructions not found in other English dialects.

*THE NATION:* Small Algonquin tribes inhabited the region when the first Europeans crossed the Atlantic Ocean. Traditionally, Vikings visited Labrador in A.D. 985 or 986, although researchers have found no definite proof of the early expedition. Vikings reached the island in 1285, but a Viking settlement, under Landa-Rolf, ultimately failed. Giovanni Caboto, called John Cabot, sighted the island in 1497 and called his discovery "New-founde-land."

The Grand Banks, one of the world's great fishing grounds, discovered soon after Cabot's voyage, attracted competing fishing fleets. Small settlements, established by the fishermen of several European countries, sprang up in the isolated coves in the 1500s despite English territorial claims. To consolidate English domination, the Crown formally annexed the island in 1583, England's first overseas possession. The French founded a rival colony on the island in 1662, but English sovereignty was confirmed in 1713. French claims to the region ended with the cession of Labrador in 1763, although they retained the two small islands of Saint Pierre and Miquelon just south of Newfoundland.

The colony grew slowly, the majority of the inhabitants living in small, isolated coastal settlements where they retained customs and speech patterns that disappeared elsewhere. An influx of Irish immigrants, fleeing famine in Ireland, settled in Newfoundland in the 1840s, giving the emerging Newfie culture a definite Irish flavor, particularly noticeable in the Newfies' music and folklore.

The British granted the island a separate legislature in 1832, and in1855 Newfoundland won dominion status, autonomy under a regional Newfie government. Four of Britain's North American provinces united to form the Dominion of Canada in 1867. The Newfies rejected British moves to add their island to Canada in 1869, preferring to retain dominion status, equal to, but separate from, Canada.

In the 1880s, ignoring vehement Newfie protests, the British government granted fishing rights in the Grand Banks, the dominion's major asset, to other fishing nations. In the 1890s, when the question of joining Canada again came up, the precarious state of the Newfie economy precluded any serious discussion of union with Canada.

Foreign access to the Grand Banks, without benefiting Newfoundland, awakened a latent nationalism. In 1904 the Newfies managed to eliminate France's special fishing rights, and in 1906 they signed a fishing agreement with the United States, the dominion's major trading partner. When war began in 1914, the Newfies put aside their grievances and joined the other British dominions in sending troops to Europe. During the war the nationalists gained support, and in 1917 the Newfies elected a nationalist government under William Lloyd, who attended the 1919 Paris Peace Conference as the head of a victorious nation.

The economy, based on fishing and mining, suffered severe reverses during the depression of the 1930s. Unable to meet interest payments on government loans, the dominion government requested aid from the imperial treasury. The aid request, incompatible with dominion status, forced the Newfies to comply when London suspended the constitution and withdrew dominion status in 1933. The state, over widespread Newfie opposition, gave up its independence and became the first member country to withdraw from the British Commonwealth.

Newfoundland's return to colonial status roused Newfie nationalism, many of the islanders blaming British policies for the state's economic problems. Nationalists called for independence and proposed an economic union with the United States, but nationalism waned with the outbreak of World War II in Europe. The site of major Allied bases during the war, the island prospered, aided by revenues brought in by thousands of American soldiers.

Dominion status, restored in 1946, failed to satisfy the two major political factions, pro-independence and pro-Canada. A plebiscite held in June 1948 gave the Newfies three choices, eventual independence, confederation with Canada, or continued dominion status. None of the choices received a majority, but a second plebiscite in July produced a slight edge for confederation. On 1 April 1949 Newfoundland joined Canada as the tenth province.

Nationalist protests and demonstrations gradually declined as confederation brought development funds and the benefits of Canada's welfare state. Modernization in the 1950s coaxed the Newfies out of hundreds of small ports and into a more urban life, but without the loss of their distinctive culture.

Newfie nationalism, dormant for nearly three decades, reemerged following the discovery of oil and natural gas in nearby waters in 1979, opening a passionate dispute between the provincial and federal governments over the control of natural resources. The resurgent nationalism sparked a parallel cultural revival. The first dictionary of the Newfie language appeared in 1982.

The depletion of the fish stocks in the Grand Banks, ironically the result of a Canadian government agreement allowing greater foreign access, signed on the fortieth anniversary of Newfoundland's union with Canada, resulted in a two-year moratorium on fishing in May 1992. The moratorium, blamed on Canadian government policies, and possibly extending until the year 2000, has affected 35,000 Newfie fishermen and has raised nationalist sentiment to levels not seen in the province since 1948–49.

*SELECTED BIBLIOGRAPHY:*

Hensen, Ben. *Newfoundland Portfolio.* 1979.
Hocking, Anthony. *Newfoundland.* 1979.
Neary, Peter F. *Newfoundland in the North Atlantic World, 1929–1949.* 1979.
Parker, John. *Newfoundland, Tenth Province of Canada.* 1950.

# NINGSIA

**Ningsia Hui; Ningxia Huizu**

*CAPITAL: Ningsia (Yinchuan)*

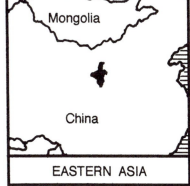

EASTERN ASIA

NINGSIA

*POPULATION:* (95e) 5,915,000 : 9,255,000 Hui (Dungans) in China. MAJOR NATIONAL GROUPS: (95e) Hui (Dungan) 70%, Han Chinese 18%, Mongol 11%. MAJOR LANGUAGES: Chinese, Arabic, Mongol. MAJOR RELIGIONS: Sunni Muslim, Buddhist, Taoist, Tibetan Buddhist (Lamaism). MAJOR CITIES: (95e) Ningsia (Yinchuan) 335,000, Wuzhong 110,000 (145,000), Zhongwei 75,000, Wuda 65,000, Pingluo 50,000, Yanchi 35,000.

*GEOGRAPHY:* AREA: 30,078 sq.mi.-77,921 sq.km. LOCATION: Ningsia occupies a highland region, the Ningsia Plateau, just south of the Alashan Desert in north-central China. Ningsia borders the Southern Mongolia* region of the Inner Mongolia Autonomous Region on the north. POLITICAL STATUS: Ningsia forms the Ningsia Hui Autonomous Region of the People's Republic of China.

*INDEPENDENCE DECLARED:* 9 August 1953.

*FLAG:* The Hui national flag is a horizontal tricolor of green, red, and black bearing a large white crescent moon near the hoist.

*PEOPLE:* The Hui, also called Dungans, are a Muslim people, descendants of early Arab, Persian, and Turkic settlers who took Chinese wives and adopted Chinese speech and culture. Now physically similar to the majority Han Chinese, the Hui are distinguished by their dress, including turbans, and their Muslim religion. Dispersed in the eighteenth century, Hui minorities live in many parts of China, with the largest concentration in the Hui heartland in Ningsia. The second largest of China's minority peoples, the Hui speak several Chinese dialects along with Arabic, the language of their Muslim religion.

*THE NATION:* Islam arrived in China by both sea and overland, with small Muslim communities established in the seventh and eighth centuries. During the rule of the Mongol Yuan dynasty, installed in China in 1260, a flood of Arabs, Persians, and Turks, fleeing the Mongol conquest of their homelands, settled in the remote region south of the Alashan Desert. The refugees gradually assimilated and adopted Chinese culture and language.

The Muslims of Ningsia expanded in the fourteenth and fifteenth centuries to convert surrounding peoples. Only nominally under the rule of the Chinese Empire, the Muslims maintained a separate state ruled by Hui sultans, a source of irritation to successive Chinese dynasties. Following the Manchu conquest of China in 1644, the Hui attempted to throw off infidel rule. Invaded by Manchu troops in 1648, the Hui fought a long and violent campaign but finally fell to the overwhelming Manchu military power.

Sporadic Hui disturbances again erupted in open rebellion in 1785. The Manchu rulers, determined to eliminate the Hui threat to their authority, loosed imperial troops on the region to carry out savage massacres, unprecedented in the East. The Hui homeland, an area larger than France, was left virtually depopulated. Hundreds of thousands fled into the desert or to other parts of China. After the Manchu campaign ended, a surviving minority slowly consolidated in a corner of their devastated former homeland. The Manchu government settled excess Han Chinese population from the eastern provinces in the region.

Excluded from government and certain professions, the Hui lived as a despised minority, suspect for their religion and for their ties to the peoples to the west. Indiscriminate attacks by Han Chinese, paralleled by a growing intolerance of their Muslim religion, provoked a renewed Hui rebellion between 1862 and 1875. Hui nationalists seized the opportunity presented by the Chinese Revolution of 1911. The nationalists drove all Chinese officials from the region and created an autonomous government, but, before they could consolidate their independence, troops loyal to the new republican government overran the region.

The weak Chinese government only occasionally exerted authority in Ningsia during the turbulent 1920s and 1930s. The Hui mobilized to protect themselves from rampaging warlords and the militias of various political factions. The Chinese National government of Chiang Kai-shek extended its authority to Ningsia in 1936 but relaxed its former harsh restraints to win Hui support as civil war with the Chinese Communists escalated. Courted by Communist agents, the Hui national leaders, ultimately rejecting the overtures, emphatically rejected the Communists' avowedly anti-religious doctrine.

The long civil war resumed after World War II. The devoutly religious Hui joined the Nationalists to fight the Communist takeover of northern China. A Communist victory in 1949 initiated a strong movement for secession or even mass emigration to another country. Hui guerrillas fighting the advancing Communists formed the Chungkuo Islam Djemiyeti (Chinese Islamic Association) in 1953. Pressed by the attempted collectivization of the Ningsia Plateau and the suppression of Muslim religious rights, Hui nationalists declared Ningsia independent of China on 9 August 1953 as the Chinese Islamic Republic.

Dubbed revisionists, splittists, and bandits, Communist troops carried out wholesale slaughter of captured Hui rebels and their suspected civilian supporters. The authorities dissolved the Hui autonomous region created in 1949 and incorporated Ningsia into the neighboring Chinese province of Kansu. After closing most mosques, Communist officials tried persuasion and pressure to separate the Hui from their Muslim religion but later instituted a campaign of harsh repression to force the stubborn Muslims to conform. In 1957 the Hui demanded the socialist self-determination preached by Communist leaders. Official reprisals against the Hui leader's calls for socialist self-government sparked a renewed Hui uprising between April and June 1958.

The defeated rebels and all the Hui lost their religious rights as the government enforced the state's official atheism. Communist officials closed all but a few of the remaining mosques and religious schools, but, in a bid to undermine Hui nationalism the Communist government reconstituted an autonomous Hui region in 1958. Only about half the Hui population in China lived within the new region's borders.

Ningsia became the scene of violent confrontations during the Cultural Revolution of the late 1960s. Zealous mobs, led by fanatical Red Guards, destroyed most of the Hui mosques, shrines, and monuments. Hui self-defense groups formed in an attempt to protect their people during the chaotic attacks on turbaned men and the forced marriage of Hui women to government functionaries. The official government policy aimed at the eradication of Islam eased only in the 1980s as China increased its efforts to establish ties to wealthy Muslim states of the Persian Gulf.

Religious tolerance, again curtailed after the crushing of the pro-democracy movement in 1989, has stimulated a renewal of Hui nationalism. The preoccupation with economic matters that has spread across China since 1990 has become a nationalist issue in Ningsia. In 1992 Hui incomes are less than the Chinese average and considerably less than that of China's favored southeastern provinces. In August 1993, the publication of a book depicting Muslims praying near a pig, anathema to Muslims, set off riots that spread to Ningsia in October. Only the rapid deployment of troops and police averted a serious crisis in the region.

*SELECTED BIBLIOGRAPHY:*

Dreyer, June. *China's Forty Millions.* 1976.
Heberer, Thomas. *China and Its National Minorities: Autonomy or Assimilation?* 1989.
Schwartz, Henry G. *The Minorities of Northern China: A Survey.* 1984.

# NISTASSIN

**Ntesinan; Ntesian; Mistassin**

*CAPITAL: Attikamagen (Schefferville)*

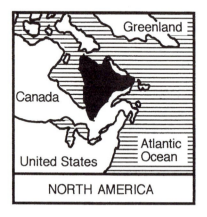

NORTH AMERICA

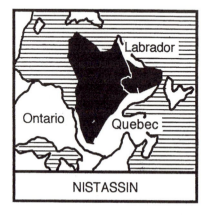

NISTASSIN

*POPULATION:* (95e) 59,000 : 18,000 Nistassine (11,000 Cree, 7,000 Montargnais and Naskapi) in Canada. MAJOR NATIONAL GROUPS: (95e) Quebecker 51%, Nistassine 30%, Labradorean 15%, Inuit 5%, other Canadian. MAJOR LANGUAGES: English, French, Cree, Montargnais, Naskapi. MAJOR RELIGIONS: Roman Catholic, Protestant, animist. MAJOR CITIES: (95e) QUEBEC: Chibougami 4,000, Attikamagen (Schefferville) 3,000, Mistassin (Baie-du-Poste) 2,000, Chisasibi (Fort-George) 2,000. LABRADOR: Labrador City 15,000, Happy Valley-Goose Bay 7,000, Sheshatshit 1,000.

*GEOGRAPHY:* AREA: 308,841 sq.mi.-800,106 sq.km. LOCATION: Nistassin lies in northeastern Canada, occupying the huge Ungava peninsula in northern Quebec* and the eastern districts of the Labrador dependency of Newfoundland.* POLITICAL STATUS: Nistassin has no official status, the region claimed by nationalists forms an unofficial region of Canada pending the resolution of land claims and negotiations on sovereignty.

*FLAG:* The Nistassine national flag, the flag of the national movement, has horizontal stripes of green, pale blue, and green, porportions 1:3:1, the stripes separated by narrow white stripes, and centered on the blue are the Nistassine national symbols in black.

*PEOPLE:* The Nistassine comprise three closely related Native American peoples, all speaking nearly identical dialects of the Cree language of the Algonquin group of languages; the Cree in the west and north, the Naskapi in the northeast, and the Montargnais, including the Innu or Eastern Montargnais, in the southeast, the latter peoples often called Eastern Crees. The three peoples, closely related culturally and linguistically, have united politically since the inception of the Quebec national movement in the 1970s to press for title to traditional lands and to coordinate their response should Quebec separate from Canada. The Quebecker minority is mostly concentrated in the urban areas and in the southeastern part of Labrador around Labrador City. The Labradoreans, mainly English-speaking, are concentrated in the Happy Valley-Goose Bay region.

*THE NATION:* The Nistassine peoples formed a powerful federation before the arrival of the Europeans in the region in the sixteenth century. Often at war with the Iroquois of Haudenosaunee* to the south, the Nistassine moved north and adapted themselves to the harsh sub-Arctic climate. The tribes learned to use every resource available in the bleak terrain, constructing dwellings of stone and driftwood covered with sod in the winter, and in the summer migrated with their herds of caribou while living in skin tents supported by wood or whale ribs. The caribou herds provided shelter, food, and clothing, and greatly influenced the Nistassine culture and traditional way of life.

European navigators sighted the coast in the late fifteenth century, with landings by John Cabot, sailing for England, in 1498, Corte-Reale of Spain in 1500, and Jacques Cartier of France in 1534. Henry Hudson, who sailed into the huge bay that bears his name in 1610–11, recorded the first European contact with the Nistassine peoples. Samuel Champlain later recorded contact with the tribes at the mouth of the Saguenay River far to the southeast. The French called the Cree bands they met Montargnais, meaning mountaineer.

The Nistassine, although a warlike people, welcomed the Europeans to their lands. Missionaries arrived in the region as early as 1615. The British established a trading post on James Bay in 1668. Encouraged by its success, Charles II chartered the Hudson's Bay Company in 1670 and granted the company a huge tract of land encompassing Hudson's Bay's enormous drainage basin. The land grant included the Cree and Naskapi homelands, but the native peoples were neither consulted nor considered. In the south the Montargnais came under French control. In the 1680s and 1690s the Europeans established treaty relations and alliances with the tribes as the competition between the two powers for control of America's rich lands and resources became a serious and often violent rivalry.

Smallpox, brought to the region by the Europeans, decimated the tribes in the eighteenth century just as the European rivalry turned to war. The Seven Years' War that began in Europe in 1756 was preceded by two years of fighting in America between the two sides and their Native American allies, the French and Indian War. All the Nistassine tribes came under British rule with the final French defeat in 1763.

The Nistassine homeland, known as Ungava, originally a possession of the Hudson's Bay Company, became a part of the Northwest Territories in 1869 and a separate territory of Ungava in 1895. In 1912 the Canadian government transferred a part of Ungava to Quebec, and in 1927 the government divided the huge area between Quebec and Labrador. The Nistassine peoples refused to recognize the partition of their homeland. Successive governments, British, French, or Canadian, simply took possession of the tribal lands and parceled them out to forestry and mining companies.

The Canadian government, after World War II, decided that the nomadic Nistassine peoples must settle. By the 1970s the Nistassine peoples lived in permanent settlements, partly in response to the government's generous subsidies. Tribal activists, beginning in the 1960s, denounced the subsidies as drains on incentive and the desire to work. Nationalists in the 1970s, galvanized by the influence of the Quebec nationalist movement, emerged from the generation that assimilation had nearly robbed of their language, culture, and way of life.

In the 1980s Nistassine nationalists launched a campaign to win cultural and linguistic rights and to press for the resolution of long-standing land claims to a vast area of traditional lands. A study published in 1984 confirmed that the incidence of suicide in the Nistassine communities was five times the Canadian average and particularly affected the young. The demands for the resolution of land claims paralleled a campaign to return the despairing Nistassine to a more traditional way of life and fueled the growth of a powerful cultural movement and a parallel national sentiment.

In the east another controversy became a national issue for the entire Nistassine nation. The Innu, or Eastern Montargnais, opposed the post–World War II establishment of a large North Atlantic Treaty Organization (NATO) base at Goose Bay, a center for flight training that the Innu claim has decimated their caribou herds and greatly affected the way of life of the Innu living around the town and the base. The Canadian government hopes to persuade NATO to choose Goose Bay for the alliance's new training center for low-altitude flights, which would raise the number of actual flights from 7,500 to over 40,000 a year. In 1988, frustrated by government inaction to their grievances, Innu activists invaded the base to publicize their plight and their demands.

Nistassine nationalism has become closely tied to Quebecker nationalism. The defeat of the 1992 Canadian constitutional referendum that would have given Native American peoples extensive rights of self-government failed to pass over the contentious issue of Quebec. The resurgence of Quebecker nationalism and their electoral victory in the province in September 1994 have stimulated the growth of Nistassine nationalism. Leaders of the three tribes have reiterated their intention to declare the region independent should Quebec secede.

*SELECTED BIBLIOGRAPHY:*

Cummings, Peter A. *Canada: Native Land Rights and Northern Development.* 1991.
Helm, June. *Handbook of North American Indians: Sub Arctic.* 1981.
Jenness, Diamond. *Indians of Canada.* 1967.
Page, Dance H. *Heritage of the North American Indian People.* 1982.

# NORMANDY

**Normandie; Normande**

*CAPITAL: Rouen*

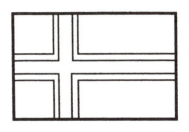

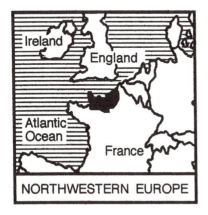

NORTHWESTERN EUROPE

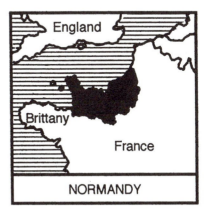

NORMANDY

*POPULATION:* (95e) 3,168,000 : 4,000,000 Normans in France. MAJOR NATIONAL GROUPS: (95e) Norman 91%, other French. MAJOR LANGUAGES: French, Norman. MAJOR RELIGIONS: Roman Catholic, Protestant. MAJOR CITIES: (95e) Le Harve 186,000 (292,000), Caen 111,000 (213,000), Rouen 99,000 (441,000), Calais 78,000 (105,000), Évreux 46,000 (62,000), Dieppe 40,000 (57,000), Alençon 32,000 (45,000), Fécamp 30,000 (53,000), Cherbourg 27,000 (92,000), Saint Lô 25,000 (36,000), Elbeuf 17,000 (54,000).

*GEOGRAPHY:* AREA: 11,519 sq.mi.-29,841 sq.km. LOCATION: Normandy lies in northwestern France, a region of coastal plains rising to the hills of Normandy in the southeast and including the Cotentin Peninsula and the Norman coast on the English Channel, locally called the Norman Channel. POLITICAL STATUS: Normandy has no official status; the region forms two regions of the French republic, Basse-Normandie and Haute-Normandie.

*FLAG:* The Norman national flag, the flag of the national movement, is a red field bearing a red Scandinavian cross, outlined in yellow. OTHER FLAG(S): The flag of the regionalist movement of Normandy is a red field bearing two yellow lions, called Norman Lions, the same lions featured on many of the personal flags of the British royal family and on flags used in the Channel Islands.

*PEOPLE:* The Normans are a French people, the descendants of Germanic Franks and, later, Norse Vikings. The Normans have retained a distinctive culture and a dialect that predates modern French and displays many Norse and

English words and forms. The Normans, true to their Scandinavian heritage, are generally taller, fairer, and more often light-eyed than the other French peoples. The largely rural Normans, in spite of the urbanization of the 1960s and 1970s, have been plagued by rural depopulation since the war. The majority of the Normans are Roman Catholic, with a Protestant minority.

*THE NATION:* The northwestern part of Roman Gaul, the coastal region declined with the Roman withdrawal from Britannia in 410 A.D. Germanic Franks, moving into the declining Roman Empire, settled the Norman coast in 486. In the sixth century the region became part of Charlemagne's Frankish Empire. The region's only large population centers evolved on the coast and in the valley of the Seine River, while rural lords held most of the land in small feudal holdings.

Norse Vikings began to raid the coastal regions in the early ninth century and from 841 controlled most of the coastal districts. The Norsemen established large colonies on the channel and pushed inland against French resistance. Unable to defeat the fierce Vikings, the French king, Charles the Simple, accepted Norse control of the region. In 911 the king recognized Rollo, the Norse chief, as the first duke of Normandy. The Norsemen, later called Normans, accepted Christianity and the French language as the price for French acceptance.

The Normans lost contact with Scandinavia but did not lose the Norse craving for adventure and conquest. On the pretext of expelling the Byzantine Greeks and Arabs from Catholic lands, the Normans conquered southern Italy and Sicily* between 1057 and 1091. Other Norman bands, under Duke William, crossed the channel to conquer Saxon England in 1066. The dukes of Normandy ruled both England and Normandy until the French conquest of the mainland Norman territories in 1204.

The Norman king of England renounced title to Normandy in 1259, but his descendants returned to the mainland to reconquer Normandy in 1346. Returned to the French by treaty in 1360, Normandy again came under English rule in 1417–18 during the Hundred Years' War, which evolved from Norman claims on both sides of the English Channel. A young Frenchwoman, Joan of Arc, burned at the stake in Rouen by the English in 1431 during the long war, became the patron saint of Normandy. In 1450 the defeated English abandoned mainland Normandy, retaining only the Norman Islands, later renamed the Channel Islands. A Norman parliament, established at Rouen in 1499 as a focus for Norman loyalty, exercised considerable regional power until the French Revolution in 1789.

Divested of all traditional privileges, the Normans turned against the French Revolution they had enthusiastically welcomed in 1789–90. Rebellion broke out in Normandy in 1793, the rebels taking the name Chouans, meaning ''owls'' in the Norman dialect. The rebel bands used owl hoots as signals and communications. The Chouans fought a bitter guerrilla war against the revolutionary forces but were ultimately defeated with great loss of life. The crushing of the Chouan revolt is still referred to by Normans as the first modern genocide.

Napoleon Bonaparte, coming to power in the aftermath of revolution and war, split France's historic regions into small departments to undermine local loyalties. Under Napoleon's reorganization of the French state, all power centralized in Paris, where it remained until the late twentieth century. The Normans again rebelled against the loss of all rights in 1815, forcing Napoleon to divert troops from the decisive final battle at Waterloo.

Normandy remained pastoral and underdeveloped. With all state functions centralized in Paris, Normans had to leave their homeland in order to excel in the arts, literature, government, or education. Resentment of the need to emigrate and the threat to their culture incited the beginning of a modest Norman national movement, one of the few in Western Europe not based on language in the late nineteenth century.

Prior to World War II, nationalist and radical political parties proliferated in Normandy, stimulated by the region's economic backwardness. In 1939 workers in Paris earned an average 40% more than their Norman counterparts.

Occupied by Nazi German troops in 1940, Normandy became part of the front line facing Britain across the channel. A concerted German campaign during the war to win Norman support by stressing common Nordic origins of the German and Norman peoples met with little success.

The first region of continental Europe to be liberated from Nazi occupation in June 1944, Normandy sustained massive damage. By the early 1950s Normandy had recovered and experienced a modest prosperity based on cross-channel trade. A regionalist movement, claiming that Paris appropriated Normandy's finest resources and most talented people, gained support after France's entry in the European Economic Community (EEC) in 1960 shifted French trade to the east and away from Normandy and the channel.

The Normans, but not the French government, supported Britain's and Ireland's bid to join the EEC, finally realized in 1973. The increasing integration of Europe has given new impetus to the growing Norman national movement. Few Normans see the sense of applying to Paris, to the east, for trade agreements with Normandy's natural trading partners, Britain and Ireland, to the west.

Granted some regional powers by the new socialist government in 1981, the national movement focused on the unification of the historic Norman territories and demands for greater economic autonomy. The survival of the declining Norman dialect has become a major nationalist issue in the 1990s. For the small, but growing, number of pro-European separatists, the survival of the Norman culture and dialect depends on achieving Norman sovereignty in a united, federal Europe of the regions.

*SELECTED BIBLIOGRAPHY:*

Collins, Martin. *Normandy.* 1986.

Douglas, David C. *William the Conqueror: The Norman Impact on England.* 1964.

Dutton, Ralph. *Normandy and Brittany.* 1953.

Jewett, S. *The Story of the Normans.* 1990.

# NORTH CHAD

**Muslim Chad; Islamic Republic of North Chad; Tchad du Nord**

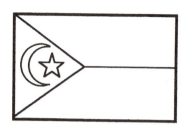

*CAPITAL: N'Djamena*

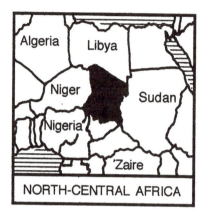

NORTH-CENTRAL AFRICA

NORTH CHAD

*POPULATION:* (95e) 3,421,000 : 2,465,000 North Chadians in Chad. MAJOR NATIONAL GROUPS: (95e) Sudanic Arabs 41% (Zagawa, Baggara, Shuwa, Oueler Shiner), Teda 27%, Wadaian 9% (Masalit, Maba, Mimi), Kanembu (Kanuri) 8%, Hausa, Fulani, Berti, Tama, Dagu, Daza, Toubou, Taureg, Hadjeraï, Baguirmi, other Chadian. MAJOR LANGUAGES: Arabic, Teda, Maba, Kanuri, Masalit, French. MAJOR RELIGIONS: (95e) Sunni Muslim 76%, animist 9%, Christian 5%. MAJOR CITIES: (95e) N'Djamena 648,000, Abéché 196,000, Ati 80,000, Biltine 63,000, Massaguet 52,000, Bokoro 47,000, Mongo 35,000, Mao 25,000, Faya 20,000.

*GEOGRAPHY:* AREA: 403,005 sq.mi.-1,044,055 sq.km. LOCATION: North Chad lies in north-central Africa, occupying the arid Tibesti Mountains in the southern reaches of the Sahara Desert in northern Chad, but with bush lands and savanna in the south around Lake Chad and the Ouaddai Plateau. POLITICAL STATUS: North Chad has no official status, the territory claimed by the Muslim nationalists includes the Chadian prefectures of Borkou-Ennedi-Tibesti, Biltine, Ouaddai, Lac, Kanem, and Batha and the northern districts of the prefectures of Salamat, Guéra, and Chari-Baguirmi.

*FLAG:* The North Chadian national flag, the flag of the national movement, is a horizontal bicolor of red over green bearing a white triangle at the hoist charged with a green crescent moon and five-pointed star. OTHER FLAG(S): The flag of the largest national organization, the Chad National Liberation Front (FROLINAT), is the same as the national flag except that the bottom stripe, crescent moon, and star are pale blue.

*PEOPLE:* The North Chadians are a Muslim people comprising dozens of distinct peoples representing several distinct cultural and linguistic groups but are united by religion and history. Most of the North Chadian peoples are of mixed Arabic, Berber, and black African descent. The largest segment of the North Chadian nation is the Sudanic Arabs, speaking Sudanic dialects of Arabic, the lingua franca of the region. Other languages widely used are the Nilo-Saharan languages and Maba. The majority of the North Chadian peoples are nomadic or seminomadic herders. A contentious claim that the North Chadians are ethnic Libyans has complicated the political and ethnic relationships in the region since the colonial period.

*THE NATION:* Known to the ancient Egyptians, the peoples of the region absorbed cultural influences from the civilizations of North Africa and the later Christian kingdoms that grew up in the area just to the east in the early Christian Era. The area south of the Sahara, mentioned by Arab historians as a region settled by nomadic pagan Arabs in the early seventh century A.D., received an influx of Berber refugees fleeing the Arab invasion of North Africa in the seventh and eighth centuries. The Arab and Berber migrants conquered or weakened the tribal states in the region, and an Arab-Berber culture spread across the region.

In the eighth century newcomers from the upper Nile Valley moved into the area and established walled city-states in the fertile lands in the south. Zagawa Arab nomads, possibly of Berber origin, conquered much of the region in the ninth century, laying the foundations for the later states that developed as regional powers in the eleventh and twelfth centuries.

Invading Muslim Arabs conquered the area and introduced Islam, traditionally in the year 1090. Controlled by a sophisticated Muslim Berber-Arab pastoral elite, the states of the region grew wealthy on the trans-Saharan caravan trade. The Muslims raided the black African tribes to the south for captives to send north to the slave markets of North Africa.

The empire of Kanem-Bornu or Kanowra,* centered on Lake Chad, conquered the numerous small warring states in the thirteenth century. Its mounted and armored warriors defeated an invasion by nomadic peoples in 1386. At the height of its power in the sixteenth and early seventeenth centuries, Kanem-Bornu controlled a vast empire in Central Africa.

The Fulani, a powerful warrior people, conquered most of the Muslim states south of the Sahara in the early nineteenth century, except for Kanem-Bornu. The Kanembu defeated the Fulani in 1812, but the effort so weakened the state that it began to disintegrate. The ancient empire was wracked by civil wars and clan and tribal conflicts when the first Europeans visited the region in 1822.

In the 1890s the Madhists, Islamic fundamentalists from present Sudan, conquered the districts in the east. In the west, Rabah Zobeir, also called Rabah Amoney, a Sudanese ex-slave turned slave trader and military chieftain, rose to power. Called the ''Napoleon of Africa,'' Rabah led a vast Muslim army west, defeating and absorbing tribes and states. Alarmed by his advance the rulers of

Kanem-Bornu requested French military aid in 1893. In 1900 a combined European military force defeated Rabah's army, and in 1902 the Europeans divided his empire between their various colonial empires.

The new French territories officially became part of Chad, a French colony south of Lake Chad since 1897. The Muslim peoples, from the beginning, rejected inclusion in a territory with the tribes they had formerly raided for slaves and booty. The French military finally subdued the Muslim tribes in 1912, and over the next year the region became part of the Chad colony. Although officially in civilian-ruled French West Africa, the Muslim northern districts of Chad remained under virtual French occupation due to the frequent uprisings.

Chad became an independent republic in 1960. The first postcolonial government, dominated by the black African tribes of the south, was rejected in the Muslim north. The French maintained a strong military presence that maintained a precarious calm, but in 1965 the Chadian government requested their withdrawal. In 1966, no longer constrained by the French presence, several Muslim leaders demanded the secession of the northern provinces and the establishment of an independent Islamic Republic of North Chad. The Front de Libération Nationale du Tchad (FROLINAT) assumed the leadership of the diverse groups. The nationalists' demands for autonomy, a larger share of power, and a fairer distribution of development funds were rejected by the French-backed Chadian government in N'Djamena.

In spite of several French-brokered truces and cease-fires and, in 1968, military intervention, rebellion spread across the region in 1970, setting off a vicious civil war. In 1978 the FROLINAT forces gained control of most of North Chad, but again the French intervened and forced negotiations. A government of national reconciliation, including Muslim leaders, fell apart, and the rebellion resumed in 1979. In March 1979 the FROLINAT forces took control of N'Djamena and drove the southern tribes from power.

In December 1980 Libyan troops intervened in the region, deepening the crisis as conflicts between various Muslim groups erupted in violence. Since 1980 the confused shifting of alliances and fighting between various Muslim factions has splintered the North Chad national movement. The repeated military intervention by the French and Libyan incursions exacerbated the chaos in the region. In October 1992 the French dispatched troops to protect a Chadian government that commands little loyalty in either Muslim North Chad or in Christian and animist Logone Chad in the south. In August 1994 a rebellion against the minority Muslim government spread across the southern provinces.

*SELECTED BIBLIOGRAPHY:*

Briggs, L. Cabot. *The Tribes of the Sahara.* 1960.

Manning, Patrick. *Francofone Sub-Sahara Africa 1880–1985.* 1988.

Thompson, Virginia, and Richard Aldoff. *The Emerging States of French Equatorial Africa.* 1960.

Timberlake, Lloyd. *Africa in Crisis.* 1989.

Trimingham, J. Spencer. *Islam in West Africa.* 1959.

# NORTH EPIRUS

Northern Epirus; Vorios Epiros;
Vorios Ipiros; Epeiros

*CAPITAL: Korytsa (Korcë)*

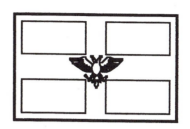

SOUTH-CENTRAL EUROPE

NORTH EPIRUS

*POPULATION:* (95e) 605,000 : 300,000 Epirote Greeks in Albania. MAJOR NATIONAL GROUPS: (95e) Epirote Greek 50%, Tosk Albanian 30%, Macedonian 13%, other Albanian (mostly Gheg). MAJOR LANGUAGES: Albanian (Tosk dialect), Greek, Macedonian. MAJOR RELIGIONS: (95e) Greek Orthodox 73%, Sunni Muslim 20%. MAJOR CITIES: (95e) Korytsa (Korcë) 77,000, Agryrokastron (Gjirokastër) 31,000, Saranda (Sarandë) 20,000, Chimarra (Himarë) 11,000, Tepelon (Tepelenë) 10,000.

*GEOGRAPHY:* AREA: 3,266 sq.mi.-8,461 sq.km. LOCATION: North Epirus lies in the southern Balkan Peninsula, a region sixty miles east to west in southern Albania, straddling the Pindus Mountains just north of the Greek border. POLITICAL STATUS: North Epirus has no official status; the region forms the departments Gjirokastër, Kolonjë, Korcë, Përmet, Sarandë, Skrapar, and Tepelenë, and the southern districts of Vlorë Department in Albania.

*INDEPENDENCE DECLARED:* 1 March 1914.

*FLAG:* The Epirote Greek national flag, the flag of the national movement, is a white field outlined in pale blue and bearing a broad, pale blue cross charged with a small, black, double-headed eagle centered. OTHER FLAG(S): The flag of the former republic is a dark blue field divided by a broad white cross centered behind a black, double-headed eagle, wings spread to the hoist and fly and holding in its claws the symbols of Epirote sovereignty.

*PEOPLE:* The Epirotes, better known as Epirote Greeks, are a Greek-speaking people, the descendants of the ancient Epirotes. Although the Epirote

Greek nationalists and the Greek government claim an ethnic Greek population of over 300,000 in the region, the Albanian government claims there are only 60,000 Greek-speaking people in Albania. Overwhelmingly Greek Orthodox by religion, the Epirote Greeks, the Orthodox Tosks, and the Macedonians form a compact Orthodox population of over half a million in predominantly Muslim Albania. Never part of modern Greece, the Epirote Greeks preserve dialects and cultural traditions that disappeared in Greece centuries ago.

*THE NATION:* Epirus, meaning "mainland" in ancient Greek, formed a separate kingdom unified by King Pyrrhus in 272 B.C. and declared a republic in 200 B.C. Overrun by the expanding Macedonian state, Epirus again became an independent kingdom following Macedonia's defeat by the Romans in 197 B.C. Rome annexed the kingdom to the growing Roman Empire in 146 B.C. Roman Epirus remained with the eastern half of the empire, Greek Byzantium, when the vast state split in A.D. 395.

Michael Angelus Commennus erected a resurgent Epirote state at the collapse of the Byzantine Empire in 1204. When the Crusaders set up a Latin state centered on the former Byzantine capital, Constantinople, Epirus remained a Greek state. The Epirotes played an important part in the preservation of Greek culture in the West.

The Turks added Epirus to their expanding empire following a long campaign, 1430–40. Administered by Greek officials under a Turkish governor, the majority of the region's Greek and Albanian Tosk populations retained their Christian religion and Greek orientation, while the majority of the Albanian Ghegs to the north converted to Islam. The Albanian language, banned by the Turks, gave way to Greek as the language of administration and daily life in the region.

Ali Pasha, the ruler of Yanina (Ioannina) in the late eighteenth century, expelled the Turks and created an independent Epirote state. The Turks soon retook the state, but with Greek independence from the Ottoman Empire in 1829, the Turkish hold on Epirus began to loosen. In 1881 the Greeks took the southern Epirus region from the declining Ottomans and pressed their claim to the Greek Orthodox districts of northern Epirus.

The First Balkan War of 1912 ended Turkish domination of the Balkans, with Albania declared independent and the Greek frontiers again expanded to the north. Greek troops, in an attempt to press Greek territorial claims, occupied the mainly Christian districts of northern Epirus. The Greek-speaking Epirotes, opposed to Albanian rule, joined by the leaders of the Orthodox Albanian Tosks, who opposed both Greek and Muslim Gheg rule, formed a joint provisional government in 1912. The joint Epirote administration repeatedly rebuffed overtures from Greece and Albania.

The Greek occupation troops withdrew under international pressure in February 1914. Under the terms of an interim agreement, the Albanian authorities would take control of the region. Rejecting the agreement, the Epirote provisional government declared the independence of the Republic of North Epirus on 1 March 1914. The resulting crisis, bringing Greece and Albania close to war, merged into the chaos of the outbreak of World War I.

Greek troops moved north to reoccupy North Epirus in December 1914 but withdrew under pressure from French and Italian troops in 1916. An autonomous state with its capital at Korytsa, supported by the French, collapsed with the French withdrawal. In 1920 Albanian troops occupied the region, and the Epirote districts were integrated into the Albanian state.

Epirote demands for regional political and religious autonomy in southern Albania were ignored or suppressed over the next decade. In 1935 the Albanian government forcibly closed Greek institutions and schools and removed all Orthodox Christians from official positions. Under the leadership of Ethem Toto, a dismissed government minister, the Epirote Christians rebelled in 1936. Intent on severing North Epirus from Albania, the rebels took control of much of the region, but the rebellion collapsed with Toto's death in 1937.

Fascist Italian troops occupied Albania in October 1939. The Epirotes again rebelled and, with Greek support, organized a provisional government, which collapsed with the German invasion of 1941. Near the end of World War II, in 1944, the Greek government reiterated its claim to the region, but in 1945 the Allied powers reestablished the prewar frontiers.

Albania's Communist government, installed in 1946, quickly suppressed all opposition. The radical Communist administration instituted decades of harsh rule and .intense assimilation pressure on the Greek Epirote minority. In 1967 the government closed all religious institutions, outlawed all public worship, and officially denied the existence of the Orthodox Christian population in North Epirus.

The collapse of Communism allowed the Epirotes, for the first time in over forty years, to organize. Demanding the same rights that the new Albanian government demanded for the Albanian minority in Kosovo* in Yugoslavia, in 1991 the Epirotes appealed to Greece. The ensuing crisis in the region polarized the positions. In 1993–94 hundreds of Greek Epirote military officers, administrators, and teachers lost their positions as the Albanian government moved to suppress the growing national movement following demands for a referendum on independence for North Epirus. The government closed Greek-language schools and institutions that the administration claimed supported Epirote separatism.

In May 1994, amid a growing crisis between Greece and Albania, the Albanian government arrested and tried for separatism several of the Epirote Greek leaders. The crisis deepened in November 1994 with government attempts to replace the Soviet-era constitution with a new constitution that the Epirotes claim restricts their rights.

*SELECTED BIBLIOGRAPHY:*

Forester, E. S. *A Short History of Modern Greece, 1821–1956.* 1958.
Pearson, Raymond. *National Minorities in Europe, 1848–1945.* 1985.
Stickney, E. P. *Southern Albania or Northern Epirus in European International Affairs, 1912–1923.* 1926.

# NORTHERN CYPRUS

**Kibris; Turkish Republic of Northern Cyprus**

*CAPITAL: Lefkosa (Nicosia)*

SOUTHEASTERN EUROPE

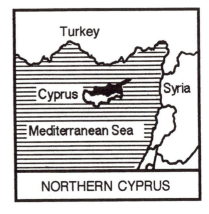

NORTHERN CYPRUS

*POPULATION:* (95e) 211,000 : 145,000 Turkish Cypriots in Cyprus. MAJOR NATIONAL GROUPS: (95e) Turkish Cypriot 68%, Turkish 29%, Greek Cypriot 2%, Armenian. MAJOR LANGUAGES: Turkish, English, Greek. MAJOR RELIGIONS: (95e) Sunni Muslim 97%, Greek Orthodox. MAJOR CITIES: (95e) Lefkosa (Nicosia) 38,000 (71,000), Gazi Magusa (Famagusta) 38,000, Girne (Kyrenia) 22,000, Morphu (Morphou) 15,000.

*GEOGRAPHY:* AREA: 1,295 sq.mi.-3,354 sq.km. LOCATION: Northern Cyprus occupies the northern part of the island of Cyprus in the eastern Mediterranean Sea forty miles south of the Turkish mainland and sixty miles west of Syria. POLITICAL STATUS: Northern Cyprus forms a self-proclaimed republic under Turkish occupation and protection. The official status of the region remains in dispute.

*INDEPENDENCE DECLARED:* 15 November 1983.

*FLAG:* The Turkish Cypriot national flag, the official flag of the republic, is a white field, with narrow, horizontal red stripes near the top and bottom, bearing a red crescent moon and red, five-pointed star.

*PEOPLE:* The Turkish Cypriots are a Turkish people, descendants of medieval settlers from the Turkish mainland. Better educated and more prosperous than the mainland Turks, the Cypriot Turks are separated from the Turks by centuries of history. The Cypriots speak a dialect of Turkish that incorporates English and Greek words. Since 1974 over 60,000 mainland Turks, called Anatolian Turks, have settled in the region, not counting the 29,000 Turkish soldiers and their families. The Turkish Cypriots are Sunni Muslims, the small Greek Cypriot and Armenian minorities are mostly Orthodox Christian.

*THE NATION:* The largest island in the eastern Mediterranean, Cyprus received colonists from most of the ancient empires that arose in the Middle East, North Africa, and Southern Europe, although the Greeks formed a majority from about 295 B.C. Conquered by the Romans in 58 B.C., the island remained a part of the eastern Roman Empire when the state divided in A.D. 395. Captured by the European Crusaders in 1191, the island became a territory of the French Lusignan family from 1192 to 1474. In 1489 the maritime empire of Venice added Cyprus to its growing empire.

Ottoman Turks invaded the island in 1562, with the last Venetian stronghold overwhelmed in 1571. The Turks imposed a harsh rule, suppressing the majority Greek Christians and settling thousands of Muslim Turks on confiscated lands. Frequent Greek rebellions, crushed with great severity, exacerbated the ethnic enmity between the island's two largest national groups.

Mainland Greece, independent of Turkish rule in 1829, supported Greek Cypriot demands for *enosis*, union with Greece. Greek volunteers aided a sporadic rebellion against Turkish rule. The Ottoman government, unable to crush the uprising, leased the island to Great Britain in 1878. Modern education and health care, introduced by the British administration, greatly benefited both ethnic groups and raised living standards on the island far beyond those of mainland Turkey or Greece. Great Britain formally annexed the island when the Ottoman Empire joined the Central Powers as war began in 1914.

In spite of the material benefits of British rule, Greek Cypriot agitation for *enosis* continued to sour relations between the island's two peoples. The Turkish Cypriots vehemently opposed inclusion in the Greek state. The dispute exploded in violent ethnic clashes in 1931 and with periodic disturbances up to World War II. A new round of violence erupted in 1954, provoked by renewed Greek Cypriot demands for union with Greece. The Turkish Cypriot minority, rejecting both Greek Cypriot domination and union with Greece, demanded *taksim*, the partition of the island between the two national groups.

Negotiations between the two groups and the British authorities broke down in 1955, when the Greek Cypriot Organization (EOKA) launched a violent campaign to drive the British from the island and achieve union with Greece by force. An agreement reached in 1959 precluded both union with Greece and partition. The compromise paved the way for Cypriot independence in 1960. The United Kingdom, Greece, and Turkey signed the independence agreement as guarantors of Cypriot peace and territorial integrity.

The Turkish Cypriots, dominated by the majority Greek population, rebelled in 1963. The uprising set off a vicious civil war and brought Greece and Turkey close to war. Greek Cypriot military officers led a coup that overthrew the island's government on 16 July 1974, the coup leaders demanding immediate *enosis*. When diplomatic efforts failed, the Turkish government, citing its obligations as a signatory to the 1959 independence agreement, launched an invasion of the island on 20 July. The 40,000 Turkish troops landed on the northern coast quickly took control of half the island. Two hundred thousand Greek Cypriots fled south, while 45,000 Turks fled north to the occupation zone.

International efforts to mediate the dispute floundered as the Turkish Cypriots demanded legal partition and declared an autonomous state in the 37% of the island under Turkish occupation. The Turkish government began to settle colonists from its underdeveloped eastern provinces on the lands abandoned by Greek refugees. Repeated attempts at negotiations failed over Turkish insistence on a bizonal federation and Greek Cypriot demands for a unitary state.

Frustrated by the lack of progress after several rounds of negotiations, the Turkish Cypriot government declared the independence of the Turkish Republic of Northern Cyprus on 15 November 1983 but left open the option of later federation. The new state, recognized only by Turkey, has continued to insist that its independence is not negotiable.

The large number of Anatolian Turks settled in the state have become a point of contention with the Turkish Cypriots. Although they share language and religion, they have little else in common. The Cypriots' world outlook and economic development had diverged from those of the mainland centuries before. Cypriot incomes, averaging 70% higher than those on the mainland, became an issue between the two Turkish peoples. The Turkish Cypriot community fear that their unique island culture will be swamped by immigration from the mainland, but an even greater fear is the loss of Turkey's military protection.

In early 1992 the United Nations put forward new proposals for a single Cypriot state made up of two zones, but again the negotiations failed. The Turkish Cypriots again reiterated that independence is not negotiable, but a federation of independent states on the island would meet the requirements of both national groups. The Greeks rejected the proposal.

In August 1991, following a new round of failed talks, the European Union complicated the situation by suggesting that Greek Cyprus join the union on its own. The union also imposed import restrictions on goods from Northern Cyprus. The European Union took 74% of Northern Cyprus's exports in 1993. The European Union's intervention exacerbated the Turkish Cypriot's sense of isolation and their determination to maintain their independence.

*SELECTED BIBLIOGRAPHY:*
Attalides, Michael. *Cyprus: Nationalism and International Politics.* 1979.
Bahcheli, Tozun. *Greek-Turkish Relations since 1955.* 1989.
Markides, Kyriaios C. *The Rise and Fall of the Cypriot Republic.* 1977.
More, Jasper. *The Mediterranean.* 1956.

# NORTH SOLOMONS

**Bougainville**

*CAPITAL: Arawa (Kieta)*

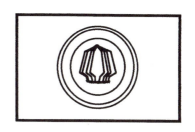

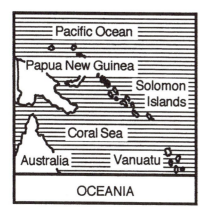

OCEANIA

NORTH SOLOMONS

*POPULATION:* (95e) 185,000 : 175,000 Bougainvillians in Papua New Guinea. MAJOR NATIONAL GROUPS: (95e) Bougainvillian 93%, Polynesian 5%. MAJOR LANGUAGES: Pidgin, Melanesian and Polynesian dialects, English. MAJOR RELIGIONS: (95e) Roman Catholic 55%, Protestant 20%, animist. MAJOR CITIES: (95e) Arawa (Kieta) 10,000, Sohano 5,000, Lemankoa 2,000.

*GEOGRAPHY:* AREA: 4,310 sq.mi.-11,165 sq.km. LOCATION: The North Solomons lie in the southwestern Pacific Ocean, forming part of the Solomon Islands group, most of which is included in the separate Solomon Islands republic just southeast. POLITICAL STATUS: The North Solomons, often called Bougainville for the largest of the islands, officially form an autonomous province of Papua New Guinea; however, their status remains in dispute.

*INDEPENDENCE DECLARED:* 1 September 1975; 17 May 1990.

*FLAG:* The North Solomons flag, the flag of the national movement, is a medium blue field charged with a centered black disc bearing a white and brown *upe*, the ceremonial headdress of the islands, within a green and white design representing *kapkap*, an abalone shell necklace.

*PEOPLE:* The Bougainvillians are a Melanesian people related to the Solomon Islanders just to the southwest but are not ethnically or culturally related to the Papuan peoples of New Guinea, Papua New Guinea's largest and dominant island. The Bougainvillians' culture is a Melanesian culture with Polynesian borrowings, known for colorful and elaborate ceremonies. The Bougainvillians speak several Melanesian dialects, along with a lingua franca used throughout the southwest Pacific, Pidgin, a patois of English. The majority of the islanders are Roman Catholic, with a large Protestant minority and smaller groups adhering to traditional religious beliefs. The Christian Bougainvillians have retained many of their pre-Christian traditions and beliefs, often mixed with the later Catholic and Protestant customs.

*THE NATION:* The islands, populated by Melanesians, were first sighted by Portuguese navigator Alvaro de Mendaña in 1567. The islands were later explored by Mendaña and others, but the Europeans made no attempt to colonize the islands, and no Europeans visited for nearly two centuries. The next Europeans to visit the islands arrived with the French Bougainville expedition in 1768. The leader of the expedition left his family name as the name of the largest island.

Fierce Melanesian resistance precluded colonization, and only a few traders and missionaries settled in the islands after 1845. Not fully explored until they came under the control of a German trading company in 1882, the islands became the object of a territorial dispute between Germany and Britain. In 1886 the European powers divided the Solomon Islands, the northern islands of the Solomon group confirmed as a German possession. Bougainville's harbors and interior mines made it one of Germany's most valuable colonies.

The Germans attempted to fortify the islands when war began in Europe in 1914, their efforts overtaken by an invasion of Allied troops. Australian civil administration of the islands was formalized at the end of the war under a 1920 League of Nations mandate. The Australians joined the North Solomons to their territory of New Guinea. Occupied by the Japanese military forces from 1942 to 1945, the islands returned to Australian administration as part of a trust territory of the new United Nations at the end of World War II.

The early missionary activity and Australian development schemes in the 1960s and 1970s made the North Solomons the most developed district of the New Guinea Trust Territory. An educated leadership formed a national movement in the 1960s. In 1968 the nationalists proposed a referendum on the choices available to the islands: independence, autonomy, or union with the neighboring British Solomon Islands.

An Australian mining consortium began to exploit Bougainville's huge copper deposits in 1972. The Bougainvillians strenuously opposed the mining operations, which they claimed abused the spirit of the land. Following several clashes, the mining company hired an anthropologist to coordinate the mining operations with the islanders' beliefs and traditions. The enormous profits from the mine, part going to the territorial government at Port Moresby, opened a dispute over the disposition of the funds. The Bougainvillians demanded a greater share of the profits for local development and for use in rehabilitating the lands desecrated by the mining operations.

The dispute over the mine was paralleled by rising ethnic tensions between the Melanesians and Papuan workers brought in from New Guinea. Violence between the two groups increased as Papua New Guinea moved toward independence. The leaders of the North Solomons, two weeks before Papua New Guinea's scheduled independence, on 1 September 1975, declared the district independent. One of the first acts of the government of Papua New Guinea, independent on 16 September, was to suspend the provincial government of the North Solomons and dispatch troops to occupy the islands.

Pro-independence violence again broke out in 1976, pushing the government to negotiate an autonomy agreement with island leaders, including the right to veto unwanted development. Secessionist sentiment declined with the restoration of provincial government. The island's copper mine developed Papua New Guinea's major source of foreign currency and provided some 20% of the country's total as revenue.

The expansion of the mine in the early 1980s renewed ethnic tensions between the islanders and the growing Papuan labor force. The Melanesians, holding all life sacred, were appalled by the almost daily Papuan murders. Ethnic tolerance turned to ethnic antagonism and racial slurs. The Bougainvillians call the Papuans Skin i Red, Redskins, while the Papuans refer to the islanders as Bilong Suspen, pidgin for as black as the remains in the bottom of a saucepan.

Growing objections to the open-pit copper mine, which offends the Bougainvillians' traditional reverence for the land, focused on the issue of damage to the island and the belief that when the copper is exhausted, they will be left with just a huge hole, a ruined landscape, and extremely polluted rivers. In 1988 island leaders demanded $12 billion to repair the damage done by the mine, one of the world's largest man-made holes, some 2,000 yards across.

Ignored by the Papuan government, the Bougainvillians rebelled, forcing the mine to close. Threatened by government troops, the rebel leaders declared Bougainville independent of Papua New Guinea on 17 May 1990. The government began an economic blockade of the island but withdrew its soldiers after several bloody clashes.

In 1992 the government again sent soldiers to end the secession, but the invasion failed and degenerated into sporadic fighting. In March 1993 the island's nationalist leaders appealed to the United Nations for the dispatch of a peacekeeping force. Negotiations, the first in three years, began in August 1993 but soon collapsed over the issues of the mine and the Bougainvillians' insistence on retaining their independence.

*SELECTED BIBLIOGRAPHY:*
Cranestone, B.A.L. *Melanesia.* 1961.
Rodman, Margaret, and Matthew Cooper, eds. *The Pacification of Melanesia.* 1983.
Siers, James. *Papua New Guinea.* 1984.
Whiteman, Darrel L. *Melanesians and Missionaries.* 1990.

# NORTHUMBRIA

**North England; Northumberland**

*CAPITAL: Newcastle upon Tyne*

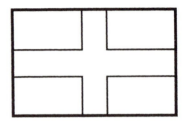

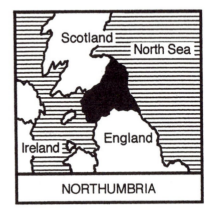

*POPULATION:* (95e) 3,071,000 : 3,496,000 Northumbrians in England. MAJOR NATIONAL GROUPS: (95e) Northumbrian 91%, Scots 5%, other English. MAJOR LANGUAGE: English (Northumbrian dialect). MAJOR RELIGIONS: Protestant, Roman Catholic. MAJOR CITIES: (95e) Newcastle upon Tyne 195,000 (1,305,000), Sunderland 181,000, Middlesbrough 160,000 (604,000), Gateshead 90,000, Hartlespool 88,000, Darlington 85,000 (108,000), Stockton-on-Tees 84,000, South Shields 84,000, Carlisle 78,000 (105,000), Barrow-in-Furness 48,000 (81,000), Durham 39,000 (94,000), Peterlee 35,000 (56,000), Blyth 34,000 (123,000).

*GEOGRAPHY:* AREA: 5,944 sq.mi.-15,401 sq.km. LOCATION: Northumbria, commonly called the North, occupies a region of rolling hills and lakes between the Irish and North Seas in northern England, just south of the border with Scotland.* POLITICAL STATUS: Designated a European region, Northumbria forms the English metropolitan county of Tyne and Wear and the non-metropolitan counties of Cleveland, Cumbria, Durham, and Northumberland.

*FLAG:* The Northumbrian flag is a horizontal bicolor of red over green charged with a centered, broad yellow cross.

*PEOPLE:* The Northumbrians, commonly called Geordies, particularly in the Tyneside region, are a northern English people speaking a dialect that developed from medieval Northumbrian, a language not influenced by the introduction of Norman French to the South in the eleventh century. The Geordie character and culture, incorporating both English and Scottish influences, retain many traits and traditions that disappeared in other parts of England. The culture of the

North developed around the ancient coal mines, mining dictated the way and rhythm of life for centuries. The Northumbrians increasingly consider themselves a distinct British people and a separate European nation.

*THE NATION:* The Celtic Ottadeni of the region between the seas came under Roman rule in the first century A.D. Their Latinized homeland formed the northern frontier of Roman Britannia. In an effort to protect the northern districts from attacks by Picts and Celts, the Romans constructed the defensive structure known as Hadrian's Wall between A.D. 120 and 123. The region, prosperous under Roman rule, declined rapidly with the collapse of Roman power and the withdrawal of the Roman garrisons from Britannia in 410.

Invaded and occupied by Germanic Angles from the European mainland in the early sixth century, the region became a separate kingdom, Bernicia. The kingdom later united with Deira, to the south, to form Northumbria, one of the seven Anglo-Saxon kingdoms of England. Converted to Christianity in 627, the kingdom experienced a golden age in the eighth and ninth centuries, a great flowering of the arts, literature, and scholarship.

The coastal areas came under Viking attack in the ninth century, the southern part of the kingdom conquered by the Norsemen in 867. The Viking invasion ended Northumbria's preeminent position in England. The Angles, maintaining a small kingdom north of the Tees River, accepted the authority of the king of Wessex in 920 and became part of the united English kingdom.

The Norman conquest of England in 1066 introduced a more centralized form of government, the North divided into counties administered by Norman nobles and the traditional liberties of the Anglo-Saxon inhabitants greatly curtailed. Reaction to authoritarian Norman rule, especially among the Anglo-Saxons, led to the reestablishment of political and personal freedom with the signing of the Magna Carta in 1215 and the creation of an English parliament in 1295.

The northern counties, forming the border with the separate Kingdom of Scotland, suffered during centuries of border wars until the two kingdoms united under the rule of the House of Stuart in 1603. Scotland joined the united Kingdom of Great Britain in 1707, ensuring the security of the Northumbrian region. Peace on the border allowed the spread of the Industrial Revolution to the North, with the rapid development of large industrial enterprises, ports, and mines, largely based on the region's important coal deposits, the world's oldest coal field and the center of Northumbrian life.

The region, far from the center of government, experienced serious unrest in the early nineteenth century with Geordie industrial workers demanding the same rights as those enjoyed by the more prosperous classes in the south. Rapid industrial expansion converted the region into a powerhouse of English industry, spurred by the expansion of the overseas British Empire. The profits from the industrialization of Northumbria, however, mostly went to the industrialists and the government based in London.

Important to the British war effort during World War I, the long conflict seriously drained the region's wealth and manpower. Severe economic problems in the 1920s converted the declining northern counties into a bastion of anti-governmental sentiment and a center of support for the new Labor Party. Economically devastated by the depression of the 1930s, the region revived during World War II. A Labor government, elected in 1945, nationalized the mining industry and introduced the British welfare system in 1948 that helped to eliminate regional economic and social differences. In 1950 the Northumbrian incomes drew equal to those of the prosperous South.

The North began a long decline following the election of a Conservative government in 1951, exacerbated by the increasing centralization of political power in London and the southeastern counties. Chronic unemployment, decaying cities, and aging industries raised social tensions and sparked a renewal of a regionalist movement and a resurgence of separate Geordie identity. The growing regional movement demanded a fairer distribution of development and investment for the perennially depressed North.

The United Kingdom's entry into the European Economic Community in 1973 further concentrated investment and development in the prosperous counties around London. By 1985 incomes in the North had fallen to 3% below the national average, while incomes in the Southeast climbed to 5% above the average, and the gap continued to widen.

Demands for autonomy and devolution of political power by the non-English nations in the United Kingdom reverberated in the Geordie North. Proposals for regional government, more responsive to local needs, have met with repeated rejections in London. Geordie regionalism grew rapidly during the 1980s amid increasing unrest and growing unemployment, up to 30% in some areas. In 1991 severe rioting swept the region, the riots highlighting the massive political and economic problems of the North.

The longest economic decline since the depression of the 1930s, blamed on the Conservative government, has raised demands for economic independence. The region, with strong support for devolution of power, increasingly looks to Europe, with a nationalist minority advocating independence within a federal United Kingdom or even within a united, federal Europe. Following the overthrow of Communism in Eastern Europe, Northumbria is often called the only remaining one-party state in Europe, a state ruled by a political party, the Conservatives, that have never won an election in the region.

*SELECTED BIBLIOGRAPHY:*

Forester, G.C.F., ed. *Northern History: A Review of the History of the North of England.* 1966.

Fraser, C. M., and K. Emsley. *Northumbria.* 1989.

Mason, Roger. *The North.* 1986.

# NUNAVUT

**Nunaavut; Tungavik Federation of Nunavut**

*CAPITAL: Iqaluit (Frobisher Bay)*

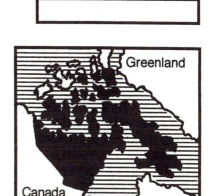

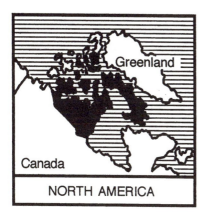

*POPULATION:* (95e) 23,000 : 25,000 Inuit in Canada. MAJOR NATIONAL GROUPS: (95e) Inuit 74%, other Canadian. MAJOR LANGUAGES: Inuktituk, English. MAJOR RELIGIONS: Protestant, Roman Catholic, animist. MAJOR CITIES: (95e) Iqaluit 3,000, Coppermine 2,000, Rankin Inlet 1,500, Eskimo Point 1,000, Baker Lake 1,000.

*GEOGRAPHY:* AREA: 770,000 sq.mi.-1,994,819 sq.km. LOCATION: Nunavut, meaning Land of the People, lies in northern Canada, occupying a huge area north of the Arctic Circle and including a number of large islands in James and Hudson Bays, mostly tundra areas north of the tree line. The islands of Nunavut in the northeast border on Kalaallit-Nunaat.* POLITICAL STATUS: Nunavut officially forms part of Canada's Northwest Territories. On 1 April 1999, Nunavut will become a self-governing Inuit homeland within the Canadian federation.

*FLAG:* The Inuit flag, the flag of the national movement, has horizontal stripes of pale blue, red, and pale blue. OTHER FLAG(S): The same flag, with the addition of a black map of Nunavut on a centered disc surrounded by the name Tungavik Federation of Nunavut in English and Inuktituk, is the flag of the largest nationalist organization.

*PEOPLE:* The Inuit, formerly called Eskimos, a name derived from the Algonquin language meaning "the eaters of raw meat," are a Native American people living mostly above the Arctic Circle. The Nunavut Inuit comprise the Baffin, Iqlulik, Caribou, Copper, Netsilik, and Mackenzie Delta bands. The Inuit speak Inuktituk, a language of the Inuit-Aleut group of languages divided into two major dialects, Yupik in the West and Inupik in the rest of the vast region. There is little cultural or dialectical variation, as the Inuit all descend from one group, the Thule Inuit, who migrated across northern America as far east as Greenland, now officially Kalaallit-Nunaat. In recent years the birthrate of the Inuit has increased, with 40% of the population now under the age of fifteen. The majority of the Inuit are Christian, with a minority adhering to traditional beliefs.

*NATION:* The ancestors of the Inuit are believed to have crossed into North America from Asia some 4,000 years ago, using a now-disappeared land bridge across the Bering Strait. The migrants adjusted to the frozen lands north of the tree line in an adaptation unequaled by any other northern ethnic group. The Thule Inuit migrated across the frozen Arctic lands of North America between A.D. 1000 and 1400, with groups leaving the main migration in present Alaska, northern Canada, the Canadian Arctic islands, and Greenland. The Inuit de scendants from this one migration give the various Inuit bands a surprising uniformity of culture and language.

Before the arrival of Europeans in the region, the Inuit were unaware that other peoples existed, beyond some sub-Arctic Indians with whom they traded. Sir Martin Frobisher became the first European to encounter the Inuit of northern Canada in 1576. The majority of the Inuit saw Europeans for the first time only in the 1770s, when Russian, Spanish, and English ships explored the Arctic regions.

The Inuit homeland, included in the Northwestern Territory in 1820, was leased to Hudson's Bay Company between 1821 and 1869. In 1876 the Canadian government organized the Keewatin District, which gradually lost its southern territories to the provinces of Ontario and Manitoba. In 1895 the Franklin District, including part of the mainland and the Arctic Islands, was organized as a separate territory.

The small Inuit population, mostly ignored until the early twentieth century, experienced a steady population growth after World War II with the decline of blood feuds and infanticide, but their lifestyle changed very little until the 1950s. The paternalistic Canadian government moved the nomadic Inuit into government housing schemes and built schools and health facilities. Increased education and contacts with the outside world promoted a new political activism in the 1960s. In 1963 Inuit nationalists put forward a plan to divide the Northwest Territories and create a self-governing Inuit homeland.

The discovery of oil, natural gas, and rare minerals in the region in the 1960s and 1970s added an economic issue to the ongoing question of land rights. The Inuit, feeling ignored and misunderstood by other Canadians, in the 1970s, mobilized to win autonomy and control of their vast Arctic homeland. Inuit delegations traveled to Ottawa and London, seeking support for the creation of a separate homeland, Nunavut. In 1979 neighboring Greenland was granted home rule by the Danish government and became a model for the Inuit of northern Canada.

The inhabitants of the Northwest Territories voted, on 14 April 1982, to divide the territories to create new provinces based on the national groups. The Inuit voted four to one for partition. In 1985 the Canadian government set tentative boundaries, the task complicated by demands for the inclusion of Inuit groups in the northeast Beaufort Sea region, Labrador, and northern Quebec.* The campaign to win autonomy politicized the Inuit, some activists favoring the Greenland-based Inuit Ataqatiqiit, which advocates an independent transpolar Inuit state. Support for nationalism increased in 1987–88 as negotiations stalled over disputed land claims and mineral rights.

In September 1989 the Canadian government finally passed the long-delayed land settlement, the biggest land transfer since the Alaska and Louisiana purchases of the nineteenth century. The agreement gives the Inuit considerable control over mineral development and sets aside lands for traditional activities such as trapping and hunting.

In the 1980s environmental groups hurt the traditional Inuit economy by successfully campaigning against seal hunting. New restrictions left once-proud Inuit hunters to go to seed on the dole and the bottle.

In 1992 the Nunavut agreement received the necessary government and voter approval. The agreement gives the Inuit outright ownership of 18% of the vast territory, most of which will remain Crown lands with joint government and Inuit control. The Inuit won the right to hunt, fish, and trap across the entire area. On 1 April 1999 Nunavut, an area three times larger than France, will become an autonomous Inuit state within Canada.

*SELECTED BIBLIOGRAPHY:*

Birket-Smith, K. *The Eskimos.* 1971.
Cumming, Peter A. *Canada: Native Land Rights and Northern Development.* 1991.
Damas, David. *Handbook of North American Indians: Arctic.* 1984.
Steltzer, Ulli. *Inuit: The North in Transition.* 1985.

# OCCITANIA

**Occitanie; Pays d'Oc**

*CAPITAL: Tolosa (Toulouse)*

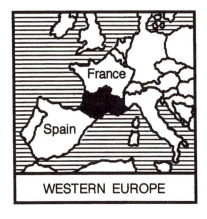

WESTERN EUROPE

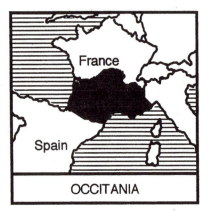

OCCITANIA

*POPULATION:* (95e) 14,868,000 : 12,000,000 Occitanians in France. MAJOR NATIONAL GROUPS: (95e) Occitan 79%, North Africans 10%, other French. MAJOR LANGUAGES: French, Occitan, Arabic, Euskara (Basque), Catalan. MAJOR RELIGIONS: Roman Catholic, Protestant, Sunni Islam, Jewish. MAJOR CITIES: (95e) Marselha (Marseille) 861,000 (1,140,000), Niça (Nice) 343,000 (462,000), Tolosa (Toulouse) 339,000 (666,000), Montpelhier (Montpellier) 213,000 (252,000), Bordèu (Bordeaux) 202,000 (701,000), Tolon (Toulon) 176,000 (437,000), Grenoble 152,000 (476,000), Ais-de-Provença (Aix-en-Provence) 152,000, Limòtge (Limoges) 144,000 (177,000), Clarmont d'Auvernha (Clermont-Ferrand) 142,000 (265,000), Nismes (Nîmes) 125,000 (142,000), Perpinyà (Perpignan) 122,000 (155,000), Avinhon (Avignon) 107,000 (180,000), Pau 86,000 (148,000), Besièrs (Béziers) 74,000 (107,000), Canas (Cannes) 74,000 (270,000), Antibol (Antibes) 73,000, Valena (Valence) 65,000 (115,000).

*GEOGRAPHY:* AREA: 83,371 sq.mi.-215,987 sq.km. LOCATION: Occitania lies in southern France, a mostly mountainous region with the Alps in the east, the Massif Central west of the Rhône River, and the Pyrenees in the southwest, with lowlands in the Rhône Valley, on the Gulf of Lions and the Mediterranean Sea, and in the west on the Atlantic Ocean. POLITICAL STATUS: Occitania has no official status; the region forms the French administrative regions of Aquitaine, Auvergne, Languedoc-Rousillon, Limousin, Provence-Alps-Côte d'Azur, and Midi-Pyrénées, and the southern departments of Rhone Alps.

*FLAG:* The Occitan flag, the flag of the national movement, is a red field charged with a red Cross of Toulouse outlined in yellow. OTHER FLAG(S): The flag of Provence has nine equal, vertical stripes of yellow and red.

*PEOPLE:* The Occitans are a Latin people, the descendants of the inhabitants of Roman Gaul, more closely related to the peoples of adjacent areas of Spain and Italy than to the northern French, called Franks by the Occitans. The Occitan language, often called Langue d'Oc, is considered the closest to the original Latin of the modern Romance languages and is the oldest of the Romance languages still in daily use. Spoken in four major dialects, Gascon, Languedocien, Provençal, and Nord, the language has a vocabulary of 160,000 words, 130,000 more than modern French. Minority populations include northern French, often called Franks, a large immigrant population mostly from North Africa, and smaller groups of Catalans and Basques, historically and linguistically part of the nations of Catalonia* and Euzkadi.*

*THE NATION:* The coastal areas originally inhabited by Celtic tribes, Greeks colonized the areas in the sixth century B.C. The flourishing Greek port cities fell to Roman rule in the second century B.C., the first Roman possessions outside Italy. Julius Caesar conquered the region in a series of wars called the Gallic Wars, 58 to 51 B.C., Gaul being the Roman name for Celt. As part of Roman Gaul, the region became a prosperous, Latinized center of Roman art and culture.

Germanic tribes invaded Gaul in the fifth century A.D., the most powerful, the Franks, settling northern Gaul in the sixth century. The region, retaining many Roman institutions and traditions, remained more advanced than the Frankish north. The major states, the County of Toulouse and the Kingdom of Arles (Provence), carried on extensive trade with North Africa, enjoying luxuries and inventions unheard of in most of Europe.

The region experienced a great cultural flowering in the eleventh and twelfth centuries. From its inception in Limousin, the budding Troubadour culture spread across the region, carried by wandering troubadours. The cultural awakening, a forerunner of the Renaissance, developed an extensive Occitan literature, marked by new forms and a striking lyric poetry. The cultural flowering coincided with the spread of an eastern religious sect, the Cathari, and the Troubadour culture and the Cathari beliefs became closely intertwined.

The Cathari sect, originating in the Balkans, gained converts in the region from the eleventh century. The converts, called Albigenses, after Albi, one of the major Cathar cities, were branded heretics by the Catholic Church. The Cathars were not heretics or even Christians, but adherents of a dualistic system believing in good and evil, body and soul, and so on. Supported by many powerful nobles the Cathar sect became a virtual state religion in many Occitan regions.

The Catholic pope sent missionaries to Occitania to stop the rapid spread of the Cathar heresy. Efforts to bring the heretics back to the church having failed, the pope proclaimed a Crusade against the Cathars in 1208. The French kingdom, to the north of the Oc states, answered the pope's call, seeing in the wealthy south a chance for conquest, expansion, and plunder. Cathar nobles, backed by Catholic Aragon, united to resist the French invasion. The holy Crusade quickly became a political war, with the Oc states as the battleground.

French knights, under the guise of stamping out heresy, devastated Occitania as refugees, both Catholic and Cathar, fled to Spain and Italy. Horrible massacres marked the French acquisition of the Oc lands. Pope Gregory IX in 1233 established a system of legal investigation in the conquered Albigensian centers, the beginning of the infamous Inquisition.

Occitania never recovered its former prosperity. The Occitan language, suppressed in favor of the French spoken in Paris, was relegated to a folk language spoken in rural areas and was finally banned in 1539. The Wars of Religion, from 1562 to 1598, again devastated the region, the massacres of Protestants echoing the earlier Cathar massacres.

The Occitans, living in the poorest part of France, began to revive their culture in the 1850s. An Occitan cultural organization, Felibrige, formed by the famed Occitan poet Frédéric Mistral in 1854, stimulated a resurgence and a new interest in the Occitan history, language, and culture. The cultural movement stimulated demands for cultural and political autonomy in highly centralized France. Between 1851 and 1871 Occitan nationalists campaigned for a federal system to replace the system of dictating all government from Paris. Mistral, in attempting to standardize the Occitan language, produced a monumental two-volume dictionary plus a collection of Occitan poetry that won him the Nobel Prize in 1904.

The Occitan movement lost support during World War I but revived after the Second World War. The legalization of the language in 1951 stimulated the rebirth of the movement. By the 1970s autonomist and nationalist sentiment in the region had begun to politicize the Occitan population. The integration of Europe in the 1970s and 1980s gave the movement focus.

Occitan nationalists claim that the region, like the Mezzogiorno in Italy, is at once colonized, neglected, and underdeveloped. The national movement in the 1990s looks back on the massacres and horrors visited on their nation by ''foreign invaders'' from northern France in the thirteenth century. Modern Occitan nationalists seek independence within a united Europe and see the Albigenses as the first Occitan nationalists.

*SELECTED BIBLIOGRAPHY:*
Brustein, William. *The Social Origins of Political Regionalism: France, 1849–1981.* 1982.
Roche, Alfonse. *Provençal Regionalism.* 1954.
Runciman, Steven. *The Medieval Manichee.* 1947.
Strayer, Joseph R. *Albigensian Crusades.* 1986.

# OKINAWA

**Ryuku Islands**

*CAPITAL: Naha*

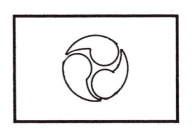

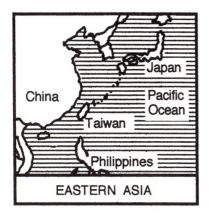

EASTERN ASIA

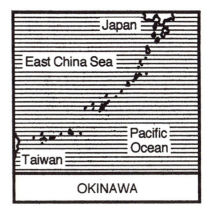

OKINAWA

*POPULATION:* (95e) 1,292,000 : 1,400,000 Okinawans in Japan. MAJOR NATIONAL GROUPS: (95e) Okinawan 83%, other Japanese. MAJOR LANGUAGES: Japanese, Nantö (Okinawan). MAJOR RELIGIONS: Buddhist, Shintoist, Christian. MAJOR CITIES: (95e) Naha 315,000 (510,000), Okinawa 110,000 (197,000), Urasoe 92,000, Ginowan 75,000, Nago 55,000 (94,000), Itoman 55,000, Naze 53,000, Gushikawa 50,000.

*GEOGRAPHY:* AREA: 1,803 sq.mi.-4,670 sq.km. LOCATION: Okinawa lies in the East China Sea, a string of islands stretching from near Taiwan* to the southern Japanese island of Kyushu. The archipelago includes three major island groups: the Sakishima Islands in the south, the Okinawa Islands in the center, and the Amami Islands in the north. POLITICAL STATUS: Okinawa forms a prefecture of Japan comprising the islands returned to Japanese sovereignty in 1972. The Amami Islands, returned to Japan in 1953, form part of Kagoshima Prefecture of Kyushu but are claimed by nationalists as part of historic Okinawa.

*FLAG:* The Okinawan national flag, the flag of the national movement, is a white field with a centered disc made up of the traditional symbols of Okinawa's Sho kings, three tear-shaped devices of red, yellow, and blue. OTHER FLAG(S): The flag of the largest national organization, the Okinawa Independence Party, is a diagonal bicolor of blue over green, upper hoist to lower fly and separated by a narrow white stripe, and bearing in a centered white disc the three devices of the Sho kings.

*PEOPLE:* The Okinawans are an Oriental people, thought to include in their ancestry the original Caucasian inhabitants of the islands, related to the Ainu of

Ho'aido,* with later admixtures of Chinese and Japanese. Generally taller and darker than the Japanese, the Okinawans speak a language akin to Ainu, the language of Japan's ancient Caucasian inhabitants. The Okinawan culture, influenced by the islands' proximity to China, the Philippines, and Southeast Asia, has revived since World War II. The Okinawans, unlike the reserved Japanese, are known for courtesy, warmth, generosity, and directness. The majority religions are Buddhism and Shintoism, with a substantial and important Christian minority.

*THE NATION:* Inhabited in ancient times by a Caucasian people, over thousands of years the islanders absorbed migrants from neighboring areas while retaining their original language and much of their ancient culture. An early kingdom, with its capital at Shuri, now a suburb of Naha, was ruled by a long line of illustrious kings, the Sho kings. From the seventh century A.D., when the Okinawans repulsed an invasion from the mainland, the Chinese constantly threatened the island kingdom. In the fourteenth century the Chinese forced the Sho kings to swear allegiance to the Chinese emperor and to pay annual tribute as a vassal state.

Influenced by Chinese culture, the kingdom entered a golden age, a great flowering of Okinawan culture, literature, and eventually political power. Throwing off Chinese hegemony the kingdom expanded to control the large island of Taiwan. The kingdom's prosperity ended with a Japanese invasion from the north in 1609. Forced to pay tribute to both China and Japan, the kingdom declined, losing Taiwan to Chinese colonization. For the next two centuries the kingdom maintained a precarious independence.

Commodore Matthew Perry of the United States landed at Naha in 1853. The Americans established friendly relations with the Okinawans and used the kingdom as a base for the eventual penetration of the hermit kingdom, Japan. During one of his visits to the islands Commodore Perry acquired an ancient Okinawan temple bell, which is now used to ring out the score at Army-Navy football games.

Japanese troops occupied Okinawa in 1872, and two years later Japan annexed the kingdom over dogged Okinawan resistance. The occupation authorities deposed the last Sho king in 1879 and instituted a policy of assimilation into Japanese culture. The Okinawan language and culture were banned. China, defeated by the Japanese in a brief 1895 war, finally recognized Japan's claim on Okinawa.

Resistance to assimilation pressure incited the growth of Okinawan nationalism after World War I, the national movement modeled on those of the ethnic minorities in Europe, including demands for autonomy and linguistic rights. Discrimination and intolerance of the Okinawan nation increased as the military hierarchy gradually took control of Japan in the 1920s and 1930s. Nationalists in the islands formed the Okinawa Independence Party in the 1930s and openly advocated secession and independence until its suppression in the late 1930s. By 1938 most of the nationalist leaders were dead or imprisoned.

Japan's military government, preparing for war, suspected the loyalty of the Okinawan population. The islands, particularly the largest, Okinawa, became heavily fortified as the tide of war turned against Japan. In early 1945 American troops invaded the islands, beginning a three-month battle to oust the Japanese. The Okinawans, forced to continue to resist the Americans long after the outcome was decided, lost over a third of their population. Fierce fighting devastated the islands. In the capital, Naha, 94% of all buildings were destroyed.

Placed under American military occupation in August 1945, the islands rapidly recovered with the aid of the occupation forces. Huge American military bases became a major source of island income. In 1953, despite Okinawan protests, the Americans returned the northern Amami Islands to Japan. The disposition of the other islands became a major source of friction between the United States and Japan.

Okinawan nationalism reemerged under the American administration. The nationalists sought American support for independence and vehemently opposed Japanese demands for sovereignty over the islands. In 1968 the islands elected their first chief executive as head of a government granted considerable autonomy. In spite of the near total destruction of their material culture during the war, the growing nationalist sentiment of the 1960s stimulated a cultural revival that drew on the undamaged, traditionally Okinawan smaller islands for the basis and inspiration of the cultural movement.

The United States and Japan, over strong nationalist opposition, but with much support in the islands, reached an agreement on the islands' return to Japan in 1971. On 15 May 1972 the United States formally ceded the islands to Japanese sovereignty.

The Okinawans, with higher incomes than the Japanese average in 1972, began to lose their economic base. Japanese businessmen descended on the islands to open polluting factories away from the environmental restrictions of the main Japanese islands. Although industrial output expanded, the Okinawans were mostly left out of the Japanese economic miracle. In the 1990s the Okinawan living standards are only 75% of those of the Japanese home islands, adding economic grievances to the growing list of nationalist issues.

Okinawan nationalism and national sentiment remain a potential force in the islands, continually stimulated by the dismal Japanese attitude to minorities. The Japanese approach, called by Okinawan nationalists a form of quiet apartheid, is summed up by the often-repeated Japanese assertion that there are no ethnic or linguistic minorities in Japan.

*SELECTED BIBLIOGRAPHY:*

Miwa, Nobuya, ed. *Water and Survival in an Island Environment: Challenge of Okinawa.* 1988.

Sakihara, Mitsugu. *A Brief History of Okinawa.* 1987.

Watanabe, O. *Okinawa Problem.* 1970.

# OROMIA

Oromo

*CAPITAL: Addis Ababa*

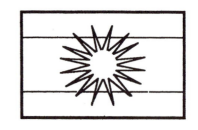

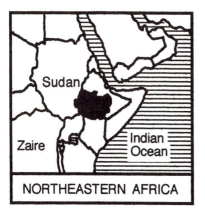

NORTHEASTERN AFRICA

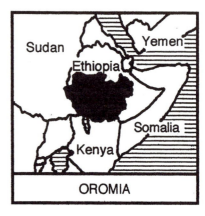

OROMIA

*POPULATION:* (95e) 34,810,000 : 22,500,000 Oromo in Ethiopia. MAJOR NATIONAL GROUPS: (95e) Oromo (Galla) 58%, Amhara 11%, Sidama 10%, Hadiyya 5%, Wolayatta 5%, Gambela, Gurage, other Ethiopian. MAJOR LANGUAGES: Oromo (Gallinya), Amhariya, Sidama, Hadiyy, Wolayatta. MAJOR RELIGIONS: (95e) Sunni Muslim 45%, animist 35%, Christian 20%. MAJOR CITIES: (95e) Addis Ababa 3,340,000, Harer 125,000, Akaki Beseka 125,000, Jimma 120,000, Nazaret 110,000, Debre Zeyit 100,000, Asela 100,000, Goba 80,000, Miesso 65,000, Awasso 60,000, Fiche 50,000, Gore 50,000.

*GEOGRAPHY:* AREA: 136,666 sq.mi.-354,058 sq.km. LOCATION: Oromia lies in southern Ethiopia, occupying the southern part of the Central Highlands and the northern extension of the Great Rift Valley. POLITICAL STATUS: Oromia has no official status; the region claimed by nationalists forms the autonomous regions of Oromo, Addis Ababa, Gambela, Harer, Sidama, Omo, and Gurage-Kemabata-Hadiya of Ethiopia.

*FLAG:* The Oromo national flag, the flag of the national movement, has three horizontal stripes of green, red, green, proportions 1:2:1, bearing a centered, sixteen-pointed yellow star. OTHER FLAG(S): The flag of the largest national organization, the Oromo Liberation Front (OLF), is the same green, red, and green flag with a centered yellow star of twenty-six points charged with a centered green tree surmounted by a small, five-pointed red star.

*PEOPLE:* The Oromo, also called Galla, are a tall, Hamitic, pastoral people related to the neighboring Somalis, but without the Arabic admixture that characterizes the Somali. The peoples collectively known as Oromo comprise sixteen major tribes and numerous subtribes and clans representing diverse cultural, linguistic, and political backgrounds. The majority of the Oromo speak a Cushitic language of the Hamito-Semitic language group with numerous dialects. An Oromo minority has adopted Amhariya or other regional languages. The primary Oromo religion is Sunni Islam, mostly in the south and east, with large animist and Christian populations in the southwest and the Central Highlands.

*THE NATION:* The Hamitic Oromo are thought to have migrated from present Somalia to the region around Lake Rudolph in the late fifteenth and early sixteenth centuries, a migration in search of grazing lands, not a political or warlike migration. The Oromo migrants traveled in individual clans, the clans united only by culture and religion, not by a central authority. Further migrations between 1550 and 1670 brought the Oromo into the Ethiopian highlands and into conflict with the Christian Amhara kingdom.

Oromo legends tell of the five fathers who established the five divisions of the Oromo Nation. In the east the Wallo Oromo adopted Islam. The Mecha and Tulema moved into the highlands, adopted Christianity, and mixed with the Semitic Amhara. In the South the Boran and Bartumma settled the less populated lands and retained their traditional Oromo culture. A number of small Oromo states grew up south of the highlands in the seventeenth century, their expansion checked by the powerful Christian Amhara states.

The Christian Ethiopian Empire conquered most of the Oromo clans in the eighteenth century, many accepting the authority of the emperor and often providing mercenary troops to the imperial army. The imperial capital, Addis Ababa, was founded in traditional Oromo territory in 1883, partly to ensure Oromo loyalty to the Ethiopian emperor.

The Ethiopians, in the late nineteenth and early twentieth centuries, conquered Jimma, Kaffa, and the other remaining Oromo states. Oromo resistance to Christian Ethiopian rule provoked frequent uprisings by the clans. A number of clans united, for the first time, in a widespread revolt in 1928–30, a forerunner of the later Oromo national movement. In 1936 Oromo nationalists led a revolt in the southwestern provinces. The Oromo rebels attempted to take several provinces into secession before their defeat by imperial troops, which included a large number of ethnic Oromo soldiers.

The Italians conquered Ethiopia in 1936. Viewed by many Oromo as liberators from Amhara rule, the clans that collaborated with the invaders faced punishment and reprisals following the Allied liberation of Ethiopia in 1941. After the end of World War II, the Ethiopian government cracked down on the growing ethnic unrest, particularly in the Oromo provinces. In the 1960s the administration outlawed all languages other than the official language, Amhariya. The language issue fueled an Oromo cultural and linguistic revival as resistance to the government edicts spread. In 1965 a nationalist uprising broke out in the southeastern provinces and soon spread across the southern Oromo territories.

The success of the rebel southern clans inspired nationalist sentiment in other Oromo regions. In 1970 several clan organizations united to form the Oromo Liberation Front (OLF), which supported the popular revolution that finally overthrew Ethiopia's feudal monarchy in 1974. Refused autonomy by the newly installed Marxist government, the OLF led a separatist campaign to establish an independent Democratic Republic of Oromia. Forced collectivization and strict Marxist control alienated the majority of the clans. The Oromo nationalist revolt spread even to the clans that had been assimilating into Amhara culture for decades.

The Communist government moved against the Oromo rebels in 1980–81, with mass arrests and the closure of churches and mosques, which the government claimed served as centers of sedition. Universal conscription, often at gunpoint, forced thousands of Oromo into the huge army fighting the ethnic insurrections in Tigre* and Eritrea in northern Ethiopia.

The OLF joined a coalition of insurgent groups in 1990. Allied to the northern rebel groups, the Oromo guerrillas moved on Addis Ababa from the south. Attacked on all sides the beleaguered Communist government began to collapse in early 1991, and in late May the Ethiopian capital fell to the rebel alliance. The rebels set up an interim government and in December 1991 granted autonomy to Ethiopia's numerous ethnic groups.

Oromo national leaders demanded a referendum on autonomy within two years, the demands splitting the national movement between the supporters of independence and those favoring autonomy within a loose federal system in Ethiopia. Territorial claims sparked violence between Oromo nationalists and rival peoples in several areas. The growing rift between the Oromo and their former allies worsened, and in June 1992 the OLF withdrew from Ethiopia's coalition government.

The Oromo alienation has prompted calls for secession. In mid-1993 the government moved against the OLF and other Oromo groups suspected of harboring separatist rebels, raising tensions in the region. The growing chaos in Ethiopia greatly increases the chances that the multiethnic state could splinter along ethnic lines. The Ethiopian government in November 1994 confirmed the right to secession by the state's various national groups. For Oromo nationalists this means that for the first time in their modern history, an independent Oromo state is a real possibility.

*SELECTED BIBLIOGRAPHY:*

Donham, Donald, and Wendy James. *The Southern Marches of Imperial Ethiopia: Essays in History and Social Anthropology.* 1986.
Hassen, Mohammed. *Oromo of Ethiopia: A History 1570–1860.* 1990.
Legum, Colin. *Horn of Africa in Continuing Crisis.* 1970.
Trimingham, J. Spencer. *Islam in Ethiopia.* 1952.

# OSSETIA

**Iryston**

*CAPITAL: Dzaujikau (Vladikavkaz)*

SOUTHEASTERN EUROPE

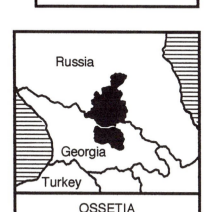

OSSETIA

*POPULATION:* (95e) 838,000 : 722,000 Ossetians (Iristi) in Russia and Georgia. MAJOR NATIONAL GROUPS: (95e) Ossetian (Iristi) 56%, Russian 17%, Georgian 11%, Ukrainian 9%, Ingush 6%. MAJOR LANGUAGES: Ossetic, Russian, Georgian, Ingush. MAJOR RELIGIONS: Russian Orthodox, Sunni Muslim. MAJOR CITIES: (95e) RUSSIA (NORTH OSSETIA): Dzaujikau (Vladikavkaz) 335,000 (449,000), Mozdok 54,000, Beslan 48,000, Alagir 38,000, Ardon 22,000. GEORGIA (SOUTH OSSETIA): Tskhinvali 42,000.

*GEOGRAPHY:* AREA: 4,595 sq.mi.-11,904 sq.km. LOCATION: Ossetia lies in southern European Russia and north-central Georgia, occupying the northern and southern slopes of the central Caucasus Mountains and the lowlands of the Terek River and its tributaries to the north. POLITICAL STATUS: Ossetia has no official status; the region forms North Ossetia, a member state of the Russian Federation, and South Ossetia, a nominally autonomous region of the Republic of Georgia.

*INDEPENDENCE DECLARED:* 12 December 1990.

*FLAG:* The Ossetian flag, the official flag of North Ossetia, is a horizontal tricolor of white, purple, and yellow. OTHER FLAG(S): The flag of the South Ossetians is a horizontal tricolor of white, red, and yellow bearing a centered white, crouching snow leopard.

*PEOPLE:* The Ossetians, calling themselves Iristi and their homeland Iryston, are an Iranian people speaking an East Iranian language of the Iranian group of the Indo-Iranian languages. The language is spoken in two major dialects, I'iron in the north and Digor in the south. The only Iranian people in the Caucasus region, the Ossetians are mainly Orthodox Christians, with a substantial Sunni Muslim minority, mostly in North Ossetia. Some thirty percent of the total Ossetian population lives outside the Ossetian regions in Russia and Georgia. The large Slav minority is concentrated in Vladikavkaz and the other cities. The Ingush minority, living in the area adjacent to Ingushetia,* have mostly fled since violence broke out in October 1992.

*THE NATION:* The ancestors of the Ossetians, the Alans or Alani, a division of the Sarmathian tribes that moved into the region as early as the seventh century B.C., traditionally settled in the Caucasus region in the fifth century B.C. The high passes of the Caucasus Mountains that united the Ossetians north and south of the mountains also served as major invasion routes between Europe and Asia. The Alani organized a state structure between the tenth and thirteenth centuries but maintained only a precarious independence against the region's numerous invaders, the Huns, Khazars, Arabs, Seljuk Turks, and Georgians.

In the twelfth century Georgia's Queen Tamara persuaded the Ossetian population to adopt Christianity, the religion of the Georgian state. The Mongols overran Georgia in the thirteenth century, the Ossetian homeland devastated in the invasion and the reckless destruction of the conquerors. In the fourteenth century the recovering Ossetians won religious freedom under the rule of the Mongol successor, the Golden Horde.

The entire Caucasus was the center of a fierce struggle for dominance by the Turkish Ottoman Empire and the Persians in the fifteenth century. The expanding Russian state to the north, taking advantage of the chaos created by the Muslim rivals, began to penetrate the region in the sixteenth century. Christian Russian influence, particularly in the Ossetian region north of the mountains, brought the Christian Ossetians some protection against the depredations of the warlike Muslim tribes of the Caucasus Mountains.

The Ossetians came under nominal Russian rule in the late eighteenth century. The key fortress of Vladikavkaz, founded in 1784, became a center of Russian expansion in the Caucasus. Resistance to Russian rule replaced the earlier good relations as tsarist bureaucrats attempted to take control of all aspects of Ossetian life. In 1794 the Ossetians rebelled, and, following their defeat, the Russians annexed their territories between 1801 and 1806. The Ossetians, through their early good relations with the Slavs, became the most advanced people in the Caucasus, favored by the tsarist authorities over their Muslim neighbors.

The Muslim Caucasian peoples, generally sympathetic to Muslim Turkey when war began in 1914, viewed the Orthodox Ossetians as Russian agents, with violence and tensions increasing as the war dragged on. The Ossetians, to protect themselves amid the spreading chaos, formed an alliance with the Terek Cossacks to the north, the dominant military power in the region. The coming of the Russian Revolution in February 1917 escalated the confusion in the Caucasus. In April 1917 the Ossetians called a national congress to establish organs of self-rule within a new democratic Russian state.

Frightened by the Bolshevik coup in October 1917, the national congress supported the creation of a joint Christian-Muslim government in the region. The alliance collapsed in December 1917, when fighting broke out between the Muslim tribes and the Cossacks in the Terek River valley. In January 1918 a council convened at Mozdok brought together the anti-Bolshevik groups in the region, the Ossetians, the Terek Cossacks, some Muslim groups, and delegates from the major Russian political organizations.

The spreading Russian civil war spilled into the region in mid-1918. Bolshevik troops allied to the Muslim Chechens and Ingush overran Russian Ossetia in November 1918. Ingush warriors captured and looted Vladikavkaz. Under the direction of the Bolshevik leader Comrade Ordzhonikidze, the Bolsheviks and Muslims unleashed a reign of terror, with Ossetian, Terek Cossack, and anti-Bolshevik Russians arrested and executed. In 1922 the new Georgian Soviet government established an autonomous South Ossetian region to win Ossetian loyalty.

The Soviet authorities created a separate North Ossetian autonomous region in 1924, and in 1936 the region became an autonomous republic with its capital at Vladikavkaz. The Ossetians remained unmoved by the overtures of the Nazi Germans who invaded the Caucasus in 1942. Their rejection of the Nazi persuasions saved them the brutal deportations suffered by neighboring Muslim peoples. In 1944 Stalin, whose mother was Ossetian, after deporting the neighboring Ingush, transferred the western district of Ingushetia to North Ossetia.

The Soviet liberalization of the late 1980s sparked a rapid and dramatic rise of nationalism among the divided Ossetian peoples. In 1988 the Ossetians in Georgia demanded secession and unification with North Ossetia, the demands setting off violent clashes in South Ossetia. Thousands of Ossetian refugees fled across the mountains to North Ossetia, their plight fanning nascent nationalism in Russian Ossetia. On 11 December 1990 the nationalist Georgian government rescinded South Ossetia's autonomy and renamed the region Shida Khartli, Inner Georgia. The following day, 12 December 1990, the region's nationalist leaders declared the independence of the South Ossetian Democratic Republic.

In 1991 the Ingush renewed their old claim to the territory transferred to North Ossetia in 1944. In May 1992, after separating from Chechenia,* the Ingush again demanded the return of the region. In October Ossetian nationalists reacted by attacking the Ingush villages in the disputed region, sending over 50,000 Ingush fleeing into Ingushetia. The conflicts with the Georgians in the south and the Ingush in the west have fueled the growth of Ossetian nationalism, but the majority work for autonomy, not full independence, fearing the loss of Russian protection in the volatile region they have inhabited since ancient times.

*SELECTED BIBLIOGRAPHY:*

Colton, Timothy, and Robert Levgold, eds. *After the Soviet Union.* 1992.
Pushkarev, Sergei. *Self-Government and Freedom in Russia.* 1988.
Rywkin, Michael. *Russian Colonial Expansion to 1917.* 1988.

# PALESTINE

**Falastin**

*CAPITAL: Al-Quds ash Sherif (East Jerusalem)*

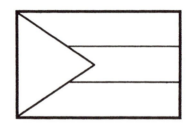

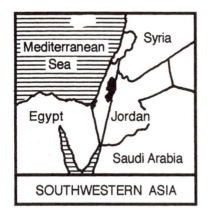

SOUTHWESTERN ASIA

PALESTINE

*POPULATION:* (95e) 1,855,000 : 2,435,000 Palestinians in Gaza, the West Bank, and Israel. The Palestinian population in the entire Middle East is 5.2 million. MAJOR NATIONAL GROUPS: (95e) West Bank and Gaza: Palestinian 94%, Israeli 6%. MAJOR LANGUAGES: Arabic, Hebrew, English. MAJOR RELIGIONS: Sunni Muslim, Christian, Jewish. MAJOR CITIES: (95e) ISRAEL: Al-Quds ash Sherif (East Jerusalem) 145,000. WEST BANK: Nabulus 210,000, Al-Khalil (Hebron) 105,000, Bayt Lahm (Bethlehem) 55,000, Ram Allah (Ramallah) 43,000 (61,000), Ariha (Jericho) 16,000 (31,000). GAZA: Ghazzah (Gaza) 175,000 (312,000), Rafah 95,000 (265,000), Khan Yunis 90,000, Jabalyah 76,000, Dayr al-Balab 45,000.

*GEOGRAPHY:* AREA: 4,998 sq.mi.-12,948 sq.km. LOCATION: Palestine lies in the Middle East, comprising the so-called Occupied Territories, the West Bank, the region west of the Jordan River, and the Gaza Strip, just north of the Egyptian border. The two areas are divided by twenty miles of Israeli territory. POLITICAL STATUS: Palestine, the areas accepted by the national leadership in 1988, forms territories under Israeli military occupation except for the Gaza Strip and the Jericho District of the West Bank, which became an autonomous Palestinian region in 1994.

*INDEPENDENCE DECLARED:* 15 November 1988

*FLAG:* The Palestinian national flag, the flag of the national movement and the official flag of the autonomous region, is a horizontal tricolor of black, white, and green bearing a red triangle at the hoist.

*PEOPLE:* The Palestinians are an Arab people, the Arab inhabitants of the area called Palestine, including present Jordan and Israel, created after World War I. The majority of the Palestinians live in other Arab countries, many in long-established refugee camps in the states bordering Israel. The Palestinian Diaspora, since 1948, has evolved a large intellectual and professional class. The Palestinian population of the Occupied Territories does not include the nearly 800,000 Palestinians who live in Israel and are Israeli citizens. The majority of the Palestinians are Sunni Muslims, with a large Christian minority. A substantial Jewish Israeli population has settled in the Palestinian territories since 1967.

*THE NATION:* The Israelites, led out of slavery in Egypt in the twelfth century B.C., eventually occupied the lands of the Canaanites. The ancient Hebrew kingdom, established in 1025 B.C., was at near constant war with the Philistines of Gaza and the coastal cities, the Philistines claimed as the ancestors of the Palestinians by some national groups. Successively part of the Assyrian, Chaldean, and Persian Empires, the region came under Roman rule in 63 B.C. Roman Judea was the scene of Christ's life and the inception of Christianity.

The Jews, refusing to accept Roman gods and culture, revolted in A.D. 70 and again in A.D. 135. The Romans finally dispersed the defeated Jews from the region. Only a small Jewish minority remained by the end of the second century. Following the dispersal, the Roman authorities renamed the province Palestine, after the earlier Philistines. By the fourth century the majority of Palestine's inhabitants had become Christians.

Poor and backward after the Roman decline, the region fell to Muslim Arab invaders in 636–40. The invaders converted most of the population to the new Islamic religion, but Jews and Christians who refused Islam were tolerated as peoples of the book (the Bible). The Muslim conquerors erected a great mosque, the Dome of the Rock, on the site of the ancient Jewish Temple of Solomon in Jerusalem, in the belief that Mohammed halted there on his flight to heaven. Angered by the stubborn Christians and Jews and their refusal to accept Islam as the logical successor to their religions, Muslim tolerance gave way to suppression.

Persecution of the Christians between 996 and 1021, particularly the destruction of churches, was partly responsible for the Christian Crusades from Europe. In 1099 the Crusaders captured Palestine and created the Latin Kingdom of Jerusalem, one of a string of Crusader states erected along the Mediterranean coast. The resurgent Muslims regained most of Palestine in 1187, and the last of the Crusader states fell to the Muslim forces in 1291.

Conquered by the Ottoman Turks in 1516, Palestine declined through three centuries of neglect and isolation. The population of the region fell to a historic low of 350,000 in 1785. Egyptian authorities, under nominal Turkish rule, took control of the province in 1831, opening the region to European influences. In 1882 Russian Jews, fleeing pogroms, joined the small Jewish minority in the area, the forerunners of the later Zionist movement, the campaign to return the Jewish Diaspora to the ancient Jewish homeland in Palestine.

In the late nineteenth century Arab nationalists became active in the region.

The movement, organized as an anti-Turkish campaign, became active in opposing further Jewish settlements. In the years before World War I, Arab nationalists focused on the creation of a separate Arab state within the multiethnic Ottoman Empire.

The British and their Allies, to win Arab support when war began in 1914, promised Palestine to a proposed united, independent Arab state. In 1917 the British and their Arab allies captured Palestine from the Turks. Pressed by their allies and influential members of the Jewish Diaspora, the British government issued the Balfour Declaration, which supported the establishment of a Jewish homeland in Palestine. At the end of the war, contrary to earlier promises, Great Britain and France carved up the former Turkish provinces.

In 1921 the British authorities split Palestine to create the Kingdom of Trans-Jordan as partial compensation for the unkept promises to their Arab allies. Tensions between Arabs and Jews, both groups having been promised the remainder of Palestine, erupted in violence in 1920–21. Bowing to Arab pressure, the British placed restrictions on further Jewish immigration to Palestine, but anti-Jewish rioting again erupted in 1929 and in 1936, when more Jews, frantic to leave Europe, began to arrive illegally.

The British Peel Commission in 1937 recommended the partition of Palestine into Arab, Jewish, and British regions, the latter to include Jerusalem and the shrines sacred to the three major religions. The Jews reluctantly agreed, but the Palestinian Arabs refused.

The Jews and many Arabs supported the British during World War II, although the Muslim religious leader of Palestine, the mufti of Jerusalem, spent most of the war as Hitler's guest in Berlin. In 1945, caught between international opinion that favored a state for the surviving European Jews, and the growing power of the oil-rich Muslim states, the British failed to satisfy either side. Unable to find a solution, the British finally turned the problem over to the new United Nations (UN) in 1947.

The UN in April 1947 approved a plan to partition Palestine into Arab and Jewish states. The Jews accepted the compromise, but the Palestinian Arabs, supported by the surrounding Arab states, rejected the plan. The Arab leaders proposed that the entire region be turned over to Arab rule with guaranteed rights for the Jewish minority.

The Palestinian Jews, supported by United Nations resolutions, declared the independence of the State of Israel on 14 May 1948. Fighting immediately broke out as the armies of the neighboring Arab states invaded. Thousands of Palestinian Arabs fled the fighting, were driven from their homes by the victorious Jews, or left the region, assured by Arab leaders that overwhelming military power would allow them to return very soon.

A UN-brokered cease-fire left much of Palestine under Israeli rule. Of the remaining districts Egypt took control of the Gaza Strip, and Jordan annexed the West Bank. The official policy of the neighboring Arab states left thousands of Palestinian refugees in squalid camps, a pool of zealously anti-Israeli fighters.

In the camps Palestinian nationalists mobilized and formed a number of organizations, the largest the Palestine Liberation Organization (PLO).

A series of inconclusive wars and skirmishes polarized attitudes on both sides. During the 1967 war, Israeli forces overran the West Bank and the Gaza Strip and, despite international pressure, refused to relinquish the territories until the Palestinians and other Arabs recognized Israel's right to exist.

The Palestinian Arabs of the Occupied Territories, not granted the same rights as the Palestinian population in Israel, remained under military rule. In 1987 the frustrated Palestinians began the *intifada*, the Palestinian uprising against Israeli military rule and the growing number of Jewish settlements constructed in the territories.

The Palestinian leadership, realizing that decades of terrorist attacks on Israeli and Western targets had achieved little and had brought international condemnation, in 1988 renounced violence and the long-held goal, the destruction of Israel. The Palestinian National Council, meeting in Algiers, proclaimed the independence of the State of Palestine on 15 November 1988. Dozens of states established diplomatic relations with the Palestinian government even though its national territory remained under Israeli military occupation.

In 1991, in the wake of the Gulf War, the first face-to-face talks were held between the Palestinians and the Israelis. A series of negotiations finally reached agreement in August 1993 on autonomy for the Gaza Strip and the Jericho District of the West Bank, the Palestinian autonomous authority to later extend to the rest of the West Bank. The contentious issue of Jerusalem, claimed as the national capital by both peoples, remains unresolved. In May 1994 Israeli troops withdrew from the new Palestinian Autonomous Area.

The PLO, almost universally recognized as the official representative of the Palestinians, is under increasing pressure from the growing Islamic fundamentalist movement, led by Hamas. The outcome of the struggle for Palestinian leadership between the fundamentalist radicals and the PLO will also determine the future of the Palestinian Nation.

*SELECTED BIBLIOGRAPHY:*

Amos, John W. *Palestinian Resistance: Organization of a National Movement.* 1981.
Catton, Henry. *Palestine: The Arabs and Israel.* 1992.
Hurewitz, Jacob C. *Struggle for Palestine.* 1968.
Muslih, Muhammad V. *The Origins of Palestinian Nationalism.* 1989.
Said, Edward W. *The Politics of Dispossession.* 1994.

# PAOH

**Pa-O; Paohland**

*CAPITAL: Hsuphang*

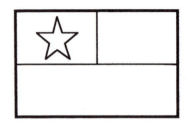

SOUTHEASTERN ASIA

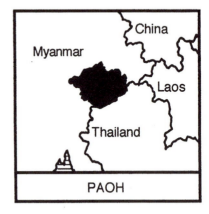

PAOH

*POPULATION:* (95e) 1,795,000 : 1,620,000 Pa-O in Myanmar and another 90,000 in adjacent areas of Thailand. MAJOR NATIONAL GROUPS: (95e) Pa-O 80%, Shan 10%, Kayah 7%, Lahu, Palaung, Lisu, other Burmese. MAJOR LANGUAGES: Pa-O, Shan, Burmese, Kayah. MAJOR RELIGIONS: animist, Christian, Buddhist. MAJOR CITIES: (95e) Mong Pan 15,000, Hsuphang 10,000, Mauk Mai 3,000.

*GEOGRAPHY:* AREA: 6,692 sq.mi.-17,336 sq.km. LOCATION: Paoh occupies the mountains and the valley of the upper Salween River just south of the Shan Plateau in eastern Myanmar. POLITICAL STATUS: Paoh has no official status; the region forms the districts of Hsuphang, Mong Pan, Mong Kang, and Mauk Mai of Shanland,* officially Shan State of Myanmar.

*FLAG:* The Pa-O national flag, the flag of the national movement, is divided horizontally, the lower half green, the upper half divided vertically into two equal rectangles, red on the fly and blue at the hoist, the blue charged with a white, five-pointed star.

*PEOPLE:* The Pa-O are a tribal people who have retained their traditional tribal and caste structures and their ancient culture in the isolation of the heavily forested mountains around the upper Salween River. The tribes collectively called Pa-O have united only in recent decades and still display great differences in culture, dialect, and political organization. The Pa-O speak a language of the Tibetan branch of the Tibeto-Burman languages. The majority of the Pa-O adhere to traditional religious beliefs, with important minorities of Christians and Buddhists, particularly in the towns.

*THE NATION:* The Pa-O are believed to have originated in eastern Tibet,* their ancestors having migrated south along the rivers in ancient times. Following the course of the Salween River, the tribes settled the valley lowlands before the sixth century A.D. Forced into the less accessible mountains by stronger peoples, the Pa-O settled in small, autonomous villages based on tribes, clans, and family groups. United only when faced with a common threat, the various groups often warred among themselves. The tribal culture, based on small units, evolved a tradition of fierce independence.

Conquered by the Shans, a Thai people, in the seventh century, the Pa-O paid annual tribute to the feudal Shan princes but mostly continued to live a traditional way of life. In the ninth century the Burmans, a people linguistically related to the Pa-O, began to penetrate the Shan states. The long rivalry for control of the region forced the majority of the Pa-O to retreat into the forests and high mountain valleys. In the seventeenth century the Pa-O came under the nominal rule of the Burman kings of the Irrawaddy delta.

The British took control of Upper Burma from the Burmese kingdom in 1886. The European authorities established a tradition of indirect rule, signing treaties with various Pa-O tribes living in the regions nominally ruled by the Shan principalities. British and American missionaries in the 1890s introduced the Pa-O tribes to Christianity and Western education. In the first decade of the twentieth century a small, educated group of chiefs' sons took the first tentative steps to try to end the endemic tribal conflicts.

During World War II, the Pa-O formed guerrilla bands behind the Japanese lines. Trained and armed by Allied officers parachuted into the region, the fierce Pa-O guerrilla bands terrorized the Japanese patrols and served as guides for Allied forces crossing their rugged terrain. The guerrillas, after the end of the war, formed the nucleus of a Pa-O national army and the growing nationalist movement.

Promised local autonomy, the Pa-O districts remained part of Shan State when Burma gained independence in 1948. Soon after independence, the Burmese government abrogated the autonomy statute. Denied the promised self-rule and rights to their traditional lands, the Pa-O rebelled in January 1949. Led by the former guerrillas, the Pa-O, with arms from China, and often allied to the Burmese Communist rebels operating in the jungle region, pursued a war against the Burmese government during the 1950s. The common goal of self-rule united the diverse tribes, and for the first time the Pa-O began to see themselves as a nation rather than as a group of unrelated tribes and clans.

The Pa-O insurgency, nearly defeated by government forces in the late 1950s, retreated into the inaccessible jungles. In 1961 the government's military commander in the region announced that the Pa-O rebellion had finally been eradicated. The next year, following the 1962 coup that brought a military government to power in Rangoon, the indiscriminate attacks by government troops on Pa-O villages reignited the nationalist movement and renewed the Pa-O insurgency.

Allied to other ethnic insurgent groups, the Pa-O leaders in 1972 put aside demands for autonomy and proclaimed the ultimate goal of independence within a federation of states what would replace Burma's brutal military government. To finance the separatist war, the Pa-O depended on modest teak logging and smuggling across the Thai border. In the 1980s, when Thai companies, granted logging concessions by the Burmese government, devastated the teak forests, many of the Pa-O tribes turned to the lucrative opium trade to finance the ongoing war with the government forces in the region.

The Pa-O's increasing involvement in drug trafficking opened rifts between the Pa-O bands and other ethnic groups. In the late 1980s fighting erupted for control of the drug trails along the Thai border. In early 1994 the Thai government sealed the border to stop the flow of drugs crossing into Thai territory.

The Pa-O, threatened by increasing violence, deforestation, and the denial of land rights, agreed to open negotiations with the government in 1994. The nationalists, after decades of fighting, continue to claim that to surrender will mean the extinction of their small nation, but armed resistance has become more difficult as arms and funds from outside their territory have begun to dry up as Thai economic interests replaces cooperation.

In December 1994 attacks by government troops, the first in over two years, renewed fighting in the region. The rebels, falling back on jungle strongholds, began to coordinate their armed struggle with the other insurgent groups under renewed attack by the government. Nationalist leaders reiterated their aim of Pa-O independence within a federation of states when the brutal military junta is finally driven from power.

*SELECTED BIBLIOGRAPHY:*

Lintner, Bertil. *Land of Jade: A Journey through Insurgent Burma.* 1990.
Nicholl, Charles. *Borderlines: A Journey in Thailand and Burma.* 1989.
Silverstein, J. *Burmese Politics: The Dilemma of National Unity.* 1980.

# PATTANI

Patani; Phatthalung; Islamic Republic
of Pattani

*CAPITAL: Pattani (Patani)*

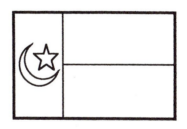

SOUTHEASTERN ASIA

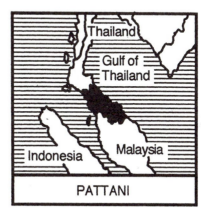

PATTANI

*POPULATION:* (95e) 4,028,000 : 2,824,000 Pattani (Pattani Malays) in Thailand. MAJOR NATIONAL GROUPS: (95e) Pattani (Pattani Malay) 66%, Thai 28%, Chinese 3%, Sakai, Semang. MAJOR LANGUAGES: Malay, Thai, English. MAJOR RELIGIONS: Sunni Muslim, Buddhist, animist. MAJOR CITIES: (95e) Hadyai (Ban Hat Yai) 174,000, Singora (Songkha) 116,000, Trang 85,000 (120,000), Yala 76,000, Pattani (Patani) 65,000, Naradhivas (Narathiwat) 53,000, Padalung (Phatthalung) 42,000, Satul (Satun) 31,000.

*GEOGRAPHY:* AREA: 11,008 sq.mi.-28,518 sq.km. LOCATION: Pattani occupies a heavily forested region of the central Malay Peninsula between the Thale Luang Lake and the Malaysian border, between the South China Sea and the Andaman Sea. POLITICAL STATUS: Pattani has no official status; the region forms the Phatthalung Division of Thailand, comprising the provinces of Narathiwat, Pattani, Phatthalung, Satun, Songkha, Trang, and Yala.

*FLAG:* The Pattani national flag, the flag of the national movement, is a horizontal bicolor of red over white with a wide vertical green stripe at the hoist bearing a white crescent moon and five-pointed star.

*PEOPLE:* The Pattani, also called Pattani Malays, are a Malay people closely related to the Malay peoples of the lower Malay Peninsula. The Pattani speak a Malay dialect with a Thai admixture; however, in the northern districts a minority has adopted the Thai language. The Pattani culture has been influenced by their long association with the Thais to the north and early contacts with the Chinese. The majority religion is Sunni Islam, the religion closely identified with the Pattani culture. There are pockets of Muslims as far north as the Isthmus of Kra. Minorities in the region include the Buddhist Thais and the small groups of aboriginal Negrito peoples, the Sakai and Semang.

*THE NATION:* The ancestors of the Malays probably originated in southern China. Small migrations began to filter down the long Malay Peninsula about 2000 B.C. The migrants settled in the coastal zones, a region of wooded lowlands and swamps. Their colonization gradually pushed the native Negrito peoples into the dense jungles in the center of the peninsula. Around the beginning of the Christian Era, Buddhist and Brahman missionaries spread new religions among the pagan population.

Small, Hindu-influenced states developed in the region. One of the small states, Langkasuka, based in the present Kedah region of Malaysia, eventually expanded to control most of the central section of the peninsula. The state grew wealthy on trade with ships arriving in its port towns from as far away as China and the western Indian Ocean. The Hinduized kings of Langkasuka are mentioned in Arab and Chinese records of the sixth through the eighth centuries.

In the second half of the eighth century the Sailendra rulers of the Sri Vijaya kingdom of Sumatra extended their influence up the peninsula to absorb Langkasuka. Pattani developed as one of the centers of the Sailendras' empire, even rivaling Palembang, the Sailendra capital, in splendor and wealth. Sailendra rule, eclipsed in Java and Sumatra, continued in Pattani where the Sailendras moved their power base.

Pattani remained a center of Sailendra influence until the Cholas, from southern India, overran the peninsula in the eleventh century. After a half century of Chola domination, the Sailendras reasserted their power in the region. Pattani regained its importance as a center of Sailendra naval power. Sailendra hegemony continued into the thirteenth century but eventually fell to the expanding Sukothai kingdom of the Thais. The Thai king, Rama Kamheng, who began his forty-year rule in 1275, conquered the northern part of the peninsula and brought the various states under nominal Thai rule.

Islam, introduced to the peninsula through the port of Malacca, the Thai's rival power to the south, spread to Pattani in the fifteenth century. The Muslim Empire centered on Malacca disputed Thai influence in the northern Malay states, but Malacca's power ended in 1511 with the Portuguese conquest of the capital city. In the north the Thais reasserted their authority over the various small Muslim states. The Islamicized Malay states maintained considerable autonomy while acknowledging the Thai kings as suzerains.

The first European ships appeared in the port cities in the sixteenth century. The first expeditions, mainly Portuguese traders, spread rumors and stories of the region's wealth and brought back the exotic spices so prized in Europe. English and Dutch expeditions explored the coasts, and from 1612 to 1623 the English maintained a trading factory at Pattani. Concentrating their activities to the south, the Europeans abandoned the region for over a century, leaving the Siamese Thais as the dominant power in the northern Malay states.

The Pattani Malays, with growing opposition to Buddhist Thai domination, rebelled several times in the seventeenth and eighteenth centuries. In the nineteenth century an increasingly centralized Siamese government gradually reduced the northern Malay states to near provincial status. In 1826 the Thais signed a treaty with the British that opened the port cities of the Siamese-controlled Malay states to British trade.

The Siamese Malay states shared in the growing commercial prosperity of the British-protected Malay states to the south but did not attain the commercial importance of the southern states. Growing British influence in Pattani and the other northern states resulted in Siam's 1909 transfer of suzerainty of Kelantan, Perlis, Kedah, and Trengganu to Great Britain. In spite of increasing European pressure, the Thais managed to retain control of the Pattani, Yala, Satun, and the other northern states.

The anticolonial movement, spreading from the British Malay States, stimulated a parallel movement in the Thai states. In the late nineteenth century the Pattani formed the first nationalist organization of Muslims under Thai rule. The resurgence of the Malays' Muslim religion spurred the movement, the Muslims nationalists vehemently opposed to rule by infidel non-Muslim Buddhists.

The Thais, nominal allies of the Japanese during World War II, gradually lost control of the region. On 8 December 1941 Japanese troops in the region took control of the Pattani region, used to launch attacks on the British states to the south. The return of the Thai authorities in 1946 marked the beginning of the modern Pattani national movement.

The Pattani nationalists demanded the self-government extended to the British Malay states in 1948, with some Pattani calls for union with the British-sponsored federation. In the 1950s, spurred by the independence of Malaya in 1957, the Pattani demanded independence from Thailand, and skirmishes with the Thai military broke out. In the 1960s separatist violence and fighting spread across the region, described by radicals as a Muslim holy war. The separatists received support from several Muslim states.

The national movement lost support in the 1970s as the Thai government allowed greater autonomy. In the 1990s the movement has again become active, partly in response to renewed Muslim militancy and Thai efforts to assimilate the Malays. In August 1993 the separatists launched a new campaign to win independence, burning Thai language schools, ambushing trains, and attacking Thai military targets.

*SELECTED BIBLIOGRAPHY:*
Insor, D. Thailand: *A Political, Social, and Economic Analysis.* 1963.
Ryan, N. J. *Malaya through Four Centuries.* 1959.
Winstedt, Richard. *The Malays, a Cultural History.* 1984.

# PIEDMONT

**Piemonte**

*CAPITAL: Turin (Torino)*

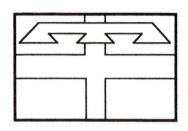

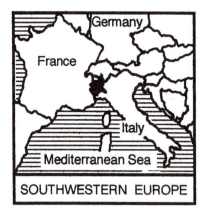

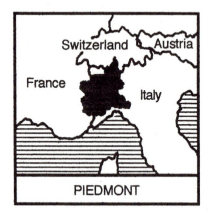

*POPULATION:* (95e) 4,283,000 : 3,750,000 Piedmontese in Italy. MAJOR NATIONAL GROUPS: (95e) Piedmontese 77%, Occitan 7%, other Italian. MAJOR LANGUAGES: Italian, Piedmontese, Occitan. MAJOR RELIGIONS: Roman Catholic, Protestant. MAJOR CITIES: (95e) Turin (Torino) 987,000 (1,713,000), Alessandria 91,000 (162,000), Novara 90,000 (149,000), Asti 89,000, Cuneo 68,000, Biella 59,000, Vercelli 52,000, Alba 37,000 (80,000).

*GEOGRAPHY:* AREA: 9,807 sq.mi.-25,406 sq.km. LOCATION: Piedmont occupies a fertile upland plain, nearly surrounded by mountains, in northwestern Italy, bordering Switzerland on the north, France on the west, and Lombardy* on the east. POLITICAL STATUS: Piedmont forms a semiautonomous region of the Italian republic.

*FLAG:* The Piedmontese national flag, the flag of the national movement, is a red field divided by a centered white cross and bearing an inverted blue crown on the top half.

*PEOPLE:* The Piedmontese are an Italian peoples of mixed Italian, French, and Occitan background, speaking a distinctive dialect of Italian that incorporates substantial borrowings from the French and Occitan languages. Nationalists claim Piedmontese is a separate language, not a dialect of Italian. One of the latest of Europe's nations to espouse nationalism, the movement is based on the language and the Piedmontese culture, a French-influenced alpine culture with values and traditions radically different from those of central and southern Italy. In the western districts there is a large Occitan minority, part of the Occitan population of Occitania* in southern France.

*THE NATION:* Settled by early Celtic peoples, the Gallic and Ligurian tribes, the region came under Roman rule between 177 and 121 B.C. Called Pedemontium, meaning "at the foot of the mountains," the Romans incorporated the region into the province of Cisalpine Gaul. The Celts adopted Roman culture, becoming a Latinized, urban population.

The prosperous district fell to invading barbarians as Roman power decayed in the fifth century A.D. Huns ravaged the region in 452, and in the sixth century Longobards (Lombards), a Germanic tribe, conquered the fertile lowlands. The Lombards incorporated the region into their kingdom, centered on the Po Valley, in 568. Modern Piedmont developed from the Lombard kingdom's western districts of Turin and Ivrea.

Conquered by Charlemagne in 774, the Franks absorbed Piedmont into the Frankish Empire, later the Holy Roman Empire. In the eleventh century parts of the region passed by marriage to Savoy.* In the fifteenth century the Savoyard state emerged as the most powerful regional force, its territories straddling the mountains that traditionally divided the Italian and French territories of Southern Europe.

The bilingual Savoy duchy, dominated by the French-speaking Savoyards, was occupied by French troops in 1536. Later restored, the duchy moved its capital from Chambéry to Turin, although the language and tone of the court remained French until the eighteenth century. In 1720 the duke of Savoy acquired the island of Sardinia* and renamed the state, taking the title King of Sardinia. In 1848 the Sardinian kingdom acquired additional territories, including the remaining Piedmontese territories.

The kingdom became a center of the Risorgimento in the 1850s, the movement to unite the numerous Italian states under the rule of the kingdom's House of Savoy. Napoleon III, for his help in uniting Italy, demanded the cession of the culturally French regions of the kingdom, Savoy, Nice, and Menton. Turin was named the capital of the newly united Italian kingdom in 1861; however, a Tuscan dialect spoken around Florence was adopted as the new national language over unwavering Piedmontese opposition. The Tuscan dialect, spoken by less than 10% and written by only 1% of Italy's population, was considered more representative of the majority of the spoken dialects than the Piedmontese language.

The Italian kingdom finally wrested Rome from papal rule in 1870, and the authorities transferred the capital of the kingdom to the more central city. The government's move to Rome dealt a severe blow to the Piedmontese and has never been forgiven. The loss of prestige and power undermined Piedmontese enthusiasm for Italian unification. A movement formed in the 1870s to protect the Piedmontese dialect from Italianization incited a literary revival and over the next decades spurred a cultural revival. The Piedmontese revival coincided with the development of a large industrial middle class that further divided the region from agrarian central and southern Italy.

Fascism gained strength in Italy after World War I, but its base lay in the poor, backward south. Nationalists and Communists gained support in industrial Piedmont, the rival ideologies leading to frequent clashes, particularly in Turin. The fascist Italian government, allied to the Axis powers, won Piedmontese backing with promises to recover the territories lost to France in 1860. The region's initial enthusiasm declined rapidly after fighting broke out on the French border in June 1940. The Italian government surrendered to the Allies in 1943. The Nazi Germans quickly occupied the northern Italian regions and treated their former allies as a conquered state.

Liberated in 1945, the Piedmontese began agitation for autonomy, the movement gaining support following the 1946 Italian referendum that eliminated the beloved monarchy that had ruled Piedmont for over 900 years. Fearing unrest in the northern regions that led Italy's postwar economic recovery, the government promised self-rule but, after numerous delays, finally granted only semi-autonomous status in 1970.

Piedmont's industries boomed in the 1950s and 1960s, attracting hundreds of thousands of workers from Italy's underdeveloped southern regions. Forced to communicate, both the workers and their Piedmontese supervisors replaced their mutually incomprehensible dialects with standard Italian in the workplace. In 1950 approximately 60% of the Piedmontese spoke only the Piedmontese dialect, the percentage dropping rapidly with the influx of southerners and the spread of mass media over the next two decades. In 1990 the majority of the Piedmontese described themselves as bilingual. Only 36% spoke Italian only, but just 17% continued to use Piedmontese as the language of daily life.

The Italian economic miracle, confined to the northern regions, raised the Piedmontese levels of industrial production and incomes to the equal of neighboring European regions but greatly increased Piedmontese frustrations with the massive and inefficient Italian state. Resentment of their taxes being squandered on the corrupt and backward south grew from the increasing integration of the northern regions into mainstream Europe in the 1970s.

A Piedmontese nationalist movement emerged in the 1980s, closely allied to other such movements evolving across the prosperous northern regions. By 1992 the alliance of northern Italian nationalists, autonomists, and separatist groups, the Northern League, had become a major political force. The Europeanization of Piedmont has fueled a strong desire to participate in the continental federation, the European Union, without the encumbrance of the huge and inefficient Italian bureaucracy or the poor, crime-ridden southern regions.

*SELECTED BIBLIOGRAPHY:*

Carello, Adrian N. *The Northern Question: Italy's Participation in the European Economic Community and the Mezzogiorno's Underdevelopment.* 1989.
Cunsolo, Ronald S. *Italian Nationalism from Its Origins to World War II.* 1990.
Smith, Denis M. *The Making of Italy 1796–1870.* 1988.

# PUERTO RICO

## Borinquen

*CAPITAL: San Juan*

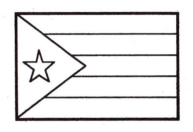

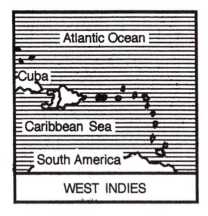

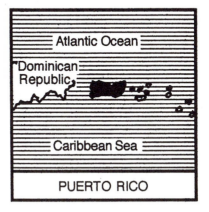

*POPULATION:* (95e) 3,676,000 : 5,500,000 Puerto Ricans in Puerto Rico and the United States. MAJOR NATIONAL GROUPS: (95e) Puerto Rican (Puertorrequeño) 97%, other American. MAJOR LANGUAGES: Spanish, English. MAJOR RELIGIONS: (95e) Roman Catholic 91%, Protestant. MAJOR CITIES: (95e) San Juan 442,000 (1,793,000), Bayamon 234,000, Ponce 198,000 (307,000), Carolina 189,000, Caguas 151,000, Mayaguez 108,000 (217,000), Guaynabo 105,000, Arecibo 96,000 (172,000), Aguadilla 33,000 (74,000).

*GEOGRAPHY:* AREA: 3,515 sq.mi.-9,106 sq.mi. LOCATION: Puerto Rico lies in the northern Caribbean Sea, the smallest and most easterly of the Greater Antilles, set between the Dominican Republic and the Virgin Islands. POLITICAL STATUS: Puerto Rico forms a self-governing commonwealth in free association with the United States.

*FLAG:* The Puerto Rican national flag, the official flag of the commonwealth, has five horizontal stripes of red and white bearing a blue triangle at the hoist charged with a single, five-pointed white star. OTHER FLAG(S): The flag of the Independence Party is a green field with a centered white cross.

*PEOPLE:* The Puerto Ricans are a Caribbean people, a mixture of the island's original inhabitants, Spanish colonists, and African slaves. Estimates of the makeup of the Puerto Rican people are 20% of European descent, 20% of African descent, and 60% of mixed background. The primary language of the island is Spanish, with English widely spoken. The bilingual majority reflects the island's culture, an amalgamation of 500 years of Spanish influence mixed with twentieth-century American modernism. Over 2 million Puerto Ricans live on the American mainland, mostly concentrated in the northeastern states and Florida. An estimated half of all Puerto Ricans spend some part of their lives away from the island, usually to live for some years in the mainland United States.

*THE NATION:* Called Borinquen, the island's original inhabitants, the Arawaks, are thought to have migrated north from the South American mainland in ancient times. Sighted by Columbus on his second voyage to the New World in 1493 and by Ponce de Leon in 1508, the island was called by the Spaniards Puerto Rico, the rich port. The Spanish founded a colony at Caparra in 1509, but were forced to abandon the settlement two years later to escape Arawak attacks. In the first four years of Spanish rule, forced labor, mistreatment, and disease decimated the Arawak population. In need of laborers to replace the disappearing native people, the Spanish authorities began to import African slaves in 1513.

The island grew rich on tropical agriculture and the treasure-laden galleons that anchored at San Juan on the long voyage to Spain. The Spanish sea routes and the port cities attracted the attentions of English and Dutch buccaneers. In the eighteenth century, as Spain's vast colonial empire declined, Puerto Rico settled into a quiet plantation existence. The colonial calm of the island ended in the 1820s, with calls by a nascent nationalist movement for Puerto Rican independence as the other Spanish American colonies threw off Spanish rule.

The abolition of slavery in 1873 exacerbated island discontent with Spanish rule, particularly among the influential planter class. The Spanish government hastily granted autonomy in 1898 to ensure the Puerto Ricans' loyalty when war began with the United States. Seven months later, in October 1898, U.S. troops occupied the island. By the terms of the peace treaty, Puerto Rico was ceded to the United States. The island remained under military occupation until a civil administration took control in 1900.

The U.S. administration, to extend military conscription to the island, granted the islanders U.S. citizenship in 1917. Thousands of conscripts, not considered white, were drafted into Negro regiments. The Puerto Ricans, particularly those of European descent, greatly resented their arbitrary classification as nonwhites.

Fleeing poverty and underdevelopment, thousands of islanders moved to the mainland in the 1920s and 1930s, most settling in separate districts of the northeastern industrial states. Discrimination against the darker, Spanish-speaking Puerto Ricans provoked the first stirrings of nationalist sentiment. During World War II, the administration again assigned Puerto Rican draftees to black regiments. The indignation of the Puerto Rican soldiers fed the growing nationalism taking hold on the island.

Armed separatist groups, formed after World War II mostly by returning soldiers, began to operate on the mainland. In 1950 Puerto Rican nationalists attempted to assassinate President Harry Truman, and in 1954 radical nationalists attacked the House of Representatives, wounding four congressmen.

Puerto Rico became a commonwealth in 1952, electing its own government and representatives in the House of Representatives and Senate, but, despite some concessions, the U.S. authorities remained firmly in control. In the 1960s the island government launched Operation Bootstrap, luring manufacturing to the island with tax incentives and low wages. By the late 1960s Puerto Rico had become the most prosperous island in the Caribbean, although average incomes remained well below those of the U.S. mainland.

Advocates of statehood gained support in the 1960s and 1970s, while the small independence movement splintered among rival groups. More militant nationalists conducted a campaign of sabotage and terrorism in the late 1970s, but failed in attempts to win widespread support for independence. Leftist groups, aided by Communist Cuba, advocated the creation of a socialist Puerto Rican republic. In September 1982 the United Nations General Assembly voted seventy to thirty to defeat a Cuban motion to label Puerto Rico an American colonial possession.

The leading political parties reflect the ongoing debate on the island's future, pro-commonwealth, pro-statehood, and a smaller independence party. Support for independence has declined since the island achieved the highest standard of living in Latin America in the 1970s. In 1989 the island's governor called for a plebiscite giving the voters three choices: enhanced commonwealth, full statehood, or independence. The plebiscite, originally scheduled for 1992, was postponed when the needed legislature stalled in the U.S. Congress.

In November 1992 elections, the pro-statehood political party won, vowing to hold a referendum on statehood in 1993. In January 1993 the legislature overturned a law making Spanish the only official language, effectively reinstating English as the island's second language. Puerto Rican voters participated in the long-postponed plebiscite in November 1993, the vote narrowly confirming their desire to maintain the island's present commonwealth status in free association with the United States.

*SELECTED BIBLIOGRAPHY:*

Carr, Raymond. *Puerto Rico: A Colonial Experiment.* 1984.

Clark, Victor S. *Puerto Rico and Its Problems.* 1975.

Davidson, Donald. *Regionalism and Nationalism in the U.S.: The Attack on the Leviathan.* 1990.

Ferre, Luis A. *The Plea of Puerto Rico.* 1980.

# PUSHTUNISTAN

**Pakhtunistan; Pakhtoonistan**

*CAPITAL: Peshawar*

*POPULATION:* (95e) 19,064,000 : 16,500,000 Pushtun (Pakhtun) in Pakistan and another 8,500,000 in neighboring Afghanistan. MAJOR NATIONAL GROUPS: (95e) Pushtun (Pakhtun) 82%, Afghan 15%, other Pakistani. MAJOR LANGUAGES: Pushtu, Punjabi, Giyari, Kohistani, English. MAJOR RELIGIONS: Sunni Muslim, Shia Muslim, Ismaili Muslim. MAJOR CITIES: (95e) Peshawar 1,173,000 (1,575,000), Mardan 236,000, Mingoara 111,000 (184,000), Charsadda 86,000 (150,000), Dera Ismail Khan 79,000, Kohat 68,000 (98,000), Abbottabad 56,000 (122,000), Nowshera 47,000 (160,000), Bannu 42,000 (75,000).

*GEOGRAPHY:* AREA: 40,377 sq.mi.-104,603 sq.km. LOCATION: Pushtunistan lies in northwestern Pakistan, a mountainous region, partly in the Himalayas, west of the Indus River on the Afghan border. POLITICAL STATUS: Pushtunistan has no official status; the region forms the North-West Frontier Province and the federally administered Tribal Areas of the Islamic Republic of Pakistan.

*INDEPENDENCE DECLARED:* 2 September 1947.

*FLAG:* The Pushtu national flag is a red field divided by a broad, vertical black stripe offset toward the hoist and charged with an overlapping white disc bearing three snowcapped green mountains set against a pale blue sky and backed by a yellow rising sun.

*PEOPLE:* The Pushtu, formerly known as Patans, are an Indo-Iranian people comprising four major divisions: the Durrani of Afghanistan, and the Pakistani groups—the Ghilzai (the highland nomads), the highland nomads called Tribals, (living along the Afghan border), and the Lowlanders (the most integrated). The divisions are further fragmented among some sixty tribal groups. The Pushtu are overwhelmingly Muslim but are divided into different, often conflicting, sects. All Pushtu honor the Pushtunwali, the strict code of honor that imposes three obligations: Nanawatai, giving asylum to any refugee, even a mortal enemy; Melmastia, extending hospitality to all strangers; Badal, obtaining revenge for a wrong.

*THE NATION:* The mountainous region, containing the main passes leading into the Indian Plain, has been a corridor for invaders for thousands of years. A center of the ancient Buddhist kingdom of Gandhara, the region was reached by the Greek soldiers of Alexander the Great. In the first century A.D. the Kushans overran the region. Fair Aryan tribes, driven from the Iranian Plain, occupied the mountains in the seventh century and created small tribal states in the high mountain valleys.

Conquered by the Muslim warriors of the Afghan Empire in the tenth century, the Pushtu tribes adopted Islam. Centuries of invasions by Afghans, Persians, Indians, and Mongols converted the Pushtu tribes into a warrior people, the best guerrilla fighters in Asia. The tribes, uniting only when threatened, more often warred among themselves.

The Afridi Pushtu rallied the tribes to defeat a Mogul army of 40,000 in the seventeenth century. Only partially subdued by repeated Mogul attacks, the Indian Moguls initiated the practice of paying local rulers to keep the peace on the volatile frontier district. The Mogul Empire declined rapidly after 1707, leaving the Pushtu to unite under the Durrani Sultanate of Afghanistan in 1747.

The Sikhs, expanding from the Punjab lowlands, drove the Durrani Pushtu from the territory east of the Khyber Pass in 1823. The Pushtu territories, along with the rest of the Sikh Empire, passed to British rule following the defeat of the Sikhs in 1849.

The British garrisoned the main towns but, unable to pacify the tribal areas, continued their predecessor's practice of paying stipends to local rulers to keep the peace. The stipends became the region's major source of legal income, with most tribal fees coming from smuggling and other prohibited activities.

Military expeditions attempted to subdue the tribes in the 1880s and 1890s, but with little success. In 1901, having failed militarily, the British authorities created a semiautonomous region, the North-West Frontier District. British garrisons in the district effectively controlled only a third of the Pushtu territory. British soldiers, dressed in the traditional red jackets, were often targeted by tribal sharpshooters. The British military finally swapped the red for uniforms made of khaki, a local Pushtu word meaning "dusty."

Pushtu resistance to British rule continued through the 1940s and World War II, forcing the diversion of units of the hard-pressed British Indian army to fight tribal uprisings. After the war, as British India moved toward independence, the Afghan government proposed that the Pushtu of the North-West Frontier District be allowed to vote for joining Afghanistan, Pakistan, or India or for separate independence. The choices offered by the British authorities allowed accession only to Muslim Pakistan or Hindu-dominated India.

Pushtu nationalists formed Khuda-i-Khidmatgar (Servants of God), popularly called the Red Shirts, and called for a nationalist boycott of the accession referendum and refused to be bound by the result of the vote, accession to Muslim Pakistan. The Red Shirts launched a terrorist campaign against the new Pakistani state and on 2 September 1947 declared the district independent as Pushtunistan, the Land of the Pushtu. Pakistani troops invaded the breakaway state, the invasion provoking violent rioting in the Pushtu cities. The Pushtu uprising became the first serious threat to Pakistan's fragile unity.

The Pakistanis, unable to fully subdue the rebellious tribes, finally adopted the earlier practice of paying local chiefs to keep the peace. Pushtu separatism, supported by Afghanistan and the Soviet Union, continued to destabilize the region in the 1950s and 1960s. In 1952, 5,000 nationalists, trained in Afghan camps, invaded the Peshawar Valley to plant the flag of Free Pushtunistan.

Beset by nationalist movements in several provinces in the 1960s and 1970s, the government outlawed political parties, banned regional assemblies, and suppressed nationalist groups. In 1971 the secession of East Pakistan, renamed Bangladesh, provoked a crisis as Pushtu nationalists pressed for the Pushtu to follow the Bengali into secession.

The Soviet invasion of Afghanistan in 1979 sent a flood of refugees into the province, the majority Afghan Durrani Pushtu closely related to the region's Pushtu population. The Afghan civil war, after the Soviet withdrawal of 1989, fired ethnic conflicts between the majority Durrani Pushtu and the large ethnic minorities in Afghanistan, the conflicts raising Pushtu nationalist sentiment in Pakistan.

The radicalization of the Muslim religion in the 1990s reverberated in the North-West Frontier Province. In November 1994 Pushtu fundamentalists took control of the tribal Malakand District and demanded the creation of an Islamic state in the region. The Pakistani government, aware of the unrest and nationalist stirrings in the region, conceded an Islamic government in Malakand District, but rejected the rebel's political demands.

*SELECTED BIBLIOGRAPHY:*
Caroe, Olaf. *The Patans, 550 B.C.–A.D. 1957.* 1958.
Jansson, Erland. *Nationalist Movements in the North-West Frontier Province, 1937–47: India, Pakistan, or Pakhtunistan.* 1981.
Moorehouse, Geoffrey. *To the Frontier.* 1984.
Wilcox, W. A. *Pakistan: The Consolidation of a Nation.* 1963.

# QUEBEC

**Québec**

*CAPITAL: Quebec (Québec)*

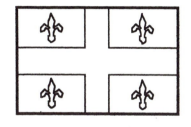

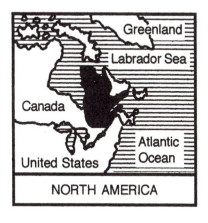

NORTH AMERICA

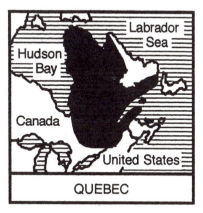

QUEBEC

*POPULATION:* (95e) 6,904,000 : 5,755,000 Quebeckers (Québécois) in Canada. MAJOR NATIONAL GROUPS: (95e) Quebecker (Québécois) 83%, other Canadian. MAJOR LANGUAGES: French (Quebec dialect) 83%, English 9%, Italian 3%, Native American languages. MAJOR RELIGIONS: (95e) Roman Catholic 88%, Protestant 10%, Jewish 1.5%. MAJOR CITIES: (95e) Montreal 960,000 (2,968,000), Laval 274,000, Quebec (Québec) 155,000 (641,000), Longueuil 130,000, Sherbrooke 71,000 (130,000), Chìcoutimi 62,000 (Chìcoutimi-Jonquière 155,000), Jonquière 60,000, Hull 54,000, Trois-Rivières 48,000 (116,000), Granby 43,000 (53,000), Saint-Hyacinthe 40,000 (52,000), Saint-Jean-sur-Richelieu 36,000 (63,000), Drummondville 26,000 (62,000), Shawinigan 22,000 (66,000).

*GEOGRAPHY:* AREA: 524,861 sq.mi.-1,359,743 sq.km. LOCATION: Quebec occupies a large part of eastern Canada, a heavily wooded region between the large Hudson and Ungava Bays on the north and the Gulf of St. Lawrence on the south. POLITICAL STATUS: Quebec forms a province of Canada.

*FLAG:* The Quebecker national flag, the official flag of the province, is a blue field divided by a centered white cross, each blue rectangle charged with a white fleur-de-lis.

*PEOPLE:* The Quebeckers, descendants of early French colonists, are a French-speaking North American people with a New World French culture unique on the North American continent. The devoutly Catholic Quebeckers speak a French dialect retaining many words and forms from the French spoken in the eighteenth century. The largest minorities in the province are the English-speaking Quebeckers concentrated in Montreal and the eastern counties, immigrant groups, mostly Italian, Ukrainian, and Polish, and Native American peoples in the north, Inuits along the coast in the far north, and Cree and related peoples in the Ungava Peninsula, the region they call Nistassin.*

*THE NATION:* The huge area, sparsely populated by diverse tribal peoples, was claimed for France by Jacques Cartier in 1534. Samuel de Champlain built a trading post on the upper reaches of the St. Lawrence River in 1608. The town that grew up around the post, Quebec, became the center of missionary and exploration activities for all the enormous colony of New France. By 1700 over 12,000 French colonists had settled in the fertile south.

French and British rivalry in North America led to a series of wars, culminating in the French defeat on the Plains of Abraham outside Quebec's city walls in 1759. New France, with its 70,000 French citizens, was ceded to British North America in 1763. With rebellion growing in the thirteen British colonies farther south, the British parliament passed the Quebec Act of 1774, which divided Canada into French-speaking Lower Canada and English-speaking Upper Canada. The division guaranteed the Quebeckers land tenure and cultural, linguistic, and religious rights.

Quebecker dissatisfaction with British rule heightened in the early nineteenth century. In 1837 the Quebeckers rebelled under the influence of Louis Papineau, the leader of the French Canadian Reform Party. The rebels, known as Patriotes, attempted to create an independent republic, Laurentia, before their final defeat in 1838. The separate province of Lower Canada, dissolved in 1840, became part of a united province called East Canada. In 1867 the province reverted to its parts and renamed Quebec, the province joined with three English-speaking provinces to form the new Canadian federation.

The Quebeckers, mostly rural, poor, and staunchly Roman Catholic, looked to Quebec as the bastion of French culture and language. Their largest city, Montreal, became one of North America's greatest immigration melting pots, with English gradually replacing French as the language of business and culture. In the late nineteenth century, responding to a growing threat to their language and culture, Quebeckers began to organize in nationalist groups to press for Quebecker political and linguistic autonomy.

Urbanized between 1901 and 1921, the massive immigration to the burgeoning cities carried with it the language and culture, particularly the all-important influence of the extremely conservative Catholic Church. The severe hardships of the Great Depression particularly affected the Quebecker areas, where families of a dozen children were common. The dominance of the church extended to all aspects of Quebecker life, books from France were censored, and women had no voting rights until 1940. The only careers open to Quebecker women remained motherhood or the convent until the liberalization of the 1960s.

After World War II, church power declined as education and greater opportunities began to spread. In the 1960s the Quebeckers finally attained a standard of living equal to that of the English-speaking North Americans. The so-called

Quiet Revolution transformed Quebec from an underdeveloped backwater into an advanced, French-speaking industrial state.

French president Charles de Gaulle, on an official visit to Canada in 1967, ignited modern Quebecker nationalism when he proclaimed, during a speech, "Vive le Québec Libre" ("Long Live Free Quebec"). De Gaulle's proclamation became the rallying cry of the nationalists. The rise of nationalist sentiment split the movement into the more moderate, seeking independence by democratic means, and militants, demanding immediate independence and willing to use any means. In 1970 the largest of the militant groups, the Front for the Liberation of Quebec (FLQ), turned to terrorism to publicize their demands.

The openly separatist Parti Québécois (PQ) won the 1976 provincial elections with vows to hold a referendum on independence. A French-only language law, passed in 1978, drove many of the province's powerful English-speaking business community to leave, raising fears that independence would aggravate Quebec's economic problems. A 1980 referendum on independence failed 58.2% to 41.8%. Following the plebiscite, the economy replaced nationalism as the province's primary concern. Young Quebeckers quickly moved into leadership positions in commerce and industry in the 1980s.

The nationalist debate resurfaced in 1986, provoked by a conflict over the controversial language law and Quebecker demands for recognition as a distinct society within Canada. Proposed changes to the federal constitution, blocked by opponents in Manitoba and Newfoundland* in 1990, stoked the nationalist resurgence.

The Quebecker nationalist movement now includes many of Quebec's successful entrepreneurs and businessmen, the sector most opposed to separation in 1980. Supported by the belief that Quebec is now an economically viable industrial state, the nationalists gained support in local elections. In late 1993 the nationalists took fifty-four of the seventy-five Quebec seats in the Canadian parliament, making the Quebec nationalists the official opposition on a Canadian national level. In August 1994, for the first time, nearly 50% of those polled favored separation and independence.

Jacques Parizeau, the leader of the PQ, in December 1994, tabled a bill in the National Assembly whose first article declared Quebec a sovereign state and outlined plans to retain the Canadian dollar and membership in NAFTA.

*SELECTED BIBLIOGRAPHY:*
Basu, Aparna. *Imperialism, Nationalism and Regionalism in Canadian and Modern Indian History.* 1989.
Chapin, Miriam. *Quebec Now.* 1955.
Esman, Milton J. *Ethnic Conflict in the Western World.* 1977.
See, Katherine O. *First World Nationalisms: Class and Ethnic Politics in Northern Ireland and Quebec.* 1988.

# RIF

**Riff; Er Ref**

*CAPITAL: Tittaouen (Tétouan)*

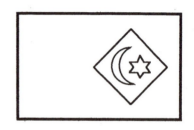

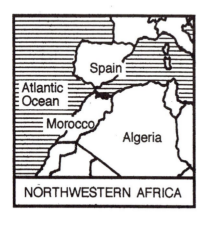

NORTHWESTERN AFRICA

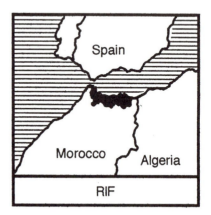

RIF

*POPULATION:* (95e) 2,560,000 : 2,300,000 Riffians in Morocco and Spain. MAJOR NATIONAL GROUPS: (95e) Riffian 77%, Spanish 4%, other Moroccan. MAJOR LANGUAGES: Tamazight (Chelna), Arabic, Spanish. MAJOR RELIGIONS: Sunni Muslim, Roman Catholic. MAJOR CITIES: (95e) MOROCCO: Tittaouen (Tétouan) 365,000, Nador 78,000, Ajdir (Al-Hoceima) 47,000, Chechaouen (Chaouan) 45,000, Tarquist 20,000. SPAIN: Rusadir (Melilla) 72,000, Sebha (Ceuta) 67,000.

*GEOGRAPHY:* AREA: 6,584 sq.mi.-17,055 sq.km. LOCATION: The Rif occupies a hilly coastal lowland in northern Morocco, including several Spanish enclaves, extending from east of Melilla to the Strait of Gibraltar just west of Ceuta and south to the Rif Mountains, which divide the region from the rest of Morocco. POLITICAL STATUS: Rif has no official status; the region forms Al-Hoceima, Nador, and the northern districts of Taza and Tétouan provinces of Morocco, the Spanish enclaves of Melilla and Ceuta, and three smaller territories.

*INDEPENDENCE DECLARED:* 19 September 1921.

*FLAG:* The Riffian national flag, the flag of the former republic, is a red field charged with a white diamond, centered on the fly, bearing a green crescent moon and six-pointed star.

*PEOPLE:* The Riffians are a Berber people, descendants of the region's pre-Arab population, divided into twenty tribal groups speaking dialects of Tamazight, called Chelna by the Arabs. More closely related to the European peoples than to the Semitic Arabs, the Riffians' high incidence of fair hair, 25% blond and 4% red, is roughly the same as in Ireland and Scotland* and would seem to validate theories that ancient Celts crossed to North Africa. Overwhelmingly Sunni Muslim, the Riffians have retained many pre-Islamic customs and traditions, including equal status for women. The substantial Arab population is concentrated in Tétouan and the west. The European population mostly lives in the Spanish enclaves on the coast.

*THE NATION:* Known to the ancient maritime peoples of the Mediterranean, the ancient Berbers traded with the Phoenicians as early as the seventh century B.C. The Carthaginian Empire, of Phoenician origin, controlled the coastal regions until its second-century B.C. defeat by the rival Romans. Following the Roman destruction of Carthage, the Berbers formed a separate kingdom called Mauretania. Roman rule extended to Mauretania in 25 B.C. and the Romans subdued the last free Berber tribes in A.D. 41–42.

Roman Mauretania, a prosperous agricultural province, suffered invasions by barbarian tribes from Europe after the Roman collapse in the fifth century. Germanic Vandals defeated the remnants of the Roman garrisons and overran the province. The wanton destruction of the wealthy region gave the world a new word, "vandalism." Thousands of Berber refugees fled to sanctuaries in the mountains. In the less accessible mountains, the Berbers created a loose tribal confederation that resisted later incursions by foreigners into the mountains.

Muslim Arabs conquered the lowlands in 683, but Arab incursions into the Berber Mountains met fierce resistance. Unable to militarily defeat the tribes, the Arabs eventually formed alliances with tribal chiefs. Isolated in the Rif Mountains, the Berbers became known as Riffians, the Arabs of the lowlands known as Fasis, meaning people of Fez. Slow to adopt the Arab's Islamic religion, the tribes molded the new faith to their ancient customs, the unveiled Riffian women retaining their pre-Islamic freedom and respect.

The coastal tribes turned to piracy in the twelfth century, their swift raiders preying on European shipping. The Portuguese, attacking the pirate bastions, seized the Riffian port of Sebha (Ceuta) in 1415, the seizure initiating the European conquest of Africa. Spanish forces conquered Rusadir (Melilla) in 1497 and took control of Ceuta from the Portuguese in 1578.

The European powers, competing for influence in Morocco, played on the traditional Arab-Berber enmity to gain influence in the eighteenth and nineteenth centuries. In 1904 Spain and France divided Morocco into spheres of influence, most of the Rif assigned to the Spanish zone. Spanish military columns moved out of the port cities in 1909, intent on subduing the troublesome Riffian tribes. Badly mauled, the Spanish retreated to the garrisons, pursued and harassed by Riffian warriors. The Spanish authorities claimed the Rif as part of the protectorate called Spanish Morocco, created in 1912, although Spanish colonial authority was restricted to the fortified ports.

Repressive Spanish rule aroused the Riffian inhabitants of the coastal towns. In 1919 Abd el Krim, a *qadi* (Muslim judge) and tribal chief, employed as a newspaper editor in Melilla, led a widespread Riffian rebellion. The Riffians annihilated a Spanish force of 60,000 at the Battle of Anual in 1921. At Chaouan 16,000 Spaniards were slaughtered, and 40,000 driven from the city. In the east, the Riffians overran Melilla, sending a flotilla of terrified refugees back to Spain.

United for the first time in centuries, the Riffians seemed invincible to the Spaniards huddled behind the walls of the few ports still in Spanish hands. Abd el Krim created a civil administration for the tribal confederation and adopted modern judicial and legislative systems. On 19 September 1921 Abd el Krim declared the independence of the Confederal Republic of the Tribes of the Rif.

Riffian tribes in the south, living on both sides of the international border, began to attack French outposts, finally drawing France into the war in the spring of 1925. A combined Franco-Spanish force, numbering over half a million, the largest European army in African history, moved on the Riffian state in late 1925. Defeated in May 1926, the Riffians surrendered, ending the twentieth century's first attempt at Berber independence.

The Riffians again rose against the Spanish authorities in 1954–55, the Riffian rebellion becoming part of the Moroccan independence movement. Granted independence in 1956, the Spanish zone, except for five small enclaves, became part of the Moroccan kingdom. Promised autonomy, the Riffians celebrated Moroccan independence but, excluded from government and under pressure to assimilate, the enthusiasm turned to resentment. In 1958 the Riffians again rebelled, only to suffer defeat by mechanized columns in 1959.

Demands for linguistic and cultural rights provoked large demonstrations in 1981. As unrest spread new demands were raised: Berber studies in the region's schools and universities and the release of Riffian nationalists jailed by the Moroccan authorities. Emigration to Europe and a government crackdown on cannabis production, the region's only lucrative export, became nationalist issues in the 1980s.

Between 1986 and 1988 Riffian unrest extended to the Spanish enclaves, with demands for Spanish nationality. The Riffians resident in the enclaves enjoy greater freedom than their kin in Morocco and represent the only Berber citizens of the European Union. In 1993 Riffian nationalists appealed to Spain, the former colonial power, to intervene to save the Riffian homeland from the ravages of emigration and depopulation.

*SELECTED BIBLIOGRAPHY:*

Coon, Carleton S. *Tribes of the Rif.* 1931.
Landau, Rom. *Moroccan Drama, 1900–1955.* 1956.
Taha, Abdulwahid D. *Muslim Conquest and Settlement of North Africa and Spain.* 1988.
Terhorst, Bernard. *With the Riff Kabyles.* 1969.

# ROMANDE

Romandie; Jura

CAPITAL: Genève (Geneva)

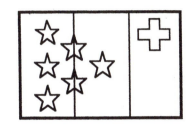

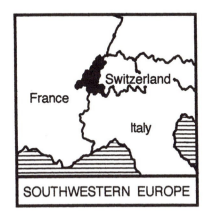

SOUTHWESTERN EUROPE

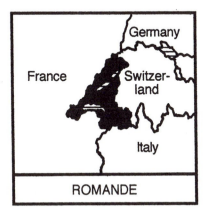

ROMANDE

*POPULATION:* (95e) 1,528,000 : 1,282,000 Romands in Switzerland. MAJOR NATIONAL GROUPS: (95e) Romand (Jurassic) 82%, other Swiss. MAJOR LANGUAGES: French, German, Italian. MAJOR RELIGIONS: (95e) Protestant 75%, Roman Catholic 23%. MAJOR CITIES: (95e) Genève (Geneva) 165,000 (441,000), Lausanne 124,000 (316,000), Bienne (Biel) 51,000 (84,000), Fribourg (Freiburg) 34,000 (62,000), Neuchâtel 32,000 (70,000), La Chaux-de-Fonds 31,000 (50,000), Sion 22,000 (34,000), Yverdon 20,000 (32,000), Montreux 20,000, Vevey 15,000 (Vevey-Montreux 66,000), Delémont 14,000.

*GEOGRAPHY:* AREA: 3,934 sq.mi.-10,191 sq.km. LOCATION: Romande lies in western Switzerland, occupying the western part of the Swiss Plateau bounded by the Jura Mountains on the west and the Pennine Alps in the south and including the lake regions around Lake Geneva, Lake of Neuchâtel, Lake Morat, and Lake Bienne (Bielersee). POLITICAL STATUS: Romande, popularly called the Swiss Romande, has no official status; the region forms the majority French-speaking cantons of Fribourg, Geneva, Jura, Neuchâtel, and Vaud and the western districts of Valais and Bern cantons.

*FLAG:* The Romande national flag, the flag of the national movement, is a vertical tricolor of blue, white, and red, bearing three white stars on the blue stripe, two stars divided vertically white and blue at the juncture of the blue and white stripes, a single blue star centered on the white stripe, and a white, square cross on the upper fly. OTHER FLAG(S): The flag of the largest national organization, the Jura Independence Movement (MIJ), is a vertical tricolor of blue, white, and red, bearing a red mountain horn on the white stripes and three white horizontal stripes on the red.

*PEOPLE:* The Romands are a Romance people speaking the Romand or Jurassic dialects of French along with the standard French of Paris. The Romand nation has been shaped more by the Protestantism and its long separate history than by ethnic or linguistic considerations. The Romands, unlike the German or Italian Swiss, do not fear losing their identity to a larger French culture. The Romand national identity, based on centuries of separate history, is that of a French-speaking Protestant people, but not a French people. The descendants of ancient Latinized Celtic tribes, the Romands have only recently become politically mobilized as a separate nation, one of the latest in Europe to define their national identity as a distinct European people.

*THE NATION:* Originally populated by Celtic peoples, Allobroges, Sequani, and Helvetii, the region around the lakes fell to the Roman legions in 58–57 B.C. Urban and sophisticated, the Latinized Celtic towns became centers of Roman culture. Barbarian tribes overran the region with the decline of Roman power. Invading Germanic Burgundians devastated the Roman towns in A.D. 442–43, followed by the Franks in 534–36. Joined to the Frankish kingdom, later the Holy Roman Empire, the Romand districts slowly recovered.

An important and prosperous part of Charlemagne's empire, the lakes region was included in the middle kingdom of Lotharingia at the division of Charlemagne's empire in 843. From 888 to 1032 the Romande became part of the successor kingdom known as Transjurane Burgundy. Divided into a number of territories, the region formed part of the Holy Roman Empire from 1032. By the thirteenth century Savoy* had gained control of the southern districts. In 1481 Fribourg became the first of the Romande states to join the Swiss alliance.

The German-speaking Bernese conquered Vaud in 1536, facilitating the southward expansion of the Protestant Reformation to the Romande. In 1538 the Genevans expelled the Protestant leader John Calvin, but by 1541 the majority accepted Calvin's doctrine. Calvin established a theocratic state at Geneva that developed as a leading political and intellectual center of Protestant Europe. Geneva's preeminence grew with the arrival of thousands of Protestant Huguenot refugees fleeing persecution and massacres in Roman Catholic France.

In the sixteenth century, threatened by Catholic Savoy and France, the states of Geneva and Fribourg formed a protective alliance with German-speaking Protestant Bern. Protected by a network of political and defensive alliances, the Romande states prospered, the old ruling classes gradually replaced by patrician elites more concerned with commerce than politics. Carefully avoiding involvement in the sporadic wars that convulsed the surrounding regions, the Romande states in the eighteenth century grew rich on trade and services.

Buffeted by the chaos and upheavals that followed the French Revolution in 1789, the Romande states became a refuge for those fleeing the revolutionary excesses. Occupied by French troops in 1798, the states were forcibly joined to

Napoleon's Helvetic Republic. In 1803 the Swiss Confederation was partly restored, including the new French-speaking canton of Vaud. Following Napoleon's final defeat in 1815, Geneva, Neuchâtel, and Valais joined the confederation. In 1848, following a nearly bloodless civil war between the Protestant and Catholic cantons, the Swiss adopted a new constitution that guaranteed cantonal autonomy.

The Swiss Confederation avoided involvement in the European wars of the nineteenth and twentieth centuries. The confederation remained a prosperous multinational and multireligious island of tolerance in the center of Europe. Switzerland's strict neutrality precluded membership in the League of Nations, the later United Nations, or any international organization. In 1959 a referendum favored an exception, and Switzerland joined the European Free Trade Association (EFTA).

Modern Romande nationalism grew from the movement of the French-speaking western districts to separate from the predominantly German-speaking Bern Canton. In 1978 the majority French-speaking districts of northwestern Bern voted to form a new canton called Jura, but the separatists failed to win enough votes in the mixed districts around Lake Bienne (Biel). The controversy opened a bitter rift between the French and German cantons of Switzerland. Nationalist organizations called not just for the separation of Jura but for the separation of the French-speaking cantons from Switzerland.

The economic realities of post–Cold War Europe propelled the Swiss into closer cooperation with its European neighbors. In May 1992 the Swiss government formally applied for membership in the European Economic Community (EEC) and in December held a referendum on a joint EEC-EFTA trading area. To the chagrin of the pro-European Romands, the referendum was defeated due to the majority opposition in the German-speaking cantons.

The growing split between the two largest national groups in Switzerland has exacerbated the Romande perception that the German Swiss are increasingly usurping Swiss identity and shunting the Romande to the margins of Swiss political life. The so-called fried potato ditch, the Rösti-Graben, has become more than just the imaginary line dividing the two peoples. For centuries Swiss identity has been defined in negative terms, not German, not French, not part of any international organization. The Romande Swiss have now begun to redefine their identity as a separate European nation.

*SELECTED BIBLIOGRAPHY:*

Coyle, Dominick J. *Minorities in Revolt.* 1982.

Lundman, B. J. *Nations and Peoples of Europe.* 1984.

Mayer, K. B. *The Population of Switzerland.* 1982.

Oechali, W. *History of Switzerland, 1499–1914.* 1922.

# ROMANISTAN

**Romanestan**

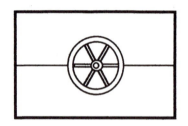

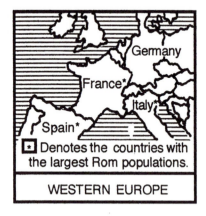

Denotes the countries with the largest Rom populations.

WESTERN EUROPE

EAST-CENTRAL EUROPE

*POPULATION:* (95e) Estimates of the world's Rom population usually vary from between 6 and 15 million, although some estimates quote figures of up to 70 million. Accurate estimates are difficult to obtain as many governments count only nomadic Rom, others misrepresent Rom population figures, and some governments even deny the existence of Rom populations in their countries. The largest Rom population, between 8 and 10 million, is in Europe, four-fifths of the total in Eastern Europe and the former Soviet Union. Other regional estimates are 600,000 in the United States and Canada, 400,000 in the Middle East, North Africa, and India, and 100,000 in Latin America. Only about a half million maintain the Rom's traditional nomadic way of life. NATIONAL GROUP: Rom or Romani (Gypsy). MAJOR LANGUAGE: Romani (Romanés), various dialects. MAJOR RELIGIONS: Christian (Orthodox, Roman Catholic, Protestant), Muslim, other sects.

*GEOGRAPHY:* LOCATION: The Rom are dispersed throughout the world, with the largest concentration in Europe. POLITICAL STATUS: In the majority of world states, the Rom have few or no rights or official status. Romanistan is the dream of creating an independent Rom state somewhere in the world as a focus and a homeland for the Rom Nation.

*FLAG:* The Rom flag, recognized by all Rom communities, is a horizontal bicolor of blue over pale green charged with a centered red wheel with six or more spokes.

*PEOPLE:* The Rom, popularly called Gypsies, a medieval corruption of Egyptian, call themselves Gajo, Rom, or Romani and refer to all other peoples as Gadje. Comprising three major divisions, Rom, Sinti, and Kale, and numerous subdivisions, the most important Rom divisions are the Gitano in Spain, Portugal, and Latin America; the Manouche in France; Sinte in Germany and Italy; Rom in Eastern Europe and the former Soviet Union; Romnichal in the British Isles; Boyash in Romania; Xoraxaya in Turkey and the Middle East; and Arfikaya in North Africa. The Romnichal and Boyash are the most numerous groups in North America. The Rom have adopted local languages and religions while retaining their separate culture and language, spoken in seventeen major and minor dialects. Intermarriage with Gadje has been limited, but some mingling over the centuries has give the Rom populations a wide range of physical appearances, from very dark to very fair.

*THE NATION:* Rom legends place their origins in Sind,* now a province in southeastern Pakistan. Although small groups of nomads are thought to have appeared in the Middle East between 600 and 500 B.C., the main migration began with refugees fleeing the Muslim conquest of Sind in A.D. 711–12. Traditionally following three different leaders, the refugees gradually coalesced in the three major Rom divisions.

Nomadic wanderers in many lands, Rom bands moved into Eastern Europe from Asia Minor in the fourteenth century, many settling as sedentary farmers or tradesmen, others hounded from place to place. Smithing and metalworking developed as the primary occupations, valuable skills to sell to settled populations. Some Rom entered Southern Europe from North Africa, probably having passed through Egypt. The name Egyptian, corrupted to Gypsy, was eventually applied to all Rom groups.

The Turkish conquest of Southeastern Europe forced many Rom to migrate to Western Europe; others fled west to escape enslavement by feudal lords. By the fifteenth century most European states had passed anti-Gypsy laws. The most abhorrent allowed enslavement or death, with bounties paid for Gypsies, dead or alive. Tales associating the Rom with the Crucifixion were used to justify the persecutions, expulsions, and suffering that followed the Rom throughout Europe. In the sixteenth and seventeenth centuries the first Rom prisoners were forcibly transported to the New World, often as slaves. The Rom in the Middle East and North Africa, where nomadic peoples were common, fared better than their kin in Europe.

In the eighteenth and nineteenth centuries the European governments treated the Rom very like the Jews, subject to special taxes, restrictions, official discrimination, and religious persecution. Only in the late nineteenth century did some European states rescind the more odious anti-Gypsy laws. Immigration to North America became one of the few options for the persecuted Rom. New restrictions and discrimination became common in Western Europe following World War I.

German law had already legalized many anti-Gypsy restrictions when the Nazis came to power in 1933. The Rom, like the Jews, were considered to be of Asiatic origin, and official Nazi persecution of the Rom escalated during the

1930s. In 1936 the first group of 400 Rom was imprisoned at the Nazi concentration camp at Dachau. Genealogical investigations, initiated in December 1938, followed a decree labeling the Rom as a menace to German society. Even persons with an eighth Gypsy blood became subject to the increasingly harsh strictures.

The German authorities arrested and deported thousands of Rom to the concentration and labor camps in Poland in 1940. By the summer of 1942 the Nazi hierarchy had decided to exterminate Europe's Gypsies. On 16 December 1942 Himmler signed a decree sending the German Rom to the extermination camp at Auschwitz. Germany's allies, Italy, Vichy France, Romania, Slovakia, and Croatia, issued similar decrees. The Gypsy Holocaust claimed some 2 million lives during World War II, most dying in massacres or of hunger and disease, but a half million Rom perished in the Nazi death camps. Not one Rom was called to witness at the German war crimes trials at Nuremberg in 1945–46.

Denied compensation by West Germany and with many of the survivors declared stateless, the Rom began to organize closer intergroup contacts and to develop ways to protect Europe's remaining Rom population. In the early 1950s Rom leaders pleaded at the United Nations for the establishment of a Rom Israel, an independent homeland to be called Romanistan. The Rom petition did not receive a sympathetic hearing.

Still surrounded by mystery, myth, and superstition, the Rom have again become the targets of ethnic hatreds released by the overthrow of Communism in Eastern Europe and the Soviet Union. The frustrations and economic hardships of converting command economies to free markets are all too often turned on the most defenseless minority, the Rom.

Rom nationalists believe that the anti-Communist revolution of 1989–91 may have opened their last opportunity to join the world community. In October 1991 a conference of European Gypsies at Rome put forward a new proposal for the recognition of the Rom as a transnational European community, a nation without a state but with the same guaranteed cultural, economic, and political rights everywhere in a united, federal European union.

*SELECTED BIBLIOGRAPHY:*
Block, Martin. *The Gypsies: Their Life and Their Customs.* 1939.
Enloe, Cynthia H. *Ethnic Conflict and Political Development.* 1986.
Starkie, W. F. *In Sara's Tents.* 1953.
Tyrnauer, C. *Gypsies and the Holocaust.* 1989.

# SABAH

**North Borneo; Minsupala Sabah**

*CAPITAL: Kota Kinabalu*

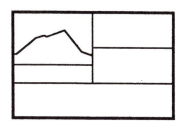

SOUTHEASTERN ASIA

SABAH

*POPULATION:* (95e) 1,760,000 : 940,000 Sabahans in Malaysia. MAJOR NATIONAL GROUPS: (95e) Sabahan 52% (Kadazan 34%, Bajau 12%, Murut 5%, Bruneis 3%, smaller groups), Malay 24%, Chinese 23%. MAJOR LANGUAGES: Kadazan, Malay, Chinese, English. MAJOR RELIGIONS: (95e) Christian 40%, Sunni Muslim 40%, Buddhist, animist. MAJOR CITIES: (95e) Sandakan 223,000, Kota Kinabalu 208,000, Tawau 104,000, Keningau 47,000, Kudat 38,000, Beaufort 32,000, Ranau 27,000.

*GEOGRAPHY:* AREA: 29,545 sq.km.-76,541 sq.km. LOCATION: Sabah, part of East Malaysia, occupies the mountainous northwest of the island of Kalimantan (Borneo) in the central Malay Archipelago. Sabah, with a 900-mile coastline on the South China, Sulu, and Celebes seas, borders Sarawak* on the southwest and Indonesian Kalimantan on the south. POLITICAL STATUS: Sabah forms a state of the Federation of Malaysia.

*FLAG:* The Sabahan flag, the official state flag, is a horizontal tricolor of blue, white, and red bearing a pale blue canton on the upper hoist, charged with a dark blue silhouette of Mount Kinabalu.

*PEOPLE:* The Sabahans, the descendants of the island's original inhabitants, include the Kadazan, also called Dyaks, the largest of the state's sixteen ethnic groups. The Kadazans are divided into the agricultural Kadazan and the seafaring Iban and are mostly Christian. Other large Sabahan groups are the Bajau and Bruneis, farmers and fishermen, and the Murut in the higher elevations. Smaller groups mostly live in the interior valleys. The Sabahans speak related languages of the Malayan branch of the Malayo-Polynesian language group. The Sabahan peoples are closely related to the indigenous peoples of Indonesian Kalimantan and the Moros of the Bangska Moro* region of the southern Philippines. The large Muslim Malay population is concentrated in the coastal areas, and the Chinese population is primarily urban.

THE NATION: Small, culturally diverse tribes, with a long history of conflict between the coastal and highland peoples, have inhabited the island since ancient times. The Kadazan and the related peoples, farmers and fishermen, evolved a society centered on longhouses, with whole villages living under one roof. Muslim sailors and merchants introduced Islam to the pagan coastal peoples in the fourteenth and fifteenth centuries. Powerful Muslim states developed in Brunei and Sulu, in the Philippine Islands to the northeast, the rival sultanates competing for domination of the tribal people of the region.

The tribal peoples had little contact with the outside world until the middle of the nineteenth century. An American, Joseph Torrey of Massachusetts, won a concession on the west coast from the sultan of Brunei in 1865, but his American trading company relinquished its claim ten years later. The British gained control of the area in 1877–79 and in 1888 established the protectorate of North Borneo.

Christian missionaries, Europeans and Americans, established mission stations across the region between the 1880s and the 1930s. The missionaries, particularly successful with the Kadazan peoples, introduced the new Christians to Western education and ideas. In the 1920s and 1930s an educated, Christian minority took over the leadership roles of many of the tribes and began to challenge the traditional domination of the Muslim minority.

The newly independent Philippines and Indonesia, just after World War II, laid claim to the British colony on historic and ethnic grounds. The outside claims to their homeland stimulated the rise of local nationalism, particularly among the Christian Kadazan. Nationalism became a potent force as the British moved to decolonize North Borneo.

A lack of trained administrators and statesmen convinced the North Borneo leaders that independence was not, at the time, a viable option. Renamed Sabah, the colony joined neighboring Sarawak, the British Malay States, and Singapore in an independent federation in 1963. Refusing to renounce its claim, Indonesia backed guerrilla bands inside Sabah and across the border in Indonesian Borneo. In 1968 the Philippines passed a bill that formally annexed the region but could not press its claim. The conflicting territorial pretensions were finally referred to the United Nations, which settled the claims in Malaysia's favor.

Resentment of Malay domination, especially of the mainland Malays, who held most state government offices, raised the question of independence in the 1970s, the situation aggravated by increasing tensions between the Christian and Muslim populations. In 1975 Sabah's Muslim leaders attempted to secede and to form a federation with the related Moros of the southern Philippines, but were blocked by the Christian groups in the state.

The development of extensive petroleum reserves in the late 1970s encouraged nationalists to again demand independence as the state's Muslim-dominated government signed away 95% of the state's oil and natural gas revenues and ran up enormous debts on showy prestige projects. The growth of Kadazan nationalism paralleled the Malaysian government's official policy of promoting ethnic Malay interests.

A Christian Kadazan, Joseph Pairan Kitingan, won over a strong Muslim opposition to become Sabah's first Christian head of state in the federation in April 1985. Allied to the Chinese minority the new state government made Kadazan and English the official languages and moved to end the Malay domination of government and the economy. In March 1986 Malay rioting broke out and quickly spread to the large refugee Muslim population from the Philippines, prompting Christian demands for the expulsion of the Philippine Moros.

A 1989 Malaysian government campaign stressing Malay predominance, coupled with growing demands for the creation of an Islamic state in Malaysia, provoked a Sabahan nationalist backlash and stimulated demands for secession from Malaysia. The government reacted with a wave of arrests of Sabahan nationalist leaders in 1990–91.

In May 1991 Muslim fundamentalist groups made important gains in mainland Malaysia and greatly increased Muslim influence in the federation government. In the 1990s many Sabahans view the Malaysian government as a proselytizing Islamic force poised to subjugate Sabah's non-Malay majority, supported by the hundreds of thousands of Muslim refugees from the Philippines settled in the region with government aid. The increasing Muslim fundamentalist power in the federation has frightened the Sabahans and stimulated a renewed nationalism. In 1992 nationalists denounced the Malaysian government's treatment of Sabah as a colony, which receives only 5% of the revenues from its oil and natural gas, its once extensive forests nearly logged out.

In February 1994, vowing to defend Sabah's identity and interests, a nationalist coalition defeated the Malaysian government's ruling party. In late March the coalition collapsed under Malaysian government pressure, and the country's ruling Malay party took control of the state government.

The perceived Muslim Malay threat has united the state's Sabahan and Chinese populations in opposition. Should Malaysia replace its beleaguered secular tradition with an Islamic government, Sabahan nationalism, buoyed by oil wealth, will become a potent threat to the future of the Malaysian federation.

*SELECTED BIBLIOGRAPHY:*

Islam, M. Nazrul. *Pakistan and Malaysia: A Comprehensive Study of National Integration.* 1989.

McKie, Ronald. *The Emergence of Malaysia.* 1979.

Rutter, Owen. *The Pagans of North Borneo.* 1929.

# SAHRAWI

**Western Sahara; Sahrawi Arab Democratic Republic**

*CAPITAL: Aaiun (Lâyoune)*

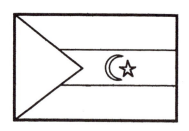

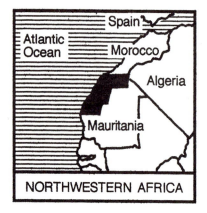

NORTHWESTERN AFRICA

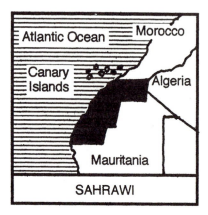

SAHRAWI

*POPULATION:* (95e) 265,000 : 300,000 Sahrawi in Morocco. MAJOR NATIONAL GROUPS: (95e) Sahrawi 53%, Moroccan 45%. MAJOR LANGUAGES: Arabic, Sahrawi, Spanish. MAJOR RELIGION: Sunni Muslim. MAJOR CITIES: (95e) Aaiun (Lâyoune) 130,000, Dakhla 40,000, Smara (Essemara) 35,000, Lemsid 20,000.

*GEOGRAPHY:* AREA: 102,703 sq.mi.-266,069 sq.km. LOCATION: Sahrawi occupies a largely desert region in northwestern Africa, bordering the Atlantic Ocean on the west, Morocco on the north, Algeria on the east, and Mauritania on the south. POLITICAL STATUS: Sahrawi, the Sahrawi Arab Democratic Republic, is recognized diplomatically by over fifty countries; however, most of the region is under Moroccan military occupation. The territorial conflict is to be decided by an often-postponed United Nations referendum.

*INDEPENDENCE DECLARED:* 27 February 1976.

*FLAG:* The Sahrawi national flag, the official flag of the republic, is a horizontal tricolor of black, white, and green bearing a red triangle at the hoist and charged with a centered red crescent moon and five-pointed star.

*PEOPLE:* The Sahrawi are a North African tribal people of mixed Berber and Arab background. Divided into numerous tribes and clans, the Sahrawi are united by history, religion, and language, a distinct dialect combining both Berber and Arabic influences. Disputes over the population estimates have become one of the major stumbling blocks to the proposed United Nations (UN) plebiscite. The Moroccan government claims the Sahrawi number no more than

175,000, while nationalists assert that there is a Sahrawi population of up to a million. Many Sahrawi live across the border in refugee camps in Algeria.

*THE NATION:* The western reaches of the Sahara Desert, populated by Berber tribes, possibly of Celtic origin, had little to interest potential invaders, even though the region was claimed by several ancient states. The Berbers, divided into a number of autonomous tribal groups, lived an isolated existence until the Arab invasion of the eighth century. Converted to Islam, the tribes adopted the social and religious structures of the Arab conquerors.

Arab Morocco, to the north, claimed the region in the tenth century, and, traditionally, Morocco's eleventh- and twelfth-century Almoravid dynasty originated in the area. The dynasty began with Abdullah ibn Yasin, who converted some of the Saharan tribes to his own reform version of Islam and led them north to conquer Morocco. The western reaches of the Sahara Desert came under nominal Moroccan rule in the sixteenth century. Although claimed as subjects of the sultan, the Saharan tribes had little contact with the Moroccan authorities.

In 1860 the Moroccan sultan granted rights in the region to Spain. In 1884 the Spanish established a protectorate comprising two territories, Saguia El Hama in the north and Rio de Oro in the south. The Spanish colonial administration, confined to the coast and several oases, was extended to the interior only in 1934, the extension possible only with the assistance of soldiers from French Morocco.

Shaikh Ma el Amin, a widely revered religious leader, led the Sahrawi resistance to Spanish rule from 1900 to 1910. This campaign later passed to his son, and the movement he began formed the basis of the nationalist movement formed in the 1950s. Tribal leaders drove the Spanish authorities from the protectorate in 1957, but with French military aid the Spanish returned in 1958. The rebellion, supported by most of the population, spread across the huge desert region and effectively restricted Spanish authority to a few garrison towns.

Morocco, independent from France in 1956, laid claim to the region on historical grounds, claiming that the tribes had traditionally paid tribute to the Moroccan sultans. Neighboring Mauritania, to the south, citing clan and family ties between the Sahrawi and the its northern tribes, also put forward a claim to the region. In 1958 the Spanish government changed the region's status to an overseas province. Spanish and French troops defeated a Moroccan attempt to take the region by force in 1959. One of the world's richest phosphate deposits, discovered at Bu Craa in 1963, gave the conflicting claims to the province economic as well as political importance.

Rebellious tribal leaders formed the Popular Front for the Liberation of Saguia El Hama and Rio de Oro (POLISARIO—Polisario Front) in 1973. Drawing recruits from the thousands of refugees from Spanish rule living in camps across the Algerian border, the rebels overran all but the main towns by early 1975. Pressured by world opinion, the Spanish government signed an agreement with the Polisario Front leaders allowing for the orderly withdrawal of Spanish troops as a prelude to Sahrawi independence. The United Nations endorsed the agreement, which would give legal sanction to the independence of the region.

The Moroccan king rejected the pact and on 6 November 1975 launched the so-called Green Revolution, an organized march of 350,000 Moroccan civilians into the Sahrawi territory. Over 200,000 had crossed the border when the Spanish authorities abruptly abandoned the province on 14 November. At UN urging, Morocco agreed to evacuate its civilian marchers but in December the Moroccan government reached an accord with Mauritania for the partition of the region. On 26 February 1976 Morocco formally annexed the northern districts, and Mauritania annexed the southern third of the territory.

The Polisario Front leaders rejected the partition as illegal and appealed to the United Nations. On 27 February 1976 the leaders declared the independence of the Sahrawi Arab Democratic Republic and launched a guerrilla war against the Moroccan and Mauritanian occupation. In 1978, following Polisario Front guerrilla attacks well inside their country, the government of Mauritania renounced its claim to the southern districts, which the Moroccans promptly occupied and annexed to the Moroccan kingdom.

The Moroccan authorities, to protect the important phosphate mining operations and the growing number of Moroccan colonists, built a 400-mile wall of sand and rock, topped with sensors and explosive mines, around the government-held lands. The Moroccans later extended the wall by another 800 miles. Attacks by Moroccan jets on towns and villages sent thousands of Sahrawi civilians into refugee camps in Algeria.

Increasing international pressure for a negotiated settlement prompted both sides, believing that they would win, to accept a proposed UN-supervised referendum. The planned referendum, which has been repeatedly postponed due to conflicting population and voter eligibility claims, has become yet another issue in the war of words that threatens to end the United Nations efforts to bring about a peaceful settlement and to avert yet another round in the ongoing Sahrawi war of independence.

*SELECTED BIBLIOGRAPHY:*

Bodington, Nicholas. *The Awakening Sahara.* 1961.

Price, David L. *The Western Sahara.* 1979.

Thompson, Virginia, and Richard Adloff. *The Western Saharans: Background to Conflict.* 1980.

# SAKHA OMUK

**Sakha; Yakutia**

*CAPITAL: Kalar (Yakutsk)*

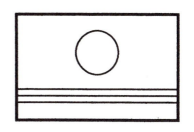

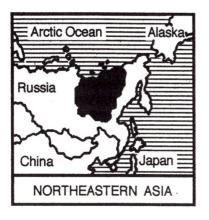

NORTHEASTERN ASIA

SAKHA OMUK

*POPULATION:* (95e) 1,125,000 : 520,000 Sakhas (Yakuts) in Russia. MAJOR NATIONAL GROUPS: (95e) Sakhalar (Yakuty) 45%, Russian 35%, Ukrainian 7%, Evenki 2%. MAJOR LANGUAGES: Russian, Yakut (Sakhalari), Even. MAJOR RELIGIONS: Russian Orthodox, animist (shamanist). MAJOR CITIES: (95e) Kalar (Yakutsk) 215,000 (280,000), Neryungeri 135,000 (190,000), Mirnyy 85,000, Nagornyy 50,000, Aldan 38,000 (73,000), Sangar 35,000, Lensk 30,000, Tommot 25,000, Pokrovsk 20,000 (45,000).

*GEOGRAPHY:* AREA: 1,198,146 sq.mi.-3,104,005 sq.km. LOCATION: Sakha Omuk occupies a vast area of northeastern Siberia* around the basin of the Lena River. Mountainous in the east and south, about 40% of the region lies within the Arctic Circle. POLITICAL STATUS: Sakha Omuk, meaning Sakha Nation, forms a member state of the Russian Federation.

*INDEPENDENCE DECLARED:* 22 February 1918.

*FLAG:* The Sakha national flag, the official flag of the republic, is a pale blue field charged with a centered white disc and bearing narrow, horizontal stripes of white, red, and green at the bottom.

*PEOPLE:* The Sakha or Sakhalar, called Yakuts by the Russians, are considered the largest group of the Altaic branch of the Turkic peoples but are actually of mixed Turkic, Mongol, and Paleo-Siberian background. The Sakha population displays two distinct physical types, Mongol and Turkic. The Sakha language, without dialects and with few regional differences, is related to the Turkic languages but with roots of about a third Turkic, a third Mongol, and a third unknown, probably adopted from the earlier Paleo-Asiatic peoples. The majority of the Sakha are Orthodox Christian, with a minority retaining the traditional shamanistic beliefs, mostly in the more remote parts of the huge Sakha homeland.

*THE NATION:* Sakha legend traces their national origin to a Tatar hero and a Buryat maiden on the shores of Lake Baikal in Buryatia.* A Turkic people, the Sakha fled the region around the lake to escape the thirteenth-century Mongol invasion. By the fifteenth century the Sakha had occupied the basin of the Lena River in the cold country far to the northeast. Herdsmen and horsemen, the Sakha adapted to the harsh conditions of their new homeland with remarkable flexibility. Unlike their Turkic relatives in Central Asia, the Sakha were never affected by the Islamic religion but kept their ancient shamanistic beliefs.

Russian explorers and traders moved into the area in the sixteenth century, trading tobacco for valuable furs to sell in European Russia. In 1632 Cossacks founded a fort at Yakutsk, and by 1710 thousands of Slavic colonists had occupied the more productive lands in the southern river valleys. Several Sakha rebellions followed the colonization and the imposition of the *yasak*, the Russian tax on the Sakha trappers.

The Slavic influx, limited to the southern districts, had little effect on the Sakha majority in the huge region until the arrival of political and criminal deportees at labor camps established in the nineteenth century. Many of the highly educated Poles and Russians exiled to Yakutia were scholars and scientists who devoted themselves to the study of the Sakha culture and language. The exiles from Europe opened a Yakut museum in 1891, and a political exile compiled the first dictionary of the Sakha language.

Schools opened by deportees and the Russian Orthodox Church aided the development of a Sakha literary language and the emergence of an educated minority before World War I. Revolutionary ideas espoused by the exiles, freedom and nationalism, found fertile ground in Yakutia, where poverty and malnutrition were endemic. Sporadic rebellions swept the region between 1905 and 1914, each quickly and severely put down.

The Yakut, as a non-European minority, were exempted from military service when war began in 1914, but, desperate for manpower, the tsarist government began to conscript Sakhas for labor battalions in 1916. Resistance to the conscription aroused antigovernment feelings and fueled the beginning of the Sakha national movement. The nationalists mobilized following the overthrow of the tsar in February 1917 and in alliance with liberal Russian political parties took control of the region as the breakdown of civil administration left the region without a government.

The Bolshevik coup in October 1917 pushed the Sakha to form an alliance with the anti-Bolshevik White forces. In alliance with the forces of General Pepelayev, the Sakhas created the Autonomous Government of the Yakut Region, turning their homeland into an anti-Communist bastion in the Far East.* Over White opposition, the Sakha national leaders declared the region independent on 22 February 1918, calling the new state Sakha Omuk. Far from the

Russian heartland in Europe, the state escaped the devastation of the Russian civil war but in 1920 it fell to the advancing Red Army.

The Soviet attempts to settle the 240,000 Sakhas on collectives provoked a widespread rebellion in November 1921, the rebellion not fully contained until 1923. To avoid further violence, the Soviet authorities accepted the necessity of a seminomadic way of life. In spite of continuing unrest and a renewed rebellion in 1928, the Sakha benefited from Soviet educational and cultural policies. After World War II, a Sakha intelligentsia abandoned their traditional way of life and moved into the professions.

The region's enormous gold, diamond, and coal deposits drew in a large Slavic population in the 1950s and 1960s. The Sakha percentage of the population dropped from 80% of the total in 1946 to less than 50% in 1965. Growing resentment of the Slav workers who came to the mines for a few years, then left, having accumulated, by Soviet standards, considerable wealth, fanned a resurgence of Sakha nationalism and demands for local control of the important mining industry.

National sentiment increased dramatically with the introduction of the Soviet liberalization of the late 1980s. The first Sakha demand in the more relaxed atmosphere, that they be allowed to de-Russify family names, opened a torrent of grievances and discussion of past abuses and oppression. Nationalists demanded that control of the lucrative mines be moved from ministries in Moscow to the local government. Militants called for the expulsion of many of the Slav workers who had settled in the region since World War II.

The Yakut government declared the autonomous republic a sovereign state in October 1990 and in the wake of the disintegration of the Soviet Union unilaterally declared the renamed Sakha Republic a full member state of the Russian Federation and extracted numerous tax concessions before consenting to sign the 1992 federation treaty. Sakha nationalist demands for independence have widespread support, but moves toward secession have been tempered by the threat of the Slav-dominated mining region to stay with Russia should Sakha Omuk secede from the federation.

*SELECTED BIBLIOGRAPHY:*

D'Encausse, Helene C. *The Great Challenge: Nationalities and the Bolshevik State, 1917–1930.* 1991.

Lied, Jonas. *Siberian Arctic.* 1960.

Pushkarev, Sergei. *Self-Government and Freedom in Russia.* 1988.

Stephen, John J. *The Russian Far East.* 1994.

Wood, Alan, and R. A. French. *The Development of Siberia's Peoples and Resources.* 1989.

# SANJAK

Sandzak; Sandzhak; Novibazar; Novi Pazar

*CAPITAL: Novibazar (Novi Pazar)*

*POPULATION:* (95e) 787,000 : 525,000 Sanjaki Muslims in Yugoslavia. MAJOR NATIONAL GROUPS: (95e) Sanjaki Muslim 65%, Serb and Montenegrin 30%, Albanian 5%. MAJOR LANGUAGES: Serbian (Sanjaki dialect), Albanian. MAJOR RELIGIONS: (95e) Sunni Muslim 69%, Serbian Orthodox. MAJOR CITIES: (95e) SERBIA: Novibazar (Novi Pazar) 47,000, Pribol (Priboj) 18,000. MONTENEGRO: Taslidza (Pljevlja) 22,000, Andrijevica (Ivangrad) 20,000,

*GEOGRAPHY:* AREA: 2,973 sq.mi.-7,702 sq.km. LOCATION: Sanjak lies in southwestern Yugoslavia, occupying the mountainous region and the Sandzhak Plateau, which straddles the border between Serbia and Montenegro.* POLITICAL STATUS: Sanjak has no official status; the historic region forms the Sandzhak regions of Serbia and Montenegro in the Federal Republic of Yugoslavia.

*FLAG:* The Sanjaki national flag, the flag of the national movement, is a white field charged with a centered shield divided diagonally green over blue, separated by a white stripe, the green bearing three white crescent moons and the blue bearing three gold stars.

*PEOPLE:* The Sanjakis are a Muslim South Slav people converted to Islam during centuries of Turkish rule. The Sanjaki dialect of the Serbian branch of the Serbo-Croatian language is, like Serbian, written in the Cyrillic alphabet. Although linguistically related to the Serbs and Montenegrins of Yugoslavia, the Sanjakis have their own culture, closely tied to their Muslim religion. The descendants of early Slav peoples and a later Turkish military aristocracy, the Sanjakis are often called Turks by their Orthodox neighbors, a derogatory term. The Serbs claim that the Muslims settled in the region in the seventeenth and eighteenth centuries.

*THE NATION:* Slavic tribes, probably originating in the present Ukraine, settled the Lim River valley and the surrounding mountains in the seventh century. The settlers accepted the authority of the Byzantine authorities, and by the ninth century the majority had adopted the Byzantines' Christian religion. In the tenth century the Slavs living in the Dinaric Alps embraced a new faith. The dualistic creed, attributed to Bogomil, a Bulgarian priest, taught that every action had two sides, good and evil, life and death, and so on. The creed, intensely nationalistic and political as well as religious, opposed Slavic serfdom, church authority, and Byzantine cultural influences. The Slav believers, known as Bogomils, were branded heretics and suffered severe and violent persecutions.

In the twelfth century a powerful Serb state emerged, the Orthodox faith an integral part of the Serb culture. The kingdom, with its capital at Raska, later called Novi Pazar by the Turks, extended its authority into the isolated Bogomil valleys. Thousands of Bogomils died in massacres and planned heretic hunts from the twelfth to the fourteenth centuries.

Just to the south of the Bogomil homeland, at Kosovo Polje, the Field of Blackbirds, a coalition of Christian forces met defeat in one of medieval Europe's largest battles in 1389. The defeat opened the way for the expansion of the Turkish Ottoman Empire in the Balkan Peninsula. In 1456 the advancing Turks occupied the Bogomil heartland in the Lim Valley.

The Bogomils, hated and persecuted by both Orthodox and Roman Catholics, largely converted to the Islamic religion of the Turks. As Muslims they became a favored minority and, with the Turkish military aristocracy settled on the lands of the annihilated Serb nobility, forming a ruling class that controlled large estates worked by Christian and Muslim serfs.

The region around the Lim Valley, administered as a separate Turkish province or *sanjak*, called the Sanjak of Novi Pazar, separated Orthodox Serbia on the east from Orthodox Montenegro to the west. Surrounded by Orthodox majority territories, the region suffered sporadic Christian uprisings during the eighteenth and nineteenth centuries. In 1718 the Austrians occupied the province but made no changes to the existing social structure before withdrawing their administration in 1739.

A widespread uprising in 1875 finally drew in Austrian military intervention and the Austrian occupation of Bosnia, Herzegovina, and Sanjak in 1878. In 1908, in partial compensation to the Ottomans for the Austrian annexation of Bosnia-Herzegovina, the Austrian authorities returned the Muslim-majority Sanjak of Novi Pazar to Turkish rule.

Serbian troops occupied the region during the first Balkan War in 1912, and in 1913 the Sanjak region was partitioned between the Serb and Montenegrin states. The Balkan wars left unresolved territorial conflicts that were partly to blame for the outbreak of World War I in 1914. The Serbs and Montenegrins, at war with the Austrians, were unable to impose changes, and the medieval social organization of the Sanjak remained intact.

In 1917, in spite of Sanjaki opposition, the region became part of the newly constituted South Slav kingdom. At the end of the war, in 1918, the Muslim landlords were ousted, and serfdom was outlawed. The Sanjaki Muslim population lost its privileged position and became a despised minority in the passionately Orthodox Christian kingdom.

Overrun by invading fascist armies in 1941, the Sanjak became the focus of ethnic fighting, reprisals, and widespread atrocities perpetrated by all sides. Following the German withdrawal in 1944, many of the Sanjaki leaders fled as Tito's Communist partisans took control of the region and systematically eliminated all opposition. Tito's division of Yugoslavia into six ethnic republics in 1946 brought Sanjak demands for a Sanjaki republic. Although the neighboring Montenegrins, with about the same ethnic population, were given their own republic, Tito refused the Muslim Sanjakis' demands.

The Sanjakis, having identified themselves only by their religion, or as Muslim Serbs or Montenegrins, up to World War II, in the decades after the war evolved a separate national identity. In the 1948 census the Sanjakis were listed as Muslims, and in 1953 they were counted as undetermined Yugoslavs. Finally recognized, along with the neighboring Bosnians, as a separate Muslim nationality in 1969, they were again counted as just Muslims in 1981.

Tito's death in 1980 began a slow unraveling of the federation he had held together. The collapse of Communism in 1989 stirred the long-dormant Sanjaki nationalism. In late 1989 and early 1990 large demonstrations demanded national rights and protested growing Serb oppression. The disintegration of the Yugoslav federation in 1990–91 fueled a Sanjaki campaign to follow the other Yugoslav national groups to independence.

The Sanjakis in late October 1991 voted for autonomy in defiance of the Serb authorities. Just hours after the polls opened, Serb police moved in to forcibly close them, but the voting continued in secret. The Sanjakis boycotted the 1992 referendum that renewed the truncated Yugoslav federation of Serbia and Montenegro. In late 1993 violent incidents broke out between Sanjaki demonstrators and radical Serb nationalists but were quickly brought under control as the Serbs feared fighting within their own borders.

In 1994 twenty-four Sanjaki nationalist leaders were arrested and put on trial, charged with plotting the secession of the Sanjak from Yugoslavia. The trial has fueled Sanjaki nationalism but has raised new fears that the violence of neighboring Bosnia will spread, making their unarmed, defenseless population vulnerable to the Serbs' "ethnic cleansing."

*SELECTED BIBLIOGRAPHY:*
Kaplan, Robert D. *Balkan Ghosts.* 1993.
Margas, Branka. *The Destruction of Yugoslavia.* 1993.

Murvar, Vatro. *Nationalism and Religion in Central Europe and the Western Balkans, Vol. 1. The Muslims in Bosnia, Hercegovina and Sandzak: A Sociological Analysis.* 1990.

# SANTA CRUZ

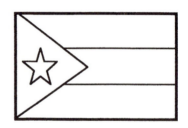

*CAPITAL: Santa Cruz*

SOUTH AMERICA

SANTA CRUZ

*POPULATION:* (95e) 2,310,000 : 1, 800,000 Cambas (Cruceños) in Bolivia. MAJOR NATIONAL GROUPS: (95e) Camba (Cruceño) 78%, Guarani 3%, Brazilian 1%, Kolla (other Bolivian) 17%. MAJOR LANGUAGES: Spanish, Portuguese, Guarani. MAJOR RELIGIONS: Roman Catholic, Protestant. MAJOR CITIES: (95e) Santa Cruz 695,000 (800,000), Trinidad 60,000, Montero 53,000, Riberalta 40,000, Robore 32,000, Buena Vista 24,000.

*GEOGRAPHY:* AREA: 222,554 sq.mi.-576,564 sq.km. LOCATION: Santa Cruz occupies the Llanos, the subtropical lowlands east of the high Antiplano, the Bolivian plateau in the Andes Mountains. POLITICAL STATUS: Santa Cruz, the area claimed by nationalists, has no official status; the region forms the Bolivian departments of Santa Cruz and El Beni.

*INDEPENDENCE DECLARED:* 8 July 1921; 22 May 1935.

*FLAG:* The Camba national flag, the flag of the former republic, is a horizontal tricolor of green, white, and red bearing a pale blue triangle at the hoist charged with a five-pointed, white star.

*PEOPLE:* The Cruceños, popularly called Cambas, are mostly of mixed European and Indian background, with a substantial unmixed population of European descent and a Guarani minority in the southeast. Physically, historically, and culturally separated from the highland Bolivian culture of the Andes Mountains, the Cambas are a lowland, tropical people. Mostly farmers in the fertile plains, a growing number of Cambas are involved in the drug trade, which is estimated to support 600,000 people directly and, indirectly, almost the entire

Santa Cruz region. The majority of the Cambas are Roman Catholic, with small Protestant, mostly Mennonite, minorities.

*THE NATION:* Sparsely populated by Native American tribes, later called Indians, the region came under the influence of the highly advanced civilizations of the Andean highlands. In the early sixteenth century Spanish explorers crossed the region but, finding little gold or treasure, moved on. The Spanish, seeking riches not land, ignored the fertile region for decades. Spanish colonists moving north from Paraguay finally settled the area in the mid-sixteenth century, founding the town of Santa Cruz in 1560. The tribal peoples, driven from the fertile plains, took refuge in the forested areas of the southeast.

Physically isolated, the inhabitants of Santa Cruz developed their own cultural traditions and a character distinct from those of the centers of Spanish activity in the highlands. Dominated by Europeans and Cholos, the offspring of mixed marriages, the region became a producer of tropical produce, its main trade links directed to the Rio Plate region to the south. In 1776 the Spanish authorities separated Santa Cruz from the Andean provinces and added the region to the La Plata colony governed from Buenos Aires, and in 1782 it was organized as a separate Spanish province.

The Cambas rebelled against Spanish rule in 1809, one of the earliest colonial rebellions in Spanish America. Two years later, in 1811, the rebels drove the Spanish authorities from the province and declared Santa Cruz an independent republic. Spanish reinforcements ended the secession, but, as rebellions spread through the Spanish Empire, the Cambas joined with the Kollas, the highlanders of the Antiplano, to fight the Spanish. In 1825 the rebels triumphed, calling their new country Bolivia. Santa Cruz, organized as a Bolivian province in 1832, split ten years later when El Beni was separated off as a separate province.

Isolated and restive under the domination of the highland Kollas, the region remained the domain of the European and mixed populations, unlike the largely Indian population of the Antiplano. The cultural differences created tensions between the two peoples that erupted in Camba rebellions in 1892 and 1904. Each Camba uprising was ended by troops sent from the highlands, increasing the Camba resentment and support for separation from Bolivia.

A renewed revolt spread across the region in 1920, resulting in a virtual military occupation by Bolivian troops. On 25 May 1921 the Cambas resumed the rebellion, which quickly escalated into a civil war. Camba nationalist leaders declared the independence of Santa Cruz on 8 July 1921, but the breakaway republic fell to Bolivian forces less than a year later. Nationalists formed the Santa Cruz National Party to work secretly for the restoration of an independent republic. In 1924 the Cambas again rose against the Bolivian occupation forces, but again suffered defeat and an intensified military occupation.

Tensions between Bolivia and Paraguay over the territory called the Gran Chaco, just south of Santa Cruz, increased in the 1920s. In 1928 the two countries both laid claim to the region, believed to have substantial petroleum reserves. Four years later, in 1932, war broke out over the region. In 1935, after three years of war, the Paraguayan government announced its support for an independent Santa Cruz. In May 1935 Camba prisoners of war requested separation from the other Bolivians. Over 150 officers and 6,000 men, released by the Paraguayans, swore allegiance to the proposed Camba state. On 22 May 1935 the leaders declared Santa Cruz independent of Bolivia. The end of the Chaco War and the negotiated partition of the Gran Chaco territory freed the Bolivians to deal with the Camba secession.

Santa Cruz remained isolated until the 1950s and the construction of a railroad linking the province to Brazil. Even though the region remained restive, and a renewed rebellion broke out in 1961, settlers spread across the fertile plains. Development accelerated in the 1960s and 1970s, based on the fertility of the land, which yielded two crops a year without fertilizer. The exploitation of the region's natural wealth attracted thousands of poor highlanders to Santa Cruz, again raising tensions between the Cambas and Kollas.

Attempts by the Bolivian government, supported by American antidrug funds and military equipment, to curtail the drug trade affected the entire region. The militarization of Santa Cruz sparked a resurgence of nationalism as Camba leaders compared the situation with the military occupation of the 1920s and 1930s. The provincial leaders denounced the government actions and declared that the drug trade would continue until a viable economic alternative became available.

The drug controversy and rising tensions between the lowland Cambas and the Kollas of the Antiplano have fueled the region's nationalist resurgence. Rich in cocoa dollars, the Cambas have established close commercial relations with neighboring parts of Brazil, particularly the Corumba region, 390 miles east of Santa Cruz. Trade with Brazil has become much more important than the region's ties to La Paz and the Andes provinces. The settlement of over 10,000 Brazilian farmers in the region since 1985 has strengthened Santa Cruz's ties to Brazil and further weakened the hold of the Bolivian government.

*SELECTED BIBLIOGRAPHY:*

Klein, Herbert B. *Bolivia: The Evolution of a Multi-Ethnic Society.* 1982.

Morales, Waltrand Q. *Bolivia: Land of Struggle.* 1991.

Osborne, Harold. *Bolivia: A Land Divided.* 1956.

Stearman, Allyn M. *Camba and Kolla: Migration and Development in Santa Cruz, Bolivia.* 1985.

# SANWI

Sefwi

CAPITAL: Aboisso

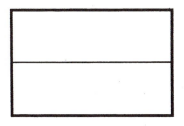

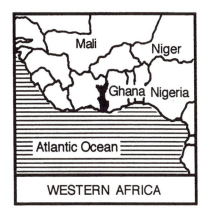

WESTERN AFRICA

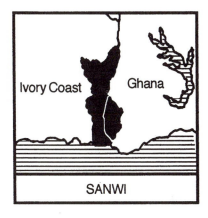

SANWI

*POPULATION:* (95e) 1,520,000 : 1,600,000 Agni (Anyi) in Côte d'Ivorie (Ivory Coast) and Ghana. MAJOR NATIONAL GROUPS: (95e) Agni (Anyi) 82%, other Ivorian, other Ghanaian. MAJOR LANGUAGES: Agni (Agni-Ashanti), French, Baule, English. MAJOR RELIGIONS: Roman Catholic, Protestant, animist, Muslim. MAJOR CITIES: (95e) IVORY COAST: Abengourou 80,000, Bondoukou 59,000, Aboisso 45,000, Agmbilékrou 30,000. GHANA: Enkyi 25,000, Sehwi Wiaso 20,000, Assini 16,000.

*GEOGRAPHY:* AREA: 11,456 sq.mi.-29,680 sq.km. LOCATION: Sanwi occupies a heavily wooded plateau between the Komoé and Tano Rivers in southeastern Côte d'Ivorie and southwestern Ghana. POLITICAL STATUS: Sanwi has no official status; the region forms the Abengourou, Aboisso, and Bondoukou departments of Côte d'Ivorie (Ivory Coast) and the western districts of Ghana's Western Province, the Nzima region west of the Tano River.

*INDEPENDENCE DECLARED:* 5 February 1960.

*FLAG:* The Agni national flag, the flag of the national movement, is a horizontal bicolor of red over yellow gold.

*PEOPLE:* The Agni, also called Anyi, are a Bantu people of the Akan subgroup, closely related to the Ashanti of neighboring Ashantiland.* Comprising six major divisions—Sanwi, Betie, Indenié, Aboure, and Abron in Ivory Coast and Nzima in Ghana—the Agni speak dialects of Agni-Ashanti, a Kwa language of the Benue-Niger language group. The Agni language, like the Chinese dialects, is a tonal language. The Agni are a matriarchal people, an Agni man inheriting his status and property from his mother's brother. The majority of the Agni are Roman Catholic, with an animist minority in the northern districts and a small Protestant minority, mostly in Ghana.

*THE NATION:* The region's original inhabitants, small Bantu tribes of herders and farmers, were absorbed by Akan peoples moving from the east between the eleventh and thirteenth centuries. Gradually brought under the rule of the expanding Ashanti, the tribes became part of the powerful Ashanti confederation in the late seventeenth and eighteenth centuries. Around 1740, following a dispute, the Agni moved westward out of the confederation and in their new homeland established four distinct kingdoms: Sanwi, the most important; the minor kingdoms of Moronou and Indenié in present Côte d'Ivorie; and Comoenou in Ghana.

The Agni kings, called *ohenes*, each possessed a royal stool, the incarnation of the sovereignty and dignity of their respective kingdoms. Centered on the divine kings, the kingship closely tied to the Agni culture and religion, the states were administered by an aristocratic bureaucracy that dominated subordinate tribes and regulated the labor of the slaves captured from less advanced peoples to the north. The kingdoms established trade and cultural ties as far away as present Nigeria while carrying on a long series of wars with the rival Baule tribe to the west.

Europeans visited the coast as early as the sixteenth century, but the Agni kingdoms had little contact with the colonial powers until the nineteenth century. In 1842 the French established a fort at Assini and signed a treaty with Sanwi providing for the cession of the land around the fort in exchange for tribute paid to the Sanwi king. A year later, threatened by the resurgent Ashanti, the Sanwi king, Amon Ndoffou, placed his kingdom under French military protection. The advancing Ashanti conquered the Nzima kingdom, Comoenou, but the French halted further Ashanti incursions. The French authorities established a protectorate over Sanwi, protectorate status extended to the inland Agni kingdoms in 1887.

The British conquest of Ashantiland in 1900 ended the threat to the kingdoms. No longer in need of French protection, the Agni tried to reassert their independence but failed to dislodge the French military. The Agni peoples, traditionally holding their lands in common, fiercely resisted French efforts to acquire land for export crops. French land taxes and demands for forced labor pushed the Agni to rebel during World War I. Agni resistance collapsed as the French artillery reduced village after village, and the rebels finally surrendered in 1916.

The Agni, their kingdoms administered as part of the French Ivory Coast after World War I, became the most advanced of the tribes in the colony and eventually the most pro-French. Under Vichy French rule following the fall of France in 1940, many Agni crossed into the British Gold Coast to join the Free French and helped to liberate their homeland in 1943. Although the Agni welcomed the returning French authorities, the kingdoms remained the focus of Agni loyalty, not the Ivory Coast colony. In 1948 severe rioting erupted over French attempts to interfere in the succession to the throne of Indenié.

Agni nationalism grew rapidly in the 1950s, fanned by conflicts with the colony's predominant Baule tribe. The Agni claimed that their treaties with France covered only military matters, and nationalists demanded separation from the Ivory Coast as a separate Agni state. Early in 1959, as it became clear that the Ivory Coast colony would become an autonomous state, King Amon Ndoffou II of Sanwi asserted the Agni's right to separate independence based on the 1843 and 1887 treaties. The king established a provisional government and sent emissaries to Paris to argue the Agni case for separation.

Their appeal to the French rebuffed, the Agni moved toward secession. In early 1960, as the Ivory Coast prepared for the independence scheduled for August, the Agni nationalists mobilized. On 5 February 1960 the king declared Sanwi independent of France and the Ivory Coast. Unable to halt Ivorian soldiers moving into the region, many Agni fled to Ghana, but the king and over 400 supporters were arrested. King Amon Ndoffou II and his head of government, Ehoumou Bile, received prison sentences of ten years followed by twenty years of banishment. In 1962 the Ivorian government, to quell ongoing separatist disturbances, released the king and the other Agni political prisoners but banned all tribal rituals.

The Ivorian recognition of the independence of the secessionist Republic of Biafra* in 1969 provoked a new crisis in Sanwi. Agni nationalists claimed the same right the government acknowledged in Biafra and prepared to declare independence. Ivorian soldiers moved in to crush the movement, carrying out a secret war denied by the Ivorian government. It is still not known how long the operation lasted or how many Agni died in the conflict and the repression that followed.

The Ivorian one-party state allowed little dissent or opposition until faced with a severe economic and political crisis in 1989–90. Agni nationalists, suppressed for nearly two decades, organized amid the growing tumult. In 1991 nationalist leaders asserted that the Agni kingdoms, separate French protectorates until forcibly incorporated in the Ivorian state in 1960, had the legal right to decide democratically to continue their ties to Côte d'Ivorie or to separate under the terms of the protectorate agreements of the nineteenth century.

The death of Félix Houphouet-Boigny on 7 December 1993, the president of Côte d'Ivorie since independence, released long-suppressed regional and tribal rivalries in the country. The rising tension, coupled with a sharp decline in prosperity since 1985, has fueled a resurgence of Agni nationalism and calls for the recognition of the Agni kingdoms.

*SELECTED BIBLIOGRAPHY:*
Kimble, G.H.T. *Tropical Africa.* 1960.
Lewis, Barbara. *The Ivory Coast.* 1990.
Mundt, R. *Historical Dictionary of the Ivory Coast.* 1987.
Zollberg, Aristide R. *One-Party Government in the Ivory Coast.* 1969.

# SAPMI

Sápmi; Sameanda; Sameadnam;
Saamiland; Lapland; Lappland

*CAPITAL: Kautokeino*

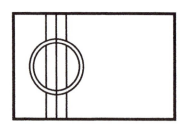

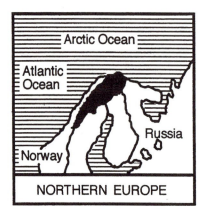

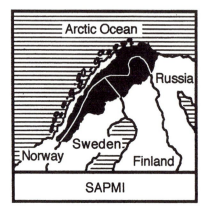

*POPULATION:* (95e) 210,000 : 100,000 Sámi (Lapps) in Scandinavia (70,000 in Norway, 22,000 in Sweden, 8,000 in Finland) and another 3,000 in Russia. MAJOR NATIONAL GROUPS: (95e) Sámi (Lapp) 44%, other Norwegian, Swede, Finn. MAJOR LANGUAGES: Sámi, Norwegian, Swedish, Finnish. MAJOR RELIGIONS: Lutheran, Orthodox. MAJOR CITIES: (95e) NORWAY: Hammerfest 8,000, Vadso 7,000, Kirenes 6,000, Kautokeino 3,000. SWEDEN: Kvikkjokk 3,000, Tärnaby 2,000. FINLAND: Sodankyla 5,000, Ivalo 3,000.

*GEOGRAPHY:* AREA: 91,130 sq.mi.-236,089 sq.km. LOCATION: Sapmi occupies the northern regions of Norway, Sweden, and Finland, a vast area of tundra and fjords mostly lying within the Arctic Circle. POLITICAL STATUS: Sapmi has no political status, the region forms Finnmark and parts of Tromso and Nordland provinces of Norway, the eastern districts of Norrbotten and Vasterbotten provinces of Sweden, and the northern districts of Finland's Lappi Province. The unofficial capital, Kautokeino, is situated in Norwegian territory close to the Finnish and Swedish borders.

*FLAG:* The Sámi national flag is a blue field with a broad red stripe at the hoist divided from the blue by narrow vertical stripes of green and yellow and bears a circle divided vertically blue near the hoist and red on the fly.

*PEOPLE:* The Sámi, called Laps or Lapps by the Scandinavians, are a European people speaking a Finnic language of the Finno-Ugric language group. The Sámi minority that has not settled in permanent homes are the last nomads in Europe. The language is spoken in three major dialects, North, South, and

East, and over fifty subdialects. Extensive intermingling has nearly erased the Sámi's Asian origins, with most not distinguishable from their Scandinavian neighbors. Sámi society, divided by labor, includes the Mountain or Reindeer Sámi; the Forest and River Sámi, hunters and fishermen; and the Sea Sámi, fishermen and whalers. The distinctive clothing and headgear, combining the bright colors of blue, red, yellow, and green, are still worn in many areas and proclaim the Sámi's home regions. Only 10% of the Sámi population still engage in reindeer herding, but that minority represents a continuation of traditional Sámi culture. The majority of the Sámi, as in the other Scandinavian nations, are Lutheran, with a small Orthodox minority mostly made up of Sámi refugees from the former Soviet Union. The total Sámi population is a matter of conflict as censuses often leave settled Sámi populations out of the calculations.

*THE NATION:* Little is known of the early history of the Sámi, a people of early Mongol origins thought to have migrated west from Central Asia in prehistoric times. Mentioned as a separate people living in the far north of Europe by the Roman historian Tacitus in A.D. 98, the Sámi, nearly 2,000 years ago, were driven north into the barren Arctic by successive waves of Slavic, Finnic, and Gothic peoples.

The Sámi pursued fishing, hunting, whaling, and, in the lands warmed by the Gulf Stream, some farming. The main activity of the Sámi tribes revolved around the vast herds of reindeer. On skis, a Sámi invention, herders traveled great distances with their herds, which provided the resources for survival in the north and became the measure of wealth.

Norwegians and Swedes conquered the western Sámi territories in the Middle Ages but left the Sámi to their traditional way of life. In the east the Sámi tribes came under the rule of the expanding Russian state in 1721. Long resistance to Christianity, finally overcome by Lutheran and Orthodox missionaries, led to the conversion of the final Sámi tribes in the eighteenth century.

Norway, which split from Sweden in 1905, counted the largest Sámi population. The second largest concentration, in the Kola Peninsula region of northwestern Russia, came under Soviet rule in 1920. Their herds collectivized and cross-border contacts with their kin forbidden, the Sámi mostly fled to the west during the Russo-Finnish War in 1940. Only a fraction of the 1939 population of 15,000 remained in the Soviet Union.

The contemporary world intruded into the Scandinavian Sámi homelands during World War II. The conflict brought bombs, tanks, and destruction to a people whose language has no word for war. Germany's early scorched policy in northern Norway in 1944 left virtually every building in Finnmark burned and the Sámi herds slaughtered. The experience of war profoundly affected the peaceful Sámi, raising the first demands for greater control of events that concerned their small and threatened nation.

The rapid increase of the region's non-Sámi population after the war began to interfere with the traditional way of life. New mining towns sprang up, and roads, power stations, dams, and parks crowded in on the Sámi grazing lands.

Faced with the differing national policies of Norway, Sweden, and Finland, Sámi activists formed the Nordic Saami Institute in 1973 to press for political and land rights.

Sámi nationalism, greatly influenced by environmental issues, grew rapidly in the 1970s. In 1983 Sámi leaders declared the sovereignty of the divided nation. In 1986 the Chernobyl nuclear disaster spread radiation across the area and made necessary the destruction of most of the Sámi reindeer herds. Two years later national leaders demanded the creation of a Sámi parliament that would have influence over planning and development of the region.

Sweden and Finland's entry into the European Union on 1 January 1995 has provoked a serious debate on the future of their nation. The Sámi nationalists have begun a campaign to join the European Union as a separate European people, not Norwegian, Swedish, or Finnish, but Sámi. Without full participation in the union as a separate nation, the Sámi are skeptical of having to meet regulations, not of their making, that take no account of the unique conditions of life in the European Arctic.

*SELECTED BIBLIOGRAPHY:*

Bosi, Roberto. *The Lapps.* 1960.
Heital, Kaija. *Lapland.* 1966.
IWGIA. *Sami Rights and Northern Perspectives.* 1990.
Zachrisson, Inger. *Lapps and Scandinavia: Archeological Finds in Northern Sweden.* 1976.

# SARAWAK

## North Kalimantan

*CAPITAL: Kuching*

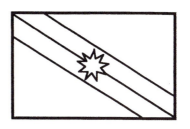

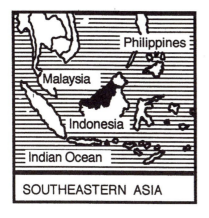

SOUTHEASTERN ASIA

SARAWAK

*POPULATION:* (95e) 1,846,000 : 1,020,000 Sarawakans in Malaysia. MAJOR NATIONAL GROUPS: (95e) Sarawakan 55% (Iban 32%, Dyak 8.5%, Bidayuh 6%, Melanau 5%, Kelabit, Kayan, Kenyah, Kajang, Murut, Bahau, smaller groups), Chinese 27%, Malay 18%. MAJOR LANGUAGES: Dyak, Chinese, Malay, English. MAJOR RELIGIONS: (95e) animist 40%, Sunni Muslim 24%, Christian 20%, Buddhist, Taoist. MAJOR CITIES: (95e) Kuching 312,000, Sibiu 181,000, Miri 126,000, Simangang 40,000, Serian 34,000.

*GEOGRAPHY:* AREA: 48,375 sq.mi.-125,325 sq.km. LOCATION: Sarawak, part of East Malaysia, occupies a tropical lowland, backed by mountains in the south and east, on the large island of Kalimantan (Borneo) in the Malay Archipelago. POLITICAL STATUS: Sarawak forms a state of the Federation of Malaysia.

*FLAG:* The Sarawakan flag, the official flag of the state, is a yellow field divided by diagonal black and red stripes upper hoist to lower fly, bearing a centered, nine-pointed yellow star.

*PEOPLE:* The Sarawakans comprise a number of related Bornean peoples. The most numerous of the Sarawakan peoples, the Dyaks, are divided into the Dyaks or Land Dyaks, and the Iban, also called the Sea Dyaks. The Dyaks and other Sarawakans often live in communal longhouses, often large enough to house a whole village. The state's indigenous peoples speak a number of related Bornean languages of the Malay-Polynesian language group. The Dyak language is the lingua franca of the region and is understood by most of the diverse groups. Large minorities in Sarawak include the Chinese in the urban areas and the Muslim Malays along the coast. The majority of the Sarawakans have retained traditional beliefs, with a large and influential Christian minority.

*THE NATION:* Sarawak, inhabited for thousands of years, received early migrants from the interior of Borneo and by sea from the Asian mainland. Divided into tribes, the inhabitants engaged in endemic warfare, particularly among the coastal and highland tribes, whose ritual head-hunting formed an integral part of tribal culture. In the fourteenth century Muslim sailors and traders introduced Islam to the coastal areas. The Muslim coastal peoples united under the powerful sultan of Brunei. By the sixteenth century the sultanate controlled most of the huge island of Borneo.

When it was visited by Magellan's expedition in 1521, tales of the opulent sultanate drew European adventurers to the island in the sixteenth and seventeenth centuries. European encroachments greatly weakened the sultanate, leading to a period of lawlessness, chaos, and piracy. A British subject, James Brooke, arrived in the sultanate in 1839. Brooke offered his military experience to the sultan and assisted the Bruneis to defeat rebel Dyak tribes and to suppress piracy. In 1841 a grateful sultan gave Brooke some 7,000 square miles of territory and the title raja of Sarawak.

Knighted by the British Crown, Sir James proceeded to create a government and to put down head-hunting and piracy. In 1850 the United States recognized Sarawak's independence, and in 1864 the United Kingdom extended diplomatic ties. Sir James's nephew, Charles Johnson, rechristened Brooke, succeeded as the second Brooke ruler. Raja Charles abolished slavery, encouraged commerce, and greatly extended the authority of his government. In 1888 the raja Charles Brooke accepted the protection of the United Kingdom.

Charles Vyner Brooke succeeded his father in 1917, inheriting one of the most prosperous states in the Far East. To celebrate the centenary of the Brooke family's rule, a new constitution was adopted in 1941. The constitution provided for a legislature and some representative government. Before the administrative changes could take effect, Japanese forces invaded the state, forcing the Brooke family to flee.

Devastated by fighting and forced labor, Sarawak, liberated in September 1945, came under British military rule. The economy in ruins, the Sarawak legislature voted eighteen to sixteen to become a British colony to avail itself of British economic assistance for the task of reconstruction. On 1 July 1946 Raja Brooke ceded Sarawak to the United Kingdom, ending over a century of rule by the legendary white rajas.

Newly independent Indonesia, including most of the island of Borneo, laid claim to Sarawak in 1949. The discovery of oil increased tensions between Indonesia and the British administration during the 1950s. British plans to include Sarawak in a proposed Malaysian federation incited strong resistance by the state's non-Malay majority. Dyaks and dissident Chinese formed nationalist organizations across the border in Indonesian territory. In 1962, with Indonesian arms, the nationalist forces invaded Sarawak in an attempt to create an independent state of North Kalimantan but were forced back by British troops.

Sarawak joined the Malaysian federation in 1963, with safeguards for the non-Malay population and with considerable local autonomy. The Indonesian government refused to recognize the federation, actively supporting attacks on the state by nationalist and Communist groups based on the border in Indonesian territory.

Vast oil reserves and bauxite production converted Sarawak into Malaysia's most prosperous state, even though a majority of the state's revenues were siphoned off for development projects in poorer mainland Malaya. Sarawakan support for secession, a growing force in the state, rose and fell with the economic and political situation in the 1970s and the early 1980s.

Government politics favoring Malaysia's Malay majority led to a rapid spread of nationalist sentiment in the 1980s. The Bornean peoples, led by the Dyaks, and the Chinese mobilized against Malay domination. The Sarawakan national organizations demanded greater linguistic, economic, religious, and political autonomy. Environmental issues, particularly the increasing deforestation sanctioned by the government, became nationalist issues.

Demands by fundamentalist Muslim Malays for the creation of an Islamic state in Malaysia raised tensions in 1989. Amid increasing demands for independence in the state, the Malaysian government cracked down on Sarawakan nationalism, with many tribal and community leaders detained in 1989–91.

Violence spread to the interior of the state where tribal peoples opposed to the massive logging operations clashed with Malay police. Sarawak's hardwood forests, at the present rate of logging, will disappear by the year 2002. The destruction of Sarawak's forests, one of the most controversial ecological attacks on a virgin forest region in the 1990s, galvanized the Sarawakan nationalists. The nationalists charge the Malaysian government with the wanton destruction of the habitat that the Sarawakan tribes have guarded for thousands of years.

*SELECTED BIBLIOGRAPHY:*

Harrison, T. *World Within.* 1984.

Hong, Evelyne. *The Natives of Sarawak.* 1986.

Islam, M. Nazrul. *Pakistan and Malaysia: A Comprehensive Study of National Integration.* 1989.

Pringle, Robert M. *Rajas and Rebels: The Ibans of Sarawak under Brooke Rule 1841–1941.* 1970.

# SARDINIA

**Sardigna; Sardegna**

*CAPITAL: Calaris (Cagliari)*

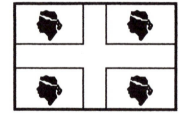

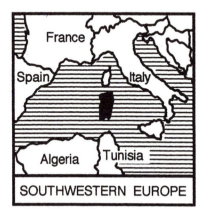

SOUTHWESTERN EUROPE

SARDINIA

*POPULATION:* (95e) 1,677,000 : 2,225,000 Sards in Italy. MAJOR NATIONAL GROUPS: (95e) Sard 80%, other Italian. MAJOR LANGUAGES: Italian, Sardinian. MAJOR RELIGION: Roman Catholic. MAJOR CITIES: (95e) Calaris (Cagliari) 211,000 (328,000), Sassari 144,000 (162,000), L'Alguer (Algero) 42,000 (57,000), Carbonia 41,000 (60,000), Nuoro 39,000, Olbia 38,000, Iglesias 36,000, Oristagni (Oristano) 35,000 (50,000).

*GEOGRAPHY:* AREA: 9,302 sq.mi.-24,098 sq.km. LOCATION: Sardinia, the second largest of the Mediterranean islands, lies some one hundred miles west of the Italian mainland and is separated by a narrow channel from the French island of Corsica* to the north. POLITICAL STATUS: Sardinia, called Sardigna in the Sard language and Sardegna in Italian, forms a semiautonomous region of the Italian republic.

*FLAG:* The Sardinian national flag, the flag of the national movement, is a white field divided by a centered red cross, each white rectangle charged with a black Moor's head in profile.

*PEOPLE:* The Sards are a Romance people, descendants of early Latin peoples and later admixtures of other Mediterranean nations, speaking a separate Romance language as close to ancient Latin as to modern Italian, with some dialects closer to Spanish or Catalan. Traditionally more soft-spoken and reserved than the Italians, the Sards nevertheless pursue violent vendettas over points of honor. A small minority, around the city of Algero, has preserved much of the culture and language brought to the island from Catalonia.* The

Sards are devoutly Roman Catholic, although church influence has decreased since World War II.

*THE NATION:* A center of early Mediterranean culture, the island's Bronze Age Nuraghic civilization flourished from about 1800 B.C., leaving behind some 30,000 stone fortresses. Around 800 B.C. Phoenicians founded trading colonies on the island's coasts; however, according to Greek legends, the island was first settled by Carthaginians under the leadership of Sardo about 500 B.C. The Romans conquered the island in 238 B.C. Thoroughly Latinized during six centuries of Roman rule, Sardinia has retained an indelible Latin imprint.

Goths and Vandals from the mainland overran the remaining Roman defenses in the fifth century A.D. The Byzantines of the Eastern Roman Empire expelled the Vandals in 533. The island remained Byzantine until the eleventh-century invasion of Muslim Arabs, called Saracens or Moors. The maritime republics of Genoa and Pisa competed for control of the island in the eleventh and twelfth centuries, finally settling for partition in 1294. Three years later, in 1297, the pope bestowed the island on the Catalan-speaking Kingdom of Aragon. In 1479 Aragon and Castile united to form the Kingdom of Spain, making Sardinia a Spanish possession. The island remained under the rule of united Spain until 1713.

The island passed to the rule of the duke of Savoy* in 1720. Taking the title king of Sardinia, the duke applied the name of the island to his extensive domains in northern Italy and southeastern France. Granted some autonomy, the island remained under the control of a small ruling elite. The ruling oligarchy's feudal privileges ended in 1835, and their resistance to modernization culminated in the withdrawal of autonomy in 1847. Sardinia, the most neglected and backward territory of the Sardinian kingdom, became part of the Italian kingdom that united under the House of Savoy in 1861.

The Sards in the late nineteenth century remained a peasant people dominated by a small, Italianized upper class. The Sard language, the language of daily life for the majority, was banned for use in education, administration, and publishing. The island's feudal conditions spawned a culture of violence and blood feuds, while banditry became a way of life for the disadvantaged Sards.

The island remained virtually unchanged by the wars that swept across Europe in the twentieth century. Only in the post-World War II period did some change begin to come to the island, mostly in the form of the growing tourist industry.

Young Sards began to take a new interest in their language and culture in the 1960s, the Sard language becoming a rallying point of the growing national movement and its use a matter of pride for the young nationalists. In 1968 Sard nationalists attempted to stir up a separatist uprising on the island, but the movement collapsed following arrests and pressure by the Italian military. More moderate nationalist organizations used threats of separatism to pressure the Italian government for more autonomy and development for the economically backward and bandit-infested island.

Sard nationalism has increased dramatically since the late 1970s, the majority of the islanders supporting moderate nationalist demands for direct and autonomous management of the available resources to meet Sardinian needs. Long neglected by the Italian government, the island's agrarian sector is still characterized by large estates, and throughout the island work is scarce, utilities are primitive, and the schools are inferior. The island's neglect has created fertile ground for support of nationalist calls for independence from the inefficient and increasingly polarized Italian state.

Militant nationalists, unable to find work on the island but refusing the island's traditional outlet, emigration, turned to violence to publicize the island's plight in the 1980s. The campaign of violence escalated in the late 1980s and early 1990s. In 1991–92 over 200 bombings rocked the island, the militants particularly targeting state-owned industries and Italian government offices.

European unification has focused nationalist demands for recognition of the Sards as a separate European people. Growing numbers of Sards look to the European Union as the island's economic salvation, hoping the union will deliver the needed aid the Italian government has long promised but has not delivered. Bills providing economic aid for the island habitually fail to pass the Italian parliament.

Pressed by the growth of nationalism in several regions, the Italian government officially recognized minority languages for use in education, administration, and commerce in November 1991. The legalization of the Sard language ends a ban on the language that has been in effect since Italian unification. To the Sard nationalists seeking recognition as a separate European people, the legalization of the language is only a first step to the realization of the Sards' national rights.

*SELECTED BIBLIOGRAPHY:*
Abulafid, David. *Italy, Sicily and the Mediterranean, 1100–1400.* 1987.
Carlyle, Margaret. *The Awakening of South Italy.* 1985.
More, Jasper. *The Mediterranean.* 1956.
Waite, Virginia. *Sard.* 1977.

# SAVOY

Savoie (Savoie and Vallée d'Aoste);
Savoia (Savoia and Valle d'Aosta)

*CAPITAL:* Chambéry

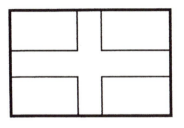

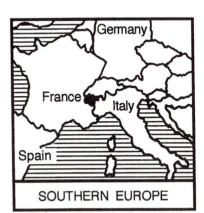

SOUTHERN EUROPE

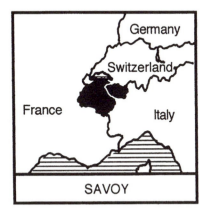

SAVOY

*POPULATION:* (95e) 1,073,000 : 985,000 Savoyards in France and Italy (910,000 Savoyards and 75,000 Valdaostans). MAJOR NATIONAL GROUPS: (95e) Savoyard (including Valdoastan) 83%, other French, other Italian. MAJOR LANGUAGES: French, Italian, Savoyard (Harpeitanya). MAJOR RELIGIONS: Roman Catholic, Protestant. MAJOR CITIES: (95e) FRANCE: Chambéry 54,000 (99,000), Annecy 48,000 (117,000), Annemasse 39,000, Thanon-les-Bains 26,000, Aix-les-Bains 24,000. ITALY: Aoste (Aosta) 38,000 (52,000).

*GEOGRAPHY:* AREA: 5,286 sq.mi.-13,694 sq.mi. LOCATION: Savoy lies in the Graian and Savoy Alps, a region of high alpine valleys in the mountains straddling the Franco-Italian border just south of Switzerland's Lake Geneva and northwest of Piedmont.* POLITICAL STATUS: Savoy forms the departments of Savoie and Haut-Savoie of the French region of Rhône-Alps and the semiautonomous Italian region of Valle d'Aosta (Vallée d'Aoste).

*FLAG:* The Savoyard national flag, the flag of the national movement, is a red field charged with a centered white cross. OTHER FLAG(S): The flag of the Valdaostans is a vertical bicolor of black and red.

*PEOPLE:* The Savoyards, also called Harpeitians or Mountain Occitans, are a Gallo-Romanic people, the descendants of Romanized alpine tribes. The Savoyards of the Aosta Valley in Italy are known as Valdaostans. Along with French and Italian, the Savoyards also speak their own Romance language, called Harpeitanya, a Franco-Provençal hybrid mixing forms and words from both Occitan (Langue-d'Oc) and French (Langue d'Oil). The language forms part of the unique Savoyard culture that combines French, Occitan, and Piedmontese influences. The majority of the Savoyards are Roman Catholic, with a small, important Protestant minority, mostly in the high alpine valleys of French Savoy.

*THE NATION:* Home to an alpine Celtic people, the Allobroges, the western Alps region fell to the Romans in 121 B.C. and became part of the Roman province of Gaul. The alpine valleys, appreciated for their cool weather and numerous thermal spas, became a favorite retreat for Roman officials and patricians of the large lowland cities.

Germanic Burgundians overran the region's last Roman defenses about A.D. 460. The Burgundians conquered the lowlands to the west in 480, the combined territories joined in the Christianized Burgundian kingdom. Franks conquered the Burgundian kingdom in 534, the Burgundian lands, including the highland region in the east. The conquered lands were absorbed into the growing Frankish kingdom, the later Holy Roman Empire of Charlemagne.

A powerful feudal lord, Count Humbert the White-Handed, expanded his small holdings in Savoy, acquiring Chambéry in 1232. His successors secured additional territories now in France, Italy, and Switzerland. The expanding bilingual Savoyard state emerged as the most powerful in the region. Raised to the status of a duchy in 1416, Savoy lost the Swiss territories between 1475 and 1536. The loss of territory shifted the center of power to the Savoyard territories in Piedmont* in Italy. In 1559 the duke moved the state's capital from highland Chambéry to Turin, in his Italian territories, although the language and tone of the court remained French until the eighteenth century.

Savoy gained control of Sicily* in 1714 and in 1720 exchanged the island for the Austrian-ruled island of Sardinia.* Duke Victor Amadeus of Savoy assumed the title king of Sardinia in 1720, applying the name to his territories in Savoy, Nice, Menton, Piedmont, and, after 1815, Liguria and Genoa. A center of the Risorgimento, the kingdom led the movement for Italian unification under the House of Savoy.

The Risorgimento, finally achieved with French aid in 1860, left only Rome and the Papal States outside the domains of the House of Savoy. Emperor Louis Napoleon of France, for his aid in the Italian unification, demanded the French-speaking parts of the kingdom, Savoy, Nice, and Menton. Only the French-speaking Aosta Valley of the former Savoyard duchy remained part of Italy.

The centralized French and Italian kingdoms banned the official use of the Savoyard language and pressed assimilation, but the culture and dialect survived as a peasant language in the high mountain valleys. By the late nineteenth century the cities and towns of Savoy had become French-speaking, and in Aosta a sizable Italian-speaking minority settled in the towns; however, in the rural areas and the high alpine valleys the Franco-Provençal dialect remained the language of daily life.

The fascist Italian regime, in power in Italy from 1922, posed the first major threat to Savoyard culture in Italy. In the 1930s the fascist authorities banned both French and Harpeitanya and ordered all names, even family names, changed to Italian.

The House of Savoy, held partially responsible for Italy's World War II defeat, was deposed following a 1946 referendum. As the new republican government began drafting a constitution, the Savoyard nationalists in the Aosta Valley demanded secession from Italy and reunification with Savoy in an independent Etat Montagne. The movement gained considerable support in Savoy, but separatist sentiment died down after the Italian government separated the Aosta Valley from Piedmont and granted some political autonomy to the region in 1948.

The opening of several tunnels in the 1960s brought an influx of outsiders and turned the region into a major commercial route between France and Italy. The rapid expansion of tourist facilities and holiday homes sparked the first calls for linguistic and cultural autonomy in the 1970s. In 1978 nationalists formed the National Savoyard Front (FNS) to work for the reunification and autonomy of Savoy. Over the next decade the nationalist aims evolved to become a movement for Savoyard independence within a united Europe.

The Savoyards, after centuries of resistance, are no longer threatened by armed invasion but are threatened by rural depopulation and the cultural and environmental impact of mass tourism. The Savoyard sense of identity remains strong, and in the 1990s there is a growing awareness that the limited autonomous powers allowed by the French and Italian governments have done little to prevent the growing loss of their unique culture or the destruction of their fragile alpine environment.

Valdaostan nationalists on 3 September 1991 set in motion the procedures for a referendum on secession from Italy, seen as a first step toward a reconstituted Savoyard state within a united European federation. In May 1993 the Valdaostan nationalists took 37.3% of the vote in local elections, the highest in their history. Radical separatists, vowing to secede and reunite with neighboring Savoy, took a surprising 5% of the vote. The militancy of the nationalists in Italian Savoy has fueled a regional movement in the Alps. In the mid-1990s the more radical nationalist groups have demanded the reunification of territories now in Italy, France, and southwestern Switzerland.

*SELECTED BIBLIOGRAPHY:*

Brustein, William. *The Social Origins of Political Regionalism: France, 1849–1981.* 1982.

Cox, Eugene L. *The Eagles of Savoy: The House of Savoy in Thirteenth Century Europe.* 1983.

Kamman, Madeleine. *Madeleine Kamman's Savoy: The Land, People and Food of the French Alps.* 1989.

Smith, Denis M. *The Making of Italy 1796–1870.* 1988.

# SAXONY

**Sachen; Saxonland**

*CAPITAL: Dresden*

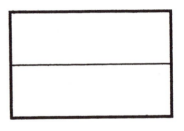

*POPULATION:* (95e) 5,201,000 : 7,750,000 Saxons in Germany. "Greater Saxony" 8,628,000. MAJOR NATIONAL GROUPS: (95e) Saxon 88%, Sorb, other German. MAJOR LANGUAGES: German (Saxon dialect), Sorbian. MAJOR RELIGIONS: (95e) Lutheran 88%, Roman Catholic 5%. MAJOR CITIES: (95e) SAXONY: Leipzig 494,000 (681,000), Dresden 488,000 (745,000), Chemnitz 301,000 (455,000), Zwickau 115,000 (156,000), Plauen 76,000 (99,000), Gorlitz 75,000 (121,000), Bautzen 53,000, Altenburg 52,000. SAXONY-ANHALT: Halle 235,000 (483,000), Dessau 103,000 (140,000), Wittenberg 52,000, Bitterfeld 20,000 (105,000). THURINGIA: Erfurt 220,000, Gera 132,000, Jena 107,000, Weimar 62,000 (92,000), Suhl 61,000 (83,000), Gotha 57,000, Eisenach 50,000.

*GEOGRAPHY:* AREA: 6,331 sq.mi.-16,402 sq.km. "Greater Saxony" 15,589 sq.mi.-40,386 sq.km. LOCATION: Saxony lies in southeastern Germany, a region of flat plains in the valleys of the river Elbe and its tributaries rising to mountains in the south, the so-called Saxon Switzerland. POLITICAL STATUS: Saxony forms a state of the Federal Republic of Germany. "Greater Saxony," the region claimed by nationalists, also includes the Halle District of the state of Saxony-Anhalt and the state of Thuringia.

*INDEPENDENCE DECLARED:* 19 November 1918.

*FLAG:* The Saxon national flag, the traditional flag of the Saxon regions, is a horizontal bicolor of white over green. OTHER FLAG(S): The flag of the Thuringian Saxons is a horizontal bicolor of white over red.

*PEOPLE:* The Saxons are a German people, the descendants of early Germanic tribes and Germanized Slavs. The Saxon dialect of High German, actually a group of nine dialects, four of them spoken only in Thuringia, is the language of daily life in the region. In spite of centuries of disunity, the Saxons have retained an inbred sense of identity that even decades of Communist rule failed to destroy. The only substantial minorities are Germans from the western half of the country who have settled in the region since 1990 and a small Slavic group in the southeastern region of Lusatia.* The majority of the Saxons are Lutherans, with a small Roman Catholic minority and a substantial number professing no religious beliefs.

*THE NATION:* The Saxon tribes were first mentioned in the second century A.D. as inhabiting the area around the mouth of the river Elbe in northwestern Germany. In the fourth and fifth centuries the Saxon tribes split, some tribal groups joining the Angles and Jutes in the invasion and conquest of Angoland (England). The remaining tribes, called the Old Saxons, followed the river Elbe south to conquer Thuringia in 531. Partially subdued by the Franks in 566, the Saxon lands were ultimately absorbed by the Frankish Empire, and Saxons were forcibly Christianized in the seventh century.

A Saxon duchy, established in the ninth century, formed one of the five stem duchies of the Germanic Holy Roman Empire. Expanding eastward, the Saxons conquered and absorbed large Slav populations between the tenth and thirteenth centuries. The Wettin dynasty, established as the ruling house of the Margravite of Meissen in 1100, extended its authority to eventually control a large part of the Holy Roman Empire. From the fifteenth century the Wettin family members divided and subdivided the land into a number of small states.

Martin Luther in 1571 pinned up a case for free choice in religion on the church door in Wittenberg. Luther's action began the momentous Protestant Reformation. The great popularity of Luther's works, written in the Saxon dialect, helped to standardize the Saxon dialects as a literary language. A Protestant stronghold during the wars of religion, in the seventeenth century Saxony emerged as one of the two most powerful of the Protestant German states, beginning a long and bitter rivalry with Brandenburg-Prussia.

The French Revolution and the rise of Napeoleon pushed Saxony into an anti-French alliance with its antagonistic Prussian neighbor. In 1806, during the Napoleonic Wars, Saxony switched sides. Napoleon raised the Saxon elector to the status of king of Saxony, but the new king's failure to abandon his French ally before Napoleon's fall cost him the northern half of his kingdom. In 1815 a triumphant Prussia annexed northern districts of Saxony.

Passionately anti-Prussian and determined to recover the lost provinces, Saxony sided with Austria during the Austro-Prussian War of 1866. Defeated by superior Prussian forces, the kingdom was forced to pay a large indemnity and to join the Prussian-dominated North German Confederation. In 1871 Saxony, under Prussian pressure, joined the German Empire.

Saxony's abundant mineral wealth stimulated rapid industrialization in the late nineteenth century. The heavy industries established in the region, manned by a large urban proletariat, became centers of socialist ideals. Important to the war effort after 1914, the industrial zones became centers of radical political movements, many supporting a 1917 movement for Saxon secession from Germany and separate peace with the Allies.

In early November 1918 King Frederick Augustus III, along with the Wettin rulers of the small Saxon duchies and principalities in Thuringia, abdicated as revolution swept defeated Germany. On 19 November, inspired by the Russian Revolution, workers and soldiers councils took control of Saxony and declared the independence of the Soviet Republic of Saxony. The new government announced sweeping nationalization and expropriations. During the months that followed, violent clashes and running battles among Communists, Saxon nationalists, and pan-German groups left thousands dead and injured.

In April 1919 the Saxon state severed all remaining ties to Germany. The action provoked an invasion of federal troops and the overthrow of Saxony's Communist government. Called Red Saxony, the region remained a center of Communist and socialist activities until the dissidents were driven underground by Hitler's Nazi troops in 1933.

Devastated in World War II, the Saxon states fell to advancing American troops in 1945. The Americans later traded control of the region to the Soviets in exchange for Allied control of six boroughs of Berlin. Included in the Communist German state created in 1949, many Saxons fled to the Western-occupied zones. As part of the official opposition to regionalist sentiment, the Saxon states were abolished in 1952 and replaced with administrative units.

Saxon nationalism, having survived over fifty years of Communist rule, resurfaced in 1989 with demands for the partition of East Germany into Saxon and Prussian states. The rediscovered Saxon identity was put aside as euphoria accompanied the rush to German unification in October 1990. Disillusionment with reunification, which was followed by mass unemployment and economic hardship, spurred a nationalist resurgence. A poll in October 1993 demonstrated the growing despair: 25% saw themselves as the losers in unification, 15% were so disillusioned that they wanted a return to Communist rule, and 20% expressed the opinion that independence for the Saxons would be a better alternative.

*SELECTED BIBLIOGRAPHY:*

Leyser, K. J. *Rule and Conflict in Early Medieval Saxony.* 1989.
Marsh, David. *Germans: A Pivotal Nation.* 1990.
Shlaes, Amity. *Germany: The Empire Within.* 1991.

# SCANIA

**Skåne**

*CAPITAL: Lund*

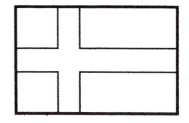

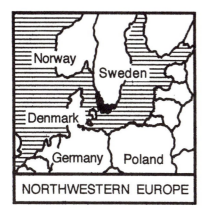

NORTHWESTERN EUROPE

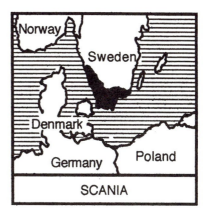

SCANIA

*POPULATION:* (95e) 1,511,000 : 1,630,000 Scanians in Sweden. MAJOR NATIONAL GROUPS: (95e) Scanian 91%, other Swedish. MAJOR LANGUAGES: Scanian, Swedish, Danish. MAJOR RELIGION: Lutheran. MAJOR CITIES: (95e) Malmo 238,000 (500,000), Helsingborg 107,000 (190,000), Lund 88,000, Halmstad 76,000 (91,000), Kristianstad 75,000 (120,000), Karlskrona 61,000 (86,000), Trelleborg 47,000 (86,000), Varberg 43,000 (62,000).

*GEOGRAPHY:* AREA: 7,452 sq.mi.-19,306 sq.km. LOCATION: Scania lies in southern Sweden, a region of flat, fertile plains, the southern point of the Scandinavian Peninsula separated by a narrow strait, the Kattegat, from Denmark to the west. POLITICAL STATUS: Scania has no official status; the region, as defined by nationalists, forms the Swedish provinces of Blekinge, Halland, Kristianstad, and Malmöhus.

*FLAG:* The Scanian national flag, the flag of the national movement, is a red field charged with a yellow Scandinavian cross.

*PEOPLE:* The Scanians are a Scandinavian people of mixed Danish and Swedish descent, their culture and language incorporating customs and influences from both along with many unique traits. The Scanian dialect, widely spoken in the region and claimed by nationalists as a separate Scandinavian language, is, in some ways, closer to Danish than to Swedish. The Scanians have a strong sense of identity and consider themselves a separate Scandinavian nation, their identity as strong as that of the larger Scandinavian peoples. The Scanians are overwhelmingly Lutheran, their Protestant religion an integral part of their culture.

*THE NATION:* The Scandinavian Peninsula, inhabited since ancient times, was occupied and settled by Germanic tribes in the sixth century A.D. The Scanian tribes settled in the coastal regions in the south and soon spread to the fertile interior. The Scanians of the overpopulated coastal regions, unable to sustain the size of the population, participated in the great Viking expansion during the eighth and ninth centuries. Scanian Vikings, searching for land and plunder, raided Britain, Ireland, and Northern Europe.

The Danish kingdom, with its capital at Lund, gained power under King Canute in the eleventh century, becoming an extensive empire that controlled Scania, Denmark, Norway, and most of England. The empire disintegrated following Canute's death in 1035 although Scania continued as the heartland of the reduced Danish kingdom.

Christianity gradually became the dominant religion in spite of fierce resistance. The archbishopric established at Lund in 1104 developed as the ecclesiastical center of all Scandinavia. The Scania region, the crossroads of Northern Europe, became a prosperous center of religious life and commerce. Danish rule of the rich Scanian provinces in the thirteenth century was increasingly challenged by the Swedes to the north.

The Union of Kalmar united Denmark, Scania, Norway, and Sweden in one kingdom in 1397. At the dissolution of the union in 1523, Denmark retained control of Scania and Norway. The Protestant Reformation, accepted by the Danes in 1534, was accepted by the Scanians two years later, ending a serious religious rift between the Scanians and the Danes.

Danish control of both sides of the Kattegat, the narrow strait between Denmark and the Scandinavian Peninsula, allowed the kingdom to halt trade and military traffic between the Baltic and North Seas during the frequent European wars. Sweden's hostile relations with the Danish kingdom centered on a desire to annex Scania to attain a natural coastal frontier and to end Danish control of the Kattegat, the entrance to the Baltic Sea.

Sporadic wars between the two kingdoms in the seventeenth century resulted in the loss of Halland to Sweden in 1645. Renewed hostilities culminated in the Swedish conquest of the remaining Scanian provinces in 1658. War again broke out in 1660, the invading Danes aided by an ultimately futile Scanian uprising against Swedish rule. The Scanians again rose when the war resumed in 1675, welcoming the closely related Danes as liberators from the hated Swedes. Swedish reprisals marked the return of the Swedish authorities to Scania when the Danes withdrew, and peace was agreed to in 1679.

Influenced by Swedish culture and language, the Scanians began to develop away from the more closely related Danes. The evolution of a distinctive Scanian culture led to a decline of pro-Danish sentiment. When the Danes again invaded the region in 1709, the majority of the Scanians remained loyal to the Swedish kingdom or adopted a neutral stance.

Devastated by the long series of wars, Scania began to recover only in the mid-eighteenth century. The end of the Scandinavian wars allowed a period of consolidation of the separate Scanian culture and language, incorporating both the earlier Danish traditions and later Swedish influences. To forestall Scanian unrest, the Swedish government relaxed cultural and linguistic restrictions in the Scanian provinces in the nineteenth century.

A Scanian revival took hold in the 1880s, reversing over two centuries of gradual assimilation. Unlike many European minorities, the Scanian revival failed to evolve a strong nationalist sentiment. The revival, more cultural than most parallel European movements, focused on the modernization of the Scanian language and a renewal of interest in Scania's folklore, crafts, and traditions. The Scanians benefited from neutral Sweden's avoidance of Europe's conflicts and its concentration on social development.

The Scanians cooperated with the Danes to save nearly all of Denmark's Jewish population during World War II. Sympathy for the Danish plight and cooperation with the Danish resistance to the Nazi occupation reestablished close ties to the Danes during and after the war. The Swedish government's murky relationship with Nazi Germany is still a controversial issue in Scania.

In the decades after the war, Sweden attained one of Europe's highest standards of living under a liberal, democratic government. The Scanians, their culture and language protected, had little motivation to espouse nationalism. However, a small movement in the 1970s began a campaign for a separate Scanian state in a Nordic confederation.

The assassination of Sweden's prime minister, Olof Palme, in 1986, followed by a series of government scandals and a sharp economic decline, politicized the formerly complacent Scanians. A resurgent national movement began to question the benefits and the social cost of Sweden's welfare state. In 1988 the first openly separatist political party formed in Scania as the debate over membership in the European Community galvanized the population.

Sweden's entry into a united Europe, strongly supported in Scania, has raised the question of sovereignty within a united Europe. The national movement in February 1994 accused the Swedish government of betrayal when the government dropped Scania from an aid blueprint during negotiations on European Union membership. The fervently pro-European Scanian nationalists have gained support for a sovereign Scania with close ties to both Denmark and Sweden in a united European federation.

*SELECTED BIBLIOGRAPHY:*

Gordon, Raoul. *Sweden: Its Peoples and Industry.* 1976.

Kirby, David. *Northern Europe in the Early Modern Period: The Baltic World 1492–1772.* 1990. Lauring, Palle. *A History of the Kingdom of Denmark.* 1960.

Loiit, Aleksander. *National Movement in the Baltic Countries during the Nineteenth Century.* 1985.

# SCOTLAND

**Alba; Scotia**

*CAPITAL: Edinburgh*

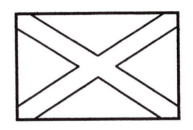

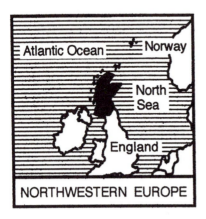

NORTHWESTERN EUROPE

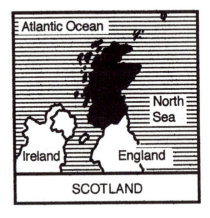

SCOTLAND

*POPULATION:* (95e) 5,187,000 : 5,755,000 Scots in the United Kingdom. MAJOR NATIONAL GROUPS: (95e) Scots 96%, other British. MAJOR LANGUAGES: English, Lallans, Eise (Gaelic). MAJOR RELIGIONS: Protestant, Roman Catholic. MAJOR CITIES: (95e) Glasgow 682,000 (1,924,000), Edinburgh 440,000 (685,000), Aberdeen 213,000 (283,000), Dundee 198,000 (235,000), Greenock 58,000 (108,000), Dunfermline 56,000 (139,000), Kilmarnock 51,000 (88,000), Ayr 47,000 (107,000), Kircaldy 46,000 (157,000 Kircaldy-Glenrothes), Glenrothes 46,000, Sterling 43,000 (94,000), Inverness 43,000, Perth 41,000 (56,000), Falkirk 38,000 (155,000), Irvine 33,000 (107,000).

*GEOGRAPHY:* AREA: 30,414 sq.mi.-78,792 sq.km. LOCATION: Scotland occupies the northern third of the island of Great Britain, which it shares with England and Wales.* Over half of Scotland's total area lies in the Highlands, north of the Scottish heartland in the valleys of the Clyde, Tay, and Forth Rivers and the southern uplands on the border with England. POLITICAL STATUS: Scotland forms a constituent state of the United Kingdom of Great Britain and Northern Ireland.

*FLAG:* The Scottish national flag, the flag of the national movement, is a blue field charged with a white saltire. OTHER FLAG(S): The traditional Scottish flag is a yellow field charged with a centered red rampant lion and bearing two thin, red stripes near the perimeter decorated with spaced, red pike heads.

*PEOPLE:* The Scots are a people of mixed ancestry, descended from the earliest inhabitants, the Picts, later Celtic migrants from Ireland, and Norsemen. The Scots speak standard English but also retain a distinctive Scots dialect, Lallans, that developed between the fifteenth and seventeenth centuries from medieval Northumbrian, a northern English language without the Norman French influence of standard English. In the Highlands the inhabitants still use the Scots' original Celtic language, Eise, and have remained largely Roman Catholic. The majority of the Scots are Protestant, mostly belonging to the separate Church of Scotland.

*THE NATION:* The Picts, of obscure origin, inhabited the northern part of the island in prehistoric times. A fierce warrior people, the Picts defeated repeated Roman attempts to penetrate their homeland. The Romans constructed a series of fortifications across the island to divide Roman Britain from the wild tribal lands to the north. Although Roman influence remained slight, missionaries spread the Roman religion, Christianity, to the region in the fifth century A.D.

Divided into four small, warring kingdoms, the region was the object of raids by Norse Vikings between the eighth and eleventh centuries. The Norsemen established colonies and ruled parts of the region. The union of the Picts and Scots, Celtic invaders from Ireland in 843, is considered the original formation of the Scottish kingdom. In 1018 the Scottish king extended his authority to the formerly independent Strathclyde kingdom.

In 1189 the English kingdom recognized the Scots' independence, but the ambiguous terms opened a long and bitter struggle between the two neighboring kingdoms. The English king, Edward I, laid claim to Scotland in 1294, provoking a war that continued until his death in 1307. His son, Edward II, gathered the largest force ever raised on the island. In 1314, 100,000 English troops moved north into Scotland, intent on conquest. Some 30,000 Scots, led by Robert Bruce, defeated the English at the Battle of Bannockburn, which secured the independence of the Scottish kingdom, but not a cessation of English interference.

The long conflict with England ended when the Scottish king, James VI, succeeded to the English throne in 1603 and combined the two kingdoms in an uneasy dynastic union. A disastrous and expensive colonial adventure forced the Scots to choose either independence and poverty or prosperity in union with England. In 1707 the Scots gave up their separate parliament and Crown and joined the United Kingdom.

The union, unpopular with many Scots, was assailed by rebellions and attempts to restore Scottish independence until the English forces decisively defeated the Scots at the Battle of Culloden in 1746. After the defeat, the British government pressed assimilation of the Scots into English culture and banned the Scots' Gaelic language.

Scottish participation in the expansion of the British Empire brought industrialization and prosperity and, in the eighteenth century, a particularly Scottish renaissance, with such names as Hume, Adam Smith, Burns, and Scott known throughout the world. By the nineteenth century the industrialized Lowlands became an urbanized, largely English-speaking region. In 1872 the compulsory teaching of English threatened the Gaelic and Lallans spoken by the majority of the Scots.

Munitions manufacture brought Scotland unprecedented wealth during World War I, but a declining economy after 1919 encouraged support for a nascent national movement. In 1928 nationalists formed the Scottish National Party to work for greater independence for the Scots. The nationalist controversy was briefly put aside during the Second World War, but the debate resumed in 1945. Many prominent Scots signed the Scottish Covenant in 1949, binding its signatories to work for Scottish home rule.

The Scottish National Party (SNP) remained a fringe party until the discovery of oil off Scotland's coast in 1971. Claiming the oil wealth for Scotland, the nationalists led a campaign for control of natural resources and the restoration of the Scottish parliament, the first step toward recovering Scotland's independence. A 1979 referendum on home rule was narrowly defeated, partly due to nationalist opposition to its continuing restrictions.

Growing economic problems and progress toward a united Europe spurred a nationalist resurgence in the 1980s. The Scots were the most pro-European of the British peoples, and support for independence within a united Europe continued to win minority support, while devolution, home rule, and a separate Scottish parliament maintained widespread support. Strong English opposition prompted many Scots to look to the nationalists. Polling of public opinion in 1990 showed 36% favored independence. A similar poll in January 1992 revealed that separatist sentiment had risen to 50%, with only 15% favoring the status quo.

Nationalist groups, determined that Scotland take its place as a separate and ancient European nation, launched a campaign in March 1992 for a referendum on Scotland's future. The nationalist plebiscite proposal would offer the Scots three choices: independence, devolution and increased autonomy within the United Kingdom, or the maintenance of the Scotland's present semiautonomous status.

In 1994 the Scottish nationalists concentrated on increasing their representation in local government bodies while continuing to campaign for independence within a federal United Kingdom or separate membership as a state of the European Union. Opinion polls, in 1994 and early 1995, show a growing economic confidence and support for increased autonomy.

*SELECTED BIBLIOGRAPHY:*
Harvie, Christopher I. *Scotland and Nationalism: Scottish Society and Politics, 1707–1977.* 1979.

Kemp, Arnold. *The Hollow Drum: Scotland since the War.* 1993.

Marr, Andrew. *The Battle for Scotland.* 1992.

Mason, Roger, ed. *Scotland and England, 1286–1815.* 1987.

Scott, Paul, ed. *Scotland: A Concise Cultural History.* 1993.

# SEQUOYAH

**Indian Territory**

*CAPITAL: Muskogee*

CENTRAL UNITED STATES

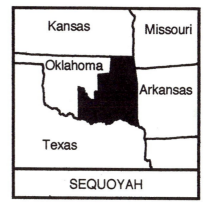

SEQUOYAH

*POPULATION:* (95e) 1,511,000 : 445,000 Sequoyahans in the United States (includes the 240,000 claiming tribal membership and the estimated 205,000 not registered as Indians). MAJOR NATIONAL GROUPS: (95e) Sequoyahan 29% (Cherokee, Creek, Chocktaw, Chickasaw, Seminole), other American. MAJOR LANGUAGES: English, Sequoyahan languages. MAJOR RELIGIONS: Protestant, Roman Catholic. MAJOR CITIES: (95e) Tulsa 370,000 (721,000), Broken Arrow 69,000, Muskogee (Sequoyah capital) 36,000 (70,000), Bartletsville 34,000 (49,000), Ardmore 23,000, Sapulpa 20,000, Okmulgee (Creek capital) 13,000, Talequah (Cherokee capital) 11,000, Wewoka (Seminole capital) 5,000, Tishomingo (Chickasaw capital) 3,000, Tushahoma (Choctaw capital) 1,000.

*GEOGRAPHY:* AREA: 31,400 sq.mi.-81,347 sq.km. LOCATION: Sequoyah lies in the south-central United States, a region of grazing and forest lands in eastern Oklahoma. POLITICAL STATUS: Sequoyah has no political status, from 1850 to 1907 the region formed the Indian Territory of the Five Civilized Tribes, now included in thirty-five counties of Oklahoma.

*FLAG:* The Sequoyahan flag, adopted in 1905, is a green field with a centered blue disc, outlined in yellow and surrounded by five white stars, bearing a large white, five-pointed star and forty-five small white stars; each point of the center star is charged with the symbols of the five tribes.

*PEOPLE:* The Sequoyahans, known as the Five Civilized Tribes, are the descendants of nations deported from the southeastern United States in the 1830s and 1840s. The most assimilated of the Native American peoples, an estimated 45% of all Sequoyahans are not registered as Indians, but retain family and

cultural ties to the officially recognized tribal structures. A minority of the Sequoyahans are black Americans, the descendants of former slaves. Most of the
Sequoyahans continue to use tribal languages, along with English. Except for
Cherokee, an Iroquoian language, the Sequoyahan languages belong to the Mus-
kogean group of the Hokan-Siouan languages. Unlike the other Native American
peoples in the United States, the Sequoyahans have no reserved tribal lands.

*THE NATION:* Known as the Mississippian Culture, the ancient nations of
southeastern North America developed a sophisticated, centralized society ruled
by an established elite of priests and chiefs. The tribes, living in fortified towns
built around large temple mounds, spread across a vast area east of the Mississippi River. The Cherokee dominated in present North and South Carolina, Tennessee, and eastern Kentucky, the Creek in central Georgia, the Choctaw in
central Alabama and Mississippi, and the Chickasaw in Alabama, northern Mississippi, and western Tennessee and Kentucky. The Seminole split from the
Creeks in the eighteenth century and moved south into central Florida.

A Spanish expedition led by Hernan De Soto came across the settled, agricultural peoples in 1539. Armed with guns, the Spaniards looted temples and
kidnapped women in the Choctaw and Chickasaw territories before moving into
the Creek Confederacy. The more warlike Creeks resisted the Europeans and
forced them to fight their way through to the Cherokee lands. Driven from the
region by the Cherokees, the Spanish leader, De Soto, died after reaching the
Mississippi River.

The tribes, under pressure from settlers moving inland from the European's
coastal settlements, established relations and alliances with the British and
French. The Cherokee and Choctaw nations maintained ambassadors at the
Court of St. James. While broken treaties, war, and disease took their toll, the
tribes increasingly adopted the lifestyle of the Europeans. The tribes lived as
well as, and usually better than, the European frontiersmen and settlers. By the
early nineteenth century education was widespread, and a majority lived much
as their American neighbors. The former tribal ruling classes established themselves as slave-owning aristocrats employing white tutors for their children.
Known as the Five Civilized Tribes, the nations dealt with the U.S. and European governments as equals.

A Cherokee named George Guess, Sequoyah to his people, saw whites re-
cording letters and set out to apply a similar system to the Cherokee language.
He devised a phonetic table of eighty-five characters, the only such invention
by a single man in history. The written language devised by Sequoyah in 1821
spread rapidly. Sequoyah's invention was used in education, publishing, and the
republican constitutions adopted by the tribes.

A number of broken treaties and land-hungry settlers began a long series of
wars, with the tribes forced to cede large tracts of land to the expanding United
States. In 1820 the Cherokees established an independent republic in northern
Georgia, but American expansion soon eroded the boundaries set out in treaties
between the nations and the American government.

President Andrew Jackson in 1830 adopted a policy of removing the Native American nations obstructing American expansion. He established a dubious legality by coercing a chief or faction to sign removal orders, and those who resisted were branded rebels, revolutionaries, and traitors subject to imprisonment or death. Sanctioned by the government, militiamen rode through the nations burning and looting and choosing the mansions, plantations, and other valuable properties they would confiscate following the removal of the lawful owners.

Driven from their homes, the tribes were herded into squalid camps where disease, starvation, and filth decimated the weakest. In 1833 the Choctaw were forced west on the so-called Trail of Tears, followed by the Chickasaw between 1833 and 1850, the Cherokee and Creeks in 1838, and the Seminole in 1842. Black slaves often accompanied the former plantation owners on the journey west. Thousands died on the forced migration to the area designated Indian Territory. Those who survived endured torments and humiliations unequaled in modern history until the twentieth century.

Generally allied to the Confederacy during the American Civil War, the tribes shared the South's defeat. In 1865 all treaties were set aside, and the tribes were restricted to the eastern part of the Indian Territory, the western districts confiscated for the settlement of other dispossessed tribes. Stripped of power, the tribal governments ceased to function except as advisory councils. Threatened by the American restrictions, the tribes began to coordinate their administrations and cooperation against the encroachments. In 1872 the five tribes founded Muskogee as the administrative capital of the tribal confederation. In 1887 the administration forced the tribes to abandon communal lands for individual plots, the large quantity of surplus land confiscated by the federal government.

Pressed by illegal land seizures, the tribal leaders met in Muskogee on 21 August 1905 to debate the region's future. The council passed bills codifying tribal law and adopted a constitution for a proposed autonomous state to be called the All-Indian State of Sequoyah, to include all the lands still designated Indian Territory. Representatives took the proposal to the U.S. Congress, which never acknowledged or acted upon the petition.

In 1906 the Congress passed the Enabling Act, which merged the Indian and Oklahoma territories and ended all tribal sovereignty. On 16 November 1907 Oklahoma was admitted to the Union as a state, and the former tribal lands were thrown open to thousands of settlers.

Neglected and ignored, the tribes began to mobilize in the 1940s, pressing their claims to former tribal lands. A cultural revival, with renewed interest in the tribes' history, culture, and languages, led to a reestablishment of tribal governments in the 1950s. Over the next decade the revival movement merged with the militant liberation movement of the 1960s.

University-educated activists in the 1960s and 1970s demanded that the U.S. government honor the treaties that recognize the five tribes as sovereign nations. In 1970 the tribal governments were again authorized to elect their own leaders.

Tribal activists joined the other Native American peoples in petitioning the United Nations to recognize the indigenous peoples of North America as sovereign nations and in demands that the red race, the only race not represented, be given seats at the world body.

The renewed emphasis on self-determination, particularly acute following the disintegration of the Soviet Union and Yugoslavia in 1991, has given the Sequoyahan activists new confidence in the fight to restore their nations to sovereignty. In October 1991, equating the deportations of the five nations to the Stalinist deportations of Soviet minorities during World War II, militants demanded the restoration of their homeland in eastern Oklahoma, including the large city of Tulsa, founded as a Creek village in the 1830s.

*SELECTED BIBLIOGRAPHY:*

Barsh, Russell, and James Y. Henderson. *The Road: Indian Tribes and Political Liberty.* 1987.

Ehle, John. *The Trail of Tears: The Rise and Fall of the Cherokee Nation.* 1988.

Foreman, Grant. *The Five Civilized Tribes.* 1935.

Hamilton, Charles. *Cry of the Thunderbird.* 1985.

Jahoda, Gloria. *The Trail of Tears.* 1975.

# SHANLAND

**Shan State; Federated Shan States**

*CAPITAL: Taunggi*

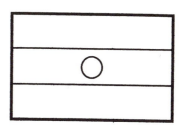

SOUTHEASTERN ASIA

SHANLAND

*POPULATION:* (95e) 5,615,000 : 3,825,000 Shans in Myanmar and another 1.5 million in adjacent areas of Thailand, Laos, and China. MAJOR NATIONAL GROUPS: (95e) Shan 48%, Burman 20%, Karen and Kayah 10%, Wa 9%, Kachin 5%, Chinese (Kokangs) 4%, Lahu, Pa-O, Palaung, other Burmese. MAJOR LANGUAGES: Shan, Burmese, Karen, Wa. MAJOR RELIGIONS: Buddhist, Christian, animist. MAJOR CITIES: (95e) Taunggi 188,000, Lashio 40,000, Namtu 33,000, Kentung 30,000, Namsang 25,000.

*GEOGRAPHY:* AREA: 60,155 sq.mi.-155,841 sq.km. LOCATION: Shanland occupies the broad Shan Plateau on both sides of the Salween River valley in northeastern Myanmar, bordering China and Laos on the east and Thailand on the south. POLITICAL STATUS: Shanland has no official status; the region forms Shan State of the Union of Myanmar.

*INDEPENDENCE DECLARED:* 3 October 1942.

*FLAG:* The Shan national flag, the flag of the national movement, is a horizontal tricolor of yellow, green, and red bearing a white disc centered on the green. OTHER FLAG(S): The flag of the largest national organization, the Shan State Progressive Party, is a red field charged with three crossed yellow arrows surrounded by a yellow cog within a wreath of yellow plant leaves. The Shan war flag, the flag used by several Shan organizations, is a pale blue field bearing three yellow mountains at the bottom and a five-pointed star on the upper hoist.

*PEOPLE:* The Shans, called Tayok in China, form one of the three main divisions of the Thai peoples. With lighter skin color than the Thai or the Burmans, the Shans are thought to have mixed with early non-Thai peoples, the mixture evident in their culture and language, a Thai language of the Sino-Thai language group. The Shans are a Buddhist people, practicing their own form of the religion. Large minorities in the state include the Burmans, mostly in the urban areas and the western districts; the Karens, Pa-O, and Lahu in the south; the Wa in the east; the Palaung and Kachins in the north, and ethnic Chinese, called Kokangs, in the eastern districts and in the towns.

*THE NATION:* Thai peoples began to migrate southeast from their original home in China, possibly as early as the first century A.D. In the seventh century the Thai tribes occupied the highland plateau, absorbing or displacing the earlier inhabitants. The Shans began to expand in the twelfth century, extending their rule into the lowlands. Their numbers increased by refugees fleeing the Mongol conquest of the Thai state of Nan Chao* in the thirteenth century, the reinforced Shans moved out to conquer most of Burma.

The resurgent Burmans expelled the Shans from the Irrawaddy delta in the fifteenth century, eventually reconquering most of northern Burma. Forced back to their highland homeland, the Shans formed thirty-four *sabwas* (principalities), dominated by an aristocratic elite. The still-powerful Shans defeated a Chinese invasion in 1766–70 but, exhausted by the struggle, declined as a power. By the nineteenth century the principalities had become tributaries of the Burman kings.

The Chinese conquered the eastern Shan territories in a bloody campaign in 1873. The Shan pleas for Burman military assistance were ignored, and the Chinese held on to their conquests in eastern Shanland. The principalities renounced their allegiance to the Burman king in the late 1870s, plunging northern Burma into chaos. The turbulence in the region gave the British a pretext for intervention.

The British annexed the Shan states in 1886, leaving the princes to rule under the supervision of British advisers and their succession subject to confirmation by the colonial authorities. Not included in British Burma, each of the Shan states maintained direct treaty relations with the British. In 1922 the states united to form the Federated Shan States but retained their separate relations with the colonial administration.

Overrun by Japanese and Thai forces during World War II, many Shans collaborated, believing Japanese promises of independence. Neighboring Thailand annexed two of the largest Shan states in 1942, and Shan nationalists declared the remaining territory independent on 3 October 1942. To placate their Burman allies, the Japanese dissolved the nationalist Shan government in December 1943. Placed under direct Burman rule for the first time in their long history, the Shans rebelled. The Shan revolt continued until the return of British rule in March 1945.

At the end of the war the British announced their intention to grant Burmese independence. Insisting on their treaty rights, the Shans demanded separate independence. Pressured by the British authorities and promised autonomy by the majority Burman government, the Shans finally agreed to inclusion in the Union of Burma. The agreement, included in Burma's constitution, allowed for Shan secession after ten years if they felt that continued association harmed their interests. Within months of Burma's independence in 1948, the new Burmese government abrogated the independence constitution and attempted to impose direct rule on the Shan federation.

The Shans, led by rival princes, produced a bewildering array of rebel forces, often fighting among themselves. The Shan princes in 1958 notified the Burmese government of their intention to secede under the terms of the 1948 independence constitution. Refusing to honor the agreement, the government retaliated by stripping the hereditary princes of their titles and privileges in 1959. The affront to their national dignity united most of the Shan rebel groups in a war against the Burmese government, which ended in a stalemate in 1960.

To finance the continuing separatist war, several Shan groups turned to the area's traditional product, opium. Called the "Shan passport to independence," the drug trade nevertheless drew in groups and organizations with little interest in the Shan nationalists' fight for secession from Burma.

The nationalists joined rebel Karens and Mons in 1969 to coordinate the insurgency against the hated Burman-dominated military government. The group later expanded to include many of the other ethnic groups fighting the Burmese military. The combined group drew up a plan to replace the military government with a loose federation of independent states in Burma. The combined group supported the pro-democracy movement that swept the country in 1988 but returned to insurgency following the crushing of the movement by the military and the overthrow of the results of a democratic election.

U Khun Sa, the most notorious of the "Golden Triangle" drug lords, in July 1994, offered to end opium poppy cultivation in Shanland in return for a withdrawal of the Burmese military troops from the region. He later offered to surrender in return for Burma's recognition of Shan independence. The legitimate nationalist organizations disavowed his offer but endorsed the call for the withdrawal of the Burmese military and the end of the drug trade that has damaged the nationalists' attempts to win international assistance in their fight for independence.

*SELECTED BIBLIOGRAPHY:*

Aung-Thwin, Michael. *The Origins of Modern Burma.* 1985.
Lintner, Bertil. *Land of Jade: A Journey through Insurgent Burma.* 1990.
Yawnghwe, Chao Tzang. *The Shan of Burma: Memories of a Shan Exile.* 1988.

# SIBERIA

Sibir

*CAPITAL: Novosibirsk*

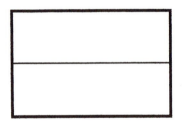

*POPULATION:* (95e) 27,155,000 : 20,500,000 Siberians (Siberyaks) in Russia. MAJOR NATIONAL GROUPS: (95e) Siberian (Siberyak) 73%, Ukrainian 7%, German 1%, other Russian. MAJOR LANGUAGES: Russian (Siberian dialects), German, Tatar, Buryat, Evenki. MAJOR RELIGIONS: Russian Orthodox, Roman Catholic, Protestant, Sunni Muslim, Buddhist, Jewish. MAJOR CITIES: (95e) Novosibirsk 1,493,000 (1,715,000), Omsk 1,236,000 (1,310,000), Krasnoyarsk 976,000 (1,080,000), Irkutsk 655,000 (804,000), Novokuznetsk 629,000 (1,458,000), Barnaul 632,000, Tyumen 519,000, Kemerovo 549,000 (752,000), Tomsk 547,000, Kurgan 385,000, Chita 378,000, Ulan-Ude 385,000 (420,000), Surgut 335,000, Nizhnevartovsk 302,000, Prokopyevsk 288,000 (440,000), Angarsk 278,000, Bratsk 276,000, Biisk 248,000, Norilsk 182,000, Rubtsovsk 179,000, Abakan 174,000, Kolchugino (Leninsk-Kuznetsk) 148,000 (243,000), Mezhdurechensk 115,000 (188,000).

*GEOGRAPHY:* AREA: 2,555,336 sq.mi.-6,620,041 sq.km. LOCATION: Siberia occupies a huge area in the central Russian Federation between European Russia and the Far East.* The territory, extending from above the Arctic Circle to the borders of Kazakhstan and Mongolia on the south, is roughly divided into two regions, the lowlands of the West Siberian Plain and the highlands of the Central Siberian Plateau. POLITICAL STATUS: Siberia has no official status; the region forms the oblasts (provinces) of Chita, Irkutsk, Kemerovo, Kurgan, Krasnoyarsk, Novosibirsk, Omsk, Tomsk, and Tyumen, the republics of Altai, Buryat, Khakass, and Tuva, and the Territory of Altay.

*INDEPENDENCE DECLARED:* 4 July 1918.

*FLAG:* The Siberian national flag, the flag of the national movement, is a horizontal bicolor of white over green. OTHER FLAG(S): The flag of a proposed United States of North Asia is the Siberian bicolor with the addition of an arc of five blue stars on the white stripe.

*PEOPLE:* The Siberians, calling themselves Siberyaks, are the descendants of Slavic settlers, deportees, and exiles, with admixtures of the region's seventy different ethnic groups. The Siberian culture, developed by the harsh conditions and frontier history, includes a number of regional dialects collectively called Siberian, a language as different from standard Russian as Ukrainian and claimed as a separate Eastern Slav language by nationalists. The historic separation of the Siberians from European Russia is demonstrated by the Siberian custom of referring to the Russian heartland as the ''mainland,'' as if Siberia were an island. The majority of the Siberians are Orthodox, although most major religions are represented in the region.

*THE NATION:* Originally inhabited by nomadic Turkic and Mongol tribes, the area remained divided until most of the southern territories united under Mongol rule in the thirteenth century. At the disintegration of the Mongol's vast empire, most of the region was included in a Tatar successor state, the Khanate of Sibir.

Cossacks crossed the Urals to conquer Sibir in 1518, the name of the conquered state applied to the entire area east of European Russia. A series of Cossack forts gradually expanded Russian territory against the resistance of the native peoples. The first settlers, mostly Cossacks and peasant serfs seeking land and independence in Siberia's vast spaces, expanded along the rivers, the only means of transport and communication.

Organized as a Russian province in 1710, Siberia became a dumping ground for deportees, political prisoners, recalcitrant serfs turned over for deportation by landlords, convicted prostitutes, and Jews who failed to pay their taxes. The deportation of Polish insurgents, revolutionaries, and captured members of antitsarist groups began in 1825.

The abolition of serfdom in 1861 freed thousands of land-hungry peasants. Offered free land in underpopulated Siberia, thousands crossed the Urals to settle the valleys of the Ob and Yenisei Rivers. The completion of the Trans-Siberian Railroad in 1891–92 facilitated settlement, and over 3 million European Slavs had migrated to Siberia by 1914. The new arrivals, generally adopting the speech and antigovernment attitudes of the earlier migrants, joined a society in many ways more similar to Canada and America than European Russia.

The Siberians, through long contact with exiled revolutionaries and political prisoners, were among the first to espouse revolutionary ideals as Russia slowly collapsed during World War I. The overthrow of the monarchy in February 1917 met with jubilation in much of the region. Exiles and revolutionaries, suddenly freed, eagerly joined the revolution.

A Siberian national movement had existed since the late nineteenth century, but with little popular support until the revolution. In August 1917 the nationalists formed a Siberian parliament. Promised autonomy, the nationalists supported Russia's new democratic government until its overthrow by the Bolsheviks in October 1917. Rejecting Bolshevik overtures, the nationalists convened the All-Siberian Congress, which authorized the formation of a national army from the thousands of Siberian soldiers deserting the front. The Siberian government severed all ties to Bolshevik Russia, and on 4 July 1918 the nationalists declared the vast region an independent republic.

An All-Russian Provisional Government, organized by ex-tsarist officers in November 1918, vehemently opposed the breakup of the Russian Empire. On 18 November allies of the rival government's head, Admiral Kolchak, overthrew the separatist Siberian government and took control of the administration. Recognized as the legitimate government by the Allies, Admiral Kolchak led the anti-Bolshevik White forces in Siberia as civil war spread across the region. In 1920 most White resistance collapsed, and by 1922 Siberia was Soviet.

The Soviet government up to World War II treated Siberia as a colony to be exploited. The site of the infamous Gulag, millions were deported to the region during Stalin's long rule, the deportees used as slave labor for mines and the construction of dams, railroads, and cities. Siberia's vast resources propelled the Soviet Union to superpower status, but the living and working conditions of ordinary Siberians barely attained the levels of developing Africa.

The Soviet liberalization of the late 1980s loosed a torrent of Siberian grievances. The Siberian nationalist movement, dormant for decades, reemerged in 1988 with demands that Siberia become the sixteenth union republic. In the aftermath of the Soviet disintegration in 1991, demands changed to republic status within the new Russian Federation, while more militant groups debated the issue of Siberian independence.

The Russian government's plans to continue closing unprofitable or unproductive mines and industries have stirred the debate over autonomy. In February 1993, responding to Siberian charges that the region is still treated as a colony, the government officially ended the practice of exiling convicted criminals to the region. The economic hardships of the Russian change to a market economy have caused a massive exodus of Russian bureaucrats, miners, and other workers back to European Russia. The Siberian nationalists, gaining strength with each perceived desertion, claim that when all the Russians have gone home the Siberians, the descendants of Cossacks, exiles, and freed serfs, will regain control of their vast and potentially wealthy homeland.

*SELECTED BIBLIOGRAPHY:*

Broderick, Benson. *East of the Sun: The Epic Conquest and Tragic History of Siberia.* 1992.

Lincoln, W. Bruce. *The Conquest of a Continent: Siberia and the Russians.* 1993.

Snow, Russell E. *The Bolsheviks in Siberia: February 1917 to March 1918.* 1986.

Threadgold, D. W. *The Great Siberian Migration.* 1957.

# SICILY

**Sicilia**

*CAPITAL: Palermo*

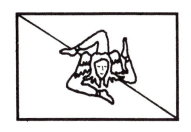

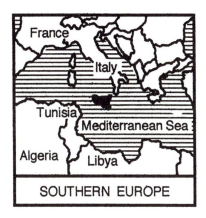

SOUTHERN EUROPE

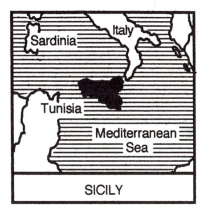

SICILY

*POPULATION:* (95e) 5,151,000 : 7,550,000 Sicilians in Italy. MAJOR NA-TIONAL GROUPS: (95e) Sicilian 94%, other Italian. MAJOR LANGUAGES: Sicilian, Italian. MAJOR RELIGION: Roman Catholic. MAJOR CITIES: (95e) Palermo 827,000 (991,000), Catania 371,000 (570,000), Messina 302,000, Siracusa 133,000, Gela 88,000, Trapani 79,000 (102,000), Agrigento 65,000 (130,000), Modica 58,000, Acireale 57,000, Marsala 56,000 (92,000), Vittoria 56,000 (89,000), Caltanisetta 55,000, Ragusa 52,000, Caltanisetta 55,000, Barcellona 45,000 (100,000).

*GEOGRAPHY:* AREA: 9,817 sq.mi.-25,432 sq.km. LOCATION: Sicily, the largest island in the Mediterranean Sea, lies off the southern Italian Peninsula and is separated from the mainland by the narrow Strait of Messina. The island, ninety miles north of the African coast, is mostly a broad plateau rising in the northwest to volcanic Mount Etna. POLITICAL STATUS: Sicily forms a semi-iautonomous region of the Italian republic.

*INDEPENDENCE DECLARED:* 10 July 1943.

*FLAG:* The Sicilian national flag, the official flag of the region, is a diagonal bicolor of red over yellow, upper hoist to lower fly, bearing three legs joined in the center behind a winged head. OTHER FLAG(S): The traditional flag of the national movement has nine horizontal stripes of yellow and red bearing a pale blue canton on the upper hoist charged with a representation of the head of Medusa.

*PEOPLE:* The Sicilians are of mixed background, descendants of the island's original Celtic and Latin inhabitants, with admixtures of the many conquerors.

The Sicilian dialect, claimed as a separate language, is a Romance language using borrowings from Greek, Spanish, and Arabic, as distinct from standard Italian as Romanian. The Sicilian culture, developed during 2,000 years of foreign rule, incorporates many customs and traditions not found on the mainland and has spawned the Mafia, Sicily's infamous export to the world. The Sicilians are devoutly Roman Catholic and among the most conservative of the Italian peoples.

*THE NATION:* Originally inhabited by Sicani, Elymi, and Siculi tribes, probably of Celtic origin, the island early divided into numerous small territories. Between the eighth and sixth centuries B.C., Greeks settled the eastern part of the island, and Carthaginians settled in the west. Syracuse, the largest and most powerful of the Greek cities, developed as a center of Greek culture and Mediterranean trade and eventually extended its influence throughout Sicily and southern Italy.

Carthaginian control of western Sicily involved the island in the conflicts between Rome and Carthage, the Punic Wars. In 241 B.C. Roman legions invaded the island, and by 215 B.C. all of Sicily had come under Roman rule. Rome's first overseas possession, the island was divided into large estates, a debilitating economic legacy that persists to the present.

Muslim Arabs, called Saracens, conquered the island from nearby North Africa in the ninth century. Sicily's Muslim rulers practiced a tolerance of the religious and ethnic minorities unknown in the rest of Europe. The enlightened Muslim government fostered education, agriculture, art, and the sciences and administered a civilized state far ahead of the European culture of the time.

The Norman conquest of Sicily mirrored the 1066 Norman conquest of England. A large force led by Roger de Hauteville left Normandy* in 1061, his forces ultimately victorious in Sicily thirty years later. Under the Hauteville dynasty, the Normans adopted much of the more advanced Saracen culture, particularly the tolerance that allowed a mixed population of Normans, Muslims, Latins, Greeks, and Jews to live in peace and to prosper. The most enlightened state in Europe from 1072 to 1266, Sicily enjoyed a golden age that was a forerunner of the later European Renaissance of the fourteenth to sixteenth centuries.

The pope, on the death of the last Hauteville heir, bestowed the kingdom on Charles of Anjou as king of Naples and Sicily. Harsh and intolerant French rule ended the brilliant Sicilian civilization of the Saracens and Normans. A 1282 Sicilian rebellion culminated in the massacre of all the French on the island, the so-called Sicilian Vespers. Freed of French rule, the Sicilians chose the king of Aragon as their new ruler in 1295. Ruled as a separate kingdom until 1409, Sicily then became part of Aragon. The merger of Aragon and Castile in 1479 in the united Spanish kingdom brought an end to all Sicilian autonomy.

Sicily remained Spanish until 1713 and was held briefly by Savoy* and Austria before coming under the Bourbon kings of the Kingdom of the Two Sicilies. Dominated by the Neopolitans of the kingdom's capital, the Sicilians rebelled in 1820, 1848–49, and 1860. During the 1860 rebellion Giuseppe Garibaldi and a thousand volunteers stormed ashore. Garibaldi relinquished his Sicilian conquests to a newly united Italian kingdom in 1861.

Sicily's feudal system, control of the land by a few large aristocratic estates, remained unchanged under Italian rule. The Mafia emerged to serve a vital purpose, offering Sicilian peasants a means of justice outside the always unequal Italian law. Carried to the Americas by Sicilian immigrants, the Mafia remained a strong force among immigrant communities.

Promised reforms, the Sicilians supported Mussolini's fascist takeover of Italy in 1922. Sicilian support of the fascists waned following government efforts to curtail the Mafia in 1927–28. Fervently antifascist by the time Italy joined World War II, a nascent nationalist movement provided fertile ground for British and, later, American agents.

Encouraged by the Allies, the nationalists carried out a guerrilla war against the Italian fascists and their Nazi allies. Welcomed as liberators, Allied troops invaded Sicily in 1943. Supported by the Allies, the nationalist leader, Turiddu Giuliano, declared Sicily independent on 10 July 1943 and began to organize the first independent Sicilian state in history.

The Allies, to persuade the Italian government to withdraw from the war, abruptly ended their support of Sicilian separatism. In late 1943 Italian troops invaded the island, finally defeating the nationalists in a vicious eight-week war. With widespread popular support, the rebels continued to fight a guerrilla war in the west of the island. In 1945 the Sicilian nationalist pled their case before the newly formed United Nations, but the Sicilian rebellion collapsed following the death of Giuliano in 1950.

Decades of neglect forced thousands to emigrate in the 1950s and 1960s, provoking Sicilian resentment and a resurgence of nationalist sentiment in the 1970s. The polarization of Italy, marked by a rise of antisouthern sentiment in the rich north, gave the movement new impetus in the 1980s. Nationalists claim that collusion between the Italian government and the Mafia has maintained an iron grip on the island since the separatist war in the 1940s. The unholy alliance kept social protest to an absolute minimum until cooperation collapsed in the late 1980s. The reemergence of the nationalists showed in the voter support for nationalist issues in the March 1994 local elections. The nationalists claim that the unholy alliance between the government and the Mafia since World War II has left Sicily a neglected dependency with incomes little more than half the Italian average.

*SELECTED BIBLIOGRAPHY:*

Abulafid, David. *Italy, Sicily and the Mediterranean, 1100–1400.* 1987.

Finley, M. I. *A History of Sicily.* 1987.

Freeman, Edward A. *A History of Sicily from Earliest Times.* 1965.

# SIKKIM

Denjong

CAPITAL: Gangtok

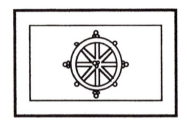

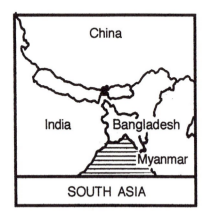

SOUTH ASIA

SIKKIM

*POPULATION:* (95e) 442,000 : 420,000 Sikkimese in India. MAJOR NA-
TIONAL GROUPS: (95e) Gorkali 66%, Bhutia 14%, Lepcha 12%, other Indian.
MAJOR LANGUAGES: Gorkali, Bhutia, Lepcha (Rong), Limboo, English.
MAJOR RELIGIONS: (95e) Hindu 58%, Buddhist (Tibetan Lamaism) 40%.
MAJOR CITIES: (95e) Gangtok 60,000, Rangpo 17,000.

*GEOGRAPHY:* AREA: 2,818 sq.mi.-7,301 sq.km. LOCATION: Sikkim, also
called Denjong, the Valley of Rice, occupies the high valleys in the Himalayas
of northeastern India just south of Tibet.* POLITICAL STATUS: Sikkim forms
a state of the Republic of India.

*INDEPENDENCE DECLARED:* 15 August 1947.

*FLAG:* The Sikkimese national flag, the flag of the former kingdom, is a
white field, bordered in red, bearing a centered gold and red Buddhist wheel.

*PEOPLE:* The Sikkimese comprise three major groups: the Gorkali, highlanders originally from Nepal; the Bhutia, originally from Tibet; and the Lepcha,
the earliest inhabitants. The Gorkali speak a Pahari language of the Indo-Iranian
languages; the Bhutia and Lepcha speak languages of the Tibeto-Burman language group. The three peoples, formerly divided by race, religion, and
language, have united since 1975, all now considering themselves Sikkimese.
The Gorkali are Hindus. The Bhutia and Lepcha adhere to the Tibetan form of
Buddhism, Lamaism.

*THE NATION:* Sikkim has been inhabited for thousands of years, even though
little is known of its ancient history. An early center of trade among China,

India, and Tibet, the region maintained ties to regions far beyond the Himalayas. The Lepcha formed a state, the Rong kingdom, ruled by the Namgyal dynasty of Tibetan origin, in the fourteenth century. Tibetan migrants, the Bhutia, settled in the kingdom in the sixteenth century, paying tribute to the Lepcha rulers.

The Bhutia's religion, Mahayana Buddhism, known as Tibetan Lamaism, became the state religion in 1630 with the conversion of the king, Pentsho Namgyal. The adoption of Lamaism strengthened religious and cultural ties to Tibet. In 1642 the king, called the Choygal, extended his rule over a large area of the Himalayan highlands, although Sikkim remained a virtual dependency of Tibet until the nineteenth century.

Sikkim lost territory to the powerful Gurkha state of Nepal in the eighteenth century. The warlike Gurkhas invaded the kingdom several times over the next century. In 1814–16 the Gurkhas were driven back with the assistance of British forces. The Gurkhas who remained in the kingdom were later called the Gorkali. In 1861 Sikkim's status as a British protected state was formalized by a treaty with the Bhutia-dominated royal government.

The king accepted British military protection against the continuing Gurkha threat, but in 1835 the British authorities forced the cession of the southern part of the kingdom to direct British rule. The British took additional territory from the kingdom in 1846 and 1849. To counter Tibetan claims to the newly ceded districts, the British encouraged immigration from Nepal, the migrants also moving into southern Sikkim. In 1861 Sikkim's status as a British protected state was formalized by treaty.

Sikkim's separate treaty relations allowed the kingdom to survive the consolidation of the Indian states in 1947. On 15 August 1947, the day the British withdrew from India, the king declared Sikkim an independent state. Political and social unrest, a result of Gorkali demands for rights equal to those of the ruling Bhutia, persuaded the king to sign a treaty of protection with India in 1950. In 1961 the Gorkali won full political and cultural rights.

In 1963 the Namgyal heir married an American, Hope Cooke, the "Grace Kelly" of the East. On 2 December 1963 the heir, Gyalsay Palden Thonduys Namgyal succeeded to the throne, and his American wife became the queen, the Gyalmo. The queen's foreign background became a political issue as political parties formed in the 1960s and demands for popular participation in government grew.

In 1965 China renewed Tibet's old claim to Sikkim, and two years later fighting broke out on the Tibetan border. Indian troops aided the Sikkimese to defend the state, and an Indian-constructed road ended Sikkim's long isolation. The Indians withdrew when the Chinese threat ended.

A deepening political crisis, aggravated by Indian-sponsored Gorkali rioting, shook the kingdom in 1971–72. In early 1973 the royal family was forced to flee, although the king returned later in the year. Unable to quell renewed Gorkali rioting, the king requested assistance from the Indian government. On 4 July 1974 the king signed the state's first constitution, gave up his absolute rule, and created a constituent assembly. The Indian military intervened as rioting again erupted, then stayed to overthrow the royal government and place the king under house arrest.

The Indians revoked the titles of the royal family and the nobility as they extended their control of the small state. A referendum of dubious legality on 15 April 1975 confirmed the abolition of the monarchy and union with India. On 16 May India annexed Sikkim, ignoring the protests of the king and the opposition of the neighboring states.

To undermine the continuing Sikkimese opposition, the Indian government sponsored the migration of Indians from the lowlands to the newly annexed region, but the migration only served to unite the three Sikkimese peoples. In 1981–83 serious disturbances shook the state as nationalists demanded the expulsion of the newcomers and the restoration of Sikkimese independence under United Nations auspices. In 1982 the exiled Choygal died in the United States.

The Indian government countered growing Sikkimese opposition by dissolving the state government and imposing direct rule from New Delhi in 1984. A year later the government restored the state government following renewed disturbances and protests. In 1990 nationalist leaders declared the annexation of Sikkim illegal and reiterated their demands for the restoration of the kingdom. The Indian government acknowledged the illegal annexation and issued an official apology but refused to discuss the kingdom's restoration. However, as a conciliatory gesture, the government opened the state to visitors, the first since 1978.

In November 1994 state elections, the Sikkimese nationalists won a substantial portion of the vote. The nationalist resurgence has become an embarrassment for the Indian government, which claims that Sikkimese nationalism has faded away under the benefits of Indian rule.

*SELECTED BIBLIOGRAPHY:*
Chopra, P. N. *Sikkim.* 1979.
Rao, P. R. *Sikkim: The Story of Its Integration with India.* 1978.
Rustomji, Nari. *Sikkim: A Himalayan Tragedy.* 1987.

# SIND

**Sindhu Desh**

*CAPITAL: Karachi*

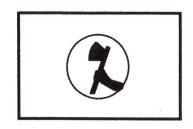

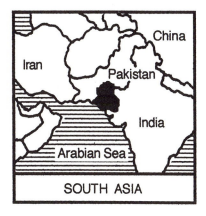

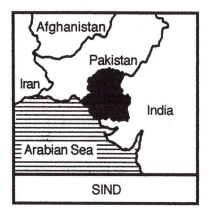

*POPULATION:* (95e) 27,040,000 : 16,650,000 Sindhi in Pakistan. MAJOR NATIONAL GROUPS: (95e) Sindhi 61%, Mohajir 27%, Pushtu 7%, Baluch 1%, other Pakistani. MAJOR LANGUAGES: Sindhi, Urdu, Pushtu, English. MAJOR RELIGIONS: (95e) Sunni Muslim 85%, Hindu 10%, Ismaili Muslim 3%. MAJOR CITIES: (95e) Karachi 7,212,000 (9,857,000), Hyderabad 986,000 (1,407,000), Sukkur 234,000, Larkhana 201,000, Mirpur Khas 182,000, Nawabshah 132,000, Shikarpur 118,000, Jacobabad 110,000, Tando Adam 100,000.

*GEOGRAPHY:* AREA: 54,407 sq.mi.-140,950 sq.km. LOCATION: Sind occupies an area of flat plains in the Indus River valley and the delta on the Arabian Sea, in southeastern Pakistan. POLITICAL STATUS: Sind forms a province of the Islamic Republic of Pakistan.

*FLAG:* The Sindhi national flag, the flag of the national movement, is a red field bearing a centered white disc charged with a black forearm and hand holding a black hatchet. OTHER FLAG(S): The flag of the Hindu Sindhi minority is a solid field of saffron orange.

*PEOPLE:* The Sindhi are a mostly rural Aryan people of mixed Aryan, Arabic, and Baluch background speaking an Indo-Aryan language, with six major dialects, written in a modified Iranian script. The urbanization of the Sindhi began only in the 1970s so that the Sindhi culture remains a rural culture, traditional and conservative. Large minorities in the region include the Mohajirs, Urdu-speaking groups originally from India who form a majority in the largest cities, Karachi and Hyderabad. The Hindu Sindhis and the Pushtu are mostly concentrated in Karachi, and the smaller numbers of Baluch and Punjabis are mostly in the areas bordering Baluchistan* and the Punjab.

*THE NATION:* Possibly the site of the subcontinent's earliest civilizations, a sophisticated civilization flourished in the Indus Valley over 4,000 years ago. Conquered by the Persians in the fifth century B.C., the culture and language of the conquerors became predominant. Sind fell to Greeks of Alexander the Great and later formed part of the Buddhist Mauryan Empire following the Greek withdrawal. Over the next centuries Sind retained considerable autonomy under the nominal rule of various states and empires. The region fragmented into a number of small states in the fifth century A.D.

Invading Arabs overran the region in 711–12. The Arabs' new religion, Islam, from its foothold in the port cities, spread to the inland districts over the next decade. Ruled as part of the Muslim Empire, the Caliphate, until the eleventh century, Sind later came under the control of Turkic peoples and in the fourteenth century became part of India's Mogul Empire. The Sindhis asserted their independence under their own emirs in the eighteenth century, the region uniting except for Khairpur, which formed a separate state in the northwest.

A British military campaign defeated the Sindhis in 1842–43. The British authorities added the conquered Sind states to the British province of Bombay. In 1861, with the exception of Khairpur, the Sindhi territories were consolidated in a single district. Religious tensions between Muslims and Hindus stimulated the growth of both Sindhi nationalism and Muslim separatism in the late nineteenth century.

Communal tensions escalated after World War I, raising Sindhi demands for separation from Hindu-dominated Bombay Province. Sporadic rioting and violence continued even after Sind became a separate province in 1937. The endemic rioting and disturbances reached serious proportions during and after World War II.

Sind, as a Muslim majority region, joined the new Pakistani state in 1947. The states of Sind and Khairpur were consolidated into a single Sind Province. Sind's eastern border became the scene of horrible massacres and violence as Hindus fled to India and Muslims to Pakistan. Multiethnic Karachi, dominated by Muslim refugees from India, the Mohajirs, was separated from Sind to form a Pakistani federal capital district. The Mohajirs' language, Urdu, the predominant language of the newly designated capital, was adopted as Pakistan's official language, even though its use was mostly restricted to the influential refugee population. The Pakistani government abolished the ancient provinces in 1955.

Politically and economically dominated by the more sophisticated, urbanized Mohajirs, the Sindhi resistance evolved a cultural and linguistic nationalism in the 1960s. In 1967 the predominantly Sindhi Pakistan People's Party formed under the leadership of Zulfikar Ali Bhutto and in 1970 won control of the Pakistani government. Bhutto's home province, Sind, was reconstituted with its capital at Karachi. The Sindhi provincial government passed a Sindhi-only language law in 1972, which exacerbated the growing rift between the Sindhis and the Mohajirs and set off serious Mohajir rioting.

The Bhutto government, vehemently opposed by Pakistan's majority Punjabis, in alliance with the Mohajirs, was overthrown by the army. In 1979 Bhutto was hanged by the military government. Bhutto's wife and daughter, Benazir, took over the Pakistan People's Party as the party of Sindhi nationalism. Bhutto became a martyred Sindhi national hero.

A growing Sindhi alienation provoked widespread nationalist and ethnic violence in 1983–85, leaving over 6,000 dead in Sindhi and Mohajir rioting. Politically dominated by the Punjabi military and economically dominated by the Mohajir minority, Sind's indigenous population turned to nationalism. In December 1986 the worst ethnic violence since 1947 swept the province, quieting only with the virtual military occupation of the Pakistani army.

Benazir Bhutto, as the leader of her father's political party, won the Pakistani elections in 1988 to become the first female prime minister of a Muslim country. Bhutto's election victory temporarily ended nationalist demands for separation from Pakistan. Disappointed by Bhutto's refusal to grant Sindhi autonomy and her political alliance with the Mohajirs, the Sindhis renewed their support for nationalist groups. The nationalist resurgence sparked renewed rioting in 1989–90.

Bhutto's government was ousted in August 1990, pushing many moderate Sindhi political groups to form closer ties to the increasingly vocal nationalists. The Pakistani government accused India of supporting Sindhi separatism to offset Pakistani aid to the nationalists of Kashmir* and Khalistan.* Sind, the most lawless and alienated of the turbulent Pakistani provinces, has become the most serious threat to Pakistan's fragile unity.

The city of Karachi, the focus of Sindhi nationalism, in late 1994 again became the scene of violent confrontations between the various national groups and between the armed groups and the Pakistani police. The city, like Pakistan itself, has become virtually ungovernable and is split between hostile national groups.

*SELECTED BIBLIOGRAPHY:*
Ali, Asghar. *Ethnic Conflicts in South Asia.* 1987.
Burki, Shahid. *Pakistan: The Continuing Search for Nationhood.* 1985.
Islam, M. Nazrul. *Pakistan and Malaysia: A Comprehensive Study of National Integration.* 1989.
Khuhro, M. J. *Sind through the Centuries.* 1982.

# SOMALILAND

### Northern Somalia

*CAPITAL: Hargeisa (Hargeysa)*

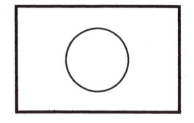

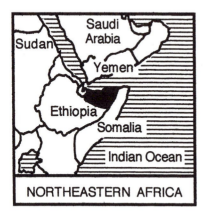

NORTHEASTERN AFRICA

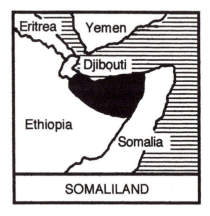

SOMALILAND

*POPULATION:* (95e) 2,915,000 : 2,650,000 Northern Somalis in Somalia and another 750,000 in adjacent areas of Ethiopia and Djibouti. MAJOR NATIONAL GROUPS: (95e) Northern Somali 90% (Issak, Dir, Issa, Darob, Gadabursi, Dolbahunta, Ogadeni), Arab 2%, other Somali. MAJOR LANGUAGES: Somali, English. MAJOR RELIGION: Sunni Muslim. MAJOR CITIES: (95e) Hargeisa (Hargeysa) 250,000, Berbera 130,000, Burco (Burao) 70,000.

*GEOGRAPHY:* AREA: 67,918 sq.mi.-175,954 sq.km. LOCATION: Somaliland occupies a semiarid region of coastal lowlands and interior plateaus bordering the Gulf of Aden region of the Indian Ocean in northwestern Somalia. POLITICAL STATUS: Somaliland's status has yet to be resolved. Officially, the region forms the Somali regions of Woqooyi, Galbeed, Togdheer, and Sanaaq and the western districts of Nugaal.

*INDEPENDENCE DECLARED:* 26 June 1960; 18 May 1991.

*FLAG:* The Somaliland flag, the official flag of the republic, is a white field bearing a green disc, often with the Shahada (There is no God but God, Mohammed is the Prophet of God) in black Arabic script around the disc. OTHER FLAG(S): The flag of the largest Northern Somali national group, the Somali National Movement (SNM), is a horizontal tricolor of red, white, and green.

*PEOPLE:* The Northern Somalis are a Hamitic people, the northern clans of the Somali, mostly Issak and Dir, but with minorities of several other clan groups, many more numerous across the borders in the region of Western Somalia* in Ethiopia or in Djibouti. The clans speak the northern dialects of Somali, a Cushitic language of the Hamito-Semitic language group. English, the language of the former colonial administration, is also widely understood and is used as a lingua franca among clans speaking mutually unintelligible dialects. The only sizable non-Somali minority in the region is the Arab population of the port cities.

*THE NATION:* Known to the ancient Egyptians as the "Country of Perfumes," little of the region's pre-Islamic history has survived. By tradition the first Muslims to arrive in the region were refugees who fled Mecca with Mohammed in 622 A.D., but, rather than continue to Medina with the prophet, they turned south to the Red Sea ports and crossed the narrow Gulf of Aden to introduce Islam to the northern Somali coast. Muslim Arabs soon followed to conquer the region, which later formed a powerful medieval Muslim sultanate.

The sultanate split into small clan states in the seventeenth century. The states mostly came under the rule of Oman and after 1832 were administered from Zanzibar.* Between the sixteenth and nineteenth centuries the clans participated in the frequent wars between the Muslim peoples and the highland Christian kingdoms of Ethiopia.

Egyptian troops occupied the coastal towns in the 1870s but were withdrawn and replaced by British troops in 1884. Three years later the British authorities established a protectorate in the northern Somali territory. The remaining Somali lands came under Italian, French, and Ethiopian colonial rule. The Somali clans, ignoring the colonial borders, moved freely across the entire region. Frequent clan wars over water and grazing rights continued well into the twentieth century.

The clans of British Somaliland rebelled in 1901, led by a Muslim religious leader known as the "Mad Mullah," Mohammad bin Abdullah Hassan. The Muslim holy war ended in defeat in 1921, and Hassan fled to Ethiopian Somalia. The focus of Somali nationalism in the 1920s and 1930s remained the reunification of the Somali clans of the Horn of Africa.

The Italians in 1936 defeated and annexed Ethiopia, combining the Somali-populated Ogaden region of Ethiopia with Italian Somaliland. In 1940, following the outbreak of World War II, Italian troops took control of British Somaliland. British forces, operating from Kenya, drove the Italians from all the Somali territories in March 1941. The British reestablished the protectorate of British Somaliland and set up military administrations in Italian and Ethiopian Somali territories. Pressed by Somali nationalists, the British presented a plan for a united Somali trusteeship territory to the new United Nations in 1946.

United Nations deliberations continued for five years. The final decision rejected the British proposal, returned the Ogaden region to Ethiopia, and placed former Italian Somaliland under Italian administration as a trust territory. The solution, rejected by Somali nationalists, provoked violence and rioting across the entire Somali region. The Somali nationalists reiterated their demand for a "Greater Somalia" to include British and Italian Somaliland, Ethiopia's Ogaden, French Somaliland, and Kenya's Northwest Province.

British Somaliland, decolonized in 1960, declared independence on 26 June

1960. The new national legislature voted for union with newly independent Italian Somaliland, the united republic proclaimed on 1 July. The union provided for substantial regional autonomy.

In 1969 a Supreme Revolutionary Council took power in a bloodless coup. The coup's leaders quickly ended regional autonomy within Somalia while demanding the unification of the Somali territories outside the state. In 1977 the Somali government launched an invasion of Ethiopia's Ogaden. At first successful, the invasion ultimately floundered when faced with Ethiopia's hastily summoned Soviet and Cuban allies.

Refugees from the Ogaden war poured into northern Somalia, most with clan and family ties to the northern clans. Amid the chaos northern leaders began to stress clan and tribal ties over pan-Somali nationalism. The increasingly leftist Somali government, dominated by the southern clans, attempted to force the northerners into Communist-style collectives. In 1981, with clan conflicts growing, several northern leaders openly espoused separatism and formed the Somali National Movement. In May 1988 open rebellion spread across the north.

Government reprisals and indiscriminate bombing of northern cities pushed the remaining northern clans to join the separatist revolt. Some 400,000 refugees fled to neighboring countries as towns and villages were pounded to rubble. Weakened by a spreading clan war in the southern provinces, demoralized government troops lost most of the north to a rebel offensive in April and May 1991. The rebel leader, Abdirahman Ahmed Ali, on 18 May 1991 declared the independence of the territory that formerly made up the protectorate of British Somaliland.

The world's refusal to grant the breakaway state diplomatic recognition hampered reconstruction and prevented the arrival of famine and development funds. Although the Northern Somalis were spared the horrors that overtook the southern clans in the 1990s, the peace remained fragile. In early 1993 clan elders met for four months to work out ways to avoid the chaos and bloodshed of Somalia from spreading to Somaliland, including the adoption of the means to elect a two-house legislature.

In August 1994 the bicameral legislature adopted a separate currency and began debate on drawing up a democratic constitution. The Somaliland legislature again pleaded for recognition of the state's independence, warning of disaster if the world continued to ignore the region. In November 1994, as predicted, violence broke out in Hargeisa and threatened to spread across the devastated republic.

*SELECTED BIBLIOGRAPHY:*

Laitin, David D., and Said S. Samatar. *Somalia: Nation in Search of a State.* 1985.
Lewis, I. M. *Nationalism and Self-Determination in the Horn of Africa.* 1984.
Samatar, Ahmed. *Socialist Somalia: Rhetoric and Reality.* 1988.

# SOUTHERN MONGOLIA

**Inner Mongolia**

*CAPITAL: Kukuhoto (Hohhot)*

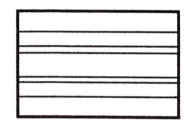

*POPULATION:* (95e) 16,862,000 : 3,570,000 Southern Mongols in China. MAJOR NATIONAL GROUPS: (95e) Chinese 75%, Mongol 21%, Hui 4%. MAJOR LANGUAGES: Chinese, Mongol. MAJOR RELIGIONS: Buddhist, Taoist, Tibetan Buddhist (Lamaism), Sunni Muslim. MAJOR CITIES: (95e) Baotou 910,000 (1,105,000), Kukuhoto (Hohhot) 605,000 (850,000), Jining 190,000, Linhe 130,000, Wuhai 115,000, Erenhot 110,000, Abnagar 110,000, Bayinhot (Bayan Obo) 105,000, Alxa Zuoqi 100,000, Fengzhen 100,000.

*GEOGRAPHY:* AREA: 117,708 sq.mi.-304,944 sq.km. LOCATION: Southern Mongolia lies in north-central China, a vast region of rolling grasslands between the border with the Republic of Mongolia and the Great Wall, the massive construction originally built to protect China from the ancient Mongols. POLITICAL STATUS: Southern Mongolia has no official status; the region forms the southern part of historic Mongolia, now included in the Inner Mongolian Autonomous Region of the People's Republic of China.

*INDEPENDENCE DECLARED:* 23 April 1934; 22 November 1937.

*FLAG:* The Southern Mongol flag, the flag of the former Southern Mongol federation, is a yellow field bearing a centered, horizontal red stripe bordered by narrow white stripes inside wider, pale blue stripes.

*PEOPLE:* The Southern Mongols are the descendants of the historic Forty-Nine Banners of Inner Mongolia, mostly belonging to the Tumet, Chahar, and Khorchin tribes. The tribes are organized in six leagues: Huna in the north, Khingan in the center, Qirin in the southwest, Jooda in the south, and Chahar and Silingol in the southeast. The Southern Mongols speak a Mongol language with four major dialects: South Mongolian, Ordos, Chahar, and Harachin. The Southern Mongols adhere to Mahayana Buddhism, also called Tibetan Lamaism. As in Tibet,* the Dalai Lama is revered as the spiritual leader. The Chinese majority has mostly settled in the area in the twentieth century, particularly after World War II.

*THE NATION:* Originally occupied by the Chahar and Tumet tribes, the immense plains south of the Gobi Desert were often overrun by other nomadic Mongol tribes. Tribal wars and raids on the settled peoples to the south brought the tribes into conflict with the ancient Chinese Empire. To contain the fierce Mongol peoples, the Chinese constructed an enormous defensive wall, the Great Wall, which extended some 1,500 miles along the northern border of the empire. The Chinese completed the massive construction in 204 B.C.

Genghis Khan, the ruler of a small tribe called the Mongols, extended his rule over neighboring tribes and in 1206 A.D. established the first unified Mongol state. A Mongol army was built into an efficient fighting force around a core of highly mobile cavalry that eventually conquered most of the known world. The vast Mongol Empire stretched from the east coast of China to the Danube River.

The empire disintegrated into several successor states in the late thirteenth century, including the Mongol dynasty, the Yuan, that ruled all of China from 1271 until the Mongols were finally expelled in 1377–78. Hostility to the Mongols helped to unite China under successive Chinese dynasties. The disintegration reached the Mongol heartland, the Southern Mongols uniting in a loose confederation of leagues (principalities), the Forty-Nine Banners of Inner Mongolia.

The Manchu, a Tungus people from the northeast, conquered the South Mongol confederation in 1635. The Manchu moved south to conquer China in 1644, the Mongol lands added to Manchu China. To blunt continuing Mongol resistance to Manchu rule, the emperor issued a decree that promised the Mongols of the Forty-Nine Banners renewed independence, under their own laws, should there be a change of dynasty in China.

Chinese immigration to the provinces of Outer China, populated by non-Chinese minorities, remained restricted until 1878. To relieve severe land pressure, the Manchu government opened the borderlands to Chinese settlement. Sporadic violence and resistance accompanied the colonization of Inner Mongolia in the 1880s and 1890s. In 1904 the Mongol demonstrations turned to rioting and spread across the region with attacks on immigration offices and Chinese settlements. The disturbances continued up to the revolution that overthrew the Manchu dynasty in 1911.

The Mongols of the Forty-Nine Banners, invoking the Manchu decree, informed the new republican government of their intention to secede. The government refused to recognize the decree and dispatched troops to suppress the national movement. In 1916 twenty-four of the Southern Mongol princes presented a memorandum to the government stating that unless the Manchu dynasty was to be restored, they were invoking the Manchu decree and intended to secede. Savage Chinese reprisals left entire principalities depopulated and thousands of Mongols dead in indiscriminate massacres.

The Japanese, in control of neighboring Manchuria* from 1931, encouraged resurgent Mongol nationalism in the 1930s. Taking advantage of chaotic conditions in China, the Southern Mongols declared the historic Forty-Nine Banners independent on 23 April 1934. The Japanese took control of the Mongol state in 1937. A Japanese-installed Mongol puppet government then declared the state's independence on 22 November 1937.

The puppet Mongol state collapsed with the Japanese defeat in 1945. A Mongol army of 80,000 moved south from the Communist Mongolian People's Republic to occupy the region. Welcomed as liberators from both the Japanese and the Chinese, the Mongols drove the last of the Japanese forces from the region and stopped the advances of both sides in the widening Chinese civil war. The Southern Mongols erected a provisional government and organized a referendum on unification with Mongolia. The Chinese Communists, embroiled in the civil war, appealed to their ally, Joseph Stalin. Stalin asserted his influence with the Mongolian government, effectively blocking Southern Mongol unification with Mongolia and forcing the withdrawal of the Mongol army from the region.

The Chinese Communists moved into the region in 1947, quickly suppressing the Southern Mongol nationalist movement. As part of the Communist's nationalities policy a theoretically autonomous Inner Mongolian region was created for the Southern Mongol people, and in 1949 the government granted the region the hypothetical right to secede from China. Government-sponsored immigration soon turned the Mongols into a minority in their traditional homeland. By 1951 the Southern Mongols were outnumbered by two to one, in 1957 they numbered only one in every eight, and in 1980 they constituted just one out of every seventeen people in the region.

Southern Mongol nationalism reemerged during the destruction and violence of the Cultural Revolution in 1966–67, but strict censorship kept details from reaching the West. The turbulence of the collapse of Communism in neighboring Mongolia in 1990–91 and the crushing of the democracy movement in China gave the resurgent nationalists new impetus. In March 1992 details leaked out to the West of growing unrest and nationalist demands for the government to honor the promise made in 1949.

*SELECTED BIBLIOGRAPHY:*
Collier, Mac. *China in Disintegration, 1912–1949.* 1977.
Orleans, Leo A. *Every Fifth Child: The Population of China.* 1972.
Rahul, Ram. *Mongolia, between China and the U.S.S.R.* 1989.

# SOUTHERN SUDAN

Imatong; New Sudan; Anyidi; Azania

CAPITAL: *Juba*

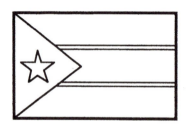

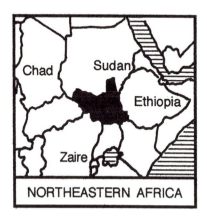

NORTHEASTERN AFRICA

SOUTHERN SUDAN

*POPULATION:* (95e) 6,940,000 : 7,000,000 Southern Sudanese in Sudan. MAJOR NATIONAL GROUPS: (95e) Southern Sudanese 96% (Dinka 43%, Nuer 18%, Azande, Shilluk, Bari, Anauk, smaller groups), other Sudanese. MAJOR LANGUAGES: Jieng, Naath, Zande, English, Arabic. MAJOR RELIGIONS: (95e) animist 67%, Christian 28%, Sunni Muslim. MAJOR CITIES: (95e) Juba 250,000, Wau (Waw) 180,000, Malakal 150,000, Abiye 135,000, Torit 50,000, Rumbek 40,000, Bor 35,000, Uwayi 30,000, Yei 20,000, Yambio 20,000.

*GEOGRAPHY:* AREA: 250,215 sq.mi.-648,225 sq.km. LOCATION: Southern Sudan lies in the southern part of Africa's largest state, Sudan, occupying a lowland region traversed by the White Nile and its tributaries and characterized by the Great Sudd Swamp and extensive rain forests. POLITICAL STATUS: Southern Sudan has no official status; the region forms the provinces of Bahr el Ghazal, Eastern and Western Equatoria, Lakes (El Buheyrat), Jonglei (Sobat), and Upper Nile of the Republic of the Sudan.

*FLAG:* The Southern Sudanese national flag, the flag of the national movement, is a horizontal tricolor of black, red, and green, the stripes divided by narrow white stripes, bearing a pale blue triangle at the hoist charged with a large, five-pointed red star.

*PEOPLE:* The Southern Sudanese people encompass a large number of black African tribes related to the peoples of the neighboring countries, but not to the Arabs and Arabized peoples of northern Sudan. The major Southern Sudanese tribes include Nilotic peoples in the northern districts, Dinka, Nuer, Shilluk, and Anauk; Nilo-Hamitic tribes in the south, Bari, Murle, Didinga, Boya, Toposa, Lotuko, Mundari, and Kabwe; and Sudanic tribes in the southwest, Azande, Kreisch, Bongo, Moro, and Madi. The majority of the Southern Sudanese people speak English as a lingua franca, as thirty-two major languages are spoken in the region. Most of the tribes retain traditional beliefs, with a large and influential Christian minority in the region.

*THE NATION:* The original "Land of the Slaves," Egyptian slavers knew the region as early as 2800 B.C. The present tribes, most believed to have settled in the region before the tenth century A.D., remained divided into tribal groups, engaging in intertribal warfare and cattle raids. Protected by formidable natural barriers and with little contact from the outside world, the tribes retained a nomadic existence adapted to the annual migrations of their cattle herds, the local measure of wealth.

Muslims, searching for slaves and ivory, began to penetrate the swampy Sudd in the 1840s, followed by European explorers who claimed the region on behalf of colonial empires. In 1874 the United Kingdom decreed an end to slavery and launched military campaigns against the Arab gangs that had already devastated many tribes.

Conflicting European territorial claims brought Britain and France close to war in 1897. Two years later Britain's territorial claim was confirmed by international agreement. Favoring indirect rule through the traditional tribal leaders, the British separated the region from the Arab-dominated northern districts of Sudan. Although Sudan officially remained a unified territory under its own colonial administration, the southern districts were effectively governed as separate territories. In 1928 the last of the southern tribes to resist British control submitted to the colonial authorities.

Tribal leaders united in 1950 to form the Southern Liberation Party, which advocated federal status within Sudan and an equal share of the development programs. Southern resistance to Arab domination became a major impediment to Sudanese independence in the 1950s. The British authorities favored a plan to give the southern tribes an opportunity to decide their own future. Under intense pressure from the oil-rich Arab states, they finally agreed to the integration of the southern provinces in a unified, independent Sudanese state in spite of the impassioned opposition of the southern tribal leaders.

Southern troops mutinied as tensions escalated in 1955 and killed their Arab officers and several hundred Arab civilians. The mutiny set off anti-Arab violence across the region. In spite of the growing crisis in the South, Sudan became independent in 1956.

The Arab-dominated Sudanese government, viewed by many southerners as the new colonial power, refused all concessions to southern self-rule. The government's uncompromising position finally provoked a widespread rebellion in 1962. The rebels soon split along tribal lines, and the national movement splintered into a number of rival groups. The largest organization, supported by the majority Dinka and Nuer tribes, attempted to create an independent state, Anyidi, in 1969. Sudan's Arab rulers finally agreed to southern autonomy and a regional parliament in 1972, ending a decade of civil war.

Relations between the southern peoples and the government deteriorated rapidly following the division of the region into three separate provinces in 1981, a clear violation of the autonomy agreement. In late 1983 the government officially extended strict Muslim Sharia law to the south, ending the last vestiges of Western law and justice. Rebellion again erupted in the region, which, with only seventeen miles of paved roads, quickly declined into a premodern condition.

The rebels, in control of all but the main towns by 1987, were unable to provide for the civilian population. In the first five years of the renewed rebellion, over 2 million fled the fighting, leaving behind over 250,000 dead of starvation and disease. Southern leaders accused the Sudanese government of blocking international aid to terrorize and starve the southern region into submission.

The lack of tribal unity, a major obstacle to final victory, led to serious splits in the rebel ranks in late 1991, mostly between factions favoring autonomy and their opponents that advocated an independent Southern Sudan. The tribal splits involved not only tribes such as the Toposa, armed by the Khartoum government, but the two largest ethnic groups, the Dinka and the Nuer. Several rival nationalist groups emerged from the movement's factional rift.

In March 1992 a government offensive, the largest in decades, pushed south on four fronts, the advance aided by the split in the rebel leadership. The southern rebellion, which has continued for all but ten of the years since Sudanese independence in 1956, was originally launched to win equality and autonomy for the southern tribes, but, with over 600,000 dead just since 1983, the conflict has became a war of survival.

In September 1993 the neighboring states of Ethiopia, Eritrea, and Uganda acted as mediators in talks between the government and the southern leaders. The negotiations collapsed almost as soon as they opened over southern demands for self-government. In February 1994 the government launched an offensive across the southern provinces. The advance, adding to the chaos already created by the southern factional fighting, created another 150,000 refugees who fled the renewed fighting. The conflict, complicated by the tribal factionalism in the South, continues to widen the gap between the two halves of Sudan.

*SELECTED BIBLIOGRAPHY:*

Deng, Francis, and Prosser Gifford. *The Search for Peace and Unity in Sudan.* 1987.
Rienner, Lynne. *Sudan, 1898–1989: The Unstable State.* 1990.
Voll, John N., and Sarah P. Voll. *The Sudan: Unity and Diversity in a Multicultural State.* 1985.
Wai, Dunstan. *The African-Arab Conflict in the Sudan.* 1981.

# SOUTH KASAI

**Kasai; Lubaland**

*CAPITAL: Mbuji-Mayi*

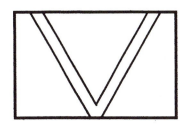

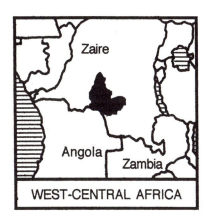

*POPULATION:* (95e) 6,365,000 : 4,650,000 Baluba (Luba) in Zaire. MAJOR NATIONAL GROUPS: (95e) Baluba (Luba) 63%, Benelulua (Lulua) 30%, other Zaïrean. MAJOR LANGUAGES: Luba-Lulua (Chiluba), French, Tetela, Songye. MAJOR RELIGIONS: Roman Catholic, animist. MAJOR CITIES: (95e) Kananga 725,000, Mbuji-Mayi 675,000 (1,200,000), Tshikapa 175,000, Kabinda 120,000, Mwene Ditu 90,000, Gandajika 75,000, Ilebo 65,000, Demba 55,000, Luebo 50,000, Mweka 50,000.

*GEOGRAPHY:* AREA: 96,256 sq.mi.-249,367 sq.km. LOCATION: South Kasai occupies the heavily wooded basin of the Kasai River and its tributaries in south-central Zaire, a region of rain forests and lowlands. POLITICAL STATUS: South Kasai has no official status; the region forms the province of Kasai Occidental and the southern half of Kasai Oriental of Zaire.

*INDEPENDENCE DECLARED:* 9 August 1960.

*FLAG:* The South Kasaian national flag, the flag of the former republic, is a green field bearing a large yellow V, centered, enclosing a red triangle. OTHER FLAG(S): The flag of the national movement is a horizontal bicolor of red over green bearing a large yellow V, the point touching the center bottom.

*PEOPLE:* The South Kasaians, comprising the Luba and Lulua tribes, speak dialects of the same Bantu language of the Benue-Niger language group. The two peoples formed one tribe until the seventeenth century, and, although they remain separate, the Luba centered on Mbuji-Mayi and the Lulua on Kananga, they have greatly increased ties and cooperation since the chaos of the 1960s.

Smaller Bantu tribes and a small European minority, mostly engaged in the important mining industry, make up the remainder of the population of the region.

*THE NATION:* Bantu peoples settled the region before the fifth century A.D., establishing numerous small clan and tribal states. In the eighth and ninth centuries an elaborate culture evolved, based on mining and trade. Kongolo, a local chief, began to expand his territory by conquering neighboring chiefdomships in the early fifteenth century. Kongolo's son, Kalala Ilunga, completed the unification of the Luba kingdom. The powerful Luba state controlled extensive territories in present Zaire and Angola, including a number of tributary states.

Around 1600 the kingdom fell to the Lunda kingdom of Katanga* but soon broke away, only to disintegrate through internal dissension and civil war. The Luba people split, the Lulua organizing as a separate tribe. A number of small successor states, tributary to the Katangan king, were visited by European explorers in the 1850s and 1860s. The Europeans reported a decayed empire rich in diamonds and other valuable minerals.

The Belgians, extending their territorial holdings east from the Congo River, penetrated the region in the 1870s and 1880s. In 1885 the Belgians formally laid claim to the Luba homeland. Their land occupied by Belgian troops in the 1890s, the Luba submitted to colonial rule. Mining companies quickly formed to exploit the rich diamond and mineral deposits.

The Luba readily adapted to European culture and education. Expanding throughout most of the Kasai region in the 1920s and 1930s, the Luba began to move into the Lulua territory. The Luba rapidly became the largest ethnic group living in the Lulua's traditional capital, Luluabourg (Kananga). While the Lulua remained a mostly rural people, the Luba urbanized and moved into positions in the local administration.

Elections for local city councils in 1957 gave the peoples of the Belgian Congo their first taste of democracy. Long prohibited, political parties quickly formed, many based on tribal and regional loyalties. Anticipation of Belgium's announced intention to grant independence to the Congo reactivated old tribal and regional rivalries.

Violence between the Luba and Lulua escalated rapidly as chaos overtook the huge Congo territory. To escape the vicious tribal violence, over a million Luba fled back to their homeland in south Kasai in 1959–60. With the Congo government unable or unwilling to protect them, the Luba increasingly espoused nationalist demands for separation. The Luba nationalist leader, Albert Kalonji, proposed a federation of autonomous states in the Congo, but the Belgian authorities ignored the suggestion in their haste to grant independence.

On 30 June 1960 Congo received its independence amid growing turmoil and violence. In Kasai, armed Lulua launched attacks on Luba areas and overran Luluabourg, setting off a vengeful civil war. The Belgian military intervened only to rescue endangered Europeans. Encouraged by the secession of neighboring Katanga, Albert Kalonji declared the independence of South Kasai on 9

August 1960. Backed by the Belgian mining companies and Belgian volunteers, the Luba retook Luluabourg and repulsed advancing United Nations troops.

Troops of the reorganized Congolese government invaded the state in December 1961. The Congolese were driven back but returned in September 1962. Thousands died in the pacification of South Kasai in the spring of 1963. Refugees fleeing into Angola formed antigovernment groups that continued to harass the border region for several years.

Mobutu Sese Seko, installed as Congo's president in 1965, received the support of the West as an anti-Communist ally in Central Africa. Mobutu established a one-party dictatorship that allowed little dissent or opposition. Over the next decades the Mobutu regime systematically looted the once-rich country, which Mobutu renamed Zaire.

Kasaian nationalism resumed in the early 1970s. By 1975 incomes and development in the region had fallen to less than half the levels of the secession period. Revenues from Kasai's industrial diamonds, some 90% of the world's total, disappeared in Kinshasa, while no new roads, construction, or maintenance was undertaken in the area for over three decades.

The termination of the Cold War tensions greatly reduced the West's automatic support of Mobutu, his former allies rapidly reducing military aid and demanding political and economic reforms. Mobutu's loosening hold on the huge country fueled the rapid growth of regional and national sentiments in many areas.

The resurgent nationalism in neighboring Katanga turned to ethnic violence in 1990. The Katangans turned on the Kasaian minority in the region. Many of the Lubas and Luluas living in Katanga were educated city dwellers, easy targets for Katangan mobs. Violent attacks on the Kasaians forced thousands to flee back to Kasai, the refugees provoking a rapid increase in Kasaian nationalism. The two South Kasaian peoples, the Luba and Lulua, have renewed ties in the face of the common threat, and both peoples have supported the growing national movement. Renewed attacks in Katanga in 1993–94 left thousands of Kasaian dead and injured and swelled the refugee population to over 30,000.

The revival of ethnic rivalries, fanned by the Mobutu regime, which claims that only President Mobutu can hold the country together, has renewed the Kasaian nostalgia for the pre-independence peace and security of the Belgian colonial period. The Kasaian's shared poverty in a region that should be one of Africa's most prosperous is the prime movement in the reconciliation of the Luba and Lulua, and the renewed violence and "ethnic cleansing" of the 1990s are fueling the renewed nationalist sentiment and calls for the revival of South Kasai.

*SELECTED BIBLIOGRAPHY:*
Ingham, Kenneth. *Politics in Modern Africa: The Uneven Tribal Dimension.* 1990.
Ngongola-Ntalaja. *Crisis in Zaire.* 1988.
Schuyler, Philippa. *Who Killed the Congo?* 1962.
Wormersley, Harold. *Legends and History of the Luba.* 1984.

# SOUTH MOLUCCAS

**Maluku Selantan**

*CAPITAL: Amboina (Ambon)*

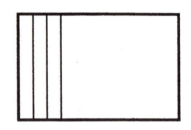

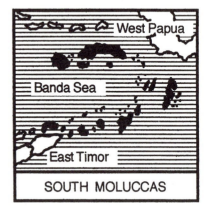

*POPULATION:* (95e) 1,296,000 : 1,250,000 South Moluccans (Ambonese) in Indonesia and another 45,000 in exile in the Netherlands. MAJOR NATIONAL GROUPS: (95e) South Moluccan (Ambonese) 97%, other Indonesian. MAJOR LANGUAGES: Ambonese, Dutch, Bahasa Indonesia. MAJOR RELIGIONS: Protestant, Roman Catholic, Sunni Muslim. MAJOR CITIES: (95e) Amboina (Ambon) 140,000 (234,000), Tual 61,000, Amahai 50,000, Saparua 33,000, Saumlaki 30,000, Namlea 20,000.

*GEOGRAPHY:* AREA: 19,266 sq.mi.-49,912 sq.km. LOCATION: The South Moluccas are an island group spread across the Banda Sea between East Timor* and West Papua* in the eastern islands of Indonesia. POLITICAL STATUS: The South Moluccas has no official status; the islands form the southern districts of the Indonesian province of Maluku (Moluccas).

*INDEPENDENCE DECLARED:* 25 April 1950.

*FLAG:* The South Moluccan national flag, the flag of the national movement, is a red field with three vertical stripes of black, white, and green at the hoist.

*PEOPLE:* The South Moluccans, also known as Ambonese, are a people of mixed Malay, Papuan, Dutch, and African background, speaking a Malayo-Polynesian language with Dutch, Portuguese, and African admixtures. The majority of the South Moluccans are Protestant, with smaller Roman Catholic and Sunni Muslim minorities. The island culture, through close contact during the colonial period, has incorporated more European influences than the neighboring Indonesian peoples. An exile community has lived in the Netherlands since the early 1950s.

*THE NATION:* The original inhabitants, a Papuan people called Afuros, were absorbed or pushed into the island interiors by ancient Malay settlers. Often ruled by the powerful Hindu empires that dominated the islands to the west, the earlier religions had mostly given way to Islam in the fifteenth century. Valued for their produce, mainly exotic spices, the islands came under the rule of the powerful Muslim Sultanate of Ternate in the northern Moluccas soon after Islam spread through the region.

The Spanish expedition led by Magellan explored the islands in 1511–12, the sailors returning to Europe telling stories of the abundant spices so prized for preserving food. The Portuguese established trading posts in 1521 and won a virtual monopoly on the spice trade after defeating Ternate in a long war, 1550–87. Portuguese missionaries, expelled from the northern islands in 1574, began the Christian conversion of the southern islands.

The Dutch expelled the Portuguese in 1605 and annexed the southern Moluccas in 1660. A separate residency of the Dutch East Indies, the islands became a center of clove production. Dissatisfied with the Ambonese as workers, the Dutch authorities imported African slaves to work the clove plantations.

Converted to Protestant sects, the Ambonese became a favored people of the Dutch colonial authorities. Ambonese moved easily into the colonial administration and the army. Better educated and more prosperous than the other East Indians, the Ambonese readily adopted much of the Dutch European culture, further widening the rift with the neighboring Muslim peoples. In 1860 slavery was abolished, the freed slaves gradually absorbed into the Christian Ambonese community.

Fervently pro-Dutch, Ambonese nationalism in the early twentieth century focused on the creation of a separate Christian state in union with the Netherlands. In 1920 students formed the first nationalist organization, called the Ambonese Union. United with the northern residency, Ternate, to form a separate government of the Moluccas in 1927, serious religious conflicts developed in the region. The conflicts were aggravated by the growth of Muslim Indonesian nationalism in the northern Ternate region.

Overrun by the Japanese in 1942, the islands became the scene of an Ambonese guerrilla war against the invaders until the Japanese surrender in 1945. At the end of the war, Indonesian nationalists laid claim to all the islands of the Dutch East Indies. Vehemently opposed to Muslim rule, the Ambonese joined the returning Dutch forces to fight the Indonesian nationalists from 1945 to 1949.

A negotiated settlement finally allowed Indonesian independence as a federation of autonomous states in 1949. The Ambonese, persuaded to join the federation, won a provision for peaceful secession if they felt their interests were jeopardized. The Indonesian government, soon after independence, began to centralize the government over the objections of the islands beyond central Java. In 1950 the Ambonese announced their intention to secede from Indonesia. The Indonesian government retaliated by dissolving the local administration and imposing direct rule from Djakarta.

The Dutch-trained Ambonese army rebelled and drove the Indonesians from the islands. On 25 April 1950 the Ambonese leaders declared the independence of the South Moluccas and appealed to the United Nations and the Dutch government. The Muslim states blocked United Nations intervention, and the Dutch refused to be drawn into yet another Indonesian war. Abandoned, the South Moluccans prepared to fight for their independence. In November 1950 Indonesian troops invaded the breakaway state, setting off heavy fighting.

The Ambonese, faced with imminent defeat in November 1951, accepted a Dutch offer of humanitarian aid. The Dutch evacuated 12,000 South Moluccans threatened by Indonesian reprisals. Another 23,000 fled to neighboring Dutch New Guinea or Portuguese Timor. The Dutch government housed the refugees in former Nazi concentration camps in the Netherlands, where rebel leaders formed a government-in-exile. The South Moluccan revolt resumed in 1956, but, with most military leaders in exile in the Netherlands, the rebellion collapsed in 1958. In 1966 the Indonesians executed the captured former president of the South Moluccas as a warning to the South Moluccan nationalists.

The South Moluccan refugees in the Netherlands resisted assimilation and continued to work for the restoration of their republic. Young South Moluccans, born in Europe, formed the South Moluccan Liberation Front (SMLF) in 1973. In December 1975 radical militants attacked the Indonesian embassy and hijacked a Dutch train, holding scores of hostages to force Dutch support for a resurrected South Moluccan republic. In 1977 the group struck again, taking over a hundred children hostage at a Dutch elementary school.

In April 1990, on the fortieth anniversary of South Moluccan independence, thousands demonstrated in the Netherlands. The nationalists, inspired by the changes brought on by the end of the Cold War, compare the multiethnic Indonesian state to the fallen Soviet Empire.

Nationalism in the islands, dormant for decades, resurfaced in the early 1990s as Muslim militancy threatened their Christian heritage. Starting in 1992, a series of attacks on churches and Christian targets in Indonesia has fueled a resurgence of separatist sentiment. In late 1994 South Moluccan nationalists in the islands formed a working group with the nationalist forces of the neighboring regions of East Timor and West Papua to coordinate their response to the increasing violence against the ethnic and religious minorities in Indonesia.

*SELECTED BIBLIOGRAPHY:*

Hawthorne, Daniel. *Islands of the East Indies.* 1977.
Hyma, Albert. *History of the Dutch in the Far East.* 1953.
Palmer, L. H. *Indonesia and the Dutch.* 1962.
Van Kaam, Ben. *South Moluccans.* 1981.

# SOUTH VIETNAM

**Viet Nam Cong Hoa; Annam**

*CAPITAL: Saigon (Ho Chi Minh City)*

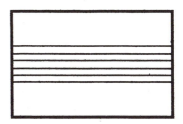

SOUTHEASTERN ASIA

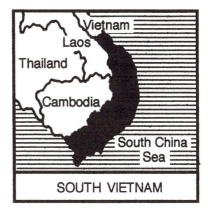

SOUTH VIETNAM

*POPULATION:* (95e) 32,977,000 : 29,500,000 South Vietnamese in Vietnam. MAJOR NATIONAL GROUPS: (95e) South Vietnamese 88%, Chinese 3%, Montagnard 3% (Moi, Muong, Man, Miao), Khmer 2%, Cham, other Vietnamese. MAJOR LANGUAGES: Vietnamese, English, French, Chinese, Khmer, Cham. MAJOR RELIGIONS: (95e) Buddhist 69%, Roman Catholic 13%, Cao Dai 10%, Hoa Hao 3%, Binh Xuyen 3%. MAJOR CITIES: (95e) Saigon (Ho Chi Minh City) 4,225,000 (6,100,000), Danang 840,000 (1,125,000), Hue 348,000 (420,000), Nhatrang 258,000, Quinhon 251,000, Longxuyen 225,000, Cantho 219,000, Camranh 201,000, Giadinh 195,000, Dalat 184,000, Bienhoa 163,000, Mytho 155,000, Phanthiet 148,000, Phuvinh 137,000, Rachgia 132,000, Vungtau 129,000, Banmethuot 122,000, Sadec 103,000.

*GEOGRAPHY:* AREA: 67,108 sq.mi.-173,854 sq.km. LOCATION: South Vietnam lies in southern Vietnam, a region of mountainous interior plateaus, the Central Highlands, and lowlands in the delta of the Mekong River and the coastal plains on the South China Sea and the Gulf of Thailand. POLITICAL STATUS: South Vietnam has no official status; the territory of the former republic forms the southern provinces of the Socialist Republic of Vietnam.

*INDEPENDENCE DECLARED:* 26 October 1955.

*FLAG:* The South Vietnamese national flag, the flag of the former republic, is a yellow field charged with three narrow, horizontal red stripes centered.

*PEOPLE:* The South Vietnamese are a Viet people speaking the southern dialects of Vietnamese, a language of the Annamese-Muong language group. Although there are only minor dialectical differences between the South and the

North Vietnamese, there are tremendous cultural and historical differences. The majority of the South Vietnamese are Buddhists, with large Roman Catholic and indigenous religious minorities. The Cao Dai sect mixes Buddhist, Islamic, and Christian teachings; the Hoa Hao and Bin Xuyen sects are based on Buddhist traditions. Large non-Viet minorities include Chinese in the urban areas, the tribal peoples of the Central Highlands, collectively called Montagnards, the Khmer in the west, and the Chams, the remnant of the highland Champa.*

*THE NATION:* The Viet peoples originated in the valley of the Red River in the North, the region conquered by the Chinese in 214 B.C. A separate Viet state, Annam, emerged in A.D. 923 and finally threw off Chinese domination in 1428. Expanding south, the Viet state, called Dai Viet, defeated the Chams in 1471, extending their authority to the area of present Danang.

The kingdom divided in 1558, with the north, later called Tonkin, ruled from Hanoi, and Annam in the south centered on Hue. The Annamese conquered the remainder of the Cham lands and in the eighteenth century conquered the Mekong River delta from the Khmers, taking control of the major city of Saigon in 1776. The Annamese dynasty was overthrown in 1778, and the south split into several small states. In 1802 a Hue general reunited the states in a reconstituted Annamese Empire.

French Catholic missionaries converted many to Catholicism in the early nineteenth century. In 1858 persecution of Catholics and mistreatment of French nationals provided a pretext for French intervention. A French military force occupied Saigon in 1859 and annexed the provinces of Cochin China between 1862 and 1867. Cochin China became a French colony in 1884, while the northern Viet states, Annam and Tonkin, became French protectorates.

A Vietnamese nationalist movement, based in northern Tonkin, became active in the early twentieth century. By 1930 the national movement, called the Vietminh, was dominated by the Communists and led by Ho Chi Minh. A guerrilla army during the Second World War, the Communists established a regime at Hanoi following the Japanese defeat. Ho Chi Minh laid claim to all of Vietnam, but the French refusal to give up Cochin China provoked war in 1946.

The French authorities supported a rival Vietnamese government in Saigon in early 1950 and in February 1950 requested U.S. military aid. By the time the French suffered a decisive defeat at Dien Bien Phu in May 1954, the United States was paying 80% of the French war costs. As a temporary expedient, Vietnam was partitioned, the south under a French- and American-supported government, and the north under Ho Chi Minh's Communists. Elections and reunification were scheduled for July 1956.

Nationalists in the south, fearing a Communist victory in the elections, declared the Republic of Vietnam independent on 26 October 1955. The new government won recognition by most of the world's non-Communist states. In 1956 war broke out between the two Vietnams, and a pro-Communist guerrilla group, the Viet Cong, began to operate in the south.

South Vietnam, in spite of despotic rule and the ongoing war, developed a dynamic capitalist economy aided by increasing American economic and military aid. U.S. troops, introduced in 1955, numbered over half a million by 1969. The war and the mounting American casualties provoked massive antiwar demonstrations and pressure to disengage. A 1973 truce, the Paris Peace Accords, formally ended the war. The U.S. troops were finally withdrawn, having suffered 57,000 casualties.

In early 1975 the North Vietnamese launched an offensive at Banmethuot. The South Vietnamese government ordered the defenders to withdraw. The withdrawal became a headlong retreat, the fleeing soldiers accompanied by hundreds of thousands of panicked civilians. In violation of the 1973 accords, the North Vietnamese rolled south, spreading chaos through the republic. Tens of thousands of southern officials, clergy, and intellectuals who failed to escape were ultimately imprisoned in reeducation camps.

Over the next decade a million South Vietnamese fled, mostly in small boats. Exile nationalists organized to aid the refugees and to work for the restoration of the republic. In 1979 the Communist government agreed to the "orderly departure" program, which has allowed some 100,000 to leave legally in exchange for foreign currency.

South Vietnamese nationalism, suppressed since 1975, reemerged in the late 1980s, strengthened by a wave of nostalgia for the former republic. The introduction of *doi moi*, economic reforms, in 1986, exacerbated the tensions between the richer, more dynamic southern provinces and the poorer, more economically backward north. In May 1992 the Vietnamese government adopted a new, highly centralized constitution to combat "archaic autonomy demands" and "localism." The authorities in March 1993 announced the arrest of a large number of South Vietnamese charged with attempting to destabilize and split Vietnam. The government crackdown on the southerners, particularly the Buddhist and Catholic clergy, provoked the largest antigovernment demonstrations in Saigon since the 1975 invasion.

The government euphemisms, the "opponent forces" and the "enemies within," are increasingly applied to the restive southerners. As economics replaced ideology as the prime nationalist issue in the 1990s, discontent and resentment fed a nationalist resurgence. Although South Vietnam is still thirty years ahead of the north in development, it has fallen way behind its former competitors during the so-called Golden Era, 1955 to 1975.

*SELECTED BIBLIOGRAPHY:*

Beresford, Melanie. *National Unification and Economic Development in Vietnam.* 1989.
Dacy, Douglas. *Foreign Aid, War and Economic Development, South Vietnam 1955–1975.* 1986.
Lindholm, R. W. *Viet-Nam: The First Five Years.* 1959.
Turley, Wm. S. *The Second Indochina War: A Short Political and Military History, 1954–1975.* 1986.

# SOUTH YEMEN

Aden

*CAPITAL: Aden*

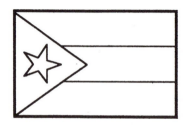

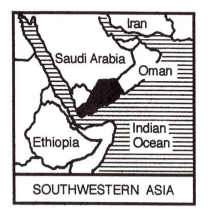

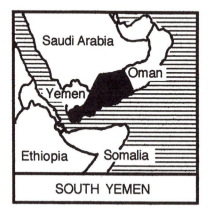

*POPULATION:* (95e) 2,532,000 : 1,950,000 South Yemenis in Yemen. MAJOR NATIONAL GROUPS: (95e) South Yemeni Arab 68%, Indian 11%, Somali 8%, Adeni Arab 7%, other Yemeni. MAJOR LANGUAGES: Arabic, English. MAJOR RELIGIONS: (95e) Sunni Muslim 91%, Christian 4%, Hindu 3.5%. MAJOR CITIES: (95e) Aden 335,000 (427,000), Mukhalla 184,000, Lahij 120,000, Seiyun 90,000, Shirh (Ash-Shirh) 55,000, Zinjibar 35,000.

*GEOGRAPHY:* AREA: 128,559 sq.mi.-333,054 sq.km. LOCATION: South Yemen lies in the southeastern Arabian Peninsula, an arid, hilly region with a sandy coast on the Arabian Sea stretching back to the highlands of Hadhramaut and the Arabian Desert beyond. POLITICAL STATUS: South Yemen has no official status; the region forms the provinces of the former republic unified with North Yemen in 1990.

*INDEPENDENCE DECLARED:* 7 September 1963; 30 November 1967; 21 May 1994.

*FLAG:* The South Yemeni flag, the flag of the former republic, is a horizontal tricolor of red, white, and black, with a pale blue triangle at the hoist, bearing a red, five-pointed star.

*PEOPLE:* The South Yemenis comprise several different groups, the South Yemenis in the southwest, the Hadhramautis in the northeast, and the Adenis, the majority in the city of Aden. The South Yemenis are a tribal people closely related to the North Yemenis but adhere to the Sunni branch of Islam; the northerners are mostly Zeidi Muslims. The Hadhramautis, or Hadranis, are the descendants of the inhabitants of a number of sultanates and emirates, the most conservative. The Adenis are the descendants of non-Yemeni Arabs who settled in Aden under British rule. The majority of the South Yemenis speak Arabic, with the Yemeni dialect the most frequently used. The legacy of British rule and the liberal policies of the former Communist government, South Yemeni women are among the most liberated in the Arab world. English is widely spoken by the Adenis and the non-Arab peoples.

*THE NATION:* In ancient times an advanced civilization evolved in the region, leaving behind extensive ruins in Hadhramaut, however, the region's early history remains a mystery. Ancient Adana, later called Aden, prospered as a port under Roman rule, but the interior tribes resisted entry by foreigners. The region declined into small tribal states in the early Christian Era. Muslim Arabs, in the first rapid expansion of Islam, overran the region and introduced the new religion to the pagan tribes between A.D. 628 and 632.

The expanding Ottoman Turks established a nominal rule over the region in 1538. Aden's port became a center of the Arab dhow trade between Africa and India and a prized way station on the newly opened European trade routes to the East. In the interior the tribal peoples were ruled by a number of sultanates and sheikdoms hostile to the outside world. Aden, under the autocratic rule of the sultans of Lahij, declined in the seventeenth and eighteenth centuries, an insignificant village when the British occupied the site in 1839.

Aden slowly revived under British rule to emerge as a major entrepôt on the Indian and Asian trade routes, particularly after the opening of the Suez Canal in 1869. The port of Aden rapidly became Britain's most important port east of Suez and a major military base. The port, populated by non-Yemeni Arabs and non-Arabs, was administered as part of British India. To safeguard the port, the British authorities, between 1882 and 1914, signed protectorate treaties with the nineteen tribal states, grouped into a distinct Aden Protectorate.

The British made Aden a separate Crown colony in 1935 and separated its government from British India in 1937. During World War II, the city, a heavily fortified naval base, was granted a legislative council with limited autonomy and in 1947 became fully autonomous. In February 1959 the western Hadhramaut states united in a British-organized Federation of South Arabia, joined by the remaining states between 1959 and 1965.

British moves to unite the federation of tribal states and the separate Aden colony provoked impassioned opposition in Aden. The sophisticated Adenis, fearing domination by the tribal majority, demanded separate independence. Nationalists organized rival groups, the Front for the Liberation of South Yemen (FLOSY) and the National Liberation Front (NLF).

In 1963 British preparations to merge Aden into the surrounding federation sparked a revolt by Adeni nationalists. On 7 September 1963 the nationalists declared Aden independent. British troops quickly ended the secession, and Aden became part of the federation, but with provision for secession after seven years if the Adenis felt that their interests were being harmed. Friction immediately provoked violence. The NLF and FLOSY nationalists mounted a terrorist campaign against the British and the federation government while fighting each other for control of Aden.

British troops withdrew from the entire federation, except turbulent Aden, in September 1967. In November fierce battles erupted in the city between the rival nationalist groups and between the nationalists and the British military. Unable to control the situation, the British withdrew from Aden. The NLF, having eliminated all rivals, seized control of the city and on 30 November 1967 declared the independence of South Yemen. The leftists in control of the city moved out to overthrow the rulers of the Hadhramaut states and to impose their version of socialism.

In 1969 a radical faction of the NLF seized control and rapidly nationalized the economy and strictly regimented daily life. The new government created the first Marxist state in the Arab world. In 1979 the government granted the Soviet Union the right to use the abandoned British naval base.

The Marxist regime, in spite of the liberalization of Muslim life, particularly the Marxist equality of women, ruined the economy. The sophisticated, urbanized Adenis abhorred the excesses of the government, labeled "Bedouin socialism." In January 1986 a coup attempt provoked fierce fighting in the city, leaving over 10,000 dead. In early 1989 the government admitted that the twenty-one-year experiment in Marxism had failed.

The collapse of Communist ideology forced the Marxist government of South Yemen to accept Yemeni unification proposed by the tribal leaders who controlled North Yemen. The economic ruins left by Marxist experimentation made the union near absorption by the north. On 22 May 1990 the two states merged. The South Yemenis, particularly the women, though impoverished, were relatively modern and vehemently resisted the control exercised by the near-feudal north.

The rifts between north and south widened immediately after unification. In the south the legacy of 137 years of British rule had shaped a separate national identity. In elections in May 1993, the more populous north prevailed. In August 1993 the southern leaders, buoyed by increasing oil revenues, pushed for the decentralization of the Yemeni government. Rebuffed by the Yemeni government, the South Yemenis moved toward secession. On 4 May 1994 fighting broke out between rival military units. On 21 May 1994 southern leaders declared the independence of South Yemen. After two months of civil war the victorious North Yemeni troops besieged Aden, bombarding the city from the hills around the port. The nationalists, though defeated by the northern military, remain a potent force in the region.

*SELECTED BIBLIOGRAPHY:*

Helfritz, Hans. *The Yemen: A Secret Journey.* 1958.
Sanger, Richard H. *The Arabian Peninsula.* 1954.
Zwemer, Samuel M. *Arabia: The Cradle of Islam, Studies in the Geography, People and Politics of the Peninsula.* 1980.

# TAHITI

**Polynesia; Society Islands**

*CAPITAL: Papeete*

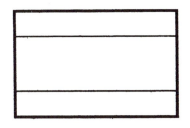

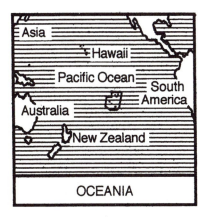

OCEANIA

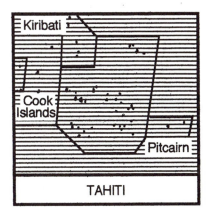

TAHITI

*POPULATION:* (95e) 212,000 : 162,000 Tahitians in French Polynesia. MA-JOR NATIONAL GROUPS: (95e) Tahitian 76%, Chinese 12%, European 10%, other Pacific Islanders. MAJOR LANGUAGES: French, Tahitian. MAJOR RE-LIGIONS: (95e) Protestant 60%, Roman Catholic 32%, Buddhist. MAJOR CITIES: (95e) Papeete 24,000 (105,000), Faa 23,000, Pirae 19,000.

*GEOGRAPHY:* AREA: 1,522 sq.mi.-3,943 sq.km. LOCATION: Tahiti, an archipelago of 130 islands, lies in the southwestern Pacific Ocean some 2,000 miles south of Hawaii.* POLITICAL STATUS: Tahiti, officially French Polynesia, forms an overseas territory of the French republic.

*FLAG:* The Tahitian national flag, the flag of the national movement, has three horizontal stripes of red, white, and red, the white twice the width of the red stripes. OTHER FLAG(S): The Tahitinui flag, the pan-Polynesian independence movement, has three horizontal stripes of blue, white, and blue with a centered cross of five gold stars.

*PEOPLE:* The Tahitians are a Polynesian people, descendants of early migrants from Southeast Asia, speaking a Polynesian language of the Malayo-Polynesian language group. On the major islands the Tahitians have some European and Chinese admixture, but on the outer islands the Tahitians have retained the traditional culture. The majority of the Tahitians belong to various Protestant sects, with an important Roman Catholic minority. The largest minorities are the Chinese, important in commerce, and the French, including those born in the islands and continental French, called Metros.

*THE NATION:* Tahitian tradition asserts that migrants from Samoa settled the islands in the fourteenth century A.D. Over the next century the settlers spread through the far-flung archipelago. Ruled by chiefs or kings, the widely separated islands often engaged in interisland warfare, the inhabitants of each island constituting a separate nation. The Polynesians constructed their villages along the water, the interiors of the islands remaining nearly uninhabited and often considered sacred.

Charted by Spanish explorer Alvaro de Mendaña in 1595, no other Europeans visited the islands until the expedition of Samuel Wallis sighted Tahiti in 1747. Captain James Cook arrived in 1769, accompanied by a party of scientists from London's Royal Society, and in their honor he named the archipelago the Society Islands. Again visited by Cook in 1773 and 1777, the idyllic islands figured in the drama of the *Bounty*, which visited the island in 1788. The inadvertent introduction of European diseases devastated the island populations, drastically reducing the population in the nineteenth century.

British and French missionaries became active in the islands in the early nineteenth century, their activities intensifying the European rivalry for influence. In 1841 Queen Pomare IV of Tahiti sought French assistance against British encroachment and two years later agreed to a French protectorate. In 1846 the queen appealed to the British in an attempt to block the French annexation of Tahiti. Queen Pomare died in 1877. Her son and heir, Pomare V, was forced to abdicate in 1880, the abdication followed by French annexation. In 1903 the various island groups were consolidated to form the colony of French Polynesia.

French economic development, accompanied by imported Chinese labor, generally ignored the native Tahitians until after World War II. The French government granted citizenship in 1946, as promised to ensure Tahitian loyalty in 1939. The authorities in the 1950s extended parts of the French welfare system to the islands.

Leftist French politicians in 1958 announced their support of an independent Tahitian republic. The proposal shocked the Tahitians, who marched in what was probably the world's first pro-colonial demonstration. In November 1958 the islanders voted to make their islands a French overseas territory administered by a governor and a territorial assembly.

The extension of French monetary subsidies and the advent of tourism dramatically raised living standards and ended the islands' long isolation during the 1960s. By the early 1970s the modernization of the islands had turned Tahiti into the most urbanized island in the South Pacific south of Hawaii.

Between 1962 and 1966 over 15,000 French soldiers, bureaucrats, and technicians arrived in the islands to prepare for French nuclear tests on Mururua Atoll, 500 miles southeast of the main island, Tahiti. The European influx and the beginning of nuclear tests spurred the growth of Tahitian nationalism. Over the next decade nationalist's demands for autonomy or independence gained widespread support in the islands.

Reports that the nuclear tests threatened the islands' health and environment mobilized the population in the 1970s and 1980s. Several nationalist groups formed and in 1976 demanded autonomy for the islands. A year later the more militant groups called for immediate independence, an end to nuclear testing in their homeland, and the repatriation of all mainland French. In 1980 elections, nearly all the island political parties, including those representing the Europeans, supported greater autonomy or independence.

The French authorities, not willing to lose the nuclear test site or the revenues from the lucrative tourist trade, rejected the autonomy demands. In 1982 a majority in the territorial assembly announced support for independence, and nationalist groups threatened a violent separatist campaign like that in Kanaki.* Fearing that the growing nationalist sentiment could erupt in violence, the French government hastily granted autonomy in September 1984. Nationalism, in the late 1980s, was tempered by the increase in the generous government subsidies that gave the islands the highest standard of living of all the islands between Hawaii and New Zealand.

The growth of militant separatist groups in the late 1980s pushed the islands toward independence. In June 1989 the nationalists called a boycott of local elections, which 90% of the voters honored. In June 1991 the imposition of new taxes set off rioting, the riots quickly turning into a mass pro-independence movement that eventually forced the resignation of the local French administration.

The desire for self-rule, seen as the only means to preserve Tahiti's ancient culture, has fueled the dramatic rise of Tahitian nationalism. However, even though there is widespread support for independence, the French monetary subsidies may prove too difficult for Tahiti's prosperous and sophisticated population to give up.

*SELECTED BIBLIOGRAPHY:*
Firth, Stewart. *Nuclear Playground.* 1987.
Levy, Robert I. *Tahitians: Mind and Experience in the Society Islands.* 1975.
Suggs, R. C. *The Island Civilization of Polynesia.* 1960.
Trumbull, Robert. *Tin Roofs and Palm Trees: A Report on the New South Seas.* 1977.

# TAIWAN

**Formosa**

*CAPITAL: Taipei*

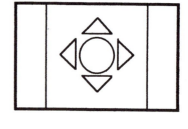

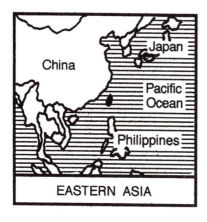

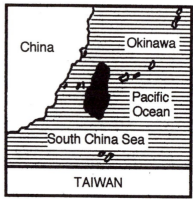

*POPULATION:* (95e) 21,336,000 : 18,200,000 Taiwanese in China. MAJOR NATIONAL GROUPS: (95e) Taiwanese 85%, Mainland Chinese 14%, Kaoshan 1%. MAJOR LANGUAGES: Taiwanese, Mandarin, Amoyese, Hakka (Kejia), English. MAJOR RELIGIONS: Taoist, Buddhist, Confusionist, Christian. MAJOR CITIES: (95e) Taipei 2,571,000 (7,504,000), Kaohsuing 1,346,000 (1,940,000), Taichung 685,000, Tainan 674,000, Chilung 408,000, Hsinchu 322,000, Chiai 280,000, Chungli 234,000, Taoyuan 211,000, Pingtung 166,000 (238,000), Changhua 166,000 (212,000), Hualien 125,000, Fengyuan 120,000 (162,000), Lukang 120,000, Yangmei 116,000, Pingchen 111,000, Chutung 110,000, Nantou 106,000, Miaoli 105,000, Shulin 100,000.

*GEOGRAPHY:* AREA: 13,895 sq.mi.-35,997 sq.km. LOCATION: Taiwan lies in the South China Sea, a large, mountainous island north of the Philippines and south of Japan and ninety miles east of the Chinese Mainland across the Taiwan Strait. POLITICAL STATUS: Officially, Taiwan forms a province of the Republic of China, since 1949 the only Chinese province controlled by the republic's government. The government of the rival People's Republic of China considers Taiwan a province in rebellion against the rightful government of China.

*INDEPENDENCE DECLARED:* 23 May 1895.

*FLAG:* The Taiwanese national flag, the flag of the nationalist movement, is a white field flanked by vertical blue stripes and bearing a centered green disc surrounded by four green triangles. OTHER FLAG(S): The flag of the Republic of China is a red field bearing a blue canton on the upper hoist charged with a white, twelve-rayed sun. The flag of the largest Taiwanese national party, the

Democratic Progressive party, is a green field divided by a centered white cross bearing a green map of the island at the center of the cross.

*PEOPLE:* The Taiwanese are a Chinese people, descendants of early migrants from the mainland provinces, speaking a Min dialect closely related to the language spoken in mainland Fujian. The island's language and culture have absorbed many non-Chinese influences from the indigenous Malay minority, the Kaoshan, the Europeans and Americans, and from the Okinawans and Japanese who controlled the island for various periods of its history. The large Chinese minority, called Mainland Chinese, arrived in 1949 and mostly speak Mandarin, the official language. The majority of the Taiwanese adhere to traditional religions; however, there is an important Christian minority.

*THE NATION:* The island, inhabited by Malay tribes related to the inhabitants of the Philippines to the south, began to receive settlers from the Chinese mainland in the seventh century A.D. In the next centuries small groups continued to cross the narrow strait, the growing Chinese population gradually forcing the Malays into the eastern mountains. In the seventeenth century thousands of refugees fleeing mainland upheavals settled on the island.

Portuguese sailors sighted the island in 1590, calling it Ilha Formosa, the Beautiful Island. In 1624 the Dutch established forts in the south and in 1641 gained control of the entire island. Koxinga, a Chinese general fleeing the Manchu conquest of China, expelled the Dutch in 1662 and established an independent kingdom. Manchu forces from the mainland conquered the island and added it to their Chinese Empire in 1683.

The Taiwanese, having developed independently of the mainland, resented Chinese domination and attempted to throw off Manchu rule in 1721. Brutally crushed by imperial troops, the uprising and its aftermath sparked a tradition of antigovernment and antimainland tendencies.

Japan, expanding rapidly during the late nineteenth century, became interested in the island's potential, one of the reasons for war with China in 1895. Resisting the cession of the island to the victorious Japanese, the Taiwanese declared the island independent on 23 May 1895 and appealed for international support to save their island from a colonial occupation. The Japanese quickly suppressed the republic and all Taiwanese opposition.

Exploited for the Japanese home market, the undeveloped island was organized with new transportation systems, industries, and cities. Without attempting mass Japanese settlement, the colonial administration pressed assimilation and the use of the Japanese language in daily life. The Kuomingtang (KMT), the National Party, in control of China following the overthrow of the Manchu dynasty in 1911, was increasingly caught up in a spreading civil war with the Chinese Communists and ignored the situation on Taiwan.

The island taken from the defeated Japanese by American troops in 1945, the Americans turned it over to their ally, the Chinese Nationalist government. The nationalists established the island as a safe base in the civil war that resumed on the mainland in 1945.

A provincial government installed by the National government used harsh measures to put down Taiwanese nationalist sentiment. In 1947, careful to profess continued support of the Nationalist government, the Taiwanese rebelled against the brutal provincial government. In spite of the rebels' appeals for the removal of the provincial authorities, the Nationalist government of Chiang Kai-Shek withdrew 10,000 troops from the fight against the Communists and sent them to pacify the island. Savage reprisals left 28,000 dead, generating Taiwanese bitterness and resentment that continue to the present.

The Communist victories in 1948 and 1949 sent a flood of refugees fleeing to the island from all over China. In December 1949 Chiang Kai-Shek's Nationalist government fled to the island. By 1950 over 2 million Nationalist supporters had arrived on Taiwan. Even though the Nationalist government controlled just one province, Taiwan, it maintained that it represented the only legitimate government of all China. The National government imposed martial law on the island, banned all political parties except the Kuomingtang, outlawed the Taiwanese language in favor of Mandarin, and persecuted Taiwanese nationalists as traitors.

The Nationalist government's increasing isolation in the 1970s, as many countries switched diplomatic recognition to the mainland's Communist government, provoked a resurgence of Taiwanese nationalism. The nationalists demanded that Taiwan, effectively independent since 1949, take its place among the countries of the world, but opposition to Taiwanese nationalism was the only point on which the Nationalists and Communists agree.

Demands for democracy in the late 1980s finally forced the government to lift martial law and the ban on the Taiwanese language in 1987. Taiwanese political parties, legalized after four decades of suppression, rapidly gained support, with calls for an end of Mainlander domination, democracy, and independence for the wealthy, industrialized state.

The island had incomes nearly equal to the mainland's in 1950, but by 1990 Taiwanese incomes were thirty times higher. Taiwanese nationalists claim that the islanders, not the Mainlanders, are responsible for Taiwan's economic miracle. Assured, rich, and unlike the Mainlanders, with no spiritual ties to the mainland, the Taiwanese see little need to maintain the Nationalist fiction that it is the only legitimate Chinese government. The often-repeated threat of a Communist invasion should Taiwan declare independence remains the major impediment to the Taiwanese desire to take their place among the nations of the world.

*SELECTED BIBLIOGRAPHY:*

Chiu, Hungdah. *China and the Quest of Taiwan.* 1973.
Copper, John F. *Taiwan: Nation-State or Province.* 1989.
Kerr, George. *Formosa Betrayed.* 1976.
Long, Simon. *Taiwan: China's Last Frontier.* 1990.

# TAMIL EELAM

Eelam

CAPITAL: Jaffna

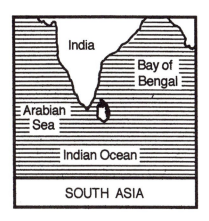

SOUTH ASIA

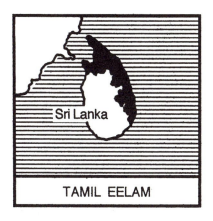

TAMIL EELAM

*POPULATION:* (95e) 4,431,000 : 3,450,000 Tamils in Sri Lanka. MAJOR NATIONAL GROUPS: (95e) Tamil 77%, Moor 12%, Sinhalese 10%. MAJOR LANGUAGES: Tamil, Sinhala, English, Arabic. MAJOR RELIGIONS: Hindu, Sunni Islam, Buddhist. MAJOR CITIES: (95e) Jaffna 170,000, Trin Komali (Trincomalee) 75,000 (100,000), Batticoloa 55,000, Kalmunai 40,000, Mullaittivu 35,000, Vavuniya 30,000, Mannar 20,000.

*GEOGRAPHY:* AREA: 7,269 sq.mi.-18,831 sq.km. LOCATION: Tamil Eelam occupies the coastal regions of the north and east of the island of Sri Lanka, just southeast of the Indian mainland. POLITICAL STATUS: Tamil Eelam has no official status; the region forms the Northern and Eastern provinces of the Democratic Socialist Republic of Sri Lanka.

*FLAG:* The Tamil national flag, the flag of the national movement, is a red field bearing a rising yellow sun at the bottom with eleven rays touching the outer edge of the flag at the top, hoist, and fly. OTHER FLAG(S): The flag of the largest nationalist organization, the Liberation Tigers of Tamil Eelam (LTTE), is a red field charged with a yellow, roaring tiger's head centered in a circle of short yellow rays.

*PEOPLE:* The Tamils are a Dravidian people, closely related to the larger Tamil population of the Indian mainland, concentrated in the state of Tamil Nadu.* The Tamils are divided into two distinct groups, the descendants of the early settlers and the Indian Tamils, brought to the island in the nineteenth century. The two groups are united by their Hindu religion and the Dravidian Tamil language. The largest minorities in the region are the Moors, Muslim descendants of Arab settlers in the east, and the Buddhist Sinhalese, part of the island's predominant population.

*THE NATION:* The island, inhabited by a primitive people, the Vedda, was conquered by Aryans from northern India in the fifth century B.C. The center of an advanced Buddhist civilization in the third century B.C., the island fell to Tamil invaders from the mainland in 253 B.C. The Hindu Tamils ruled the island as an aristocratic elite until the resurgent Buddhists overthrew Tamil rule in 101 B.C.

The Tamils of the mainland Chola Empire invaded and conquered the north of the island in A.D. 1017. The invaders spread across the northern districts and down the eastern coast, bringing the regions into the Hindu Tamil kingdom. In the twelfth century most of the remaining Sinhalese fled the Tamil kingdom, moving into the south and west as the Tamils expanded into the central districts of the island.

The Portuguese, taking advantage of the island's ethnic and religious conflicts, took control of several coastal areas in the north. The Portuguese gradually extended their authority and the Dutch ousted them from the entire island in 1658. The French and British established footholds on the island in the late eighteenth century, with the island coming under British colonial rule in 1796.

The British added the Tamil north to the Madras government on the mainland until 1833. United with the Buddhist Sinhalese south, the two parts of the island were organized under a separate colonial administration. Plantation agriculture, introduced in 1815, required additional labor with thousands of Tamils brought to Ceylon from the mainland between 1830 and 1850. To differentiate the newcomers, they were called Indian Tamils. Christian missionaries, restricted to the Tamil-populated Jaffna Peninsula, gave the Tamils a head start in education, heightening ethnic tensions as the Tamils advanced more rapidly than the Sinhalese.

The resentment of the majority Sinhalese manifested itself in bloody pogroms and the seizure of Tamil lands. The attacks on the Tamils continued up to World War II. Only the British presence prevented even more violent ethnic confrontations. The dour and hardworking Tamils prospered under British rule. Ethnic Tamils held most of the clerical and administrative jobs in the British colonial government.

The British began to dismantle the empire after World War II, granting Ceylon independence in 1948. The Sinhalese-dominated government immediately disfranchised the Indian Tamils, which greatly curtailed Tamil voting power and political strength. Official discrimination and a law establishing Sinhala as the only official language provoked serious clashes and rioting in 1956, 1958, and 1961. Determined to protect Tamil interests, Tamil national leaders petitioned the government for limited autonomy, backed by a nonviolent campaign for linguistic and cultural rights.

A new constitution approved in 1972 changed the island's name to Sri Lanka and institutionalized Buddhism as the state religion, completely ignoring Tamil rights. Moderate nationalists led a nonviolent resistance that government ministers dismissed as a mere nuisance. Militant nationalists, seeing no progress by non-violent means, demanded independence for the north and east of the island in 1975. Anti-Tamil rioting swept the island in 1975–76, with Sinhalese mobs attacking Tamil areas, murdering, raping, and looting Tamil businesses and homes. In retaliation the militant Tamil nationalists, led by the Liberation Tigers of Tamil Eelam, launched a terrorist campaign against Sinhalese domination.

Anti-Tamil rioting resumed in 1981–83, the worst ethnic violence in over thirty years of confrontations. Too late to stop the violence overtaking the island, the Sri Lankan government in 1984 offered the Tamils limited concessions and power-sharing. The Tamil leaders rejected the limited offer and repeated their demands for autonomy and an end to Sinhalese settlement in Tamil districts. Attempts to reach a negotiated settlement collapsed in 1985.

Heavy fighting between separatists, armed by Tamil sympathizers in India, and the Sri Lankan military swept the northern districts in 1986. To avert civil war, the Indian government brokered a compromise that provided for the disarming of the Tamil rebels under an Indian military force that would temporarily occupy the Tamil region. The pact, accepted by most Tamil groups, was rejected by the LTTE.

The Indian troops, at first viewed as the saviors of the Tamils, by late 1987 were seen as oppressors. Skirmishes between LTTE guerrillas and the Indian troops turned into running battles. Badly mauled by the separatist forces and no longer welcomed by the Sri Lanka government, the Indian government withdrew its troops in 1989–90.

The LTTE took control of much of the region as the Indians left, battling rival Tamil groups. Violence erupted between Tamils and the Muslim Moors unwilling to accept their rule in the Eastern Province, which, unlike the majority Tamil Northern Province, is 40% Tamil, 33% Moor, and 27% Sinhalese. By June 1990 over 30,000 had died in the ongoing conflict.

The LTTE extended the war to the Indian mainland, on 21 May 1991 assassinating Rajiv Gandhi, the prime minister of India during the Indian occupation of Tamil Eelam in the 1980s. In April 1993 an LTTE suicide assassin blew up Sri Lanka's president Ranasinghe Premadasa. The Tamil campaign for independence has become one of the world's most violent and long-lasting separatist wars and seemingly one of the most intractable.

*SELECTED BIBLIOGRAPHY:*

Leary, Virginia. *Ethnic Conflict and Violence in Sri Lanka.* 1981.
McGowan, William. *Only Man Is Vile: The Tragedy of Sri Lanka.* 1993.
Seevaratnam, Ned. *The Tamil Nationalist Quest and the Indo-Sri Lanka Accord.* 1989.
Spencer, Jonnathan. *Sri Lanka: History and the Roots of Conflict.* 1990.

# TAMIL NADU

**Tamilnad**

*CAPITAL: Madras*

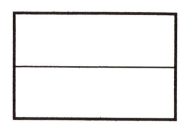

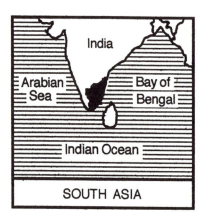

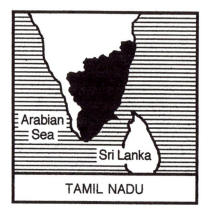

*POPULATION:* (95e) 57,714,000 : 62,500,000 Tamils in India. MAJOR NATIONAL GROUPS: (95e) Tamil 83%, other Indian. MAJOR LANGUAGES: Tamil, Telugu, Kannarese, Malayalam, English. MAJOR RELIGIONS: (95e) Hindu 91%, Sunni Islam, Christian. MAJOR CITIES: (95e) TAMIL NADU: Madras 3,996,000 (6,802,000), Madura (Madurai) 1,153,000 (1,274,000), Koyambattur (Coimbatore) 1,131,000 (1,200,000), Selam (Salem) 431,000 (532,000), Tiruchchirappalli 425,000 (873,000), Tuttukkudi (Turicorin) 237,000 (313,000), Thanjavur (Tanjore) 228,000, Nagercoil 211,000 (285,000), Velluru (Vellore) 203,000 (315,000), Dindigul 204,000, Tiruppur 189,000 (260,000), Tirunelveli 181,000 (460,000), Erode 171,000 (358,000), Kuddalur (Cuddalore) 159,000 (261,000), Ambattur 148,000, Rajapalaiyam 134,000 (245,000). PONDICHERRY: Puttucheri (Pondicherry) 184,000 (342,000).

*GEOGRAPHY:* AREA: 50,178 sq.mi.-129,996 sq.km. LOCATION: Tamil Nadu lies in southeastern India, a broad plain backed by mountains, the Eastern Ghats, which extend from the northeastern border to the Nigiri Hills in the southwest. POLITICAL STATUS: Tamil Nadu forms Tamil Nadu State and the union territory of Pondicherry of the Republic of India.

*FLAG:* The Tamil national flag, the flag of the national movement, is a horizontal bicolor of red over black.

*PEOPLE:* The Tamils are an ancient Dravidian people, generally smaller and darker than the Aryan peoples of northern India, speaking a Dravidian language with a literary tradition that goes back over 2,000 years. The majority of the

Tamils are Hindu; however, the Tamil Hindu rites and strictures are much less rigid than the Brahminism prevalent in the northern Aryan Indian states, with a less structured caste system and more liberal interpretation of Hindu traditions. Religious minorities include Sunni Muslims and Christians. Ethnic minorities in the region are mostly related Dravidian peoples and some 3 million tribal people.

*THE NATION:* Once dominant in almost all of present India, the Dravidian peoples of the vast Indo-Gangetic Plain were driven south by invasions of Aryan tribes from the Iranian Plateau between 2000 and 1700 B.C. The Aryan northerners adopted the religion of the Dravidians, but developed a form of Hinduism that enshrined the rigid caste system and elaborate priestly ritual rejected by the Dravidian peoples moving south to escape Aryan rule.

Powerful Tamil kingdoms, Pandya and Chola, emerged in the fifth century B.C. The Tamils halted Aryan incursions from the north while expanding their rule in the Dravidian south. Under powerful Chola kings the Tamils crossed the narrow strait to conquer the Buddhist island of Sri Lanka in A.D. 1017 and expanded to control vast areas of southern India. For over three centuries the Chola kings supported a flourishing social and economic life and a great flowering of Hindu Tamil culture. A declining power in the thirteenth century, in 1279 the kingdom fell to invading Muslims. A century later the resurgent Tamils drove the Muslims from their homeland.

The Portuguese established the first European base on the coast in 1519, beginning centuries of European encroachment. In 1639 the English opened a post at Madras, and the French founded a base at Pondicherry in 1673. The long European rivalry ended with the French expulsion from all but two small enclaves in 1763. The center of British power in southern India, Madras developed rapidly as one of the three cornerstones of British India.

The stability and peace of British rule generated an important Tamil cultural revival in the late nineteenth century, notable for a quality literature drawing on ancient traditions. A parallel growth of Tamil nationalism took hold in the early twentieth century. The first distinctly Tamil interest group formed in 1921. The first openly secessionist movement was espoused by a Tamil political party in 1925.

Tamil particularism gave way to Indian nationalism in the 1930s. The province of Madras, made a separate autonomy within British India in 1937, joined independent India as a state a decade later, in 1947. With the Indian government dominated by the Aryan northern states, Tamil nationalism resurfaced in the late 1940s with demands for autonomy. Nationalists in the 1950s promoted a united Dravidian state in southern India, but neighboring Dravidian peoples, with memories of past Tamil domination, rejected the proposal. Tamil nationalism gained support following the separation of the non-Tamil districts of Madras State into distinct linguistic states between 1953 and 1956.

The Dravida Munnetra Kazagham (DMK), anti-Aryan and anti-Brahmin, was formed by a coalition of nationalist and cultural groups in the late 1950s. Opposition to Hindi, a language spoken only in northern India, as India's national language, stimulated DMK support for secession. In 1965, following a series of violent pro-independence demonstrations in the region, the Indian prime minister, Jawaharlal Nehru, made the advocating of secession a criminal offense. The DMK, in order to operate legally, changed its focus to Tamil autonomy, the change ending the first serious threat to Indian unity in 1966.

The DMK won control of the state legislature in 1967 elections. The DMK-dominated state government curtailed the teaching of Hindi in the state, and in 1968 the legislature voted to change the state's name to Tamil Nadu, the Tamil Nation. In 1976 the Indian government dissolved the Tamil Nadu state government and accused the Tamil DMK of corruption and support for separatism. The government action began a long period of tensions between the Tamils and the Indian administration.

The Indian government's covert support for the separatists of Tamil Eelam* in Sri Lanka, while refusing to discuss greater Tamil autonomy in India, escalated the tensions in the 1980s. The government detained over 10,000 Tamils following antigovernment rioting in 1984, and two years later 19,000 were arrested after the disturbances and rioting resumed. In 1987 the Indian government intervened militarily in Sri Lanka, supposedly to protect the island's Tamil population. The Indian troops were soon involved in a war with the island's Tamil separatists. Reaction in Tamil Nadu raised nationalist sentiment to levels not seen since the secessionist crisis of 1965–66.

In January 1991 the federal government again imposed direct rule on Tamil Nadu and Pondicherry, accompanied by 15,000–20,000 arrests to prevent antigovernment violence. Rajiv Gandhi, the prime minister of India during the occupation of northern Sri Lanka in 1987–89, was assassinated by a Sri Lankan Tamil while on a visit to Tamil Nadu in May 1991, reportedly with the active participation of Indian Tamil nationalists. The assassination demonstrated the strengthening ties between nationalists on both sides of the Gulf of Mannar, the narrow body of water that separates the Indian Tamils from their kin in Sri Lanka. Since 1992 the Indian and Sri Lankan governments have increased their cooperation to oppose the growing Tamil nationalist movement in both countries.

SELECTED BIBLIOGRAPHY:

Chitty, Simon Casie. *Tamil Plutarch.* 1987.

Embree, Ainslee T. *India's Search for Identity.* 1988.

Fraser, T. M. *India, Culture and Change.* 1968.

Indhu, Rajagopal. *Tyranny of Caste: The Non-Brahmin Movement and Political Development in South India.* 1984.

Seevaratnam, Ned. *The Tamil National Quest and the Indo-Sri Lanka Accord.* 1989.

# TANNU TUVA

**Tuva Ulus; Touva; Urjanchai;
Uryankhai**

*CAPITAL: Kysylchoto (Kyzyl)*

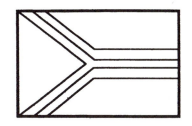

NORTHEASTERN ASIA

TANNU TUVA

*POPULATION:* (95e) 317,000 : 245,000 Tuvans in Russia and another 35,000 in adjacent areas of Mongolia. MAJOR NATIONAL GROUPS: (95e) Tuvan (Tuvinian) 65%, Russian 28%, Mongol 3%. MAJOR LANGUAGES: Tuvan, Russian, Mongol. MAJOR RELIGIONS: Lamaism (Tibetan Buddhist), Russian Orthodox. MAJOR CITIES: (95e) Kysylchoto (Kyzyl) 99,000, Turan 34,000, Ak-Douvarak (Kyzyl-Mazalyk) 15,000 (30,000).

*GEOGRAPHY:* AREA: 65,830 sq.mi.-170,544 sq.km. LOCATION: Tannu Tuva, geographically in the center of the Asian continent, occupies the valley of the lower Yenisei River in southern Siberia,* the valley surrounded by the Sayan Mountains on the north and the Tannu-Ula Mountains on the Mongolian border. POLITICAL STATUS: Tannu Tuva, officially called Tuva Ulus, forms a member republic of the Russian Federation.

*INDEPENDENCE DECLARED:* 18 December 1911; 14 August 1921.

*FLAG:* The Tuvan national flag, the official flag of the republic, is a blue field bearing a yellow triangle at the hoist outlined by narrow white stripes that extend in parallel stripes to the fly.

*PEOPLE:* The Tuvans are a people of mixed Turkic and Mongol background, physically resembling the Mongols but speaking a Turkic language of the North Turkic language group. Culturally and physically, the Tuvans are related to the Kyrgyz people of Kyrgyzstan in Central Asia and the neighboring peoples of Altai-Khakassia.* Traditionally herders, the Tuvans comprise several divisions, one of which, the Urjankhai, inhabits adjoining areas of Mongolia. The Tuvan religion is Lamaism, and the Dalai Lama of Tibet* is revered as the spiritual leader of the Tuvan nation. The only large minority in the region is the Slavs, mostly concentrated in the urban areas.

*THE NATION:* The region has been inhabited since ancient times, although little is known of its early history. The remains of an extensive irrigation system indicate a formerly settled agricultural society. The Tuvans were first mentioned in the chronicles of travelers of the tenth century A.D. A herder people living in clan groups ruled by hereditary or elected chiefs, the Tuvans inhabited the grasslands of the mountains north of the Silk Road, the ancient trade route between China and the Mediterranean.

Conquered by the Mongols of Genghis Khan in the thirteenth century, the Tuvans lived under Mongol rule for three centuries. The Mongol domination greatly changed the Tuvans' Turkic culture and physical appearance. The Tuvan tribes regained their independence in the sixteenth century but retained strong cultural and religious ties to the Mongol peoples. In 1757 the Manchus, the rulers of China, took control of the Tuvan territories. Called Urjanchai, the region was incorporated into the Manchu province of Mongolia.

Russians began to move into the territory as Manchu control weakened in the 1870s. Over the next decades several thousand Russians settled in the fertile river valleys. Russian influence gradually replaced Manchu authority. Tuvan nationalists, with Russian support, organized a government during the 1911 Chinese Revolution, which ended the Manchu dynasty. On 18 December 1911 the Tuvans declared the independence of the region from China. The state, called the Urjanchai Republic, rejected Chinese and Mongol claims and maintained a precarious independence up to World War I.

The Tuvans, bowing to the demands of the republic's influential Russian population, accepted Russian protection against renewed Chinese and Mongol claims when war began in Europe in 1914. The protectorate, administered as part of Russia's Altai region, reasserted its independence when revolution swept through Russia in 1917.

Local Bolsheviks in early 1918 supported a socialist revolution in the state, the conflict drawing the Tuvan homeland into the spreading Russian civil war. Devastated by over two years of heavy fighting, the state finally fell to Soviet rule in 1920. The Soviet authorities overthrew the feudal Tuvan lords, and on 14 August 1921 Tuvan and Russian socialists declared the state an independent people's republic.

Conflicting Mongol and Chinese claims and Soviet moves to annex Tannu Tuva pressed the Tuvans to reassert their independence in 1924. The dispute was turned over to an international mixed claims commission appointed to determine the state's future. The commission reaffirmed Tuvan independence in 1926, the state's sovereignty confirmed by treaties with neighboring states. In 1931 the Soviets forced the government to disfranchise the traditional ruling class and to reorganize as a Communist state, the world's third.

Tannu Tuva remained an independent Communist state until Soviet troops occupied the capital city in October 1944 during World War II, leading to the Soviet annexation of the country in 1945. Included in the Soviet Russian Federation as an autonomous province, the region remained a center of Tuvan agitation. The Tuvans won greater cultural freedom when the Soviet government raised the province to the status of an autonomous republic in 1961.

The liberalization of the 1980s allowed the Tuvans to reestablish long-forbidden ties to the neighboring peoples. The area was closed to foreigners for over two decades, but the ban was finally lifted in 1988, facilitating contacts with the outside world.

Tuvan nationalism gained support in the newly liberal atmosphere organized in opposition to the local Communist government. In June 1990 large demonstrations rocked the capital, the demonstrators demanding the dismissal of the local government and denouncing the illegal annexation of their state in 1945. In July and August 1990 demonstrators regularly clashed with Soviet police dispatched to regain control of the republic. The clashes left hundreds dead and injured. Over 3,000 ethnic Slavs fled the escalating violence in the republic.

The disintegration of the Soviet Union in 1991 raised demands for the resurrection of the Tuvan's former independent republic. In September 1991 Tuvan nationalist leaders acknowledged that, after nearly half a century of Soviet rule, the Tuvans suffered from a lack of trained administrators and that immediate independence would be impossible. However, pressed by the nationalist demands, the Tuvan government unilaterally declared Tannu Tuva a full republic within the Russian Federation as a first step to the restoration of the Tuvans' independence.

Local presidential elections in March 1992 consolidated the nationalist movement's influence in the republic. The growing national movement, while avoiding an open break, is gaining experience as the republic gradually slips from Moscow's control in the 1990s. The republic has developed close ties to the neighboring Republic of Mongolia since the ethnically and historically related Mongolians began to democratize in 1990.

Sacred scrolls, spirited away and hidden in 1921, were returned to a reopened Tuvan religious center in Kyzyl in late 1992. The return of the scrolls, the symbol of Tuvan religious devotion and sovereignty, is seen as yet another step to the restoration of the republic's former independence.

*SELECTED BIBLIOGRAPHY:*

Brodrick, Benson. *East of the Sun: The Epic Conquest and Tragic History of Siberia.* 1992.

Lattimore, Owen. *Mongol Journeys.* 1941.

McCagg, William O., and Brian D. Silver, eds. *Soviet Asian Ethnic Frontiers.* 1979.

Wood, Allen, and R. A. French. *The Development of Siberia's Peoples and Resources.* 1989.

# TATARSTAN

Tataria; Idel-Ural

*CAPITAL: Kazan*

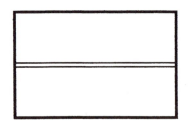

*POPULATION:* (95e) 4,353,000 : 6,620,000 Tatars in Russia. MAJOR NA-TIONAL GROUPS: (95e) Tatar 50%, Russian 41%, Udmurt 4%, Chavash 3%, Mari 2%. MAJOR LANGUAGES: Tatar, Russian, Chavash. MAJOR RELI-GIONS: Sunni Muslim, Russian Orthodox. MAJOR CITIES: (95e) Kazan 1,132,000 (1,234,000), Naberezhnyy Chelny 466,000 (529,000), Nizhnekamsk 207,000, Almetyevsk 137,000, Zeleny Dol (Zelenodolsk) 98,000 (143,000), Bugulma 92,000 (118,000), Novaya Pismyanka (Leninogorsk) 73,000, Chistopol 68,000, Elabuga (Yelabuga) 62,000 (115,000), Menzehinsk 50,000.

*GEOGRAPHY:* AREA: 36,255 sq.mi.-93,924 sq.km. LOCATION: Tatarstan lies in eastern European Russia, occupying the valleys of the Volga and Kama Rivers and rising to wooded uplands in the east. POLITICAL STATUS: Tatar-stan forms a member republic of the Russian Federation.

*INDEPENDENCE DECLARED:* 24 January 1918.

*FLAG:* The Tatar national flag, the official flag of the republic, is a horizontal bicolor of red over green, the colors separated by a narrow white stripe. OTHER FLAG(S): The flag of the Tatar national movement is a diagonal bicolor of green over red, divided lower hoist to upper fly, and bearing a centered yellow crescent moon, horns pointing down, and a five-pointed, yellow star.

*PEOPLE:* The Tatars, including the closely related Mishar, are a Turkic peo-ple speaking a West Turkic language of the Turkic group of Altaic languages. Russia's largest non-Slav minority, the Tatars are the most northerly of the Muslim peoples, although a majority of the Tatar population lives outside the republic, many in the now independent former Soviet Central Asian republics. Since 1991 there has been an influx of Tatars from the other areas of the former Soviet Union. An Orthodox Christian minority, the Kreshen, number 320,000 and have helped to maintain historic Tatar ties to the neighboring Finnic and Slav Christian peoples. The large Russian population is concentrated in the cities, although many are tied by marriage to the Tatar majority.

*THE NATION:* Nomadic Turkic tribes, the Tata, inhabited northeastern Mongolia in the fifth century A.D. Migrating west, the Tata first appeared in the lower Volga River basin in the eighth century. From the ninth to the twelfth centuries the Tatars formed a national state in the region, with its capital at Bolgary Velikiye. Mixing with the Finnic and Bulgar peoples of the Volga region, the Tatars' physical aspect became more European with each generation. Traders and migrants from the south converted the Tatars to Islam, traditionally in A.D. 922.

Conquered and absorbed by the Mongol Golden Horde in 1236, the Tatars participated in the Mongol conquests farther west. Following the disintegration of the enormous Mongol Empire, the Tatars established a successor state in the Volga-Kama region in 1445, the Khanate of Kazan. In 1502 the Tatars defeated the remnant of the Golden Horde and expanded west to the Ural Mountains. The powerful khanate extracted tribute from the Slav states west of the Urals as the price for their continued independence. Rich on tribute and trade, the khanate fostered a great flowering of Tatar culture, arts, and literature.

The Tatars' former vassals, the Russians, led by Ivan IV, called the Terrible, the grand duke of Moscow, invaded and conquered Kazan in 1552–53. Even though Ivan ruthlessly suppressed the Tatars' Islamic religion, the family of the last khan and the Tatar aristocracy were absorbed into the tsarist aristocracy, greatly facilitating the annexation of the vast region. The most advanced of the Turkic peoples, the Tatars became the middlemen between the imperial government and newly conquered Turkic peoples over the next three centuries. The Tatar administrators and officials dispersed to many parts of the expanding empire.

Tatar resistance to Russification and forced conversion to Orthodox Christianity generated sporadic revolts in the seventeenth and eighteenth centuries. The revolts prompted the tsarist administration to settle loyal Slavs in the region. In 1708 Kazan became the center of the Slavic colonization of the Volga basin. Thousands of Slav colonists settled in the area over the next century.

The resilient Tatars, despite steady pressure to assimilate, tenaciously clung to their language and culture. Their Islamic religion, banned for two centuries, was again allowed during the reign of Catherine the Great in the eighteenth century.

The Tatars by the 1880s had evolved a large middle class, the first Turkic people to do so. The high literacy rate and well-developed national culture stimulated a national revival in the late nineteenth century. The first openly nationalist group formed in 1906, advocating independence, socialism, and the expulsion of the Slavs from traditional Tatar lands.

Exempted from conscription until 1916, the Tatars felt little of the effects of World War I until revolution swept the empire in February 1917. As civil government collapsed, Tatar nationalists and moderate Slav Mencheviks took control of the region. Vehemently opposed to the atheism of the Bolsheviks following the October 1917 coup and threatened by advancing Bolshevik forces, the Tatar leaders declared independence on 24 January 1918. In April the Bolsheviks overran the breakaway state and suppressed the Tatar national movement.

Aided by the anti-Bolshevik Czech Legion, the nationalists routed the Bolsheviks. With the other non-Russian peoples of the Volga, the Tatars formed a federation, declared independent on 30 September 1918 as civil war spread through the area. In 1920 the victorious Soviets took control of the Tatar lands, which were absorbed into the new Soviet Russian Federation as an autonomous republic.

The discovery of extensive petroleum reserves during World War II hastened industrialization but drew in a large influx of Slav workers. By 1975 the Tatar population of the republic had fallen to just 37% of the total. Minority status quickened a national revival that converged with the liberalization of Soviet life in the late 1980s.

The disintegration of the Soviet Union in August 1991 sparked huge pro-independence rallies in Kazan. A referendum on sovereignty resulted in a vote of 61% favoring greater independence. The Tatar national movement led a campaign for separation, but more moderate groups advocated some form of continued ties to Russia. In March 1992 the Tatar government refused to sign a new federation treaty, and in November the Tatar parliament approved an amendment declaring Tatarstan a sovereign state freely associated with the Russian Federation.

The Tatar national leaders, in spite of growing pressure, stubbornly insisted that Tatarstan's relations with Russia and other states must be governed by treaty. In July 1993 the Tatars negotiated twelve bilateral treaties with Russia. In February 1994 the Tatar leaders of the republic approved the treaty that normalizes relations with the Russian Federation. The treaty, revised through two years of often acrimonious negotiations, covers a number of the points that the Tatars insisted on, including the recognition of Tatarstan as a sovereign state freely associated with the federation and includes a clause recognizing the republic's right to legal secession from the federation.

*SELECTED BIBLIOGRAPHY:*
Pushkarev, Sergei. *Self-Government and Freedom in Russia.* 1988.
Rorlich, Azade-Ayse. *The Volga Tatars: A Profile in National Resilience.* 1986.
Rywkin, Michael. *Russian Colonial Expansion to 1917.* 1988.

# TEREK

**Stavropolye; Stavropol**

*CAPITAL: Stavropol*

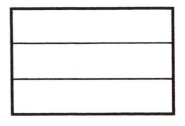

SOUTHEASTERN EUROPE

TEREK

*POPULATION:* (95e) 2,992,000 : 1,050,000 Terek Cossacks in Russia. MA-JOR NATIONAL GROUPS: (95e) Russian 45%, Terek Cossack 34%, Ukrainian 16%, Chechen 2%. MAJOR LANGUAGES: Russian, Cossack, Ukrainian. MAJOR RELIGIONS: Russian Orthodox, Sunni Muslim. MAJOR CITIES: (95e) Stavropol 337,000 (375,000), Nevinnomysk 117,000, Pyatiagorsk 115,000 (161,000), Kislovodsk 110,000, Yessintuki 85,000, Mineralny Vody 79,000, Georgiyensk 62,000, Budyonnovsk 58,000, Svetlograd 54,000.

*GEOGRAPHY:* AREA: 25,676 sq.mi.-66,518 sq.km. LOCATION: Terek occupies the Stavropol Plateau and the Terek River basin between the Kuma and Kuban Rivers in southern European Russia. POLITICAL STATUS: Terek has no official status; the region forms Stavropol Krai (territory) of the Russian Federation.

*INDEPENDENCE DECLARED:* 4 March 1918.

*FLAG:* The Terek national flag, the flag of the former republic, is a horizontal tricolor of black, green, and red. OTHER FLAG(S): The flag of the Terek Cossack national movement is a blue field crossed by a wavy, diagonal white stripe upper hoist to lower fly.

*PEOPLE:* The Terek Cossacks, the third largest of the Cossack peoples of Russia, are a Slavic people of mixed Slav and Caucasian background, speaking a dialect of the Cossack language that incorporates Russian, Ukrainian, Caucasian, and Turkic elements. Not recognized by the Russian government as a separate cultural or national group, the Terek Cossack claim to national status is based on their history, dialect, and geographic location. The Terek Cossacks are concentrated in the east and southeast of the territory; the remainder of the population is mostly Slav, Russian, and Ukrainian, with small Muslim minorities in the southern districts.

*THE NATION:* The Russians began to expand into the Muslim lands between the Black and Caspian Seas in the sixteenth century. The Slavs captured the region traversed by the lower Volga River in 1554–56, and pushed into the North Caucasus region in 1557. Although claimed by Russia in 1598, the Ottoman Turkish resistance to the Russians delayed colonization for over two centuries. In 1770 Cossacks established a fort at present Stavropol, which became the center of the Slavic colonization of the North Caucasus.

The Cossacks spearheading the Russian expansion governed themselves, under elected leaders called atamans, in return for military service and an oath of personal loyalty to the Russian tsar. The Cossacks moving south from Stavropol took the name of the river that marked their southern boundary, the Terek. In 1861 the Terek Cossack lands were combined with the newly conquered highlands of the Caucasus Mountains to form Terek Province. The lands of the Muslim Chechen and Ingush peoples north of the river were confiscated, and the Muslims were driven into the mountains.

The Cossack communities, holding their land in common, became large-scale landlords in the late nineteenth century. The abolition of serfdom in Russia sent a wave of landless peasants to the region, most settling on the Cossacks' communal lands as tenant farmers. The better educated and more prosperous Cossacks dominated a large area of the North Caucasus up to World War I, the Terek Cossacks charged with keeping the Muslims tribes included in Terek Province under close military control.

Formed into elite military units when war began in 1914, the Terek Cossack units sent to the front were decimated. In February 1917 the discontented Terek Cossacks, freed from their oath to the tsar by revolution, began to desert and return to their homeland. In March 1917 the Terek Cossacks elected a new ataman and formed a military government to fill the void as the tsarist civil government collapsed.

The Muslim peoples and the Terek Cossacks put aside decades of tensions as a new force threatened them both. The Bolshevik coup in October 1917 forced the peoples of the region to participate in a cooperative government. On 20 October 1917 the government declared its sovereignty as a temporary expedient, until a legitimate Russian government could be reestablished. The cooperative state, called Terek-Dagestan, collapsed in December 1917 as fighting broke out between the Terek Cossacks and the Chechen-Ingush, the Muslim tribes attempting to recover lands lost to the Cossacks in the eighteenth and nineteenth centuries.

The Terek Cossack military government on 4 March 1918 declared Terek independent of Bolshevik Russia. The Terek leaders tried to ensure the security of their new republic by proposing a union of the states seceding from Russia or, failing that, a federation with the Cossack Don* and Kuban* republics.

In November 1918 invading Bolsheviks overran the republic, beginning a reign of terror against the anti-Bolshevik groups. The Soviet authorities confiscated Cossack properties, and the lands were redistributed to the pro-Bolshevik Russians and their Chechen-Ingush allies. The Soviets allowed the looting of Cossack towns and villages while thousands faced eviction and persecution. In January 1919 the anti-Bolshevik forces drove the Soviets from the Terek, but by 1920 the victorious Red Army had regained military control of most of the region.

The Soviet authorities ended all the Cossacks' traditional privileges and dismantled the Terek Cossack military structure. The Terek Cossack leaders who failed to escape were deported or executed. The Soviets banned the use of the Cossack language and reclassified the Cossacks as ethnic Russians, carefully suppressing their separate history and culture. In 1936 the Cossacks were again allowed military training and to serve in the Red Army.

Fervently anti-Soviet, thousands of Terek Cossacks joined the Germans' anti-Communist crusade during World War II, often facing Cossacks serving in the Soviet forces. The German advance on the Caucasus reached Terek in 1942, the invaders often welcomed as liberators from hated Soviet rule. The Soviet authorities meted out punishment for the collaboration with deportations and mass executions in 1944–46, the oppression continuing until Stalin's death in 1953.

A Cossack cultural and national revival, begun among exile groups in Europe and the United States, started to slowly penetrate the closed territory in the 1960s and 1970s. The exile publication of the first Cossack dictionary, along with works on Cossack culture and history, stimulated a renewed interest in the suppressed Terek nation.

The revival accelerated in the late 1980s, the renewed national sentiment reviving the traditional hostility between the Terek Cossacks and the Chechen Muslims of Chechenia* to the south. In April 1990 serious ethnic clashes erupted as the conflict, frozen but not resolved by Communist rule, again became a factor in the politics of the region.

The disintegration of the Soviet Union in August 1991 split the growing national movement. One faction, centered on Stavropol, demanded official recognition as a separate people and republican status within the reconstituted Russian Federation. The other faction, based in the old Terek Cossack capital, Vladikavkaz, now in Ossetia,* resumed the ancient Cossack tradition of defending Russia's southern frontier with the Muslim lands. In July 1993 the Stavropol regional parliament began a continuing debate on whether to declare the territory a republic and to restore the name Terek, banned by the Soviets in 1920.

*SELECTED BIBLIOGRAPHY:*

Cresson, William P. *The Cossacks: Their History and Culture.* 1919.
Glaskow, Wasili G. *History of the Cossacks.* 1968.
McNeal, Robert H. *Tsar and Cossack: 1855–1914.* 1987.

# TIBET

**Böd; Pö; Xizang**

*CAPITAL: Lhasa*

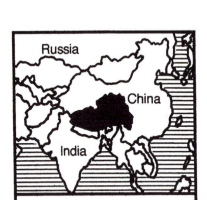

ASIA

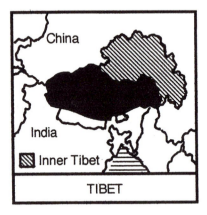

TIBET

*POPULATION:* (95e) 2,295,000 : 6,500,000 Tibetans in China. "Greater Tibet" 13,500,000. MAJOR NATIONAL GROUPS: (95e) Tibet (Outer Tibet) Tibetan 77%, Chinese 22%. MAJOR LANGUAGES: Tibetan, Chinese. MAJOR RELIGIONS: Tibetan Buddhist (Lamaism), Buddhist, Taoist. MAJOR CITIES: (95e) OUTER TIBET: Lhasa 225,000, Gyangtse (Jiangzi) 90,000, Shigatse (Xigaze) 70,000, Naquka (Heihe) 50,000. INNER TIBET: Sining (Xining) 525,000, Miyikai (Dukou) 245,000, Shwakingse (Xichang) 175,000, Yaan 95,000, Tarchendo (Kanding) 75,000, Tangar (Huangzhong) 70,000, Golmud 50,000.

*GEOGRAPHY:* AREA: 471,660 sq.mi.-1,221,917 sq.km. "Greater Tibet" 852,038 sq.mi.-2,207,352 sq.km. LOCATION: Tibet occupies the vast Tibetan Plateau in the Himalayas of southwestern China, the world's highest inhabited area. POLITICAL STATUS: Tibet forms the Xizang Autonomous Region of China. "Greater Tibet," the historic regions of Outer and Inner Tibet, also includes the province of Qinghai and the western districts of Sichuan Province.

*INDEPENDENCE DECLARED:* 18 February 1912.

*FLAG:* The Tibetan national flag has a central yellow sun with twelve red and blue stripes or rays at the top, hoist, and fly; a white triangle at the bottom, its point touching the center of the sun, is charged with two white dragons holding the national symbols; the flag is bordered on all but the fly by narrow yellow stripes.

*PEOPLE:* The Tibetans are a Mongoloid people speaking a Tibeto-Burman language of the Shino-Tibetan language group. An isolated mountain people, the Tibetans are the heirs of an ancient civilization but are more defined by their religion, a variant of Mahayana Buddhism known as Tibetan Buddhism or Lamaism. The Tibetan religion is closely tied to the Tibetan culture and way of life. Prior to the imposition of Communist rule, Tibetan life revolved around the yearly religious calendar. The majority of China's Tibetan population lives in the region formerly known as Inner Tibet, the designated autonomous region covering only the area formerly called Outer Tibet. Since 1959 a massive influx of ethnic Chinese has been settled in both regions in government-sponsored migrations.

*THE NATION:* Nomadic tribes, possibly originating in Ladakh* to the southwest of the massive plateau, created a sophisticated theocratic kingdom following the introduction of Buddhism around A.D. 630. The Buddhist religion merged with the pre-Buddhist demonolatry to produce a unique system of beliefs and rituals. The Tibetan kingdom expanded in the eighth century into the Mongol lands to the north and the lowlands south of the Himalayas. The expansive kingdom first established relations with China during the T'ang dynasty (618–906), beginning centuries of resistance to Chinese incursions and conquest.

Invading Mongols conquered much of Inner Tibet in the thirteenth century, eventually extending their influence to mountainous Outer Tibet. In 1270 the Mongol emperor of China, Kublai Khan, was converted to Lamaism by the abbot of the Sakya Lamasery. The abbot later returned to Outer Tibet to become Tibet's first priest-king. Tibet's religious leaders in the sixteenth century accepted the reform sect of Mahayana Buddhism, Gelugpa (the Victorious Order of the Yellow Hat), under the spiritual leadership of the Dalai Lama. Tibet's hostility to outsiders earned it the appellation the ''Hermit Kingdom.''

Manchu China, having incorporated Inner Tibet, established nominal rule over Outer Tibet in 1720. Over the next century the British gained control of the vassal kingdoms south of the Himalayas. When the Tibetans rebuffed a demand for trade concessions, the British dispatched an expedition to occupy the country in 1903–4. The British occupation force coerced the Dalai Lama to sign a treaty that opened several Tibetan cities to outsiders.

The Manchus, to reinforce their claim, sent a Chinese force to Tibet in 1910, the invaders driving the Dalai Lama and many followers into exile in British India. The Chinese Revolution that overthrew the Manchu dynasty in 1911 seriously weakened the occupation. Tibetan soldiers ultimately succeeded in driving the Chinese from the kingdom. The thirteenth Dalai Lama returned from exile in India to declare Tibet independent of republican China on 18 February 1912. The Tibetans, in control of Outer Tibet, laid claim to the historic territory of Inner Tibet still under Chinese rule.

Organized as a Buddhist theocracy ruled by the Dalai Lama, only 3% of the Tibetan population controlled all the land, distributed among noble families, feudal lords, and some 6,000 lamaseries. Of the Tibetan majority 5% were slaves, 20% Buddhist monks, and the remainder serfs attached to the feudal estates and lamaseries.

Tensions between Tibet and China, primarily over the Chinese treatment of the Tibetan majority in Inner Tibet, continued from 1912 to 1951. The small Tibetan army successfully resisted Chinese invasions in 1918 and 1931–33 but lost additional Tibetan territory north of the Yangtse River. China's growing civil war and the later war with Japan eased pressure on the kingdom in the 1930s and 1940s.

The Chinese civil war, suspended during the last years of World War II, resumed in 1945. Four years later the Chinese Communists emerged victorious and set about consolidating their authority. On 30 October 1950 the Chinese army invaded Tibet, the Communists forcing the Dalai Lama to accept Chinese garrisons on the borders.

The supreme Communist leader, Mao Tse Tung, announced his intention to change the Tibetan majority population of Inner Tibet to a Chinese majority of five to one. To that end he launched a massive, government-sponsored migration of Han Chinese to the region in 1954. In 1956 the Tibetans in the colonization region revolted, determined to reunite their region with Outer Tibet under the rule of the Dalai Lama. The revolt spread to Outer Tibet in 1959. In March 1959 the Chinese army invaded, driving the Dalai Lama and 87,000 refugees into exile in India.

Determined to crush the Tibetan culture, the Communist government ordered the destruction of 6,125 ancient lamaseries, murdered over 100,000 Tibetans in mass executions, and began to settle millions of ethnic Chinese in the traditionally Tibetan lands. During the upheavals of the Cultural Revolution, from 1966 to 1976, most of the remaining shrines and lamaseries were reduced to rubble by zealous Red Guards. The priceless collections of ancient manuscripts stored in the lamaseries were publicly burned. Of the 6,254 lamaseries in existence in 1959, only 13 survived the onslaught.

The exiled Dalai Lama for over three decades has continued to lead a non-violent campaign to save the Tibetan nation from genocide. An estimated 1 million Tibetans have been killed since the Chinese occupation in 1959, but the Tibetans continue to defy the Communist authorities. Pro-independence demonstrations in Lhasa in 1988 spread across the region to cities in Inner Tibet in 1989. The authorities countered the nationalist upsurge with thousands of arrests and increased suppression. In 1989, over fiery Chinese protests, the Dalai Lama was awarded the Nobel Peace Prize, an acknowledgment of his and his nation's peaceful campaign to regain their lost freedom. In September 1994 the Dalai Lama again warned China that the Tibetans could turn to armed rebellion if the government oppression continues.

In Mach 1995 the Dalai Lama put forward a plan for a referendum of all Tibetans, both those living under Chinese rule and those living in exile, to determine their wishes for the future of their threatened nation. The Chinese government condemned the plan and the Tibetan's efforts to involve the United Nations and other international bodies as just another ploy to win independence for Tibet.

*SELECTED BIBLIOGRAPHY:*

Heberer, Thomas. *China and Its National Minorities: Autonomy or Assimilation?* 1989.
Nowak, Margaret. *Tibetan Refugees: Youth and the New Generation of Meaning.* 1984.
Richardson, H. E. *A Short History of Tibet.* 1962.
Rinpoche, T. T. *Buddhist Civilization in Tibet.* 1988.

# TIGRE

**Tigray**

*CAPITAL: Mekele*

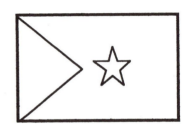

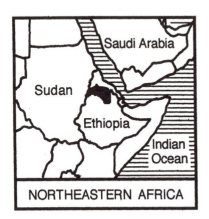

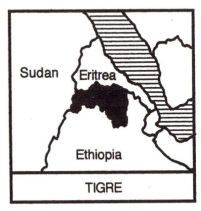

*POPULATION:* (95e) 5,010,000 : 7,020,000 Tigreans in Ethiopia. MAJOR NATIONAL GROUPS: (95e) Tigrean 82%, other Ethiopian. MAJOR LANGUAGES: Tigrean, Amhariya. MAJOR RELIGIONS: Coptic Christian, Sunni Muslim. MAJOR CITIES: (95e) Mekele 105,000 (140,000), Adwa 65,000, Adigrat 40,000, Aksum 30,000, Maychew 25,000.

*GEOGRAPHY:* AREA: 39,372 sq.mi.-102,000 sq.km. LOCATION: Tigre occupies a mountainous region in the Ethiopian highlands east of the desert Danakil Depression in northwestern Ethiopia, just south of the border with Eritrea. POLITICAL STATUS: Tigre forms an autonomous region of the Ethiopian republic.

*INDEPENDENCE DECLARED:* 11 September 1943.

*FLAG:* The Tigrean national flag, the flag of the national movement, is a red field bearing a yellow triangle at the hoist and a yellow, five-pointed star near the point of the triangle.

*PEOPLE:* The Tigreans are a Semitic people, descendants of ancient migrants from the Arabian Peninsula. Considered the closest to the original settlers, the tall, handsome Tigreans have intermarried less than the other Semitic peoples of Ethiopia and have retained a Semitic language closely related to Old Ethiopian, the language spoken in the fourteenth century. The majority of the Tigreans are Coptic Christians, with a minority, the Jabarti, that have adopted Sunni Islam and form a trading class that has maintained the Tigrean's close contacts with neighboring Muslim peoples.

*THE NATION:* The Tigreans claim descent from the Sabeans of ancient

Sheba, the legendary monarchy on the Arabian Peninsula. Tigrean tradition has Sabean migrants, led by Menelik, the son of Israel's King Solomon and the queen of Sheba, arriving in the region traditionally around the year 1000 B.C. Menelik is credited with bringing the Ark of the Covenant to Aksum, the capital of the Semitic kingdom known as the Aksumite Empire.

Authentic records from the first century A.D. confirm the early Ethiopian state centered on Aksum, the empire controlling present Tigre and parts of Sudan. Frumentius of Tyre, called Abba Salama by the Aksumites, converted the Aksumite king to Christianity in A.D. 330. The Semitic Christian peoples of the empire, spreading across the Ethiopian highlands, evolved as two separate peoples, the Tigreans in the north, and the Amhara in the west and south.

The introduction of Islam to the region in the seventh century confined the Christian peoples to the highlands, a Christian island surrounded by hostile Muslim states. In the eighth century Muslims overran Tigre, and the center of Christian power shifted south to the Amhara lands. The Christian reconquest of Tigre, led by the Amhara, relegated the resurrected kingdom to a secondary position in the Amhara-dominated empire.

The Tigreans increasingly shifted their culture and loyalty away from the Amhara during the intense civil strife in the empire in the seventeenth and eighteenth centuries. In the early nineteenth century Tigre broke away under its *ras* (prince), Mikhail Suhul. Tigre was reconquered by Theodore, an Amhara chief, who was later crowned Ethiopian emperor in 1855. In 1868 the succession passed to the *ras* of Tigre, only to be usurped by the Amhara leader, later known as Menelik II, with Italian assistance. Increasing tensions between the two peoples culminated in a Tigrean uprising in the 1880s. The imperial army sent against them defeated the Tigrean rebels. The Tigrean prince and many leaders were exiled, and reprisals decimated the Tigrean nobility.

Threatened by Italian expansion from their colony in Eritrea, the Tigreans joined the Amhara to defeat an Italian invasion in 1895, the first major defeat of a European force in northeastern Africa. Determined to erase the shame of their 1895 defeat, a mechanized Italian army returned to defeat the feudal Ethiopians in 1935.

British forces from Kenya liberated Ethiopia early in World War II. Ethiopia's emperor, Haile Selasse, returned in 1941 amid rising Tigrean demands for special status and the right of their *ras* to return to Tigre. Their appeals ignored, the Tigreans rebelled in 1943, intent on separating from Ethiopia under their *ras*. In early September the rebels drove the government troops from Mekele and on 11 September 1943 declared Tigre independent.

Fearing the destabilization of the entire Horn of Africa, the British occupation forces in neighboring Eritrea aided the imperial forces to reconquer the breakaway state. Continued Tigrean resentment and resistance evolved into a modern liberation movement. In the 1970s the government moved against the nationalists, forcing the movement underground.

The Tigreans initially supported the 1974 revolution that overthrew the feudal monarchy. The anti-Christian stance of the new Marxist government soon rekindled the Tigrean rebellion. In 1975 the Tigray People's Liberation Front (TPLF) was formed as a coalition of nationalist, Marxist, and democratic groups to lead the Tigrean insurrection. By 1978 the Tigreans had driven the Ethiopian forces from 90% of Tigre. Drought and famine, exacerbated by government refusal to allow relief supplies to enter rebel areas, took thousands of lives in the 1970s and 1980s. In spite of ideological differences and splits between the pro-autonomy and pro-independence factions, the Tigreans continued to advance against the Soviet-supported Ethiopian forces.

Abandoned by their Soviet allies during the turmoil in the Soviet Union in 1989, the Ethiopian military began to crumble. An alliance of insurgent groups, led by the Tigreans, moved on the Ethiopian capital, Addis Ababa, in 1990–91. In late May 1991 the rebels occupied the city and overthrew the hated Communist government. The rebel coalition established a loose confederation of ethnic regions.

In 1992–93 the coalition government of Ethiopia began to split along ethnic lines. The Oromos and others withdrew from the government as ethnic violence and tensions returned to the multiethnic state. In the Tigrean heartland nationalists began a campaign to win support for the independence of Tigre, including the territories taken from the Tigreans after the 1943 rebellion, in a federation of independent states.

The Tigrean national movement, split between the faction that supports a federal system in Ethiopia and a militant faction seeking to follow Eritrea to independence, remains the most important component in Ethiopia's post-Communist government. Tigre's position as an island of calm in the chaotic Ethiopian state is increasingly threatened, the condition of the Tigrean homeland the major point of difference between the two factions.

In December 1994 the Tigrean-dominated Ethiopian government approved a new constitution that allows any of the new federation's ethnic regions to secede peacefully if a referendum proves that independence is the wish of the region's majority. The pro-independence faction of the Tigrean national movement publicly welcomed the new legality, but Tigrean leaders admitted that with Tigrean autonomy support for independence has waned since 1991.

*SELECTED BIBLIOGRAPHY:*

Levine, Donald M. *Greater Ethiopia: The Evolution of a Multiethnic Society.* 1977.
Lewis, I. M. *Nationalism and Self-Determination in the Horn of Africa.* 1984.
McCann, James. *From Poverty to Famine in Northeast Ethiopia.* 1987.
Sauldie, Madan M. *Ethiopia: The Dawn of the Red Star.* 1983.

# TOGOLAND

**Eweland**

*CAPITAL: Lomé*

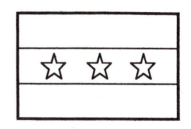

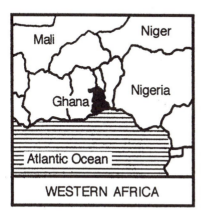

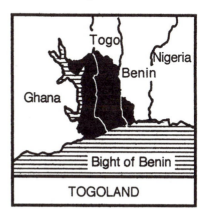

*POPULATION:* (95e) 4,310,000 : 3,955,000 Ewe in Togo, Ghana, and Benin. MAJOR NATIONAL GROUPS: (95e) Ewe 73%, Mina 10%, Kabye, Avatime, Fon. MAJOR LANGUAGES: Ewe, English, French, Mina, Fon. MAJOR RELIGIONS: (95e) Christian 48%, animist 47%, Sunni Muslim 5%. MAJOR CITIES: (95e) TOGO (TOGOLAND): Lomé 423,000 (610,000), Palimé 66,000, Atakpamé 48,000, Anécho 33,000, Tsévié 26,000, Tabligbo 21,000. GHANA (WESTERN TOGOLAND): Ho 88,000, Keta 51,000, Aflao 32,000, Hohoe 29,000, Anloga 22,000. BENIN (EASTERN TOGOLAND): Lokossa 35,000, Grand Popo 20,000.

*GEOGRAPHY:* AREA: 18,431 sq.mi.-47,749 sq.km. LOCATION: Togoland occupies the coastal region of West Africa between the Volta and Koutto Rivers in southeastern Ghana, southern Togo, and southeastern Benin. POLITICAL STATUS: Togoland has no official status; the region forms the Volta Province of Ghana (Western Togoland), the Togolese prefectures of Des Plateaux and Maritime (Togoland), and the Mono Province of Benin (Eastern Togoland).

*FLAG:* The Ewe national flag, the flag of the national movement, has three horizontal stripes of green, red, and green, bearing three yellow, five-pointed stars on the red stripe.

*PEOPLE:* The Ewe are an Akan people traditionally divided into 120 clans and subgroups. United as a nation only in the twentieth century, the formerly disparate Ewe clans share a common culture and language, a Kwa language of the Niger-Congo language group that became a literary language under German rule before World War I. An energetic commercial people, the famous Ewe market women dominate local commerce across the region. The Ewes are about half Christian, mostly in the urban areas, and half animist.

*THE NATION:* Small tribal and clan groups, thought to have originated in the Niger River valley in the twelfth century, settled the coastal regions between the fourteenth and sixteenth centuries. Organized as small chiefdomships, the Ewe never developed the state structures of the neighboring Kwa peoples. Habitually raiding neighboring peoples for slaves and plunder, the Ewe were known over a wide region for their ferocity and aggressiveness.

Visited by Portuguese explorers in 1482, several European nations soon established trading posts in the area they called the Slave Coast. The Ewe clans, raiding into Ashantiland* in the west and the Fon state of Dahomey in the east, sold thousands of captives to the Europeans. The slave trade dominated Ewe activities until the European powers outlawed the trade in the nineteenth century.

European and American missionaries arrived in the Ewe lands in the 1840s, their mission quite successful among the coastal Ewe clans. Mission education produced the beginning of a national sentiment among the numerous clans. The ties of a common language and culture began to break down the historic barriers between the clans.

The European competition for colonies divided the Ewe lands in the late nineteenth century. In 1884 the Germans announced the establishment of a protectorate called Togo, meaning ''beyond the sea'' in the Ewe language. Ten years later the borders of the protectorate were delimited, with small parts of Eweland included in the French and British possessions to the east and west of German Togo.

British and French troops moved into the protectorate when war began in Europe in 1914. Taken from defeated Germany in 1919, parts of Togoland were occupied by the French and British, the partition formalized by the creation of League of Nations mandates in 1922.

The partition of their homeland, already divided once in 1894, marked the beginning of Ewe national awareness. Sporadic demonstrations and unrest accompanied demands for reunification up to World War II. After the war, over heated Ewe opposition, the division of Togoland was reconfirmed as the old British and French mandates became trust territories of the new United Nations.

Ewe nationalists organized and in 1946 formed a coalition of nationalist and cultural groups, the All-Ewe Conference, which established permanent committees to work for the reunification of an independent Togoland within its 1914 borders. In 1947 Ewe nationalists presented their case to the United Nations General Assembly, but action on the Ewe appeals was blocked by the British and French governments.

French Togoland became an autonomous unit of the French Union in 1956, the same year that the United Nations organized a plebiscite in British Togoland on the question of annexation by the British Gold Coast. The overwhelming no vote in the Ewe southern districts lost to the yes vote of the more numerous non-Ewe tribes of the northern districts. The Gold Coast, including former British Togoland, became the first sub-Saharan European colony to win independence, in 1957.

The Ewes of Ghana's Trans-Volta Togoland refused to accept the incorporation of their homeland in Ghana. In 1958 the Ewes rebelled, the uprising spreading to the Ewe population in the west, in the territory incorporated into the Gold Coast in 1894. Forced underground by government police actions, the national movement grew with widespread Ewe support.

French Togoland gained independence in 1960, taking the name Republic of Togo. The first president of the republic, Sylvanus Olympio, began his career serving as the Ewe national spokesman at the United Nations in 1947. Support for Ewe reunification grew as Togo's diplomatic relations with neighboring Ghana and Dahomey (later Benin) deteriorated. Separatist groups, operating in Ghana since the 1950s, became active in Togo after a 1967 coup overthrew the Ewe-dominated government and installed a military regime controlled by the Kabye, a northern Hamitic tribe.

The international border between Ghana and Togo is often closed as the two governments alternate support and suppression of Ewe nationalist groups operating on each other's territory. The end of the Cold War and the growing demands for multiparty democracy in Africa have fueled a resurgence of Ewe nationalism. The nationalists in all three Togoland territories have coordinated their demands for an end to the divisions imposed on their nation by European colonialism.

Economic grievances and tensions between the Bantu Ewe and the Hamitic Kabye in Togo have revived popular support for Ewe reunification. Increasing ethnic violence and the growing number of Ewe refugees fleeing the excesses of Togo's Kabye-dominated military, are increasing the region's instability and spreading unrest among the Ewe populations of all three states.

In the Ewe heartland in Togo, the split between the Bantu south and the Hamitic north, drawing in the allied and related tribes in both regions, has become the scene of violent ethnic clashes involving the military. Elections in 1993, boycotted by the Ewes and the other Bantu tribes, returned the northern military dictatorship to power with the support of the northern tribes. The movement for the separation of the Ewe and Bantu south in Togo continues to reverberate in the Ewe territories in Ghana and Benin.

*SELECTED BIBLIOGRAPHY:*

Asiwaju, A. I. *Partitioned Africans: Ethnic Relations across Africa's International Borders, 1884–1984.* 1985.

Bourret, F. M. *Ghana: Road to Independence, 1919–1957.* 1960.

Pedler, F. J. *West Africa.* 1959.

Stevens, Gareth. *People and Nations of Africa.* 1988.

# TORO

Toroland; Ruwenzururu; Ruwenzuru

*CAPITAL: Fort Portal*

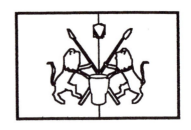

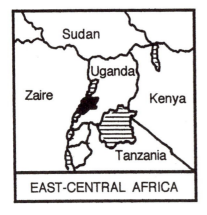

EAST-CENTRAL AFRICA

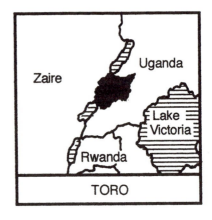

TORO

*POPULATION:* (95e) 1,421,000 : 830,000 Batoro (Toros), 410,000 Bakonjo (Konjos), and 185,000 Baamba (Ambas) in Uganda. MAJOR NATIONAL GROUPS: (95e) Batoro (Toro) 56%, Bakonjo (Konjo) 28%, Baamba (Amba) 9%, other Ugandan. MAJOR LANGUAGES: Lutoro, Lukonjo, Luamba, Swahili, English. MAJOR RELIGIONS: Christian, animist. MAJOR CITIES: (95e) Fort Portal 55,000, Kasese 30,000, Kyenjojo 20,000, Kilembe 20,000.

*GEOGRAPHY:* AREA: 5,233 sq.mi.-13,556 sq.km. LOCATION: Toro occupies a region of rolling grasslands west of the Ruwenzori Mountains in southeastern Uganda just east of the border with Zaire. POLITICAL STATUS: Toro forms the southern district of Uganda's Western Province. In 1993 the kingdom was partially restored.

*INDEPENDENCE DECLARED:* 13 February 1963.

*FLAG:* The Toro national flag, the flag of the kingdom, is a vertical bicolor of blue and yellow bearing a centered brown drum backed by crossed white spears and flanked by erect lions, the drum surmounted by a red ceremonial mask. OTHER FLAG(S): The flag of Ruwenzuru, representing the Konjo and Amba, is a horizontal tricolor of blue, green, and yellow bearing a white disc on the upper two-thirds charged with a black monkey on a brown branch.

*PEOPLE:* United historically, Toro's people comprise three ethnically distinct tribes: the Toro, descendants of tall Hamitic herdsmen; and the Bantu peoples of the Ruwenzori Mountains in the west, the Konjo and Amba, peoples closely related to the peoples across the border in Zaire. Until the 1960s intermarriage between the tribes was forbidden, and only since the 1970s has a sense of shared nationhood become widespread. The three tribes speak closely related Bantu languages of the Benue-Niger language group. The majority are Christian, a minority adhering to traditional beliefs based on ancestor worship.

*THE NATION:* Bantu agriculturists settled the lowlands, probably before A.D. 1100, settling in autonomous villages united only by culture and tradition. Around 1,500 tall Hamitic herdsmen conquered the region around the highland lakes. The invaders created a large, centralized kingdom dominated by a Hamitic aristocracy. The warlike nomads relegated the more advanced Bantu to a lower class of serfs, craftsmen, farmers, and herdsmen forbidden to own cattle, the measure of Hamitic wealth.

Nilotic invaders from the north conquered the kingdom in the sixteenth century. The Nilotes divided the region into a string of small independent kingdoms. The area west of the Blue and Ruwenzori Mountains formed the kingdom of Bunyoro.* About 1830 a Nyoro prince broke away from the kingdom and, with his followers, created a separate kingdom in the southern districts south of Lake Albert.

The prince, the first *omukama* (king) of Toro, controlled the lowlands but only nominally ruled the mountainous west. The inhabitants of the region in the Ruwenzori Mountains, the Konjo and Amba, considered primitive by the cultured lowlanders, acknowledged the authority of Toro's government while maintaining only minimum contact.

European explorers visited the kingdom in the 1850s, amazed to find a sophisticated culture and state system. Over the next decades the kingdom established trade relations with the British and allowed Protestant and Roman Catholic missions to operate. The majority of the kingdom's inhabitants converted to Christianity. The growing Christian presence began to undermine the king's power, traditionally based on the magic and rituals of the old religion.

The kingdom signed a diplomatic treaty with the British authorities in 1890. Five years later, reacting to interest by other European powers, the British declared Toro a protected state. The king finally signed the protectorate agreement in 1900 and, with British assistance, consolidated his authority and in 1906 brought the mountain tribes under direct Batoro rule. The Rukurato, the Toro parliament, became a partly elected legislature under British influence, allowing the Konjo and Amba some say in the government of the kingdom.

Long isolated from the central authority of the kingdom, the Konjo rebelled in 1919. The Konjo rebels repulsed the king's troops but met defeat when British forces were dispatched to the kingdom. Even though serfdom and slavery gradually disappeared, the dominant Toros continued to discriminate against the Ruwenzuru peoples in education, administration, and economics. The discrimination, only partly ethnic and cultural, was accentuated by the inaccessibility of the Ruwenzuru people's mountain homelands.

The colonial authorities gradually reduced the power and independence of the kingdom, although in 1949 legislation passed recognizing the king's right to regulate local government within the protectorate of Uganda. Encouraged by the British, who believed that Ugandan independence was still decades away, the kingdom became the focus of Batoro nationalism and identity. In 1953 the royal government demanded federal status and the extension of the Lutoro language to all the kingdom's schools.

The issue of Toro nationalism intensified as independence for Uganda neared in the late 1950s. The rapid growth of Batoro nationalism paralleled the growing nationalism of the Konjo and Amba, a reaction to increasing assimilation. The two mountain peoples demanded separation from Toro and the creation of a separate Ruwenzuru district within Uganda. The threat to the kingdom's territorial integrity raised Toro demands for recognition as an independent state before future relations with Uganda were regulated. On the eve of Ugandan independence, the kingdom adopted a new constitution that ignored the Ruwenzuru people's demands for official recognition of the kingdom's three peoples.

In 1962 the kingdom accepted semifederal status within the newly independent Ugandan state. Toro nationalists, somewhat mollified by official recognition of the kingdom, blocked Konjo and Amba efforts to separate in a distinct district. In early 1963 the mountain tribes rebelled and on 13 February 1963 declared Toro independent as the Kingdom of Ruwenzururu, their claims to the entire Toro kingdom based on historic possession.

Uganda's government, dominated by northern tribes, had little sympathy for the traditional Bantu monarchies in the southern districts. In 1967 the government abolished the kingdoms as centers of local nationalism and separatism, and in 1970 the Ruwenzuru rebels were finally defeated. The government, taken over by Idi Amin in 1971, gained infamy as Africa's most brutal. A strong secessionist movement in Toro ended in 1972 with the murder or disappearance of the majority of Toro's leadership.

A Bantu-supported resistance movement finally took control of devastated Uganda in 1986, forming the country's first government controlled by the southern Bantus. The relative freedom, after two decades of terror and destruction, rekindled Toro nationalism. The three Toro peoples, finally united by shared hardships since 1970, support the movement.

In July 1993, with government approval, the Toro kingdom was partially restored, and Patrick Olimi Kaboyo took the throne as the new *omukama*. The Konjo and Amba initially refused to relinquish the former royal lands they had occupied, but in March 1994 senior members of the Ruwenzuru movement acknowledged the new king, officially ending the conflict that had begun three decades before.

*SELECTED BIBLIOGRAPHY:*
Gukiina, Peter. *Uganda: A Case Study in African Development.* 1972.
Ingham, Kenneth. *The Making of Modern Uganda.* 1962.
Karugire, Samuel R. *A Political History of Uganda.* 1980.

# TRANSYLVANIA

**Erdély; Ardeal; Transilvania**

*CAPITAL: Kolozsvár (Cluj-Napoca)*

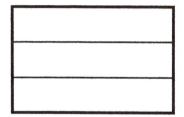

SOUTH-CENTRAL EUROPE

TRANSYLVANIA

*POPULATION:* (95e) 6,820,000 : 2,300,000 Hungarians in Romania (1,800,000 Szekely, 500,000 Magyar). MAJOR NATIONAL GROUPS: (95e) Vlach (Romanian) 48%, Hungarian 33% (Szekely 26%, Magyar 7%), Rom (Gypsy) 14%, German 2.5%, Serb, Tatar, Ukrainian, other Romanian. MAJOR LANGUAGES: Romanian (Vlach dialect), Hungarian, German. MAJOR RELIGIONS: Roman Catholic, Uniate, Orthodox, Protestant, Jewish. MAJOR CITIES: (95e) Brassó (Brasov) 360,000 (464,000), Kolozsvár (Cluj-Napoca) 341,000, Temesvár (Timisoara) 328,000, Nagyvárad (Oradea) 218,000, Arad 196,000, Nagyszebén (Sibiu) 182,000 (242,000), Maros-Vásárhely (Tîrgu-Mures) 181,000, Szatmar-Nemetí (Satu-Mare) 135,000, Nagybánya (Baia-Mare) 148,000, Resiczabánya (Resita) 133,000, Vajdahunyád (Hunedoara) 115,000 (230,000), Medias 101,000, Gyulafehérvár (Alba-Iulia) 73,000 (113,000).

*GEOGRAPHY:* AREA: 38,590 sq.mi.-99,975 sq.km. LOCATION: Transylvania, called Erdély in Hungarian, Ardeal in the Vlach dialect, and Transilvania in Romanian, occupies the eastern extension of the Great Hungarian Plain, divided from the Romanian heartland by the Carpathian Mountains and the Transylvanian Alps. POLITICAL STATUS: Transylvania has no official status; the region forms the historic provinces of Transylvania, Crisana-Marmures, and Banat, now divided into sixteen counties of Romania.

*INDEPENDENCE DECLARED:* 28 October 1918.

*FLAG:* The Transylvanian national flag, the flag adopted in 1918, is a horizontal tricolor of red, green, and white.

*PEOPLE:* The Transylvanians comprise three distinct peoples: the Szekely, originally a Turkic people; the Magyars, ethnic Hungarians; and the majority Vlach, one of the three main divisions of the Romanian peoples. The Szekely and Magyar speak Hungarian and are mostly Roman Catholic or Protestant. The Vlach speak a dialect of Romanian that is without the Turkic and Slavic influences of standard Romanian and are primarily Uniate Catholic or Romanian Orthodox. The Transylvanian population, one of Europe's most complex ethnic mixtures, also includes a large Rom or Gypsy population and numerous smaller minorities. The Transylvanian peoples have lived together in the region for over a thousand years.

*THE NATION:* The area was a Roman colony from A.D. 107, and the Romans' Latin tongue remained following the destruction of the Roman culture by barbarian invasions in the third century. The Szekely, a Turkic-speaking nomadic people, occupied the region in the ninth century, before or with the Magyars, a Finno-Ugric people from beyond the Urals. War with neighboring peoples pushed the majority of the Magyars farther west across the great, flat plain. Incorporated into the expanding Magyar kingdom in 1003, the Szekely gradually adopted the Hungarian language but retained much of their earlier culture.

Twelfth-century Hungarian kings promoted development of the region by inviting German colonists to settle the underpopulated districts. Many of the region's cities began as German settlements. Granted some autonomy, the first parliament was attended by delegates of the Szekely, Magyar, and German peoples in 1229. The three peoples formed the so-called Privileged Nations, the nobility and upper classes that dominated a large class of serfs and workers, mostly Romanian-speaking Vlach.

The invasion of Europe by the Ottoman Turks divided the medieval Hungarian kingdom in the sixteenth century. Austria took control of western Hungary; the Ottomans, central Hungary and Transylvania. Ruled by its own princes under nominal Turkish administration, the Transylvanian principality experienced a period of peace and a flowering of its distinct culture in the seventeenth century. The Turks formally ceded the state to Austria in 1699.

Their privileges threatened by Austrian rule, the Szekely rebelled, delaying complete Austrian control until 1711. The Austrian bureaucracy progressively broke down Transylvania's independence, even though the ''privileged'' nations continued to maintain their own militias, civil organizations, and religious hierarchies. An Austrian attempt in 1763 to press the Szekely into service as a border militia provoked a second serious revolt. The Vlach petitioned the Austrians for recognition as the fourth Transylvanian nation, but the regional parliament, the Diet of Transylvania, rejected the Vlach demands.

An attempt by the Szekely and Magyars to throw off Austrian rule and join an independent Hungarian kingdom in 1848 ended with the repeal of all the region's remaining autonomous rights. Following the compromise of 1867, which created the Dual Monarchy, the Austrians transferred Transylvania to the Hungarian kingdom.

The province, about half ethnic Romanian, was promised to Romania as an incentive to join the Allies during World War I. The three Transylvanian nations, rejecting Romania's claim, organized as Austria-Hungary collapsed in defeat in late 1918. On 28 October 1918 the Diet, following a vote, declared Transylvania independent, countered by a Vlach proclamation of union with Romania on 1 December 1918. The conflict provoked a brief war between Hungary and Romania in 1919. Occupied by Romanian troops, Hungary formally ceded Transylvania to Romania in 1923.

Tensions in Romania mounted with the Romanian suppression of thousand-year-old institutions. Initial Vlach enthusiasm for union declined as disputes erupted between the Westernized, Catholic "New Province" Romanians and the Orthodox "Old Kingdom" administrators sent from Bucharest. In 1929 the Romanian government placed restrictions on the Transylvanians' language and religious rights and pressed assimilation on the Vlachs.

The territorial conflict remained, even though Romania and Hungary joined the Axis powers during World War II. Axis mediation awarded some two-thirds of Transylvania to Hungary in 1940, the dispute bringing the two allies to war in 1944, which opened the way for Soviet occupation of both countries. At war's end, the Soviet-installed Romanian government expelled many Germans, suppressed Hungarian language institutions, and in 1948 forcibly merged the Vlach's Uniate Catholic hierarchy into the Communist-approved Romanian Orthodox Church.

Decades of oppression and Communist experimentation impoverished the rich agricultural region but failed to destroy the Transylvanians' resistance. In December 1989 government attempts to silence a Hungarian Protestant minister in Timisoara sparked a revolution that quickly swept Romania's Communist dictator from power. The arrival of some democracy reopened the old disputes in Transylvania. In March 1990 radical Romanian nationalists, formerly supported by the Communist government, provoked attacks on Hungarians in Tîrgu-Mures, the worst violence since World War II.

The violence horrified all the Transylvanian peoples and proved a catalyst for change. Although discrimination continues openly in many areas, the Transylvanians have begun to work together to preserve the region's tense peace. Moderates of all the Transylvanian nations regard the region's ethnic diversity as a triumph that would allow a sovereign Transylvania to play an important role in an integrated European federation.

*SELECTED BIBLIOGRAPHY:*

Fischer-Galati, Stephen, ed. *Romania.* 1957.

Illyes, Elemer. *National Minorities in Romania: Change in Transylvania.* 1982.

Pearson, Raymond. *National Minorities in Eastern Europe, 1848–1945.* 1985.

Twedeanu, Emile. *Modern Romania: The Achievement of National Unity.* 1988.

# TRIESTE

**Trst**

*CAPITAL: Trieste*

SOUTH-CENTRAL EUROPE

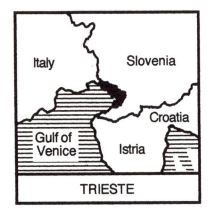

TRIESTE

*POPULATION:* (95e) 270,000 : 300,000 Triestines (Triestini) in Italy. MAJOR NATIONAL GROUPS: (95e) Triestine 72%, Slovene 10%, Friuli 8%, Austrian 4%, other Italian. MAJOR LANGUAGES: Italian, Slovene, Furlan, German. MAJOR RELIGIONS: Roman Catholic, Protestant, Jewish. MAJOR CITIES: (95e) Trieste 226,000 (270,000), Muggia 15,000.

*GEOGRAPHY:* AREA: 81 sq.mi.-211 sq.km. LOCATION: Trieste occupies a narrow coastal plain on the Gulf of Trieste, an extension of the Adriatic Sea, in northwestern Italy. Surrounded by Slovenian territory, Trieste is connected to the rest of Italy by a narrow land corridor. POLITICAL STATUS: Trieste and its suburbs form a province of the Italian region of Friuli-Venezia Giulia.

*INDEPENDENCE DECLARED:* 10 February 1947.

*FLAG:* The Triestine national flag, the flag of the former state, is a red field charged with a white, spearlike halberd.

*PEOPLE:* The Triestines are an Italian people of mixed ethnic background, their language and culture the product of centuries of close contact with Germanic and Slav peoples. The city, Italy's most un-Italian, is a crossroads of languages and cultures. The population of the province includes the majority Triestines, an Italian people speaking a unique dialect that incorporates borrowings from neighboring languages: the Slavic Slovenes, related to the people of neighboring Slovenia; the Friuli, a Rhaeto-Romanic people more numerous in the adjoining Italian region of Friulia*; and Austrians, the remnant of a formerly larger Austrian population.

*THE NATION:* A small Friuli town, Trieste came under Roman rule in 177 B.C. The port, fortified and expanded, served as the outport and protection for the more important Roman commercial city of Aquilea, twenty-two miles northwest. Overrun by barbarian tribes as Roman power collapsed, Trieste superseded Aquilea, whose inhabitants fled to the islands of the Venetian Lagoon in A.D. 452. Slavic migrants occupied the region around the port in the sixth century. Trieste, retaining its Latin culture, formed a bulwark on the newly established linguistic and cultural frontier.

Incorporated in the Carolingian Empire in 788, Trieste remained in the later Holy Roman Empire while the hinterland to the west and south came under Venetian rule. An episcopal see, the bishop of Trieste ruled the city from 948 to 1202, when the city became a free imperial city. Following two centuries of struggle against rival Venice, Trieste finally accepted autonomy under Austrian rule in 1342.

Austria's most important outlet to the sea, Trieste developed as the primary port and naval base of the vast multiethnic Hapsburg empire. The city's rapid expansion replaced the essentially Italian town with long, straight, Austrian-designed boulevards lined with stately and ornate Hapsburg architecture. A free port from 1719, Trieste's importance increased with the extension of Austrian administration to surrounding Venetian territory in 1797. In 1867 Trieste became the capital of the newly created crownland of Kustenland, a province of mixed Italian, Slovene, Croat, Friuli, and Austrian populations.

The Italia Irredenta movement, formed after Italian unification in 1870, dedicated to the recovery of Italian-populated regions outside the kingdom, gained Italian support in Trieste in the late nineteenth century. In 1910 serious anti-Austrian demonstrations erupted in the city, the Italian-speaking protesters demanding union with Italy.

The Allies during World War I included the city, Austria's primary naval base, in the list of territories offered to Italy as an incentive to declare war on Austria-Hungary in 1915. The city authorities rejected Italian claims, but with Austria's looming defeat rival nationalisms clashed in the region, and chaos engulfed the city.

Triestine nationalists took control of the city. Rejecting plans to separate the Italian majority city from its non-Italian hinterland, the local legislature in October 1918 voted to form a separate republic, Venezia Giulia, an Italo-Slovene state that would incorporate Trieste, the Julian region to the north, and the Istrian Peninsula. The independence movement ended with the occupation of the region by Italian troops on 3 November. Formal annexation by the Italian kingdom followed in 1920 despite impassioned opposition in the region.

Trieste's economic importance declined rapidly with the departure of thousands of Austrian civilians. The fascist Italian government after 1922 pressed the Italianization of the polyglot region. To counter Slav claims and to reduce the Triestine majority, the government sponsored immigration from the culturally and dialectically distinct regions of southern Italy.

The city's long decline reversed with the outbreak of World War II, but the long-smoldering tensions flared as antifascist- and Yugoslav-supported Communist groups clashed in Trieste. In the spring of 1945 Tito's Yugoslav Communist partisans occupied Trieste. Thousands of the region's inhabitants, real or imagined fascist collaborators and anti-Communists, were rounded up. Many of the detainees, men, women, and children, were thrown alive into an abyss in the Corso Mountains during the forty days of Tito's terror. Liberated by British troops, Italy's failure to protect the region against the Communist terror stimulated the growth of modern Triestine nationalism

Conflicting postwar Italian and Yugoslav claims to Trieste went to the new United Nations in 1946. A compromise, grudgingly accepted by the claimants and welcomed by the Triestines, created a Free Territory of Trieste. The state, under United Nations protection, was proclaimed independent on 10 February 1947. The region flourished as a neutral trading state in the early years of the Cold War. The majority of the population vehemently opposed the partition of the state between Italy and Yugoslavia in 1954.

Outstanding territorial claims delayed the treaty formalizing the division of Trieste until 1975. The signing of the treaty incited a Triestine revival, led by a populist coalition that denounced the accord and demanded autonomy. Steadily gaining support as the provincial population and economic importance declined, the nationalists blamed Trieste's growing problems squarely on Italy's notoriously inefficient and corrupt government.

The overthrow of Communism in 1989 ended Trieste's long isolation as ties to old ''Mitteleuropa'' resumed. The only Italian city to have lost population since 1965, Triestine nationalists seized on the rapid changes sweeping Europe as a last chance to avert stagnation as a neglected Italian backwater. Since 1990 nationalist factions have put forward several proposals, the revival of the independence of 1947–54, autonomy within a federal Italy, or a European region grouping the province of Trieste with its traditional hinterland in a neutral free zone open to the European Union and the fledgling democracies in Central and Eastern Europe. The one point all of the factions share is a desire to be free of Italy's huge and hugely inefficient government that they claim stifles Trieste's potential. In local elections in November 1993 the nontraditional parties, including nationalists, autonomists, and federalists, took more than 50% of the vote in the city and province of Trieste.

*SELECTED BIBLIOGRAPHY:*

Grindrod, Muriel. *The Rebuilding of Italy.* 1955.

Novak, Bogan C. *Trieste Nineteen Forty-One to Nineteen Fifty-Four: The Ethnic Politics and Ideological Struggle.* 1970.

Raval, Roberto G. *Between East and West: Trieste, the United States and the Cold War 1941–1954.* 1988.

# TRIPURA

Tippera

CAPITAL: Agartala

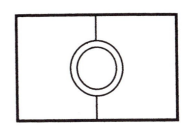

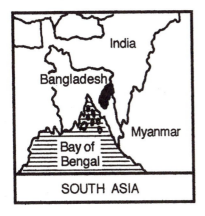

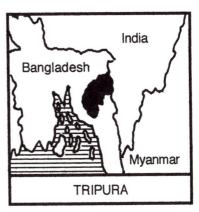

POPULATION: (95e) 3,035,000 : 2,125,000 Tripuri in India. MAJOR NA-
TIONAL GROUPS: (95e) Tripuri 70%, Bengali 23%, Miethei, Kuki, Chakma.
MAJOR LANGUAGES: Bengali 59%, Kokbarak 35%, Meithei, Bodo, Kuki-
Chin. MAJOR RELIGIONS: (95e) Hindu 70%, Sunni Muslim 25%, Christian
5%. MAJOR CITIES: (95e) Agartala 202,000, Kailashahar 40,000.

GEOGRAPHY: AREA: 4,027 sq.mi.-10,433 sq.km. LOCATION: Tripura occupies a mountainous area of northeastern India, an enclave surrounded on three
sides by Bangladeshi territory. POLITICAL STATUS: Tripura forms a state of
the Republic of India.

FLAG: The Tripuri national flag, the flag of the national movement, is a
vertical bicolor of red and yellow bearing a centered white disc outlined in green.

PEOPLE: The Tripuri are an Indian people of mixed Bengali and Tibeto-
Burman background. The majority of the Tripuri are now Bengali-speaking, with
a large minority retaining the Tibeto-Burman language called Kokbarak. The
majority of the Tripuri are considered settled, although 29% of the population
is classed as tribal, mostly Tripuri, but some twenty separate tribes live in the
state. The majority of the Tripuri are Hindu, the religious practices often mixed
with pre-Hindu traditions and customs. A large Muslim minority is mostly ethnic
Bengali. The smaller Christian minority is made up of tribal converts.

THE NATION: Lowland Aryan peoples penetrated the high mountain valleys,
inhabited by diverse tribes, around the fourth century A.D. The Aryans settled
in the region and in the late seventh century established the state of Tripura,

one of the subcontinent's earliest Hindu states. The Bengali language, brought to the state by migrants from the lowlands to the south, gradually became the predominant language. Bengali cultural influence and extensive intermarriage changed the tribal structure of the kingdom. The Tripuri evolved a sophisticated, settled society in the isolated high valleys.

The Bengali population of the surrounding lowlands converted to Islam in the tenth century, separating and isolating the Hindu kingdom. The Mankiya dynasty, founded in 1280, strengthened the state's defenses against Bengali incursions from the lowlands. The Bengalis finally overran the state in 1625, incorporating Tripura as a dependency of the Muslim Bengali state. British officials, from their expanding base in Bengal, visited Tripura in 1725, calling the highland region Hill-Tippera.

Soldiers of the Muslim Mogul Empire conquered Tripura in 1733 but allowed the kingdom to retain nominal independence as a tributary state. In 1765 the Moguls detached part of the kingdom, called the district of Tippera, as a separate, Mogul-ruled region. The Mogul action turned the Tripuri against their Muslim overlords. The power of the Moguls effectively ended in 1803 with the British rapidly taking control of former Mogul territories. In 1808 Tripura established direct treaty relations with the British Empire. The maharaja formally ceded the district of Tippera, taken by the Moguls in 1765, to the British, to become a separate district of British Bengal.

The kingdom preserved its traditional feudal system as a separate British protectorate and ally. During World War I the maharaja furnished troops to aid his British ally. During World War II, Tripuri enthusiasm for Britain noticeably waned until a Japanese thrust into Indian territory nearly reached Tripura. Spurning Japanese overtures and promises of independence, the Tripuri rallied to the Allied cause.

The British authorities, soon after the end of World War II, began preparations to grant independence to British India. The huge region, divided into predominantly Hindu India and Muslim Pakistan, became the scene of increasing violence. The numerous British protectorates could decide which of the two new states they wished to join, but other choices or demands were adamantly opposed by the British, Indians, and Pakistanis.

Predominantly Hindu, Tripura favored India, but as it was considered too small to maintain itself as a separate state, the British recommended that Tripura become part of Assam.* The Tripuri vehemently rejected the recommendation on historic, linguistic, and ethnic grounds. Resisting British and Indian pressure, Tripura remained under nominal British protection when India and Pakistan became independent in August 1947. The British withdrawal, and increasing threats from neighboring Muslim East Pakistan ultimately pressed the Tripuri government, over fiery nationalist protests, to accede to India on 15 October 1949, ending 1,300 years of separate existence. The nationalists denounced the accession and Indian rule as illegal.

Administered directly from New Delhi as a separate territory, the Tripuri continued to reject proposals for union with neighboring Assam. In 1956 the government granted the region some autonomy as a union territory. Tripuri nationalists, never reconciled to Indian rule, continued to agitate for greater independence. Included in the Northeastern Areas Reorganization Act of 1971, Tripura became a full state of the Indian union.

Muslim Bengalis, in search of arable land, began to migrate to the fertile Tripuri valleys in 1951, raising religious and ethnic tensions in the region. The Indian government's inability or unwillingness to stem the illegal immigration in the 1960s and 1970s spurred the growth of Tripuri nationalism. Members of a Tripuri cultural group formed the first avowedly separatist organization in 1978. Gaining support in the state and with ties to other nationalist organizations in India's turbulent northeastern region, the Tripuri nationalists called for an end to India's illegal control of Tripura and the expulsion of all Bengali migrants.

The national movement also exacerbated tensions between Tripura's settled, Bengali-speaking population and the tribal peoples in the mountain regions of the state. Although both groups vehemently opposed the Muslim Bengali migration, they failed to agree on tribal rights and the future administration of the state. The Communist Party, not involved in the factional dispute, won state elections in 1978 with promises to restore lands taken by the growing number of illegal immigrants.

The tribal peoples, frustrated with inaction, attempted to reclaim stolen lands in the late 1970s and early 1980s. The resulting ethnic and religious conflict spread across the state leaving over 800 dead in violent clashes. The continuing clashes and the growing Tripuri separatist campaign in the 1980s focused on the migrant Bengali population. Over 200,000 Bengalis fled the violence to the protection of camps set up by the Indian government.

The Tripuri nationalists agreed to end the insurgency in 1988, but religious violence reactivated the separatist campaign in 1989. A nationalist boycott of state elections in June 1991 allowed India's predominant Congress Party to take control of the state. In late 1991 party cadres attacked Tripuri nationalists and burned the headquarters of legal opposition parties while the Congress Party-controlled police turned a blind eye. The growing violence provoked the tribal factions to demand the creation of a separate tribal state within Tripura. The increasing polarization of the state's population has hampered the nationalists and autonomists in their efforts to win greater independence. In April 1993 the Communists again took power after winning state elections.

*SELECTED BIBLIOGRAPHY:*
Chanra, B. *Nationalism and Colonialism in Modern India.* 1979.
Das, N. K. *Ethnic Identity, Ethnicity, and Social Stratification in North-East India.* 1989.
Karotempral, S., ed. *The Tribes of Northeast India.* 1984.

# TYROL

**Tirol; Tirolo**

*CAPITAL: Innsbruck*

SOUTH-CENTRAL EUROPE

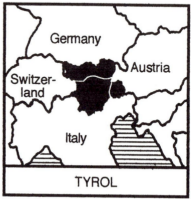

TYROL

*POPULATION:* (95e) 1,901,000 : 1,750,000 Tyroleans in Austria and Italy (633,000 Tyroleans, 493,000 Trentines, 362,000 Vorarlbergers, 262,000 South Tyroleans). MAJOR NATIONAL GROUPS: (95e) Tyrolean 92%, other Austrian, other Italian. MAJOR LANGUAGES: German (Tirolese dialect), Italian (Trentino dialect). MAJOR RELIGIONS: Roman Catholic, Protestant. MAJOR CITIES: (95e) AUSTRIA: Innsbruck 115,000 (176,000), Dornbirn 43,000 (117,000), Bregenz 27,000 (55,000), Feldkirch 22,000 (41,000), Lustenau 21,000. ITALY: Trento (Trent) 104,000 (165,000), Bozen (Bolzano) 97,000 (168,000), Roverto (Rofreit) 41,000 (72,000), Meran (Merano) 34,000 (93,000), Brixen (Bressanone) 18,000.

*GEOGRAPHY:* AREA: 11,143 sq.mi.-28,868 sq.mi. LOCATION: Tyrol occupies a mountainous region of high alpine valleys in the Alps in western Austria and northwestern Italy. POLITICAL STATUS: Tyrol forms the Austrian states of Tyrol and Vorarlberg and the Italian region of Trentino-Alto Adige.

*INDEPENDENCE DECLARED:* 3 November 1918; 24 April 1919.

*FLAG:* The Tyrolean national flag is a horizontal bicolor of white over red bearing, on a centered white disc, the national symbol, the red Tyrolean eagle. OTHER FLAG(S): The Tyrolean eagle centered on a white field is the flag of the South Tyrol. A horizontal bicolor of red over white is the flag of the Trentino.

*PEOPLE:* The Tyroleans are an alpine people comprising the Tyroleans and South Tyroleans, speaking the Tirolese dialect of German, in the center and north; the Vorarlbergers, speaking a dialect related to Swiss German, in the north; the Vorarlbergers, speaking a dialect related to Swiss German, in the northwest; and the Trentines (Trentinos, Trentini), speaking a Gallo-Italic dialect of Italian, in the center and south. The various groups share over a thousand years of coexistence, a collective history as Tyroleans, their Roman Catholic religion, and a common alpine culture that superseded the linguistic diversity.

*THE NATION:* The mountainous region north of Roman Italy came under Roman rule in the year 15 B.C. The region's Celtic inhabitants readily adopted the Romans' Latin speech and culture, becoming influential citizens of the vast empire. In the fifth and sixth centuries Germanic tribes overran the region, absorbing or dispersing the Romanized Celts. Called Tirol for a castle of that name, now in Italian Tyrol, the region became Germanic in language and culture. In the eighth century the Franks absorbed the region into their growing empire, the forerunner of the Holy Roman Empire.

The southern Tyrolean districts came under the rule of the powerful bishops of Trent and Brixen in the eleventh century. In the north the counts of Tyrol and Montfort gained control of the Tyrolean districts. In 1342 the Tyrolean peoples adopted a constitution, the first of its kind in Europe. The Hapsburgs gained control of part of Tyrol in 1363 and eventually extended their rule to Vorarlberg, which they added to their Tyrolean territory in 1523.

The secularized bishoprics of Trent and Brixen were awarded to Austria in 1802, during the upheavals of the Napoleonic Wars. Three years later a defeated Austria ceded all of Tyrol to Napoleon's ally, Bavaria.* Andreas Hoffer, now a Tyrolean national hero, united the diverse Tyrolean peoples to drive the Bavarians and French from the region. Hoffer was captured and executed in 1809, but his followers held out in mountain strongholds until Tyrol returned to Hapsburg control in 1815. The rebellion strengthened the ties among the Tyrolean peoples.

Italian irredentism, the movement to incorporate Italian-speaking parts of the Austro-Hungarian Empire into newly united Italy, gained some support after 1878. The majority of the Italian-speaking Trentines, separated from Italian influence since the fourteenth century, remained markedly unaffected by calls to Italian unity. Progressive and prosperous, in the 1880s and 1890s Tyrol was one of the few regions of the vast Hapsburg Empire where ethnic strife remained virtually unknown.

Italy, promised the Italian-speaking areas of Austro-Hungary, joined the Allies in 1915. Italy's entry into World War I turned Tyrol's pristine alpine valleys into battlefields and opened a rift between the German and Italian-speaking Tyroleans. A growing national movement, opposed to the war and rejecting Italian territorial claims, gained support. In October 1918 the Tyroleans took control of the administration. In the northwest the Vorarlbergers voted for secession and an alliance with Switzerland, and on 3 November 1918 declared their independence, but the Allies quickly moved to block the secession.

Tyrolean nationalists, citing point number ten of U.S. president Wilson's Fourteen Points, independence for the non-Austrian peoples of the empire, rejected both Austrian and Italian claims to the region. When it became clear that Italy was determined to annex the southern districts, the nationalists declared Tyrol independent on 24 April 1919. The nationalists began to erect a confederation of Swiss-style autonomous cantons, but again the Allies intervened to prevent secession. At the Paris Peace Conference the Allies assigned Tyrol and Vorarlberg to the new Austrian republic. The mainly Italian-speaking Trentino and South Tyrol, with its 250,000 German-speaking Tyroleans, came under the authority of the Italian kingdom.

The fascist Italian government, installed in 1922, and the leftist Austrian government pressed assimilation in their respective Tyrolean territories. In the south, despite promises of autonomy, the fascist authorities closed all Tyrolean institutions and in 1926 ordered the Tyroleans to change all place-names and family names to Italian. Government sponsored immigration from the backward, culturally and dialectically distinct southern Italy raised tensions, not only with the German-speaking Tyroleans in South Tyrol but also between the immigrants and the alpine Trentino Tyroleans.

The tensions reverberated in Austrian Tyrol. A militia sent from "Red Vienna" to suppress the Tyrolean national movement brought the region close to civil war in the early 1930s. The German annexation of Austria, in 1938, welcomed in the anti-Austrian, but pro-German, Tyrol, proved a disaster for the region. The German annexation of South Tyrol, following Italy's World War II surrender in 1943, briefly reunited the region, and over 60,000 Tyroleans had moved to the north Tyrol before Germany's defeat in 1944.

A democratic postwar Austrian government began to champion the cause of the German-speaking South Tyroleans. Agreements between Austria and Italy provided for limited autonomy in 1964, the accord designed to head off a growing campaign of violence and sabotage by South Tyrolean nationalists in Italy.

The increasing integration of Europe and the reunification of Germany stimulated a resurgence of Tyrolean nationalism in the 1990s. The possibility of reunification within a federal Europe has stimulated nationalist sentiment across the region. Resentment of the mass migration from southern Italy, beginning in the 1950s, has reversed decades of assimilation and reinforced the Trentine participation in the common alpine nationalism. On 15 September 1991 nationalists from all the Tyrolean areas demonstrated on the frontier at the Brenner Pass, demanding a referendum on reunification of Tyrol within a united Europe. Faced with rising nationalism, the Italian government agreed to greater autonomy in 1992.

Austria became a member state of the European Union on 1 January 1995, effectively uniting the two halves of the Tyrolean nation within the union. For the nationalists seeking a politically united and autonomous Tyrol within a European federation the fact that both Italy and Austria belong to the European Union does not alter their goal.

*SELECTED BIBLIOGRAPHY:*

Levy, Miriam. *Governance and Grievance: Hapsburg Policy and Italian Tyrol in the Eighteenth Century.* 1988.

Proctor, Alan. *The Tyrol.* 1986.

Shepard, Gordon. *The Austrian Odyssey.* 1957.

# UDMURTIA

**Votyakia; Votskaya**

*CAPITAL: Izhevsk*

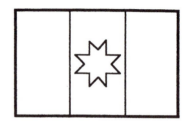

EASTERN EUROPE

UDMURTIA

*POPULATION:* (95e) 1,657,000 : 1,120,000 Udmurts in Russia. MAJOR NA-
TIONAL GROUPS: (95e) Russian 48%, Udmurt 41%, Tatar 8%, Mari 1%,
Bashkir 1%. MAJOR LANGUAGES: Russian, Udmurt, Tatar. MAJOR RELI-
GIONS: Russian Orthodox, Sunni Muslim, animist. MAJOR CITIES: (95e)
Izhevsk 685,000 (760,000), Sarapul 114,000 (145,000), Votinsk 111,000
(134,000), Glazov 110,000 (135,000), Mozhga 55,000, Igra 42,000.

*GEOGRAPHY:* AREA: 15,869 sq.mi.-41,111 sq.km. LOCATION: Udmurtia
lies in eastern European Russia, a highland region between the Vyatka and Kama
Rivers and the foothills of the Ural Mountains. POLITICAL STATUS: Udmurtia
forms a member state of the Russian Federation.

*FLAG:* The Udmurt national flag, the official flag of the republic, is a vertical
tricolor of black, white, and red bearing a red, eight-pointed star, representing
the sun, centered on the white.

*PEOPLE:* The Udmurts are a people of the eastern branch of the Finno-Ugric
peoples speaking a Finno-Permian language of the Finno-Ugric language group.
The Udmurts comprise two major divisions: the Udmurts in the south and the
Besmerians, possibly of Chavash origin but speaking an Udmurt dialect, in the
north. The Udmurt portion of the republic's population has begun to increase,
possibly due to a large number who have switched their ethnic classification
from Russian back to Udmurt. The Udmurts, forming 52% of the population in
1939, had fallen to 32% in 1959, the drop due to a mass Slav influx during
World War II and the number of Udmurts who listed themselves as ethnic

Russians during the Stalin era. The Udmurts are mostly Russian Orthodox, but with a minority that has retained traditional beliefs.

*THE NATION:* Udmurt tradition traces the origins of their nation in the region back to Neolithic times. A tribal people practicing a shamanistic religion revolving around veneration of ancestors, the Udmurts controlled a large territory north of the Volga River until the conquest of their territory by the Bulgar Chavash people in the eighth century. In the early Middle Ages, influenced by the Chavash, the Udmurts settled in agricultural villages.

Russian explorers from the Novgorod republic explored the northern Udmurt districts in the early twelfth century, and in 1174 Novgorodian colonists founded fortified settlements north of the Vyatka River. The Udmurts fiercely resisted the Slav colonization but gradually lost ground to the Slavs and abandoned their traditional lands in the north.

Mongols, advancing from the southeast, devastated the Udmurt lands in 1236–37, forcing many Udmurts to take refuge in the unconquered Slavic region to the north. At the breakup of the Mongol Golden Horde in the fourteenth century, the southern Udmurts were included in the Tatar-dominated Khanate of Kazan. The Udmurts in the north came under the control of the Slavic Vyatka Republic. By the late fourteenth century most of the Udmurts had accepted the Christian religion brought to the region by Orthodox monks.

The northern Udmurts came under Russian rule in 1489 following the conquest of Vyatka by the expanding duchy of Moscow. The conquest of Kazan in 1552 reunited the Udmurt peoples under Russian rule, although Udmurt rebels continued to fight the Russians until 1558. The Udmurts, including the large Orthodox population, suffered a harsh Russian colonial rule. By the seventeenth century most Udmurts were tied to large Russian estates as serfs, unpaid agricultural workers. Kept in ignorance and poverty, the Udmurt's only escape was the lower ranks of the Orthodox priesthood.

The majority of the Udmurt population lived in isolation until World War I. The small Udmurt population in the Kama River area produced the first educated minority, the spark that began an Udmurt cultural revival in the late nineteenth century. In 1910 the first literary works appeared in the Udmurt language, the development of a separate literary language accelerating the cultural and national revival.

Thousands of illiterate Udmurt soldiers, sent to the front in 1914, began to desert and return home following the overthrow of the tsar in February 1917. The returning soldiers formed a self-defense force as civil government collapsed. In the summer of 1917 the Udmurts convened a national congress. The delegates voted for autonomy in a federal, democratic Russia as promised by government agents. The Bolshevik coup in October ended the debate and thrust the non-Russian peoples of the Volga basin into closer cooperation. The Udmurts began to erect a state as part of a federation of non-Russian states in the region.

Bolshevik forces occupied Udmurtia in March 1918. The Soviets quickly suppressed the Udmurt national movement and transferred the capital of the region from the Udmurt city of Glazov to the mostly Russian industrial city of Izhevsk. To win Udmurt support, the authorities distributed the lands of the great Russian estates to the former Udmurt tenant farmers. Following the Soviet victory in the Russian civil war, the authorities established an autonomous province on 5 January 1921.

The Soviet authorities quickly suppressed a revolt stemming from the confiscation of the lands distributed to the Udmurts in 1918. Soviet agricultural confiscation and policies exacerbated the growing hunger in the region. In 1920–22 thousands of Udmurts perished from famine and disease. In the 1930s the remaining Udmurt lands were confiscated and collectivized, their dispossessed owners forced to settle on government communes.

In spite of the harshness of Soviet rule, the Udmurts advanced in education and culture, particularly after gaining republic status in 1934. In 1922 only 22% of the region's population were literate, and only 10% of that small number were ethnic Udmurts. By the time World War II began in June 1941, Udmurt literacy had become widespread.

Part of the Ural industrial region, Udmurtia received industries and populations displaced by the war farther west. The influx reduced the Udmurts to a minority in their homeland, their minority status stimulating the first stirrings of modern Udmurt nationalism. In the 1970s the Udmurts urbanized, the populations of many towns doubling between 1969 and 1979. Urbanization produced a modern generation of Udmurts, little aware of their unique history and educated in Russian. Udmurt assimilation, well advanced by 1980, began to reverse as young Udmurts began to take a new interest in their culture in the 1980s.

The Soviet liberalization of the late 1980s accelerated the reculturation of the Udmurts. Cultural and nationalist groups formed, demanding official status for their language, the opening of a specifically Udmurt university, and a change from the Russian Cyrillic alphabet to the Latin alphabet used in the West.

The republican government, pressed by the growing Udmurt national movement, declared the republic a sovereign state in October 1990. The Udmurt parliament declared that federal laws were valid in the republic only when confirmed by the parliament. Following the disintegration of the Soviet Union in August 1991, militants advocated independence within a Volga federation, but the majority of the Udmurts fear the uncertainties of independence while asserting their rights within the Russian Federation. The moderate nationalist groups believe that real autonomy will ensure that the Udmurts have not replaced Soviet domination with an equally oppressive Russian domination.

*SELECTED BIBLIOGRAPHY:*

Colton, Timothy, and Robert Levgold, eds. *After the Soviet Union.* 1992.

Kozlov, Viktor. *The Peoples of the Soviet Union.* 1988.

Smal-Stocki, Roman. *The Captive Nations: Nationalism of the Non-Russian Nations and Peoples.* 1960.

# URALIA

**Urals; Uralsk**

*CAPITAL: Yekaterinburg (Sverdlovsk)*

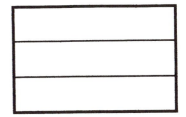

*POPULATION:* (95e) 13,357,000 : 12,000,000 Ural Russians (Uralnaks) and 135,000 Ural Cossacks in Russia. MAJOR NATIONAL GROUPS: (95e) Ural Russian (Uralnak) 73%, Russian 13%, Ural Cossack 10%, Ukrainian 3%. MAJOR LANGUAGES: Russian, Ukrainian, Cossack. MAJOR RELIGIONS: Russian Orthodox, Roman Catholic. MAJOR CITIES: (95e) Yekaterinburg (Sverdlovsk) 1,381,000 (1,658,000), Chelyabinsk 1,161,000 (1,363,000), Perm 1,109,000 (1,208,000), Nizhniy Tagil 440,000, Magnitogorsk 435,000, Kurgan 385,000, Kamensk-Uralsk 213,000, Zlatoust 208,000, Berezniki 205,000 (269,000), Miass 170,000 (279,000), Kopeysk 159,000, Pervouralsk 143,000 (240,000), Solikamsk 111,000, Nadezhdinsk (Serov) 103,000, Troitsk 100,000, Asbest 84,000 (132,000), Korkino 80,000 (138,000).

*GEOGRAPHY:* AREA: 198,571 sq.mi.-514,433 sq.km. LOCATION: Uralia lies in west-central Russia on both sides of the Ural Mountains that divide Europe from Asia, occupying the steppe lands and the foothills in eastern European Russia and the vast plain east of the mountains, the Ural Steppe, in western Siberia.* POLITICAL STATUS: Uralia has no official status; unilaterally declared a member republic of the Russian Federation, the Russian government has not recognized the declaration. Officially, the region forms the oblasts (provinces) of Perm, Yekaterinburg, Chelyabinsk, and Kurgan.

*FLAG:* The Uralnak national flag, the flag of the national movement, is a horizontal tricolor of black, yellow, and green. OTHER FLAG(S): The flag of the Ural Cossacks is a horizontal bicolor of pale blue over yellow.

*PEOPLE:* The Ural Russians, calling themselves Uralnaks, are the descendants of early Cossack settlers, freed serfs, and later Slav settlers transferred wholesale to the region before and during World War II, speaking a Russian dialect with marked admixtures of Ukrainian, Cossack, and Turkic borrowings. The Ural Cossacks are a Cossack people, one of eleven Cossack communities in Russia. Historically and physically removed from the European Russian heartland, the Uralnaks and Cossacks see themselves as Ural Slav peoples, the descendants of pioneers and later groups unwanted in European Russia. The majority of the Ural peoples are Russian Orthodox, with an influential Roman Catholic minority, mostly groups deported from Russia's western provinces during and after World War II.

*THE NATION:* The original inhabitants of the region, Finnic Permian peoples in the north and Turkic tribes in the south, came under loose Mongol rule in the thirteenth century. The Tatars, absorbed into the Mongol hordes, gained control of much of the region with the breakup of the Mongol Empire in the fourteenth century. The powerful Tatar khanates of Kazan and Sibir extracted tribute from the Slavs west of the Ural Mountains, as far west as Moscow.

Known to the medieval Slavs as the Stone Belt, Slav explorers and fur traders from the Novgorod republic began to penetrate the region in the twelfth century. The expanding Russian state, the Moscow duchy, extended its authority west of the mountains in the fifteenth century, and in 1552 the Russians overthrew the Tatar Khanate of Kazan. The conquest of Kazan and the subsequent conquest of Sibir in 1581 opened the way for European colonization. Russian colonists settled the western slopes of the Urals, founding the town of Perm, named for the Permian peoples, in 1568. The region's mineral wealth led to the establishment of the first ironworks in the 1630s.

The colonization and exploration of the region, undertaken from Perm, absorbed or displaced the earlier populations. Ural Cossacks moved out to found a string of forts on the eastern slopes and the Ural Steppe beyond. The Cossacks established Yekaterinburg in 1721, Nizhniy Tagil in 1725, and Chelyabinsk in 1736. The Yekaterinburg region was annexed by Russia between 1726 and 1762; the southern districts, after 1731.

The rugged, mountainous region, far from the centers of Russian life, grew slowly in the eighteenth and early nineteenth centuries. The freeing of the serfs in 1861 brought an influx of land-hungry colonists. The freed serfs, allowed to take possession of parcels of land, received little practical government help and suffered incredible hardships. The colonists evolved a strong antigovernment, anti-European attitude that exists to the present. The construction of the Trans-Siberian Railroad in the 1890s to Kurgan opened the way to the mass colonization of the Ural Steppe and the high plateau of the middle Urals.

The thousands of Ural conscripts sent to the front when war began in 1914 mostly deserted and returned home following the Russian Revolution in February 1917. The returnees, bitter and disillusioned, enthusiastically joined the revolution. After the Bolshevik coup overthrew the provisional government of Russia in October 1917, various armed bands roamed the region, pro-Bolshevik, anti-Bolshevik, and a small separatist group made up of deserters and Cossacks trying to protect their homeland from the spreading civil war.

The Bolsheviks in March 1918 took control of most of the region. The Czech Legion, Czech and Slovak prisoners of war trying to return to Europe via the Trans-Siberian Railroad through Siberia, became stranded. They established their headquarters at Chelyabinsk, which became a haven for the various anti-Bolshevik factions in the region as the legion fought the Bolsheviks for control of the vital railroad and the Urals industrial zone.

The last Russian tsar, Nicholas II, and his family, transported east as prisoners of the provisional government, fell into the hands of the members of the Ural Soviet. Held prisoner in Yekaterinburg, the former imperial family became the object of an anti-Bolshevik White offensive. As the rescuers neared, the Soviet authorities, possibly on Lenin's orders, executed the entire family on 16 July 1918. By 1920 the Urals region had come under firm Soviet rule.

Soviet economic experimentation and the crushing of anti-Soviet groups in European Russia kept a steady stream of deportees arriving in Urals in the 1920s and 1930s. After 1929 many of the remaining tracts of land were forcibly colonized by Kulaks, former free farmers persecuted and deported from the European provinces.

The beginning of World War II in June 1941 drastically changed the region. During the course of the war much of the heavy industry and the needed workers and their families, threatened by the Nazi advance, were transferred to the Urals region. The rapid increase of population required an administrative reorganization. In 1943 Chelyabinsk and Sverdlovsk were organized as separate administrative provinces.

The liberalization of Soviet life in the late 1980s opened a torrent of grievances in the region, from neglect and disdain by European Russia to the massive pollution doing great harm to the health of the inhabitants. Demands for an end to the economic control by ministries in Moscow led to other demands for political as well as economic autonomy. In June 1993 the government of Yekaterinburg Oblast unilaterally declared the region a member republic of the Russian Federation, and by October the other Ural provinces had voted to join the revolt. To pressure Moscow to accept their bid for greater independence, the provinces began to withhold taxes and block government directives. In December 1993 Russia's president Boris Yeltsin dismissed the provincial leader of Yekaterinburg, Eduard Rossel. Ministers in Moscow have labeled the region a separatist center that threatens Russia's territorial integrity.

*SELECTED BIBLIOGRAPHY:*

Broderick, Benson. *East of the Sun: The Epic Conquest and Tragic History of Siberia.* 1992.

Colton, Timothy, and Robert Levgold, eds. *After the Soviet Union.* 1992.

McAuley, Alistair, ed. *Soviet Federalism: Nationalism and Economic Decentralization.* 1991.

# VENETO

### Venetia; Venezia

*CAPITAL: Venice (Venezia)*

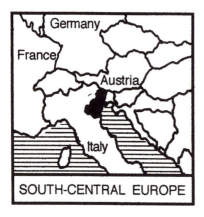

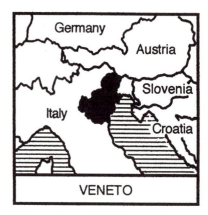

*POPULATION:* (95e) 4,423,000 : 3,600,000 Venetians in Italy. MAJOR NA-
TIONAL GROUPS: (95e) Venetian 78%, other Italian. MAJOR LANGUAGES:
Italian, Venetian, German. MAJOR RELIGIONS: Roman Catholic, Protestant.
MAJOR CITIES: (95e) Verona 293,000 (426,000), Padua (Padova) 247,000
(310,000), Mestre 207,000, Vicenta (Vicenza) 125,00 (183,000), Travise (Tre-
viso) 88,000, Fossa (Chioggia) 81,000 (104,000), Rovige (Rovigo) 70,000
(92,000), Venice (Venezia) 65,000 (448,000), Bellun (Belluno) 49,000 (76,000).

*GEOGRAPHY:* AREA: 7,096 sq.mi.-18,383 sq.km. LOCATION: Veneto oc-
cupies a flat plain rising to the Carnic Alps in the north, just east of the Adriatic
Sea in northeastern Italy. POLITICAL STATUS: Veneto forms a region of the
Italian republic.

*FLAG:* The Venetian national flag, the flag of the national movement, is a
yellow field charged with a red square on the hoist bearing the Lion of Venice
in yellow and, outlined in a yellow and red design, the same design reflected
in six horizontal stripes on the fly.

*PEOPLE:* The Venetians are a northern Italian people speaking, along with
standard Italian, a distinctive dialect that has incorporated influences from the
neighboring Slav and Germanic peoples. Venetian nationalists claim the dialect
as a separate Romance language. The dialect is spoken by 60% of the Venetian
people and is used by 35% of the population as the language of daily life.
Venetian culture, like the language, has been influenced by neighboring nations
and the peoples of the once-extensive Venetian Empire and is quite distinct

from the standard Italian culture of central and southern Italy. The majority of the Venetians are Roman Catholic, with a Protestant minority, mostly in the mountainous districts in the north.

*THE NATION:* The region, inhabited by an Illyrian people, the Veneti, came under Roman rule in the second and first centuries B.C. Organized as a Roman province, two cities dominated the region, Aquileia, at the head of the Adriatic in the northeast, and Padua, second only to Rome itself in wealth and culture. Barbarian tribes invaded the collapsing empire in the fifth century A.D. In 452 the Huns, led by Attila, moved across the province, destroying everything in their path. The inhabitants of the once-flourishing city of Aquileia, to escape the destruction, fled to the 118 islands of the Venice Lagoon.

The small island communities united in 697 to elect the first *doge* (duke) to rule over the unified island state. Well situated to control the flourishing maritime trade, the island communities grew and prospered. In the ninth century the central islands joined to form the city of Venice. Over the next century Venice broke free of Byzantine rule and began to expand its mainland territories. The Venetians won control of the plains east of the Adige River and expanded to conquer the islands and coastal regions of Dalmatia across the narrow Adriatic.

The fourth Christian Crusade, led by the Venetian *doge*, instead of moving on to free the Holy Land from Muslim rule, turned on the Byzantine capital, Constantinople. The treasures looted from Christendom's largest and wealthiest city financed Venice's rise to power. Venice emerged from the venture as the ruler of a colonial empire made up of several Mediterranean islands and parts of the Greek mainland.

In 1380–81 Venice defeated the rival Republic of Genoa to become the premier Mediterranean maritime power. In the fifteenth century Venice extended its rule to the former free cities of the eastern Po Valley to become an extensive Italian state, one of the wealthiest and most powerful in Europe.

The emergence of the Turkish Ottoman Empire in the East challenged Venetian dominance of the Mediterranean. Sporadic wars between the fifteenth and eighteenth centuries gradually shrank the republic's overseas empire as colony after colony fell to Turkish rule. Even though the republic declined in power, its cities experienced a great flowering of culture and arts between the fourteenth and sixteenth centuries, the Renaissance.

The republic, in spite of frantic efforts to maintain its neutrality, fell, without a shot, to Napoleon's forces in 1797. Napoleon traded most of the Venetian districts to Austria in exchange for territories in the Low Countries. Briefly joined to Napoleon's Kingdom of Italy from 1805 to 1814, Venice returned to Austrian rule following Napoleon's final defeat.

The Venetians, led by Daniele Manin, rebelled against Austrian rule in 1848. The rebels proclaimed Venetian independence as the Republic of St. Mark. Opposed to Venetian moves to unite with the Kingdom of Sardinia,* Manin resigned but returned in 1849 to lead Venetian opposition to the reimposition of Austrian rule. The Kingdom of Italy, united in 1860–61 under the Sardinian king, sided with Prussia in the Austro-Prussian War of 1866. As a reward, Prussia backed the Italian annexation of the Venetian territories from defeated Austria.

The new Italian kingdom adopted a Tuscan dialect spoken around Florence as its national language. The dialect, very unlike the Venetian dialect, was generally rejected in the region. Linguistic nationalism increased as Veneto industrialized in the late nineteenth century, bringing the first migrants from southern Italy, part of the same migration that sent millions of southern Italians to the Americas. The first recorded incidence of violence between the migrants and anti-immigrant Venetians took place in Verona in 1889.

The Italian fascist government launched a campaign to eradicate Italy's many regional languages in 1922, the campaign largely unsuccessful in Veneto. After World War II, 60% of the Venetian population still used the Venetian dialect in daily life. The percentage began to decline only with the arrival of mass media in the 1950s and 1960s. The postwar economic boom in northern Italy further eroded the use of the Venetian dialect. Standard Italian became the lingua franca used by Venetian supervisors and the thousands of southern Italians moving north to work in the booming industries in the 1960s and 1970s.

Anti-immigrant sentiment and violence began to grow in the 1970s, along with an increasing frustration with the notoriously inefficient and overstaffed government in Rome. Moves toward European integration raised fears that Veneto and the other industrialized northern regions would be unable to compete in Europe while hampered by Rome's bloated bureaucracy and the need to channel northern taxes and massive development aid to the corrupt and backward southern regions.

Venetian nationalism, exemplified by the dramatic spread of national sentiment in the late 1980s and early 1990s, is still mainly autonomist, the majority of the nationalists favoring political and economic autonomy within a federal Italy. In late 1994 nationalists in the city of Venice accused members of the Italian government of having more interest in looting the public purse than in the neglected heritage of Venice and other decaying historic cities. The massive corruption and crime scandals that have reached the highest circles of the Italian government and the economic elite have spurred the growth of Venetian nationalism and calls for a separate Veneto state within a united, federal Europe.

*SELECTED BIBLIOGRAPHY:*

Carello, Adrian N. *The Northern Question: Italy's Participation in the European Economic Community and the Mezzogiorno's Underdevelopment.* 1989.

Mayne, R. J. *The Community of Europe.* 1962.

Morris, James. *The World of Venice.* 1985.

Smith, Denis M. *The Making of Italy 1796–1870.* 1988.

# VOLGA

**Volga Germany**

*CAPITAL: Engels (Pokrovsk)*

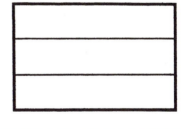

*POPULATION:* (95e) 1,358,000 : 950,000 Volga Germans in Russia. The total German population in Russia, Kazakhstan, and other former Soviet republics is estimated to number over 2 million. MAJOR NATIONAL GROUPS: (95e) Russian 85%, Ukrainian 10%, Volga German 3%, Kazakh. (1941: Volga German 67%, Russian 20%, Ukrainian 12%). MAJOR LANGUAGES: Russian, Ukrainian, German (various dialects). MAJOR RELIGIONS: Russian Orthodox, Roman Catholic, Protestant. (1941: Protestant 65%, Orthodox 17%, Roman Catholic 14%, Mennonite 4%.) MAJOR CITIES: (95e) Balakovo 220,000, Engels (Pokrovsk) 195,000 (242,000), Nikolaevsk (Pugachev) 45,000, Yershov 33,000, Katrinenstadt (Marks) 30,000.

*GEOGRAPHY:* AREA: 10,888 sq.mi.-28,207 sq.km. LOCATION: Volga, formerly called the German Volga Republic, occupies the rolling steppe lands in the valley of the middle Volga River on the arbitrary divide between Europe and Asia. POLITICAL STATUS: Volga has no official status; the region forms the eastern districts of Saratov Oblast. The Russian and German governments have agreed to the re-creation of an autonomous Volga German state in the region they occupied before 1941, but as yet nothing more has been accomplished.

*FLAG:* The Volga German flag, the flag of the republican movement, is a horizontal tricolor of red, pale blue, and black.

*PEOPLE:* The Volga Germans originated with eighteenth-century colonists from the southern German states. The Germans still retain dialects and cultural traits that long ago disappeared in Germany, and their culture has absorbed many Slav influences, the differences setting them apart from both the Germans and the Russians. The German population, deported from the Volga and Black Sea regions in 1941, have lived in Siberia* and Kazakhstan for over fifty years and have begun to succumb to assimilation. In 1989 only 60% of the ethnic Germans listed German as their first language; however, since the collapse of the Soviet Union and the reunification of Germany, a rapid reculturation has taken hold in the German-populated areas.

*THE NATION:* Tsarina Catherine II of Russia, known as Catherine the Great, was born in the southern German state of Anhalt-Zerbst in 1762. To strengthen her empire and to exploit the rich agricultural lands newly won from Turkic and Tatar peoples, the tsarina issued an invitation to the inhabitants of the German states to settle in the region. Catherine's manifesto, issued in 1763, guaranteed the colonists and their descendants free lands, exemption from military service, freedom of religion, local autonomy, use of their own languages, and many other incentives designed to appeal to the industrious German peasants.

Catherine's invitation, particularly appealing to the peoples of the southern German states that had suffered extensive devastation during the just-ended Seven Years' War, provided a less costly alternative to emigration to America. Between 1764 and 1768 thousands of German colonists settled the newly conquered frontier districts north and east of the Black Sea. Some 27,000 Germans moved farther east to establish over a hundred farming communities along the middle course of the Volga River.

The colonists, isolated and self-sufficient, prospered as farmers and merchants in close-knit communities having little to do with the neighboring Slav villages. Dialects, cultures, and traditions that gradually changed or disappeared in Germany continued in the region, eventually forming part of a distinctive, Slav-influenced German culture.

Catherine's successors progressively abolished the Germans' privileges. By 1870 all of Catherine's guarantees had disappeared. Over the next decade an official policy of assimilation and Russification closed German schools, publications, and institutions. The authorities introduced military conscription. Resistance to assimilation and conscription led to the growth of national sentiment in the 1880s and 1890s. The German national movement evolved as a cultural campaign to preserve their language and culture but also became anti-government.

Suspected of pro-German sentiment when war began in 1914, the tsarist government imposed harsh new restrictions on the Germans. In 1916 the government issued a decree ordering the deportation of all Germans, the order to be implemented in April 1917. The decree, suspended when revolution swept Russia in February 1917, was finally rescinded, along with all other tsarist decrees, by the Bolsheviks who overthrew the Russian provisional government in October 1917.

The Volga Germans organized an autonomous administration as the civil government of the region collapsed. Nationalists, in control of the government, prepared to declare independence and to seek assistance from the German military units occupying Russian territory farther to the west, but in late 1917 Bolshevik forces overran the Volga region. The first ethnic group to be organized under the Soviet nationalities program, a Volga German autonomous region was authorized and in 1919 became an autonomous republic. Outside the republic the Soviet authorities created seventeen autonomous districts for the scattered German populations. Created as a model showcase to encourage the spread of Communism in Germany, the Volga Republic suffered harsh repression when post-World War I Communist uprisings failed in Germany. The Stalinist terror eased only when the Soviet Union signed a friendship treaty with Nazi Germany in 1939.

The Nazi invasion of the Soviet Union in June 1941 ended the short period of leniency. Stalin accused all Soviet Germans of collaboration. In August 1941 the 440,000 Volga Germans and between 250,000 and 350,000 mostly Black Sea Germans were shipped east in closed cattle cars. The deportees, often without food or shelter, were dumped at rail sidings across Siberia and Central Asia under close KGB control.

Another 350,000 Germans, living in areas overrun by the German armies, were evacuated to Germany. Over 200,000 of the evacuees, rounded up by Soviet troops in defeated Germany in 1945, were forcibly repatriated and sent directly to slave labor camps, where they remained until granted amnesty after Stalin's death in 1953.

Not rehabilitated with the other deported peoples in 1956–57, the Germans were finally exonerated in 1964 but were not allowed to return to their homes in European Russia. Their petitions and appeals constantly rebuffed, the exiles developed a sense of grievance that stimulated the growth of nationalism. In 1975 a Volga German national movement formed to work for the reestablishment of an autonomous German homeland on the Volga. Improved relations between the Soviet Union and Germany allowed a small number to emigrate, but the numbers were limited by Germany's inability to absorb all who wished to leave.

Demands for the resurrection of the autonomous republic increased during the Soviet liberalization of the late 1980s. Cool to the idea of yet another minority nationalism, the Soviet authorities refused. The nationalists again raised the demand following the Soviet disintegration in 1991. The new Russian authorities, badly in need of Germany's political and financial assistance, in a series of meetings with German officials finally agreed. The long delay in implementing the accord has stimulated more militant groups and demands and has provoked the emigration of over 100,000 a year to Germany in the 1990s.

*SELECTED BIBLIOGRAPHY:*

Curran, Alfred A. *Soviet-German Nationalism.* 1986.

Ingsborg, Fleischhauer, and Benjamin Pinkus. *The Soviet Germans: Past and Present.* 1986.

Koch, Frederick C. *The Volga Germans: In Russia and the Americas 1763 to the Present.* 1987.

Nekrich, Alexander. *The Punished Peoples.* 1978.

# WAH

**Wa; Wa States**

*CAPITAL: Namton*

SOUTHEASTERN ASIA

WAH

*POPULATION:* (95e) 620,000 : 450,000 Wa in Myanmar and another 100,000 in adjacent areas of Thailand and China. MAJOR NATIONAL GROUPS: (95e) Wa 70%, Shan 20%, Lahu, Palaung. MAJOR LANGUAGES: Wa (Lawa), Shan, Burmese. MAJOR RELIGIONS: animist, Buddhist, Christian. MAJOR CITIES: (95e) Namton 15,000, Man Hpang 10,000.

*GEOGRAPHY:* AREA: 9,090 sq.mi.-23,549 sq.km. LOCATION: Wa occupies the basin of the upper Salween River and the surrounding highlands of the Shan Plateau in northeastern Myanmar. POLITICAL STATUS: Wa has no official status; the region claimed by nationalists forms the former Wa States and the adjoining Wa-populated areas of Myanmar.

*FLAG:* The Wa national flag, the flag of the national movement, has horizontal stripes of pale blue, red, and pale blue, the red twice the width of the blue stripes and charged with a white, nine-pointed star.

*PEOPLE:* The Wa, called Lawa in Thailand and Va in China, are believed the original inhabitants of the Shan Plateau region and form nine clan or tribal groups. A Mon-Khmer people, the Wa are ethnically and linguistically related to the Mon of Honsawatoi* and the Khmer of Cambodia. Until the early twentieth century head-hunting formed an integral part of the Wa culture and religion, the skulls used to fertilize fields and believed to ensure good crops and good health. The Wa speak a Palaung-Wa language of the Mon-Khmer language group written in a Latin alphabet devised by missionaries. The majority of the Wa adhere to traditional beliefs, with Buddhist and Christian minorities.

*THE NATION:* From their origins in eastern Tibet,* the Mon-Khmer peoples migrated south along the Mekong and Salween Rivers. The Wa settled the mountains along the upper Salween, probably between the fifth and third centuries B.C. According to Wa tradition, they once inhabited the plateau lowlands, but stronger peoples drove them into the mountains. A primitive tribal people, the Wa, unlike most of the other peoples of the region, never came under the religious or cultural influences of India or China.

The Shans, a Thai people, overran the Wa territory in the seventh century. The conquerors from southeastern China imposed their social order on the tribes, creating small Wa states ruled by an aristocratic elite. Allied to the Shans, the fierce Wa warriors helped to defeat a Mongol invasion in the thirteenth century.

The Shan declined in the early nineteenth century, leaving the Wa States virtually independent as vassal states of the Burman king. In the 1870s the Wa and Shan princes renounced their allegiance to the Burman king, the resulting chaos giving the British a pretext to intervene in the region. Following the third Anglo-Burman war in 1885–86, the region came under British rule, the newcomers often welcomed as liberators from oppressive Burman rule.

The British established separate treaty relations with the Wa princes, the treaties formalizing their status as British protectorates not included in British Burma. Many Wa clans, particularly in the less developed northern states, resisted the imposition of British rule until 1889. British attempts to stamp out ritual head-hunting, an integral part of the Wa's culture and religion, met fierce resistance. Although the states remained semi-independent under their traditional rulers, the British retained the right to confirm the succession of the rulers.

The colonial authorities consolidated the Wa and Shan States in 1922 to form the Federated Shan States. The federation, under the responsibility of a British commissioner, was structured to separate the Wa States as an administrative unit under the authority of the British commissioner as adviser to the courts of the various Wa princes.

The European influence, particularly the impact of the missionaries who arrived in the states in the 1920s, gradually ended the ancient practice of head-hunting. The missionary education, in the Wa language, using a Latin alphabet devised for the purpose, introduced the Wa to the ideas and power of European nationalism and fostered a sense of unity among the various tribes and clans. In 1930 the first Wa national organization formed to promote and protect the Wa language and culture in the Wa States and the surrounding areas.

The Wa generally supported the British during World War II, acting as guides for Allied patrols and fighting the Burman, Shan, and Thai allies of the Japanese. The occupation of the region by the Japanese and their allies forced the Wa to retreat into the mountains, where they formed guerrilla groups that terrorized enemy patrols. In December 1943 the Japanese authorities placed the Wa States under the direct rule of their Burman allies, the first time in history that the Burmans were able to impose their rule directly on the fiercely independent Wa tribes. The Burmans, who switched to the Allied cause in 1944, maintained their control of the region following the Japanese defeat and the return of the British in 1945.

Preparations for the independence of Burma after the war stimulated Burman demands for the inclusion in the Burmese state of all the territories that were tributary to the medieval Burman kings. In 1948, without their consent, the British included the Wa States in the territories ceded to the new Union of Burma.

In 1959 the government deposed the Wa princes, setting off a rebellion in the region. The Wa rebels, holding the strategic passes, formed alliances with insurgent Shans, who controlled the lowlands, and the Lahu tribes, in control of the mountain tops. The Wa insurgency spread to the formerly neutral Wa tribes following the takeover of the Burmese state by a brutal military regime in 1962.

Wa ties to the related tribes in China gave them a natural sanctuary and a conduit for military aid and arms. The Wa insurgents, armed by the Chinese Communists, formed an alliance with the Chinese-supported Burmese Communist rebels active in the region. To finance the ongoing war, the Wa turned to the region's traditional crop, opium. In 1972, in the midst of a fierce rivalry with the Shan insurgents for control of the opium-producing eastern Shan Plateau, the Wa leaders, for the first time, openly espoused a separatist platform and independence in a federation of states to replace the Burmese military regime.

The crushing of the pro-democracy movement in Burma in 1988 pushed to Wa to adopt a less doctrinaire and more openly nationalist ideology. In April 1989 the Wa tribesmen, accounting for 80% of the membership of the insurgent Communist Party of Burma (CAB), rebelled and drove the Communist leaders across the border into China, and later in 1989 signed a cease-fire with the military government.

The lucrative drug trade sparked a minor war with the Shanland* drug lord, Khun Shan, in 1990. The violent fighting for control of the drug trails along the Thai and Chinese border left hundreds dead. In April 1991 the fighting became so fierce that the Thai military intervened to drive both the Wa and Shan drug traffickers deeper into Myanmar and away from the sensitive Thai border.

The Wa insurgency in the 1990s has split between the groups fighting for autonomy or independence and the groups fighting to protect their contraband drug trade. Violence between the two groups has seriously weakened the Wa national movement since 1992.

*SELECTED BIBLIOGRAPHY:*
Lintner, Bertil. *Land of Jade: A Journey through Insurgent Burma.* 1990.
Smith, Martin. *Burma, Insurgency and the Politics of Ethnicity.* 1988.
Tinker, Hugh. *The Union of Burma.* 1961.

# WALDENSIA

**Valli Valdesi; Waldensian Valleys**

*CAPITAL: Torre Pelice*

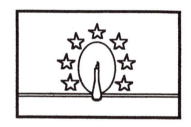

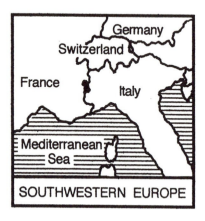

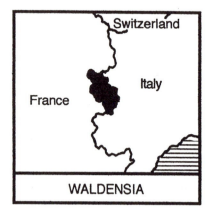

*POPULATION:* (95e) 61,000 : 32,000 Waldensians (Waldenses/Valdese) in Italy and another 15,000 in the Rio Plate region of Argentina and Uruguay. MAJOR NATIONAL GROUPS: (95e) Waldensian 50%, Occitan 34%, other Italian. MAJOR LANGUAGES: Italian, Occitan, French. MAJOR RELIGIONS: Waldensian, other Protestant, Roman Catholic. MAJOR CITIES: (95e) Luserna 9,000 (16,000), Torre Pelice 6,000, Villar Persosa (Val Persosa) 5,000.

*GEOGRAPHY:* AREA: 1,136 sq.mi.-2,943 sq.km. LOCATION: Waldensia lies in the Cottian Alps, occupying seven valleys traversed by the Pellice and Germanesca Rivers, on the French border southwest of Turin in northwestern Italy. POLITICAL STATUS: Waldensia has no official status; the region forms a historic area in the Italian region of Piedmont.*

*FLAG:* The Waldensian flag is a blue field with a narrow, red horizontal stripe at the bottom divided from the blue by a narrow white stripe. In the center is a black candle with an oval of yellow light around the flame surrounded by seven white stars.

*PEOPLE:* The Waldensians are a division of the Occitan people who inhabit northwestern Italy and the Occitania* region of southern France but are historically and religiously distinct as the oldest surviving Protestant nation in the world. The Waldensians speak a dialect of Occitan, along with Italian, and many also speak French. The descendants the followers of the first Protestant religious dissidents in the twelfth and thirteenth centuries, the Waldensians became a nation through centuries of persecution and isolation. The Waldensian culture, protected by their self-imposed isolation, combines the original Occitan Latin culture with influences from the Piedmontese and the Romande* in Switzerland.

*THE NATION:* In the latter half of the twelfth century, in 1170, a wealthy merchant in Lyon, Pietro Waldo, also called Valdo or Valdesius, ceded his fortune to his family and took a vow of poverty. He began a life of religious devotion and poverty, vowing vengeance on the money he believed had reduced him to a form of slavery and made him more obedient to it than to God. Dedicating his life to meditation, he soon gained a following, known as the "Poor of Lyon."

Waldo and his followers questioned religious doctrine and attempted to return Christianity to the simplicity and purity of the early Christian Era. They demanded of the church hierarchy the freedom to worship in their regional Occitan vernacular and, to that end, published the Bible in the dialect. Waldo advocated a return to the era when the church and the Bible dealt only with religious matters and rejected the papacy, purgatory, indulgences, and the opulence of the mass. Contrary to prevalent church teachings, Waldo laid great stress on gospel simplicity.

The outspoken condemnation of the corruption and opulence of the Roman Catholic Church gained Waldo and his followers powerful enemies. In 1179 Pope Alexander III forbade Waldo and his followers to preach. The dissidents' refusal to comply prompted the church leaders to excommunicate them as heretics, but, as they believed that they acted according to pure religious doctrine, they were not swayed by threats or the church's official condemnation. In 1215 the pope formally declared Waldo and his believers heretics, and the congregations were forcibly dispersed.

Driven from Lyon, the dissidents separated: Waldo himself fled to Bohemia, where he died in 1217. In spite of church edicts that forbade Waldensian contacts with Catholic believers, the movement continued to win followers. Many of the Waldensians suffered torture, burnings, and crusades of extermination called up by the church authorities. Many Waldensian communities in France and Italy were virtually wiped out. In 1487, at the instigation of Pope Innocent, most of the Waldensian colonies in Dauphine, west of the Alps, were massacred. The Waldensian survivors fled to a seven-valley redoubt in the high Cottian Alps in Piedmont.

In the late fifteenth century the Waldensian valleys came under the authority of Savoy.* Pressed by the Inquisition, the duke of Savoy led the first systematic attempt to annihilate the Waldensians in 1494. The duke's troops overran many Waldensian towns, murdering and pillaging. Waldensian women threw themselves off high cliffs to escape the shame of rape by the rampaging soldiers. The Waldensians, although numerically fewer and more poorly armed, eventually repulsed the ducal troops and forced the duke to grant a peace treaty lasting forty years.

The religious strife spreading through Europe, the Reformation, in the sixteenth century again threatened the Waldensians. In 1532 the Waldensians joined the Protestant movement and thus reignited official church enmity. In 1550 anti-Waldensian attacks reached a peak of ferocity and cruelty. The persecution continued through the Thirty Years' War in the early seventeenth century. In 1685 the French king insisted that his cousin, the duke of Savoy, deal with the Waldensians as he had dealt with the Protestant Huguenots. The duke's Catholic soldiers swept through the Waldensian valleys, killing thousands in horrible massacres. Most of the captives were imprisoned in cruel, crowded conditions. Only 3,000 Waldensians survived the duke's bloody crusade.

The survivors, after their release from the duke's prisons, migrated to Switzerland or other parts of Protestant Europe. In 1689 a small band of Waldensians left their homes near Geneva and, in what is called the ''Glorious Return,'' fought their way back to their ancestral valleys. The Waldensians defeated the forces sent against them and liberated their valleys, one after another. The Waldensian victory ended the wars and massacres, but not the persecution they suffered as church-labeled heretics. The recuperation of their beloved valleys began a long process of revival and renewal of the Waldensian nation.

Real freedom for the Waldensians came only in 1848, when King Charles Albert of Sardinia* granted them full civil rights within his kingdom. In spite of the official rehabilitation, the continuing hardships and hatred they faced drove many to emigrate. In the latter half of the nineteenth century many left for South America to begin anew. A group of Waldensians settled in the United States at Valdese, North Carolina.

The Waldensians, before and during World War II, actively opposed Italy's fascist government with its enforced religious and national conformity so alien to their ideas of freedom. Many joined partisan units during the war, and the communities suffered official reprisals, particularly after the German occupation of northern Italy in 1943. Whole villages were destroyed in retaliation for the Waldensians' unbending opposition to fascism.

The small nation knew peace only after World War II. In 1979 the 130 congregations in Italy federated with the Methodist Church of Italy and moved to end their centuries of self-imposed isolation. The Waldensians began to participate in national and international religious affairs, and began to organize their national life as a separate people.

In the 1990s, although not threatened by neighboring peoples, the Waldensians are threatened by unconstrained development, particularly alpine tourism. An active movement to win greater say over development projects in the 1980s evolved a more militant activism to save their unique culture and traditions from extinction. The Waldensians have become the latest of Europe's ethnic and religious mosaic to emerge as a separate nation.

SELECTED BIBLIOGRAPHY:

Symcox, Geoggrey. *Victor Amadeus II: Absolutism in the Savoyard State 1675–1730.* 1983.

Whale, J. S. *The Protestant Tradition.* 1955.

Wye, J. A. *History of the Waldenses.* 1880.

# WALES

## Cymru

*CAPITAL: Caerdydd (Cardiff)*

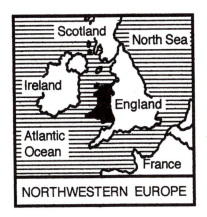

NORTHWESTERN EUROPE

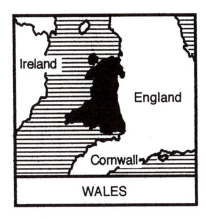

WALES

*POPULATION:* (95e) 2,911,000 : 3,075,000 Welsh (Cymry) in the United Kingdom. MAJOR NATIONAL GROUPS: (95e) Welsh (Cymry) 88%, English 11%, other British. MAJOR LANGUAGES: English, Welsh (Cymraeg). MAJOR RELIGIONS: Methodist, Anglican, Roman Catholic. MAJOR CITIES: (95e) Caerdydd (Cardiff) 251,000 (655,000), Swansea 162,000 (292,000), Casnewyyd-ar-Wysg (Newport) 119,000 (333,000), Pont ap Hywel (Pontypool) 90,000, Rhondda 65,000, Islwyn 64,000, Llanelli 53,000, Y Barry-Y Rhos (Barry) 52,000, Cwnbran 50,000, Caerffili (Caerphilly) 50,000, Port Talbot 40,000 (133,000), Wrescam (Wrexham) 40,000 (53,000), Merthyr Tudful (Merthyr Tydfil) 38,000 (50,000), Bae Colwyn (Colwyn Bay) 27,000 (120,000), Hawarden 20,000 (63,000).

*GEOGRAPHY:* AREA: 8,016 sq.mi.-20,766 sq.km. LOCATION: Wales lies in the extreme west of the island of Great Britain, a large rectangular peninsula between the Irish Sea and the Atlantic Ocean west of the land border with England. POLITICAL STATUS: Wales forms a separate principality of the United Kingdom.

*FLAG:* The Welsh national flag is a horizontal bicolor of white over green, bearing the Welsh national symbol, a red dragon, centered.

*PEOPLE:* The Welsh, calling themselves Cymry and their country Cymru, are a Celtic people with a vigorous and unique culture. English is now the first language of Wales. Only 60,000 Welsh speak just the Welsh language, and only a quarter of the population is bilingual although the numbers are increasing. The language, Cymraeg, belongs to the Brythonic branch of the Celtic languages and has a long literary history. The language has been revived since World War II as part of the Welsh cultural resurgence. The majority of the Welsh belong to the Protestant Methodist Church, the religion closely tied to the Welsh culture.

*THE NATION:* Celtic tribes, originally from the European mainland, populated the western mountains by the early Bronze Age. Under nominal Roman rule from 55 B.C., the highland tribes retained their culture and language, while the Celtic lowlands to the east became Latinized in culture and speech. The declining Roman Empire gradually abandoned Britannia in the early fifth century. In 410 the Romans withdrew the military garrisons.

Invaded by Germanic tribes from Northern Europe, the Celtic defenders fell back on the less accessible areas to the west, the peninsulas of Wales and Cornwall,* and eventually crossed the channel to Brittany.* The Anglo-Saxon invaders called the native Celts *waelisc*, meaning "foreign." The invaders were unable to conquer the Celts, but their advance separated the Celtic populations north and south of the Bristol Channel.

The Welsh, calling themselves Cymry, or compatriots, defeated all attempts to invade their peninsular strongholds. In the sixth century the scattered bands united to form a viable nation. A Welsh king, Hywel Dda, in the tenth century collected Welsh law and custom in a unified code for the kingdom.

The Norman invaders from continental Europe conquered England in 1066, but fierce Welsh resistance halted their invasion at the Welsh border. The Norman leader, William the Conqueror, declared himself lord of Wales in 1071, even though the Normans gained only a foothold in south Wales in 1093. Dissension in Norman England eased the military pressure on Wales in the twelfth century, the respite stimulating a great flowering of medieval Welsh culture. For over 200 years the Welsh repulsed sporadic attempts to conquer their homeland but ultimately failed to stop the English onslaught. Wales fell to English rule in 1282. Edward I of England in 1301 named his eldest son and heir Prince of Wales.

Harshly treated by the English and resentful of unjust laws and administration, the Welsh rebelled under the leadership of Owen Glyndwr (Glendower) in 1400. Initially successful, the Welsh rebels formed a government and created a representative parliament, one of the first in Europe. Defeated nine years later, the victorious English gradually curtailed the principality's rights and in 1536 joined Wales to England in a political union.

English, made the official language of the principality, provoked fierce resistance. The Protestant Reformation, particularly the English version, also fueled Welsh opposition. In the late eighteenth century most of the Welsh finally accepted Protestantism, but not the Anglican sect of England. The Welsh adopted the teachings of John Wesley, derisively called the Methodist for his methodical attention to study and religious duty. The Methodist creed became closely tied to the reviving Welsh culture over the next century.

The industrialization of south Wales in the late nineteenth century brought an influx of English industrial workers. Between 1870 and 1911 over 120,000 English migrated to the southern counties. The Welsh industrial expansion continued through World War I, but a serious decline began in 1918. The grave economic problems of the 1920s aroused Welsh nationalist sentiment. In 1925 nationalists formed Plaid Cymru, the Welsh National Party.

The spread of education in English after World War II decreased the number of Welsh able to speak their own language. The percentage of Welsh speakers declined by half during the 1950s. The decline of the language and culture stimulated the emergence of a modern nationalist movement based on the effort to save the language and culture from extinction.

An organized campaign to win some say in local administration spurred the growth of nationalism in the 1950s and 1960s. In 1964 the British government created a specific Welsh affairs office in London, with a separate government secretary for Wales. The nationalists denounced the offices as continued colonialism. In 1966 Plaid Cymru, advocating national status within a federal United Kingdom, elected its first member to the British Parliament.

European integration in the European Economic Community pushed the continent's Celtic nations to reestablish ancient ties. Annual congresses, folk festivals, and cultural exchanges increased and revitalized the Celtic cultures in the 1970s and 1980s. The renewed pan-Celtic ties gave the Welsh a reinforced determination to win self-rule and equal status for the Welsh language in education and administration.

A referendum on the devolution of administrative power to a Welsh parliament went down in defeat in 1979. The groups opposed to the devolution stressed British, as opposed to Welsh, nationalism. Discontent with the result of the referendum, militant nationalists launched a campaign of arson, burning holiday homes and real estate offices dealing with the people buying them, the "foreigners" from across the English border.

Economic success in the 1980s and 1990s has enhanced the Welsh confidence that their country no longer needs the monetary subsidies that have tied Wales to England for centuries. In January 1992 nearly three-quarters of the Welsh demonstrated support for devolution and a separate Welsh assembly, for the nationalists a first step toward the goal of a separate Welsh state in an integrated Europe. The rising tide of Welsh nationalism won a concession on the language. In May 1992 the British government finally granted Welsh equal status with English in the principality.

*SELECTED BIBLIOGRAPHY:*
Davies, John. *A History of Wales.* 1993.
Ellis, Peter B. *The Celtic Revolution.* 1988.
Rees, J. F. *Studies in Welsh History.* 1947.
Williams, David. *A Short History of Modern Wales.* 1962.

# WALLONIA

**Wallonie; Wallony; Walonia**

*CAPITAL: Namur*

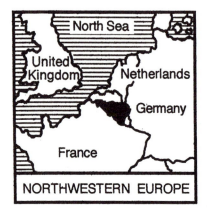

NORTHWESTERN EUROPE

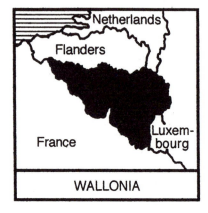

WALLONIA

*POPULATION:* (95e) 4,330,000 : 3,905,000 Walloons in Belgium, and another 200,000 in adjacent areas of France. MAJOR NATIONAL GROUPS: (95e) Walloon 88%, German 2%, other Belgian. MAJOR LANGUAGES: French, Walloon, German, Flemish. MAJOR RELIGIONS: Roman Catholic, Protestant. MAJOR CITIES: (95e) Charleroi 203,000 (510,000), Liège 189,000 (887,000), Namur 104,000 (151,000), Mons 89,000 (253,000), La Louvière 76,000 (176,000), Tournai 58,000 (80,000), Veviers 52,000 (105,000), Ath 37,000 (50,000).

*GEOGRAPHY:* AREA: 6,502 sq.mi.-16,844 sq.km. LOCATION: Wallonia occupies a region of low plains rising to wooded hills, the Ardennes, in southern Belgium. POLITICAL STATUS: Wallonia forms an autonomous region of the Kingdom of Belgium.

*FLAG:* The Walloon national flag, the official flag of the region, is a yellow field bearing a red rooster centered. OTHER FLAG(S): The flag of the Walloon Germans is a white field bearing a red lion rampant surrounded by a ring of nine blue flowers.

*PEOPLE:* The Walloons are a Latin people, the most northerly of the Latin peoples in Europe. The Walloons tend to be shorter and darker than the Flemish of northern Belgium. The Walloons speak French, the official language of the region, and 450,000 also still speak Walloon, a dialect closer to Old French than standard modern French. The language is described as a Romance language with a Celtic substratum and Germanic influences. The language has a substantial literature, but no official status in Wallonia. A large Walloon population

inhabits the eastern part of France's Nord Department and has retained its separate culture and dialect. The Walloons are overwhelmingly Roman Catholic.

*THE NATION:* Inhabited by Celtic peoples, the Belgae, the area fell to Roman
rule in 57 B.C. The Celtic inhabitants of the Roman province of Belgica, under
Roman rule for over 400 years, became thoroughly Latinized, adopting Latin
culture and language.

Germanic Franks invaded the province as Roman power crumbled in A.D.
358, quickly overrunning the remaining Roman defenses in Belgica and moving
on into Gaul. The areas to the north and south of them settled by the Germanic
invaders, the Latin-speaking population took refuge in the Ardennes. The pressure of the Germanic settlers gradually pushed the Latins to a line approximating
the present linguistic frontier between the Walloons in southern Belgium and
the Flemish of the northern provinces.

The region split into a number of small, independent states soon after Charlemagne's Frankish Empire was divided by his heirs in 843. Reunited in the
fifteenth century under the House of Burgundy, the provinces passed by marriage to the Hapsburgs in 1477. Rule of the provinces, called the Low Countries,
passed from the Austrian Hapsburgs to the Spanish Hapsburgs in 1555. The
southern districts of the Hapsburg province of Hainault, with a large Walloon
population, came under French rule in 1678.

Napoleon took the provinces from the Spanish in 1792 and annexed the provinces to the French state in 1801. The Congress of Vienna, convened in 1815
to reorganize Europe at the end of the Napoleonic Wars, added the Roman
Catholic former Hapsburg provinces to the predominantly Protestant Dutch kingdom. A shared antipathy to Protestant rule united the Walloons and Flemish in
a revolt against Dutch rule in 1830. Supported by the United Kingdom and
France, the Catholic provinces in Flanders* and Wallonia united in a separate
kingdom called Belgium in 1831.

The Walloon dialect remained the language of administration for the first three
decades of Belgian independence, but French gradually took precedence in the
1860s. Industrialized Wallonia dominated the kingdom in the nineteenth century.
The French language became the predominate dialect in Wallonia and Brussels
and was the only official language of the kingdom. Prosperous and assured,
Wallonia thrived in the 1870s and 1880s, easily dominating the rural, agricultural Flemish provinces. The Walloon culture experienced a flowering of art and
literature, the cultural revival centered on the Walloon metropolis, Liège.

Flemish assertiveness after World War I challenged Walloon domination of
the kingdom. United only by a common religion, the language issue emerged
as the kingdom's primary preoccupation in the 1920s and 1930s. Amid growing
cultural and linguistic tensions the Belgian government finally recognized Flemish as an official language for some uses in the late 1930s, ending over 400
years of Walloon domination.

The tension between the two peoples escalated after World War II, fanned
by economic changes. Wallonia's outdated heavy industries declined rapidly,

while new industries shifted to Flanders nearer the Flemish port cities. The shift of economic and political power to Flanders fed a growing Flemish nationalist movement, stimulating Walloon nationalism in response. In 1961 Walloon socialists demanded a new state structure, with local autonomy for the two Belgian nations.

Attitudes hardened in the 1970s as both nations demanded greater political and economic autonomy. Linguistic nationalism provoked violent clashes and mass demonstrations. Teaching the Walloon language in regional schools won government permission in 1983. In August 1990 Wallonia and Flanders won major autonomy, opening a bitter debate over control of the Belgian capital, Brussels. The mainly French-speaking, but not Walloon, inhabitants of the capital evidenced little interest in the dispute, while the predominantly Flemish suburbs agitated for the metropolitan area's inclusion in Flanders.

The continuing communal dispute made Belgium all but ungovernable as administrations formed and fell on the linguistic and autonomy issues. In 1988 a bitter dispute prevented agreement on the component parties of a coalition, leaving Belgium without a constitutional government for over four months. In 1989 the Brussels metropolitan area became a third Belgian autonomous region, the compromise reluctantly accepted by the Walloon and Flemish authorities, while demanding new powers for their two regions.

A serious constitutional crisis in late 1991 again left Belgium without an effective administration, the crisis bringing the dissolution of the kingdom ever closer. Nationalists on both sides proposed that Brussels, the center of European integration, become a separate European capital district, with Wallonia and Flanders independent states within a federal Europe. The nationalists claim that the European option would formalize the division that has virtually turned Belgium into a geographic area occupied by two separate nations.

The devolution of additional powers to the regions in February 1993 effectively partitioned Belgium. Walloon authority, including the southern part of Brabant, called Barents, was augmented by the implementation of a federal state in mid-1993. The few powers left to the Belgian government, powers that will eventually become European responsibilities, are the only official ties left between Wallonia and Flanders. When the Belgian government surrenders the responsibilities to the European government, Belgium will effectively cease to exist, and Wallonia and Flanders will become separate states in a federal Europe.

*SELECTED BIBLIOGRAPHY:*

Enloe, Cynthia H. *Ethnic Conflict and Political Development.* 1986.

Esman, Milton J. *Ethnic Conflict in the Western World.* 1977.

Fitzmaurice, John. *The Politics of Belgium: Crisis and Compromise in a Plural Society.* 1983.

Lijphart, Arend, ed. *Conflict and Coexistence in Belgium: The Dynamics of a Culturally Divided Society.* 1981.

# WESTERN SOMALIA

## Ogaden

*CAPITAL: Hara (Harer)*

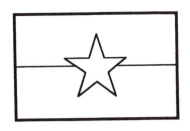

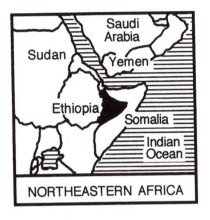

NORTHEASTERN AFRICA

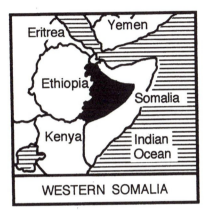

WESTERN SOMALIA

*POPULATION:* (95e) 4,340,000 : 3,700,000 Western Somalis in Ethiopia. MAJOR NATIONAL GROUPS: (95e) Western Somali 82%, Oromo 10%, other Ethiopian. MAJOR LANGUAGES: Somali (western dialects), Oromo (Galli-nya), Harari, Amhariya. MAJOR RELIGIONS: Sunni Muslim, Coptic Christian. MAJOR CITIES: (95e) Dire Dawa 155,000, Hara (Harer) 140,000, Jijiga 50,000, Kersa 30,000, Korahe 20,000.

*GEOGRAPHY:* AREA: 132,370 sq.mi.-342,927 sq.km. LOCATION: Western Somalia lies in southeastern Ethiopia, occupying the semi-arid Ogaden Desert and the highlands in the Ahmar Mountains in the northwest. POLITICAL STATUS: Western Somalia has no official status; the area forms the Ethiopian regions of Somali, Harer, and a small part of Oromo.

*FLAG:* The Western Somali national flag, the flag of the national movement, is a horizontal bicolor of red over green bearing a centered, five-pointed, white star. OTHER FLAG(S): The flag of the largest national organization, the Western Somali Liberation Front (WSLF), is a vertical bicolor of black and red bearing a centered, five-pointed, white star.

*PEOPLE:* The Western Somalis are a Muslim Somali people of mixed Somali and Oromo background encompassing the Western Somali clans, the Darod and Harari around Harer, the Dir around Dire Dawa, the Issa, Issak, and Gadabursi in the north, the Ogadeni in the south and southwest, the Abo in the south, the Hawiye in the southwest, the Marahan in the southeast, and the Dolbahuna in the east. The clans speak the western dialects of Somali, a Cushitic language of the Hamitic language group. The Western Somali dialects are written in the Ethiopian alphabet, not the Arabic used by the other Somali peoples.

*THE NATION:* Nomadic Hamitic tribes have roamed the Ogaden Desert since ancient times. The tribes, autonomous nomadic groups, often warred over water and grazing lands. Even though the clans spoke dialects of the same Somali language, the desert peoples remained free of the coastal Somali states to the east. Islam, introduced to the Somali port cities by Arab traders, spread to the inland tribes in the seventh and eighth centuries. The new religion established a strong bond between the various clan and tribal groups. The clans united to defeat an Oromo expansion from the west in the fifteenth and sixteenth centuries, the western Somali clans later mixing with the newly converted Muslim Oromo tribes.

The Muslim peoples, led by Ahmed Gran, waged holy war on the Christian Ethiopian kingdom in the highlands to the west from 1529 to 1542 but failed to take the Christians' mountain strongholds. With military support from the Portuguese, the Christians rallied and drove the Muslims back to the Ogaden. The war between the Muslims and Christians set off centuries of sporadic warfare in the region.

The Ethiopians conquered Harer, the traditional capital of the Western Somali clans, in 1887. The Ethiopians used the city as a base to extend Ethiopian rule in the Ogaden as part of the colonization of the Somali lands. France, Italy, and the United Kingdom took control of the coastal Somali tribes. The Western Somali clans united in 1899 to launch a twenty-one-year holy war against Christian Ethiopian rule. Ultimately defeated in 1920, the Ethiopian imperial government began a program to separate the western clans from their kin under European rule, including a ban on the traditional Arabic script used by the other Somali groups.

The Italians, from their coastal bases, moved out to conquer Ethiopia in 1936 and, during World War II, took control of British Somaliland.* United under one government for the first time in their history, the Somali peoples evolved a pan-Somali nationalist movement dedicated to the creation of a "Greater Somalia" from the five colonial Somali territories.

British troops from Kenya drove the Italians from the Horn of Africa in 1941. The British placed the Ogaden under military rule but returned the territory around Harer and Dire Dawa to Ethiopian administration. In April 1942 the Dir and Darob clans rebelled, the revolt the beginning of the modern Western Somali national movement. The British disarmed the Ogaden clans and restricted their movement but opened their lands and water resources to the still armed clans of neighboring British Somaliland. The Western Somali resentment of the coastal clans pampered by the British escalated the growth of Western Somali nationalism.

The British authorities in 1946 proposed to the new United Nations (UN) a plan for a trusteeship to encompass British Somaliland, former Italian Somaliland, and the part of Ethiopian Somaliland under British military rule. The plan, blocked by the Ethiopian government, was discarded, although the disposition of the Somali territories continued to be debated by the UN General Assembly throughout the late 1940s. In 1948 nationalists demanding separate independence for Western Somalia led demonstrations and clashed with the British occupation troops.

The United Nations recommended a return to the prewar borders in 1950, including the return of Western Somalia to the rule of the feudal Ethiopian state. Vehemently opposed to Ethiopian rule, the clan elders appealed to the British authorities. The British delayed the transfer of authority until 1954 but were ultimately obliged to relinquish control to the Ethiopians. In 1955 harsh Ethiopian restrictions provoked widespread violence in the region.

Independent Somalia, formed from British and Italian territories in 1960, agitated for the unification of all ethnic Somalis in an expanded ''Greater Somalia.'' The Western Somali clans, never part of the coastal Somali states, felt little affinity with the Somali republic, although a majority supported a loose federation of Somali states. The national question divided the clans between those favoring Somalia, the advocates of separate independence, and the minority that had prospered under Ethiopian rule.

Western Somali rebels, drawn from the northern clans and armed by Somalia, launched a separatist war against Ethiopian rule. The fighting intensified with the installation of a Communist regime in Addis Ababa in 1974. In 1976 the rebellion spread to the southern clans, seriously threatening Ethiopia's hold on the Ogaden. In July 1977 the army of the Republic of Somalia invaded the Ogaden in support of the separatists. The Western Somali rebels, backed by the Somali troops, nearly succeeded in separating the Ogaden from Ethiopia before the intervention of Communist Cuban and Soviet troops bolstered the Ethiopians.

The war generated hundreds of thousands of refugees and exacerbated the instability of the Horn of Africa. In 1981 a clan congress committed itself to the creation of an independent free state of Western Somalia. Civil war in Somalia in 1988 and the declaration of independence of the northern clans in Somaliland in 1991 administered the final blows to the long-held Somali dream of a ''Greater Somalia.''

In May 1991 a coalition of ethnic insurgent groups overthrew Ethiopia's Communist government. In December 1991 the new coalition government created a federation of ethnic-based regions. The regions, allowing major autonomy, also created new conflicts. The Western Somali dispute with the Oromos over control of Dire Dawa and Harer erupted in serious fighting in 1992–93. The Western Somali national movement by late 1993 encompassed twelve separate nationalist groups supporting various autonomist and separatist views.

*SELECTED BIBLIOGRAPHY:*

Laitin, David D., and Said S. Samatar. *Somalia: Nation in Search of a State.* 1985.

Legum, Colin. *Horn of Africa in Continuing Crisis.* 1979.

Lewis, I. M. *Nationalism and Self-Determination in the Horn of Africa.* 1984.

Samatar, Ahmed. *Socialist Somalia: Rhetoric and Reality.* 1988.

# WESTERN UKRAINIA

**Galicia; Halychnya**

*CAPITAL: Lwiw (Lvov)*

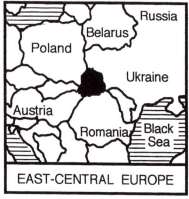

EAST-CENTRAL EUROPE

WESTERN UKRAINIA

*POPULATION:* (95e) 6,824,000 : 5,280,000 Western Ukrainians in Ukraine. MAJOR NATIONAL GROUPS: (95e) Western Ukrainian 77%, Polish 7%, Russian 2%, Moldovan 1.5%, other Ukrainian. MAJOR LANGUAGES: Ukrainian, Polish, Russian. MAJOR RELIGIONS: (95e) Uniate Catholic 64%, Ukrainian Orthodox 10%, Roman Catholic 8%, Protestant 3%, Russian Orthodox. MAJOR CITIES: (95e) Lwiw (Lvov) 850,000 (1,026,000), Cernivci (Chernovtsy) 284,000, Stanislaviv (Ivano-Frankovsk) 270,000, Ternopil (Ternopol) 234,000, Drohobych (Drogobych) 106,000, Cervonohrad (Chervonograd) 79,000 (118,000), Kalus (Kalush) 71,000, Kolomyja (Kolomyya) 70,000, Stryj (Stry) 66,000, Boryslav (Borislav) 48,000 (94,000).

*GEOGRAPHY:* AREA: 22,329 sq.mi.-57,847 sq.km. LOCATION: Western Ukrainia occupies a flat plain, traversed by the Dniestr River and its tributaries, rising to the Carpathian Mountains in southwestern Ukraine. POLITICAL STATUS: Western Ukrainia has no official status; the region, the historic region of Galicia, forms the Ukrainian oblasts of Lwiw, Cernivci, Ivano-Frankivs, and Ternopil.

*INDEPENDENCE DECLARED:* 14 November 1918; 30 June 1941.

*FLAG:* The Western Ukrainian flag, the flag of the national movement, is a horizontal bicolor of red over black. OTHER FLAG(S): The historic flag of Galicia, used by several Western Ukrainian nationalist organizations, is a horizontal bicolor of red over green.

*PEOPLE:* The Western Ukrainians are an East Slav people, ethnically part of the Ukrainian nation but historically, culturally, and religiously distinct. The region's language, the southwestern dialect of Ukrainian, is quite different from the Russianized southeastern dialect spoken in Kiev and the eastern provinces. The Western Ukrainian culture, through centuries of Austrian and Polish rule, is a Central European culture and is notably free of the strong Russian influences in the culture of central and eastern Ukraine. The majority of the Western Ukrainians belong to the Byzantine rite Uniate Catholic church, with an Orthodox minority split between the Autocephalous Orthodox Church, an independent Ukrainian Orthodox sect banned in 1930, the official Ukrainian Orthodox Church, and the Russian Orthodox Church.

*THE NATION:* Populated by East Slav tribes during the Slav migrations in the sixth century A.D. the region early came under the influence of the non-Slav peoples to the west. The Slavs of the upper Dniestr River basin became part of Kievan Rus, the first great East Slav state, in 1054. Within fifty years Kievan Rus had fragmented into twelve principalities. The most southerly of the principalities, Galicia, lay on the frontier between the Latins and Byzantines.

Separated from Russian territory by the Mongol invasion of the thirteenth century, Galicia eventually came under Tatar rule in 1324. The Poles liberated and annexed the region in 1349, and in 1386 Galicia became part of the merged Polish-Lithuanian state. The Roman Catholic Poles, intent on converting the state's Orthodox subjects, agreed to a compromise in 1596. The Orthodox Ukrainians formed a union with Rome and accepted the pope as their spiritual leader but retained the Byzantine religious rite and their own hierarchy, their priests preserving the right to marry.

Galicia, with a mixed population of Ukrainians and Poles, became part of Austria as a result of the first Polish partition in 1772. The southeastern area around Cernivci, the region of Bukovina, was added to Austrian Galicia three years later. Better educated and less restricted than the Ukrainians under Russian rule, the Western Ukrainian culture and language developed separately, influenced by Vienna and Krakow, not Kiev or Moscow.

Lemburg (Lwiw) emerged as the principal center of Ukrainian nationalism in the Hapsburg Empire in the nineteenth century. The Uniate Church, closely tied to Western Ukrainian culture, provided the focus of Western Ukrainian nationalism.

A border region on the frontier with Russia, Galicia became a battleground when war began in 1914. As Austro-Hungarian defeat neared in October 1918, Western Ukrainian nationalists organized to oppose Polish and Romanian claims on the region. On 14 November 1918 nationalist leaders declared the independence of Galicia. Romanian troops invaded the new state to occupy the southeastern region of Bukovina, but a hastily organized national army repulsed the Poles in 1919. Threatened on all sides, the Western Ukrainians voted for union with newly independent Ukraine despite vigorous opposition to the union on religious and cultural grounds. After the Soviet occupation of central and eastern Ukraine, Polish troops overran the region during the Polish-Soviet War in 1919.

The Paris Peace Conference, convened after World War I, citing religious affinities, assigned most of Galicia to Poland.

The Soviets, as part of the secret Nazi-Soviet pact signed in 1939, occupied the eastern provinces of Poland in November 1939 and in 1940 took Bukovina from Romania. The region's ties to Rome and the West provoked severe repression, with over a million Western Ukrainians killed or deported, including all those with the smooth hands of the intellectual.

In June 1941 the Nazis launched an invasion of their Soviet ally, and, as Soviet authority collapsed, Western Ukrainian nationalists emerged from hiding to take control of the region. On 30 June 1941 the nationalists declared Western Ukrainia an independent state, but the Nazis ignored the proclamation and occupied the region. The Germans suppressed the national government and sent the region's leaders to concentration camps. Separated from the eastern Ukraine and eventually promoted as an ally in the Nazis' anti-Communist crusade, many Western Ukrainians joined the Germans to fight the hated Soviets.

Retaken by the Red Army in 1944, another half million Western Ukrainians faced deportation or imprisonment between 1945 and 1949. Stalin accused the entire Uniate Catholic population, including the Metropolitan of Lwiw, of collaboration with the Nazis. Forced to renounce its ties to Rome, the Uniate Church was absorbed by the official Russian Orthodox Church. While Russian Orthodoxy received state subsidies, Ukrainian Uniate Catholic priests, nuns, and laymen filled Stalin's slave labor camps.

The church, forced underground, became a center of clandestine Western Ukrainian nationalism from the 1950s to the liberalization of the late 1980s. The Uniate Church functioned openly after 1987 and received official sanction in 1988. The legalization of the church opened bitter disputes between the Uniates and Orthodox over church properties confiscated in 1946, the controversy becoming part of the growing rift between the strongly nationalist Western Ukraine and the traditionally pro-Russian central and eastern regions.

Ukrainian independence, enthusiastically supported in the western provinces, achieved during the disintegration of the Soviet Union in 1991, temporarily submerged the east-west rifts. In the 1990s economic hardships exacerbated the split between the two halves of the country, the nationalists versus the unionists of eastern Ukraine seeking renewed ties with Russia. In Ukrainian presidential elections in July 1994, the pro-Russian victor received less than 4% of the vote in the region, the danger of civil war in Ukraine moving closer. Nationalist leaders reiterated their readiness to go it alone and to suffer the initial hardships of independence.

*SELECTED BIBLIOGRAPHY:*

Armstrong, John A. *Ukrainian Nationalism.* 1990.

Markovits, Andrei, and Frank E. Sipyn. *Nation Building and the Politics of Nationalism: Essays on Austrian Galicia.* 1982.

Ramet, Pedro. *Cross and Commissar: The Politics of Religion in Eastern Europe and the U.S.S.R.* 1987.

Sullivant, R. S. *Soviet Policies in the Ukraine, 1917–1957.* 1962.

# WEST PAPUA

Irian Jaya; West Irian

*CAPITAL: Hollandia (Djayapura)*

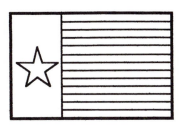

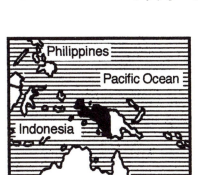

*POPULATION:* (95e) 1,958,000 : 1,530,000 Papuans in Indonesia. MAJOR NATIONAL GROUPS: (95e) Papuan 78%, Javanese 20%, other Indonesian. MAJOR LANGUAGES: Papuan, Bahasa Indonesian, Javanese, Dutch. MAJOR RELIGIONS: animist, Christian, Sunni Muslim. MAJOR CITIES: (95e) Hollandia (Djayapura) 125,000, Sorong 40,000, Kaimana 25,000.

*GEOGRAPHY:* AREA: 159,355 sq.mi.-412,836 sq.km. LOCATION: West Papua occupies the western half of the island of New Guinea, a region of low coastal plains surrounding high central mountains west of the international border with Papua New Guinea. POLITICAL STATUS: West Papua has no official status; the region forms Irian Jaya province of Indonesia.

*INDEPENDENCE DECLARED:* 9 December 1975.

*FLAG:* The West Papuan national flag, the flag adopted in 1975, has thirteen horizontal stripes of blue and white bearing a wide, vertical red stripe at the hoist charged with a white, five-pointed star.

*PEOPLE:* The West Papuans, part of the island's Papuan population, are divided among numerous tribes and language groups. Considered some of the least developed of the world's peoples, the Papuans had little contact with the outside world until the twentieth century. The majority of the Papuans adhere to traditional beliefs; a minority, mostly in the urban areas, are Christian. A large Javanese population, settled in the province in government-sponsored migrations, is Muslim and forms part of Indonesia's dominant Javanese ethnic group.

*THE NATION:* Inhabited for thousands of years, the island's early inhabitants settled in autonomous villages. Never united under a central authority, each small tribe developed its own distinct culture and language. First sighted by Dutch navigators in 1606, the island, without the economic incentives of the islands farther west, was generally ignored until the early years of the nineteenth century.

The Dutch, from their East Indies colony, laid claim to the southern coastal region west of the 141st meridian in 1828. In 1848 the Dutch extended their territorial claims to preclude claims by the British and Germans in possession of the eastern part of New Guinea. The three European powers formally divided the island in 1895. The Dutch claim to the eastern 47% of the island's territory was confirmed by treaties with Germany and the United Kingdom.

Generally neglected in favor of the rich Indonesian islands, only a few coastal trading bases represented Dutch authority in the region. The bases, centers of Christian missionary activity, became the nucleus of a small, educated Papuan minority. The Christian-educated Papuans became the spokesmen in dealings with the colonial authorities and began to foster a sense of Papuan unity that gradually diminished the endemic feuds and tribal wars. Dutch administration and missionary activity slowly penetrated the interior of the island, although many Papuans would not see a European until well into the twentieth century.

Technically a part of the Dutch East Indies, the colonial administration set Dutch New Guinea aside as a restricted area, prohibiting migration to the island from the overcrowded Indonesian islands. Culturally, linguistically, and religiously separated from the other Dutch island possessions, the island effectively became a distinct Dutch possession.

A brutal Japanese occupation during the Second World War ended in 1945 but left the Papuans with an enduring hatred of all Asians. Thousands of Papuans, freed from forced labor, virtual slavery under the Japanese, welcomed the return of the Dutch after the war.

The Dutch administration, forced to recognize Indonesian independence in 1949, rejected the Indonesian claim to Dutch New Guinea. In spite of Indonesian and international pressure to decolonize New Guinea, the Dutch refused to relinquish control so long as the Papuans wished them to stay. United Nations (UN) efforts to mediate an acceptable compromise failed. The Papuans adamantly refused inclusion in Indonesia, even with guarantees of autonomy. A Dutch plan for Papuan independence, prepared in 1959–60, was blocked by Indonesia's Communist and Third World supporters in the UN General Assembly.

In April 1961 the Dutch created a Papuan legislature and granted some self-government. The Indonesians denounced the Dutch preparations for autonomy as yet another ploy to win separate independence for the Papuans and launched a surprise attack on the province, setting off heavy fighting.

The United States brokered a compromise that placed the territory under United Nations administration on 1 April 1962, with provision for a plebiscite to determine the wishes of the Papuans. The United Nations administration, ignoring the agreement and Papuan protests, turned the territory over to Indonesia following a vote in the General Assembly in 1963, with provision that Indonesia hold the plebiscite before 1969.

In August 1969 the Indonesian military government organized the UN-mandated referendum, but only a few handpicked tribal chiefs who had prospered under Indonesian rule were allowed to participate. Outraged by the United Nations betrayal and the excesses of the Indonesian military, Papuan nationalists led a widespread rebellion that pitted Stone Age warriors against the American-equipped Indonesian army.

The Indonesians, determined to hold the province and its newly discovered petroleum reserves, launched a campaign of brutal suppression. Indonesian troops attacked undefended Papuan villages and expelled the Christian missionaries who denounced the measures. Pursued by helicopter gunships, thousands fled to mountain sanctuaries or crossed the border to refugee camps in Papua New Guinea.

Papuan leaders appealed to the United Nations but were ignored. On 9 December 1975 the leaders signed the Serui Declaration, a unilateral declaration of the independence of the Republic of West Papua. The proclamation stimulated renewed Indonesian suppression. By 1984 over 100,000 Papuans had died in the conflict, most of the dead innocent villagers killed in indiscriminate bombardments and mass executions.

The Indonesian government, with the financial assistance of several well-intentioned international aid agencies, has settled hundreds of thousands of ethnic Javanese in the province. The mass expulsion of the Papuan populations from the best and most productive lands preceded the implementation of the government-sponsored transmigration program. The program has proved a human and ecological disaster for the region and threatens to obliterate the Papuan people.

Ignored by the world, the war in West Papua has continued for over two decades. Faced with genocide, a more radical generation of Papuan leaders vow to pursue the war until their nation is either free or extinct.

*SELECTED BIBLIOGRAPHY:*

Matthiessen, Peter. *Under the Mountain Wall.* 1962.
Osborne, Robin. *Indonesia's Secret War: The Struggle in Irian Jaya.* 1985.
Otten, Mariel. *Transmigracy: Indonesian Resettlement Policy 1965–85.* 1986.
Siers, James. *Papua New Guinea.* 1984.

# YORUBALAND

**Western Nigeria**

*CAPITAL: Ibadan*

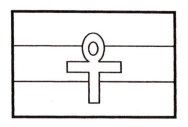

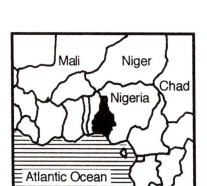

WEST-CENTRAL AFRICA

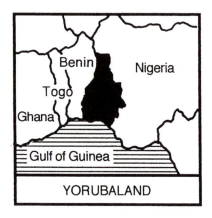

YORUBALAND

*POPULATION:* (95e) 29,269,000 : 25,500,000 Yorubas in Nigeria. MAJOR NATIONAL GROUPS: (95e) Yoruba 83%, other Nigerian. MAJOR LANGUAGES: Yoruba, English, Ibo, Edo. MAJOR RELIGIONS: Christian, Sunni Muslim. MAJOR CITIES: (95e) Lagos 7,120,000 (10,928,000), Ibadan 2,302,000 (3,515,000), Ogbomobsho 705,000, Oshogbo 411,000 (619,000), Ilorin 395,000, Abeokuta 366,000, Ilesha 320,000, Mushin 315,000, Ado-Ekiti 293,000 (532,000), Iwo 293,000, Ede 251,000, Ife 246,000, Ikire 224,000, Shomolu 220,000, Ila 216,000, Ikerre 210,000, Oyo 185,000 (284,000), Iseyin 183,000, Ilobu 176,000, Offa 170,000, Shaki 153,000, Ikirun 142,000 (249,000), Ilawe-Ekiti 142,000, Ikorodu 139,000, Ondo 135,000.

*GEOGRAPHY:* AREA: 43,502 sq.mi.-112,701 sq.km. LOCATION: Yorubaland lies in southwestern Nigeria, a region of savanna and forest lands between the middle Niger River and the Gulf of Guinea. POLITICAL STATUS: Yorubaland has no political status, the region forms the Nigerian states of Kwara, Lagos, Ondo, Oshun, Oyo, and western Kogi.

*FLAG:* The Yoruba national flag, the flag of the national movement, is a horizontal tricolor of green, yellow, and red bearing a centered black Ankh, an ancient Egyptian symbol resembling a cross topped by a circle. OTHER FLAG(S): The flag of the former Western Region is a dark blue field bearing a large white disc offset toward the hoist charged with a yellow Yoruba sword backed by a green design.

*PEOPLE:* The Yoruba are a people of mixed Hamitic and Bantu descent speaking a Kwa language of the Niger-Congo language group. Claiming ultimate descent from ancient Egyptians and the Nile Valley, the Yoruba have the only strong urban tradition found in sub-Saharan Africa, with 65% of the Yoruba living in cities. Even though the Yorubas are mainly Christian in the south and Muslim in the north, religion is less important than clan and tribal ties. The name Yoruba is now applied to all persons who speak Yoruba dialects and share in the common Yoruba culture but originally designated only the inhabitants of the old Oyo kingdom, the related peoples designated by the name of their respective kingdoms.

*THE NATION:* The Yoruba tradition has all the Yoruba peoples descended from a common ancestor, Oduduwa, the first man the Supreme Being let down from heaven on a chain to create the earth. Claiming descent from the ancient Egyptians and the Meroe civilization of the upper Nile, the Yoruba are believed to have settled their present homeland around 1,000 years ago. Little is known of the region's early history, although the system of divine kings is thought to have developed in the ninth century A.D. In the eleventh century the Yoruba began to coalesce in independent city-states. Ife, the oldest existing Yoruba city, dates from about 1300. All Yoruba chiefs trace their ancestry to Ife and consider the *oba* (king) of Ife as their ritual superior.

Portuguese navigators visited the coastal cities in the late fifteenth century. Commercial relations developed, with the Yoruba trading slaves and agricultural produce for European trade goods. The Portuguese were soon followed by English, French, Dutch, and Danish traders and explorers. The Yoruba coastal states satisfied the growing European demand for slaves by raiding the interior states.

The expanding power of the Oyo kingdom superseded Ife in the seventeenth century. Over the next hundred years, Oyo united the numerous Yoruba kingdoms in a powerful empire. Muslim Fulani tribes invaded the empire in the early nineteenth century, overrunning the northern states, which mostly converted to Islam.

Civil war, fought with European firearms, devastated the empire, and Muslim incursions and the slave trade finally destroyed Yoruba unity. The empire split into numerous smaller states, many founded by refugees fleeing the Muslim conquest of the northern states in the 1820s and 1830s. One of the new city-states, Ibadan, finally defeated the Muslim Fulani invaders in 1840.

The British gradually gained a predominant position in the Yoruba states. In 1807 the British navy attempted to end the slave trade, but the lucrative business continued for another seventy years. In 1861 the British annexed Lagos and began to intervene in the Yoruba wars in the 1880s. Over the next decade British authority extended to all of Yorubaland, partly by force but often by the treaties that offered British protection.

Ruled indirectly through the traditional chiefs, the Yoruba states were divided between Lagos colony and the protectorates of Southern and Northern Nigeria. As early as 1908 Yoruba nationalists demanded a united Yoruba state in British Nigeria. In an attempt to promote unity and end inter-Yoruba conflicts, the region's leaders turned to the myth of a common ancestor, Oduduwa. A Yoruba ethnic consciousness gradually developed, the resulting unity blurring differences in religion, history, and culture.

Yoruba nationalism grew dramatically during World War II. In 1945 a group of Yoruba students in London formed Egbe Omo Oduduwa (Society of the Children of Oduduwa) to work for a united Yoruba state within the British Empire. From 1948 the movement gained substantial support, fanned by the increasing tensions among Nigeria's three largest ethnic groups: the Yoruba, the Ibo in the southeast, and the Muslim Hausa-Fulani in the north.

Nigeria became independent as a federation of three regions in 1960, the three largest ethnic groups immediately engaged in an acrimonious three-way scramble for power. A general breakdown of law and order in 1965, the product of the ongoing regional rivalries, aroused Yoruba secessionist sentiment. In July 1966 the Yorubas moved toward secession but were blocked by northern troops loyal to the Muslim-dominated government deployed to occupy Lagos and other important Yoruba cities.

In 1967 the Ibos of the southeast declared the independence of the Republic of Biafra,* the secession prompting nationalist demands of Yorubaland to follow. Deterred by the Muslim occupation troops and the potential loss of the benefits of Biafra's oil wealth, the Yoruba ultimately rejected secession and supported the federal cause in the civil war of 1967–70.

Yoruba nationalism resurfaced in 1970 over a perceived conspiracy of the Muslims and the defeated Ibo to exclude the Yoruba from important government positions. Continued domination of the Nigerian government by the Muslim-controlled military fueled Yoruba nationalism in the 1980s. The political resistance was aggravated by severe economic problems. The standard of living in Yorubaland fell by 15% between 1980 and 1986.

The Muslim-dominated military government, pressed by international opinion, allowed free presidential elections in June 1993. For the first time in thirty-four years of independence, a Yoruba, Chief Mashood Abiola, won the election. The election was annulled by the military government, effectively robbing the Yorubas of the victory and perpetuating the Hausa-Fulani hold on Nigeria. The dramatic increase of Yoruba national sentiment, particularly after Chief Abiola was put on trial for treason, raised separatist tensions to the level of the 1960s. A growing number of Yorubas see independence as the only way to end over three decades of domination of the Yoruba homeland by Nigeria's northern Muslims.

*SELECTED BIBLIOGRAPHY:*

Anifowase, F. O. *The Violence and Politics in Nigeria: A Case-Study of the Tiv and Yoruba.* 1982.

Coleman, James S. *Nigeria: Background to Nationalism.* 1971.

Igiehon, Noser. *To Build a Nigerian Nation.* 1987.

Irukwu, J. O. *Nigeria at the Crossroads.* 1983.

# YUCATAN

## Mayaland

*CAPITAL: Tihoo (Merida)*

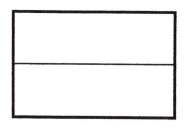

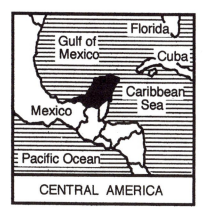

CENTRAL AMERICA

YUCATAN

*POPULATION:* (95e) 2,777,000 : 3,800,000 Mayas in Mexico and another 6,100,000 in Guatemala, Honduras, and Belize. MAJOR NATIONAL GROUPS: (95e) Mayan 88%, other Mexican. MAJOR LANGUAGES: Mayan, Spanish. MAJOR RELIGIONS: Roman Catholic, animist. MAJOR CITIES: (95e) Tihoo (Merida) 596,000, Kimpech (Campeche) 202,000, Ciudad del Carmen 154,000, Chetumal 95,000, Cancun 86,000, Progresso 63,000, Chichimila (Valladolid) 58,000, Motul 46,000, Tizimun 34,000, Ticul 30,000.

*GEOGRAPHY:* AREA: 54,170 sq.mi.-140,336 sq.km. LOCATION: Yucatan occupies a large peninsula in southeastern Mexico, mostly a flat tableland projecting into the sea between the Caribbean Sea and the Gulf of Mexico. POLITICAL STATUS: Yucatan forms the Mexican states of Campeche, Quintana Roo, and Yucatan.

*INDEPENDENCE DECLARED:* 3 April 1916; 3 July 1924.

*FLAG:* The Mayan national flag is a horizontal bicolor of pale blue over red.

*PEOPLE:* The Maya peoples, the descendants of the great Mayan Empire, inhabit a large area of southern Mexico and Central America. The Maya of the Yucatan Peninsula primarily speak Yucatec, with minorities speaking Itzá and Quiché, languages of the Penutian language group. Yucatec is the most important of the fifteen major Mayan dialects. The Maya are mostly poor farmers, the majority speaking little or no Spanish. The Mestizo middle class and the small upper class, mostly of pure Spanish descent, are concentrated in Merida and the resort cities. The Mayan majority are Roman Catholic, mixing the Christian beliefs with many pre-Christian religious traditions and customs.

*THE NATION:* The early history of the Maya peoples is obscure although scholars agree on three major epochs in Mayan history: the Preclassic Era from about 1500 B.C. to A.D. 300, the Classic Era from about 300 to 900, and the Postclassic, 900 to 1697. Preclassic Mayan civilization, centered in present Guatemala, developed a sedentary agricultural society, well advanced in the arts and sciences. During this period the Maya invented an extremely accurate calendar, hieroglyphic writing, and major works of art. In the early Classic period Mayan culture spread over a much wider area. During the Postclassic Era the center of Mayan civilization shifted to the city-states of the Yucatan Peninsula.

Scientists estimate that the Maya numbered some 14 million in the eighth century, mostly south of the Yucatan Peninsula. The collapse of Mayan civilization in the late Classic Era led to the abandonment of the southern cities as two large migrations from Guatemala and Honduras moved north to the peninsula, traditionally settled in 899.

The settlers constructed new cities on the peninsula, which became centers of the flourishing Postclassic period. In the ninth and tenth centuries Toltec invaders from central Mexico overran the peninsula. Even though Toltec influence disappeared by about 1200, Mayan culture was drastically changed by such Toltec practices as human sacrifice. A federation of the three major city-states of the peninsula in the late thirteenth century began a long period of stability and prosperity.

The stability crumbled around 1440 as a fierce civil war ended the federation. Whole populations fled, leaving behind abandoned cities and towns. A series of natural disasters further weakened the Maya amid the continuing civil war. The Itzá, the probable founders of Chichén Itzá, migrated to the region of Lake Petén in present Guatemala around 1450.

A shipwrecked Spanish sailor in 1511 taught a Mayan girl to speak Spanish. The girl, Malinche, rechristened Marina, served as the interpreter for Cortez after 1519. Using Campeche as their base, the Spanish launched an expedition against the Maya in 1531–35. The last Mayan strongholds fell to the Spanish in 1546. The Itzá, the last free Mayan nation, were driven from their capital at Tayasal in 1697, their defeat ending all Maya independence.

The Spanish systematically destroyed the Mayan culture and religion. Zealous Catholic missionaries gathered and burned all Mayan books and records, with only a few scattered examples surviving. The inventors of advanced mathematics, astronomy, arts, and sciences were reduced to a subject people, often enslaved and forced to work on Spanish plantations.

The newly independent Mexican state claimed the Yucatan Peninsula as part of its national territory in 1821. One of the wealthiest areas of Spanish America, with sisal plantations worked by Mayan debt slaves, the region's Spanish landowners rejected the Mexican claims. Regional leaders, considering the peninsula a separate Central American state during Spanish rule, declared the region independent in 1839. Mexican troops sent from the capital ended the secession in 1843. The secession aroused the downtrodden Maya. A rebellion against the cruel European and Mestizo landlords erupted in 1847. The revolt quickly escalated to civil war, called the War of the Castes, in 1847–48.

Revolution and civil war from 1914 to 1919 left Mexico virtually without a central government. A revolt in Yucatan in 1916, led by Felipe Carillo, effectively separated the region from the weak Mexican state. On 3 April 1916 Carillo declared the independence of the Socialist Republic of Yucatan, a year before Lenin proclaimed a socialist state in Russia.

The Mayas again rebelled in 1923, while renewed political chaos preoccupied the Mexican government. An alliance of Mayan and Mestizo leaders declared Yucatan independent of Mexico on 3 July 1924. The new government, for the first time since the Spanish conquest, made the Mayan language an official language. Quickly defeated and returned to Mexican government control, the peninsula was administratively divided.

The legacy of large estates, effectively excluding the Mayas from participation in the region's economy, remained a well-established pattern of dominance and subordination into the 1960s. Newly discovered petroleum reserves and the growing importance of tourism began to change the Mayas' situation in the 1970s. A renewed interest in their rich heritage raised demands for equal rights and attention to the many cultural and economic grievances. A Mayan rebellion begun in 1975 in neighboring Guatemala sparked the growth of a more militant Mayan nationalism in Mexico.

The Mayas' habits, culture, and outlook differ drastically from those of the largely Mestizo Mexicans. A refusal to assimilate has obliged non-Maya to learn the language in order to live or work in the region. Merida, alone of the large Mexican cities, is effectively bilingual. As part of the Mayan cultural revival of the 1970s and 1980s, a language academy was established in Merida to standardize and modernize contemporary usage.

The Maya began casting aside their legendary patience in the 1990s, particularly after a rebellion broke out among the related peoples of Chiapas in 1993–94. Nationalist groups began to call for Mayan autonomy and pressed for land and cultural rights.

Mexico's entry into the North American Free Trade Agreement (NAFTA) stimulated a debate on the region's future. NAFTA offered economic backing for autonomy. As close to New Orleans or Miami as it is to Mexico City, Yucatan began to move away from Mexico's tight economic control, with growing demands for economic autonomy adding to the strengthening national sentiment in the Yucatan.

*SELECTED BIBLIOGRAPHY:*

Carey, James C. *The Mexican Revolution in Yucatan, Nineteen Fifteen to Nineteen Twenty-Four.* 1984.

Lockwood, C. C. *The Yucatan Peninsula.* 1989.

Mallan, Chicki. *Yucatan Handbook.* 1990.

# ZANZIBAR

**Zanzibar and Pemba**

*CAPITAL: Zanzibar*

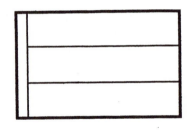

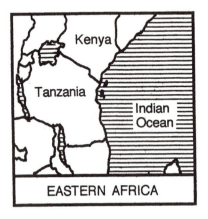

EASTERN AFRICA

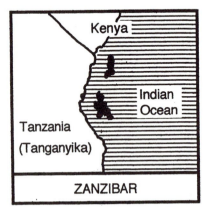

ZANZIBAR

*POPULATION:* (95e) 641,000 : 600,000 Zanzibaris in Tanzania. MAJOR NATIONAL GROUPS: (95e) Zanzibari 92% (Shirazi 64%, black African 12%, Arab 10%, Asian 6%), other Tanzanian. MAJOR LANGUAGES: Swahili, Arabic, English. MAJOR RELIGIONS: (95e) Sunni Muslim 77%, Christian, Hindu. MAJOR CITIES: (95e) Zanzibar 152,000, Chake Chake 33,000.

*GEOGRAPHY:* AREA: 950 sq.mi.-2,461 sq.mi. LOCATION: Zanzibar, comprising two large islands, Zanzibar and Pemba, and a number of small islands, lies in the Indian Ocean twenty-two miles east of the East African coast. POLITICAL STATUS: Zanzibar forms an autonomous state of the United Republic of Tanzania.

*INDEPENDENCE DECLARED:* 9 December 1963.

*FLAG:* The Zanzibari national flag, the official flag of the state, is a horizontal tricolor of blue, black, and green bearing a narrow white, vertical stripe at the hoist. OTHER FLAG(S): The flag of the former sultanate, still used by a number of nationalist organizations, is a red field bearing a centered green disc charged with a golden stem bearing two cloves.

*PEOPLE:* The Zanzibari nation comprises several distinct groups. The largest component is the Shirazi, named for early Persian traders from the city of Shiraz, claiming mixed black African and Persian descent. The major Shirazi groups are the Hadimu and Tumbatu of Zanzibar and the Pemba of Pemba Island. The African population is mostly descended from former slaves, augmented by recent arrivals from the mainland. The Arabs, descendants of early colonists, formerly made up a ruling elite. Pakistanis, Indians, and Goans are the largest groups of the Asian population. The primary language of the islands is Swahili, a hybrid language of mixed Arabic and Bantu influences spoken by most of the Zanzibaris of all backgrounds. The majority of the Zanzibaris are Sunni Muslim, with important Christian and Hindu minorities.

*THE NATION:* The islands, known to the early maritime nations of the Indian Ocean, were visited by Persian and Indian traders as early as the first century A.D. Merchants from the city of Shiraz, attracted by the sheltered harbor, established a colony at Zanzibar. The colony, probably founded in the seventh century, became the center of a large Persian migration between the tenth and twelfth centuries.

Arabs trading in the islands from the eleventh century expanded their operations from Zanzibar to the coastal regions of East Africa, founding a string of Arab trading towns and cities. Arab merchant adventurers penetrated far into the African interior, returning with slaves, ivory, and gold for sale in the Arab coastal cities and Zanzibar.

Portuguese explorer Vasco da Gama rounded the Cape of Good Hope in 1499, at the head of the first European expedition to penetrate the Indian Ocean. Da Gama returned to Europe to tell of an opulent island state, easy prey for the better-armed Europeans. A Portuguese squadron conquered Zanzibar and parts of the African mainland in 1503. The Portuguese later consolidated the conquered mainland settlements in the colony of Mozambique.

Omani Arabs from the eastern Arabian Peninsula ousted the Portuguese from Zanzibar in 1698. The Omanis ruled the islands as a vassal state of the powerful sultanate of Muscat, although the Arabs generally ignored the island province until the nineteenth century. Sultan Sayyid Zaid, recognizing the value of the fertile islands, introduced clove production from the Molucca Islands of the Dutch East Indies. In 1832 the sultan transferred the capital of his possessions from Arabia to the flourishing and economically more important Zanzibar.

A rigidly stratified society evolved, dominated by the Arab aristocracy and a large Asian merchant class. Vast Arab clove plantations, worked by African slaves, supported a culture famed for its wealth and extravagance. The importation of black African slaves from the mainland turned Zanzibar into one of the world's largest slave markets.

British pressure finally forced Zanzibar and Muscat to separate into two realms in 1861, the islands increasingly under British influence. The Zanzibari sultanate retained the islands and an extensive mainland coastal territory. Unable to resist European encroachments, the sultan closed the slave markets in 1873 and between 1887 and 1890 sold or ceded the mainland territories to Germany and the United Kingdom. An agreement between Germany and the British in June 1890 allowed the British to proclaim Zanzibar a protectorate.

History's shortest war broke out in Zanzibar in 1896. A British admiral anchored his fleet off Zanzibar so his men could watch a cricket match. The fleet so angered the sultan that he declared war and sent his only warship against the

British fleet. The British promptly sank the Zanzibari ship and shelled the sultan's palace. The sultan sued for peace, ending the so-called Cricket War, which lasted exactly thirty-seven minutes and twenty-three seconds.

The islands were considered an essentially Arab country, and the British authorities maintained their existing social order, effectively excluding the mixed-race Shirazi and the Africans from participation in the sultan's political life. A legislative assembly convened in 1926 reaffirmed the Arab domination of the island protectorate.

Political parties organized in the 1950s split along ethnic lines. The most important of the parties, the Arab- and Asian-supported Zanzibar National Party, soon had a powerful rival in the Afro-Shirazi party of the disadvantaged majority. Supported by the Arab and Asian minority, the sultan declared Zanzibar independent on 9 December 1963.

A Communist-inspired coup overthrew the sultanate government and declared Zanzibar a people's republic on 12 January 1964. In a few days of savagery, over 5,000 Arabs and Asians were murdered, their women raped, and their estates and businesses looted and burned. The sultan fled into exile, accompanied by thousands of terrified refugees.

A radical island government nationalized the clove industry and confiscated the remaining Arab and Asian properties. In October 1964 Zanzibar merged with mainland Tanganyika to form a united, socialist republic. The excesses of the revolution and opposition to the merger with the mainland incited the formation of a Zanzibari national movement, which gained support as socialist experimentation impoverished the islands.

The Tanzanian government, to avert a nationalist crisis, granted autonomy in 1979. The economic hardships and the widening rift between Zanzibar and the bankrupt mainland in the 1980s pushed even the former revolutionaries to reconcile their differences with exile and nationalist groups. In 1990 a coalition of Zanzibar's ethnic and cultural groups demanded a referendum on independence, claiming that the merger with the mainland, based on a now dead ideology, has transformed Zanzibar from a bustling economic power to a poor, neglected colonial appendage. The state, once accounting for half the world's clove production, has seen its exports fall from 18,000 tons in 1967 to less than 2,000 tons in 1991.

In January 1992 the Tanzanian government approved multiparty democracy but outlawed political parties based on tribal or regional interests. The restriction, denounced by the Zanzibaris, opened new rifts with the mainland. Constitutional reforms and wrangling since October 1993 and a campaign by the mainly Christian mainlanders for a separate Tanganyika government, have brought the breakup of the Tanzanian union ever closer.

*SELECTED BIBLIOGRAPHY:*

Anany, Samuel G. *A History of Zanzibar: A Study in Constitutional Development, 1934–1964.* 1970.

Bailey, Martin. *Union of Tanganyika and Zanzibar: A Study in Political Integration.* 1973.

Middleton, John, and Jane Campbell. *Zanzibar: Its Society and Politics.* 1985.

# ZETLAND

### Shetland and Orkney Islands

*CAPITALS: Kirkwall and Lerwick*

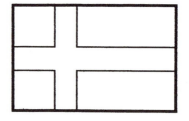

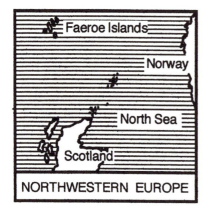

NORTHWESTERN EUROPE

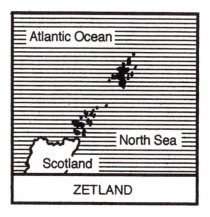

ZETLAND

*POPULATION:* (95e) 43,000 : 25,000 Shetlanders and 22,000 Orcadians in the United Kingdom. MAJOR NATIONAL GROUPS: (95e) Shetlander 52%, Orcadian 45%, other British. MAJOR LANGUAGE: English (island dialects). MAJOR RELIGIONS: Protestant, Roman Catholic. MAJOR CITIES: (95e) Lerwick 7,000, Kirkwall 6,000.

*GEOGRAPHY:* AREA: 927 sq.mi.-2,401 sq.km. LOCATION: The islands, the most northerly territory of the United Kingdom, form a long archipelago north of the mainland of Scotland.* The Orkney Islands, comprising some one hundred islands and islets, make up the southern group, the closest island only ten miles north of the mainland. The Shetland Islands, seventy islands and islets, lie fifty miles north of the Scottish mainland. POLITICAL STATUS: Zetland has no official status; the Shetland and Orkney Islands form administrative regions of Scotland in the United Kingdom.

*FLAG:* The Zetland national flag, the flag of the national movement, is a dark blue field charged with a white Scandinavian cross.

*PEOPLE:* The Shetlanders and Orcadians, who call themselves Islanders, are the descendants of early Viking settlers with a later Scottish admixture. Ethnically, the Islanders are more closely related to the peoples of Iceland and the Faeroe Islands* than to the other peoples of the British Isles. The island dialects, Shetlandic and Orcadian, claimed as dialects of a separate Zetland language, are virtually unintelligible to mainlanders and combine Old Norse, Celtic, and English influences. Culturally, the Islanders remain more Scandinavian than Scottish, many of the earlier Norse traditions and customs having survived to the present.

*THE NATION:* The islands, originally settled by Bronze Age Picts from the mainland, came under Norse Viking rule in the eighth century as part of the Viking expansion in the North Atlantic. By the ninth century Scandinavian colonists had settled many of the islands, the earlier inhabitants absorbed into Viking culture. Annexed by Harold Fairhair, the first king of Norway, the islands were organized as a separate earldom in 875. Details of the Norse conquest and settlement are recounted by the *Orkneyinga Saga*, a Norse epic.

The islands, called Zetland, meaning "high land," remained a Norwegian dependency until the Norwegian kingdom, along with its possessions and dependencies, passed to Denmark in 1397. The Danish king, Christian I, in 1468 pledged the islands to James III of Scotland as security for the dowry of Margaret of Norway on her marriage to the Scottish king. King James, not in receipt of the dowry, annexed the islands to his kingdom in 1472.

Scotland's union with England in 1707 began a long campaign in the islands for separation from Scotland and for a distinct legal status within the United Kingdom. The Islanders demanded the political and economic autonomy that would recognize their distinct culture and history, a status similar to the autonomy granted Mannin* or the Channel Islands. Relative isolation and a small population facilitated the efforts to preserve the islands' unique culture and dialects, even though the English language spread to the isolated islands in the eighteenth and nineteenth centuries.

The islands developed as the United Kingdom's major fishing region, while excess population left for the mainland, keeping the population nearly constant during the early decades of the twentieth century. The relative prosperity of the region renewed the island campaign to win separate legal status.

The population of the islands began to drop after World War II and the decline of the fishing industry. The Islanders, forced to leave in search of work, denounced the lack of opportunities as the result of their colonial political status. The discovery of oil in the North Sea off the islands in 1970 reversed the population decline. The islands became a center of the North Sea oil industry, with oil workers from many parts of the world brought in by the British and international oil companies.

Their culture and way of life threatened by the massive influx of oil workers and companies, the Islanders began to mobilize. Nationalist organizations demanded autonomy and separate legal status to protect their unique culture and to give them local control over the ecological damage done by the oil companies. In 1979 the Islanders threatened secession as their pristine islands were practically overrun by the oil companies going after the rich oil deposits in the North Sea.

The region's oil wealth, which stimulated Scottish nationalists to demand that the British government leave the control of the booming industry to the Scots, also roused island demands that the Scots keep their hands off Zetland's oil. The nationalist upsurge, with growing support for island control of development and the offshore oil fields and demands for a fairer share of the oil revenue, added another element to the dispute between Scotland and the government of the United Kingdom over control of natural resources.

Scottish nationalism, advocating independence within a united Europe, stimulated Zetlander sentiment for separation from Scotland in the 1980s and 1990s. The Islanders, culturally and historically distinct, in numerous polls expressed their preference for separate legal status within the United Kingdom; a large minority favored eventual independence within a European federation. Many supported calls for separate status within the United Kingdom, while the pro-Scottish opinion was a distant third. In the 1990s the pro-European sentiment is gaining support with the realization that future European regulations and funding will be more important to the islands than decisions made in either Edinburgh or London.

The Shetlanders and Orcadians, part of Scotland through a quirk of history, mostly oppose Scottish nationalism and, if loose ties to the United Kingdom are not possible, look with some confidence to independence. An independent Zetland within a European framework, including the part of the North Sea oil production within their territorial waters, valued at around $18 million a day, would be a viable, even wealthy, sovereign state.

*SELECTED BIBLIOGRAPHY:*

Schei, Liv K., and Gunnie Moberg. *Shetland Story.* 1988.
Simpson, Grant. *Scotland and Scandinavia 800–1800.* 1990.
Tudor, John R. *The Orkneys and Shetland: Their Past and Present State.* 1963.

# ZORAM

## Chin

*CAPITAL: Haka (Falam)*

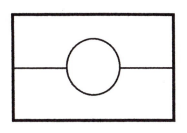

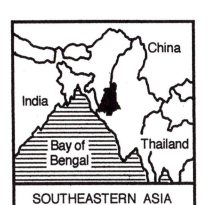

SOUTHEASTERN ASIA

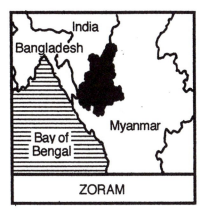

ZORAM

*POPULATION:* (95e) 1,576,000 : 860,000 Zomi (Chin) in Myanmar and another 300,000 in adjoining areas of India and Bangladesh. MAJOR NATIONAL GROUPS: (95e) Zomi (Chin) 55%, Mizo 4%, Arakanese 2%, Kuki 2%, other Burmese. MAJOR LANGUAGES: Burmese, Zomi (Chin), English. MAJOR RELIGIONS: (95e) Buddhist 38%, animist 37%, Christian 19%, Sunni Muslim 5%. MAJOR CITIES: (95e) CHIN STATE: Haka (Falam) 55,000, Tiddim 20,000. MAGWE DIVISION: Pakokku 95,000, Gangaw 30,000. SAGAING DIVISION. Mawlaik 40,000.

*GEOGRAPHY:* AREA: 26,146 sq. mi.-67,735 sq.km. LOCATION: Zoram occupies the region of northwestern Myanmar east of the Irrawaddy and Chindwin Rivers, an area of river lowlands rising to the Chin, Pakokku, and Chindwin hills in the west. POLITICAL STATUS: Zoram has no official status; the region claimed by nationalists forms Chin State, the Pakokku District of Magwe Division, and the Upper Chindwin District of Sagaing Division of the Union of Myanmar.

*FLAG:* The Zomi national flag, the flag of the national movement, is a horizontal bicolor of white over pale blue bearing a large, centered red disc.

*PEOPLE:* The Zomi, called Chin by the Burmans, speak a Kuki-Chin language of the Tibeto-Burman language group, the only regional language in Myanmar written in the Latin alphabet. The language, with forty-four dialects, is closely related to the Mizo and Kuki languages spoken by the ethnically related Mizo and Kuki minorities and spoken in neighboring areas of India. Less than 60% of the Zomi inhabit the area designated Chin State; the remainder inhabit the mountains east of the state and in northern Arakan,* and a sizable minority lives in the river lowlands, among a large ethnic Burman population.

*THE NATION:* The Zomi originated in eastern Tibet* in the eighth century. Pushed south by invasions of stronger peoples, the Zomi tribes took refuge in the mountainous areas west of the Irrawaddy plains. Organized in autonomous tribes, the Zomi never evolved a state structure, the various tribes uniting only when faced with an outside threat.

The Zomi tribes came under pressure from the expanding Burman kingdom in the seventeenth century. The tribes often became involved in the wars between the Burmans and the states to the north of the Zomi homeland in present India. In the 1820s the tribes came under nominal Burman rule, a tributary to the Burman kings, but aside from paying tribute and a nominal allegiance, the tribes remained effectively independent in their isolated hills.

The British claimed the region following the third Anglo-Burmese war in 1885. The victorious British formally annexed the Zomi territory on 1 January 1886. Ruled directly by a separate British administration, the Zomi territory remained a distinct political entity not legally a part of British Burma.

Christian missionaries arrived soon after the last tribes submitted to British authority in 1891. The Christians introduced European education and made some important converts among the families of local chiefs. In the early twentieth century a Christian-educated minority began to take power in the region and to promote unity among the disparate tribes.

The fierce Zomi warriors, recruited by the British for their colonial forces, became the best soldiers in the colonial army. Elite Chin military units maintained British authority in turbulent Burma but several times rebelled when the British attempted to assert their colonial rights in the Zomi homeland.

The Christian leadership in the early 1920s began to reject traditional tribal authority and to stress Zomi unity. An emphasis on the shared culture and language, written in a Latin alphabet devised by missionaries, marked the beginning of the Zomi nationalist movement in the 1920s and 1930s.

The Zomi, loyal British allies during World War II, demanded separate independence as the British prepared India and Burma for independence after the war. Arguing that their homeland had never formed part of British Burma, nationalists pressed for separation but finally settled for autonomy in a loose Union of Burma in 1948. The battle-hardened Chin soldiers formed the nucleus of the Burmese army and were largely responsible for saving Rangoon from capture by Karen rebels in 1949.

Some sentiment for independence emerged in the 1950s as the Burmese government became more authoritarian. Even though the government refused to implement fully the 1948 autonomy agreement, the Chins, now calling themselves Zomi, remained one of the few non-Burman ethnic groups not in rebellion against the state.

In 1961 the Burmese government passed a controversial religious law that made Buddhism the official state religion. The law deeply offended the Christian and animist Zomi, who had fought to preserve a secular state in Burma. Their demands for negotiations on the religious issue rebuffed, the Zomi rebelled. A national army, organized from Zomi units deserting the Burmese military, backed Zomi demands for political and religious freedom.

A Burmese military government, installed after a 1962 coup, dropped all pretense of federalism and attempted to impose military rule on the Chin Hills Special Division, the Zomi heartland. Fierce fighting erupted, but the Burmese soldiers failed to penetrate the Zomi's mountain strongholds. The Zomi leaders put aside their differences to demand the consolidation of the Zomi-populated areas of Magwe, Sagaing, and Arakan in an independent Zomi state. In 1964 the remaining uncommitted Zomi tribes joined the growing separatist war. By the mid-1970s, for the first time in their history, the Zomi had united as a nation.

The military pressure on the Zomi eased in 1988, with many Burmese military units pulled back to Rangoon to combat massive popular demonstrations demanding democracy. The brutal crushing of the democracy movement freed the military to resume the offensives against the ethnic insurgencies in the country. An offensive against the Zomi, launched in 1989, led to the fiercest fighting of the separatist war in 1991–92.

The Zomi leadership, closely allied to other insurgent groups in Myanmar and in neighboring Indian states, advocates independence within a federation of sovereign states that would replace Myanmar's brutal military government. More militant nationalists contend that independence would be the first step to the consolidation of an expanded Zomi state to include all the related peoples in Myanmar and India.

*SELECTED BIBLIOGRAPHY:*

Lintner, Bertil. *Land of Jade: A Journey through Insurgent Burma.* 1990.
Silverstein, Josef, ed. *Independent Burma at Forty Years.* 1989.
Von der Mehden, Frederick R. *Religion and Nationalism in Southeast Asia: Burma, Indonesia and the Philippines.* 1968.

# ZYRIA

**Komi and Komi-Permyak**

*CAPITAL: Syktyvkar*

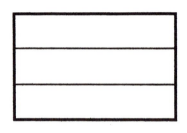

NORTHEASTERN EUROPE

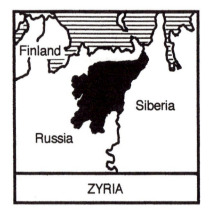

ZYRIA

*POPULATION:* (95e) 1,397,000 : 565,000 Komi in Russia. MAJOR NA-
TIONAL GROUPS: (95e) Russian 48%, Komi (including Komi-Permyak) 38%,
Ukrainian 7%, Belarussan 4%. MAJOR LANGUAGES: Russian, Komi, Ukrain-
ian. MAJOR RELIGIONS: Russian Orthodox, Roman Catholic. MAJOR
CITIES: (95e) KOMI: Syktyvkar 291,000 (360,000), Vorkuta 132,000
(242,000), Chibyu (Ukhta) 122,000 (220,000), Zheloznodorozhnyy 87,000,
Pechora 75,000, Inta 65,000, Sosnogorsk 57,000, Mikun 40,000. KOMI-PER-
MYAK: Kudymkar 39,000.

*GEOGRAPHY:* AREA: 173,282 sq.mi.-448,917 sq.km. LOCATION: Zyria
occupies the basins of the Pechora, Vychegda, and upper Kama Rivers, a region
partly above the Arctic Circle in northern European Russia. POLITICAL
STATUS: Zyria has no official status; the region forms the Komi Republic, a
member state of the Russian Federation, and the autonomous region of Komi-
Permyak, officially part of Russia's Perm Oblast.

*FLAG:* The Komi national flag, the official flag of the republic, is a horizontal
tricolor of blue, green, and white.

*PEOPLE:* The Komi, also called Permians, are a Finno-Ugric people with
two major divisions, the Zyrians or Komi Zyranes and the Permyaks or Komi
Otir. Both Komi divisions speak dialects of the same Finno-Permian language,
which is written in its own alphabet of mixed Latin and Cyrillic letters. The
most northerly of the Finnic peoples, the Komi culture has been influenced by
contact with the non-Finnic peoples of Russia's far north. The Komi are mostly

Orthodox Christians, as are the majority of the large Slav population. A Slav minority, mostly descendants of political exiles from Russia's western districts, are Roman Catholic.

*THE NATION:* Migrations of early Finnic peoples in the seventh and eighth centuries A.D. moved as far west as present Finland and Estonia. The ancestors of the Komi broke off from the main migration and turned north into the forest zone to settle the fertile river valleys. The Permian tribes, isolated in their northern homeland, developed a separate Finnic culture and language. Living in small clan groups the Permians gradually divided into two groups, the Zyrians (Zyrane) in the north and the Otir (Permyak) in the south.

The Permians, calling themselves Komi, came under the rule of the Slavic republic known as Great Novgorod in the thirteenth century. Formerly practicing a form of ancestor worship, the Komi converted to the Orthodox Christianity introduced to the clans by Saint Stephen in the 1360s and 1370s. Saint Stephen, the Komi's patron saint, is called the ''Enlightener of the Komi'' and is revered for opening the Komi homeland to the world outside.

The Russians of the rival Muscovite duchy began to penetrate Novgorodian territory in 1450 and finally conquered Novgorod between 1471 and 1478. Although more blond and Nordic than the Russians, the Komi were subjected to prejudice and a harsh colonial regime. The Russians suppressed the Komi language and culture, but not their Orthodox faith, and forced assimilation. In the eighteenth century the authorities opened the southern Komi districts to Slavic colonization, while setting aside the forest and Arctic zones as a place of exile for criminals and tsarist political prisoners.

A Komi cultural revival in the late nineteenth century emphasized their language, particularly the distinguished tradition of oral epics and folk literature. The revival began to reverse centuries of forced assimilation. A parallel movement, heavily influenced by the attitudes and ideals of the large population of political exiles, evolved a Komi national sentiment, antigovernment and anti-Russian.

The outbreak of World War I reinforced the growing antitsarist movement. Many young Komi took refuge in the forests to escape conscription. The overthrow of the tsar in February 1917 raised Komi expectations that the abuses and wrongs of the past would finally be addressed. A Komi congress in the summer on 1917 voted for autonomy in a new democratic Russia and sent a formal petition to the provisional government.

The Bolshevik coup in October 1917 swept away the remaining Russian authority in the region. Virtually independent, the Komi began to organize the institutions of self-rule. In early 1918 Bolshevik troops of the new Soviet government invaded the region. Allied Anglo-American interventionist forces, landed in the north, encouraged the Komi to organize a national state to combat Bolshevik influence in the important region.

Aided by the numerous freed political prisoners and members of the interventionist force, the Komi created a number of cultural and governmental institutions. To disseminate information over the large territory, a Komi alphabet was devised to fit the Komi's Permian language. In 1919 the interventionist forces withdrew from the region, opening the way for the Soviet reoccupation of the Komi state.

The Soviets created a Zyrian autonomous province in 1921 and a separate autonomous area for the Komi-Permyak in the southeast in 1925. The population of the regions, 92% Komi in 1926, expanded rapidly during the Stalinist years. The Gulag, a vast chain of slave labor camps built to exploit the high-quality coal discovered in the Pechora Basin and to provide labor for the construction of logging roads and mills, swallowed up thousands of prisoners. Northern Zyria, a region so forbidding that it had been rejected as place to send prisoners by Tsar Nicholas I, by the mid-1930s had a population of over 100,000 prisoners.

The region gained new importance during World War II as threatened industries and populations shifted east. In 1943 the Vorkuta-Kotlas Railway was completed across the region, entirely built by slave labor. The opening of the rail link began a period of spectacular growth. The population of the Komi region quadrupled between 1939 and 1949. By the end of World War II the Komi formed only a large minority in their homeland.

The Soviet reforms of the late 1980s provoked massive strikes by the region's coal miners to punctuate demands for higher pay and better working conditions in 1989–90. The strike and the disturbances by miners, already handsomely paid by Komi standards, loosed a torrent of Komi grievances and demands that Komi mistreatment be addressed by the republic's Chamber of Deputies. Economic demands gave way to political demands, including calls for the reunification of the Komi lands divided by Stalin between 1925 and 1929.

The disintegration of the Soviet state in August 1991 fueled a dramatic increase in the Komi's national awareness. The republican government in November 1991 unilaterally declared Komi a constituent republic of the renewed Russian Federation and reiterated an earlier demand for the reunification of the Komi homeland in one state.

Komi national organizations, formed mostly since 1991, have become increasingly nationalistic. Since 1993 the nationalists have waged a nonviolent war of symbols in the region. Denouncing the new Russian flag as a symbol of colonialism, as offensive as the former red banner of the Communists, nationalists routinely tear down the Russian flag and raise the banner of Komi nationalism in its place. The Komi flag, representing the nationalists' aspirations, has come to symbolize the nationalists' contention that the region's coal, timber, oil, and natural gas would sustain the same flag flying over an independent Komi republic.

*SELECTED BIBLIOGRAPHY:*

Allworth, Edward. *Soviet Nationality Problems.* 1971.

Duik, Nadia, and Adrian Karatnycky. *The Hidden Nations: The People Challenge the Soviet Union.* 1990.

Kozlov, Viktor. *The Peoples of the Soviet Union.* 1988.

# Declarations of Independence by Nonstate Nations since 1890

| | |
|---|---|
| Republic of Rio Grande do Sul (Geralia) | 8 September 1892 |
| Republic of Hawaii | 4 July 1894 |
| Republic of Taiwan | 23 May 1895 |
| Gagauz Republic | 19 January 1906 |
| Urjanchai Republic (Tannu Tuva) | 18 December 1911 |
| State of Tibet | 18 February 1912 |
| Republic of North Epirus | 1 March 1914 |
| Socialist Republic of Yucatan | 3 April 1916 |
| Hashemite Kingdom of Hejaz | 27 June 1916 |
| Terek-Dagestan Republic (Dagestan) | 20 October 1917 |
| Republic of Flanders | 11 November 1917 |
| Bashkurd Republic (Bashkortostan) | 29 November 1917 |
| Chechen Republic | 2 December 1917 |
| Taurida Republic (Crimea) | 10 December 1917 |
| Republic of the Don | 10 January 1918 |
| Tatar Republic (Tatarstan) | 24 January 1918 |
| Confederated Republic of Altay (Altai-Khakassia) | 26 January 1918 |
| Republic of the Kuban | 16 February 1918 |

| | |
|---|---|
| State of Sakha Omuk | 22 February 1918 |
| Terek People's Republic | 4 March 1918 |
| Abkhaz Republic | 8 March 1918 |
| Southwestern Caucasian Republic (Ajaristan) | 18 April 1918 |
| Republic of North Caucasia (Circassia) | 11 May 1918 |
| Crimean Democratic Republic | 16 May 1918 |
| Karachay Republic | 18 May 1918 |
| Far Eastern Republic | 23 May 1918 |
| Kalmyk Republic | 12 June 1918 |
| Republic of Siberia | 4 July 1918 |
| Idel-Ural Federation | 30 September 1918 |
| Republic of Transylvania | 28 October 1918 |
| Republic of Vorarlberg (Tyrol) | 3 November 1918 |
| Western Ukrainian Democratic Republic | 14 November 1918 |
| Soviet Republic of Saxony | 19 November 1918 |
| Democratic and Socialist Republic of Bavaria | 22 November 1918 |
| Republic of Lusatia | 1 January 1919 |
| Buryat Republic | 11 February 1919 |
| Free State of Tyrol | 24 April 1919 |
| Republic of North Ingermanland (Ingria) | 23 January 1920 |
| Far East Republic | 6 April 1920 |
| Persian Soviet Socialist Republic of Gilan (Gilan) | 20 May 1920 |
| Adzharian Muslim Republic (Ajaristan) | 12 February 1921 |
| Republic of Abkhazia | 4 March 1921 |
| Republic of Eastern Karelia | 21 April 1921 |
| Republic of Santa Cruz | 8 July 1921 |
| People's Republic of Tannu Tuva | 14 August 1921 |
| Confederal Republic of the Tribes of the Rif | 19 September 1921 |
| Free State of Chukotka | 28 October 1921 |

| | |
|---|---|
| Republic of Yucatan | 3 July 1924 |
| State of Manchuria | 8 February 1926 |
| Nan Chao Federation | 12 January 1927 |
| Solon Republic (Eastern Mongolia) | 15 December 1928 |
| Republic of Manchuria | 4 February 1929 |
| Republic of Euzkadi | 14 June 1931 |
| Manchukuo (Manchuria) | 18 February 1932 |
| Islamic Republic of East Turkestan | 23 January 1934 |
| Mongolian Federation (Southern Mongolia) | 23 April 1934 |
| Republic of Catalonia | 4 October 1934 |
| Republic of Santa Cruz | 22 May 1935 |
| Federation of the Mongol Borderlands (Southern Mongolia) | 22 November 1937 |
| Republic of Carpatho-Ukraine | 2 March 1939 |
| Alawite Republic of Latakia | 28 June 1939 |
| Republic of Western Ukrainia | 30 June 1941 |
| Kingdom of Montenegro | 13 July 1941 |
| Kalmyk National Republic | 7 August 1942 |
| Karachai National Republic | 11 August 1942 |
| Federated Shan States | 3 October 1942 |
| Republic of Sicily | 10 July 1943 |
| Republic of Tigray (Tigre) | 11 September 1943 |
| East Turkestan Republic | 31 January 1945 |
| People's Republic of Eastern Mongolia | 15 January 1946 |
| Kurdish People's Republic (Kurdistan) | 22 January 1946 |
| Republic of the Faeroe Islands | 18 September 1946 |
| Free Territory of Trieste | 10 February 1947 |
| Federal Republic of Nagaland | 14 August 1947 |
| Kingdom of Sikkim | 15 August 1947 |
| Khanate of Kalat (Baluchistan) | 15 August 1947 |
| State of Travancore (Kerala) | 15 August 1947 |
| State of Pushtunistan | 2 September 1947 |

| | |
|---|---|
| Republic of Kawthoolei | 14 June 1949 |
| State of Aceh | 11 February 1950 |
| Republic of South Moluccas | 25 April 1950 |
| Chinese Islamic Republic (Ningsia) | 9 August 1953 |
| Republic of Vietnam | 26 October 1955 |
| Khanate of Kalat (Baluchistan) | 20 June 1958 |
| Kingdom of Sanwi | 5 February 1960 |
| State of Somaliland | 26 June 1960 |
| Republic of Katanga | 11 July 1960 |
| Mining State of South Kasai | 9 August 1960 |
| Kingdom of Buganda | 31 December 1960 |
| Ruwenzuru Republic (Toro) | 13 February 1963 |
| State of Aden (South Yemen) | 7 September 1963 |
| Sultanate of Zanzibar | 9 December 1963 |
| State of Champa | 19 February 1964 |
| Republic of Mizoram | 6 July 1966 |
| Republic of Biafra | 30 May 1967 |
| Republic of Benin | 18 August 1967 |
| Democratic People's Republic of Yemen (South Yemen) | 30 November 1967 |
| Republic of Cabinda | 1 August 1975 |
| Republic of the North Solomons | 1 September 1975 |
| Democratic Republic of East Timor | 28 November 1975 |
| Republic of West Papua | 9 December 1975 |
| Sahrawi Arab Democratic Republic | 27 February 1976 |
| Turkish Republic of Northern Cyprus | 15 November 1983 |
| State of Khalistan | 30 April 1986 |
| State of Palestine | 15 November 1988 |
| Republic of Bougainville (North Solomons) | 17 May 1990 |
| South Ossetian Democratic Republic (Ossetia) | 12 December 1990 |
| Somaliland Republic | 18 May 1991 |

| Dniestr Moldavian Republic (Dniestria) | 2 September 1991 |
| Kosovo Republic | 11 October 1991 |
| Chechen Republic | 2 November 1991 |
| Republic of Artsakh | 31 December 1991 |
| Democratic Republic of Crimea | 5 May 1992 |
| Republic of Abkhazia | 23 July 1992 |
| Democratic Republic of Yemen (South Yemen) | 21 May 1994 |

The names of states and the dates of independence are often a matter of confusion or dispute. The state names are subject to translation and interpretation, and the dates of independence are subject to confusion with declarations of sovereignty or intent, the date the event was reported or the declaration report received, or the differences in the calendars in use at the time.

# Geographic Distribution and National Organizations Listed by Nation

**AFRICA**

Algeria: Azawad; Kabylia.

Angola: Cabinda; Musikongo.

Benin: Togoland.

Cameroon: Bamilekeland; Kanowra.

Chad: Kanowra; North Chad.

Congo: Musikongo.

Côte d'Ivorie: Sanwi.

Djibouti: Adal.

Equatorial Guinea: Bioko.

Eritrea: Adal.

Ethiopia: Adal; Oromia, Tigre, Western Somalia.

Ghana: Ashantiland; Sanwi; Togoland.

Kenya: Masailand.

Mali: Azawad.

Morocco: Rif; Sahrawi.

Niger: Azawad; Kanowra.

Nigeria: Benin; Biafra; Calabar; Hausa; Kanowra; Yorubaland.

Portugal: Madeira.

Senegal: Casamance.

Somalia: Somaliland.

South Africa: KwaZulu-Natal.

Spain: Canary Islands; Rif.

Sudan: Darfur; Southern Sudan.

Tanzania: Masailand; Zanzibar.

Togo: Togoland.

Uganda: Ankole; Buganda; Bunyoro; Toro.

Zaire: Katanga; Musikongo; South Kasai.

Zambia: Barotseland.

Zimbabwe: Matabeleland.

## National Organizations by Nation

ADAL: Afar Liberation Front (ALF); Afar National Liberation Movement (ANLM); Afar-Saho Liberation Party; Afar Democratic Revolutionary Party (ARDU); Front for the Restoration of Unity and Democracy (AROD); Popular Front for Liberation (PFL); Popular Movement for the Liberation of Djibouti (MPLD); Front for the Restoration of Rights and Legality (AROD); Organisation des Masses Afars (OMA); Parti Populaire Djiboutien (PPD).

ANKOLE: Ankole-Kigezi Association; Federal Democratic Movement; Kumayana Movement; People's Congress.

ASHANTILAND: Ashanti Confederation; Ashanti United Party (AUP); Federal Party; Movement for Freedom and Justice (MFJ); National Liberation Movement (NLM); United Kotoko Society.

AZAWAD: Azawad United Front (FUA); Front for the Liberation of Eastern Sahara (FLES); Islamic Front for the Liberation of Azawad (FIAA); National Liberation Front of Azawad; Popular Movement of Azawad (MPA); Popular Movement for the Liberation of Azawad (FPLA); Islamic Front of Azawad (FIIA); Revolutionary Movement of the Blue Men (Morehob); Revolutionary Army of the Liberation of Azawad (AKLA); Armée Révolutionnaire de Libération du Nord-Niger (ARLN); Front de Libération de Tamoust (FLT); Front de Libération de l'Aïr et l'Azaouad (FLAA); Front Patriotique de Libération du Sahara; Front Islamique-Arabe de l'Azaouad (ARLA).

BAMILEKELAND: Bamileke Independence Front (FIB); Cameroon Anglophone Movement (CAM); Kumaze; Social Democratic Front (SDF); Union Bamileke.

BAROTSELAND: Movement for an Independent Barotseland (MIB); Barotse National Council; Itenge; National Party.

BENIN: Otu Edo; Ogbomi Society; Great Benin Movement; Edo National Union.

BIAFRA: Adami Oha Society; Ibo Federal Union (IFU); Keep Biafra Alive (KBA); Adami Oha Veterans Association; People's Party.

BIOKO: Front for the Liberation of Bioko (FIB); Eri Democratic Front (FDE); Bubi National Group (GNB); Movement Fernando Póo.

BUGANDA: Buganda National Council (BNC); Democratic Party (DP); Federal Democratic Movement (MOFEDE); Kabaka Yekka Party (King Only Party); Remember Buganda.

BUNYORO: Federal Bunyoro Movement; Independence Revolutionary Movement; Ruhuga Society; Mubende Banyoro Party; Kitara Bunyoro.

CABINDA: Front for the Liberation of the Enclave of Cabinda (FLEC); Popular Front for the Liberation of Cabinda (MPLC); National Union for the Liberation of Cabinda (UNLC); Movement for the Liberation of Cabinda (MOLICA).

CALABAR: Brotherhood of the Cross and the Star; Ekpe Society; Ibibio Union; National Independence Party (NIP).

CANARY ISLANDS: Canary National Congress (CNC); Canary Nation; Movement for the Autonomy and Independence of the Canary Archipelago (MAIAC); Canary People's Union (UPC); Movement for the Independence of the Canary Islands (MIIC); Canary National Assembly (ACN); Asamblea Majorera (AM); Union Nacionalista de Izquerida.

CASAMANCE: Movement of the Democratic Forces of the Casamance (MFDC); Casamance United National Movement (MNCU); Front Nord; Front Sud.

DARFUR: Darfur Development Front (DDF); Fur National Movement (FNM); Sony Liberation Movement (SLM).

HAUSA: Islamic Republican Movement; Moslem Brotherhood; Islamic Legion; Northern Elders; Islamic Movement; Northern People's Congress (NPC).

KABYLIA: Socialist Forces Front (FFS); Algerian Human Rights League (LADH); Union for Culture and Democracy (RDC); Sons of the Martyrs of the Revolution; Berber Cultural Movement (MCB); Rassemblement pour la Culture et la Démocratie (RCD).

KANOWRA: Bornu Youth Movement (BYM); Kanem-Bornu; Kanowra People's Party (KPP); Islamic League; Movement for Kanembu Freedom (MLK).

KATANGA: Confederation of Tribal Associations of Katanga (CONAKAT); Rally for Independence; Democratic Front; Congolese National Liberation Front (FLNC); Union for Democracy and National Social Progress; Union of Federalists and Independent Republicans (UFERI); Rebirth Katanga; Katanga Gendarmes.

KWAZULU-NATAL: Inkatha Yenkululeko Yesikwe; Inkatha Freedom Party (IFP); Natal People's Conference; Natal Democratic Party; Amasinyora; KwaZulu Police (KZP).

MADEIRA: Madeira Archipelago Liberation Front (FLAMA); Madeira Liberation Organization (OLM); Independence Movement of Madeira-Europe (MIME).

MASAILAND: Masai Democratic Congress; Masai United Front (MUF); Masai National United Movement; National Liberation Front of United Masailand (NLFUM).

MATABELELAND: Zimbabwe African People's Union (ZAPU)/Zimbabwe People's Revolutionary Army (ZIPRA); Democratic League; United National Federal Party (UNFP); Forum Party (FP); Committee for a Democratic Society (CODESO); Zimbabwe Active People's Unity Party.

MUSIKONGO: Association for the Maintenance, Unity, and Expansion of the Kikongo Language (ABAKO); Congolese National Movement (MNC); Kongo Popular Movement of Musikongo (MPKM); Matswa; Ngwizako-Ngwizani a Kongo; Union pour la Démocratie et le Progrès Social National.

NORTH CHAD: North Chad National Movement (MICN); Chad National Liberation Front (FROLINAT); Armed Forces of the North (FAN); Chadian Armed Forces (FAT); Mouvement pour la Démocratie et le Dévelopement (MDD); Forces Armées Occidentales (FAO).

OROMIA: Oromo Liberation Front (OLF); Islamic Front for the Liberation of Oromia (IFLO); Oromo People's Democratic Organization (OPDO); United Oromo People's Liberation Front (UOPLF); Oromo Abo Liberation Front (OALF).

RIF: Rif Movement for Liberation and Liquidation (MRPLL); Popular Movement (MPR); Neapolis; Averroes; Democratic Union of the Peoples of the Rif (UDPR); Organisation Nacional del Rif (National Organization of the Rif).

SAHRAWI: Government of the Sahrawi Arab Democratic Republic (SADR); Popular Front for the Liberation of Saguia El Hama and Rio de Oro (POLISARIO—Polisario Front).

SANWI: Sanwi Liberation Front (FLS); Agni Students Association; Agni Union; Rassemblement des Forces National du Sanwi (RFNS); Parti pour la Libération de l'Sanwi.

SOMALILAND: Somali National Movement (SNM); United Somali Party (USP); United Somali Front (USF); Somali Democratic Front (SOA).

SOUTHERN SUDAN: Southern People's Liberation Front (SPLF)/Southern People's Liberation Army (SPLA); Azania Liberation Front (ALF); Anyidi Movement; Sudan African Liberation Front (SALF); Forces of Unity; SPLA-Unity; Liberation Front for Southern Sudan; Sudan African National Union (SANU); South Sudan Independence Movement.

SOUTH KASAI: Front for the Liberation of Occupied South Kasai (FLKSO); Union of Federalists and Independent Republicans (UFERI); Kasai Democratic Front.

TIGRE: Tigray People's Liberation Front (TPLF); Tigray National Organization; Relief Society of Tigre (REST); United Independence Movement of Tigre.

TOGOLAND: Togoland Congress (TC); National Liberation Movement of Western Togoland (NLMWT); Togolese Liberation Movement (TLM); All-Ewe Conference; Ewe Unionist Association; Ewe National Movement; National Movement of Mono-East Togoland (MNMTE).

TORO: Toro People's Organization; Ruwenzuru Movement; Ruwenzururu; Federal Democratic Movement (FDM); Christian Democratic Party (CDP); Ruwenzuru Kingdom Freedom Movement.

WESTERN SOMALIA: Western Somali Liberation Front (WSLF); Western Somali United Democratic Union (WSUDU); Issa Gugiera Liberation Front; Ogaden National Liberation Front (ONLF); Somali Abo Liberation Front (SALF); Harer National League; Issa and Gurgura Liberation Front; Yem Nationality Movement; Ethnic Somalis' Democratic Movement.

YORUBALAND: Egbe Omo Oduduwa; Yoruba Action Party (YAP); Yoruba United Party (YUP); All-Yoruba National United Party (AYNUP).

ZANZIBAR: Bismillah Party; Maendelo Zanzibar; Kamahuru; Movement for a Democratic Alternative (MDA); National Movement of Zanzibar (MNZ); Zanzibar National Party (ZNP); Zanzibar Voice.

## THE AMERICAS AND OCEANIA

Bolivia: Santa Cruz.

Brazil: Geralia.

Canada: Haida Gwaii; Haudenosaunee; Newfoundland; Nistassin; Nunavut; Quebec.

Chile: Araucania.

Colombia: Antioquia.

Denmark: Kalaallit-Nunaat.

France: Guadeloupe; Guiana; Kanaki; Martinique; Tahiti.

Honduras: Mosquitia.

Indonesia: West Papua.

Mexico: Yucatan.

Nicaragua: Mosquitia.

Papua New Guinea: North Solomons.

United States: Dinetah; Haida Gwaii; Haudenosaunee; Hawaii; Lakota; Puerto Rico; Sequoyah.

### National Organizations by Nation

ANTIOQUIA: Latino National Movement (MLN); Patria Libre; Pro-Antioquia; Popular Militia; United Antioquia Movement (MAU); Antioquian Rebels; Antioquia Libre (Free Antioquia); Movimento Antioquia Soberana (MAS).

ARAUCANIA: Ad Mapu (Mapuche People's Liberation Organization); Aukiñ Wall Mapu (Council for the Land); Central Cultural Mapuche; Party of the Land and Identity; Pelondugun Society.

DINETAH: Dine Bii Coalition (Coalition for Navajo Liberation); Dine Land Movement; Dine Bikeyah.

GERALIA: Front of the Three (FT); Geralia Movement; Movement of the Democratic South (MSD); Southern Party; Republic of the Pampas (GRP); Party of National Construction (PCNG); Southern Party (PS); Movimento Nacional de Las Pampas (MNP); Partido de Construcão Nacional (PNC); Partido Federalista (PF).

GUADELOUPE: Counseil National de la Resistance Guadeloupéine; Mouvement Populaire pour une Guadeloupe Indépendante; Union Populaire pour la Libération de la Guadeloupe (GPU); Revolutionary Alliance of the Caribbean.

GUIANA: Fo non Libéré Guyane; Action Démocratique Guayanaise (ADG); Forces Démocratique Guayanaise (FDG); Mouvement pour la Décolonisation et l'Emancipation Sociale; Parti National Populaire Guyanais (PNPIG); Parti Socialiste Guyanais (PSG); Union de Travailleurs; Revolutionary Alliance of the Caribbean.

HAIDA GWAII: Council of the Haida Nation; Sgan Gwaii; Alaska Native Brotherhood; Assembly of First Nations.

HAUDENOSAUNEE: Iroquois Confederation; American Indian Movement (AIM); Assembly of First Nations; Ganiekeh Movement; Mohawk Nation; Haudenosaunee Runners Society.

HAWAII: Ka Lahui Hawai'i (Hawaiian Nation); Polynesian Sovereignty Movement; Lokahi aki paa (Unity); National Movement of the Hawaiian Peoples; National Homeland Movement.

KALAALLIT-NUNAAT: Atassut; Inuit Ataqatiqiit; Issittup-partii-a; Suimut; Inuit Transpolar Movement; Ohana Council.

KANAKI: Kanak Socialist Liberation Front (FSLK); Front Uni de Libéracion Kanak (FULK); National Kanak Socialist Liberation Front (FLNKS); Union Caledonienne (UC); United Front for Kanak Liberation (FUKL); Libération Kanak Socialiste (LKS).

LAKOTA: Lakota Nation; Lakota Treaty Council; American Indian Movement (AIM); Paha Sapa Liberation Movement (PSLM).

MARTINIQUE: Mouvement Indépendente Martiniquais (MIN); Parti Progressiste Martiniquais.

MOSQUITIA: Moskito-Sumo-Rama Asala Takanka (MISURATA); Kisan Group; Misura; Yamata; Sukawala; Pana-Pana.

NEWFOUNDLAND: Newfie Independence Movement (NIM); Party for an Independent Newfoundland; National Liberation Movement of Newfoundland (NLMN).

NISTASSIN: Innu Campaign against the Militarization of Ntesian; Labrador Innu Association; Assembly of First Nations.

NORTH SOLOMONS: Bougainville Revolutionary Government (BRG)/Bougainville Revolutionary Army (BRA); Independence Movement of the North Solomons; Melanesian Alliance.

NUNAVUT: Inuit Circumpolar Conference; Nunavut Constitutional Forum; Tungavik Federation of Nunavut; Inuit Tapirisat.

PUERTO RICO: Puerto Rican Independence Party; Armed Forces of National Resistance (FALN); Armed Liberation Commandos (CAL); Armed Volunteers of the Puerto Rican Revolution; Boricua Popular Army-Los Macheteros; Puerto Rican Independence Party (PIPR); Partido Socialista Puertorriqueño (PSP); Partido Communista Puertorriqueño (PCP); Democratic Popular Party (PDP).

QUEBEC: Parti Québécois (PQ); Quebec Liberation Front (FLQ); Bloc Québécois (BQ); Democratic Rally for Independence; Popular Liberation Front (FLP); Quebec Liberation Front (FLQ); Societé Saint-Jean Baptiste; Parti Action Québécois (PAQ); Action Démocratique de Québec.

SANTA CRUZ: Conference of Campesino Unions; National Liberation Army (ELN); Santa Cruz National Party; Santa Cruz National Confederation (CNSC); Accíon Nacionalista (AN); Frente Patriótica de Santa Cruz Libre (FP).

SEQUOYAH: Four Mothers Society; Five Nations Treaty Council; American Indian Movement (AIM); Sons of Sequoyah.

TAHITI: Ai'a Api (New Land); Free Tahiti Party (PTL); Front for Internal Autonomy (FAI); Ia Mana te Nunaa; Polynesian Liberation Front (FLP); Te Nunaa Ia Ora; Pupu Here Ai'a; Tahitinui; Pupe Here Ai'a te Nunaa la Ora.

WEST PAPUA: All-Papua Conference; Operasi Papua Merdeka (Free Papua Movement); Melanesian Socialist Party; West Papuan Government-in-Exile.

YUCATAN: Army of the Poor; Mayan Language and Nation; Movement for Mayan

Rights (MDM); Petenero Inde Front; Mayan Unity; National Heritage; Partido de Accion Nacional; Zapatista National Liberation Army (EZLN).

## ASIA

Afghanistan: Baluchistan.

Bangladesh: Kaderia.

China: Eastern Mongolia; East Turkestan; Manchuria; Nan Chao; Ningsia; Southern Mongolia; Taiwan; Tibet.

India: Assam; Gorkhaland; Jharkhand; Kashmir; Kerala; Khalistan; Ladakh; Meghalaya; Meithei Laipak; Mizoram; Nagaland; Sikkim; Tamil Nadu; Tripura.

Indonesia: Aceh; East Timor; South Moluccas.

Iran: Arabistan; Baluchistan; Gilan; Kurdistan.

Iraq: Assyria; Kurdistan.

Israel: Palestine.

Japan: Okinawa.

Lebanon: Mount Lebanon.

Malaysia: Sabah; Sarawak.

Myanmar: Arakan; Honsawatoi; Kachinland; Kawthoolei; Kayah; Nagaland; Paoh; Shanland; Wah; Zoram.

Oman: Dhofar.

Pakistan: Baluchistan; Kashmir; Ladakh; Pushtunistan; Sind.

Philippines: Bangska Moro.

Russia: Altai-Khakassia; Buryatia; Chukotka; Far East; Hasava; Ho'aido; Koryakia; Sakha Omuk, Siberia; Tannu Tuva; Uralia.

Saudi Arabia: Hejaz.

Sri Lanka: Tamil Eelam.

Syria: Assyria; Jebel ed Druze; Kurdistan; Latakia.

Thailand: Pattani.

Turkey: Kurdistan.

Uzbekistan: Karakalpakstan.

Vietnam: Champa; South Vietnam.

Yemen: South Yemen.

## National Organizations by Nation

ACEH: Aceh Merdeka (Free Aceh); Aceh National Liberation Front (ANLF); Hassan Tiro Group; National Liberation Front of Aceh-Sumatra (NLFAS).

ALTAI-KHAKASSIA: Abakan-Altai; Altai United Front; Confederal Nation of Altai-Khakass.

ARABISTAN: Arab Front for the Liberation of Ahvaz (AFLA); Popular Front of Ahvaz (PFLA); Popular Liberation Front of Arabistan (PLFA); Group of the Martyrs; Chararshanbeh-e-Siah (Black Wednesday); Movement for the Liberation of Ahvaz (MLA); Movement for the Liberation of Arabistan.

ARAKAN: Arakan Liberation Party (ALP)/Arakan Liberation Army (ALA); Arakan League for Democracy; Arakan Liberation Front (ALF); Arakan Rohingya Patriotic Front (ARIO); Rohingya Patriotic Front (RPF); National United Front of Arakan (NUFA); Mujahadin; Rohingya Solidarity Organization (RSO); Arakan Rohingya Islamic Front (ARIF).

ASSAM: All-Assam Gana Sangram Parishad (AAGSP); Assam People's Front; Free Assam; United Liberation Front of Assam (ULFA); All-Assam Students Union (AASU)/All-Assam Students Union Volunteer Force (AASUVF); Asom Gana Parishad.

ASSYRIA: Assyrian Democratic Union; Bet Nahrain Democratic Party (BNDP); International Confederation of the Assyrian Nation; Student Representative Council; Assyrian Quest.

BALUCHISTAN: Baluchistan Liberation Front (BLF); Baluch People's Liberation Front (BPLF); Baluchistan People's Democratic Organization (BPDO); World Baluch Organization; Popular Front for Armed Resistance (PFAR); Baluchistan National Front (BNF); Front of Nimruz; Popular Movement; Tehrik-i-Istiqalal; Jamboary Watan Party (JWP); Balochistan National Alliance; Baluchistan Liberation Front (BLF); Baluch Pesh Merga (Baluch Volunteer Force).

BANGSKA MORO: Moro National Liberation Front (MNLF); Moro Islamic Front (MILF); Bangska Moro Islamic Party; Bangska Moro Army (BMA); Bangska Moro National Liberation Front (BMNLF); Moro Autonomist Movement; Abu Sayaff; Mindanao Independence Movement.

BURYATIA: Sinechiel (Renewal); Buryat Pan-Mongol Movement; Society of the Scepter of Indra; Buryat Mongol People's Party; All-Buryat People's Congress; People's Alliance; All-Buryat People's Parliament.

CHAMPA: Cham Islamic Organization (OIC); Cham National Liberation Movement (MNLC); Liberation Front of Highland Champa (FLHPC); United Front for the Struggle of Oppressed Races (FULRO).

CHUKOTKA: Chukot National Movement; People's Movement of Northeast Asia; Association of Northern Minorities.

DHOFAR: Popular Front for the Liberation of Oman and Dhofar (PFLOD); Dhofar Liberation Front (DLF); Popular Front for the Liberation of the Occupied Arabian Gulf (PFLOAG); Front for the Liberation of Oman and the Arab Gulf (FLOAG).

EASTERN MONGOLIA: Eastern Mongol Leagues; Solon Democratic League; Pan-Mongol Democratic Union; United Herdsmen and Farmers Party; Independence Party; United Mongol Party of Eastern Mongolia; Believer's Party.

EAST TIMOR: East Timor Liberation Movement (MLTE); National Council of Resistance: East Timor Committee; Timorese Democratic Union (UDT); Revolutionary Front of Independent East Timor (FRETILIN); National Council of the Maubere Resistance.

EAST TURKESTAN: Eastern Turkish National Revolutionary Front; Eastern Turkish Party; East Turkestan Cultural Association; Front for the Liberation of Uigherstan;

Islamic Party of East Turkestan; National Liberation Front; Turki National Front; Joint National Liberation Front of East Turkestan.

FAR EAST: Far Eastern People's Front; Far Eastern Union; Republican Movement; Zemyak; Alliance of Pacific Peoples; Far East Independence Movement.

GILAN: Gilaki National Movement; Hizb-i Jangali (Jungle Party); Jangli Movement; Jangli Mudajahedine. .

GORKHALAND: Gorkha National Liberation Front (GNLF); Gorkhaland Independence Movement; Gorkhaland People's Party (GPP); Darjeeling Hill Development Council.

HASAVA: Hasava United Movement; Nenets National Movement; Association of Northern Minorities.

HEJAZ: Hashemite Movement; Hejaz Reform Movement; Hizbollah fil Hijaz (Hejaz Party of God).

HO'AIDO: Untari; Ainu Association of Hokkaido; Ainu Liberation Movement of Ho'aido.

HONSAWATOI: Mon National Defense Organization (MNDO); Mon National Democratic Front; New Mon State Party (NMSP)/Mon National Liberation Army (NMLS); Mon People's Front (MPF); For a Democratic Honsawatoi (DH).

JEBEL ED DRUZE: Druze National Unity; Juhal Movement; Progressive Socialist Party (PSP); Sons of al-Atash; National Liberation Front of United Druzistan; Druze National Liberation Front (FNLD).

JHARKHAND: Adivasi Liberation Front (AFL); Chota Nagpur Plateau Praja Parisad; Jharkhand Militia; Jharkhand Mukti Morcha (JMM); Jharkhand Party; Jharkhand Freedom Movement.

KACHINLAND: Kachin Independence Organization (KIO)/Kachin Independence Army (KIA); Kachin National Defense Organization (KNDO); Kachin State National Congress for Democracy.

KADERIA: Jana Samity Samity (JSS)/Shanti Bahini (Force of Peace); Kaderia Bahini (Army of Free Kaderia); Parbottya Chattyram Jana Sarghati Samity; National Movement of Free Kaderia (NMFK); Kaptai Self-Defense Organization.

KARAKALPAKSTAN: Kara-Kalpak United Front; Republican Movement of Karakalpakstan; People's National Party; Islamic Renaissance Party; Equality.

KASHMIR: Allah Tigers; All Pakistan Jammu and Kashmir Conference; Hizbul Mujaheddin; Jammu and Kashmir Liberation Front (JKLF); Jammu and Kashmir Plebiscite Front (JKPF); Kashmir Liberation Front (KLF); Muslim Jambaz Force; Muslim Liberation Front (MLF); Muslim United Front (MUF); People's League; World Kashmir Freedom Movement; Student's Liberation Front (SLF); Al-Umar Mujaheddin; Moslem Liberation Front; Islamic Students League; Jaanbaz Force; Hezbollah; Northern Areas Platform.

KAWTHOOLEI: Karen Independence Movement (KIM); Karen National Liberation Front (KNLF); Karen National Union (KNU)/Karen National Defense Organization (KNDO); Karen People's Liberation Organization (KPLO); Karen State National Organization (KSNO); Karen National United Party (KNUP)/Karen National Liberation Army (KNLA); Karen Independence Movement (KIM).

KAYAH: Kayah New Land Party (KNLP); Karenni National Progressive Party (KNPP)/ Karenni Revolutionary Army (KRA); Kayah State Nationalities League for Democracy; Democratic Organization for Kayah National Unity; Moslem Liberation Organization; United Karenni States Independence Army (UKSIA).

KERALA: Kerala Socialist Party (KSP); Kerala Christian Association; Moplah Association; Muslim League; Left Front; Revolutionary Socialist Party; Islamic Sevak Sangh.

KHALISTAN: Akali Dal; All-India Sikh Students Federation; Babbar Khalsa; Khalistan Commando Force; Khalistan Liberation Army; Khalsa Dal; Panthic Committee; Pure Tigers; Khalistan Liberation Force (KLF); Council of Khalistan.

KORYAKIA: Association of Northern Minorities; Chav' Chüv; Koryak Republican Movement.

KURDISTAN: Committee for the Defense of the Kurdish Nation; Democratic Party of Iranian Kurdistan (KDPI); Revolutionary Leadership of the Kurdistan Democratic Party of Iran (RLKDPI); Free Kurdistan Campaign; Komalah Party; Kurdish Democratic Party; Kurdish Workers Party (PKK); National Liberation Front of Kurdistan; Patriotic Front of Kurdistan (PUK); People's Party; Riz Qari; People's Labor Party; National Liberation Front of Kurdistan (ERNK).

LADAKH: Ladakh Buddhist Association; Ladakh Youth Association (LYA); Movement for Culture and Education; People's Movement for Free Ladakh.

LATAKIA: Alawite Democratic Union; Alawiyah Movement; Red Knights.

MANCHURIA: Kao Kang Memorial League; Northeastern Development Front; Manchu Heritage National Party.

MEGHALAYA: All-Party Hill Leaders Conference; Hill People's Union; Hill People's Democratic Party; United Meghalaya Parliamentary Party; United Meghalaya People's Forum; Meghalaya Democratic Front (MDF); Hill State Population's Democratic Party.

MEITHEI LAIPAK: Manipur People's Party; People's Liberation Army (PLA); Revolutionary Army of Kuneipak; Revolutionary Government of Manipur (RGM).

MIZORAM: Mizo National Front (MNF)/Mizo National Army (MNA); Republic of Mizoram (ROM).

MOUNT LEBANON: Christian Independence Movement; Lebanese Forces; Phalange Militia; National Independence Movement of the Enclave of Mount Lebanon (MNIEJL); Bloc National; Christian Social Democratic Party; Al-Kata'el (Phalangist Party); Lebanese Front; Guardians of the Cedars; Social Democratic Party.

NAGALAND: Nagaland People's Council; Naga National Council (NNC); Naga National Liberation Front (NNLF); Nationalist Socialist Council of Nagaland; Naga Hill Regional Progressive Party.

NAN CHAO: Democratic United Front; Tai Zhuang Federation; United Nationalities Democratic Movement; Chao Fah Movement.

NINGSIA: Chungkuo Islam Djemiyeti (Chinese Islamic Association); Gazavat; Islamic Democratic Party (IDP); Moslem Brotherhood.

OKINAWA: New State Organization; Okinawa Independence Party; Okinawa Independence League; Ryuku Islands Movement.

PALESTINE: Palestine Liberation Organization (PLO)/Palestine Liberation Army (PLA); HAMAS/Ezzedin al Qassim; Fatah; Palestine Liberation Front (PLF); Palestine National Council (PNC); Popular Front for the Liberation of Palestine (PFLP); Islamic Jihad; Black September; Palestine Democratic Front (PDF); Hezbollah.

PAOH: Pa-O National Organization (PONO)/Pa-O National Army (PONA); Pao Shan Independence Party; Union Paoh National Organization.

PATTANI: Pattani United Liberation Organization (PULO); National Revolutionary Front (NRF); Islamic Republic of Pattani (IRP); Muslim Liberation Front.

PUSHTUNISTAN: Awami Action Committee; Awami National Party (ANP); Khidai Khedmantgar (God's Servitors); Pakhtoon Khawa Milli Awanu Party; Pakhtoon wa Qaumi Party; Azad Pushtunistan; Khuda-i-Khidmatgar; Mazdoor Kissan Party; National Democratic Party; Pakhtun Front (PF).

SABAH: Kadazan National Movement; Parti Bersatu Sabah (PBS); Parti Kadazan Asli Sabah (PKAS); Pribumi National Liberation Movement (PNLM); Sabah People's Union; United Sabah National Organization (USNO); Bersatu Rakyat Jelata Sabah (BERJAYA).

SAKHA OMUK: New Nation Assembly; Republican National Party; Sakha Omuk (Sakha Popular Front); Republican Movement; Sakha National Independence Party.

SARAWAK: Parti Bansa Dayak Sarawak (PBDS); North Kalimantan Liberation Front (NKLF); North Kalimantan People's Forces; Sarawak Native People's Party; People's Justice Movement (ARAK): Sarawak National Action Party (SNAP); Sarawak United People's Party (SUPP); Sarawak National Party (SNP).

SHANLAND: Shan State Progressive Party (SSPP)/Shan State Army (SSA); Shan United Revolutionary Army (SURA); Mongtai Revolutionary Army (MUA); Pao Shan Independence Party; Shan State Kokang Democratic Party; Shan Nationalities League for Democracy; Shan National Army (SNA); Shan State Army Eastern (SSAE); Shan State Restoration Council.

SIBERIA: All-Siberian Democratic Union; Katchan; Siberian Republican Alliance; Siberskoye Zemlyachestvo (Autonomy Movement); Sibir; Free Siberia; Democratic Siberia; Siberia First.

SIKKIM: Movement for the Restoration and Independence of Sikkim; Sikkim National Party; Sikkim Sangram Parisad; Sikkim Democratic Front.

SIND: Jamaat-i-Islami; Jiya Sind (Free Sind Movement); Sind National Liberation Front; Sind National Liberation and Independence Movement; Sind People's Movement; Sindhi National Alliance; Sindu Desh (Sind Nation).

SOUTHERN MONGOLIA: Democratic Union; People's Revolutionary Party; Ulanfu Revolutionary Association; United Leagues of Mongolia; League of the Forty-Nine Banners; Independence Party.

SOUTH MOLUCCAS: Ambonese Liberation Movement (ALM); Ambonese Union; South Moluccas Liberation Front (SMLF); Maluku Merdeka.

SOUTH VIETNAM: National Liberation Front of South Vietnam: Vietnam Anti-

Communist League; Quoc Han (Black April); Vietnam Religious Alliance; Front for the Struggle of Oppressed Races (FULRO); Vietnamese Refugees Association.

SOUTH YEMEN: Yemeni Socialist Party (YSP); League of the Sons of Yemen (LSY); Aden Socialist Action Party (ASAP); Democratic Forum.

TAIWAN: Democratic Progressive Party (DPP); Formosa Independence Movement; New Nation Alliance; New Constitution Alliance; Organization for Taiwan Nation-Building; Taiwan Independence Movement; World United Formosans; Taiwan Democratic Party; Formosa Movement.

TAMIL EELAM: People's Front of the Liberation Tigers (PFLT)/Liberation Tigers of Tamil Eelam (LTTE); People's Liberation Organization of Tamil Eelam; Eelam People's Revolutionary Liberation Front (EPRLF).

TAMIL NADU: All-India Ana Dravida Munnetra Kazhagam (AADMK); Dravida Munnetra Kazagham (DMK); Tamil Liberation of Front of Tamil Nadu; Free Tamil Movement.

TANNU TUVA: Tuvan People's Alliance; Uryanchai Banner League.

TIBET: Tibetan National Movement; Tibetan Government-in-Exile; Tibetan Youth Congress; World Tibetan Organization; Tibetan People's Assembly; Campaign for Tibet.

TRIPURA: Revolutionary Socialist Party (RSP); Tripur`Sena; Tripura National Volunteers (TNV)/Tripura National Volunteer Army (TNVA).

WAH: Wa National Organization (WNO)/Wa National Army (WNA); United Wa States Army; Wa States Independence Movement; Wa States Organization; Wah Democratic League; Wa National Development Party.

ZORAM: Chin National Organization (CNO)/Chin National Army (CNA); Zomi National Front; Zomi National Congress; Chin National League for Democracy.


## EUROPE

Albania: North Epirus.

Austria: Tyrol.

Azerbaidzhan: Artsakh.

Belgium: Flanders; Wallonia.

Croatia: Istria.

Cyprus: Northern Cyprus.

Denmark: Faeroe Islands.

Finland: Aland; Sapmi.

France: Alsace; Brittany; Catalonia; Corsica; Euzkadi; Flanders; Normandy; Occitania; Savoy.

Georgia: Abkhazia; Ajaristan; Meskhtekistan; Ossetia.

Germany: Bavaria; Lusatia; Saxony.

Italy: Friulia; Ladinia; Lombardy; Piedmont; Sardinia; Savoy; Sicily; Trieste; Tyrol; Veneto; Waldensia.

Moldova: Dniestria; Gagauzia.

Netherlands: Friesland.

Norway: Sapmi.

Portugal: Azores.

Romania: Transylvania.

Russia: Bashkortostan; Chavashia; Chechenia; Circassia; Dagestan; Don; Hasava; Ingria; Ingushetia; Kalmykia; Karachai-Balkaria; Karelia; Königsberg; Kuban; Mari-El; Mordvinia; Ossetia; Tatarstan; Terek; Udmurtia; Uralia; Volga; Zyria.

Slovenia: Istria.

Spain: Catalonia; Euzkadi; Galicia.

Sweden: Sapmi; Scania.

Switzerland: Grischun; Romande.

Ukraine: Carpatho-Ukraine; Crimea; Western Ukrainia.

United Kingdom: Cornwall; Gibraltar; Mannin; Northumbria; Scotland; Wales; Zetland.

Yugoslavia: Kosovo; Montenegro; Sanjak.

## National Organizations by Nation

ABKHAZIA: Abkhaz National Council; Aiglara (Unity); Apsua Movement; Confederation of Caucasian Highland Peoples; Government of the Republic of Abkhazia.

AJARISTAN: Ajar Islamic Front; Republican National Party.

ALAND: Aaland Independence Party; Alänsk Center; Liberlerna på Aland.

ALSACE: Alsatian National Movement (MNA); Autonomist Front; Free Alsace; Heimatbund; Language and Culture; Black Wolves Alsatian Combat Group; Union pour L'Alsace (UPA); Association of Fidelity to the Alsatian Homeland.

ARTSAKH: Armenian Pan-National Movement (APM); Dashnaktsutium Party; Artsakh Youth League; Nagorno-Karabakh Committee.

AZORES: Azores National Movement (MNA); Front for the Liberation of the Azores (FLA); National Liberation Front (FNL); Social Democratic Party.

BASHKORTOSTAN: Party of Free Bashkortostan: Bashkort Popular Front (BPF); Bashrevkom; Republican Party; Assembly of Turkic Peoples.

BAVARIA: Christian Social Union (CSU); European National Movement; Bavarian Catholic Alliance.

BRITTANY: Araok Breizh (Forward Brittany); Breton Democratic Union (UDB); Breton Liberation Front (BLF)/Breton Liberation Army (BLA); Emgann; Breton Popular Aid; Front for Socialism and Liberation; Givenn Ha Du (Black and White); Republican Army; Front Breton; Pobl.

CARPATHO-UKRAINE: League for the Liberation of Carpatho-Ukraine; Ruthene National Council; Ruthenian-Ukrainian Union; Transcarpathian People's Front; Society of Carpathian Ruthenians; Sub-Carpathian Republican Party.

CATALONIA: Convergence and Union (CIU); Movement for the Defense of the Nation (MDT); La Crida a la Solidaritat (The Call to Solidarity); Republican Left of Catalonia

(ERC); Catalan Liberation Front (FLC); Unió Valenciana (UV); Unió Mallorquin (UM); Terra Lliure (Free Land); Socialist Liberation Party; Catalunya Lliure; Patronat Catalan Pro Europa; Unitat Catalana.

CHAVASHIA: Chävash Jen; Chavash Popular Front; Tavas; Front for the Unification of Chavashistan.

CHECHENIA: Chechen National Council; Confederation of Caucasian Highland Peoples; Muridic Brotherhood; Chechen National Movement; Islamic Renaissance Party; Nakh Congress; Vainakh National Organization; All-National Congress of the Chechen People.

CIRCASSIA: Yapeqhe Tcerqes (Forward Circassia); Circassian United Front: Solidarity of the Three; Kabardinian People's Congress; Sons of Sausryko; Mountain People's Alliance; Islamic Revival Party; Confederation of Caucasian Highland Peoples; Cherkess National Congress.

CORNWALL: Cornish National Movement (CNM); Cornish National Party (CNP); Stannary Court; Mebyon Kernow (Sons of Cornwall); Democratic Party of Cornwall; Celtic League; Cornish Language Board; Celtic Society.

CORSICA: Action for the Renaissance of Corsica; A Riscossa; Accolta Natiunali Corsa (ANC); Luta per l'Indipendenza; A Cuncolta/Corsican National Liberation Front (FLNC); Regional Action Committee; Union of the Corsican People (UPC); Movimentu per l'Autodeterminazione; Resistenza; National Liberation Army of Corsica.

CRIMEA: Crimean Tatar National Movement; Crimea; Crimean Tatar Youth Union; Committee for the Return of the Exiled Crimean Tatars; Incentive Group; Mili Firka; Milli Mejlis; National Movement of the Crimean Tatars; National Movement of Tatars; Organization of the Crimean Tatars National Movement; Republican Movement of Crimea (RDK).

DAGESTAN: Dagestan People's Front; Islamic Revival Party; Confederation of Caucasian Highland Peoples; Tariqat; Democratic Party of United Dagestan.

DNIESTRIA: Dniestrian Republican Guard; Communist Party of Trans-Dniestria; Government of Cis-Dniestrian Moldova (GCM).

DON: Don Cossack Movement; Free Cossackia; Union of Cossacks; Union of Cossack Military; Edinstvo.

EUZKADI: Basque National Party (PNV); Euzkadi ta Azkaltazuna (ETA); Herri Batasuna; Euzkal Zizentasuna; Eusko Alkartasuna; Iparretarrak (IK); Iraultaz; Commandos de Iparreuskadi (Commandos of North Euzkadi); Lurraldea; Euskadiko Eskerra; Iraultza; Elkarri.

FAEROE ISLANDS: Home Rule Party; People's Party; Republican Party; Socialist Independence Party.

FLANDERS: Davidsfonds; Volksunie; Independence Organization of Flanders; Taal Aktie Komitee (TAK); Vlaamsebloc (VB); Stop Euro-Brussels; Flemish Military Order; Flemish Union of France; Joris van Severn Group; Flemish Liberal Democratic Party (VLD).

FRIESLAND: Frisian National Organization; Fryske Kultuerried; In Fryske Akysjeploesch; Friskie Najonale Party (FNP).

FRIULIA: Moviment Friül (Friuli National Movement); Doxa; Union Furland (UF); Liga Friül (Friulian League).

GAGAUZIA: Gagauz Khalki (Gagauz Nation); Gagauz Language Society; Republican Movement; Gagauze Republic; Gagauz Halky.

GALICIA: Union of the Galician People (UPG); Galiza Ciebe (Free Galicia); Armed Galician League (LGA); Galician National Block (BNG); Galician Popular Front (FPG)/Guerrilla Army of the Free Galician People (EGPGC); Galician National Party; Movement for National Liberation (MLN); Asamblea do Povo Unido.

GIBRALTAR: Association for the Advancement of Civil Rights (AACR); European Movement; Gibraltar National Party (GNP); Gibraltar Social Democrats (GSD); Gibraltar Socialist Labor Party (SGLP).

GRISCHUN: Grischa National Movement; Pro-Europa; Gray League.

INGRIA: Inkeri Popular Front; Movement for Culture and Language.

INGUSHETIA: National Galgai; Islamic Revival Party; Ingush Self-Defense Force; Ingush National Congress; Federation of Caucasian Highland Peoples.

ISTRIA: Istrian Union; Istrian Democratic League; Istarski Demokratski Sabor (IDS); Istrian People's Party (IPP); Istrian Democratic Assembly (IDA); Unione Istriana; Unione degli Italiani (UDI); United Istria; Istrian Democratic Diet (DDI).

KALMYKIA: Kalmyk Banner Organization (KBO); Kalmyk Buddhist Association; Kalmyk National Congress; Movement for an Independent Khal'mg Tangch.

KARACHAI-BALKARIA: Karachai-Balkar National Council; National Council of the Balkar People; National Council of the Karachai People; Volunteer Force of Free Karachaistan; Confederation of the Caucasian Highland Peoples; Malkar Respublika.

KARELIA: Karelian People's Front; Party of Democratic Karelia; Karelian Association; National Movement of Eastern Karelia; United Karelia; Karel Federation of Finland; Social Democratic Party; All-Federation Society for Karelian Unification and Independence.

KÖNIGSBERG: Russo-German Society; Königsberg National Memorial Association; Königsberg Movement; Königsberg Free Zone Movement; Reconciliation; Movement for a Free Republic.

KOSOVO: Albanikos; Council for the Defense of Human Rights in Kosovo (CPHRK); Kosovo National Liberation Movement; Lidhji Kosovare (Union of Kosovo); Democratic League of Kosovo (DLK); Parliamentary Party of Kosovo; Social Democratic Party.

KUBAN: Black Sea Popular Front; Edinstvo; Kuban Citizen's Committee; Kuban Cossack Movement; Kuban Self-Help Organization; Union of Cossacks.

LADINIA: Patrje Ladin; Ladin National Movement; Lega Europa; Alpine League; Lega Montana Cadorina.

LOMBARDY: Lega Lombarda (Lombard League)/Lega Nord (Northern League); Autonomous Lombard Unions; Alpine League; Armed Nucleus for Northern Separatism; Centro Filogical Milanesa; List for Milan.

LUSATIA: Domowina (Nation); Lusatian League; Macica Serbska; Sorb Democratic Union; Lusatian State Movement; New Forum.

MANNIN: Manx National Movement (MNM); Yu Trooar; Mec Vannin (Sons of Mannin); Celtic League.

MARI-EL: Mari Popular Front; Kugu Sorta; Marii Civic Union; Mari People's Democratic Party; Social Party of Marii El.

MESKHTEKISTAN: Meskhtekian National Movement; Vakhtan (Motherland).

MONTENEGRO: Alliance of Reform Forces; Democratic Coalition; National Party; Liberal Union; Democratic Party of Socialists; People's Party; Social Democratic Party; Liberal Alliance Party; Montenegrin Association; Alliance for Montenegrin Independence; Monarchist League; Peace and Democracy; Restoration.

MORDVINIA: Democracy and Independence; Mordva Front; Peoples Front of Mordvinia.

NORMANDY: Flag and Country; Normandy United Movement (MUN).

NORTH EPIRUS: Democratic League of North Epirus; Omonia (Harmony); Struggle for North Epirus; North Ipiros Liberation Front.

NORTHERN CYPRUS: Government of the Turkish Republic of Northern Cyprus; National Salvation Party; New Cyprus Party; Democratic Struggle Party; Free Democratic Party; Communal Liberation Party; National Identity Party; Republic Party; Social Democratic Party; New Dawn Party; Free Democratic Party; Republican Turkish Party; National Unity Party.

NORTHUMBRIA: Campaign Group; Council of the North; National Movement of the North (NMN); Northern Affairs Council.

OCCITANIA: Farem Tot Petar; Félibriseñ Occitane Autonomy Movement; Regió Occitania; Occitania Movement; Solidarité 13; Volem Viure al Pais (VVAP); Partit Occità; Institut d'Estudis Occitans; Il Movimento Autonomista Occitano.

OSSETIA: Ossetian National Council; Adaemon Nejkhas (Ossetian Popular Front); South Ossetian Self-Defense Committee; Ossetian Republican Party; Iryston.

PIEDMONT: Piemonte Libera (Free Piedmont); Lega Piemonte (Piedmont League); Lega Nord (Northern League); Armed Nucleus for Northern Separatism.

ROMANDE: Coordinating Committee of Suisse Romande National Institutes; Pro-Europa; Jura National Liberation Front (FNLJ); National Movement of Romande Europe; Mouvement Indépendiste Jurassien (MIJ).

SANJAK: Muslim Alliance Party; Merhamet; Muslim Democratic Union; Muslim Democratic Reform Party; Party of Democratic Action; Sanjak Equality Party; Democratic Coalition of Muslims; Sanjak Defense Forces.

SAPMI: Norsk Samers Riksforbund; Sami Lis'to; Sámiid Konfereanssas (Nordic Sámi Conference); Sami Komitet Severna; Svenska Samernas Riksförbund.

SARDINIA: Partito Sardo d'Azione (Sardinian Action Party); Sardigna Libertade; Nazione Sarda; Partidu Indipendentista Sardu; Revolutionary Sardinian Army; Sardinian Party (PS); Sardinian Separatists; Free Europe Alliance; Su Populu Sardu.

SAVOY: Autonomic Union; Free Zone Movement; Syndicat Autonome Valdotain; National Savoyard Front (FNS); Progressive Democratic Party; Union Valdotaine; Savoy Movement; Pour la Vallée D'Aoste; Union Valdotaine; Moveman Harpitanya (MH).

SAXONY: Nur fur Sachen; Saxon National Movement; Saxony United Movement; United Land Movement; Citizen's Movement for a Europe of Nations.

SCANIA: Befria Skåne (Free Scania); Scania United Left; Skånepartier (Scania Party); Pro Europe: Sjöbo Party.

SCOTLAND: Common Cause; Constitutional Movement; Democracy for Scotland; Scotland United; Scottish Labor Action; Scottish National Party (SNP); Tartan Army; Scottish Constitutional Convention.

SICILY: Movement for a Free Sicily (MSL); Republican Party of Sicily; Sicilian Independence Committee; Sons of Guiliano; La Rete (The Network).

TATARSTAN: Tatar Public Center; Ittifaq (National Independence Party); Harbi Shuro; Democratic Party of Tatarstan; Tatar National Council; Tangechebar; Party of Free Tatarstan; Assembly of Turkic Peoples.

TEREK: Free Cossackia; Terek Cossack Movement; Terek Cossack Volunteer Movement; Union of Cossack Military; Edinstvo; Historic Land Association; National Liberation Movement of the Stavropole Plateau.

TRANSYLVANIA: December 17 Association; Free Youth of Transylvania; Partidul Crestin Democrat; Hungarian Democratic Alliance; Transylvanian World Federation; Women's League for Peace and Freedom; Hungarian Party (RMDSZ); Magyar Democratic Union of Romania (RMDS); All-Transylvanian National Union.

TRIESTE: Lista per Trieste (Trieste List); Lega Triestina (Trieste League); Trieste Green Movement; Associazione per Trieste (Trieste Autonomy Movement).

TYROL: Andreas Hoffer Bund; Ein Tirol (One Tyrol); Heimatbund; Lega Trentina (Trent League); Pro-Vorarlberg; South Tyrolean German Group; Alpine League; Trentino-Tyrol Autonomist Party of Trentino; Union Für Süd Tirol; Tiroler Schützbund; Tirol; Südtirol Schützenbund; Südtirol Volkspartei (SVP); Union for a United Tirol.

UDMURTIA: Udmurt National Movement; Udmurt National Center; Republican National Party; Committee for the Defense of Udmurt Interests.

URALIA: Movement of Ural Sovereignty; Ural Republican Movement; Uralia Association.

VENETO: Consorzio Venezia Nuova; Lega Veneta (Venetian League); Lega Nord (Northern League); Liste Venetes (Venetian Lists); Refundación Veneto; Union Veneto Livre; Armed Nucleus for Northern Separatism.

VOLGA: Council of the Volga Germans; Russian German's Council; Volga German Republican Movement; Wiedergeburt (Rebirth); Heimat.

WALDENSIA: Waldensian Synod; Waldensian Church; Communita Montana Val Pellice.

WALES: Plaid Cymru (Welsh National Party); Cadwyr Cymru (Keepers of Wales); Cefn; Free Wales; Meibion Glendwr (Sons of Glendower); Mudiad Amddiffyn Cymru (Free Welsh Army); Workers Party of the Welsh Republic.

WALLONIA: Democratic Front; Francofone Democratic Front (FDF); Walonia Libre (Free Wallonia); Front National (FN); Parti Wallon (PW); Walloon Rally (RW); Front Indépendantiste Wallon (FIW).

WESTERN UKRAINIA: Incentive Group of Western Ukrainia; Lion Society; Democratic Block; Galician Assembly; Ukrainian Catholic Defense Committee; Free Galician League; Ukrainian Helsinki Association; Ukrainian Popular Front (RUKH); Ukrainian Interparty Assembly; Ukrainian Conservative Republican Party; Galician Ukrainia.

ZETLAND: Orkney and Shetland Association; Zetland United; Island Liberation Front (ILF); Orkney Movement; Shetland Movement.

ZYRIA: Coordinating Council of Democratic Parties; Heritage; Permian People's Front; Komi People's National Organization; Party of Unity and Independence.

## TRANSNATIONAL

Romanistan

## National Organizations

ROMANISTAN: Democratic Union of the Roms; International Romany Union; Rom International Committee; World Romani Congress; Eurom; Union of the Rom.

# Index

The page numbers set in **boldface** indicate the location of the main entry.

## About the Author

JAMES MINAHAN is an independent researcher and free-lance writer living in Barcelona, Spain.